Lecture Notes in Business Information Processing

485

LNBIP reports state-of-the-art results in areas related to business information systems and industrial application software development – timely, at a high level, and in both printed and electronic form.

The type of material published includes

- Proceedings (published in time for the respective event)
- Postproceedings (consisting of thoroughly revised and/or extended final papers)
- Other edited monographs (such as, for example, project reports or invited volumes)
- Tutorials (coherently integrated collections of lectures given at advanced courses, seminars, schools, etc.)
- Award-winning or exceptional theses

LNBIP is abstracted/indexed in DBLP, EI and Scopus. LNBIP volumes are also submitted for the inclusion in ISI Proceedings.

Rim Jallouli · Mohamed Anis Bach Tobji ·
Meriam Belkhir · Ana Maria Soares ·
Beatriz Casais
Editors

Digital Economy

Emerging Technologies and Business Innovation

8th International Conference, ICDEc 2023
Braga, Portugal, May 2–4, 2023
Proceedings

 Springer

Editors
Rim Jallouli 🆔
ESEN, University of Manouba
Manouba, Tunisia

Mohamed Anis Bach Tobji 🆔
ESEN, University of Manouba
Manouba, Tunisia

Meriam Belkhir 🆔
University of Sfax
Sfax, Tunisia

Ana Maria Soares 🆔
University of Minho, CICS.NOVA
Braga, Portugal

Beatriz Casais 🆔
University of Minho, CICS.NOVA
Braga, Portugal

ISSN 1865-1348   ISSN 1865-1356 (electronic)
Lecture Notes in Business Information Processing
ISBN 978-3-031-42787-9   ISBN 978-3-031-42788-6 (eBook)
https://doi.org/10.1007/978-3-031-42788-6

This Springer imprint is published by the registered company Springer Nature Switzerland AG
The registered company address is: Gewerbestrasse 11, 6330 Cham, Switzerland

Paper in this product is recyclable.

Preface

The proliferation of new technologies, such as Artificial Intelligence (AI), blockchain, and the Internet of Things (IoT), has accelerated the digital transformation, bringing new opportunities, challenges, and risks not only for organizations but also for society at large. According to Gartner, the top strategic technology trends for 2022 include AI, virtual reality, IoT, blockchain, and 5G, shaping three strategic orientations, namely (1) engineering trust by integrating and processing data more securely across cloud and non-cloud environments, (2) sculpting change through scaling and accelerating the organization's digitalization, and (3) accelerating growth by maximizing value creation and enhancing digital capabilities (www.information-age.com).

AI is rapidly establishing itself as one of the most important technologies for digital innovation, and its value is expected to continue growing in the years to come. Indeed, the value of the global artificial intelligence market is expected to reach $407 billion in 2027, from $86.9 billion in 2022, growing at an annual growth rate of 36.2% during the forecast period (www.researchandmarkets.com/report/artificial-intelligence).

Moreover, the global IoT market is projected to reach $1.386 billion by 2026, growing at an annual growth rate of 10.6% between 2021 and 2026. Based on 'Research and market Report', the global virtual reality market is expected to reach $57.55 billion by 2026. Moreover, according to the report published by Allied Market Research, the global 5G IoT market was valued at $1.45 billion in 2020 and is projected to reach $285.28 billion by 2030, registering an annual growth rate of 69.8% from 2021 to 2030.

The eighth International Conference on Digital Economy (ICDEc 2023) sought to explore these opportunities and challenges and to foster a deeper understanding of digital transformation and its implications for economy and society. This edition was held from May 2nd to May 4th, 2023, at the University of Minho, School of Economics and Management in Braga, Portugal, and brought together a diverse group of approximately 40 researchers and practitioners from various disciplines to discuss emerging technologies and business innovation. The conference attracted a diverse audience of scholars, professionals, and students interested in digital transformation, including those from the fields of business, economics, computer science, engineering, and social sciences.

The conference focused on exploring the challenges and opportunities presented by the digital economy, as well as the latest research and developments in emerging technologies and business innovation. Throughout the conference, participants engaged in lively discussions and exchanged ideas on various topics related to the digital economy. The conference proceedings showcase a selection of papers presented at ICDEc 2023, providing valuable insights into the latest developments and challenges in the field.

The conference program included keynote speeches, plenary sessions, and presentations of accepted papers, covering a range of topics, including e-learning, emerging technologies such as artificial intelligence, blockchain, and the internet of things, as well as business innovation topics such as digital transformation, e-commerce, and data analytics.

During the conference, three keynote speakers were present: Justin Paul, Professor at the University of Puerto Rico and Editor-in-Chief of the International Journal of Consumer Studies, Boutheina Ben Yaghlane Ben Slimane, Full Professor of Business Intelligence at the University of Carthage, Tunisia, and Ricardo Oliveira, cybersecurity advisor at Eurotux Group, Portugal, shared their insights and expertise on the challenges and opportunities of digital transformation. Justin Paul discussed the path, process, potential, and problems of digital transformation. Boutheina Ben Yaghlane Ben Slimane focused on the biggest digital transformation challenges facing organizations, while Ricardo Oliveira shared his knowledge on the challenges of cybersecurity and called for applied research. These presentations and discussions facilitated knowledge sharing and collaboration among participants from various fields, providing them with new insights and perspectives on the digital economy.

The ICDEc community has been steadily expanding, drawing an increasing number of contributors from various backgrounds. The remarkable level of participation witnessed in this installment brought together authors and guests from all five continents, presenting a wide collection of scientific contributions characterized by their exceptional quality. The diversity and the record number of submissions and reviewers from diverse regions of the world made the review process highly competitive.

The proceedings of the ICDEc 2023 contain 26 accepted papers presented during the conference, out of 72 submissions. They reflect a wide range of covered topics and contexts and illustrate the latest research and insights into the ongoing digital transformation. Moreover, they offer a valuable resource for researchers, practitioners, and students interested in exploring the implications of digital transformation on the economy. The contributions of the researchers and practitioners who participated in ICDEc 2023 demonstrate the importance of collaboration and interdisciplinary approaches in navigating the challenges and opportunities of the digital economy. We hope this volume will serve as a valuable resource for scholars, policymakers, and practitioners seeking to understand the complex and evolving landscape of the digital economy.

The steering committee and the editors would like to express their heartfelt gratitude to the University of Minho for graciously hosting ICDEc 2023 and providing a beautiful and welcoming venue for this conference. They would also like to extend their sincerest thanks to the organizers for their tireless efforts, which have made this event possible and successful. Special appreciation is also due to all the sponsors and scientific partners who supported this event, as well as the authors who made valuable contributions to this edition of the conference.

The editors would like to convey their appreciation to the reviewers who dedicated their time and expertise to ensure the quality of the selected papers included in the proceedings. Based on the feedback from the program committee, the acceptance rate was 36%, and the papers received an average of 3.1 double-blind reviews. The insights provided by the reviewers to improve ongoing research and the quality of the manuscripts were an essential feature, adding value to this conference.

Finally, a special acknowledgement is extended to the keynote speakers, conference chairs, and organizing committee for their valuable contributions to the success of the conference.

We hope this proceedings volume serves as a source of inspiration for future generations of scholars and practitioners working in the field and guides further research and innovation in this exciting and rapidly evolving area.

Rim Jallouli
Mohamed Anis Bach Tobji
Meriam Belkhir
Ana Maria Soares
Beatriz Casais

Organization

General Chairs

Ana Maria Soares	University of Minho, Portugal
Beatriz Casais	University of Minho, Portugal

Program Chair

Meriam Belkhir	University of Sfax, Tunisia

Steering Committee

Rim Jallouli	University of Manouba, Tunisia
Mohamed Anis Bach Tobji	University of Manouba, Tunisia

Advisory Board

Anton Nijholt	University of Twente, The Netherlands
Deny Bélisle	Université de Sherbrooke, Canada
Farid Abdallah	Australian College of Kuwait, Kuwait
Gunnar Piho	Tallinn University of Technology, Estonia
Leith Campbell	RMIT University, Australia
Olfa Nasraoui	University of Louisville, USA
Osmar Zaïane	University of Alberta, Canada
Sehl Mellouli	Université Laval, Canada
Vasile Alecsandru Strat	University of Economic Studies, Romania

Organization Committee

Eya Laffet	University of Manouba, Tunisia
Roula Jabado	Lebanese International University, Lebanon
Teissir Ben Slema	University of Manouba, Tunisia

Finance Chair

Ismehene Chahbi	University of Manouba, Tunisia

Publication Chair

Meriam Belkhir	University of Sfax, Tunisia

IT Chair

Nassim Bahri   One Way IT, Tunisia

Country Chairs

Ali Afshar	Eqbal Institute of Higher Education, Iran
Ana Maria Soares	University of Minho, Portugal
Codruta Mare	Babeş-Bolyai University, Romania
Dyah Ismoyowati	University of Gadjah Mada, Indonesia
Emrah Bilgic	Iskenderun Technical University, Turkey
Hamid Doost Mohammadian	FHM University of Applied Sciences, Germany
Hamid Mcheick	Université du Québec à Chicoutimi, Canada
Hamish Simmonds	Monitor Deloitte, Australia
Javier Rodriguez Ruiz	University of Guadalajara, Mexico
Jean-François Berthevas	University of La Rochelle, France
Kristian Dokic	Polytechnic in Pozega, Croatia
Mohammad Makki	International University of Beirut, Lebanon
Mohammed El Amine Abdelli	University of Salamanca, Spain
Sayda Elmi	University of Singapore, Singapore
Tatiana Lezina	University of Saint Petersburg, Russia
Thabo Gopane	University of Johannesburg, South Africa

Program Committee

Adriana Davidescu	Bucharest University of Economic Studies, Romania
Amine Dhraief	University of Manouba, Tunisia
Emira Derbel	Buraimi University College, Oman
Amna Abidi	INETUM, France
Ana Maria Soares	University of Minho, Portugal
Ana Sousa	University of Minho, Portugal
Anton Nijholt	University of Twente, The Netherlands
António Azevedo	University of Minho, Portugal
Arem Saai	University of Gafsa, Tunisia
Aymen Hajkacem	University of Tunis, Tunisia
Barbara Pisker	Polytechnic in Pozega, Croatia
Beatriz Casais	University of Minho, Portugal
Carlos Henrique Cabral Duarte	Brazilian Development Bank, Brazil
Chiheb-Eddine Ben N'Cir	University of Jeddah, Saudi Arabia
Claude Diderich	innovate.d llc, Switzerland
Codruta Mare	University of Babeş-Bolyai, Romania
Dorra Guermazi	University of Manouba, Tunisia
Driss Reguieg Issaad	Association Algérienne de Marketing, Algeria

Dyah Ismoyowati	Universitas Gadjah Mada, Indonesia
Ebba Ossiannilsson	The Swedish Association for Distance Education, Sweden
El Ouakdi Jihene	University of Manouba, Tunisia
Faiza Djidjekh	University of Biskra, Algeria
Fatma Smaoui	University of Tunis, Tunisia
Frank Emmert-Streib	Tampere University, Finland
Gabriela Grosseck	West University of Timisoara, Romania
Gina Gaio Santos	University of Minho, Portugal
Gunnar Piho	Tallinn University of Technology, Estonia
Hamid Doost Mohammadian	FHM University of Applied Sciences, Germany
Hamish Simmonds	University of Melbourne, Australia
Hasna Koubaa	University of Manouba, Tunisia
Ibticem Ben Zammel	University of Manouba, Tunisia
Imen Boukhris	University of Tunis, Tunisia
Javier Rodriguez Ruiz	University of Guadalajara, Mexico
Joel Vaz	University of Lusíada, Portugal
Jonas Kötter	Universität Osnabrück, Germany
Karim Grissa	University of Lorraine, France
Karima Dhaouadi	University of Manouba, Tunisia
Klimis Ntalianis	University of West Attica, Greece
Lilia Khrouf	University of Manouba, Tunisia
Longzhu Dong	University of Wisconsin-Eau Claire, USA
Maher Georges Elmashhara	Católica Porto Business School, Portugal
Malgorzata Pankowska	University of Economics in Katowice, Poland
Manh Tuan Nguyen	University of Economics and Business, Vietnam
Marco Escadas	University of Minho, Portugal
Maria Antónia Rodrigues	ISCAP, Portugal
Maria de Lurdes Martins	University of Minho, Portugal
Mbaye Fall Diallo	Lille University, France
Mercedes Galan-Ladero	University of Extremadura, Spain
Meriam Belkhir	University of Sfax, Tunisia
Michael Georg Grasser	Medical University of Graz, Austria
Moetez Khemiri	University of Manouba, Tunisia
Mohamed Anis Bach Tobji	University of Manouba, Tunisia
Mohamed Aymen Haj Kacem	ISG, Tunisia
Mohamed Shaker	BUC, Oman
Mohammad Makki	Saint Joseph University of Beirut, Lebanon
Mona Chabbeh	University of Tunis, Tunisia
Myriam Elghali	University of Manouba, Tunisia
Naima Lassoued	University of Manouba, Tunisia
Nassim Bahri	University of Manouba, Tunisia
Nessrine Benjeddou	University of Manouba, Tunisia
Nessrine Omrani	Paris School of Business, France

Nizar Abdelkafi	University of Milan, Italy
Nizar Hariri	Saint Joseph University of Beirut, Lebanon
Norhene Chabchoub	University of Manouba, Tunisia
Olga Pereira	University of Minho, Portugal
Elisabetta Raguseo	Grenoble Ecole de Management, France
Reaan Immelman	University of Johannesburg, South Africa
Riadh Bouslimi	University of Manouba, Tunisia
Rim Jallouli	University of Manouba, Tunisia
Rui José	University of Minho, Portugal
Sayda Elmi	Yale University, USA
Shaker Mohammed	Buraimi University College, Oman
Susana Marques	University of Aveiro, Portugal
Tatiana Lezina	Higher School of Economics, St. Petersburg, Russia
Teissir Benslama	University of Manouba, Tunisia
Thabo J. Gopane	University of Johannesburg, South Africa
Tharwa Najjar	University of Gafsa, Tunisia
Thouraya Mellah	University of Manouba, Tunisia
Waël Louhichi	ESSCA School of Management Paris, France
Yamna Ettarres	University of Manouba, Tunisia
Zeineb Ayachi	University of Manouba, Tunisia

Organizers 2023

ASSOCIATION TUNISIENNE D'ÉCONOMIE NUMÉRIQUE

UNIVERSITY OF MINHO (SCHOOL OF ECONOMICS AND MANAGEMENT)

University of Minho
School of Economics and Management

Scientific Partners 2023

 ÉCOLE SUPÉRIEURE
D'ÉCONOMIE NUMÉRIQUE

  UNIVERSITE DE
LA MANOUBA

 LABORATOIRE DE
RECHERCHE
OPÉRATIONNELLE,
DE DÉCISION ET DE
CONTRÔLE DE
PROCESSUS

 BUCHAREST BUSINESS SCHOOL

Contents

Digital Economy

Online Session

Digital Transformation

Barriers to Digital Transformation in SMEs: A Quantitative Study

Henning Brink[1]($\boxtimes$) ⓘ and Sven Packmohr[2] ⓘ

[1] BOW, Osnabrück University, Osnabrück, Germany
henning.brink@uos.de
[2] DVMT, Malmö University, Malmö, Sweden
sven.packmohr@mau.se

Abstract. Digital transformation (DT) is a trending topic in nearly all industries. Enterprises digitalize processes, offer digital services and products, and enhance the customer experience. However, complex barriers hinder the ability of entrepreneurial-oriented small and medium-sized enterprises (SMEs) to advance in digital transformation. Using a questionnaire, we collected and analyzed data on the barriers to digital transformation in SMEs. The data revealed a heterogonous picture of SMEs regarding digital transformation and barriers. Based on 195 completed questionnaires, we demonstrated a significant negative influence of organizational and technical barriers and missing skills on digital transformation success. The identified predictors can explain 58% of the variance in the transformation process based on 195 respondents. We could not demonstrate a significant relationship to digital transformation success for the three additional barrier dimensions individual, lack of standards, and lack of laws. Nevertheless, respondents perceive the existence of a lack of standards and laws as well as individual barriers. Our results indicate that addressing organizational barriers is an excellent way to start a DT journey.

Keywords: Digital Transformation · Barriers · Quantitative Research · SME

1 Introduction

Digital transformation (DT) brings significant and universal contributions to enterprises [1]. Previous studies emphasized contributions such as improved competitive advantages [2] or workplace environments [3]. The advantages and threats introduced by DT challenge businesses [4]. Due to the high number of stakeholders and technologies and the differences between the focus of enterprises, it is complex and challenging for businesses to comprehend DT. The adverse effects of DT vary based on the type of interaction between individuals and technology, and these challenges could hinder progress [5]. The current research aims to define all the barriers observed in this process. Barriers are "those things that hinder, slow, or stop the process of DT" [6]. The decision-makers and users of technology in enterprises should know the potential obstacles to DT and their origin. They should be able to describe these threats [7] to allow managers to intervene and implement adequate solutions.

© The Author(s), under exclusive license to Springer Nature Switzerland AG 2023
R. Jallouli et al. (Eds.): ICDEc 2023, LNBIP 485, pp. 3–17, 2023.
https://doi.org/10.1007/978-3-031-42788-6_1

According to the Organization for Economic Cooperation and Development (OECD), Small and medium-sized enterprises (SMEs) are the vital entrepreneurial actors in most economies as they employ most of the workforce and play an essential part in value creation and supply networks [8]. However, large corporations embrace their digital journeys better than SMEs. Hypothetically, large corporations have easier access to resources [9]. Thus, SMEs typically need a more entrepreneurial mindset to compensate for resource shortcomings [10]. Even before the pandemic, SMEs were lagging in their digital business strategies. The pandemic forced the application of digital tools but slowed down conceptual work. Now, SMEs need to catch up [11]. Several definitions for SMEs exist, distinguishing between the number of employees, turnover, and balance sheet total. The European Union defines SMEs as entrepreneurial-oriented corporations with fewer than 250 employees, including single entrepreneurs, and either generate an annual turnover lower than EUR 50 million or display an annual balance sheet total lower than EUR 43 million [12].

SMEs cannot exclude themselves from the megatrend of digitalization. Editorial articles have suggested the need for more empirical studies on DT [13]. However, comparing 99 relevant papers on barriers to DT, only 22 adopted a quantitative approach. Thus, we respond to this call with an empirical study on barriers to DT in SMEs to help the field mature. Furthermore, SMEs need guidance in their DT work. Especially, empirically tested results showing significant influences of barriers are of importance. Hence, we investigate the following research problems: Which barriers to digital transformation do SMEs perceive? How significant is the barriers' influence on the digital transformation process?

This paper aims to quantify and analyze the impact of perceived barriers on DT. DT is a phenomenon including "interactions between social entities and information technology" [14]. Thus, we follow a socio-technical view [15, 16] and use it within a well-adjusted questionnaire. With its help, we can analyze the impact of several perceived barriers to the implementation of DT. The questionnaire was employed to collect quantitative data from 195 respondents.

In the next section, we present the theoretical foundation for the research. After, we introduce the research approach and present the findings. Following an in-depth discussion of the results, we conclude by addressing the contribution and limitations of the study findings.

2   Related Work

DT has become a catchphrase with several definitions. Reis et al. [17] provided an aggregated DT definition: "as the use of new digital technologies that enable major business improvements and influences all aspects of customers' life." This definition included four comprehensive elements—technology, value creation, structure, and finance—reflecting the concept's complexity [18]. DT introduced a threat to the adequate management of current organizations [7]. Compared to the IT-Enabled Organizational Transformation (ITOT) that prioritizes the support of value propositions, DT focuses on a redefinition of value propositions [19]. For the Business Model Canvas (BMC), DT would impact the design of value propositions, located at the center of the canvas. Thus, DT "leverages digital resources to create differential value" [20]. Since DT affects the staple of business models, it presents further barriers compared to ITOT.

Generally, a barrier is an obstacle "that keeps people or things apart or prevents communication or progress" [21]. Hanelt et al. [22] considered the barriers to DT as "tensions that result from interweaving physical and digital layers into business models." Thus, industries with physically asset-bound business models, such as manufacturing industries, experience stronger barriers than those with weaker physical facilities like banking and insurance. We transformed these definitions into factors that hinder or slow down DT. Therefore, our research determined the DT process as the dependent variable [23].

Leaders should guide their organization during the DT process. Managing barriers is critical since they could hinder or slow down the DT process. Since DT offers endless possibilities, such as through ubiquitous access to information and communication [5], managers should embrace the DT barriers with a holistic approach. When managers integrate physical and digital layers, barriers could become facilitators. Corporations that cannot integrate both assets cannot achieve long-term gains and could fall behind. The barriers to DT relate to their opposites, namely the facilitators. If a corporate DT process advances or environmental factors change, barriers could become facilitators or vice versa [24]. Thus, further research is required on both aspects to acquire a holistic view of the development of DT processes.

SMEs cannot exclude themselves from the megatrend of digitalization. However, they generally have less access to resources, which makes it harder to follow a digital transformation process. Especially in crises, they have less room to maneuver, as they often focus on niches and smaller production quantities. Thus, they can use economies of scale to a minor degree. Cost savings need to be realized through efficiency gains, for which digitalization has a high potential. However, limited resources and know-how, combined with a missing exploration attitude, hinder SMEs from professionalizing their IT departments, scaling the IT infrastructure, and implementing emerging technology for efficiency gains [25]. Besides difficulties, structural advantages affect SMEs' DT positively. Mostly, hierarchies in SMEs are flat, allowing them to make decisions faster. Moreover, SME employees have tighter bonds with each other, making communication quick. In sum, these characteristics make SMEs more flexible in reacting to changes. Forms of changed value creation and closer customer contact are aspects of DT in which SMEs can excel [26].

Historically, research on DT barriers originated in innovation research [27]. We conducted a systematic literature review to identify the studies on DT barriers [13]. In total, we identified 99 studies. Of these, 62 adopted a qualitative research design, 22 a quantitative approach, and 15 a mixed methodology. Evaluating the studies using qualitative methods, we found overlaps in their findings. A more specific overview of DT barriers in SMEs revealed the following insights. Horváth and Szabó [28] identified significant barriers such as dependency on the local workforce, focus on niche markets, unconsciousness about business models, and shortcomings in monitoring opportunities in technological and market developments. Additional results showed implementation hurdles such as the absence of skilled labor, inappropriate work culture, and unclear economic benefits [29]. In addition to these internal barriers, studies also include external barriers, for example, in legal policies [30] or regarding the perspective of customer-related barriers [31].

One of the quantitative studies revealed six cause and two effect groups of barriers using a questionnaire study [32]. Several barriers negatively correlate with digital readiness, but a non-significant one with digital practice. Another study showed that understanding the relevance of digital technologies affects corporate globalization strategies [33]. Further, a study among Romanian SMEs indicated that knowledge, education, and strategic approach were barriers independent of the company's size and industry [34]. By using the instrument of multicollinearity, [35] identified a lack of enthusiasm and skepticism towards the necessity to digitalize as barriers of attitude. Surveying the skills of employees, another study found that 80% of employers question the adequacy of the training of their workforce [36]. Moreover, between 34% (in trade) and 69% (in manufacturing) of SMEs perceived barriers of the technical infrastructure [37]. Often, barriers are presented as unordered lists of the employment of a specific technology [38].

The barriers approach has been adopted in various research studies, such as technology-assisted business models, closer customer contact, or operations [39, 40]. In several studies on multiple contexts, the authors determined external and internal clusters to classify barriers. Internal clusters focused on barriers associated with organizational issues, such as supply chain, organizational culture and staff, IT systems, and management [41].

As our review shows, some quantitative studies exist, but need to be broadened. In our current study, we use a questionnaire based on a socio-technical approach to generate quantitative results. This approach is consistent with Jones et al. [42] who described DT as an "organization-wide change effort."

3   Method

In this study, we investigated the current state of research on DT with a literature review. As presented in the theoretical development section, we identified a few quantitative studies on SMEs and their barriers to DT. The literature review was carried out in the first quarter of 2021 using the search string "digital transformation AND barriers" as well as its synonyms in the databases AIS Electronic Library services, EBSCO, and Scopus [13]. Following the suggestions by Webster and Watson [43], we identified 99 relevant papers on barriers and DT. Out of these, roughly 15 focused explicitly on SMEs in different countries and different sectors, as presented before.

To solve the research problem, we used a questionnaire (see Table 2) that we developed through an exploratory sequential mixed-method approach [44]. We invited questionnaire respondents through calls to personal contacts and on professional networking sites, potentially resulting in many respondents from the DACH region. In this region, the automotive sector is a rather prominent one [45]. Thus, we employed a convenience sampling technique, which belongs to the non-probability methods [46]. Non-probability sampling is less prone to bias than probability sampling; but it allows a valid exploration of a field [47]. For the selection of participants, we referred partly to the EU's definition of SMEs [12]. Only participants who work in a company with less than 250 employees were considered. In total, 195 questionnaires complying with this condition were completed and employed in our statistical analysis.

Table 1. Questionnaire Sample.

Sector (%)	Automotive (40), Mechanical & plant engineering (15), ICT (10), Energy (6), Logistics (5), Tourism (4), Health (3), Other (12), Not stated (5)
Position (%)	Executive (11), staff w/ personnel responsibility (25), Staff w/o personnel responsibility (47), Intern (7), Other (6), Not stated (4)
Company size (%)	50–249 (58), 10–49 (30), 9 or fewer employees (12)

We were able to generate a diverse sample for the quantitative surveys. The respondents were employed in the automotive, farming, building, trade, or food industries. The largest group of participants comprised employees without personnel responsibility, followed by those with non-supervisory responsibilities, executive managers, and interns. Furthermore, the participants were employed by companies of different sizes. Table 1 presents the survey sample in detail.

After data collection, we analyzed the data in SPSS [48] using various statistical analyses, which are presented in more detail in the results section. The questionnaire items were assessed on a 5-point Likert scale ranging from "I disagree" to "I agree." To prevent bias generated by asking exclusively about barriers, we formulated 18 items in the questionnaire with positive wording. In the later analysis, all items were poled in a negative direction.

Table 2. Questionnaire [44].

Dimension	(Code) Item
DT Process	(DT1) Company has no roadmap to offer smart products/services. (DT2) Company offers customers significantly improved smart products/services. (DT3) Company has no roadmap to use smart products/services internally. (DT4) Company offers improved digital support for my work. (DT5) Company is moving straight ahead in terms of a DT. (DT6) Company still uses traditional methods for production/services
Individual Barriers	(IND1) DT is intimidating to me. (IND2) I control the digital workspace and the data generated. (IND3) I am afraid that, during my work, data is generated in the background allowing conclusions about my work behavior. (IND4) Traceability of my data does not influence my work behavior. (IND5) More jobs will be lost than gained through DT. (IND6) DT will harm my job prospects. (IND7) I strongly advocate DT as I expect process gains

(*continued*)

Table 2. (*continued*)

Dimension	(Code) Item
Organizational Barriers	(ORG1) Senior management supports DT and is visibly engaged. (ORG2) We have no new roles in managing digitalization projects. (ORG3) A clear strategy for DT is communicated. (ORG4) Errors are used to improve work processes. (ORG5) We strive to learn and improve to master DT constantly. (ORG6) There is an openness to new ideas. (ORG7) We do not have enough resources to manage DT
Technical Barriers	(TEC1) My work suffers from a poor data connection. (TEC2) My work suffers from insufficient data interfaces. (TEC3) While exchanging information, my company fears data theft. (TEC4) My confidential work data is sufficiently protected. (TEC5) Company's infrastructure can handle DT. (TEC6) Company's infrastructure is flexible for future developments
Lack of Standards	(ST1) Different data is more effectively integrated into my digital workspace through DT. (ST2) There are enough standards to manage DT effectively
Lack of Laws	(LA1) Legislation sufficiently protects companies in the digital world. (LA2) There are not enough laws to protect me in the digital workspace
Missing Skills	(SKL1) My IT knowledge is adequate to keep up with DT. (SKL2) Company's IT knowledge is adequate to keep up with DT. (SKL3) There is a knowledge lack about the potential of DT. (SKL4) There is a knowledge lack to use digital technologies effectively. (SKL5) I would like to be more involved in the decision-making on the implementation of new technologies. (SKL6) Company should provide more training on technology skills

4   Results

To determine which barriers prevent a DT in SMEs, we analyzed the data from the quantitative survey—first descriptively and then inductively.

Since each dimension consists of a bundle of items, we first checked the internal consistency of the dimensions. For this purpose, we performed a reliability analysis and determined the value of Cronbach's alpha. Cronbach's alpha describes the degree of interdependence of the items and the extent to which items of a dimension measure the same construct, and it can range from 0 to 1 [49]. Since we examined aggregate dimensions during the study, we calculated Cronbach's alpha values to measure the internal consistency of the dimensions and to ensure the validity of the results. The analysis showed unsatisfactory values for the dimensions "individual barriers" and "lack of standards" in the first round. Hence, we increased the internal consistency for individual barriers by deleting item "IND2," and the minimum threshold of 0.6 was exceeded. Unfortunately, it was not possible to increase the internal consistency for the dimension "lack of standards". Therefore, the validity of the analysis results relating to this dimension cannot be assured. All other dimensions show higher Cronbach's alpha values and are retained unchanged in the analysis.

The descriptive analysis of the questionnaire data revealed a wide range of responses. For example, the responses on the assessment of the DT process of a company show a minimum of 1.17, which corresponds to a non-existent digital transformation, and 5.00 of the maximum possible agreement on a perceived successful DT. However, the average score is 3.29 with a standard deviation of 0.79, revealing a vast difference among respondents' companies regarding DT. It indicates that some companies cope better with DT than others. The following analysis of the responses to the barrier dimensions influencing the DT process may provide some insight into this.

There was a similar response behavior regarding barrier dimension items. The answers cover a wide range, and the standard deviation varies from 0.62 to 0.90. Differences can also be observed in the mean values. For example, in terms of individual barriers, respondents indicated relatively low levels of existing barriers on average, with a score of 2.39. In contrast, in the case of missing skills, the respondents perceived somewhat distinct barriers on average, reflected by the value of 3.15. The mean values of the other dimensions range between these two values (as shown in Table 3).

Since we not only wanted to find out which barriers were perceived by the respondents and to what intensity but also wanted to understand why some companies have made more progress in DT than others, we calculated the correlation and performed a regression analysis. According to the Spearman correlation test, there are significant correlations between the barriers and DT. Furthermore, a solid negative significant correlation is observable between organizational barriers and DT [50]. Regarding technical barriers, lack of standards, and missing skills, we found a moderate negative correlation with DT. Further, the findings indicate a weak negative correlation between individual barriers and lack of laws. However, only the correlation with the individual barriers is significant. Table 3 shows the analysis in detail.

Unlike simple linear correlation, multiple linear regression allows us to understand the cause-effect relationship. Therefore, using a stepwise inclusion regression, we tested the extent to which the presumed barriers influence DT in the sample. As a result, we were able to demonstrate a significant negative influence of three barrier dimensions on DT (see Table 4).

The regression model containing the barrier dimensions as independent variables and the DT process as a dependent variable reports an R^2 of 0.589 and an adjusted R^2 of 0.582. These values indicate that three of our six barrier dimensions can significantly explain the DT process variance [51]. The largest impact on the DT process is observable through organizational barriers. As the perception of the organizational obstacles increases, the expected degree of DT decreases. This relationship is similar for technical barriers and missing skills, although the effect sizes are smaller.

With our sample, we could not provide statistically significant results regarding the relationship of the lack of standards and laws and individual barriers on DT. Therefore, these variables were excluded in the stepwise inclusion process in the regression due to lack of significance.

Table 3. Descriptive Statistic and Correlation.

Descriptive Statistic									Spearman's Correlation with DT Process	Cronbach's Alpha
Dimension	Minimum	Maximum	25th percentile	50th percentile	75th percentile	Mean	Deviation	Variance		
DT Process	1.17	5.00	2.83	3.33	3.83	3.29	0.79	0.63	1.00	0.79
Individual Barriers	1.00	4.00	2.00	2.33	2.83	2.39	0.62	0.38	− 0.17*	0.61
Organizational Barriers	1.00	5.00	2.00	2.54	3.14	2.58	0.78	0.62	− 0.70**	0.83
Technical Barriers	1.00	4.67	2.33	2.83	3.33	2.84	0.76	0.58	− 0.52**	0.75
Lack of Standards	1.00	5.00	2.00	2.50	3.00	2.60	0.74	0.55	− 0.38**	0.37
Lack of Laws	1.00	5.00	2.50	3.00	3.50	3.04	0.90	0.81	− 0.09	0.64
Missing Skills	1.00	5.00	2.67	3.12	3.67	3.15	0.72	0.52	− 0.59**	0.73

*p < 0.05 significant, **p < 0.01 significant.

Table 4. Regression analysis

Dimensions	Unstandardized Coefficients		Standardized Coefficients	Sig.
	B	Std. Error	Beta	
(Constant)	5.829	.180		.000
Organizational Barriers	− .549	.061	− .542	.000
Missing Skills	− .209	.071	− .188	.004
Technical Barriers	− .162	.063	− .153	.010
Individual Barriers	Excluded variable (due to stepwise inclusion process)			.783
Lack of Standards	Excluded variable (due to stepwise inclusion process)			.121
Lack of Laws	Excluded variable (due to stepwise inclusion process)			.060

5 Discussion

Using a questionnaire, we collected and analyzed data on the barriers to digital transformation in SMEs. The data revealed a heterogonous picture of SMEs in terms of DT and barriers. Based on 195 completed questionnaires, we demonstrated a significant negative influence of organizational and technical barriers and missing skills on DT success. However, we could not demonstrate a significant relationship to DT for three additional barrier dimensions (individual barriers and lack of standards or laws). Nevertheless, as our descriptive analysis shows, some of the respondents to the questionnaire indicated the existence of barriers in these three dimensions. In the following, we will discuss the results and compare findings from the literature.

The largest significant negative influence on DT success derives from the organizational barriers in our sample. Other publications have also described these types of barriers as hindering DT success in SMEs [29, 30, 52, 53]. On the other hand, Horváth and Szabó [28] argued that organizational factors might not be major barriers in smaller and more entrepreneurial enterprises. They concluded that organizational resistance might be more significant in large companies. Our results confirm this assumption to some extent. The mean value and the percentiles of organizational barriers indicate that most SMEs in our sample perceive fewer organizational barriers regarding resistance to change. Nevertheless, companies in our sample face a high degree of organizational barriers, which, according to the regression, is associated with a lack of DT success. Therefore, small companies should still critically reflect on organizational barriers. A case study by Amaral and Peças [29] also highlighted the importance of cultural barriers. Moreover, Westerman et al. [54] emphasized the importance of a clear strategy for securing engagement as well as sufficient resource allocation. The relevance of a communicated DT strategy is reflected in our results.

Missing skills is another dimension we found to have a significant negative impact on DT. This dimension of DT barriers was most frequently agreed upon in the responses to our questionnaire. Since missing skills show a significantly low influence in the regression but have the highest mean and distribution according to the percentiles, we can assume that companies further advanced in DT also struggle with missing skills, albeit somewhat. Missing skills have also been discussed as a barrier in other publications [34, 53]. On the one hand, DT requires increased abstraction and problem-solving skills as well as the ability to work with digital technologies among all employees; on the other hand, some employees also need more in-depth technical knowledge for implementation [10]. Another quantitative study showed that employers perceive a lack of skills such as data analysis, interaction with smart devices, and reading layout designs on an employee level [36]. Our results indicate that the employees also perceive missing skills and a lack of appropriate training as DT barriers.

As entrepreneurs and SMEs are often financially constrained, digital transformation is a challenge, especially in implementing new technologies [10]. Our study found a significant negative relationship between DT and technical barriers by questioning participants about IT infrastructure, security aspects, and data interfaces and connections. These barriers have also been identified in other publications as crucial barriers to DT success [52]. In our study, on average, technical barriers are experienced slightly more often than organizational barriers but a bit less than missing skills. A study among Ukrainian SMEs has shown that almost half of the companies surveyed do not take precautions regarding information security and cyber defense [37]. The authors attribute this to a lack of willingness to invest at the management level. Our findings suggest that companies with more advanced DT might have overcome these problems, resulting in a more robust perception of data security.

We did not detect a significant effect of individual barriers on DT in the regression. However, a low negative correlation could be measured using spearman's correlation. For the dimension of the individual barriers, we asked questionnaire respondents about their attitudes toward DT. The descriptive analysis shows the lowest mean values, standard deviation, and 75th percentile. Different factors could cause the results. Since the questionnaire had to be completed online, participation was voluntary, and the call for participation was placed on professional social networks, some respondent bias is possible. Nevertheless, the descriptive statistics indicate that the respondents in our sample have a fundamentally positive attitude toward DT. Other studies have shown that individual barriers may exist among employees [30]. Horváth and Szabó [28] stated that some employees fear losing their jobs due to digitalization. Our results do not contradict these findings. However, this particular group seems to be small in our sample. A different study supports our findings of low salience of individual barriers. According to this study, only 10% of the managers surveyed report resistance to digitization from staff in SMEs [37].

The lack of standards and laws are non-significant dimensions of the regression analysis. The dimension of lack of standards has a very low Cronbach's alpha value, which limits the interpretation. The literature in the context of SMEs mentions the lack of norms and standards, as well as unresolved legal matters, as DT barriers [29, 34]. Especially concerning data protection and security, a lack of standards slows down DT. Governments should strive to set national and international standards [55]. On the other hand, the means and percentiles indicate that the respondents perceive a lower lack of standards in our sample. We surveyed a broad base of individuals from different positions and departments. However, the lack of standards is more visible for IT staff, representing only a subset in our sample.

Khanzode et al. [32] found that the lack of a political framework has a strong negative influence on the implementation of Industry 4.0 in SMEs. Meanwhile, the descriptive results of our study show a mixed pattern and a high inconsistency among participants. The different impacts of the legal framework could explain this inconsistency. On the one hand, a lack of legislation can lead to uncertainty; on the other hand, restrictive laws hinder, for instance, the adoption of big data [56]. But a legal obligation to adopt a particular technology might hinder free competition. Nevertheless, laws can act as drivers if appropriately designed, for example, by requiring state-of-the-art software in some areas and sectors [37].

In sum, we were able to show a significant negative relationship between the perception of barriers and the perception of the DT process. On an aggregated level, comparable empirical results can be observed in a study by Stentoft et al. [57] on Industry 4.0 readiness and practice. They concluded that barriers reduce Industry 4.0 readiness in SMEs.

6 Limitations and Contributions

In this study, we systematically tested the influence of barriers to DT using a holistic and far-reaching dataset. Our dataset was collected via a questionnaire that provided measurements in six broad barrier dimensions. In line with other studies, we confirmed the importance of organizational, technical, and skill-related barriers with an adequate explanatory power of roughly 60%. However, we also found that individual barriers and lack of laws and standards are minor barrier dimensions.

The findings indicate that some companies have overcome a certain degree of organizational and technical barriers, as well as missing skills. As a result, they appear to have moved DT forward. This is an essential contribution for SMEs as efforts to overcome barriers will likely pay off. Of course, SMEs face problems besides DT, such as financial issues [10]. Nevertheless, according to Bollweg et al. [35], overcoming barriers can be a starting point for the entrepreneurial journey toward a digitized SME. In the long run, this means more financial stability and higher profits [54]. Our results indicate that addressing organizational barriers is an excellent way to start.

Although studies are conducted carefully, each research is bound by limitations. The first limitation is based on our voluntary-response sampling strategy, which belongs to the non-probability sampling methods. Also, our sampling provoked a focus on the DACH region due to personal networks. These aspects are susceptible to bias [47]. As mentioned in the discussion, our sample indicates a bias regarding the respondents' attitudes toward DT. Also, we cannot evaluate if several participants stem from the same enterprise and overrepresent a particular perception. Further data collection based on a probability sampling strategy could obtain a more representative picture. Further, a sample focusing more on high-level executives could add rigor to understanding the external barriers. Another limitation is related to the sample size. Although the size is sufficient for the requirements of the statistical analyses, the sample is likely not representative of the entire SME landscape. Further data collection could enable sector-specific studies, for example, or focus on relating the results to sociodemographic variables, such as departmental affiliation, age, or executive responsibility. Since it can be expected that the DT will progress, a longitudinal study could examine how the degrees of the barriers change over time. The study results and the discussion conclusions also revealed that the questionnaire does not cover all possible barriers. Further qualitative research can contribute to closing the research gap.

References

1. Schwab, K.: The Fourth Industrial Revolution. Crown Business, New York (2017)
2. Mithas, S., Tafti, A., Mitchell, W.: How a firm's competitive environment and digital strategy posture influence digital business strategy. Manag. Inf. Syst. Q. **37**, 511–536 (2013)
3. Dery, K., Sebastian, I.M., van der Meulen, N.: The digital workplace is key to digital innovation. MIS Q. Exec. **16**, 135–152 (2017)
4. Nguyen, D.K., Broekhuizen, T., Dong, J.Q., Verhoef, P.C.: Digital readiness: construct development and empirical validation. In: ICIS 2019 Proceedings (2019)
5. Vial, G.: Understanding digital transformation: a review and a research agenda. J. Strateg. Inf. Syst. **28**, 118–144 (2019). https://doi.org/10.1016/j.jsis.2019.01.003
6. Vogelsang, K., Liere-Netheler, K., Packmohr, S., Hoppe, U.: Barriers to digital transformation in manufacturing: development of a research agenda. In: Proceedings of the 52nd Hawaii International Conference on System Sciences, pp. 4937–4946 (2019)
7. Pabst von Ohain, B.: Leader attributes for successful digital transformation. In: ICIS 2019 Proceedings (2019)
8. OECD: Enhancing the Contributions of SMEs in a Global and Digitalised Economy. OECD Paris, Paris (2017)
9. Johannesson, P., Sinha, J., Packmohr, S., Brink, H.: Comparing barriers to digital transformation between small and medium-sized and large enterprises. Presented at the 21st IADIS International Conference e-Society, Lisbon, Portugal (2023)
10. Marcon, É., Marcon, A., Le Dain, M.-A., Ayala, N.F., Frank, A.G., Matthieu, J.: Barriers for the digitalization of servitization. Procedia CIRP **83**, 254–259 (2019). https://doi.org/10.1016/j.procir.2019.03.129
11. Streim, A., Meinecke, C.: Deutsche Unternehmen geben sich eine Drei im Fach "Digitales" (2020). https://www.bitkom.org/Presse/Presseinformation/Deutsche-Unternehmen-geben-sich-eine-Drei-im-Fach-Digitales
12. Commission, E.: User Guide to the SME Definition. Publications Office of the EU, Luxembourg (2015)
13. Varwig, T., Brink, H., Packmohr, S.: A systematic literature review on barriers to digital transformation: insights and implications for overcoming. Presented at the 37th EBES Conference, Berlin (2021)
14. Schmid, A.M., Recker, J., vom Brocke, J.: The socio-technical dimension of inertia in digital transformations. Presented at the Hawaii International Conference on System Sciences (2017). https://doi.org/10.24251/HICSS.2017.583
15. Hirsch-Kreinsen, H.: Digitization of industrial work: development paths and prospects. J. Labour Mark. Res. **49**, 1–14 (2016)
16. Leonardi, P.M.: Materiality, sociomateriality, and socio-technical systems: what do these terms mean? How are they related? Do we need them? In: Materiality and Organizing: Social Interaction in a Technological World, p. 384. OUP Oxford (2012)

17. Reis, J., Amorim, M., Melão, N., Matos, P.: Digital transformation: a literature review and guidelines for future research. In: Rocha, Á., Adeli, H., Reis, L.P., Costanzo, S. (eds.) World-CIST 2018. AISC, vol. 745, pp. 411–421. Springer, Cham (2018). https://doi.org/10.1007/978-3-319-77703-0_41
18. Hess, T., Matt, C., Benlian, A., Wiesböck, F.: Options for formulating a digital transformation strategy. MIS Q. Exec. **15**, 123–139 (2016)
19. Wessel, L., Baiyere, A., Ologeanu-Taddei, R., Cha, J., Blegind Jensen, T.: Unpacking the difference between digital transformation and IT-enabled organizational transformation. JAIS **22**, 102–129 (2021). https://doi.org/10.17705/1jais.00655
20. Bharadwaj, A., El Sawy, O., Pavlou, P., Venkatraman, N.: Digital business strategy: toward a next generation of insights. Manag. Inf. Syst. Q. **37**, 471–482 (2013)
21. The Oxford Dictionary: Meaning of barrier in English (2021). https://www.lexico.com/definition/barrier
22. Hanelt, A., Piccinini, E., Gregory, R.W., Hildebrandt, B., Kolbe, L.M.: Digital transformation of primarily physical industries-exploring the impact of digital trends on business models of automobile manufacturers. In: Wirtschaftsinformatik, pp. 1313–1327 (2015)
23. Klötzer, C., Pflaum, A.: Toward the development of a maturity model for digitalization within the manufacturing industry's supply chain. In: Proceedings of the 50th Hawaii International Conference on System Sciences, pp. 4210–4219 (2017). https://doi.org/10.24251/HICSS.2017.509
24. Hadjimanolis, A.: The barriers approach to innovation. In: Shavinina, L.V. (ed.) The International Handbook on Innovation, pp. 559–573. Pergamon, Oxford (2003). https://doi.org/10.1016/B978-008044198-6/50038-3
25. Spalinger, D., Grivas, S.G., de la Harpe, A.: TEA - A technology evaluation and adoption influence framework for small and medium sized enterprises. In: Abramowicz, W., Paschke, A. (eds.) BIS 2018. LNBIP, vol. 339, pp. 433–444. Springer, Cham (2019). https://doi.org/10.1007/978-3-030-04849-5_38
26. North, K., Varvakis, G. (eds.) Competitive Strategies for Small and Medium Enterprises. Springer, Cham (2016). https://doi.org/10.1007/978-3-319-27303-7
27. Piatier, A.: Barriers to innovation. F. Pinter, London, Dover, N.H (1984)
28. Horváth, D., Szabó, R.Z.: Driving forces and barriers of industry 4.0: do multinational and small and medium-sized companies have equal opportunities? Technol. Forecast. Soc. Change **146**, 119–132 (2019). https://doi.org/10.1016/j.techfore.2019.05.021
29. Amaral, A., Peças, P.: SMEs and industry 4.0: two case studies of digitalization for a smoother integration. Comput. Ind. **125**, 103333 (2021). https://doi.org/10.1016/j.compind.2020.103333
30. Orzes, G., Rauch, E., Bednar, S., Poklemba, R.: Industry 4.0 implementation barriers in small and medium sized enterprises: a focus group study. In: 2018 IEEE International Conference on Industrial Engineering and Engineering Management (IEEM), Bangkok, pp. 1348–1352. IEEE (2018). https://doi.org/10.1109/IEEM.2018.8607477
31. Peillon, S., Dubruc, N.: Barriers to digital servitization in French manufacturing SMEs. Procedia CIRP **83**, 146–150 (2019). https://doi.org/10.1016/j.procir.2019.04.008
32. Khanzode, A.G., Sarma, P.R.S., Mangla, S.K., Yuan, H.: Modeling the industry 4.0 adoption for sustainable production in micro, small & medium enterprises. J. Clean. Prod. **279**, 123489 (2021). https://doi.org/10.1016/j.jclepro.2020.123489
33. Stentoft, J., Rajkumar, C.: The relevance of industry 4.0 and its relationship with moving manufacturing out, back and staying at home. Int. J. Prod. Res. **58**, 2953–2973 (2020). https://doi.org/10.1080/00207543.2019.1660823
34. Türkeş, M., Oncioiu, I., Aslam, H., Marin-Pantelescu, A., Topor, D., Căpuşneanu, S.: Drivers and barriers in using industry 4.0: a perspective of SMEs in Romania. Processes **7**, 153 (2019). https://doi.org/10.3390/pr7030153

35. Bollweg, L., Lackes, R., Siepermann, M., Weber, P.: Drivers and barriers of the digitalization of local owner operated retail outlets. J. Small Bus. Entrep., 1–29 (2019). https://doi.org/10.1080/08276331.2019.1616256
36. Koshal, A., Natarajarathinam, M., Johnson, M.: Workforce training and industry 4.0 adoption in warehouses at SMEs. In: 2019 ASEE Annual Conference & Exposition Proceedings, p. 33669. ASEE Conferences, Tampa, Florida (2019). https://doi.org/10.18260/1-2--33669
37. Shevtsova, H., Shvets, N., Panychok, M., Sokolova, H.: Digitalization of small and medium-sized enterprises in Ukraine. In: 2020 61st International Scientific Conference on Information Technology and Management Science of Riga Technical University (ITMS), Riga, Latvia, pp. 1–5. IEEE (2020). https://doi.org/10.1109/ITMS51158.2020.9259313
38. Bilgeri, D., Wortmann, F.: Barriers to IoT business model innovation. In: Proceedings of the 13th International Conference on Wirtschaftsinformatik, pp. 987–990 (2017)
39. Chesbrough, H.: Business model innovation: opportunities and barriers. Long Range Plan. **43**, 354–363 (2010). https://doi.org/10.1016/j.lrp.2009.07.010
40. Dremel, C.: Barriers to the adoption of big data analytics in the automotive sector. In: Proceedings of the 23rd American Conference on Information Systems (AMCIS), Boston, pp. 1–10 (2017)
41. Henriette, E., Feki, M., Boughzala, I.: Digital transformation challenges. In: Mediterranean Conference on Information Systems (MICS), pp. 1–7 (2016)
42. Jones, M.D., Hutcheson, S., Camba, J.D.: Past, present, and future barriers to digital transformation in manufacturing: a review. J. Manuf. Syst. **60**, 936–948 (2021). https://doi.org/10.1016/j.jmsy.2021.03.006
43. Webster, J., Watson, R.T.: Analyzing the past to prepare for the future: writing a literature review. MIS Q. **26**, xiii–xxiii (2002)
44. Brink, H., Packmohr, S.: Identifying barriers to digital transformation and measuring their impact - a mixed-method study. In: PACIS 2022 Proceedings (2022)
45. Orth, M.: Industrial Germany: six strong numbers. www.deutschland.de/en/topic/business/germanys-industry-the-most-important-facts-and-figures. Accessed 25 Mar 2023
46. Etikan, I.: Comparison of convenience sampling and purposive sampling. AJTAS **5**, 1 (2016). https://doi.org/10.11648/j.ajtas.20160501.11
47. Stern, M.J., Bilgen, I., McClain, C., Hunscher, B.: Effective sampling from social media sites and search engines for web surveys: demographic and data quality differences in surveys of Google and Facebook users. Soc. Sci. Comput. Rev. **35**, 713–732 (2017). https://doi.org/10.1177/0894439316683344
48. George, D., Mallery, P.: SPSS for Windows Step by Step: A Simple Guide and Reference. 11.0 update, 2003. Allyn & Bacon, Boston (2016)
49. Tavakol, M., Dennick, R.: Making sense of Cronbach's alpha. Int. J. Med. Educ. **2**, 53–55 (2011). https://doi.org/10.5116/ijme.4dfb.8dfd
50. Ratner, B.: The correlation coefficient: its values range between +1/−1, or do they? J. Target Meas. Anal. Mark. **17**, 139–142 (2009). https://doi.org/10.1057/jt.2009.5
51. Cohen, J.: Statistical Power Analysis for the Behavioral Sciences. Routledge, New York (1988). https://doi.org/10.4324/9780203771587
52. Karim, S., Al-Tawara, A., Gide, E., Sandu, R.: Is big data too big for SMEs in Jordan? In: 2017 8th International Conference on Information Technology (ICIT), Amman, Jordan, pp. 914–922. IEEE (2017). https://doi.org/10.1109/ICITECH.2017.8079968
53. Rauch, E., Dallasega, P., Unterhofer, M.: Requirements and barriers for introducing smart manufacturing in small and medium-sized enterprises. IEEE Eng. Manag. Rev. **47**, 87–94 (2019). https://doi.org/10.1109/EMR.2019.2931564
54. Westerman, G., Tannou, M., Bonnet, D., Ferraris, P., McAfee, A.: The digital advantage: how digital leaders outperform their peers in every industry. MITSloan Management and Capgemini Consulting, MA, vol. 2, pp. 2–23 (2012)

55. Vidas-Bubanja, M., Bogetić, S., Bubanja, I.: International standards: an important component of a successful digital transformation of the national economy. JEMC **9**, 72–81 (2019). https://doi.org/10.5937/JEMC1901072V

56. Pappas, I.O., Mikalef, P., Giannakos, M.N., Krogstie, J., Lekakos, G.: Big data and business analytics ecosystems: paving the way towards digital transformation and sustainable societies. Inf. Syst. E-Bus. Manag. **16**, 479–491 (2018). https://doi.org/10.1007/s10257-018-0377-z

57. Stentoft, J., Jensen, K.W., Philipsen, K., Haug, A.: Drivers and barriers for industry 4.0 readiness and practice: a SME perspective with empirical evidence. Presented at the Hawaii International Conference on System Sciences (2019). https://doi.org/10.24251/HICSS.2019.619

Introduction of 3G Mobile Internet and Its Effect on Start-Up Formation: A Case of Palestine

Kirill Sarachuk$^{(\boxtimes)}$ (ID), Amer Baniodeh, and Magdalena Missler-Behr

Chair of Planing, Innovation and Business Administration, Brandenburg University of Technology Cottbus-Senftenberg, Erich-Weinert-Str. 1, 03046 Cottbus, Germany
kirill.sarachuk@b-tu.de
https://www.b-tu.de/fg-planung

Abstract. The ongoing digitalisation forces both induviduals and firms to keep up with modern technologies, invest in digital literacy and up-to-date skills. However, some regions suffer from poor Internet quality and remain digitally underdeveloped. A prominent example is Palestine which lacks digital freedom due to the restrictions posed by Israel authorities, but also faces a number of internal problems that hamper entrepreneurship. In our paper, we tried to find out whether the recent introduction of 3G mobile Internet in 2018 boosted the business activity in Palestine. Results of our survey of technologically driven start-up founders and experts working closely with them demonstrated that recent improvements in Internet quality are positively associated with the business development, though this effect is largely offset by poor legislative base and low investments in human capital in Palestine.

Keywords: internet · entrepreneurship · ICT · Palestine

1 Introduction

Few decades ago, the successful adoption of cutting-edge information and communication technologies (ICT) and their integration into existing business models were seen as competitive advantage. Nowadays entrepreneurs cannot stay out of modern technologies such as mobile and broadband internet connections, especially if they would like to cope with unexpected crises (like economic recessions or recent COVID-19 pandemic), achieve a greater market share or simply survive. Newer ICTs offer new opportunities and interesting business solutions, enhance the productivity [3,20] and innovation activity of firms [50], contribute to the technological improvements [23] etc. Not only businesses but also authorities understand the urgency of digitalisation as an important way to overcome the challenges and try to force the digital transformation process.

Supported by Graduate Research School of BTU Cottbus-Senftenberg.

R. Jallouli et al. (Eds.): ICDEc 2023, LNBIP 485, pp. 18–32, 2023.
https://doi.org/10.1007/978-3-031-42788-6_2

Rich scientific literature on effects of ICT, surprisingly, does not link too much provision of better digital technologies with start-up rates [38], mainly due to complexity of analysis or data limitations. Furthermore, existing studies focus mainly on Europe and United States while other areas remain rather unattended. For instance, there is a lack of scientific research on MENA region, which turned into an attractive market for many investors and entrepreneurs in recent years. An interesting case here is Palestine which, opposite to well-performing Saudi Arabia or UAE, faces multiple challenges from extremely high unemployment rates nearly 25% to the overall difficult economic situation [31]. The recent introduction of 3G mobile Internet there was perceived as a possible impulse to entrepreneurship as new businesses could focus not only on local market but rather on whole MENA region with a bundle of similarities between its countries.

To understand whether the recent digital transformations in Palestine could be positively associated with business activity, we surveyed founders of ICT and technologically driven start-ups and employees working in close cooperation with such firms. Albeit our results are based on a small number of completed surveys, we still were able to conclude that recent digital changes in West Bank encouraged more potential founders to start their own business in the area. We also identified several important challenges for setting up an own company in Palestine, as well as the way how firms adopt and use digital technologies.

The rest of the paper is organised as follows. Section 2 provides the literature background. Section 3 follows with an overview on the case of Palestine and introduces the hypotheses. Section 4 describes the methodology and data. In Sect. 5, we present and discuss the results of our survey and in concluding Sect. 6 we add some remarks and highlight the limitations to our study.

2   Literature Background

2.1   The Economic Impact of ICTs

General economic benefits of better ICTs were well studied in scientific literature, even for pioneer studies on dial-up and DSL era [18,19]. Scholars mention, though, several barriers in the adoption of digital technologies, such as lack of competence among managers [21], shortages in skills [36] and higher transition or education costs [27], so a positive effect of ICTs could be observed only in presence of high-skilled workforce, or so-called skill complementarity effects [4].

Besides a macro economical perspective, multiple studies argue about the positive impact of ICTs at the firm-level, for example in terms of better decision making in resource allocation [25], which however is highly dependent on organisational structure of firms [11]. Other findings link broadband and economic gains of firms with their innovative activity [50], development of infrastructure [23] or higher employment rates [24].

Yet we do not know much whether ICTs are beneficial for higher entry rates: there is no consensus on whether better digital infrastructure necessarily encourage potential entrepreneurs to set up their businesses. Some positive findings were observed for firms located in rural and remote areas [8,22], albeit other scholars counter-proved that such an effect is barely visible because of increased local competition [44]. Some scholars found positive externalities in case of adjacency to the core regions and/or metropolitan areas [13], although it does not guarantee benefits for potential entrepreneurs [39]; there is no such need for speed, as it might see at first glance [37].

2.2   Studies on ICTs in Palestine

Recent research on Palestine and its challenges focuses mostly on the human rights violations and the simmering political conflict in the area. Some scholars also recognize a positive relationship between economic growth and investments in digital infrastructure [2,40], but focus more on entire MENA region [10] rather than on specific cases.

Two reasons may explain this exclusion: first and main is the insufficient (or totally absent) data that is required to derive some valuable results; second is that many scholars tend to be biased because of the historical background of Palestine and its relations with Israel and, thus, misunderstand or misinterpret the outcomes. The latter is connected with an issue that Palestinian economy works under many restrictions and constraints imposed by the state of Israel, most visible is the limitation on freedom of movement for people and goods and control over land[1]. Still, ICTs may offer a unique opportunity to Palestinian entrepreneurs as a medium to grow globally, but due to the existing 'unfair competition' among the Israel telecommunication providers Palestinian cellular network companies are unable to cover the whole territory while Israel operators benefit from a full area coverage, as follows from the World Bank Report [35].

The role of ICTs in Palestine dates back to mid-1980s when few local entrepreneurs started to develop accounting and word processing software. Oslo Agreements (1995) and the creation of Palestinian National Authority (PNA) fostered the demand for digital solutions and hardware, both from the government and private sector, universities and non-profit organizations [45]. However, the contribution of ICT sector to the GDP in Palestine still remains low compared to neighboring countries, despite an increase from 0.1% in 1994 to 3.3% in 2018 [29].

3   The Palestinian Case: Background Information

Palestine underwent a long way since 2016 where it was ranked 170th out of 189 world economies in terms of ease of starting a business, while its actual ranking is closer to the middle [47]. Still, its economy remains underdeveloped and mainly because of the several restrictions and barriers that hinder the Palestinian ICT sector from developing and reaching its full potential.

---

[1] United Nations (UN) reports that Israel controls more than 60% of the Palestinian lands and most of the roads (and borders) between Palestinian areas so all the imports and exports pass Israel customs resulting in double taxation for Palestinians.

Previously we mentioned that Palestine lacks a full autonomy to develop own services and infrastructure as every improvements should be agreed upon Israel authorities. In ICT domain that suggests vast control measures over broadband access in Palestinian territories and imports of specific telecommunication equipment that hampers technological advancements. For instance, local cellular operators were not allowed to launch the high-speed internet 3G in the West Bank until 2018, waiting almost 10 years for a permission [35]. Furthermore, both Palestinian territories (West Bank and Gaza Strip) remain poorly interconnected as Israel heavily limited the number of fiber optics connections [7].

Next, the absence of an independent regulatory agency slows down the development of the ICT sector in Palestine. In 2009, the PNA approved a new telecommunication law manifesting the creation of an independent authority which has not been established so far, so all operational issues, licensing, and pricing remain under the control of the Ministry of Telecommunications and Information Technology (MTIT). The lack of regulations can create a negative impact on the long-term growth of the ICT sector in Palestine, as the environment remains uncertain for local and international investors [9].

Weak intellectual property rights (IPR) protection is another issue that scares off potential investors. In theory, Palestine acknowledges patents and copyright protection, but the existing norms rely on very old laws issued in the first half of 20th century. Local authorities have introduced several important legislative changes, but due to the political situation the enforcement is still absent [28]. Obviously that strong IPR protection helps in creating new businesses and supports innovation but also enhances competition and raises the quality and variety of products and services [6].

In addition, the population literacy rate in Palestine is assumed to be very high (99% for people aged 15–54, see [30]) and the educational system produces enough graduates, but generally less specialized due to a lack of internships and training programs at universities [28]. PITA in their report 2014 show that there is an obvious gap between university outputs and the ICT market needs in Palestine: while nearly seventy percent of ICT students expressed their dissatisfaction with the quality of their education system, the majority of ICT employers complain about poor technical and business skills of graduates.

The scientific literature is full of examples how ICT contribute to the entrepreneurship [5,42], increase employment. [41] and GDP growth per capita [46]. Still, while the global community is looking forward to 5G technology, Palestine just celebrated the introduction of 3G in January 2018. Still, even from that point local entrepreneurs could start benefiting from the newest opportunities. One year after 3G technology reached Palestine, the ICT adoption rate has increased remarkably: more than 72% of individuals above 18 years old have smartphones in Palestine and are active internet users [29]. This may be regarded as a turning point for Palestinian entrepreneurs and, as expected, it should foster more business ideas and initiatives and, respectively, higher tech start-up creation rates.

Hypothesis 1. Despite all challenges, ICTs made it easier for Palestinian entrepreneurs to start their own business.

Hypothesis 2. Mobile internet adoption has a positive effect on entrepreneurship, mainly in terms of firm-level productivity and business communication.

The Palestinian entrepreneurial milieu is growing steadily since 2009, but despite the good level of education among the Palestinian start-up founders (55% holding a bachelor's degree and nearly 20% a higher degree at the time of founding), their experiences and skills are perceived as insufficient and problematic for investors, according to the World Bank Report 2018. Higher levels of entrepreneurship in Palestine may be driven by a higher level of unemployment (25% nationwide as reported by PCBS, 2019), thus representing a so-called necessity entrepreneurship[2]. Cowling and Bygrave (2002) suggest that when unemployment rates are high, necessity entrepreneurship rates will be high as well. Similarly, Llisteri et al. (2006) found that high unemployment rates were a major factor for the Latin American entrepreneurship scene.

Hypothesis 3. The entrepreneurship scene in Palestine could be mainly categorized as *necessity entrepreneurship*.

The Palestinian market, however, is too small itself and has a limited space for new companies, their growth and sustainability. That may explain why local companies focus on international markets to sell their products and services. MENA region suits perfectly for expansion, primarily because of a similar cultural background and consumer behavior, but also due to a higher ICT penetration in society (1.2 mobile subscriptions per inhabitant, see a report by World Bank, 2019, and the number of users is expected to double until 2023 [14]. Still, MENA region also suffers from the same problems as Palestine: recent study of PwC 2019 on decision-makers from 200 private businesses across the Middle East clearly demonstrates that more than half of the ventures suffer a lack of in-house talents to achieve the full benefits of ICTs. Furthermore, most of them address these issues by collaborating with start-ups to increase the skills of their workforces. Those opportunities could be vital for some Palestinian tech start-ups and outsourcing companies.

4   Data Collection

The lack of research and reliable data on ICT and entrepreneurship in Palestine was among of the main motives behind this research. Regretfully, we could not

---

[2] Scientific literature distinguishes entrepreneurship based on the motive behind it when entrepreneurs create businesses because they saw opportunities (opportunity entrepreneurship). On the contrary, entrepreneurs may start their own businesses because they could not find other suitable alternative sources of income (necessity entrepreneurship).

find too much official data on firm dynamics as well as on broadband usage. As the result, we finally opted for a digital survey: first, due to the ongoing SARS-CoV-2 pandemic which made face-to-face communication completely unable; secondly, because of the accessibility issues in Palestine (that may explain why we refused phone interviews or something similar); third, an online data collection simplified the process.

The data was gathered was between March and May 2020. We distributed the surveys to 112 potential participants, including 63 founders of technologically driven start-up companies who have started a new business after 3G internet was launched, and 49 employees of business incubators, coworking spaces and non-profit organisations who work closely with start-ups and could provide several interesting insights. Totally, 53 surveys were completed - 33 from start-up founders and 20 from experts. Nearly 80% of all participants were under 35 years old that means a huge domination of a younger generation (in both groups). A vast majority of the start-ups in our sample are based in Ramallah City, the rest - in other cities like Jineen, Nablus, and Jerusalem. In fact, we failed to reach any participant in the Gaza Strip: the ICT infrastructure there remains almost completely dependent on Israel authorities [1], contrast to the West Bank regime with more digital freedom.

Our online survey was divided into two different parts. First part included only multiple-choice answers along with three 10-point Likert scale questions measuring the perception on internet quality and complexity of finding an own business. In this part, the respondents were asked to express their general opinion on the role of ICTs in Palestine, reasons for setting up an own firm and factors that affect productivity. The second part contained both multiple-choice and free-answer questions and was aimed at getting more details to the questions formulated in part one, for instance, how interviewees personally assess the role of Israel in ICT provision in Palestine and, consequently, economic development of the region. The first part was distributed to both respondent group, while the second part - to firm founders only.

5   Results and Discussion

5.1   General View on Challenges and Barriers for Start-Ups

We first refer to the questions that were distributed to all participants in our survey. First, we asked our respondents how they evaluate the five following aspects (see Fig. 1) that affect start-up in Palestine. Weak IPR protection system was named by nearly two-third of all respondents as poorly developed, given this aspect has a very high importance for Palestinian founders as they do not have too much manoeuvring options and fear of losing the first competitive advantage [6]. Almost every respondent claimed at least satisfactory skills of their employees (nearly 60% reported for good or very good skills) which somehow contradicts with the survey made by PITA 2014. Still, it is to mention that we included technologically driven start-ups for our survey which require more competent workforce and usually search for qualified graduates.

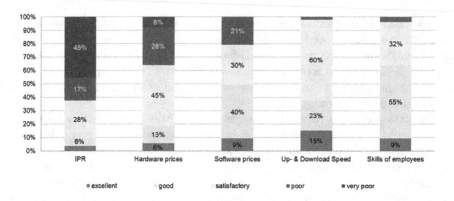

Fig. 1. Importance of particular aspects for potential founders (N = 53)

An interesting insight was the remarkable difference in perceived prices for software (seem to be good for nearly half of participants) and hardware which are perceived as a more expensive thing. The reason for that is that hardware increases in price while passing Israel customs with exceeding tariffs, while most software licenses could be purchased easier and at universal price, or even obtained freely. A further building block for many companies, namely quality of internet connection speed, is not perceived as poor, but rather satisfactory which still indicates that the need for speed is present in the area.

Next, we looked in more details which of those mentioned in existing scientific literature on Palestine challenges indeed seem to be the most important for entrepreneurs (Fig. 2). Responds clearly demonstrate that the respondents' answers support the existing paper trails, before all with respect to the lack of funding and regulations, as well as market imperfections. We also mentioned that outdated legislative norms in Palestine decrease the attractiveness for foreign investors. In addition, existing policies focus mainly on huge investors, thus neglecting those the entrepreneurs who would like to start businesses from scratch [43] and making imperfection, at least for technologically driven startups. Also given a set of restrictions with respect to the transportation of people and goods outside Palestine, local entrepreneurs have very limited possibilities to exchange knowledge and ideas globally. Finally, political instability poses huge risks not only for Palestinian entrepreneurs but also for foreign companies and individuals.

All the aforesaid may possibly explain why, in addition to mentioned problems, nearly 80% of respondents filed problems in financial transactions: some payment systems (like PayPal) are still unavailable or operate with severe restrictions, so businesses in Palestine carry excessive fees [12]. Along with that, more than $\frac{3}{4}$ of respondents see substantial challenges in unexperienced mentors as they generally have almost no practical experiences in a successful start-up ecosystem. The underdeveloped ICT infrastructure is also reported by more

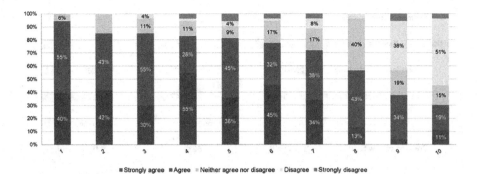

Fig. 2. Challenges for start-ups in Palestine (N = 53). Legend: 1 - Lack of funding, 2 - Lack of regulations, 3 - Market shortages, 4 - Political instabilities, 5 - Financial transactions, 6 - Unexperienced mentors, 7 - No freedom of movement, 8 - Poor ICT infrastructure, 9 - Expensive labour, 10 - Lack of skilled workers

than a half of founders as a problem from business milieu, while lack of skilled workers and cost of labour in Palestine seem to be of less importance.

We addressed one more question to evaluate the impact of 3G internet connection on business environment (Fig. 3). Both founders and employees agreed on that the introduction of 3G mobile internet had a severe impact both on firm-level productivity and communication between companies, but also was a prerequisite for new business models, E-commerce and, hence, creation of new start-ups. Additionally, we received some verbal feedback from founders expressing the latter notion in a clearer way:

> *Internet is a core customer channel tool ≪ ⋯ ≫ important for easier connectivity, better targeting for businesses when it comes to advertising. We were able to provide more services. ≪ ⋯ ≫ 3G enabled ≪ ⋯ ≫ multiple interactions with consumers immediately ≪ ⋯ ≫, as well as capability to expand the scope of work & enhance systematic working procedures.*
>
> *The business community became more connected. ≪ ⋯ ≫ More opportunities for e-commerce businesses to rise because of more people having access to the internet all the time.*

Most respondents believe that ICT made it more transparent, easier, and simpler for entrepreneurs to start their own business in Palestine and mentioned the appearance of many novel business ideas, while just nearly twelve percent doubt about it. However, almost all those surveyed believe that newer ICT will have a significant and positive impact on the economic development in Palestine in the future, albeit existing internal and external challenges, including political instability, lack of competition, and corruption still have a negative impact on the ICT sector itself.

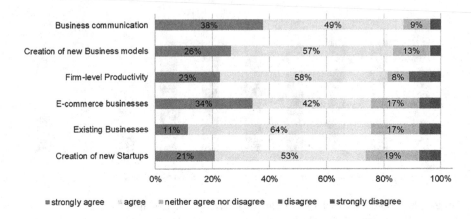

Fig. 3. Effects of 3G mobile internet on business environment (N = 53)

5.2 Entrepreneurial Milieu in Palestine: The View of Start-Up Founders

A next portion of questions was distributed to start-up founders only; prior to all, we tried to investigate the motives behind business creation. Cowling and Bygrave (2002) suggested that a high unemployment rate, as in case of Palestine, may serve as an indicator of necessity entrepreneurship. However, while just one founder confessed that he was unemployed and because of that he decided to start an own business, almost all others mentioned unique opportunities or their wish to create a solution to solve the problem they experienced before:

> *With the emergence of 3G internet, I thought it was a great opportunity to start a business. In particular, some services were not present in Palestine ≪ ··· ≫ and I personally experienced a problem that needed a solution.*
> *Some of my colleagues I used to work with were not satisfied with their jobs and started to look for opportunities to start their own businesses. I decided to try my hand at entrepreneurship too ≪ ··· ≫ as Palestine needs modern IT solutions.*
> *I had lost my job not long before ≪ ··· ≫ and had no choice but to try to start my own firm.*

Two interesting outcomes may be derived from the aforesaid: first, most technological start-ups in Palestine are opportunity- rather than necessity-driven; second, most entrepreneurs tend to create firms to solve problems and deliver better and faster products and (or) services. As far as opportunity entrepreneurship correlates more with growth-oriented businesses [17], that may be foreseen as a positive sign for entrepreneurial milieu in Palestine. Still, as we focused on ICT-based start-ups, that does not necessary apply, for instance, to low-tech companies as well, where the outcome may be totally different[3]. More than half

---

[3] We asked additionally both experts and founders how they evaluate the complexity of setting up an own company. Less than 20% of respondents evaluate the efforts

of founders also reported three major environmental challenges for start-ups in Palestine: cost restraints, resistance to change and lack of relevant know-how. Surprisingly, only a small proportion mentioned such issues as technological risks or corruption, probably due to the fact that it has already become the accepted norm in society and is not perceived as a serious problem.

Then, we asked our surveyed start-up founders to estimate whether the MENA market could be a suitable area for expansion. Most of respondents mentioned language, cultural and consumer behavior similarities that serve as deciding factors for tech-oriented companies while choosing MENA region as a place for expansion (Fig. 4). Furthermore, nearly 70% of Palestinian entrepreneurs believe that in some countries of MENA region consumers have a higher willingness to pay which also plays well when consumers in the area share further similar behavior so companies can better understand the needs).

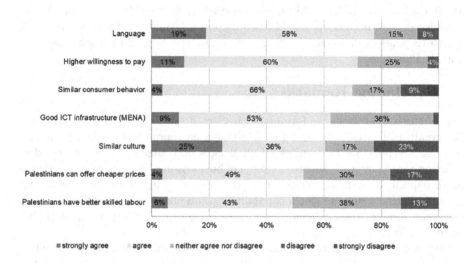

Fig. 4. What makes MENA region a good market for Palestinian Startups? (N = 33)

Regarding the ICT, few surveyees believe that the MENA region's ICT infrastructure is in unsatisfactory condition for Palestinian start-ups. That corresponds with the report of PwC (2020) stating that the area has very good ICT infrastructure and the citizens are early technology adopters and consumers. However, most start-up founders (60%) mentioned some relevant barriers in ICT adoption, mainly resistance to change and cost restraints, as employees and stakeholders may try to resist the transformation, so resilient organizations need to be able to overcome it with minimal costs to adapt to the new environments and circumstances [16]. With respect to the costs of ICT adoption, the negative

---

as 'easy' while almost a half mentions that firm creation is a very complex process compared to the neighbouring countries.

role of Israel authorities was mentioned by nearly half of respondents. In addition, the existing barriers hamper the development of skills (mentioned by 45% of founders) and cause gaps in relevant know-how because employees' competences remain outdated. Still, many projects are aimed at improving the ICT skills and the relevant know-how exist in Palestine, for instance, PITA's efforts to close the gap between the universities output and the ICT sector demand by doing workshops and training programs with ICT students.

Finally, we also asked about the usage of digital technologies for businesses. In most companies it is generally limited to the basic tools as Google or Microsoft cloud services (75%) and online advertisement tools (nearly half of surveyed people); complex tools and programming languages are used much less. However, internet is used more frequently to reach the customers: via social media (90%), e-mails (75%) or online ads (67%) rather than with the help of traditional ways like phone calls (48%), newspapers and magazines (18%) or radio and TV (12%), albeit the word of mouth (76%), like everywhere in the MENA region, is still considered as an important way of reaching potential clients. However, just every fourth respondent claimed that their website or app is used to reach customers outside Palestine.

6 Concluding Remarks

Out of three hypothesis we formulated in Sect. 3, we were able to confirm two. Before all, ICTs made it easier for Palestinian entrepreneurs to start their own business (Hypothesis 1) despite all challenges and difficulties. Many founders insist on that they were able to create new business models even without having much capital, as well as received the possibility to target customers and consumers in other countries. Such capabilities could enable other entrepreneurs to overcome some of the challenges and make it possible for new business models to survive in such environments.

Moreover, even Palestine was one of the last countries celebrating the introduction of mobile 3G internet, it was a turning point for potential firm founders (Hypothesis 2) and helped local firms to have a better reach and more accurate targeting, but also dropped the communication costs. That stays in line with existing research [6,41] and, as expected, when more advanced technologies like 4G and subsequent 5G finally reach the country, the overall impact on entrepreneurship may be even more pronounced. However, just better digital infrastructure is not enough, and we believe that local authorities should target the challenges and barriers to ICT adoption first, as well as make more efforts towards digital transformation in schools, universities, and governmental organisations. In addition, currently not too much ICT and technologically driven firms try to reach customers outside Palestine (at least in MENA region with similar cultural background), so we may expect that local authorities have to encourage founders to focus at least on compatible markets which seems to be a more strategic solution, especially in the earlier expansion stages.

We failed, however, to find any proof to the hypothesis that entrepreneurship in Palestine is mostly necessity-driven, given a high unemployment rate, which somehow contradicts the existing studies [26]. Moreover, most of the surveyed founders said that their main motive was a unique opportunity they saw before starting an own business. That could be explained twofold: the first reason is a large influence of Israel that hampers business communication and limits funding options; secondly, our survey focused on ICT- and technologically based start-ups where a firm creation is more complex, and the entry barriers are high. Along with that, our results represent mostly the city of Ramallah and the West Bank which have a lower unemployment rate compared to other cities and territories in Palestine (as Gaza strip).

In our paper we did not focus on the role of Israel in influencing entrepreneurship and broadband provision in Palestine much. Although this question was also included in our survey, we mentioned that many scholars tend to remain biased because of the complex political and historical background between Palestine and Israel, so we decided to leave this question outside of this study. Still, nearly a third of respondents filed the excessive control of Israel authorities and their indirect responsibility for the lack of available funding in Palestine, unattractiveness of Palestinian market for foreign investors, which could be an interesting topic for future researchers:

> *Israel ≪ ··· ≫ has a massive negative effect on economic development in Palestine. They control borders and the flow of raw materials for various industries. That is why many investors ≪ ··· ≫ decline from investing in Palestine.*
>
> *≪ ··· ≫ funding is scarce ≪ ··· ≫ and expansion is narrow as well, not to mention other geopolitical and economic factors ≪ ··· ≫ that definitely increase the already existing slim chances of success.*
>
> *A negative influence is tied to the growing Palestinian ICT outsourcing business towards Israel. Outsourcing ≪ ··· ≫ rather kills the talent with small and fragmented tasks.*

Some limitations apply to our research as well. Firstly, the sample size was relatively small to draw plausible conclusions. However, we must confess we reached only those technologically driven firms whose credentials were found in public domain (there is no centralised information about the firm dynamics), and their number was very modest. Secondly, our sample represents the West Bank start-ups and not the Gaza strip, which could create a gap of perceptions because both the political and the economic situation in Gaza is very different from the West Bank. Moreover, most of the participants were from Ramallah, a capital city with high concentration of businesses and government offices, while entrepreneurs in different locations face different kinds of challenges and perceive things differently. In addition, the time frame of the study could be a limitation as well, as we conducted our research during the SARS-CoV-2 pandemic. Finally, the lack of studies on entrepreneurial issues in Palestine and raw data made it harder to get more objective pieces of evidence. Nevertheless, we believe that our paper could be the basis for further research, probably with much more reliable data sources.

References

1. AbuShanab, A.: Connection interrupted: Israel's control of the Palestinian ICT infrastructure and its impact on digital rights. In: The Arab Center for the Advancement of Social Media (2018)
2. Aghaei, M., Rezagholizadeh, M.: The impact of information and communication technology (ICT) on economic growth in the OIC countries. Econ. Environ. Stud. (E&ES) **17**(2), 257–278 (2017)
3. Airaksinen, A., et al.: Information Society: ICT impact assessment by linking data from different sources (2008)
4. Akerman, A., Gaarder, I., Mogstad, M.: The skill complementarity of broadband internet. Q. J. Econ. **130**(4), 1781–1824 (2015)
5. Alderete, M.V.: Mobile broadband: a key enabling technology for entrepreneurship? J. Small Bus. Manag. **55**(2), 254–269 (2017)
6. Alfarraj, A.: Intellectual Property Protection in Emerging Economies and Trade Related Intellectual Property Rights. Available at SSRN 2878138 (2016)
7. Arafeh, N., Bahour, S., Abdullah, W.: ICT: the shackled engine of Palestine's development. Al-Shabaka Policy Brief **9** (2015)
8. Atasoy, H.: The effects of broadband internet expansion on labor market outcomes. ILR Rev. **66**(2), 315–345 (2013)
9. Avasant. Palestinian ICT Market Penetration, Final Report. Report (2013)
10. Bahrini, R., Qaffas, A.A.: Impact of information and communication technology on economic growth: evidence from developing countries. Economies **7**(1), 21 (2019)
11. Bloom, N., Sadun, R., Van Reenen, J.: It ain't what you do, it's the way that you do IT.-testing explanations of productivity growth using US affiliates. Centre for Economic Performance, London School of Economics, pp. 167–201 (2005)
12. Butcher, M.: PayPal Brushes-off Request from Palestinian Tech Firms to Access the Platform. TechCrunch (Web Page, 9 September 2016) (2019)
13. Capasso, M., Cefis, E., Frenken, K.: Spatial differentiation in industrial dynamics. The case of the Netherlands (1994–2005). Tijdschrift voor economische en sociale geografie **107**(3), 316–330 (2016)
14. Cisco. Cisco annual internet report (2018–2023): White paper (2020)
15. Cowling, M., Bygrave, W.D.: Entrepreneurship and unemployment: relationships between unemployment and entrepreneurship in 37 nations participating in the Global Entrepreneurship Monitor (GEM) 2002. In: Babson College, Babson Kauffman Entrepreneurship Research Conference (BKERC) (2002)
16. Dayton, B.W.: Managing crises in the twenty-first century. Int. Stud. Rev. **6**(1), 165 (2004)
17. Fairlie, R.W., Fossen, F.M. Opportunity versus necessity entrepreneurship: two components of business creation (2018)
18. Greenstein, S.M., Spiller, P.T.: Modern telecommunications infrastructure and economic activity: an empirical investigation. Ind. Corp. Change **4**(4), 647–665 (1995)
19. Grimes, A., Ren, C., Stevens, P.: The need for speed: impacts of internet connectivity on firm productivity. J. Product. Anal. **37**(2), 187–201 (2012)
20. Haller, S.A., Lyons, S.: Broadband adoption and firm productivity: evidence from Irish manufacturing firms. Telecommun. Policy **39**(1), 1–13 (2015)
21. Kezar, A., Eckel, P.: Examining the institutional transformation process: the importance of sensemaking, interrelated strategies, and balance. Res. High. Educ. **43**(3), 295–328 (2002)
22. Kolko, J.: Broadband and local growth. J. Urban Econ. **71**(1), 100–113 (2012)

23. Koutroumpis, P.: The economic impact of broadband on growth: a simultaneous approach. Telecommun. Policy **33**(9), 471–485 (2009)
24. Lehr, W.H., et al.: Measuring broadband's economic impact (2006)
25. Linton, I.: The Benefits of Using ICTs in Business & Finance (2018)
26. Llisterri, J.J., et al.: Is youth entrepreneurship a necessity or an opportunity. Inter.-American Development Bank, Washington DC (2006)
27. Muehlemann, S., Leiser, M.S.: Hiring costs and labor market tightness. Labour Econ. **52**, 122–131 (2018)
28. Paltrade. Information and Communication Technology (ICT) Services: The State of Palestine National Export Strategy. Report (2014)
29. PCBS. Household Survey on Information and Communications Technology, 2019: Main Findings. Report (2020)
30. PCBS. Literacy Rate of Persons (15 Years and Over) in the West Bank. Report (2019)
31. PCBS. The Labour Force Survey Results Third Quarter Round. Report (2019)
32. PITA. Comparative Study: The Palestinian Education System vs. The Needs of the Private ICT Sector. Report (2014)
33. PwC. Convenience is key: insights from the Middle East consumer. Report (2020)
34. PwC. Middle East Private Business Survey 2019. Report (2019)
35. Rossotto, C.M., Lewin, A., Decoster, X.: The telecommunication sector in the Palestinian territories: a missed opportunity for economic development (2016)
36. Saleh, A.S., Burgess, L.: Factors impacting the adoption and use of ICT in the Malaysian SME sector. In: 11th International Business Research Conference: Sydney, Australia, pp. 1–24 (2009)
37. Sarachuk, K., Mißler-Behr, M.: Broadband development and firm creation: Dif-in-dif estimates for Germany. Creat. Innov. Entrep. **31**, 250–258 (2022)
38. Sarachuk, K., Mißler-Behr, M.: ICT, economic effects and business patterns: a text-mining of existing literature. In: Proceedings of the 2020 the 3rd International Conference on Computers in Management and Business, pp. 40–45 (2020)
39. Sarachuk, K., Missler-Behr, M., Hellebrand, A.: Ultra high speed broadband internet and firm creation in Germany. In: Rodionov, D., Kudryavtseva, T., Skhvediani, A., Berawi, M.A. (eds.) SPBPU IDE 2020. CCIS, vol. 1445, pp. 40–56. Springer, Cham (2021). https://doi.org/10.1007/978-3-030-84845-3_3
40. Sassi, S., Goaied, M.: Financial development, ICT diffusion and economic growth: lessons from MENA region. Telecommun. Policy **37**(4–5), 252–261 (2013)
41. Shapiro, R.J., Hassett, K.A.: The Employment Effects of Advances in Internet and Wireless Technology: Evaluating the Transitions from 2G to 3G and from 3G to 4G (2012)
42. Tiarawut, S.: Mobile technology: opportunity for entrepreneurship. Wirel. Pers. Commun. **69**(3), 1025–1031 (2013)
43. Touqan, T.: Hard Time for Start-Ups: The Legal and Regulatory Environment for Entrepreneurs in Palestine (2016)
44. Whitacre, B., Gallardo, R., Strover, S.: Broadband's contribution to economic growth in rural areas: moving towards a causal relationship. Telecommun. Policy **38**(11), 1011–1023 (2014)
45. Wihaidi, R.: The Palestinian ICT sector: a three-year outlook based on economic indicators. In: PITA: The Palestine Information and Communications of Companies. Retrieved August 17 (2009) (2014)
46. Williams, C., et al.: The economic impact of next-generation mobile services: how 3G connections and the use of mobile data impact GDP growth, pp. 77–80 (2013)

47. World Bank. Doing Business 2020. Report (2020)
48. World Bank. Tech startup ecosystem in West Bank and Gaza: findings and recommendations. Report (2018)
49. World Bank. World Development Report 2019: The Changing Nature of Work. Report (2019)
50. Xu, X., Watts, A., Reed, M.: Does access to internet promote innovation? A look at the US broadband industry. Growth Change **50**(4), 1423–1440 (2019)

Unpacking Differences in Perceptions of Barriers to Digital Transformation – A Socio-Demographic Analysis

Sven Packmohr[1] ⓘ, Fynn-Hendrik Paul[2] ⓘ, and Henning Brink[2](✉) ⓘ

[1] DVMT, Malmö University, 20506 Malmö, Sweden
sven.packmohr@mau.se
[2] BOW, Osnabrück University, 49074 Osnabrück, Germany
{fynn-hendrik.paul,henning.brink}@uos.de

Abstract. Digital Transformation (DT) is gaining attention in all industries. It also impacted non-profit sectors and higher education. DT evolves when connectivity technologies merge with physical assets, possibly altering value creation processes. These alterations aim to positively impact effectiveness, business models, and customer connection. However, companies face several barriers on their DT journey. It is essential to grasp the properties of these barriers to enable companies to find ways to overcome them. Therefore, we examined existing research on barriers and identified the gap. Using data from interviews and online surveys, our study unpacks the differences in the perception of barriers regarding the categories of company size, responsibility level, and employee age. To generate our results, we used a qualitative content analysis to generate frequencies of 29 barrier characteristics in seven dimensions from 1,436 statements by 525 survey participants. The most prominent barrier dimensions across all categories are Corporate Culture and Structural Mismatch. Together, they account for 35–50% of the total barrier perceptions. Moreover, the barrier characteristic deficient IT infrastructure scores somewhat similarly in all categories, with around 11% on average. Our research contributes to identifying similarities in the different categories and paves the way for higher generalizability.

Keywords: Digital Transformation · Barriers · Company Size · Responsibility Level · Employee Age

1 Introduction

The progress in digitalization and the correlation between digitalization and value creation have driven digital transformation (DT). The interplay between information and communication technologies through DT has altered business processes and workflows. Thus, this transformation was described as a trend that introduced significant alterations in "traditional ways of doing business by redefining processes and relationships"

[1]. Based on this approach, DT encompasses technological and software products that allow for advances in strategy and business models, processes, and customer contact. DT intersects with the discipline of Information Systems (IS) [2].

Through a combination of smart products and services, DT allows for enhanced servitization [3]. The development of digital platforms and facilities to capture real-time data leads to optimizing processes and opens-up new business models [4]. Accordingly, corporate DT expectations are high due to opportunities in efficiency, productivity, competition, and customer relations [5]. DT alters workplace settings, leading to improvements in employee functions and competencies [3]. Thus, DT is the base for competitive advantages. It accelerates the growth of digital pioneers, creating more value and profit for stakeholders [6].

However, the realization of these expectations is not easy. Corporations experience hindrances in grasping the potential of DT [7]. In practice, the adoption, diffusion, and development of re-engineered and digitalized processes encounter several barriers [8]. Thus, corporations could underestimate the efforts necessary to drive digital innovations [9]. When corporations do not recognize and handle these barriers, they will fail to accomplish their DT potential [10].

Studies that report the factors of failure are less common than those reporting success factors [9]. Thus, we aimed to address this gap in the literature by focusing on the factors of failure that could decelerate, halt, or change the DT process. We considered these failures as *barriers* [11]. The nature of these barriers, their causations, and related stakeholders should be recognized to identify the countermeasures required to reduce the undesirable effects. Currently, only a few of the digital readiness and maturity models provide advice to overcome these barriers [12]. At the same time, there is a lack of knowledge of the effects of the advised countermeasures. Hereto, our work is one step toward a more structured approach. First, we need a sociodemographic perspective on the perception of barriers to develop stakeholder-specific countermeasures in the next step. For this contribution, we posed the following research question: How differently do socio-demographic criteria describe the existence of barriers to digital transformation in corporations?

In this current study, we look at how barriers are perceived according to company size, level of responsibility linked with the job role, and the individuals' ages. Our work contributes to a wider discussion of differences in barriers in the IS community. This study evaluates barriers with a structured approach. Thus, it lays the groundwork for future hypothetical models of influence between the analyzed characteristics. The present study findings could be used by industrial corporations to plot DT barriers and to plan effective countermeasures to ensure successful DT based on corresponding socio-demographic characteristics. Moreover, our results would further advance readiness and maturity models. With our results, these models can be better adapted to different types of companies and job roles.

We adopted the following procedures to answer the research problem: The next section briefly presents related work. The qualitative data collection and research design, including the coding procedure, are described in the third section. The fourth section takes up the associations between barriers and participants' characteristics. The paper ends with the discussion and conclusion sections, including the study's limitations.

2   Related Work

The interest in DT research and practice has enlarged in recent years. Comprehensive definitions frame DT as "a process that aims to improve an entity by triggering significant changes to its properties" [10] using combinations of different technologies. Other definitions focus on improved offers through digital services and products while simultaneously enhancing the customers' experience based on digitizing processes [13]. Specifically, these improvements were linked to value creation, organizational structure, and distribution of finances [7]. Orchestrating all these improvements leads to high complexity in DT and, thus, to difficulties in managing its requirements [14]. There are differences between DT and IT-enabled organizational transformation (ITOT). For instance, DT defines new value propositions, whereas ITOT backs current propositions [15]. On the other hand, ITOT is similar to DT in employing digital resources to obtain a different value creation [16]. As new definitions of value propositions become complex, the number of barriers increases more in DT than in ITOT. Often, barriers originate in leadership or environmental factors [9]. Since DT is inevitable, managers should overcome the barriers to DT. They can reduce these barriers by recognizing the methods to better integrate physical and digital elements. Further, since barriers to DT are complex, managers should embrace a holistic DT tactic.

To examine previous study results on barriers to DT, we conducted a systematic literature review [17]. The review was directed by a search string that included the keywords "digital transformation" and "barriers" and their synonyms on Scopus, EBSCO, and AIS Electronic Library services. The search revealed 562 papers (excluding duplicates). After the first screening for relevance and availability of full-text, 148 articles were identified. After several in-depth qualitative controls, finally, 99 appropriate studies were determined [18]. The number of studies indicates the significance of the field.

The majority of the literature listed barriers to a specific technology [19]. Certain studies adopted interpretative approaches and grouped barriers based on internal and external perceptions [20], whereas others adopted temporal approaches based on short-term orientation and strategies [21] or different sizes of enterprises [22]. Further studies were based on more structured approaches that employed interpretive structural analysis to model inter-barrier dependencies [23–25]. A few studies even presented recommendations for overcoming these barriers. These recommendations were in the form of solutions or actions to overcome a particular barrier [26]. However, these studies did not focus on multifaceted interdependencies between barriers and recommendations. Examples included educational facilities to improve employee know-how [27] or external technical expert requirements of IoT implementation with systemic complexities [28], which lacked the investigation of complex causalities.

Earlier studies that aimed to identify barriers adopted research approaches that focused on technology-enhanced business models, better customer contact, or operational organization [29]. Often, these studies possess limited generalizability. Therefore, we did not focus on specific technologies. Instead, this study aimed to explore differences between characteristics. Being able to compare these characteristics across socio-demographic categories allows for distinguishing between specific and general implications. Thus, our holistic analysis might lead to increased generalizability [30].

3   Method

To solve the research problem, we collected data through interviews and online surveys. Thereafter, a barrier model was developed using triangulation [31] in the first stage, and an analysis of the frequencies of mentions by survey participants was performed in the second stage.

In the first stage, a triangulation approach was adopted to cultivate a DT barrier model based on comprehensive data [32] that included a cross-section of two data series [33]. The first data series was acquired through interviews with specialists involved in or responsible for DT initiatives in their companies. We conducted 46 semi-structured interviews between March 2017 and October 2018 using common interview guidelines. The participants were recruited through calls to personal and professional acquaintances via social network platforms. We asked the participants about the DT barriers they perceived in their companies; they were asked to introduce their companies, the current status of DT, and potential barriers. We obtained a diversified sample that would allow the most comprehension [32] by interviewing participants in diverse industries and positions. The interviewees were employed in the DACH region (Germany, Austria, and Switzerland).

We transcribed the interviews and investigated the transcripts with an inductive coding approach [34]. The codes associated with the barriers were iteratively aggregated and revised. Throughout the coding, a socio-technical perspective was adopted to capture a broad range of aspects with the aim of a holistic analysis [30]. These procedures led to an initial DT barrier model. Table 1 revises the five dimensions and their characteristics [31].

Table 1. Initial barrier model.

Dimensions	Characteristics
Missing skills	IT knowledge, information about and decision on technologies, process knowledge
Technical barriers	dependency on other technologies, security (data exchange), current infrastructure
Individual barriers	fear of data control loss, fear of transparency/acceptance, fear of job loss
Organizational & cultural barriers	keeping traditional roles/principles, no clear vision/strategy, resistance to cultural change/mistake culture, risk aversion, lack of financial resources, lack of time
Environmental barriers	lack of standards, lack of laws

Next, we triangulated the initial model to confirm and improve it. We collected further qualitative data using an anonymous online survey to achieve this. We recruited 340 participants with the same method employed to determine the interviewees. Although non-random sampling is a valid procedure for investigating a domain, it could lead to bias [35]. Thus, further participants from four companies, who responded to social network calls, were also included. The random sampling approach was adopted in this data collection phase. Therefore, a further 185 participants voluntarily finished the same survey.

Table 2. Questionnaire sample.

Criteria	Attribute [Relative share of participants]
Sector	Automotive [18%] l Construction [13%] l Finance & Insurance [14%] l Food [7%] l Information and communications technology [3%] l Mechanical & plant engineering [9%] l Wholesale [16%] l Other [20%]
Position	Manager [6%] l With personnel responsibility [26%] l Without personnel responsibility [59%] l Other [9%]
Employees	>= 1,000 [35%] l 250–999 [17%] l 0–249 [45%] l Not stated [3%]
Age	<31 [33%] l 31–40 [20%] l 41–50 [19%] l >50 [17%] l not specified [11%]

Thus, 525 completed surveys were collected with both random and non-random sampling methods between December 2019 and April 2021. The majority of the participants (60%) lived in German-speaking nations. The sample included participants from European and non-European nations (e.g., Turkey and the US), leading to cross-national data. From Table 2, we can state the dominance of the automotive sector and SMEs. Also, most participants do not possess responsibility for staff. Most of them fall in the youngest age group of under 31.

The survey yielded 1,436 statements on barriers. The survey data were coded with the deductive approach based on the dimensions and properties determined in the initial model. Since not all 1,436 statements could fit the initial model, we adjusted and extended the model [36]. Individually, each author openly coded the 466 non-fitting statements. Then, we and invited colleagues discussed and aggregated the codes to determine adjusted dimensions and properties. Thus, we followed guidelines to ensure trustworthiness [37]. With our improved coding guidelines, all 1,436 statements were deductively re-coded with the improved coding guidelines. This approach led to a valid triangulated DT barriers model that included social and technical dimensions [8].

The model included 29 DT barriers divided into seven dimensions (cf. Table 3). The dimensions broadly cover barriers of missing skills, technology, organizational misalignment, corporate culture, structural mismatch, regulatory restrictions, and market restrictions [31].

In the second stage, we analyzed the frequencies of stated DT barriers according to socio-demographic categories: company size, level of responsibility linked to the job role, and the employees' ages using the coded data from the first stage. Company size is categorized into companies with less than 250 employees (small- and medium-sized enterprises, SMEs), with 250 to 999 employees (medium to large enterprises, MLEs), and with more than 999 employees (large enterprises, LEs). In terms of the level of responsibility, we distinguished between executives, employees with personnel responsibility (PR), and employees without PR. Regarding the employees' ages, we grouped them into younger than 31, between 31 and 40, between 41 to 50, and older than 50. Finally, we presented the relative proportions of the respective DT barriers per socio-demographic category in Table 3.

4   Results

Table 3 shows the results of our study. Horizontally, we distinguish between the different analysis categories company size, level of responsibility in a company, and employee age. We did not survey years of professional experience but opted for general experience through age. Namely, since age includes study time, we considered it a good proxy for general experience. Vertically, Table 3 shows the identified dimensions and characteristics, which break down the broad dimension into more specific aspects. Each cell in the table shows the relative occurrences of a certain characteristic in the statements of a specific class of company size, responsibility, and employee age.

Regarding the barrier dimensions in general, Corporate Culture and Structural Mismatch dominate with high frequencies across the different categories. Especially within LEs, Corporate Culture is perceived as more of a barrier (27.41%) than in SMEs (21.73%) and MLEs (22.9%). Looking at the characteristics of Corporate Culture, sticking to the status quo greatly hinders enterprises. It accounts for more than half of the overall dimensional score. Regarding Structural Mismatch, SMEs and LMEs rank these barriers as slightly higher (24.17% and 24.66%, respectively) than LEs (22.59%). In particular, the characteristics lack of financial and personnel resources greatly impact the dimension Structural Mismatch. SMEs tend to have a slightly higher value regarding financial resources (9.88%) compared to MLEs (8.37%) and LEs (8.89%). Personal resources pose a higher problem for MLEs (10.13%) compared to SMEs (7.45%) and LEs (6.85%). Regarding individual characteristics within dimensions, insufficient training and learning is the major barrier to the Missing Skills dimension. Interestingly, here MLEs show the lowest value (6.61%) compared to SMEs (8.97%) and LEs (8.70%).

Within the Technical Barriers dimension, the characteristic deficient IT infrastructure ranks high among all enterprises (around 11%). SMEs experience more barriers in being restricted regarding regulations (2.58%). At the same time, they perceive market restrictions as a smaller problem (3.04%).

Within the level of responsibility category, Structural Mismatch and Corporate Culture are the dominating dimensions—with frequencies of 41.97% for Executives, 47.12% for employees with PR, and 48.89% for those without PR. Executives and employees with PR score around 22% on the dimension Corporate Culture. At the same time, employees without PR score higher, with 25.13%. Within the dimension Corporate Culture, sticking to the status quo is the major characteristic. Here as well, executives and employees with PR show rather similar results (12.35% and 12.92%, respectively). Again, those without PR score higher, with 14.08%. In the dimension Structural Mismatch, the characteristic lack of financial resources sticks out among the other characteristics. Lack of personal resources is a minor problem among executives (3.70%). Furthermore, regarding Technical Barriers such as deficient IT structure, executives show a lower frequency (9.87%) than the other two groups (11.24% and 10.92%).

On the other hand, executives perceive higher Missing Skills (17.27%). They are especially worried about insufficient training and learning (11.11%), compared to the

Table 3. Barriers to digital transformation in terms of company size, job role, and age.

Dimension	Characteristics	Company Size			Level of Responsibility			Age			
		<250	250–999	>999	Executives	PR	w/o PR	<31	31–40	41–50	>50
Missing Skills	Missing organizational knowledge	1.98%	3.53%	1.30%	1.23%	2.39%	1.91%	1.07%	1.71%	2.09%	4.82%
	Missing DT potential knowledge	2.43%	1.32%	1.48%	1.23%	1.67%	2.14%	2.57%	2.39%	2.09%	0.80%
	Missing implementation knowledge	1.52%	2.20%	1.11%	2.47%	0.48%	1.80%	2.14%	0.34%	1.39%	1.61%
	Missing user technology knowledge	2.43%	1.76%	3.15%	1.23%	2.39%	2.59%	1.28%	4.10%	3.83%	2.41%
	Insufficient training & learning	8.97%	6.61%	8.70%	11.11%	8.61%	8.11%	8.35%	9.22%	7.67%	8.03%
	Overall	**17.33%**	**15.42%**	**15.74%**	**17.27%**	**15.54%**	**16.55%**	**15.41%**	**17.76%**	**17.07%**	**17.67%**
Technical Barriers	Deficient IT infrastructure	11.09%	10.57%	10.74%	8.64%	11.24%	10.92%	8.78%	12.29%	11.15%	13.25%
	Isolated systems	1.98%	4.85%	1.11%	1.23%	1.91%	2.03%	1.28%	2.73%	3.14%	2.01%

(continued)

Table 3. (*continued*)

Dimension	Characteristics	Company Size			Level of Responsibility			Age			
		<250	250–999	>999	Executives	PR	w/o PR	<31	31–40	41–50	>50
	Security issues	2.74%	0.44%	1.67%	0.00%	2.63%	1.91%	1.93%	1.37%	1.39%	3.61%
	Missing technical support	1.06%	1.76%	0.74%	0.00%	2.15%	0.68%	1.50%	0.68%	0.00%	2.81%
	Overall	**16.87%**	**17.62%**	**14.26%**	**9.87%**	**17.93%**	**15.54%**	**13.49%**	**17.07%**	**15.68%**	**21.68%**
Organizational Misalignment	Lacking DT roadmap	3.95%	5.29%	5.19%	6.17%	5.74%	3.83%	4.07%	3.07%	6.27%	5.62%
	Immature decision-making	1.98%	2.20%	2.22%	2.47%	1.91%	2.25%	1.50%	2.73%	1.74%	4.02%
	Lack of change management	5.17%	2.64%	3.70%	4.94%	5.26%	3.94%	5.57%	3.75%	4.18%	4.02%
	Lack of communication	3.19%	4.85%	3.70%	3.70%	2.87%	3.83%	3.21%	3.41%	3.48%	4.82%
	Overall	**14.29%**	**14.98%**	**14.81%**	**17.28%**	**15.78%**	**13.85%**	**14.35%**	**12.96%**	**15.67%**	**18.48%**
Corporate Culture	Deficient innovative spirit	2.58%	1.76%	2.96%	0.00%	1.91%	2.93%	2.78%	4.10%	0.35%	1.20%
	Missing error culture	1.22%	0.88%	1.48%	1.23%	1.67%	1.13%	0.43%	1.37%	1.74%	2.81%

(*continued*)

Table 3. (*continued*)

Dimension	Characteristics	Company Size			Level of Responsibility			Age			
		<250	250–999	>999	Executives	PR	w/o PR	<31	31–40	41–50	>50
	Sticking to the status quo	12.31%	15.42%	13.89%	12.35%	12.92%	14.08%	17.34%	10.92%	8.36%	10.44%
	Diffuse fears & insecurities	4.10%	3.96%	7.78%	8.64%	5.02%	5.41%	3.64%	3.75%	9.41%	5.22%
	Silo thinking	1.52%	0.88%	1.30%	0.00%	1.20%	1.58%	1.07%	1.71%	1.74%	1.20%
	Overall	**21.73%**	**22.90%**	**27.41%**	**22.22%**	**22.72%**	**25.13%**	**25.26%**	**21.85%**	**21.60%**	**20.87%**
Structural Mismatch	Bureaucracy	1.82%	1.76%	2.59%	2.47%	0.96%	2.70%	3.43%	0.34%	2.44%	1.20%
	Process complexity	2.28%	1.32%	1.67%	0.00%	1.67%	1.91%	2.14%	1.71%	2.09%	0.80%
	Lack of financial resources	9.88%	8.37%	8.89%	11.11%	10.05%	8.56%	11.13%	8.87%	9.41%	6.43%
	Lack of personnel resources	7.45%	10.13%	6.85%	3.70%	8.85%	7.77%	6.64%	10.92%	8.71%	4.02%
	Over-aged employee structure	2.74%	3.08%	2.59%	2.47%	2.87%	2.82%	3.64%	3.41%	1.74%	1.61%
	Overall	**24.17%**	**24.66%**	**22.59%**	**19.75%**	**24.40%**	**23.76%**	**26.98%**	**25.25%**	**24.39%**	**14.06%**

(*continued*)

Table 3. (*continued*)

Dimension	Characteristics	Company Size			Level of Responsibility			Age			
		<250	250–999	>999	Executives	PR	w/o PR	<31	31–40	41–50	>50
Regulatory Restrictions	Restrictive laws	0.76%	0.00%	0.00%	1.23%	0.00%	0.45%	0.86%	0.00%	0.00%	0.40%
	Volatile & obscure legislation	0.91%	0.44%	0.93%	1.23%	0.48%	0.90%	0.43%	0.68%	1.74%	0.40%
	Lack of political engagement	0.91%	0.00%	0.56%	0.00%	0.72%	0.68%	1.28%	0.68%	0.00%	0.40%
	Overall	**2.58%**	**0.44%**	**1.49%**	**2.46%**	**1.20%**	**2.03%**	**2.57%**	**1.36%**	**1.74%**	**1.20%**
Market Restrictions	Lacking customer pull	0.91%	2.20%	1.30%	4.94%	0.96%	1.01%	0.86%	0.34%	1.74%	3.21%
	Restrictive value network	1.37%	0.00%	1.48%	4.94%	0.48%	1.13%	0.64%	1.37%	1.05%	2.01%
	Volatile technology environment	0.76%	1.76%	0.93%	0.00%	0.96%	1.01%	0.43%	2.05%	1.05%	0.80%
	Overall	**3.04%**	**3.96%**	**3.71%**	**9.88%**	**2.40%**	**3.15%**	**1.93%**	**3.76%**	**3.84%**	**6.02%**

other two groups (8.61% and 8.11%). Executives also perceive a slightly elevated level of Regulatory Restrictions (2.46%) and a significantly elevated level of Market Restrictions (9.88%).

Regarding age, we split the age groups relatively evenly, with a difference of roughly ten years. Again, the most prominent dimensions are Structural Mismatch and Corporate Culture. However, the importance of both dimensions decreases with age increase. For Structural Mismatch, the values approximately range from 27% to 14%. For Corporate Culture, the decrease is 4.39% in total (from 25.26% to 20.87%). The categories of lack of financial resources and lack of personal resources have a major impact on Structural Mismatch. The youngest age group (under 31) shows the highest perception of a lack of personal resources (11.13%). The other two age groups (31–40 and 41–50) show a rather similar perception (8.87% and 9.41%, respectively). The age group above 50 shows the lowest level of concern regarding personal resources (6.43%). Regarding lack of personal resources, the youngest and the oldest age groups have a rather similar view of this barrier, giving it low importance (6.64% and 4.02%, respectively), whereas the middle age groups seem to value it as a more important problem (10.92% and 8.71%). Within the Corporate Culture dimension, again, sticking to the status quo is the major obstacle. Interestingly, younger employees see this as a bigger obstacle, resulting in a frequency of 17.34%. This differs by nearly 9% from the frequency of the group with the lowest perception, the age group 41–51 (8.36%). On the contrary, the age group 41–51 views diffuse fears and insecurity as more important (9.41%). Further, across the age groups, insufficient training and learning are considered a major characteristic of the dimension Missing Skills (ranging from 7.67 to 9.22%). The problem of deficient IT infrastructure is the major obstacle of the Technical Barriers dimension according to all age groups. Especially in the age group above 50, the frequency shows a high value of 13.25%. For the overall Technical Barriers dimension, the observations increase with age—from 13.49% for the youngest age group up to 21.68% for the oldest. When it comes to market restrictions, the age group above 50 shows a rather high rate of concern (6.02%).

5 Discussion

The results reveal a strong impact of the barrier dimensions Corporate Culture and Structural Mismatch across all three categories.

When it comes to LEs, they tend to see Corporate Culture as the most fundamental barrier. Compared to Structural Mismatch, Corporate Culture is more informal and harder to change the larger the organization is. Especially within a DT journey, companies face a higher demand for change. Often, changes meet heavy opposition and vanish over time. To cope with cultural change, scholars recommend a reflexive approach requiring consistency and expressiveness [38]. In contrast, structural mismatch takes up the more formal organizational aspects of a company, which can be described through policies or procedures. It seems to be less of a barrier for LEs than for SMEs and MLEs. The reason can be found in hierarchical structures: in general, LEs tend to have stricter hierarchies than SMEs. Formal tools like Balanced Scorecard support the management of organizational structures [39] and were adopted in a DT setting [40]. Interestingly, the

Balanced Scorecard has the potential to provide a double-loop learning [41]. Meaning, managers can enhance their mental models of the business system, which entails the corporate culture. Thus, even if culture is seen as a more informal and structural mismatch as more formal, these aspects cannot be treated separately from each other.

Previous research indicates a lack of financial resources is hindering SMEs [42], which is confirmed in our study, showing it is more of a hindrance in SMEs than LEs. Often, LEs are publicly listed, which gives them a larger pool of financing possibilities. Surprisingly, the lack of personal resources scores higher in MLEs than in SMEs, which also struggle when it comes to human resources [43]. At the same time, MLEs perceive less hindrance from insufficient training. This could be an indicator that MLEs are more proactively educating their workforce to make up for shortcomings in the labor market. LEs could avoid a lack of personal resources by applying more financial resources. MLEs could attract talent with a more personal work environment and individual career paths. For SMEs, legal regulations are harder to track due to a lack of resources [44]. Often, they operate more locally or are active in single markets [45], giving them slightly better means to cope with market regulations.

For the category level of responsibility of the participants, there are slight differences in the degrees of perception between executives, employees with RP, and those without RP regarding the barrier dimensions Corporate Culture and Structural Mismatch. Analyzing Corporate Culture, employees without RP see it as a greater problem, whereas the executives and employees with RP share a similar, slightly lower level of concern. It is the executives' and employees with RP's responsibility to shape the corporate culture [46]. If the barrier is of more importance to employees without RP, it could indicate that reflexive learning [38] or double-loop learning [39] is not implemented well enough. When it comes to Structural Mismatch, there is a greater overlap between employees with RP and those without. If we interpret structural mismatch as a representation of the more formal organization, it becomes clear that executives bother less about these issues. This is especially visible through their low concern for the lack of personnel resources. Here, their approach might be to just contract the workforce needed or delegate it to the human resources department [47]. Instead, executives experience elevated barriers in questions regarding regulations, especially market regulations, as their task requires a strategic perspective [48]. In addition, technical barriers are out of scope for the executives, which is natural considering their responsibility within companies [49].

Moreover, within the category of age, both Corporate Culture and Structural Mismatch score high. Interestingly, both dimensions decrease with age. We did not survey the duration of the actual employment of our participants. Nevertheless, the decrease could be a strong indicator that elderly and more experienced employees have adapted better to problems in these two dimensions. As the culture influences employee commitment [50], elderly employees are exposed to this influence longer. In contrast, younger employees may see a stronger conflict between their own culture and their career goals in the formal structure in which they experience a mismatch. Generation Z employees in particular should be given a realistic job preview to manage their expectations [51]. A reverse trend can be seen for Technical Barriers, which are rather low for younger employees and high for elderly employees. However, the groups are rather even when it comes to insufficient training and learning. We could expect higher values for the elderly group here, as more training and learning could help in lowering the perception of insufficient IT, especially as age has proven to be a contextual moderator impacting the relationship between skills and training and DT [52].

Although the age group 50+ perceives a low Structural Mismatch, their perception of Organizational Misalignment is much higher. In this dimension, more strategic aspects are present. The high perception of Organizational Misalignment might be connected to the elevated view of Market Restrictions. Their experience helps them see problems in the market, which in turn is connected to organizational misalignment. This approach is considered the market-based view [53]. For companies, the ability to notice market restrictions is major. Further educating the age group 50+ and fostering technical capabilities could be an important step to balancing market- and resource-based views [54]. It is important to keep in mind that age might correlate with the level of responsibility; age and experience often lead to higher responsibility.

In general, across all categories, IT infrastructure is seen as an obstacle at roughly the same rate, around 11%. Thus, it stresses the claim that DT is about human barriers [55].

6 Conclusions and Implications

Regardless of the size of a company, the position or age of an employee, corporate culture, and structural mismatch are perceived as major barriers to DT. Thus, by conducting this study, we can generalize the independence of these barrier dimensions from the socio-demographic factors. It leads to the conclusion that culture and structure are universal problems within a huge range of companies. Further, our results support the claim that DT is not a technical problem [55], as these barriers are perceived as relatively low but consistent across the different categories. Our results confirm a rather distinct perception of barriers between the age groups under 31 and above 50. This aspect shows that having a diverse workforce can be an asset, especially when it comes to the ability to recognize and solve different barriers.

We conducted a qualitative content analysis [56] by coding open statements from data collected through a survey. Thereafter, we descriptively calculated frequencies to explore the results on an aggregated level. The coding procedure might pose problems regarding validity. For instance, other researchers might set up the dimension and categories differently. However, we can ensure a high level of validity through our triangulation approach and the huge number of statements we used in this study. We were expecting more variation in the frequencies; nevertheless, 29 characteristics will automatically lead to smaller frequencies than fewer characteristics. Indeed, our work covers a broad range of aspects.

For further development, we see more work regarding the interrelations between different barriers as important. We hypothesize that an interrelation between market restrictions and organizational misalignment exists. Further, our results show a rather low perception of the importance of DT roadmaps with executives. This finding might need further exploration, as other scholars stress the importance of this task at the executive level [57]. Even more essential is further research on *overcoming* barriers to DT, as the most common corporate countermeasure is avoidance or implementation of ad-hoc solutions [9]. The combination of barrier characteristics and perception categories could be the groundwork for exploring which countermeasures could be applicable for which type of company, for which type of responsibility, or for which type of employee age.

References

1. Dehning, B., Richardson, V.J., Zmud, R.W.: The value relevance of announcements of transformational information technology investments. Manag. Inf. Syst. Q. **27**, 637–656 (2003). https://doi.org/10.2307/30036551
2. Laudon, K.C., Laudon, J.P.: Management Information Systems: Managing the Digital Firm. Pearson, New York (2020)
3. Kagermann, H., Wahlster, W., Helbig, J.: Recommendations for implementing the strategic initiative industrie 4.0. acatech – National Academy of Science and Engineering (2013)
4. Benlian, A., Hilkert, D., Hess, T.: How open is this platform? The meaning and measurement of platform openness from the complementors' perspective. J. Inf. Technol. **30**, 209–228 (2015). https://doi.org/10.1057/jit.2015.6
5. Schwab, K.: The Fourth Industrial Revolution. Crown Business, New York (2017)
6. Gnamm, J., Kalmbach, R., Schertler, M.: Digitalization must be given top priority (2018). https://www.bain.com/insights/digitalisierung-ist-chefsache-2018/
7. Hess, T., Matt, C., Benlian, A., Wiesböck, F.: Options for formulating a digital transformation strategy. MIS Q. Exec. **15**, 123–139 (2016)
8. Hirsch-Kreinsen, H.: Digitization of industrial work: development paths and prospects. J. Labour Mark. Res. **49**, 1–14 (2016)
9. Hadjimanolis, A.: The barriers approach to innovation. In: Shavinina, L.V. (ed.) The International Handbook on Innovation, pp. 559–573. Pergamon, Oxford (2003). https://doi.org/10.1016/B978-008044198-6/50038-3
10. Vial, G.: Understanding digital transformation: a review and a research agenda. J. Strateg. Inf. Syst. **28**, 118–144 (2019). https://doi.org/10.1016/j.jsis.2019.01.003
11. Vogelsang, K., Liere-Netheler, K., Packmohr, S., Hoppe, U.: Barriers to digital transformation in manufacturing: development of a research agenda. In: Proceedings of the 52nd Hawaii International Conference on System Sciences, pp. 4937–4946 (2019)
12. Jones, M.D., Hutcheson, S., Camba, J.D.: Past, present, and future barriers to digital transformation in manufacturing: a review. J. Manuf. Syst. **60**, 936–948 (2021). https://doi.org/10.1016/j.jmsy.2021.03.006
13. Reis, J., Amorim, M., Melão, N., Matos, P.: Digital transformation: a literature review and guidelines for future research. In: Rocha, Á., Adeli, H., Reis, L.P., Costanzo, S. (eds.) WorldCIST 2018. AISC, vol. 745, pp. 411–421. Springer, Cham (2018). https://doi.org/10.1007/978-3-319-77703-0_41
14. Pabst von Ohain, B.: Leader attributes for successful digital transformation. In: ICIS 2019 Proceedings (2019)
15. Wessel, L., Baiyere, A., Ologeanu-Taddei, R., Cha, J., Blegind Jensen, T.: Unpacking the difference between digital transformation and IT-enabled organizational transformation. JAIS **22**, 102–129 (2021). https://doi.org/10.17705/1jais.00655
16. Bharadwaj, A., El Sawy, O., Pavlou, P., Venkatraman, N.: Digital business strategy: toward a next generation of insights. Manag. Inf. Syst. Q. **37**, 471–482 (2013)
17. Webster, J., Watson, R.T.: Analyzing the past to prepare for the future: writing a literature review. MIS Q. **26**, xiii–xxiii (2002)
18. Varwig, T., Brink, H., Packmohr, S.: A systematic literature review on barriers to digital transformation: insights and implications for overcoming. Presented at the 37th EBES Conference, Berlin (2021)

19. Bilgeri, D., Wortmann, F.: Barriers to IoT business model innovation. In: Proceedings of the 13th International Conference on Wirtschaftsinformatik, pp. 987–990 (2017)
20. Henriette, E., Feki, M., Boughzala, I.: Digital transformation challenges. In: Mediterranean Conference on Information Systems (MICS), pp. 1–7 (2016)
21. Kumar, P., Singh, R.K., Kumar, V.: Managing supply chains for sustainable operations in the era of industry 4.0 and circular economy: analysis of barriers. Resour. Conserv. Recycl. **164**, 105–115 (2021). https://doi.org/10.1016/j.resconrec.2020.105215
22. Khanzode, A.G., Sarma, P.R.S., Mangla, S.K., Yuan, H.: Modeling the industry 4.0 adoption for sustainable production in micro, small & medium enterprises. J. Clean. Prod. **279**, 123489 (2021). https://doi.org/10.1016/j.jclepro.2020.123489
23. Karadayi-Usta, S.: An interpretive structural analysis for industry 4.0 adoption challenges. IEEE Trans. Eng. Manag. **67**, 973–978 (2020). https://doi.org/10.1109/TEM.2018.2890443
24. Abdul-Hamid, A.-Q., Ali, M.H., Tseng, M.-L., Lan, S., Kumar, M.: Impeding challenges on industry 4.0 in circular economy: palm oil industry in Malaysia. Comput. Oper. Res. **123**, 105052 (2020). https://doi.org/10.1016/j.cor.2020.105052
25. Agrawal, P., Narain, R., Ullah, I.: Analysis of barriers in implementation of digital transformation of supply chain using interpretive structural modelling approach. J. Model. Manag. (2019). https://doi.org/10.1108/JM2-03-2019-0066
26. Dudenredaktion: Handlungsempfehlung. https://www.du-den.de/node/63055/revision/63091
27. Westerman, G., Calméjane, C., Bonnet, D., Ferraris, P., McAfee, A.: Digital transformation: a roadmap for billion-dollar organizations. MIT Center for Digital Business and Capgemini Consulting, vol. 1, pp. 1–68 (2011)
28. Zaychenko, I., Smirnova, A., Shytova, Y., Mutalieva, B., Pimenov, N.: Digital logistics transformation: implementing the Internet of Things (IoT). In: Schaumburg, H., Korablev, V., Ungvari, L. (eds.) TT 2020. LNNS, vol. 157, pp. 189–200. Springer, Cham (2021). https://doi.org/10.1007/978-3-030-64430-7_16
29. Dremel, C.: Barriers to the adoption of big data analytics in the automotive sector. In: Proceedings of the 23rd American Conference on Information Systems (AMCIS), Boston, pp. 1–10 (2017)
30. Sarker, S., Chatterjee, S., Xiao, X., Elbanna, A.: The sociotechnical axis of cohesion for the IS discipline: its historical legacy and its continued relevance. MIS Q. **43**, 695–719 (2019). https://doi.org/10.25300/MISQ/2019/13747
31. Brink, H., Packmohr, S., Paul, F.-H.: Extending a socio-technical model of the barriers to digital transformation through data triangulation. In: 2022 8th International Conference on Information Management (ICIM), Cambridge, United Kingdom, pp. 68–74. IEEE (2022). https://doi.org/10.1109/ICIM56520.2022.00020
32. Yin, R.K.: Case study Research: Design and Methods. SAGE, Los Angeles (2014)
33. Fetters, M.D., Molina-Azorin, J.F.: The journal of mixed methods research starts a new decade: principles for bringing in the new and divesting of the old language of the field. J. Mixed Methods Res. **11**, 3 (2017). https://doi.org/10.1177/1558689816682092
34. Mayring, P.: Qualitative Content Analysis: Theoretical Foundation, Basic Procedures and Software Solution. Beltz Verlag, Klagenfurt (2014)
35. Stern, M.J., Bilgen, I., McClain, C., Hunscher, B.: Effective sampling from social media sites and search engines for web surveys: demographic and data quality differences in surveys of Google and Facebook users. Soc. Sci. Comput. Rev. **35**, 713–732 (2017). https://doi.org/10.1177/0894439316683344
36. Azungah, T.: Qualitative research: deductive and inductive approaches to data analysis. QRJ. **18**, 383–400 (2018). https://doi.org/10.1108/QRJ-D-18-00035
37. Nowell, L.S., Norris, J.M., White, D.E., Moules, N.J.: Thematic analysis: striving to meet the trustworthiness criteria. Int. J. Qual. Methods **16**, 160940691773384 (2017). https://doi.org/10.1177/1609406917733847

38. Alvesson, M., Sveningsson, S.: Changing Organizational Culture: Cultural change Work in Progress. Routledge (2015). https://doi.org/10.4324/9781315688404
39. Kaplan, R.S.: Conceptual foundations of the balanced scorecard. In: Handbooks of Management Accounting Research, pp. 1253–1269. Elsevier (2009). https://doi.org/10.1016/S1751-3243(07)03003-9
40. Yamamoto, S.: A strategic map for digital transformation. Procedia Comput. Sci. **176**, 1374–1381 (2020). https://doi.org/10.1016/j.procs.2020.09.147
41. Li, C.-H., Yang, W.-G., Shih, I.-T.: Exploration on the gap of single- and double-loop learning of balanced scorecard and organizational performance in a health organization. Heliyon **7**, e08553 (2021). https://doi.org/10.1016/j.heliyon.2021.e08553
42. Eggers, F.: Masters of disasters? Challenges and opportunities for SMEs in times of crisis. J. Bus. Res. **116**, 199–208 (2020). https://doi.org/10.1016/j.jbusres.2020.05.025
43. Eller, R., Alford, P., Kallmünzer, A., Peters, M.: Antecedents, consequences, and challenges of small and medium-sized enterprise digitalization. J. Bus. Res. **112**, 119–127 (2020). https://doi.org/10.1016/j.jbusres.2020.03.004
44. Sirur, S., Nurse, J.R.C., Webb, H.: Are we there yet?: Understanding the challenges faced in complying with the general data protection regulation (GDPR). In: Proceedings of the 2nd International Workshop on Multimedia Privacy and Security, Toronto Canada, pp. 88–95. ACM (2018). https://doi.org/10.1145/3267357.3267368
45. Dosi, G., Moschella, D., Pugliese, E., Tamagni, F.: Productivity, market selection, and corporate growth: comparative evidence across US and Europe. Small Bus Econ. **45**, 643–672 (2015). https://doi.org/10.1007/s11187-015-9655-z
46. Kane, G.: The technology fallacy. Research-technology. Management **62**, 44–49 (2019). https://doi.org/10.1080/08956308.2019.1661079
47. Fenech, R., Baguant, P., Ivanov, D.: The changing role of human resource management in an era of digital transformation. J. Manag. Inf. Decis. Sci. **22**, 166–175 (2019)
48. Drucker, P.F.: The Theory of The Business. Harvard Business Review Press, Boston (2017)
49. Kane, G.C., Palmer, D., Phillips, A. N., Kiron, D., Buckley, N.: Achieving Digital Maturity. MIT Sloan Management Review and Deloitte University Press (2017)
50. Ramdhani, A., Ramdhani, M.A., Ainisyifa, H.: Model conceptual framework of corporate culture influenced on employees commitment to organization. Int. Bus. Manag. **11**, 826–830 (2017)
51. Schroth, H.: Are you ready for gen Z in the workplace? Calif. Manag. Rev. **61**, 5–18 (2019). https://doi.org/10.1177/0008125619841006
52. Trenerry, B., et al.: Preparing workplaces for digital transformation: an integrative review and framework of multi-level factors. Front. Psychol. **12**, 620766 (2021). https://doi.org/10.3389/fpsyg.2021.620766
53. McGee, J.: Market-based view. In: Cooper, C.L. (ed.) Wiley Encyclopedia of Management, p. 1. Wiley, Chichester (2015). https://doi.org/10.1002/9781118785317.weom120075
54. Makhija, M.: Comparing the resource-based and market-based views of the firm: empirical evidence from Czech privatization. Strateg. Manag. J. **24**, 433–451 (2003). https://doi.org/10.1002/smj.304
55. Tabrizi, B., Lam, E., Girard, K., Irvin, V.: Digital Transformation is Not About Technology (2019). https://hbr.org/2019/03/digital-transformation-is-not-about-technology

56. Mayring, P.: Qualitative Inhaltsanalyse – Abgrenzungen, Spielarten, Weiterentwicklungen. In: Forum Qualitative Sozialforschung/Forum: Qualitative Social Research, vol. 20, no. 3. Qualitative Content Analysis I (2019). https://doi.org/10.17169/FQS-20.3.3343
57. Zaoui, F., Souissi, N.: Roadmap for digital transformation: a literature review. Procedia Comput. Sci. **175**, 621–628 (2020). https://doi.org/10.1016/j.procs.2020.07.090

Sustainable Business Models Beyond the Carbon Footprint – A Review of Perceived Sustainability Dimensions in Practical BMI Based on Case Studies

Marc Gebauer[1] , Bejtush Ademi[2] , and Julia Braun[1]([✉])

[1] Brandenburg University of Technology Cottbus-Senftenberg (BTU), Cottbus, Germany
`julia.braun@b-tu.de`
[2] Norwegian University of Science and Technology (NTNU), Trondheim, Norway

Abstract. Sustainability has become an important goal of business model innovation for managers and researchers alike. Nonetheless, we do recognize a strong focus on the carbon footprint. Since sustainability consists at least of the three dimensions economy, ecology and social, we provide a structured literature review on the dimension researchers and managers do work with. In a first step we develop a framework of sustainability dimensions researchers have provided the literature with. In the second step we search the literature for cases of sustainable business model innovation and analyze the results with the framework of sustainability dimensions. A main finding is, that companies from our sample of cases generally long for more than one SDG. This article provides a collection of very recent case studies of SBMI.

Keywords: Sustainable Business Models · SDGs · PRISMA · Case Studies

1 Introduction

The 26th UN Climate Change Conference in Glasgow emphasized the important role of businesses in sustainable development [1]. Sustainable development is transforming business priorities, requiring them to integrate societal and environmental goals into their mission [2]. This is driven by four main factors: 1) their significant contribution to global problems, 2) their crucial role in addressing challenges, 3) stakeholder pressure [3], and 4) the potential for competitive advantage embedded in sustainability.

To integrate sustainability, businesses continually engaged in sustainability-related initiatives [4] and included sustainability as a performance measurement [5]. Businesses invested towards compliance with International Organization for Standardization (ISO) standards, engagement in corporate social responsibility (CSR) activities, shared value creation (SVC), shared value initiatives (CVI), sustainable development (SD), and sustainable business model innovation (SBMI) [6]. Further, businesses are measuring their performance using the framework introduced by Elkington [7], reporting on economic, environmental and, social dimensions.

Both business leaders and scholars are increasingly experimenting with business models aiming to address sustainability challenges [8] and are turning towards sustainable business model innovation. This is often referred to as innovation for sustainable business models [2]. Sustainable business models put sustainability at the core of the business strategy, which then "shape[s] the driving force of the firm and its decision making" [9].

Although businesses are engaging in sustainability, the progress toward sustainable development has been slow [10]. Even though a rising number of businesses are focusing on sustainability and social responsibility and showcasing their positive impact on the environment and society, the global community is still falling short of achieving sustainable development goals (SDGs) [11]. Research shows that businesses have a tendency to focus solely on carbon footprint and neglecting other aspects of sustainability, and call for a holistic approach to sustainability integrating economic, environment and social aspects [12].

This paper reviews the current state of research on SBMI and its connection to sustainability pillars and the UN SDGs. A literature review analyzes case studies on companies' SBMI efforts to address sustainability and the SDGs. Specifically, we focus on identifying the sustainability pillar and SDGs case companies focus on and what SBMI patterns they follow in their efforts to address sustainability and SDGs. Therefore, this study addresses the following research question (RQ) with its three sub questions:

RQ: How do practitioners pursue sustainability and SDGs through sustainable business model?

- *What pillars of sustainability are aimed at?*
- *What SDGs are being focused on by the investigated companies?*
- *Which countries and industries are the investigated companies from and which patterns of SBMI they apply ?*

This paper contributes to the existing research and business practitioners in multiple ways. For example, with a framework that includes SBMI, pillars, SDGs and business model types, the related industry as well as the country is presented for further re-search. Furthermore, it shows that existing companies do not focus exclusively on the CO_2 footprint in terms of sustainability. For practical application in companies, a collection of current case studies is also presented, which could serve as motivating examples.

This article is structured as follows. The following section discusses the theoretical background focusing on key relevant concepts. In Sect. 3, we thoroughly present our literature review process, elaborating on the screening process and analysis of the selected research papers. In Sect. 4, we present our main findings. The discussion of our findings and concluding remarks are presented in Sect. 5.

52   M. Gebauer et al.

2 Theoretical Background

2.1 Sustainability and Sustainable Development

Sustainable development has become the central focus of nations, businesses, non-governmental organizations, and societal and environmental activists [13]. It is considered a fundamental shift toward understanding the relationship between humanity, society, the environment, and economic growth [14]. The increasing world population, changes in consumption behaviors, inequality, poverty, and depletion of the ecosystem represent the world's critical challenges, which make sustainable development a priority [15].

The concept of sustainable development is highly contested and attracts multiple meanings and interpretations [13, 14]. The first official and most common definition of sustainable development is from Brundtland Commission [16]. In the Brundtland Commission report (1987), sustainable development was defined as *"development that meets the needs of the present without compromising the ability of future generations to meet their own needs."* [17] This is a broad and ambiguous definition. Giddings and Hopwood [13] claim that ambiguity of the definition may be intentional as it could potentially result in the broader acceptance of the concept.

The sustainable development concept has multiple dimensions, among which economic, environmental and societal are most widely discussed [18]. Brundtland's definition of sustainable development incorporates economic, environmental and social as the *"three main aims of sustainable development"* [19]. Sustainable development helps bring to light the interconnection between economic, environmental and social dimensions and reconcile their differences and trade-offs [13].

Economic Sustainability. Historically the economic dimension of sustainability has been prioritized over societal and environmental ones. [13] That is mainly based on Friedman's argument [20] that a firm's sole responsibility is maximizing economic profitability for shareholders, not society or the environment. The economic dimension of sustainability focuses on the profitability, financial resilience, stability, and long-term viability of the business.

Environmental Sustainability. Even though a relatively young concept, various definitions of environmental sustainability are found. Goodland [21] provides a short but broad definition saying that environmental sustainability refers to the *"maintenance of natural capital."* Sutton [22] defines environmental sustainability as the *"ability to maintain things or qualities that are valued in the physical environment, [which] includes the natural and biological environments."* Building on the definition of sustainable development provided in Brundtland Report, Morelli [23] defines environmental sustainability as *"meeting the resource and services needs of current and future generations without compromising the health of the ecosystems that provide them."*

Social Sustainability. Social sustainability was introduced relatively late in the sustainable development discussions [24], but it quickly became a priority. The broadness of the definition of sustainable development provided in the Brundtland Report, including people's needs and the environment as part of economic development, served as the basis for the development of social sustainability within the sustainable development agenda [25]. Although there is no unified definition of social sustainability, a common definition is the one developed by Polèse and Stren [26]: *"[...] development (and/or growth) that is compatible with the harmonious evolution of civil society, fostering an environment conducive to the compatible cohabitation of culturally and socially diverse groups while at the same time encouraging social integration, with improvements in the quality of life for all segments of the population."* This definition confirms that social sustainability addresses a wide range of social concerns, such as diversity, cohabitation, equity, and safety.

2.2 Sustainable Development Goals

On September 2015 United Nations proposed 17 SDGs aiming *"to end poverty (economic sustainability), protect the planet (environmental sustainability), and ensure prosperity for all (social sustainability)"* [27]. To achieve these goals, UN has presented a 2030 agenda, which includes specific targets and indicators for each SDG[1]. This agenda applies to a wide range of stakeholders such as governments, business community, and civil society, and calls for action to engage toward a more sustainable world [28]. The 17 SDGs are interlinked to address the three pillars of sustainability. Most of the SDG are multidisciplinary as many of the goals address two of the three pillars of sustainability, while only a few of them address all three [27].

2.3 Business Models and Sustainable Business Model Innovation

Business models as a term has been widely accepted and used among scholars and business practitioners. It refers to the logic of a company that creates, delivers, and captures value [29]. Business models explain how a company operates by elaborating on the value proposition, processes performed, resources employed, and profit formula [30].

Business models are a source of innovation and play a crucial role in addressing sustainability and SDGs. Existing research finds business model innovation more effective in addressing sustainability compared to other sustainability initiatives. Sustainability can be incorporated in all building blocks of a business model by including sustainability aspect into value proposition, value creation and delivery, and value capture [31]. Further, business model innovation can lead to digital business models, which help businesses address sustainability by incorporating digital technologies [32]. As such, sustainable business model innovation has emerged as a research stream and has gained momentum in recent years [28].

To accelerate development and innovation of sustainable business models it is important to understand different archetypes of sustainable business models [38]. Bocken and Short [38] recognized eight sustainable business model archetypes grouped in three categories: technological, social, and organizational. Under technological are three archetypes: maximizing material and energy efficiency, creating value from waste, and

---

[1] A detailed list of the goals, targets, indicators, and actions is presented in UN's official website. https://sdgs.un.org/goals.

substituting with renewables and natural processes. Under social are three archetypes: delivering functionality rather than ownership, adopting a stewardship role, and encouraging efficiency. Under organizational are two archetypes: repurposing for society and environment and developing scale up solutions.

Researchers have identified multiple business model innovation patterns for sustainability. Lüdeke-Freund et al. [33] have identified 45 patterns to support innovation of sustainable business models. Those patterns are grouped based on multiple dimensions, including revenue and pricing, financing, eco-design, circularity, supply chain, and other patterns.[2] [34].

Figure 1 shows the context in which this article is situated and provides an overview of the relationship between the terms described above and portrays them in their logical connection.

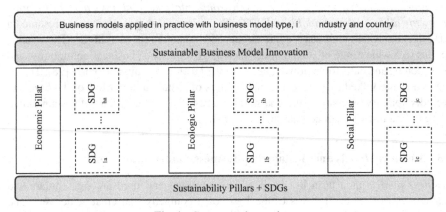

Fig. 1. Context and overview

The SDGs are assigned to the respective pillars and form the three pillars of the SBMI.

3   Methodology

To answer the question of how practitioners pursue SBMI we rely on secondary data. The scientific literature on the topic was searched for case studies of real companies longing for sustainable business models and business model innovation. Therefore, we rely on the methodology of PRISMA[3] which is generally accepted and partly demanded by the scientific community [35]. The PRISMA procedure consists of three overall steps. Those are identification, screening and working with the included articles. Starting with the identification we worked with the scientific databases Scopus and web of science.

---

[2] For more details read F. Lüdeke-Freund, H. Breuer, and L. Massa, *Sustainable business model design: 45 patterns*, Berlin, 2022.

[3] For further information see PRISMA's official website in www.prisma-statement.org/.

On the 17th of October 2022 we conducted the search.[4] Our procedure is summarized in Fig. 2.

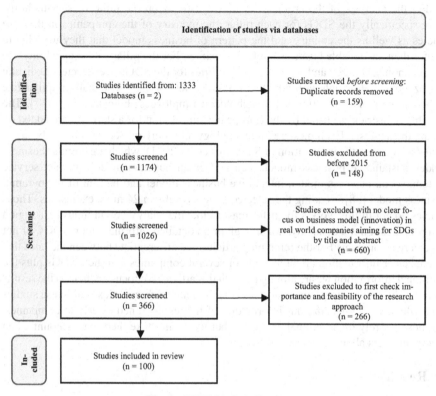

Fig. 2. PRISMA flow diagram

After excluding duplicates, we ended up with 1174 papers for further screening. Following Mio et al. [36] we excluded articles from before 2015. Thus, we were left with 1026 articles for screening. We decided to look for articles, which directly show a focus on business models or business model innovation having sustainability goals which are described or analyzed in case studies of real companies. Therefore, the abstract needed to include the terms business model or business model innovation, case study, and sustainability or more specific pillars or goals belonging to sustainability for being selected. Additionally, the given terms needed to be connected logically in the sense of our article and its research question. To prepare for an independent review of three reviewers, we went through the first ten articles together to secure the same mutual understanding of our screening rules.

---

[4] Research Strings used in the analysisTS = ("business model*" AND sustainab* AND innovat* AND (case OR "case stud*")) (728 results on web of science) & TS = ("business model*" AND sustainab* AND innovat* AND (case OR "case stud*")) (805 results on scopus).

As a result, we found 366 articles that are suitable for the purpose of this article. After that, we checked the importance and the feasibility of our approach, and we focused on the latest 100 articles.

For the analysis of the articles, we chose to focus on the pillar of sustainability, more specifically the SDGs for each pillar, the industry of the companies in the case studies as well as the country and the pattern of business model that they use plan to use for their sustainable business model innovation. For the pillars of sustainability, we used economy, ecology and social. As possibilities for the SDGs, we selected the listing of Lozano and Huisingh with nine to 14 possibilities for each sustainability pillar like "Operations: Noise" or "Internal Stakeholders: Employees' human rights" [37]. The possible industries are listed by the European Commission for a start and are added on during the analysis. Examples are biotechnology and tourism. As patterns for business models, we chose the proposition of Sinkovics et al. (2021), which are circular business model, sustainable business model, lean and green business model, product service system, social business model, integrative business model and bottom of the pyramid business model [38]. Reading the selected papers results in 24 more exclusions. Those articles do not fit this work's focus for reasons like the analysis of an industry, a region or a project but not a company, not enough or no detailed information on SDGs, or not about a real company. For the remaining articles, we differentiate between the ones that give us clear information about a single or several companies and their SDGs plus the additional information we are aiming for with this article. We focus on them in the results section. The remaining group of articles contain quite often complex multi-case studies from which we hardly find our information of interest assigned clearly to companies. On those we rely on additional examples, but we do not take them into account when giving numbers about categories of our results.

4 Results

In the case studies from our analysis the companies stem from all over the world. Starting with Europe, e.g. from Poland [39], Italy [40] and Switzerland [41], over Asia, e. g. from China [42], India [43] and Thailand [44], South America, e. g. from Brazil [45], and Afrika, e. g. from Burkina Faso [46], and North America, e.g. Canada [47]. We do find an interest of companies in sustainable development documented recently by researchers from nearly every inhabited continent. 26 of the articles we found present companies with a focus on European companies. 15 are set in Asia and six in South America.

Concerning the industries that our case study companies operate in; we also see a diverse picture. Examples of the industries are energy [39], raw materials, minerals, and forest-based industries [46], tourism [48], the automotive industry [49], construction [50], health [51], cosmetics [52], logistics [53], food and drink industry [54] and textiles, fashion, and creative industries [55].

In our analysis we do not find articles with case studies of companies focusing specifically and only on their carbon footprint concerning the three sustainability dimensions. We additionally came across articles focusing on two or even three sustainability pillars. That, in a very general sense, means that at least some companies, same as researchers, work with a comprehensive approach for sustainability in their value creation and capture.

Companies focusing mainly on one sustainability pillar, according to the case studies we chose to analyze, are, contrary to some expectations, not only focused on reducing their carbon footprint, or, in the case of our SDGs, on "operations: emissions and effluents including greenhouse gases". In three cases we do find hints for e.g., the pillar of ecology in, they aim for better operations concerning energy [56] or energy and production [39] and wastes and recycling as well as on supply chain improvements [40]. Two out of three of those cases rely on circular business models to reach their goals. For the third one we assigned the pattern of a sustainable business model.

The cases in which we find companies aiming for two sustainability pillars all include the economic pillar. This pillar is paired with the ecology pillar in 19 and eight with the social pillar of our most fitting articles. The combination with the ecological pillar includes SDGs such as "earnings, value creation, and shareholders" and "operations: wastes and recycling" for a circular business model [57], "earnings, value creation, and shareholders", "operations: co-efficiency and cleaner production" and "operations: products and eco-products" in a lean and green business model [58], "earnings, value creation, and shareholders", "operations: eco-efficiency and cleaner production" and "land use and remediation" with a product-service system business model [59] and others with the generally with the same type of business models. The examples of our article setting with the combination of the economic and the social pillar so include SDGs like "operations: energy" and "external stakeholders: supply chain" in a sharing economy business model [60], "market presence", "external stakeholders: products" and "internal stakeholders: employees' wages, work hours and benefits" in a bottom of the pyramid business model [61]. More social SDGs we find are "external stakeholders" in a social business model [62], "external stakeholder: supply chain" in a product-service system business model [54], "operations: production" in a product-service system business model [63] and "external stakeholders: communities" and "activities pertaining to or connecting internal and external stakeholders: health and safety" in a social business model [64].

The 20 cases in which we find evidence for all three sustainability pillars usually rely on a sustainable business model by the latter's definition. Examples of the SDGs we found evidence for, are "operations: emissions and effluents including greenhouse gases", "activities pertaining to or connecting internal and external stakeholders: health and safety" and "external stakeholders: supply chain" [46], "earnings, value creation, and shareholders", "operations: products and eco products" and "external stakeholders: products" [41], "earnings, value creation, and shareholders", "operations: water and wastewater treatment" and "internal stakeholders: employees' development, training and education" [42], "earnings, value creation, and shareholders", "operations: products and eco-products" and "external stakeholders: communities" [44, 65], "earnings, value creation, and shareholders", "operations: emissions and effluents, including greenhouse gases" and "external stakeholders: supply chain" [45]. Additionally, a circular business model with "operations: eco-efficiency and cleaner production", "operations: emissions and effluents, including greenhouse gases" and "operations: products and eco-products" is found [48].

Table 1 shows four selected examples of our research.

Table 1. Selected examples of our research

[Reference]	Main sustainability Pillar(s)	Examples of detected SDGs	Examples from the articles	Industry + Country	Business Model
[56]	ecologic (and economic)	operations: energy,	*"Value propositions[: ...] ecological application activities [...] energies off-shore wind-farm"*	energy, Italy	circular business model
[57]	economic, ecologic	earnings, value creation, and shareholders and operations: wastes and recycling	*"REDUCE [...] the content of plastic in packaging [...] REUSE [...] of EPS [...] RECYCLE [...] Of bio compostable plastic"; "...it points at our future growth and new business."*	packaging, Europe e.g., Italy	circular business model
[61]	economic, social	market presence, external stakeholders: products and internal stakeholders: employees' wages, work hours and benefits	*"...HPS took advantage of its initial frugal socio-technical configuration to serve BoP markets driven by economics of scale..."*	energy, India	bottom of the pyramid business model
[42]	economic, ecologic, social	earnings, value creation, and shareholders, operations: water and wastewater treatment and internal stakeholders: employees' development, training and education	*"National Environmental Excellence Enterprise Award was presented to HXW for establishing a green sewage treatment model, achieving maximum pollutant removal without affecting the life of surrounding residents."*	water treatment, China	sustainable business model

It contains the main sustainability pillars, examples of the detected SDGs, examples from the articles, the industry and country of the company as well as the business model of the company.

5 Discussion and Conclusion

Sustainability is an important goal that has already arrived in business practice. This is of particular importance in order to achieve the goals set by the 26th UN Climate Change Conference. Based on case studies from the literature, a brief overview of the actual application of sustainable business model innovation could be given in this article. Contrary to our expectations including a slow and one-dimensional development to increase sustainability in business model innovation by reducing their CO_2 footprint we find a lot of multi-dimensional cases with several SDGs being successfully aimed for. The companies in our exploratory sample of articles are based on all inhabited continents, except from Australia where we have no evidence. They also belong to a number of different industries; thus, we cannot draw a conclusion to exceptionally sustainable industries from our small sample of cases. With a focus on a first set of 100 articles after screening and for an exploration of our research question, we did find a heterogeneous picture, not numerous enough for significant correlation calculations. A set of ten in-depth cases for a qualitative and deeper analysis might have been valuable to explore the research question with case study approach in a brief journal article as well. However, what we do find with our analysis, is that companies from the chosen sample generally long for more than one SDG. In some cases, especially of companies with evidence for all three sustainability pillars, we recognized more than three SDGs[5], which exceeds the planned capacity of our analysis table for the latter.

This research about the actual sustainability of companies might be biased since we were explicitly looking for sustainable business model innovation which we found documented by other researchers with analytical frameworks for sustainability. We do not relate them with other companies, following only more traditional economic goals. And the authors of our case studies might also have documented a positive interpretation of the companies' sustainability approaches possible exceeding their actual strategies due to their analytical framework looking for sustainability. Nonetheless, we can state that multi-dimensional sustainability cannot only be found in research but also in practical business models.

Further research could add to our article by broadening the scope of the cases to develop quantitative insights including correlations from sustainability pillars and SDGs to the type or pattern of business models, the industries and the countries that the companies operate in. Additionally, SDGs and innovation drivers might be correlated with the type of ownership the company's operate in.

References

1. Minatogawa, V., et al.: Towards systematic sustainable business model innovation: what can we learn from business model innovation. Sustainability **14**(5), 2939 (2022)
2. Laasch, O.: An actor-network perspective on business models: how 'being responsible' led to incremental but pervasive change. Long Range Plann. **52**(3), 406–426 (2019). https://doi.org/10.1016/j.lrp.2018.04.002

---

[5] For example [46, 49, 66].

3. Ademi, B., Klungseth, N.J.: Does it pay to deliver superior ESG performance? Evidence from US S&P 500 companies. J. Glob. Responsib. **13**(4), 421–449 (2022). https://doi.org/10.1108/JGR-01-2022-0006

4. Zahid, A., Klungseth, N.J., Andersen, B.: The role of sustainable project management in facilities management. In: CIB W070 Facility Management and Maintenance 2023 IOP Conference Series: Earth and Environmental Science (2023). https://iopscience.iop.org/journal/1755-1315/ahead. Of print - to be published 2023

5. Ademi, B., Klungseth, N.J.: Addressing sustainability: setting and governing sustainability goals and targets. In: CIB W070 Facility Management and Maintenance 2023 IOP Conference Series: Earth and Environmental Science (2023). https://iopscience.iop.org/journal/1755-1315/ahead. Of print - to be published 2023

6. Betti, G., Consolandi, C., Eccles, R.G.: The relationship between investor materiality and the sustainable development goals: a methodological framework. Sustainability **10**(7), 2248 (2018). https://doi.org/10.3390/su10072248

7. Elkington, J.: Chapter 1 - Enter the triple bottom line. In: Henriques, A., Richardson, J., NetLibrary, I. (eds.) The Triple Bottom Line, Does It All Add Up?: Assessing the Sustainability of Business and CSR, London, Sterling, VA, pp. 1–16. Earthscan (2004)

8. Bashir, H., Jorgensen, S., Pedersen, L.J.T., Skard, S.: Experimenting with sustainable business models in fast moving consumer goods. J. Clean. Prod. **270**, 122302 (2020). https://doi.org/10.1016/j.jclepro.2020.122302

9. Stubbs, W.: Strategies, practices, and tensions in managing business model innovation for sustainability: the case of an Australian BCorp. Corp. Soc. Responsib. Environ. Manag. **26**(5), 1063–1072 (2019). https://doi.org/10.1002/csr.1786

10. Ritala, P., Huotari, P., Bocken, N., Albareda, L., Puumalainen, K.: Sustainable business model adoption among S&P 500 firms: a longitudinal content analysis study. J. Clean. Prod. **170**, 216–226 (2018). https://doi.org/10.1016/j.jclepro.2017.09.159

11. Dyllick, T., Muff, K.: Clarifying the meaning of sustainable business: introducing a typology from business-as-usual to true business sustainability. Organ. Environ. **29**(2), 156–174 (2016). https://doi.org/10.1177/1086026615575176

12. Budde Christensen, T., Wells, P., Cipcigan, L.: Can innovative business models overcome resistance to electric vehicles? Better place and battery electric cars in Denmark. Energy Policy **48**, 498–505 (2012). https://doi.org/10.1016/j.enpol.2012.05.054

13. Giddings, B., Hopwood, B., O'Brien, G.: Environment, economy and society: fitting them together into sustainable development. Sustain. Dev. Bradf. West Yorks. Engl. **10**(4), 187–196 (2002). https://doi.org/10.1002/sd.199

14. Hopwood, B., Mellor, M., O'Brien, G.: Sustainable development: mapping different approaches. Sustain. Dev. Bradf. West Yorks Engl. **13**(1), 38–52 (2005). https://doi.org/10.1002/sd.244

15. Broman, G.I., Robert, K.H.: A framework for strategic sustainable development. J. Clean. Prod. **140**, 17–31 (2017). https://doi.org/10.1016/j.jclepro.2015.10.121

16. Maltz, E., Schein, S.: Cultivating shared value initiatives: a three CS approach. J. Corp. Citizsh. **2012**(47), 55–74 (2012). https://doi.org/10.9774/GLEAF.4700.2012.au.00005

17. Brundtland, G.H.: Brundtland report. Our common future. Com. Mund. (1987)

18. Pawłowski, A.: How many dimensions does sustainable development have? Sustain. Dev. Bradf. West Yorks Engl. **16**(2), 81–90 (2008). https://doi.org/10.1002/sd.339

19. Bradley, P., Parry, G., O'Regan, N.: A framework to explore the functioning and sustainability of business models. Sustain. Prod. Consum. **21**, 57–77 (2020). https://doi.org/10.1016/j.spc.2019.10.007

20. Friedman, M.: The social responsibility of business is to increase its profits. Found. Bus. Thought, 221 (1970)

21. Goodland, R.: The concept of environmental sustainability. Annu. Rev. Ecol. Syst. **26**(1), 1–24 (1995). https://doi.org/10.1146/annurev.es.26.110195.000245

22. Sutton, P.: A perspective on environmental sustainability. Pap. Vic. Comm. Environ. Sustain., 1–32 (2004)

23. Morelli, J.: Environmental sustainability: a definition for environmental professionals. J. Environ. Sustain. **1**(1), 2 (2011)

24. Eizenberg, E., Jabareen, Y.: Social sustainability: a new conceptual framework. Sustainability **9**(1), 68 (2017). https://doi.org/10.3390/su9010068

25. Vallance, S., Perkins, H.C., Dixon, J.E.: What is social sustainability? A clarification of concepts. Geoforum **42**(3), 342–348 (2011). https://doi.org/10.1016/j.geoforum.2011.01.002

26. Polèse, M., Stren, R.E., Stren, R.: The Social Sustainability of Cities: Diversity and the Management of Change. University of Toronto Press (2000)

27. Dalampira, E.-S., Nastis, S.A.: Mapping sustainable development goals: a network analysis framework. Sustain. Dev. **28**(1), 46–55 (2020). https://doi.org/10.1002/sd.1964

28. Kostoska, O., Kocarev, L.: A novel ICT framework for sustainable development goals. Sustainability **11**(7), 1961 (2019)

29. Foss, N.J., Saebi, T.: Fifteen years of research on business model innovation: how far have we come, and where should we go? J. Manag. **43**(1), 200–227 (2017). https://doi.org/10.1177/0149206316675927

30. Johnson, M.W., Christensen, C.M., Kagermann, H.: Reinventing your business model. Harv. Bus. Rev. **86**(12), 50–59 (2008)

31. Barth, H., Ulvenblad, P.-O., Ulvenblad, P.: Towards a conceptual framework of sustainable business model innovation in the agri-food sector: a systematic literature review. Sustainability **9**(9), Article no. 9 (2017). https://doi.org/10.3390/su9091620

32. Bican, P.M., Brem, A.: Digital business model, digital transformation, digital entrepreneurship: is there a sustainable 'digital'? Sustainability **12**(13) (2020). https://doi.org/10.3390/su12135239

33. Lüdeke-Freund, F., Carroux, S., Joyce, A., Massa, L., Breuer, H.: The sustainable business model pattern taxonomy—45 patterns to support sustainability-oriented business model innovation. Sustain. Prod. Consum. **15**, 145–162 (2018). https://doi.org/10.1016/j.spc.2018.06.004

34. Lüdeke-Freund, F., Breuer, H., Massa, L.: Sustainable business model design: 45 patterns. Authors, Berlin (2022)

35. Panic, N., Leoncini, E., de Belvis, G., Ricciardi, W., Boccia, S.: Evaluation of the endorsement of the preferred reporting items for systematic reviews and meta-analysis (PRISMA) statement on the quality of published systematic review and meta-analyses. PLoS ONE **8**(12), e83138 (2013). https://doi.org/10.1371/journal.pone.0083138

36. Mio, C., Panfilo, S., Blundo, B.: Sustainable development goals and the strategic role of business: a systematic literature review. Bus. Strategy Environ. **29**(8), 3220–3245 (2020). https://doi.org/10.1002/bse.2568

37. Lozano, R., Huisingh, D.: Inter-linking issues and dimensions in sustainability reporting. J. Clean. Prod. **19**(2–3), 99–107 (2011). https://doi.org/10.1016/j.jclepro.2010.01.004

38. Sinkovics, N., Gunaratne, D., Sinkovics, R.R., Molina-Castillo, F.-J.: Sustainable business model innovation: an umbrella review. Sustainability **13**(13), 7266 (2021). https://doi.org/10.3390/su13137266

39. Samborski, A.: The energy company business model and the European green deal. Energies **15**(11) (2022). https://doi.org/10.3390/en15114059

40. Pizzi, S., Leopizzi, R., Caputo, A.: The enablers in the relationship between entrepreneurial ecosystems and the circular economy: the case of circularity.com. Manag. Environ. Qual. **33**(1), SI, 26–43 (2022). https://doi.org/10.1108/MEQ-01-2021-0011

41. Daub, C.-H., Gerhard, C.: Essento insect food AG: how edible insects evolved from an infringement into a sustainable business model. Int. J. Entrep. Innov. **23**(4), 280–290 (2022). https://doi.org/10.1177/14657503211030802

42. Guo, L., Cao, Y., Qu, Y., Tseng, M.-L.: Developing sustainable business model innovation through stakeholder management and dynamic capability: a longitudinal case study. J. Clean. Prod. **372** (2022). https://doi.org/10.1016/j.jclepro.2022.133626

43. Malik, A., Pereira, V., Budhwar, P., Varma, A., Del Giudice, M.: Sustainable innovations in an indigenous Indian Ayurvedic MNE. J. Bus. Res. **145**, 402–413 (2022). https://doi.org/10.1016/j.jbusres.2022.03.009

44. Suriyankietkaew, S., Krittayaruangroj, K., Iamsawan, N.: Sustainable leadership practices and competencies of SMEs for sustainability and resilience: a community-based social enterprise study. Sustainability **14**(10) (2022). https://doi.org/10.3390/su14105762

45. de Assis, T.F., de Abreu, V.H.S., da Costa, M.G., D'Agosto, M.A.: Methodology for prioritizing best practices applied to the sustainable last mile—the case of a Brazilian parcel delivery service company. Sustainability **14**(7) (2022). https://doi.org/10.3390/su14073812

46. Fritz, M.M.C., Lara-Rodriguez, J.S.: Mercury-free artisanal and small-scale gold mining: proposing a community-business model canvas. Extr. Ind. Soc. Int. J. **9** (2022). https://doi.org/10.1016/j.exis.2021.101039

47. Lehoux, P., Silva, H.P., Denis, J.-L., Miller, F.A., Sabio, R.P., Mendell, M.: Moving toward responsible value creation: business model challenges faced by organizations producing responsible health innovations. J. Prod. Innov. Manag. **38**(5), 548–573 (2021). https://doi.org/10.1111/jpim.12596

48. del Vecchio, P., Malandugno, C., Passiante, G., Sakka, G.: Circular economy business model for smart tourism: the case of Ecobnb. EuroMed J. Bus. **17**(1), 88–104 (2022). https://doi.org/10.1108/EMJB-09-2020-0098

49. Lanzilotti, C.O., Pinto, L.F.R., Facchini, F., Digiesi, S.: Embedding product-service system of cutting tools into the machining process: an eco-efficiency approach toward sustainable development. Sustainability **14**(3) (2022). https://doi.org/10.3390/su14031100

50. Lu, W., Du, L., Tam, V.W., Yang, Z., Lin, C., Peng, C.: Evolutionary game strategy of stakeholders under the sustainable and innovative business model: a case study of green building. J. Clean. Prod. **333**(2022). https://doi.org/10.1016/j.jclepro.2021.130136

51. Gao, S., Ma, X., Zhao, X.: Entrepreneurship, digital capabilities, and sustainable business model innovation: a case study. Mob. Inf. Syst. **2022** (2022). https://doi.org/10.1155/2022/5822423

52. Swain, S., Patoju, S.K.S.: Global enterprises: contemporarisation of khadi products in India. CASE J., 1–16 (2022). https://doi.org/10.1108/TCJ-12-2021-0214

53. Oliveira-Dias, D., Kneipp, J.M., Bichueti, R.S., Gomes, C.M.: Fostering business model innovation for sustainability: a dynamic capabilities perspective. Manag. Decis. **60**(13), 105–129 (2022). https://doi.org/10.1108/MD-05-2021-0590

54. Morioka, S.N., Holgado, M., Evans, S., Carvalho, M.M., Rotella Junior, P., Bolis, I.: Two-lenses model to unfold sustainability innovations: a tool proposal from sustainable business model and performance constructs. Sustainability **14**(1) (2022). https://doi.org/10.3390/su14010556

55. Rovanto, I.K., Bask, A.: Systemic circular business model application at the company, supply chain and society levels-a view into circular economy native and adopter companies. Bus. Strategy Environ. **30**(2), 1153–1173 (2021). https://doi.org/10.1002/bse.2677

56. Basile, V., Capobianco, N., Vona, R.: The usefulness of sustainable business models: analysis from oil and gas industry. Corp. Soc. Responsib. Environ. Manag. **28**(6), 1801–1821 (2021). https://doi.org/10.1002/csr.2153

57. Zucchella, A., Previtali, P., Strange, R.: Proactive and reactive views in the transition towards circular business models. A grounded study in the plastic packaging industry. Int. Entrep. Manag. J. **18**(3), 1073–1102 (2022). https://doi.org/10.1007/s11365-021-00785-z

58. Schiavon, O.P., May, M.R., Mendonça, A.T.B.B.: Dynamic capabilities and business model innovation in sustainable family farming. Innov. Manag. Rev. **19**(3), 252–265 (2022). https://doi.org/10.1108/INMR-07-2021-0136

59. Ding, J.-P., Li, J.-H., Liu, J.-H., Zhang, W.-F., Jia, X.-P.: ICT-based agricultural advisory services and nitrogen management practices: a case study of wheat production in China. J. Integr. Agric. **21**(6), 1799–1811 (2022). https://doi.org/10.1016/S2095-3119(21)63859-5

60. Reuter, E.: Hybrid business models in the sharing economy: the role of business model design for managing the environmental paradox. Bus. Strategy Environ. **31**(2), SI, 603–618 (2022). https://doi.org/10.1002/bse.2939

61. Bandi, V., Sahrakorpi, T., Paatero, J., Lahdelma, R.: The paradox of mini-grid business models: a conflict between business viability and customer affordability in rural India. Energy Res. Soc. Sci. **89**(2022). https://doi.org/10.1016/j.erss.2022.102535

62. Tian, X., Wang, Y.: A case study of the evolution mechanism of social enterprise business models: from living according to the situation to expanding territory. Transform. Bus. Econ. **21**(2), 361–383 (2022)

63. Doherty, B., Kittipanya-Ngam, P.: The role of social enterprise hybrid business models in inclusive value chain development. Sustainability **13**(2) (2021). https://doi.org/10.3390/su13020499

64. Best, B., Miller, K., McAdam, R., Moffett, S.: Mission or margin? Using dynamic capabilities to manage tensions in social purpose organisations' business model innovation. J. Bus. Res. **125**, 643–657 (2021). https://doi.org/10.1016/j.jbusres.2020.01.068

65. Venturelli, A., Caputo, A., Pizzi, S., Valenza, G.: A dynamic framework for sustainable open innovation in the food industry. Br. Food J. **124**(6), 1895–1911 (2022). https://doi.org/10.1108/BFJ-03-2021-0293

66. Ferlito, R., Faraci, R.: Sustainable hybrid business model of benefit corporation: the case of an Italian film production company. Sustainability **14**(10) (2022). https://doi.org/10.3390/su14105836

E-Learning and Digital Competencies

Student-Centered Design and Evaluation of a Learning Analytics Dashboard

Alena Rodda$^{(\boxtimes)}$ (iD)

Osnabrueck University, Katharinenstr. 3, 49074 Osnabrueck, Germany
alena.rodda@uni-osnabrueck.de

Abstract. The digitization of teaching at universities has increased significantly in recent years, with online and hybrid courses becoming more popular. These formats allow students a high degree of autonomy, but also require them to work independently and organize themselves. However, students often lack these skills. Learning analytics (LA) evaluations, provided as dashboards, can help students to continuously monitor their learning progress and compare themselves to their peers. Nevertheless, the student perspective has often been underrepresented in LA research. There is also a lack of standardized knowledge and processes for implementing LA and making LA information available to end users. This paper aims to develop and evaluate a LA dashboard for a university course based on the requirements of the students, using data from a university's learning management and examination system. Three dashboard versions are designed and evaluated quantitatively and qualitatively in a study with 114 participants. The results will be discussed, along with limitations and potential future research directions.

Keywords: Learning Analytics · Dashboards · Information Design

1 Introduction

The digitization of teaching at universities has developed rapidly in the last decade, also due to the Covid-19 pandemic [1]. In addition to traditional in-person teaching, online teaching formats, both synchronous and asynchronous, are becoming increasingly common, as are forms of hybrid teaching, in which students are taught partly online and partly face-to-face. Online and hybrid courses are characterized, among other things, by the fact that they allow students a high degree of autonomy [2]. Students work autonomously on online materials, such as texts, videos and assessments, and can manage their time flexibly. However, this type of learning requires that students are able to work independently and organize themselves. In practice, though, these skills are often not sufficiently available [3, 4]. In addition, online-only teaching formats, as often used during the Covid-19 pandemic, may cause students to feel isolated and lonely [5]. Lack of motivation and higher dropout rates can be a consequence [5, 6]. Learning analytics (LA) evaluations can be used to help students continuously monitor their own learning progress and compare themselves to their peers [7]. LA can be defined as "the measurement, collection, analysis, and reporting of data about learners and their contexts, for purposes

R. Jallouli et al. (Eds.): ICDEc 2023, LNBIP 485, pp. 67–80, 2023.
https://doi.org/10.1007/978-3-031-42788-6_5

of understanding and optimizing learning and the environments in which it occurs" [8] (p. 32). The data is collected from student interactions with the online portals, such as the learning management system (LMS) [9, 10]. Based on descriptive and predictive models, the data is then processed and made available to users in real-time or delayed, with the aim of supporting student learning [11]. LA reports are usually provided to students in the form of LA dashboards (LADs), to provide an easy access and to help students understand their data better with the help of visualizations [12, 13].

Students are both the primary data providers and the primary users of LADs, and it is therefore especially important to consider their demands in the design process. This can increase motivation, satisfaction and commitment when using LADs [5]. However, the students' perspective has so far been underrepresented in research [12]. In addition, there is a lack of overall standardized knowledge and processes to implement LA [11] and to make the information available to end users [14]. The goal of this paper is therefore to develop and test an LAD for a university course together with students based on their requirements. In doing so, we will address the following research question: *Which information and functionalities should be included in an LAD and how could an LAD be designed?* For this purpose, the students' requirements, which have already been identified in an explorative study with 139 participants [15], will be briefly presented first. Thereafter, a data base using the LMS and examination system of a German university is created in the form of a data mart. The data is used for the development of three dashboard versions, which are later evaluated quantitatively and qualitatively in a study with 114 students. In the quantitative evaluation the System Usability Score and the Short Visual Aesthetics of Websites Inventory are used.

As this paper examines the intersection of LA and information design, the paper begins by providing an overview of these concepts in Sect. 2. Section 3 details the requirements, the process of collecting and preparing data, as well as the development of three dashboard versions that are designed to meet the needs of students. The evaluation method and results of the study are presented in Sect. 4. The analysis and interpretation of the results are discussed in Sect. 5. The final Section provides a conclusion, that includes the limitations of the study and suggests areas for further research.

2 Theoretical Foundations

2.1 Learning Analytics

The increasing adoption of online learning has many benefits and was without alternative during the Covid-19 pandemic, but it also leads to new educational challenges [16]. Online learning relies on a more independent learning model that contradicts widely accepted socio-constructivist theories of learning [17]. Students may feel isolated because of the reduced contact to their peers and teachers [5]. Some feel disoriented in the online space, can get overwhelmed by the large amount of learning materials or lose track of their own performances [5, 6]. This may result in a loss of motivation, poorer academic performance, and higher dropout rates [5, 6]. At the same time, online learning creates vast amounts of educational data, that could be used for LA with the aim of easing some of the problems mentioned above. The student data can be divided into three categories: Socio-demographic data, previous academic data and learning activity data [10]. Socio-demographic data contains information about the students themselves, such as their age and gender. The previous academic data includes past academic performances, like standardized test scores, grade point averages (GPAs), and the number of credit points. Interactions of students with the content in LMS, or their communications with peers and teachers, can be summarized in the category of learning activity data [9, 10]. Other sources of data, such as social media platforms, can also be used to expand the LA dataset. LA data can be analyzed in a variety of ways. Analyses include descriptive modeling of the current state and predictions of the future state [11] for individuals, as well as on a course level or on a departmental level [8].

LA can support students and teachers to self-reflect, provide an overview of current strengths and weaknesses, improve teaching and learning methods, and give students orientation as well as a sense of belonging [8, 11, 18]. Although many more promising benefits of LA have been shown in literature, there are some challenging aspects of implementing LA in practice [11, 19]. Many ethical concerns have been raised [20]. LA could invade students' privacy [10], or be used for analyses (later on) that students never actively agreed to [21]. Universities need to address issues such as consent, data privacy and security, length of data retention, and access to data [5, 19]. Another problem is the integration of the various structured and unstructured data, since LA data usually come from several different data sources. The universities' systems are mostly not designed for LA purposes and they are often not interoperable [19]. The systems are often managed by different departments. As a consequence, the data integration and cleaning is complex and can result in a loss of data [11]. There can also be issues concerning the quality of the data. Cross-university comparisons tend to fail due to the lack of standardized key indicators [19]. For universities, the collection and preparation of data thus represents an enormous effort, which is associated with high costs [11, 19].

2.2 Dashboard Design

Dashboards are a key tool in Business Intelligence (BI) [22], that provide visual representations of important information to help users make informed decisions [13]. There are several important aspects to consider when designing a dashboard, including their *functional scope, scope of the information*, and the *visual representation* [13]. The *functional scope* of a dashboard depends on its intended use, as it can provide warnings or recommendations for action, as well as more detailed information through drill-down functionalities and mouseover effects [13, 23]. It is important to find a balance between providing enough functionality to be useful, but not so much that it becomes overwhelming for users. The *scope of the information* presented on a dashboard is also important, as it determines how users perceive and use the information system and the tasks associated with it [24]. If users cannot understand or interpret the information, it can lead to incorrect decisions [25] and frustration [26]. It is therefore crucial that dashboards are designed in a way that is clear, concise, and easy to understand. A dashboard should offer enough information for users to make informed decisions, but not provide too much information, as users might feel distracted or confused. In terms of *visual representation*, there are many design options to choose from, but there are no strict guidelines to follow. However, the way information is presented can significantly impact how it is understood and used by users [13, 27]. Factors such as the use of color, font, and the arrangement of elements can influence user behavior. There are some general recommendations for visualizations, such as using bar charts rather than pie charts, and using color to highlight important information [28]. When it comes to LADs, the information presented often includes resource usage, time spent in the LMS, assessment data, and comparisons between students [23]. When creating LADs, it is necessary to assure that students with no prior knowledge of analytics and reporting can benefit from the data. LADs should offer clear insights on how to improve student learning and should be designed to be transparent so that students are able to understand how their data are being used [5].

3 Development of a Learning Analytics Dashboard

3.1 Requirement Analysis

In order to create an LAD for students, the requirements for such a system have to be defined first. The requirements are based on an exploratory mixed-method study with 139 students of a BI course at a German university [15]. The course was taught in a hybrid format, which means that students were given access to learning materials through an LMS and participated in face-to-face activities that included group work and case studies using current software. The study consisted of two parts: An online questionnaire and a task in which participants were asked to create their own LAD in Tableau using a synthetic data set. The dashboards were analyzed according to their functional and informational scopes, as well as their visualizations (see Table 1).

The findings revealed that 84% of the participants wanted an LA dashboard for their courses, with the desired functions being the ability to compare their performance to that of other students, forecast final grades, receive alerts about potential threats to passing the course or achieving personal goals, and receive recommendations for elective subjects or additional courses. The majority of participants also asked for the opportunity to monitor their own learning progress and proposed additional functions including lists of typical mistakes, and countdown timers for due dates. The majority of students preferred regular updates of LA data, with self-assessment results, midterm exam scores, and homework exercise scores ranking as its most crucial components. The information used on the dashboards was mainly academic and learning activity data. Socio-demographic attributes were largely rejected. Tables and bar charts were the most commonly used visualizations. The most frequently used colors were blue, red, green, yellow, and orange. Green or blue were used to present good performance, while yellow or orange were used for average and red for bad performance [15].

3.2 Data Collection

The data for the creation of the dashboards for this paper was sourced from two different systems at the university, the LMS (StudIP) and the examination system (HISinOne). In order to evaluate the student data, an Oracle Structured Query Language (SQL) server was established and the provided data was imported. A data model was created, which comprises 12 tables, containing a total of 56,155 data entries, related to 155 students enrolled in the BI course. All of these students gave their explicit written consent for

Table 1. Requirements for Learning Analytics Dashboards

Category	Meta-Requirements	Specific Requirements
Functional Scope	*Performance Notifications and Hints*	Display of students' individual performance Display of comparisons to peers Analyses based on topics Prediction of final grade Possibility for self-input Summary of common errors Alerts to warn students if "at-risk" Recommendations for other courses Countdown for deadlines Notifications Daily updates of data
Scope of Information	*Demographic Data Academic Data* *Learning Activity Data*	Name GPA Credit points Number of semesters Self-assessment scores Exercise scores Midterm score Final exam score Bonus points LMS Logins Video usage Time expenditure Attendance
Visual Presentation	*Type of Visualization* *Colors Used*	Bar chart Table Line graph Blue Red Green Yellow Orange

the data to be analyzed. The integration of the data presented a challenge, as there has previously been no use of LA at the university, and the systems are not designed for this purpose. The BI course consists of both a lecture and exercise event, hosted on the LMS. The data had to be merged and cleaned, followed by the integration of the examination data. In order to protect the privacy of individuals, a technique known as hash anonymization was employed, in which sensitive information is replaced with a hash value (a fixed-size string of characters).

3.3 Design of the Learning Analytics Dashboard

Based on the requirements and the available student data, a team of five students and one lecturer developed three different LAD versions. These were later tested and compared (Sect. 4). For the design of each element, the data set of an average performing student in week 6 (out of 12) is used as a base. The same data is used for all elements in each of the three versions to ensure consistency. All implementable features were included. For this paper, the dashboard versions had to be translated into English and be optimized for readability. Figure 1 shows an overview of dashboard version 1.

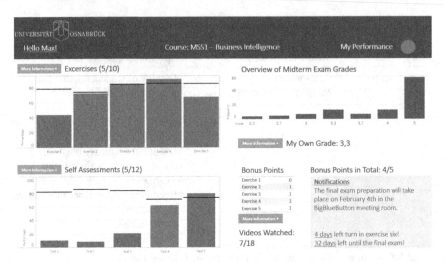

Fig. 1. Learning Analytics Dashboard Version 1

Located at the top is a blue menu bar that contains the university's logo, a greeting, and the name of the course. The circle on the top right displays an evaluation of the student's current performance in the course (green indicates good performance, orange indicates an average performance, and red indicates a poor performance compared to the other students in the class). On the top left, there is a bar chart with an overview of the scores achieved on homework exercises completed so far. The bars are again colored green, yellow, or red depending on the performance, and the black lines show the average scores of the course. The visualization at the bottom left of the dashboard is designed similarly to the visualization just described. The bar chart contains the scores from self-assessment tests. On the right side of the dashboard, users will find the results of the most recent tests, in this case those of a midterm exam. An overview of bonus points, videos watched, current notifications, and upcoming deadlines is also provided. The dashboard includes multiple mouseover effects for quick additional information, such as on "my performance" and the individual bars and lines of the bar charts. Figure 2 shows examples of the mouseover effects. The dashboard also features drill-downs labeled "more information +" which, when clicked, open a separate page containing additional information and visualizations. Figure 3 shows an example for a more detailed view of the midterm exam. Additionally, clicking on the user's name will bring up a page containing personal academic data, such as the user's field of study, the current academic term, the GPA, and the credit points earned so far.

All three versions of the dashboard contain the students' main requirements. Differences can be observed in the layout and the presence of certain elements. For example, video statistics are displayed only in versions 1 and 3. Version 3 is the only version that allows users to enter their own data, such as their assessment of their performance in the current week. However, it does not include demographic data (such as "hello Max"), academic data, or the student's current performance assessment ("my performance").

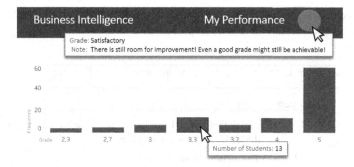

Fig. 2. Mouseover Effects

Question Titel	Own Score	Max. Score
Common Data Warehouse Model	3,00	3,00
Independent Data Marts	4,00	6,00
Metadata Classes	0,00	3,00
Extract, Transform, Load (ETL)	2,00	4,00
Structured Query Language (SQL) Part 1	4,00	8,00
Structured Query Language (SQL) Part 2	2,00	2,00
Informatica Mappings Part 1	2,00	4,00
Informatica Mappings Part 2	3,00	4,00
Online Analytical Processing (OLAP)	2,00	2,00
Exception Reporting	2,00	4,00
Multiple Choice	6,00	10,00

Less Details -   Midterm Exam Detail View

Fig. 3. Drill-Down for More Information (My Own Grade - Midterm Exam)

4 Evaluation

4.1 Design of the Study

The three different versions of the LAD will be tested using different sample groups. The goal is to evaluate design and content differences between the versions. The participant group consists of business and information systems students who had previously completed a Business Intelligence course, resulting in a relatively homogeneous group. Participants were randomly and evenly distributed among the versions and were motivated to participate by the offer of bonus points for a course or the chance to participate in a voucher raffle. An online questionnaire was used for the evaluation. Upon entering the study, the participants were first presented with a welcome page and instructions. They were then able to try out the dashboard using Tableau Public. After a minimum of 5 minutes, they could also access the questionnaire on the dashboards, allowing them to focus solely on the dashboard beforehand. The questionnaire, created in LimeSurvey, was composed of five parts: 1) The System Usability Scale (SUS), 2) the Short Visual Aesthetics of Websites Inventory (VisAWI-S), 3) questions on functionality and design, 4) open-ended questions, and 5) demographic questions. Closed questions were rated on a 5-point Likert scale, with a range of 1 (do not agree) to 5 (fully agree). Table 2 shows the structure of the questionnaire and sample items.

Table 2. Overview of Questionnaire and Sample Questions

Part	# Items	Sample Questions
1 - SUS	10	I think that I would like to use this system frequently. I thought the dashboard was easy to use
2 - VisAWI-S	4	The color composition is attractive The layout appears professionally designed
3 - Elements and Functionality	15	I find the midterm exam section very good As a student, I find the LA dashboard useful
4 - Open Questions	2	What other functions would you like to see in the dashboard? What would you change about the dashboard?
5 - Demographics	4	How old are you? What is your gender?

The SUS questionnaire was utilized for the first part of the evaluation. The SUS is a standardized measure of the usability of a product, specifically software, and is composed of 10 items [29]. Higher scores indicate higher usability. The SUS is widely used in the field of human-computer interaction and has been shown to be a reliable and valid measure of usability [30]. In order to assess both the usability and aesthetics of the dashboard, the VisAWI-S questionnaire was used for the second part of the evaluation. The VisAWI-S is a 4-item questionnaire that asks users to rate the visual appeal of a website or system. Research has demonstrated that this measure of visual aesthetics is both reliable and valid [31]. The third part of the questionnaire included closed questions about the individual elements of the dashboard, their functionality, and the design. These items were formulated based on relevant literature. The fourth part of the questionnaire contained open-ended questions about functionality and suggestions for improvement. The fifth part of the questionnaire provided questions about the participants' age, gender, course of study, and highest degree.

4.2 Results of the Quantitative Questions

The following quantitative analyses were conducted using the statistical software program R. A total of 114 students took part in our study, with 39 evaluating the first version, 37 evaluating the second version, and 38 evaluating the third version. The gender distribution among participants was 62% male and 36% female, with two participants not specifying their gender. The age range of participants was between 20 and 37 years, with an average age of 24.17. The majority of participants were undergraduate students in information systems or graduate students in business. The highest level of education completed by the majority was either a high school or a bachelor's degree. The Cronbach's Alpha was 0.88 for the SUS and 0.81 for the VisAWI-S, indicating a good reliability of the questionnaire [32]. The Mann-Whitney U test was used to determine whether there were statistically significant differences, as the Shapiro-Wilk test indicated that a normal distribution could not be assumed [33, 34].

The mean value on the SUS for all three dashboards was 81.05, with a score range of 0 (worst value) to 100 (best value). The standard deviation was 15.5. The first version received the highest mean score, at 85.06, while the second version had the lowest mean score, at 78.78. The third version had a slightly higher mean score, at 79.14 (see Fig. 4). The average rating of the three versions on the SUS is within the good range, with the first version even approaching the "excellent" category [30]. There were statistically significant differences in scores for certain items between versions 1 and 3. Specifically, for item 5 ("I found the various functions in the dashboard were well integrated"), version 1 had a mean score of 4.1, while version 3 had a mean score of 3.5. Additionally, there were statistically significant differences in scores for items 8 ("I found the dashboard very cumbersome to use") and 9 ("I felt very confident using the dashboard") between version 1 (mean scores of 1.43 and 4.4, respectively) and version 2 (mean scores of 1.94 and 3.94, respectively). These findings suggest that there may be improvements that could be made concerning the integration and usability of the dashboard in future versions. It is noteworthy that the ease of use of the dashboard received high ratings, with mean scores of 4.31 and 4.44 for items 3 ("I thought the dashboard was easy to use") and 7 ("I would imagine that most people would learn to use this dashboard very quickly"), respectively.

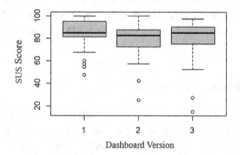

Fig. 4. SUS-Score of the Dashboard Versions

On the VisAWI-S scale, the mean value across the three dashboards was 3.55, with a score range of 1 (worst value) to 5 (highest value). The first version received the highest score, at 3.73, followed by the third version with a mean of 3.49 and the second version with a mean score of 3.42 (see Fig. 5). The mean rating on the VisAWI-S scale was slightly lower than the benchmark alternatives, but still within reach [35]. According to the ratings, the overall color scheme was rated most positively (with an overall mean score of 3.9), while the versatility of the layout was rated least positively (with an overall mean score of 3.37). These findings suggest that there is room for improvement concerning the aesthetics of the dashboard, especially concerning the layout.

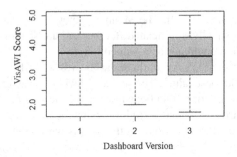

Fig. 5. VisAWI-S-Score of the Dashboard Versions

The third part of the survey assessed the satisfaction with each individual element of the dashboard. The elements were generally rated positively, with a median of 4 out of 5 for the majority. Three elements, the "overview of midterm grades", "own grade," and "current announcements" were rated even higher, with a median of 5. The element for self-input (version 3) was evaluated with the lowest score, a median of 3. There were statistically significant differences in the rating of certain elements among the three versions of the dashboard. In particular, satisfaction with the "exercises," "self-assessment tests," "own grade in midterm exam," and "current performance" elements varied. In all cases, version 1 received higher ratings than the other two versions. The drill-down and mouseover effects, as well as the number of functions and elements included in the dashboard, received positive ratings with a mean of 4. 19% of the participants missed certain functions in the dashboard, which will be discussed in further detail in Sect. 4.3. Of the participants, 97% considered the LAD to be useful, and 95% said they would use it regularly.

4.3 Results of the Qualitative Questions

At the end of the survey participants were asked to answer to open questions. In regard to additional functions that would improve the use of the dashboard, participants came up with many ideas. These included, for example, a direct connection between the dashboard and the university's LMS (n = 6), which was deemed very important for accessing links, files, and other resources. The other requested features included a more detailed view of the videos watched and progress made (n = 4), breakdowns of final grades (n = 7), a help menu with details about the teacher's contact information and office hours (n = 3), and an overview of errors summarized by topic or assignment (n = 8). Additionally, students highlighted the importance of a final grade prediction function (n = 8).

Related to the second open question of what participants would change about the dashboard, the most common response related to a more appealing and modern dashboard design (n = 27), with clearer structures and areas, as well as a navigation menu and different pages. Participants also mentioned a need for more detailed comparisons with their peers in order to understand where they stand in relation to them (n = 9). There were also several comments on the "exercises" element, including suggestions to make the mouseover effect more similar to that of the "self-assessment tests" element and to better display the average of all students in the course (n = 5). Participants also suggested that the elements related to the midterm exam should be more hierarchically organized using drill-downs (n = 4). In general, there were many recommendations to use drill-downs more frequently to create hierarchies of information (n = 8). There was also feedback to make the element "my performance" more transparent in terms of how the assessment is calculated, so that students can better understand it can be influenced by their actions (n = 4). While the feedback from all participants was very similar across the different versions of the dashboard, there is one exception regarding the "self-input" feature. This was only available on version 3, as a text field with an input option. This element was rated the lowest in the questionnaire with a score of 3. While several participants said that they would like the ability to indicate in the dashboard how they rate their own performance, the function would take up too much space and should only appear a once a week, possibly as a pop-up window (n = 3).

5 Discussion

One key finding of this study is the importance of considering the perspective of students in the design and implementation of LADs. The scores on the SUS and VisAWI-S indicate that the dashboard is generally easy to use and aesthetically pleasing. The feedback provided by participants regarding the specific information and functions they would like to see in the LADs highlights the importance of meeting the needs and preferences of students in order to ensure their commitment and success.

There were also some differences in the evaluation of the same elements across versions of the LADs, with version 1 generally receiving the highest scores. This suggests that certain design and features may be more effective at meeting the needs and preferences of students than others. A revised version of the dashboard could be based on version 1. The layout should be more professionally modified, as the VisAWI-S-Score still leaves room for improvement, especially concerning the diversity facet and craftsmanship. This was also illustrated by the results of the qualitative evaluation. The LAD can be improved by making it look more organized, such as by grouping related elements and arranging them according to importance. More detailed information through drill-downs and a prediction of the final grade should also be included. The comparison to peers should be expanded on a more detailed level. The LAD should include a function for self-input, however, according to the qualitative results, it does not need to be constantly presented on the dashboard but rather pop up once a week.

Based on the results of our study, several design principles for LADs can be derived. First, it is important to consider the perspective of students throughout the whole design and development process, as this can increase student motivation, satisfaction, and commitment to use an LAD [5]. This includes involving students in the requirements engineering and design process, gathering their feedback and input, and testing LADs with student users to ensure that they are effective and user-friendly. Second, LADs should provide detailed information and functionalities related to the students' progress and performance. This involves information about test results and their progress compared to peers, as well as an assessment of their current performance, and the final grade. Providing this information can help students track their progress and understand what they need to do to improve. Third, LADs should be easy to use and aesthetically pleasing, which can help increase student engagement and commitment to using them. This includes designing LADs with clear navigation, intuitive interfaces, and visually appealing layouts. Finally, the results highlight the value of incorporating features such as drill-downs and mouseover effects, as well as the importance of providing a variety of elements in the LADs. By considering these design principles, it is possible to create LADs that are effective at promoting student engagement, performance, and success.

6 Conclusion, Limitations and Further Research

In summary, the use of LADs has the potential to support students in monitoring and understanding their learning progress, and improve their motivation and satisfaction. However, it is important to consider students' perspectives in the design process to ensure that the LADs meet their needs and expectations. The results of this study show that the first version of the dashboard received the highest ratings in terms of usability, visual aesthetics, and functionality, while the second and third versions scored lower in these areas. In particular, the first version was appreciated for its clear layout, ability to compare progress with peers, and drill-down and mouseover effects. It can be used as a basis for further developments. The qualitative results showed that students would generally like to have an LAD for their courses, but it should offer a more detailed overview of their progress, including a breakdown of final grades and a help menu.

This study has several limitations that should be considered when interpreting the results. While the sample size is sufficient for a usability study, it may not be representative of the entire student population. Furthermore, the study was conducted at a single German university, and the results may not be generalizable to other institutions or countries. To address these limitations and extend the findings of this study, future research could examine the long-term effects of LADs on student performance and dropout rates, as well as explore the implementation and use of LADs in different educational contexts. Additionally, it would be useful to explore the potential of integrating LADs with other tools such as artificial intelligence and gamification to enhance the user experience. Further research in this area would be valuable in order to determine the effectiveness and potential benefits of such integrations.

References

1. Zhao, Y., Watterston, J.: The changes we need: education post COVID-19. J. Educ. Change **22**, 3–12 (2021)
2. Kim, M.K., Kim, S.M., Khera, O., Getman, J.: The experience of three flipped classrooms in an urban university: an exploration of design principles. Internet High. Educ. **22**, 37–50 (2014)
3. Lai, C.-L., Hwang, G.-J.: A self-regulated flipped classroom approach to improving students' learning performance in a mathematics course. Comput. Educ. **100**, 126–140 (2016)
4. Mason, G.S., Shuman, T.R., Cook, K.E.: Comparing the effectiveness of an inverted classroom to a traditional classroom in an upper-division engineering course. IEEE Trans. Educ. **56**, 430–435 (2013)
5. Ferguson, R.: Learning analytics: drivers, developments and challenges. Int. J. Technol. Enhanc. Learn. **4**, 304–317 (2012)

6. Mazza, R., Dimitrova, V.: Visualising student tracking data to support instructors in web-based distance education. In: 13th International World Wide Web, pp. 154–161 (2004)
7. Jovanović, J., Gašević, D., Dawson, S., Pardo, A., Mirriahi, N.: Learning analytics to unveil learning strategies in a flipped classroom. Internet High. Educ. **33**, 74–85 (2017)
8. Long, P., Siemens, G.: Penetrating the fog: analytics in learning and education. Educ. Rev. **46**, 31–40 (2011)
9. Greller, W., Drachsler, H.: Translating learning into numbers: a generic framework for learning analytics. Educ. Technol. Soc. **15**, 42–57 (2012)
10. Ifenthaler, D., Schumacher, C.: Student perceptions of privacy principles for learning analytics. Educ. Technol. Res. Dev. **64**, 923–938 (2016)
11. Nguyen, A., Tuunanen, T., Gardner, L., Sheridan, D.: Design principles for learning analytics information systems in higher education. Eur. J. Inf. Syst. **30**, 541–568 (2021)
12. Ifenthaler, D.: Are higher education institutions prepared for learning analytics? TechTrends **61**(4), 366–371 (2016). https://doi.org/10.1007/s11528-016-0154-0
13. Yigitbasioglu, O.M., Velcu, O.: A review of dashboards in performance management: implications for design and research. Int. J. Account. Inf. Syst. **13**, 41–59 (2012)
14. Vieira, C., Parsons, P., Byrd, V.: Visual learning analytics of educational data: a systematic literature review and research agenda. Comput. Educ. **122**, 119–135 (2018)
15. Droit, A., Rieger, B.: Learning analytics in the flipped classroom – learning dashboards from the students' perspective. In: Proceedings of the 53rd Hawaii International Conference on System Sciences, pp. 100–107 (2020)
16. Gašević, D., Dawson, S., Siemens, G.: Let's not forget: learning analytics are about learning. TechTrends **59**, 64–71 (2015)
17. Bayne, S., Ross, J.: The pedagogy of the Massive Open Online Course (MOOC): the UK View (2014)
18. Ellis, C.: Broadening the scope and increasing the usefulness of learning analytics: the case for assessment analytics. Br. J. Edu. Technol. **44**, 662–664 (2013)
19. Daniel, B.: Big Data and analytics in higher education: opportunities and challenges. Br. J. Edu. Technol. **46**, 904–920 (2015)
20. Sclater, N.: Learning Analytics Explained. Routledge, New York (2017)
21. Prinsloo, P., Slade, S.: Student vulnerability, agency and learning analytics: an exploration. J. Learn. Anal. **3**, 159–182 (2016)
22. Negash, S., Gray, P.: Business intelligence. In: Handbook on Decision Support Systems, vol. 4, pp. 175–193 (2008)
23. Schumacher, C., Ifenthaler, D.: Features students really expect from learning analytics. Comput. Hum. Behav. **78**, 397–407 (2018)
24. Popovič, A., Hackney, R., Coelho, P.S., Jaklič, J.: Towards business intelligence systems success: effects of maturity and culture on analytical decision making. Decis. Support Syst. **54**, 729–739 (2012)
25. Janssen, M., van der Voort, H., Wahyudi, A.: Factors influencing big data decision-making quality. J. Bus. Res. **70**, 338–345 (2017)
26. Hancock, P.A., Warm, J.S.: A dynamic model of stress and sustained attention. Hum. Factors **31**, 519–537 (1989)
27. Anderson, J.C., Mueller, J.M.: The effects of experience and data presentation format on an auditing judgment. J. Appl. Bus. Res. **21**, 53–63 (2011)
28. Klerkx, J., Verbert, K., Duval, E.: Learning analytics dashboards. In: Handbook of Learning Analytics, pp. 143–150. Society for Learning Analytics Research (SoLAR) (2017)
29. Brooke, J.: SUS: a 'quick and dirty' usability scale. In: Jordan, P.W., Thomas, B., McClelland, I.L., Weerdmeester, B. (eds.) Usability Evaluation in Industry, pp. 207–212. CRC Press (1996)
30. Bangor, A., Kortum, P.T., Miller, J.T.: An empirical evaluation of the system usability scale. Int. J. Hum. Comput. Interact. **24**, 574–594 (2008)

31. Moshagen, M., Thielsch, M.: A short version of the visual aesthetics of websites inventory. Behav. Inform. Technol. **32**, 1305–1311 (2013)
32. Cronbach, L.J.: Coefficient alpha and the internal structure of tests. Psychometrika **16**, 297–334 (1951)
33. McKnight, P.E., Najab, J.: Mann-Whitney U test. In: Weiner, I.B., Craighead, W.E., Corsini, R.J. (eds.) The Corsini Encyclopedia of Psychology, p. 960. Wiley, Hoboken (2010)
34. Shapiro, S.S., Wilk, M.B.: Approximations for the null distribution of the W statistic. Technometrics **10**, 861 (1968)
35. Thielsch, M.T., Spieth, J.-H., Jahn, M., Hirschfeld, G., Koller, F.: Der VisAWI im Praxiseinsatz: Best Practices, neue Benchmarks und neue Entwicklungen. UP14-Vorträge. German UPA (2014)

Competences for Digital Transformation in Companies – An Analysis of Job Advertisements in Germany

Frieda Ernst, Mana Ghofrani, Carlo Sahrmann, Paul Schwegmann,
Henning Brink(✉) ⓘ, and Fynn-Hendrik Paul ⓘ

BOW, Osnabrück University, 49069 Osnabrück, Germany
{henning.brink,fynn-hendrik.paul}@uos.de

Abstract. Digital transformation (DT) offers major improvement of a business by significantly changing its characteristics through the combination of information, computing, communication, and connectivity technologies by using new digital technologies. To take advantage of these opportunities, certain competences are required. However, not all of the required competences can be fulfilled by the current employees. To fill these gaps, companies are looking for employees with different competence sets on employment websites. Most studies analyzing competences for DT are conducting interviews, questionnaires, or performing literature reviews which disregards the actual requirements of companies looking for employees to conquer DT. To better understand what competences companies are looking for in the labor market, we conducted a content analysis of job advertisements on StepStone. Using text mining, data mining, and a subsequent manual analysis of 3,138 job advertisements posted on a relevant employment website, we were able to derive 23 different competences relevant to DT.

Keywords: digital transformation · competences · model

1 Introduction

Globalization and economic trends present companies with challenges that cannot be solved without digital technologies [1]. Companies need to adapt their thinking and actions to the new conditions which cannot solely be mastered by only automating their processes. Digital transformation (DT) is therefore inevitable for companies [2]. Although there is no universally accepted definition, various sources agree that DT includes the "process of reinventing a business to digitize operations and formulate extended supply chain relationships" [3], "the fundamental transformation of the entire business world through the establishment of new technologies based on the internet with a fundamental impact on society as a whole" [4] and "results from the need to use new technologies to stay competitive in the Internet age, where services and products are delivered both online and offline" [5].

To advance DT in companies, qualified employees are required, which leads to an increase in jobs related to DT. While in 2020 38.3% of companies planned to meet these

© The Author(s), under exclusive license to Springer Nature Switzerland AG 2023
R. Jallouli et al. (Eds.): ICDEc 2023, LNBIP 485, pp. 81–96, 2023.
https://doi.org/10.1007/978-3-031-42788-6_6

requirements by hiring contractors, 34.5% aimed to expand their current workforce [6]. These vacancies are then adverted on employment websites. This paper aims to analyze the job advertisements (job ads) to better understand what competences are needed to drive the DT from a company's perspective. We intend to answer the following research question: Which competences are companies seeking to accelerate DT?

To answer this research question, we conducted a content analysis based on 3,138 gathered job ads in Germany posted on the employment website StepStone. Based on roles and competences extracted from job ads, we develop and link a competence and role model resulting in a competence-role-matrix.

The paper is structured as follows: The theoretical background is explained in chapter two. This is followed by an explanation of the research methodology, after which the study results are presented in chapter four. These results are discussed in chapter five and summarized in chapter six to provide recommendations for subsequent studies.

2 Theoretical Background

DT is the improvement of a business by significantly changing its characteristics through the combination of information, computing, communication, and connectivity technologies by using new digital technologies [7]. DT has a socio-technical impact on the entire company [7]. DTs of companies redefine the value proposition and create new organizational identities [8]. Therefore, all departments of a company are influenced and have to face changes such as the use and implementation of new digital technologies, processes, and structures as well as related financial barriers [9].

Since DT is not about replacing employees with computers, but rather about the additional help computers can provide to complete tasks or speed up work processes [10], employees need certain competences to interact with the new technologies. These digital competences have become more relevant in recent years which led to a dynamization of the job market [11]. Nowadays, Digital competences have become an integral part of the working environment and are widely used and also accepted by the workforce in various business segments [13–15]. DT is a process of organizational change that is driven by digital technologies [7]. Therefore, the spectrum of competences required for the success of a DT goes beyond the technology-oriented competences. Most papers focus on digital competences rather than competences for DT. DT competences are captured by a broad variety of definitions. Osmundsen defines DT competences as "a firm's bundle of its collective competences (skills, knowledge, expertise, experience, and other employee attributes) that are essential for a DT, and includes the firm's ability to combine these attributes in responding to and managing the DT." [16], while another study concludes that the relevant competences for DT are digital vision, digital knowledge, failing fast, empowerment, and managing diverse teams [17].

The lack of qualified DT specialists is a big challenge for businesses in Germany [18]. This leads to more job ads being published on relevant employment websites. Although the research field on DT continues to grow and the DT competences are an important part of this change, there are few studies on this topic. Most researches deal with competences required for specific jobs or job fields, for example, the digital skills of teachers and their change throughout the COVID-19 pandemic [19] or the need for digital skills in the field of marketing and e-commerce [20]. Some researchers take a deeper look at the competences that are needed when using certain technologies such as the collaboration of employees with artificial intelligence [21] while other papers are limited to specific countries or regions, for example, the IT competences resulting from the digital changes in the United Arab Emirates [22] or the DT competences required in the Norwegian energy sector [16]. Especially papers that focus on Germany are rare, even though the DT gains more and more importance. This development is represented by the Digitalization Index which is generated every year to show the level of digitalization in Germany. While this index was 100 points in 2020, it rose to the score of 108.9 points in 2022 [23]. A major driver of this increase was the COVID-19 pandemic because most of the businesses of various branches had to completely rearrange their way of working [24]. Nevertheless, digitalization in Germany is still behind expectations and the European average [25]. Competences for DT are increasingly required.

3 Research Approach

While conducting this research we followed the approach of a content analysis using text mining, data mining, and a subsequent manual analysis of the data to identify competences and match them to relevant roles in a resulting role-competence matrix.

We first had to select an appropriate employment website. We examined several employment websites, whereby we paid attention to the relevance and structure of the website. We selected "StepStone.de" [26], one of the largest employment websites in Germany, since the HTML structure adheres to a fixed form and most job ads are divided into the sections like "Title", "About us", "Tasks", "Profile", and "We offer". This allows us to analyze the job ads in a structured way. The search string "Digital* Transformation" was chosen to limit the list of results to the job ads that are relevant to DT. With this string, we can ensure that the search results contain digital transformation as a coherent term and all German and English results are included. Additionally, we set the region to "Germany" to only include national job advertisements.

To automatically extract the information from each job ad on the employment website we decided to use the web scraping tool Octoparse [27]. By using URL detection, all matching job ads can be passed through and due to the consistent HTML structure of the pages on StepStone, the contents of the job ads can be saved and assigned to the previously mentioned sections like "Title or "Profile". During our data collection period in December 2022, we extracted 3,375 job ads, of which 3,138 were still relevant after excluding duplicates and incomplete advertisements. As a result, we have obtained an Excel table in which each row represents a job ad, consisting of the column headers "Title", "Your Profile", "Tasks", "Employer" and "Type of employment".

In the next step, the text analysis & mining software Wordstat [28] was used to analyze the extracted data. This unsupervised method of text mining is particularly suitable for systematically mining large amounts of data. Since this has the disadvantage that texts cannot be analyzed in as much depth as with manual text analysis, it is helpful to combine the advantages of automatic content analysis with those of manual analysis [29]. To achieve this, the results of the first, automated analysis with Wordstat are further interpreted and aggregated by the authors in a second step.

We first identified job roles in the data by analyzing and clustering the "Title" header of the extracted job ads. By using the nonnegative matrix factorization (NMF) Wordstat forms topics by identifying patterns in word frequencies and using these patterns as a basis [30]. NMF allows the "automatic identification of semantic features and document clusters in a heterogeneous text collection" [31]. Wordstat was able to identify 44 topics representing different job roles. The 44 generated topics, however, still showed many similarities or relations between them regarding the naming or the related keywords. Therefore, these 44 topics were further aggregated by the authors using inductive manual analysis [29]. Here, the approach of the qualitative derivation of possible superordinate categories was used. The authors independently took a deeper look at the topics and the keywords included. Mayrings [32] approach involves first paraphrasing, then generalizing and finally reducing the given text. This detailed work with the already existing topics helped to develop individual lists of possible final topics. As a final step, an exchange about the different lists formed by each author took place. By identifying similarities and differences between the authors' suggestions, it was possible to discuss and merge and/or rename the topics until a consensus among the authors was reached. Finally, 12 job roles were derived.

In addition to the job roles, we analyzed the required competences. We followed the same methodical procedure as for the job roles. First, Wordstat automatically determined topics of competences by analyzing the "your profile" column. This resulted in 80 topics representing the different competences. Again, the topics showed many similarities or relations between them regarding the naming or the related keywords. By analyzing the given 80 topics and the related keywords using inductive manual analysis [29] aggregated topic lists were formed by each author. The suggestions were compared and discussed. Finally, it was possible to compile a final list of 23 competence topics.

The competence and role models both are illustrated in tables including the respective titles of competences or roles, a selection of the keywords filtered out of the job ads, the coherence, and the relative frequency. The coherence refers to the consistency between the keywords and how well-connected these are [33].

Finally, we combined the results of the job roles and competences analysis in a matrix (see Table 3). The matrix shows the percentage values of competences per role clarifying the relationship and importance of a specific competence for a certain role.

4 Results

In the following, we will present the results. First, the competences and the roles are described. The description of both is in descending order of frequency of mention in the job ads. Finally, we will connect both in a matrix and show the relationships.

Table 1 shows the competence topics derived from our research approach. With an occurrence of 80.43%, the overall most required competence is a university degree. This competence is composed of various degrees of university education in different disciplines like computer science, business informatics, economics, physics, mathematics, and engineering up to and including a doctoral degree. The second most required competence is a high affinity for languages, especially German and English. This competence is required in 70.00% of all cases and often includes the requirements to speak or write the languages fluently as shown by the keywords. An apprenticeship is required for 59.40% of all analyzed job ads. This ties in with the university degree because both competences describe an educational qualification. The high values for both of these competences could be explained by the fact that some job ads specifically required a university in addition to an apprenticeship or, in some cases, listed both while one of the qualifications is sufficient.

The first soft skill in Table 1 is professionalism with a frequency of 47.16% of overall job ads. The topic describes a high level of responsibility, reliability, and commitment. The fifth competence is practical experience, which can be linked to competences one and three. With a relative frequency of 44.39%, it is only marginally less frequently required and includes experience levels from internships up to actual work experience. Competence number six, fast perception, is the second most frequently required soft skill with a relative occurrence of 41.71%, and includes the competences necessary for problem-solving. These competences begin with the "analysis" and extend to the process of finding "creative solutions" as shown in the keywords. Communication skills are required in 37.06% of all analyzed job ads and are closely linked to language skills. Communication skills enable the applicants to communicate constructively, effectively, and consciously [34] and are closely related to an applicant's interpersonal skills and ability to work in a team. For teamwork skills, it is important that the applicants can communicate their results and show high social and intercultural competence. In this context, the competence of communication is relevant both internally when dealing with colleagues and externally when dealing with customers. Competence number 8, flexible working environment, is mentioned in 36.68% of all job ads and means a high level of mobility and flexibility and extends to business trips, both nationally and internationally. The ninth competence, productivity software, marks the first appearance of software skills and includes the office suite applications for instance in the Microsoft 365 package. With an occurrence of 34.96%, it is the last competence to be mentioned in over one-third of all job ads.

Agile software development refers to approaches in the software development process that are intended to increase the transparency and speed of change [35]. This leads to faster deployment of the developed system while minimizing risks and missteps in the development process. In this context, candidates are expected to have experience with a wide range of tools such as Scrum and Kanban. Agile methods occupy the tenth place of the required competences with an occurrence of 16.22%. Shortly behind with a frequency of 15.65% is the second mention of a specific software skillset, SAP. This includes the different components of the modular SAP architecture such as Finance (FI), Controlling (CO), Sales & Distribution (SD), Materials Management (MM), and SAP HANA, a multi-model database. Awareness of DT is only required in 12.14% of all job ads and is therefore the twelfth most requested competence. Another soft skill, a confident appearance, is mentioned in 12.01% of all cases and includes sovereignty and professionalism. Competence 14, programming languages (6.28%), and 17, JavaScript Typescript (3.66%), are two very closely linked topics and include programming languages as well as database knowledge. Together with competence 21, CI/CD (2.29%), they form an agile software development skillset. Database- and cloud-computing platforms are mentioned in 5.51% of all cases. Knowledge of business processes is mentioned

Table 1. Competences for DT.

Code	Topic	Keywords	Coherence	Cases (rel.)
C1	University degree	University of applied sciences; Higher education; Business administration; Economics; Computer science; Successfully completed degree; Degree; Computer science; Computer engineering; Doctorate	0.724	80.43
C2	Languages	English skills; Word; Written; German; Fluent; Language; Written; Skills; English; Language skills	0.351	70.00
C3	Apprenticeship	Apprenticeship; Completed; Commercial; Qualification; Vocational training; IT specialist	0.401	59.40
C4	Professionalism	Sense of responsibility; Reliability; Commitment; Self-initiative; Motivation; Commitment; Independence; Structured way of working; Familiarize with topics; Commitment Help	0.375	47.16
C5	Practical experience	Experience; Internships; Practicum; Work Experience	0.268	44.39
C6	Fast perception	Complex relationships; Creative solutions; Finding solutions; Technical relationships; Efficient to prepare; Quick analytical skills	0.442	41.71
C7	Communication skills	Communicative; Team; Project team; Skills; Communication; Social competence; Inter-cultural competence	0.555	37.06
C8	Flexible working environment	Mobility; Flexibility; Willingness to travel; Business travel; National; International; Driver's license class; Hybrid work; International travel	0.248	36.68

(*continued*)

Table 1. (*continued*)

Code	Topic	Keywords	Coherence	Cases (rel.)
C9	Productivity software	OFFICE; MS; Excel; PowerPoint; Word; applications; handling; user skills; Power BI; BIG DATA	0.513	34.96
C10	Agile methods	Scrum; Kanban; Prince; Agile methods; design thinking; experience	0.396	16.22
C11	SAP	FI; CO; SD; MM; SAP; Modules; HANA	0.394	15.65
C12	Awareness of DT	Transformation; Digital; Trends; Digital; Current; Technologies	0.278	12.14
C13	Confident appearance	Appearance; confident; sovereign; convincing; professional; personal; convincing	0.232	12.01
C14	Programming languages	Python; SQL; JAVA; Programming Languages; Databases; javascript; programming languages	0.249	6.28
C15	Cloud computing	AWS; Azure; Cloud; Microsoft; Cloud Technologies	0.333	5.51
C16	Knowledge of business processes	Accounting; controlling; business administration; auditing; corporate finance; due diligence	0.312	4.91
C17	Javascript/Typescript	HTML; CSS; Javascript; Web; Javascript Typescript	0.409	3.66
C18	Operating systems	Server; Windows; Linux; Client; Active; Microsoft; Network	0.334	3.03
C19	Machine learning	Machine learning; Data; Analytics; Product; Advanced analytics; Deep; Learning	0.316	2.90
C20	Cyber security	Cyber; Expert; University; Digital; Advanced training; Business	0.382	2.61
C21	CI/CD	CI; CD; CI CD PIPELINES	0.332	2.29

(continued)

Table 1. (*continued*)

Code	Topic	Keywords	Coherence	Cases (rel.)
C22	Social media	Social; Media; Content; Marketing; Platform	0.207	1.34
C23	Wiki software	Jira; Confluence; Git	0.217	1.34

in 4.91% of all cases and includes competences regarding accounting and controlling as well as business administration. The software related competences number 18, operating systems (3.03%), 19, machine learning (2.90%), 20, cyber security (2.61%), and 23, wiki software (1.34%) form a highly specialized competence model and are only required in a fraction of the analyzed job ads. Together with relevant software, social media skills are the least required competence with a relative frequency of 1.34%, and include the use of social media, particularly in the area of content creation and marketing.

We were able to create a set of 12 final job roles as shown in Table 2. The most frequent job role, with an occurrence of 15.52%, is consultant, which groups all consultants and senior consultants. Therefore, management consulting plays an important role in the labor market.

The second largest cluster is project staff (9.24%), combining product owners, agile coaches, and project managers, followed by software developer/SAP developer with 6.15%. This cluster contains all possible professions related to software development, programming, and solution architecture.

The fourth most frequent job ads are for financial professionals with an occurrence of 5.90%. Next up is customer service professional (4.08%), which includes customer success, SAP Academy, and account managers. Data analyst/scientist is also represented with a frequency of 3.38%. This role deals with data analytics, data scientists, and cyber security. It is followed by supply chain management professionals, which fill 3.35% of cases. The eighth position in the role model is system engineer (2.96%) including system engineering, IT specialists, and jobs in the IT sales department. The cluster (Online-)marketing professional, which deals with all the job descriptions concerning marketing and commerce, has a frequency of 1.75%, followed by Human Resources (HR) professional (1.37%) grouping business partners and HR business partners. The penultimate position in our role model is filled by lawyer/attorney with 1.12% and the least frequent cluster formed is commercial clerk (0.57%) concluding internal sales and office work.

The clusters of the role model cover only 55.39% of the total role designations. 44.61% of the job descriptions we worked with could not be classified in the model. Even the given clusters show low frequencies and very low coherences, suggesting a very large variety of different roles and job titles dealing with DT.

To create the matrix shown in Table 3, we examined over 17,000 mentions of the 23 required competences which are distributed over 3,138 job ads. The matrix shown in Fig. 3 is sorted in descending order by the average frequency of the correlating competence. The overall most relevant combination is language with lawyer with an occurrence of 100%. This is followed by a university degree with financial professionals (93.51%)

Table 2. Roles for DT.

Code	Topic	Keywords	Coherence	Cases rel.
R1	Consultant	Senior; Manager; Associate; Consultant; Advisor; SAP; Public Sector; Energy Consulting; Risk Management; Risk Consulting; Business Administration; Process Manager	0.091	15.52
R2	Project staff	Owner; Product; Platform; Analyst; Agile; Digital; Consultant; Project Manager; Digital Transformation	0.116	9.24
R3	Software developer/SAP developer	Developer; Frontend; Web; Software; Development; Java; SAP; Backend; Platform; Microsoft; BI; Azure; C; Solution Architect; Cloud	0.102	6.15
R4	Financial professional	Financial; Services; Consulting; Technology; Banking; Capital; Controlling; Accounting; Tax Consulting; Tax; Auditing; Pricing	0.170	5.90
R5	Customer service professional	Academy; Success; Customer; Executive; Sales; Account; SAP Academy; Account Manager	0.341	4.08
R6	Data analyst/scientist	Data; Scientist; Analytics; Science; Analyst; Datacenter; Network; IT; Infrastructure; Cloud; Cyber Security; IT Security	0.077	3.38
R7	Supply chain management professional	International Trade Management; Foreign; Wholesale; Merchants; Supply; Chain; Management; Service; Business; Experience	0.087	3.35
R8	System engineer	System; Engineer; Integration; IT; Software; Requirements	0.072	2.96

(continued)

Table 2. (*continued*)

Code	Topic	Keywords	Coherence	Cases rel.
R9	(Online) Marketing professional	Marketing; Online; Commerce; Content; Manager; Communication; Media; Corporate; Innovation; Content	0.084	1.75
R10	HR professional	Partner; Development; HR; Business; Talent; Learning	0.112	1.37
R11	Lawyer/Attorney	Lawyer; Attorney; Fully Qualified Lawyer;	0.116	1.12
R12	Commercial clerk	Commercial; Administrator; Clerk; Internal Sales; Systems; Office; Controller; Project	0.030	0.57

Table 3. Competence-Role-Matrix.

	Roles											
	R1	R2	R3	R4	R5	R6	R7	R8	R9	R10	R11	R12
C1	86.45%	90.00%	70.47%	93.51%	64.06%	70.5%	68.57%	80.65%	78.18%	79.07%	88.57%	83.33%
C2	81.11%	75.86%	78.24%	78.92%	73.44%	68.87%	76.19%	62.37%	78.18%	74.42%	100.00%	44.44%
C3	63.04%	63.45%	51.30%	56.76%	56.25%	52.83%	40.00%	65.59%	56.36%	58.14%	25.71%	83.33%
C4	47.64%	35.52%	32.64%	58.92%	39.84%	37.74%	60.00%	43.01%	40.00%	55.81%	65.71%	55.56%
C5	56.47%	50.34%	27.98%	58.92%	35.94%	38.68%	28.57%	36.56%	49.09%	51.16%	68.57%	44.44%
C6	52.98%	41.03%	29.02%	64.32%	44.53%	29.25%	40.00%	33.33%	47.27%	32.56%	80.00%	44.44%
C7	48.25%	40.34%	27.46%	50.81%	39.06%	42.45%	45.71%	31.18%	40.00%	46.51%	62.86%	16.67%
C8	52.36%	38.28%	32.64%	51.35%	35.16%	21.70%	32.38%	29.03%	16.36%	23.26%	54.29%	11.11%
C9	29.36%	28.28%	23.83%	33.51%	32.03%	32.08%	38.10%	24.73%	34.55%	41.86%	25.71%	44.44%
C10	23.82%	12.41%	18.13%	17.30%	26.56%	16.98%	15.24%	7.53%	14.55%	11.63%		16.67%
C11	21.15%	31.38%	25.91%	5.95%	10.94%	12.26%	12.38%	18.28%	9.09%	6.98%		11.11%
C12	15.20%	7.93%	9.84%	22.16%	14.84%	15.09%	10.48%	13.98%	9.09%	25.58%	11.43%	
C13	12.32%	22.76%	10.36%	14.59%	15.63%	5.66%	12.38%	4.30%	10.91%	13.95%	2.86%	
C14	4.31%	7.24%	23.32%	7.03%	0.78%	15.09%	7.62%	16.13%	1.82%			
C15	3.29%	5.52%	29.02%	1.62%	3.91%	12.26%	1.90%	12.90%	5.45%	2.33%		
C16	9.45%	3.45%	1.04%	27.57%	1.56%		2.86%	1.08%		4.65%		16.67%
C17	1.85%	2.07%	26.42%	1.62%		1.89%	2.86%	8,60%	9.09%			
C18	3.49%	4.83%	1.55%		1.56%	11.32%	3.81%	2.15%	9.09%	4.65%		
C19	1.44%	2.41%	6.22%		0.78%	11.32%	3.81%	10.75%				
C20	0.82%	0.34%	13.99%	0.54%		4.72%		12.90%	1.82%			
C21	3.29%	5.86%	1.04%	2.16%	3.13%	13.21%	2.86%	2.15%				
C22	0.21%	0.69%	1.55%	0.54%	0.78%		0.95%		25.45%			
C23	0.41%	4.14%	4.15%	0.54%	1.56%	0.94%	0.95%	2.15%				5.56%

(Competences)

and university degree with project staff (90.00%). It should be noted that a university degree is the most commonly required competence among all job roles. Another trend seems to be that the different roles often require the same competences in their job ads where university degree, language, and apprenticeship are the three most frequently requested competences with an average of up to 79.43%. This is then followed by 7 additional competences, where productivity software seems to act as a divider between commonly requested and higher specialized competences with an average of 33.03%. Further down in the matrix we begin to see competences like SAP which is most commonly requested in customer service professionals (26.56%) or Agile methods which are mostly required in the job role (online) marketing professional with an occurrence of 26.42%. The software developer/SAP developer is the role with the highest combined percentages regarding the required software skills such as programming languages (23.32%), cloud computing (29.02%), and wiki software (4.15%). Also conspicuous are the overall high percentages for financial services professionals except for the software skills.

5 Discussion

The results will be discussed in the following by starting with the competence model, continuing with the role model, and ending with the matrix.

The most frequent competences in our model are academic degrees, speaking different languages, apprenticeships, and working independently, showing that the more common competences are nonetheless the most required ones. These results are reflected in other studies as well. According to Gilli et al., an academic degree is necessary for nearly every leading role [36]. In other professions, educational background is also cited as one of the most sought-after competences, e.g. in jobs related to Big Data [37]. Our second most frequent competence, speaking different languages, is not often represented in other studies. In the job ads speaking English and German is often required. This was predictable, as we analyzed data from a German employment website. In other countries, it is to be expected that the required (foreign) language skills will vary. Nevertheless, speaking foreign languages is mentioned in the competence model from Kateryna et al. as well [38]. Their model divides the competences into cognitive, social and behavioral, and digital skills, while the digital skills are the most specific and least ones [38]. This underlines the importance of the general competences that are not specifically related to DT but still emphasizes a change in the set of required competences due to the inclusion of digital competences.

These specific competences can be found in the lower ranks of our model. Other approaches also do not see subject-specific competences as relevant as the more general competences mentioned above [36, 39]. Some of our more specific competences are for example the handling of SAP. A study on business software offers for Industry 4.0 engages in the variety of application fields for SAP delivering solutions to almost every requirement concerning intra- or inter-company processes [40]. SAP applications became an important part of the professional environment and thus the knowledge to handle these applications is an often-requested competence. Many competences that focus on the use of software occupy lower-ranked, more specific places in our competence model. In this context, programming languages such as JavaScript are another often requested competence. According to Jony et al., JavaScript was the most required competence in the internet and communication technology sector until 2017 [41]. Even though it lost the leading position, it still is a significant competence.

One of the most requested competence in other studies is communication, a cognitive skill that is required in many different kinds of jobs [11, 36, 42]. In our model, it is mentioned in less than 50% of the job descriptions. Management competence, which is listed as one of the most important competences in various papers [21, 43, 44], only ranks sixteenth in our model. "Organizations seeking managers for their DT efforts consider general managerial and leadership skills more important than specific technological skills" [36]. The differences regarding the relevance of certain competences can be explained by the different roles considered in the studies. The studies mostly focus on manager jobs while our research includes various roles in the context of DT.

To better understand how the relevance of certain competences varies depending on the underlining role, we generated a role model based on the considered job ads. Next to some larger job role topics, such as financial professional, the model contains many specific job descriptions forming an independent role, for example, lawyer which occurs very often and thus fills the ninth place.

The most frequently mentioned job role is the consultant. An important characteristic of consultants is the contact with many different companies and clients [45], leading to a high need for adaptability. Therefore, consultant services must keep up with other companies to succeed in this rapidly evolving environment. The second most frequent role of project staff combines product owners, agile coaches, and project managers. Other studies also examined the required competences for product owners and established a model, where soft skills such as communication and analytical skills are among the most important competences [46]. This also applies to our matrix in which the combination of project staff and language results in values of 75.86% and 40.43% for the combination with communication skills. Projects demand a high level of creativity, complexity, and innovation to ensure competitiveness. Currently, this innovation refers to the application of new technologies in the context of DT [47]. Another often-mentioned job role is the software developer/SAP developer, which deals accurately with digital technologies and therefore has a direct link to DT. The demand for professionals in internet and communication technology jobs rises [38], with a movement to more specific jobs such as computer systems engineers or architects noticeable [41]. Comparable roles are also represented in the lower ranks of our role model. The fourth place in our model, financial professionals, is also often found in the context of DT. According to Kim et al., companies in the financial sector have to "secure competitiveness while adapting to the constantly changing domestic and international financial market environments by actively and autonomously using the latest and most advanced digital technologies" [48]. The DT of the finance sector is additionally accelerated through the changing and modernized regulations [49].

Nevertheless, the role model only covers 55.37% of all job titles in the job ads, leading to a big number of job titles with low frequencies that could not be classified. The big variety of roles indicates the importance of DT in different business fields. "Digital business ecosystems, which in the past were only a topic of interest for IT and software industries, are becoming more and more inseparable from regular business ecosystems and increasingly relevant across sectors as digital technologies diffuse through industries and society" [50]. The introduction of digital technologies and the rising amount of interdependencies forces companies, that never had to deal with IT-related matters, and even legacy firms to follow this trend [51].

The results from the role and the competence model are combined in the matrix. Our findings indicate the subdivision of DT competences into a basic set of competences including the knowledge of languages, independency, fast perception, communication skills, flexible working, confidence, and the handling of productivity software, and the more specific competences including SAP, agile methods, awareness of DT, programming languages, cloud computing, knowledge in business processes, JavaScript, cyber security, operating systems, CI/CD, machine learning, social media, and wiki software. Comparable findings can be found in the competence model of Mavlutova et al. in which a distinction between basic, distinctive, and specific competences is made [52]. Gurcan speaks of soft competences showing parallels to our basic competences and business-orientated and analytical competences being the more specific ones [37].

6 Conclusion and Implications

Companies are looking for employees with competences to drive the DT. In this study, we analyzed 3,138 job ads. We were able to identify 23 different topics representing competences and 12 distinct roles. The relation between the competences and the roles is illustrated in the matrix and underlines the importance of the set of basic competences, which are highly required in every job role. The specific competences, mostly more in-depth digital competences, are only requested in a few individual roles.

This study has contributions to both academia and business. The competence model developed allows academia to gain a deeper understanding of what competences are currently needed in companies. Based on this, existing competence models based on other data sources can be extended. Companies, on the other hand, receive a collection of different competences that can be used to critically review whether necessary competences for DT are present in the company or not. Decision-makers in companies should push the development of the missing competences to master the DT.

However, this study is not without limitations. Employment websites offered a variety of HTML structures, from which only a few worked well enough with web scraping tools. This has reduced the choice of suitable employment websites resulting in only job ads from Stepstone being analyzed. Furthermore, only job ads in Germany have been analyzed in this study. Another limitation of this study is related to the quality of the job ads. The analysis of job ads involves the risk of shortcomings concerning the reliability and validity of the results [36]. Regarding the identified roles, it should be noted that these are not necessarily clear-cut, and a small number of job ads could be assigned to multiple roles. Other researchers might obtain a different allocation. Recruiters and HR managers must be able to identify required competences in the company and transfer them into specific job ads [53]. It is further possible that the term "digital transformation" is only used as a buzzword in some job ads, but that the actual jobs have no reference to it.

In future research, the database should be expanded by including more job ads. This could be done by widening the scope of the study to a broader spectrum of (non-German-speaking) countries. Furthermore, a longitudinal study could be conducted to investigate whether the required competences change over several points in time. Conducting data triangulation, e.g., by including interviews with experts, could overcome the described disadvantages of using only job ads for the model development.

References

1. Agostini, L., Galati, F., Gastaldi, L.: The digitalization of the innovation process: challenges and opportunities from a management perspective. Eur. J. Innov. Manag. **23**, 1–12 (2020). https://doi.org/10.1108/EJIM-11-2019-0330
2. Siebel, T.M.: Digital Transformation: Survive and Thrive in an Era of Mass Extinction. RosettaBooks (2019)
3. Bowersox, D.J., Closs, D.J., Drayer, R.: The digital transformation: technology and beyond. Supply Chain Manag. Rev. **9**(1), 22–29: ILL (2005)
4. Rasch, M., Koß, R.: Digital Controlling: Digitale Transformation im Controlling (2015). https://www.pwc.de/de/digitale-transformation/assets/pwc-studie-digitale-transformation-im-controlling.pdf
5. Mergel, I., Edelmann, N., Haug, N.: Defining digital transformation: results from expert interviews. Gov. Inf. Q. **36**, 101385 (2019). https://doi.org/10.1016/j.giq.2019.06.002
6. The Future of Jobs Report 2020 (2020). https://www3.weforum.org/docs/WEF_Future_of_Jobs_2020.pdf
7. Vial, G.: Understanding digital transformation: a review and a research agenda. J. Strateg. Inf. Syst. **28**, 118–144 (2019)
8. Wessel, L., Baiyere, A., Ologeanu-Taddei, R., Cha, J., Jensen, T.: Unpacking the difference between digital transformation and IT-enabled organizational transformation. J. Assoc. Inf. Syst. (2020)
9. Hess, T., Matt, C., Benlian, A., Wiesböck, F.: Options for formulating a digital transformation strategy. MIS Q. Exec. **15**, 123–139 (2016)
10. Kolade, O., Owoseni, A.: Employment 5.0: the work of the future and the future of work. Technol. Soc. **71**, 102086 (2022). https://doi.org/10.1016/j.techsoc.2022.102086
11. Kowal, B., Włodarz, D., Brzychczy, E., Klepka, A.: Analysis of employees' competencies in the context of industry 4.0. Energies **15** (2022). https://doi.org/10.3390/en15197142
12. Vuorikari, R., Kluzer, S., Punie, Y.: DigComp 2.2: The Digital Competence Framework for Citizens - With new examples of knowledge, skills and attitudes. https://doi.org/10.2760/115376. https://publications.jrc.ec.europa.eu/repository/handle/JRC128415. Accessed 31 Jan 2023
13. Vasilev, V.L., Gapsalamov, A.R., Akhmetshin, E.M., Bochkareva, T.N., Yumashev, A.V., Anisimova, T.I.: Digitalization peculiarities of organizations: a case study. Entrep. Sustain. Issues **7**, 3173–3190 (2020). https://doi.org/10.9770/jesi.2020.7.4(39)
14. Nazeha, N., Pavagadhi, D., Kyaw, B.M., Car, J., Jimenez, G., Car, L.T.: A digitally competent health workforce: scoping review of educational frameworks. J. Med. Internet Res. **22** (2020). https://doi.org/10.2196/22706
15. Wang, B., Ha-Brookshire, J.E.: Exploration of digital competency requirements within the fashion supply chain with an anticipation of industry 4.0. Int. J. Fash. Des. Technol. Educ. **11**, 333–342 (2018). https://doi.org/10.1080/17543266.2018.1448459
16. Osmundsen, K.S.: Competences for digital transformation: insights from the Norwegian energy sector. Presented at the Proceedings of the Annual Hawaii International Conference on System Sciences (2020)
17. Imran, F., Shahzad, K., Butt, A., Kantola, J.: Leadership competencies for digital transformation: evidence from multiple cases. In: Kantola, J., Nazir, S., Salminen, V. (eds.) AHFE 2020. AISC, vol. 1209, pp. 81–87. Springer, Cham (2020). https://doi.org/10.1007/978-3-030-50791-6_11
18. Winter, J., Frey, A., Biehler, J.: Towards the next decade of industrie 4.0 – current state in research and adoption and promising development paths from a German perspective. Sci **4**, 31 (2022). https://doi.org/10.3390/sci4030031

19. Velandia Rodriguez, C.A., Mena-Guacas, A.F., Tobón, S., López-Meneses, E.: Digital teacher competence frameworks evolution and their use in Ibero-America up to the year the COVID-19 pandemic began: a systematic review. Int. J. Environ. Res. Public Health **19** (2022). https://doi.org/10.3390/ijerph192416828

20. Kovács, I., Keresztes, É.R.: Young employees' perceptions about employability skills for e-commerce. Economies **10** (2022). https://doi.org/10.3390/economies10120309

21. Anton, E., Behne, A., Teuteberg, F.: The humans behind artificial intelligence–an operationalisation of AI competencies (2020)

22. Alzarooni, A., Lataifeh, M.: Exploring the relationship between IT competence and digital transformation within government projects in the UAE. Presented at the Proceedings of the 2022 IEEE International Conference on Communications, Computing, Cybersecurity and Informatics, CCCI 2022 (2022). https://doi.org/10.1109/CCCI55352.2022.9926598

23. Büchel, J., Engels, B.: Digitalisation of the economy in Germany: digitalisation index 2022 (2022)

24. Bellmann, L., et al.: Digitalisierungsschub in Firmen während der Corona-Pandemie. Wirtschaftsdienst **101**, 713–718 (2021). https://doi.org/10.1007/s10273-021-3005-3

25. Benchmarking Digitalisierung in Deutschland. https://www.ifo.de/en/publications/2021/monograph-authorship/benchmarking-digitalisierung-deutschland. Accessed 09 Feb 2023

26. StepStone. https://www.stepstone.de/. Accessed 01 Feb 2023

27. Octoparse. https://www.octoparse.com/. Accessed 01 Feb 2023

28. Wordstat. https://provalisresearch.com/products/content-analysis-software/. Accessed 01 Feb 2023

29. Waldherr, A., Wehden, L.-O., Stoltenberg, D., Miltner, P., Ostner, S., Pfetsch, B.: Induktive Kategorienbildung in der Inhaltsanalyse: Kombination automatischer und manueller Verfahren. 20 (2019)

30. Kobayashi, V.B., Mol, S.T., Berkers, H.A., Kismihók, G., Den Hartog, D.N.: Text mining in organizational research. Organ. Res. Methods **21**, 733–765 (2018). https://doi.org/10.1177/1094428117722619

31. Pauca, V.P., Shahnaz, F., Berry, M.W., Plemmons, R.J.: Text mining using non-negative matrix factorizations. In: Proceedings of the 2004 SIAM International Conference on Data Mining (SDM), pp. 452–456. Society for Industrial and Applied Mathematics (2004). https://doi.org/10.1137/1.9781611972740.45

32. Mayring, P.: Qualitative Inhaltsanalyse: Grundlagen und Techniken. Beltz, Weinheim u.a. (2010)

33. Aletras, N., Stevenson, M.: Evaluating topic coherence using distributional semantics. In: Proceedings of the 10th International Conference on Computational Semantics (IWCS 2013) – Long Papers, pp. 13–22. Association for Computational Linguistics, Potsdam, Germany (2013)

34. Tkalac Verčič, A., Verčič, D., Sriramesh, K.: Internal communication: definition, parameters, and the future. Public Relat. Rev. **38**, 223–230 (2012). https://doi.org/10.1016/j.pubrev.2011.12.019

35. Betta, J., Boronina, L.: Transparency in project management – from traditional to agile (2018)

36. Gilli, K., Nippa, M., Knappstein, M.: Leadership competencies for digital transformation: an exploratory content analysis of job advertisements. Ger. J. Hum. Resour. Manag. **37**, 50–75 (2023). https://doi.org/10.1177/23970022221087252

37. Gurcan, F.: Extraction of core competencies for big data: implications for competency-based engineering education (2019)

38. Kateryna, A., Oleksandr, R., Mariia, T., Iryna, S., Evgen, K., Anastasiia, L.: Digital literacy development trends in the professional environment. Int. J. Learn. Teach. Educ. Res. **19**, 55–79 (2020). https://doi.org/10.26803/ijlter.19.7.4

39. Horlacher, A., Hess, T.: What does a chief digital officer do? Managerial tasks and roles of a new C-level position in the context of digital transformation. In: 2016 49th Hawaii International Conference on System Sciences (HICSS), pp. 5126–5135 (2016). https://doi.org/10.1109/HICSS.2016.634

40. Cocca, P., Marciano, F., Rossi, D., Alberti, M.: Business software offer for industry 4.0: the SAP case. Presented at the (2018). https://doi.org/10.1016/j.ifacol.2018.08.427

41. Jony, S.S.R., Kano, T., Hayashi, R., Matsuda, N., Rahman, M.S.: An exploratory study of online job portal data of the ICT sector in bangladesh: analysis, recommendations and preliminary implications for ICT curriculum reform. Educ. Sci. 12 (2022). https://doi.org/10.3390/educsci12070423

42. Klus, M., Müller, J.: Identifying leadership skills required in the digital age. SSRN J. (2020). https://doi.org/10.2139/ssrn.3564861

43. North, K., Hermann, A., Ramos, I., Aramburu, N., Gudoniene, D.: The VOIL digital transformation competence framework. Evaluation and design of higher education curricula. In: Lopata, A., Butkienė, R., Gudonienė, D., Sukackė, V. (eds.) ICIST 2020. CCIS, vol. 1283, pp. 283–296. Springer, Cham (2020). https://doi.org/10.1007/978-3-030-59506-7_23

44. González-Varona, J.M., López-Paredes, A., Poza, D., Acebes, F.: Building and development of an organizational competence for digital transformation in SMEs. J. Ind. Eng. Manag. (JIEM) 14, 15–24 (2021). https://doi.org/10.3926/jiem.3279

45. Bode, M., Daneva, M., van Sinderen, M.J.: Characterising the digital transformation of IT consulting services–results from a systematic mapping study. IET Softw. 16, 455–477 (2022). https://doi.org/10.1049/sfw2.12068

46. Daneva, M., Wang, C., Hoener, P.: What the job market wants from requirements engineers? An empirical analysis of online job ads from the Netherlands. Presented at the International Symposium on Empirical Software Engineering and Measurement (2017). https://doi.org/10.1109/ESEM.2017.60

47. Adikari, S., Mcdonald, C., Lynch, N.: Design science-oriented usability modelling for software requirements (2007). https://doi.org/10.1007/978-3-540-73105-4_41

48. Kim, E., Kim, M., Kyung, Y.: A case study of digital transformation : focusing on the financial sector in South Korea and overseas. Asia Pac. J. Inf. Syst. 32, 537–563 (2022). https://doi.org/10.14329/apjis.2022.32.3.537

49. Bank, E.C.: The future of finance and the outlook for regulation. https://www.ecb.europa.eu/press/key/date/2017/html/ecb.sp171109.en.html. Accessed 09 Feb 2023

50. Hanelt, A., Bohnsack, R., Marz, D., Antunes Marante, C.: A systematic review of the literature on digital transformation: insights and implications for strategy and organizational change. J. Manag. Stud. 58, 1159–1197 (2021). https://doi.org/10.1111/joms.12639

51. Kopalle, P.K., Kumar, V., Subramaniam, M.: How legacy firms can embrace the digital ecosystem via digital customer orientation. J. Acad. Mark. Sci. 48, 114–131 (2020). https://doi.org/10.1007/s11747-019-00694-2

52. Mavlutova, I., Volkova, T.: Digital transformation of financial sector and challengies for competencies development. Presented at the 2019 7th International Conference on Modeling, Development and Strategic Management of Economic System (MDSMES 2019), October 2019. https://doi.org/10.2991/mdsmes-19.2019.31

53. Ahmed, S.: Desired competencies and job duties of non-profit CEOs in relation to the current challenges: through the lens of CEOs' job advertisements. J. Manag. Dev. 24, 913–928 (2005). https://doi.org/10.1108/02621710510627055

How Can Learning Analytics Enhance Online Teaching? A Teacher's Perspective

Alena Rodda(✉) (iD)

Osnabrueck University, Katharinenstr. 3, 49074 Osnabrueck, Germany
`alena.rodda@uni-osnabrueck.de`

Abstract. This paper examines the perspectives of teachers on the use of Learning Analytics (LA) to enhance online teaching in higher education institutions during the post-Covid era. The increasing shift towards online teaching as a result of the pandemic has presented a number of challenges for teachers. As online teaching is likely to remain a part of the higher education landscape, it is important to understand teachers' views on the topic. This study explores how LA could support teachers in their online teaching. For this purpose, we conducted 18 interviews with instructors from German and Dutch universities about the changes that online teaching has led to, opportunities and threats of LA, the information teachers require about their students, and the ability of LA to enhance the advantages of online teaching and mitigate its disadvantages. Our results show that teachers' opinions of LA are generally positive and that they would use LA if it were available in form of an intuitive and interactive dashboard. LA also offers the possibility to alleviate many of the problems in online teaching identified by the instructors.

Keywords: Online teaching · Learning Analytics · Higher Education · E-Learning

1 Introduction

The increasing digitization of universities, which was accelerated by the Covid-19 pandemic, has led to a significant shift toward online teaching [1]. While this transition was necessary, it also presented a number of challenges for teachers at higher education institutions (HEIs) [2]. As online teaching is likely to remain a part of the higher education landscape even after the pandemic, it is important to understand how teachers are evaluating their experiences with online teaching and whether Learning Analytics (LA) can be used to improve its quality and efficiency. LA refer to the process of collecting, analyzing, and reporting information about learners and their learning environment in order to understand and optimize learning [3]. From the perspective of teachers, limited research has been conducted to understand their perceptions of LA [4]. Studies show that teachers who have not worked with LA before often feel confused about what it is and how it could benefit their teaching practice [5]. The lack of participation of important stakeholders, such as teachers, in the development of LA systems, can be considered a

R. Jallouli et al. (Eds.): ICDEc 2023, LNBIP 485, pp. 97–110, 2023.
https://doi.org/10.1007/978-3-031-42788-6_7

significant ethical problem [6]. The inadequate involvement of teachers in the process of development can hinder the widespread adoption of LA in HEIs [7]. Therefore, this study aims to investigate the relationship between online teaching and LA in the post-Covid era from the teachers' perspective by answering the following four research questions: *1) What advantages and disadvantages do teachers see in online teaching compared to face-to-face teaching? 2) Which information do teachers require about their students to help them improve their online teaching and in what ways should this information be provided to them? 3) To what extent are LA suitable to enhance the identified advantages of online teaching and mitigate its disadvantages?* To answer these questions, a qualitative study with 18 teachers from multiple universities was conducted. We used a semi-structured questionnaire, which consists of three parts, covering the positions of the interviewees, their experiences with online teaching, perceived advantages and disadvantages of online teaching compared to in-person teaching, and questions about opportunities and threats, data requirements, presentation formats, and timeliness of LA (Sect. 3). The data collected was analyzed according to Mayring's qualitative content analysis [8]. The results will be used to answer the first two research questions in Sect. 3. The third research question will be discussed by using the results of the interviews and examining them in the light of current literature in Sect. 5. The paper finishes with a conclusion and outlook on future research.

2 Theoretical Background

2.1 Online Teaching

Online teaching is becoming a popular and convenient way to deliver education and facilitate learning [9]. It refers to the process of delivering educational content and instruction to students over the internet [10, 11]. Online teaching can take many different forms, including asynchronous (self-paced) instruction, where the students complete coursework on their own time and synchronous (real-time) instruction, where the teacher and students are online at the same time [12]. Asynchronous e-learning allows learners to balance education with work, family, and other commitments. It is most commonly supported by the usage of videos, reading materials, and discussion boards [12]. Synchronous e-learning, on the other hand, can create a sense of community and engagement, as it allows for real-time interaction and communication, for example by using video-conferencing and chats [12]. Online teaching is particularly beneficial for students and teachers who are unable to attend traditional in-person classes due to location, mobility, or personal circumstances [12]. It can also be cost-effective for students, allow a more student-centered and self-paced approach to learning and can grant unlimited, world-wide access to knowledge [13]. However, it is important to note that online teaching is not without its challenges. There are, for example, concerns about the decline of face-to-face interactions between students and teachers. This lack of personal interaction can negatively impact the effectiveness of online teaching [14]. Online teaching also comes with a significant workload for teachers [13]. The quality of online teaching is highly dependent on the quality of materials. It is important that teachers are well-trained and have the necessary technical skills to create and deliver engaging and interactive online learning materials and experiences [2]. The sudden transition to online teaching during the COVID-19 pandemic has highlighted existing problems in HEIs, such as poor online teaching infrastructure, the inexperience of teachers in using digital instructional formats, and lack of technical support [13, 15]. These challenges impact the effectiveness of online teaching for students and teachers [13]. Hodges et al. (2020) differentiate between well-planned online teaching and the teaching that has been hastily implemented as a response to the COVID-19 pandemic, which they refer to as "emergency remote teaching" [1].

2.2 Learning Analytics

The increase in online teaching and continuous developments in the field of data analytics have led universities to consider how the data generated in educational systems, such as learning management systems (LMS), can be analyzed and used to improve learning and teaching practices [16]. This educational data includes information about the users themselves, their interactions with systems, communication with others, and information about courses and learning objectives [17]. By processing the data with the help of descriptive and predictive models, teachers can gain insights about the students, their learning behavior and their usage of course materials [18]. This can support teachers to make informed decisions in order to improve learning and teaching environments [19]. From the student's point of view, LA can provide insights into their own learning habits and allow them to adjust their learning behavior [3]. Many teachers and institutions recognize the potential value of LA in improving both teaching and learning [5]. For example, in a survey of 250 teachers at an Australian university, 70% agreed that using LA would benefit their courses [20]. However, concerns have been raised about data protection [21], the invasion of privacy and the need to ensure that LA is used ethically [22]. Many teachers also express skepticism about the utility of LA [5]. They have concerns about their ability to interpret the feedback provided, potential negative impact on students' behavior, and the extra workload that LA requires [5, 20]. The usage also poses the risk of inaccurate predictions or misinterpretations [23], as a result of flawed or inadequate data [24]. LMS capture only a limited aspect of the learning process and do not provide a comprehensive perspective that takes into account all possible factors that affect a student's success or failure [25].

3 Methodology

For the present study, a qualitative research design was adopted, comprising semi-structured interviews with 18 teachers from German and Dutch universities. The participants were research and teaching assistants, postdoctoral researchers, and professors with an average teaching experience of 9 years, of which an average of almost 3 years was in online teaching. 7 participants have initial, limited experience with LA while the remainder has no experience with LA. The questionnaire was systematically developed [26] and contained 15 questions divided into three groups. The first group of questions covered the positions and responsibilities of the interviewees, as well as their experiences with in-person and online teaching. The second group of questions focused on the perceived advantages and disadvantages of online teaching compared to in-person teaching. The third group of questions addressed LA, including questions about opportunities and threats, data requirements, evaluations, presentation formats, and timeliness. The interviews were conducted following the dramaturgical model proposed by Myers and Newman [27]. Prior to the interview, a brief introduction to the research topic of online teaching and LA was provided. The average duration of the interviews was 40 min. All interviews were recorded and transcribed for further analysis. The transcripts were analyzed using Mayring's qualitative content analysis to develop categories [8] by using the software MAXQDA. After an intensive reading of the interviews the initial categories were created, using the interview guide as a first point of reference. The transcripts were coded and the coded text segments were systematically processed. If necessary, categories and subcategories were adapted during a second cycle of "fine" coding. The results were then interpreted and translated into English for the purpose of this research.

4 Results

In the following, the advantages (Sect. 4.1) and disadvantages (Sect. 4.2) that teachers see in online teaching compared to in-person teaching will be addressed. Afterwards, the opportunities (Sect. 4.3) and risks (Sect. 4.4) of LA from the perspective of teachers will be presented and their requirements for a LA Systems (Sect. 4.5) will be described.

4.1 Advantages of Online Teaching

To begin, we will examine the changes that have occurred due to the transition to online teaching. The interviewees were asked about the advantages of online teaching. Their answers were classified into four categories: 1) Flexibility, 2) quality of teaching, 3) technology use, and 4) independent learning. Table 1 shows a brief overview of the categories and subcategories, which are described in more detail in the following text.

Table 1. Advantages of Online Teaching

Category	Subcategory
Flexibility	Independence in place and time, family friendliness
Quality of teaching	Revision of old materials, careful creation of new contents
Use of technology	Interactive learning, integration of external resources, real-time feedback, reuse of materials, documentation, collaboration with other HEIs, online exams
Independent learning	Students own pace, consideration of individual needs, independent working skills

The most commonly mentioned benefit of online teaching (n = 15) is the flexibility it provides for teachers. The ability to teach remotely eliminates the need for long commutes, and in the case of asynchronous online teaching, allows for temporal flexibility as well. This flexibility can make the work of teachers more family-friendly, as they can more easily attend to the needs of children or other dependents (n = 4).

Another benefit noted by several teachers (n = 4) is the improvement in the quality of instruction. The transition to online teaching could provide an incentive for teachers to thoroughly review and revise course material. Participants noted that this is especially beneficial for courses that have been in existence for an extended period, as the materials may have been reused over time. Additionally, the interviewees report placing a special emphasis on their rhetoric and the clarity of the content when creating videos, while they tend to spontaneously reference slides during in-person lectures (n = 3). As a result, these participants perceived online teaching as more efficient (n = 3).

According to the participants, the implementation of technology could facilitate the effective transmission of knowledge (n = 5). The ability to view and pause videos multiple times could allow students to better comprehend the material (n = 5). It was also mentioned, that the opportunity for students to actively participate and share screens during synchronous instruction can contribute to a more interactive and diverse learning experience (n = 5). In addition, the technical infrastructure, if used right, could enable the seamless integration of external resources like guest lectures from experts, external videos, and software, enriching the teaching even further (n = 2). Group work could be conducted virtually through the use of breakout rooms, eliminating the need for long setup times and suitable rooms (n = 3). Anonymous surveys could be utilized to collect real-time feedback during online lectures (n = 4). Many teachers also reported the reuse of online materials as an important advantage, as videos and other content could be used for other courses or in future semesters (n = 8). The same applies to FAQs and other forms of documentation, which may also be beneficial in the event of personnel changes, as much remains easily comprehensible through documentation (n = 2). Participant 05 said: "We have recorded all our lectures as videos. That means that the course is basically no longer dependent on me as a person. As a faculty, you often have a change of staff, especially because teaching assistants only stay for maybe 3–4 years [...] and with that there is always a loss of knowledge. Now we have practically everything recorded for the posterity. Accordingly, if I would leave now, we would not have that loss of knowledge." In addition, the interviewees state that online teaching offers the opportunity to develop and deliver courses in collaboration with other universities (n = 2). The potential use of online exams was also cited as an improvement by some (n = 3). The process of room planning, the creation and printing of exam materials, and the provision of supervision would get mostly eliminated. In some cases, automatic grading becomes possible, which could save time. It was also noted that multiple teachers could grade online exams simultaneously, eliminating the risk of lost exams through the transfer of paper copies (n = 2). Also, there are more control mechanisms in online exams, such as the reconciliation of points, which can reduce human error (n = 3).

The potential to enhance student independence was stated as another advantage of online instruction (n = 3). Students would have the ability to determine their own learning times and pace, enabling them to more effectively tailor their learning to their individual needs. Through this process, they could also develop autonomous working skills. This may lead to increased motivation and a more independent learning approach (n = 2).

4.2 Disadvantages of Online Teaching

In addition to the improvements due to online teaching, respondents also identified several negative aspects. They can be classified into the following five categories: 1) Social interaction, 2) student behavior, 3) effort, 4) quality of teaching, and 5) technical problems. Analogous to Table 1, Table 2 again briefly presents the categories and subcategories, with detailed explanations following in the next paragraph.

Table 2. Disadvantages of Online Teaching

Category	Subcategory
Social Interaction	Weaker relationship, little interaction, lack of feedback, loss of visual cues
Student behavior	Passive behavior, procrastination
Effort	High expenditure of time, technical training
Quality of teaching	Formalization of teaching, reuse of materials
Technical problems	Software and hardware problems

All respondents mentioned the decline in social interaction or lack of contact with students as a negative aspect of online teaching (n = 18). The interviewees felt they no longer had a sufficient relationship with their students. Many reported that there is little interaction in their courses (n = 12). Some participants also described a lack of feedback on their teaching (n = 8), making it difficult to understand student perceptions and identify potential problem areas. The absence of feedback also makes it challenging to assess student mood and engagement (n = 2). Many respondents also described the loss of visual cues as a deterioration (n = 13). Facial expressions and gestures, such as head shaking, nodding, yawning, etc. were all described as important cues for instructors during in-person lectures. They provide valuable hints, even in large groups, and cannot be adequately replaced through the use of cameras during synchronous teaching. Another important consideration, that was noted by the participants, is that informal conversations during breaks were no longer possible (n = 5). These conversations, however, were described as crucial for exchanging information and building relationships, including forming learning groups, sharing documents, or asking instructors about other courses or thesis topics (n = 5). Interviewees also reported observing an increasing sense of isolation among students (n = 2).

The alteration in student behavior was also identified as a negative aspect by several participants (n = 7). Students were reported to be more passive, asking fewer questions and participating less (n = 4). Participant 06 mentioned: "For me, the biggest difference is that students actually participate in in-person teaching […]. In online teaching, it has happened not only once that no student has actually said anything during the whole 90 min, and as a teacher you feel like you are talking to your own screen for 90 min, because not one student turns his camera or microphone on." A decrease in student motivation was also mentioned (n = 3). According to some interviewees, the flexibility of online teaching could negatively affect those students who are unable to self-motivate and learn independently (n = 3), resulting in procrastination (n = 2). Two respondents also noted the phenomenon of "Zoom fatigue," which refers to the exhaustion that can result from excessive use of videoconferencing.

Another issue mentioned by participants (n = 8) was the increased time and effort required to transition from in-person to online teaching. This involves familiarization with technology, adaptation of teaching materials, and consideration of how to effectively deliver the content online. The process of recording videos, in particular, requires a significant amount of effort (n = 5). Participant 10 stated: "In one semester, we had to work completely with recordings due to technical problems [...] with video conferences. I have to say that the effort tripled or quadrupled because of all the preparations." Furthermore, exams and assessments must also be adapted to the online format, as some tasks may not be feasible in an online setting (n = 2).

Some respondents also worried about a decline in the quality of teaching (n = 4). The formalization of teaching through the use of online videos, exercises, and assessments may lead to a loss of creative formats and a less intimate atmosphere in courses (n = 3). In addition, due to the lack of feedback (n = 4) or for convenience (n = 2), content may be simply repeated from semester to semester without further development.

Technical issues were also cited as a negative aspect of online teaching (n = 6). These problems may arise in the preparation and provision of content, as well as in the use of conference tools, hardware such as cameras, microphones, and internet connections. These issues could cause frustration for both teachers and students.

4.3 Chances of Learning Analytics

In the third part of the questionnaire, the interviewees were asked about the opportunities of LA for their teaching. The responses were grouped into the following categories: 1) Overview of student activities, 2) detection of problem areas and patterns, 3) quality of teaching, 4) student learning, and 5) automated feedback (see Table 3).

Table 3. Chances of Learning Analytics

Category	Subcategory
Overview of student activities	Overview, insights into learning behaviors, transparency, connection
Detection of problem areas and patterns	Early identification of problems or poorly addressed content, patterns for success or failure, comparisons over time
Quality of teaching	Adaption of content, optimization of courses, feedback, continuous evaluation of changes
Student learning	Increased motivation and satisfaction, less procrastination
Automated feedback	Recommendation for actions, data-driven decision support

Several teachers (n = 9) emphasized the potential of LA in providing a better overview of student activities, including their collaboration, weaknesses, and strengths. Through LA, instructors could gain insights into the learning behavior of their students and understand how they are using course content (n = 3). Participants also noted that LA provide transparency on the students and their previous knowledge (n = 2). LA could also help instructors to feel more connected to their students (n = 4).

Another frequently mentioned opportunity of LA (n = 11) is its ability to identify problem areas early on in the teaching process which allows instructors to make adjustments early in the semester (n = 6). For example, teachers could offer additional explanations, materials, or consultation hours based on information provided by LA. Based on the data, they could also ask students why certain content has been little or poorly addressed (n = 3). Participants emphasized that they could then provide early and individualized support to at-risk students who are struggling with the course content or pace (n = 4). Through the application of LA, patterns in student learning behavior and success could be identified and used to adapt teaching strategies (n = 3). By analyzing data, such as that from exercises and exams, participants hope they could determine the usefulness of preparatory materials and the relationship between student engagement and academic performance (n = 3). For example, teachers could analyze whether students who are very active in the LMS or in discussion forums, achieve better exam grades. These patterns could also be used to make predictions about students' future course performances and to review previously established learning goals (n = 3). According to some interviewees, LA could be used to compare student performance and usage of course materials across the semester, allowing also for the assessment and documentation of courses over a longer period of time (n = 4).

The benefits mentioned so far form the foundation for the opportunity most frequently mentioned by participants (n = 14), the ability to optimize the content and the delivery of teaching based on data analyses. This can include aligning content, improving comprehensibility, and adjusting the pace of the course. These adjustments could be made in real-time during lectures through the use of surveys and quizzes (n = 3), throughout the semester (n = 14), or after the semester has ended (n = 8). LA can enable continuous improvement of the quality of teaching (n = 8) by making it more audience-oriented, needs-based, and personalized (n = 6). For example, extra teaching materials could be provided and tailored to the needs of specific groups of students, based on their prior experiences and performances (n = 5), potentially making courses more attractive in general (n = 3). LA data could also serve as feedback to support self-reflection among teachers (n = 5), and could be used to adapt not only content, but also teaching methods and formats (n = 5). These changes could then be re-evaluated using LA data (n = 6) and might also encourage instructors to try out new innovative concepts (n = 3).

Many respondents (n = 8) believe that tailoring teaching to student needs and providing teachers with an overview through LA could improve student learning and satisfaction. LA may also provide students with the opportunity to self-assess and track their progress (n = 5) and compare their performance to that of their peers (n = 2), potentially increasing motivation and reducing procrastination (n = 2). Participant 15 compares learning with workouts: "I definitely see an opportunity for the students themselves, to be motivated by LA. They see: Okay, I have generated progress, I am now at

67%, I only have 33% to go. I am also like that when I am running, I know I have to run 6 km and I am at kilometer 4 and I think to myself: I have already done two thirds, I can get this done. And that is the same with learning".

Automated feedback and recommendations for action through LA were also mentioned as an opportunity, as they could alleviate some workload for teachers (n = 2) and serve as a basis for data-driven decision support (n = 2). Participant 09 states, "I need clear implications from the data that is shown to me. If this and that is the case, then do this. There needs to be more of a decision support to the data that tells me, so to speak, what I can do with this information. That's not currently there, but I think that's where it could go." LA may also lead to time savings (n = 2) and help detect attempts at cheating in online exams (n = 2).

4.4   Threats of Learning Analytics

The teacher's responses about the possible threats of LA were classified into five categories, as shown in Table 4. The categories are: 1) Data protection, 2) focus on data, 3) impact on teachers, 4) discrimination against students, and 5) impact on students.

Table 4. Threats of Learning Analytics

Category	Subcategory
Data protection	Data protection, security, invasion of students' privacy
Focus on data	Unreliable or meaningless data, excessive weighing of key figures, misinterpretation,
Impact on teachers	Effort and resources, overwhelming amount of data, lack of technical expertise, demotivation
Discrimination against students	Different behavior towards students, self-fulfilling prophecies, discrimination
Impact on students	Constant feeling of being monitored, pressure, frustration

The most frequently mentioned threat (n = 15) was related to data protection, given the large amount of student data that is collected and analyzed through LA. Issues such as consent, data security, data storage duration, and access to data need be carefully considered when implementing LA. Most of the interviewees (n = 13) felt that data protection is the responsibility of the HEI, not of individual teachers. However, some participants also expressed concern that overly strict privacy policies could hinder the effective use of LA (n = 4). In addition, interviewees feared that the use of LA in general could be perceived by students as an invasion of their privacy (n = 4).

Another frequently named threat (n = 12) is the risk to place too much emphasis on data. Some participants pointed out that the data collected may not be meaningful in representing student learning behavior (n = 4). Participant 15 stated: "If I have someone who likes to watch the videos, but then they download the videos and work with the accompanying materials and print it out, then I cannot see exactly if the person really, actually learned or not because they just have a different learning path." Another concern was the potential for excessive weighting of key figures (n = 5), as it could be challenging to determine which metrics are most relevant for drawing meaningful conclusions. Participant 03 said: "When you use metrics, you set incentives and then people always fulfill what is required by a metric and not what is intended by it. That is totally absurd, but it always happens relatively quickly." The danger of misinterpretation of data by teachers was also mentioned by several participants (n = 10), potentially leading to false adjustments of teaching based on incorrect assumptions. Several respondents stressed the importance of not blindly relying on data (n = 4). There is also a danger of continuing to optimize courses based on the data, but not providing any new content (n = 2). This could be because the data is only ever based on what already exists.

Another potential threat from the point of view of the participants was the high investment of resources and time required for the evaluation and adaptation of courses (n = 9). This could possibly lead to a decrease in the quality of teaching, if teachers do not have sufficient time for their core tasks anymore (n = 5). The level of difficulty and time required for analyses varies depending on how clearly and effectively they are presented to instructors. Some participants also expressed concerns about feeling overwhelmed by the amount of information (n = 2) or being at a disadvantage due to a lack of technical expertise (n = 2). Additionally, teachers may find LA demotivating if they see, for example, that elaborately produced materials are not being used (n = 2).

There are also concerns from participants that LA could lead to changes in the perception of individual students or the entire group (n = 9). Some teachers fear that they may evaluate students differently based on data, or that they may subconsciously or consciously evaluate students less favorably if they are less active (n = 9). Participant 14 describes this as follows: "That would be a kind of self-fulfilling prophecy, where you see students who are perhaps not so good at the beginning, for whatever reason, that you might then evaluate them negatively in exams in advance. Or in the case of the good people, you say they are great anyway, you do not need to teach them anything more." There is also a potential for discrimination based on demographic data or prior performance, depending on the data and algorithms used (n = 3).

On the student side, participants worried that the use of LA may lead to feelings of being monitored or controlled, which could increase pressure (n = 6) and frustration (n = 4). Students may also feel pressured to alter their natural learning behavior in order to perform well in LA evaluations (n = 3).

4.5 Requirements for the Usage of Learning Analytics

In the final part of the survey, all respondents (n = 18) indicated that they would be interested in using LA. All respondents also expressed a desire for a dashboard to display the relevant data and analyses. This dashboard should be clearly arranged, intuitive and easy to understand (n = 6). It should also offer a range of filter options (n = 4) and be customizable (n = 5) to meet the specific needs of the user. Participant 02 mentioned: "I would like to have a dashboard which I can configure individually for myself, because I think every teacher has his own perspective or special information that is weighted more heavily than something else. So, if I had the possibility to see the data that really interests me, where I say, okay, maybe these are current pain points for me in teaching, that is what

I want to track and work on first right now, that would be perfect." Additionally, several teachers (n = 4) suggested that the dashboard should be integrated into the university's LMS (n = 4). Some respondents (n = 3) also requested access to raw data so they could create their own analyses.

Regarding the frequency of data collection and display, the majority of respondents (n = 13) preferred weekly evaluations, while others (n = 5) preferred daily evaluations. Several teachers (n = 7) also emphasized the importance of real-time evaluations in addition to these. It was also suggested that the data should be aggregated at the end of the semester and compared to data from previous semesters, allowing for analyses over the course of time (n = 6). Though not all respondents provided specific information on the data and evaluations they would like to see, the following were among those mentioned: Usage data for course content (n = 9), including video usage, results and time spent on tasks and self-study assessments (n = 5), total time spent in the LMS (n = 4), students' prior knowledge (n = 4), as well as number and content of discussion contributions (n = 2). Suggested evaluations included an overview of common errors by topic (n = 6), correlation between final grades and the completion of assignments (n = 5), identification of at-risk students (n = 5), an overview of the learning progress (n = 3), identification of learning styles (n = 2), and networks between students (n = 2).

5 Discussion and Conclusion

5.1 Discussion of the Results

In this section, we first take a look at the advantages and disadvantages of online teaching as perceived by the interviewees. Afterwards, the potential for LA to enhance the advantages and mitigate the disadvantages of online teaching is explored, using current literature to demonstrate and substantiate the potentials of LA. Finally, other noteworthy findings from the interviews will be discussed.

When examining the responses on the changes in teaching brought about by the shift to online teaching, it is notable that the teachers listed more disadvantages than advantages, and provided longer explanations for the disadvantages, especially in relation to the interaction with students. Other commonly named challenges were the increased time and effort to prepare online courses and technical issues. It is worth noting that 12 participants had no prior experience with online teaching before the Covid-19 pandemic and were forced to transition to it due to lockdowns of universities. The lack of prior experience and technical knowledge may have contributed to their negative views [9, 13]. With the rushed transition to online teaching during the pandemic, there was little time to explore the potential benefits [1]. Among the participants with prior experience in online teaching (n = 6), more potentials were identified, such as interactivity, the inclusion of external sources, and the promotion of independent learning.

We now examine, based on current literature, the extent to which the benefits and disadvantages of online teaching described by the participants can be enhanced or diminished by the use of LA. In terms of improving the quality of online teaching, LA can help instructors to reflect on their own practices and identify areas for improvement [18], as well as try out new forms of online teaching and evaluate their effectiveness based on educational data [28]. LA can also reinforce the benefits of technology-based feedback and documentation of courses, by providing a rich set of data and analyses on student performance, and the effectiveness of exercises in preparing students for exams [18, 28]. In addition, LA can support independent learning by providing students with continuous feedback on their own performance, helping them identify areas for further study, and motivating them through comparisons with others [3]. LA can also help address several of the identified disadvantages of online teaching, including the declining social inter-action, student behavior, and the quality of teaching. In terms of social interaction, LA could indirectly promote greater interactions among students by providing motivation through LA dashboards or data-based hints, as well as through the use of an interaction rate [3]. LA can provide instructors with detailed feedback on the processing of course content, allowing problem areas to be identified and addressed early on [3]. This can help to partially compensate for the loss of visual cues that often occurs in online teaching [7]. In terms of passive student behavior and procrastination, LA can be very effective in improving outcomes by providing students with constant feedback on their performance and progress, and enabling instructors to intervene with at-risk students early on [3]. As for the quality of teaching, LA can motivate teachers to improve their courses through feedback and summative assessments at the end of the semester [18], reducing the risk of relying solely on pre-existing materials.

Overall, the participants in the study showed a positive attitude towards the use of LA. All respondents saw opportunities in its application and expressed a desire to use LA in their own teaching, as long as the data was made available to them in an easily accessible and intuitive format, e.g., in the form of a dashboard with various filtering and customization options. While many of the respondents expressed concern about data protection, they did not see this as a threat to themselves, as they believed it was the responsibility of the institution to address these issues. The extent to which the identified opportunities can be implemented in practice depends on a number of factors, including the data collected by the institution, the availability of resources to integrate and clean the data, and the ease of access for users. Many universities are currently not equipped to handle these tasks [17, 18]. As for the threats, they can be mitigated through appropriate measures, such as using established models for LA adoptions at universities that include guidelines for data storage and use [24], and involving all stakeholders from the beginning of the development [21]. Universities can also provide support in the form of facilities and staff to help teachers use of LA. Training courses about data analyses for teachers could reduce discrimination and focus on data alone [24].

It is worth noting that participants in the study had different attitudes towards the use of LA. Some saw the greatest potentials in monitoring and controlling student behav-ior, including minimizing procrastination and tracking the progress of weaker students. Others saw greater value in using LA to support student self-reflection and to provide feedback to instructors on the effectiveness of their teaching. These different perspec-tives may be influenced by the teachers' underlying attitudes towards their students. As participant 17, who had the most extensive experience with online teaching and LA of all the participants, noted: "The desire for control is already there. Now some also want to know who has not read this or not done that? They want be able to sanction that. That has a lot to do with the basic attitude towards students. If I think that students are designed for optimization and are looking for the most favorable way to get through somehow, be it by cheating and deception, then I am also inclined to want to use the data to find exactly such things. If, on the other hand, I focus more on things like autonomy, freedom, personal responsibility, because I believe that students can do that and want to do that, then I can use LA to improve what I as a teacher have to offer".

5.2 Conclusion and Outlook

In summary, the present study aims to investigate the relationship between online teaching and LA from the perspective of teachers. The results show that the participating teachers had a positive attitude toward LA. They saw LA as a valuable tool to support online teaching, but had concerns about privacy, unreliable or meaningless data, and the effort and resources that LA requires. The study revealed that teachers require detailed, specific, and actionable data about their students in order to make informed decisions to improve their teaching. The data should be summable at different times, such as daily or weekly overviews, and end-of-semester summaries. It should also be comparable to data from previous years. Furthermore, participants preferred for the information to be presented in form of an intuitive and customizable dashboard. These findings highlight the importance of including teachers early on in the development of LA systems. Furthermore, the results of the study suggest that LA could play a valuable role in addressing many of the disadvantages of online teaching by providing insights into student learning and engagement and can help to improve the quality of teaching.

References

1. Hodges, C.B., Moore, S., Lockee, B.B., Trust, T., Bond, M.A.: The difference between emergency remote teaching and online learning. Educ. Rev. (2020)
2. Huber, S.G., Helm, C.: COVID-19 and schooling: evaluation, assessment and accountability in times of crises-reacting quickly to explore key issues for policy, practice and research with the school barometer. Educ. Assess. Eval. Account. **32**, 237–270 (2020)
3. Long, P., Siemens, G.: Penetrating the fog: analytics in learning and education. Educ. Rev. **46**, 31–40 (2011)
4. Howell, J.A., Roberts, L.D., Seaman, K., Gibson, D.C.: Are we on our way to becoming a "helicopter university"? academics' views on learning analytics. Technol. Knowl. Learn. **23**, 1–20 (2018)
5. Corrin, L., Kennedy, G., Mulder, R.: Enhancing learning analytics by understanding the needs of teachers. In: Proceedings of Electric Dreams, pp. 201–205 (2013)
6. Colvin, C., Rogers, T., Wade, A., Dawson, S., Gasevic, D., et al.: Student retention and learning analytics: a snapshot of Australian practices and a framework for advancement. Australian Government - Office for Learning and Teaching (2015)
7. Ferguson, R.: Learning analytics: drivers, developments and challenges. Int. J. Technol. Enhanc. Learn. **4**, 304–317 (2012)
8. Mayring, P.: Qualitative content analysis - theoretical foundation, basic procedures and software solution, Klagenfurt (2014)
9. Adedoyin, O.B., Soykan, E.: Covid-19 pandemic and online learning: the challenges and opportunities. Interact. Learn. Environ., 1–13 (2020)
10. Tallent-Runnels, M.K., et al.: Teaching courses online: a review of the research. Rev. Educ. Res. **76**, 93–135 (2006)

11. Means, B., Toyama, Y., Murphy, R., Bakia, M., Jones, K.: Evaluation of evidence-based practices in online learning: a meta-analysis and review of online learning studies. US Department of Education (2009)
12. Hrastinski, S.: Asynchronous & synchronous e-learning. Educause **31**, 51–55 (2008)
13. Zhang, W., Wang, Y., Yang, L., Wang, C.: Suspending classes without stopping learning: China's education emergency management policy in the COVID-19 outbreak. J. Risk Financ. Manag. **13**, 1–6 (2020)
14. Joshi, O., Chapagain, B., Kharel, G., Poudyal, N.C., Murray, B.D., Mehmood, S.R.: Benefits and challenges of online instruction in agriculture and natural resource education. Interact. Learn. Environ. **30**, 1402–1413 (2022)
15. Bozkurt, A., Sharma, R.C.: Emergency remote teaching in a time of global crisis due to CoronaVirus pandemic. Asian J. Distance Educ. **15**, i–vi (2020)
16. Greller, W., Drachsler, H.: Translating learning into numbers: a generic framework for learning analytics. Educ. Technol. Soc. **15**, 42–57 (2012)
17. Ifenthaler, D.: Are higher education institutions prepared for learning analytics? TechTrends **61**(4), 366–371 (2016). https://doi.org/10.1007/s11528-016-0154-0
18. Nguyen, A., Tuunanen, T., Gardner, L., Sheridan, D.: Design principles for learning analytics information systems in higher education. Eur. J. Inf. Syst. **30**, 541–568 (2021)
19. Gašević, D., Dawson, S., Siemens, G.: Let's not forget: learning analytics are about learning. TechTrends **59**, 64–71 (2015)
20. Kregor, G., Breslin, M., Fountain, W.: Experience and beliefs of technology users at an Australian university: keys to maximising e-learning potential. Australas. J. Educ. Technol. **28** (2012)
21. Ifenthaler, D., Schumacher, C.: Student perceptions of privacy principles for learning analytics. Educ. Technol. Res. Dev. **64**, 923–938 (2016)
22. Pardo, A., Siemens, G.: Ethical and privacy principles for learning analytics. Br. J. Educ. Technol. **45**, 438–450 (2014)
23. Siemens, G.: Learning analytics: envisioning a research discipline and a domain of practice. In: Dawson, S. (ed.) Proceedings of the 2nd International Conference on Learning Analytics and Knowledge, pp. 4–8. ACM, New York (2012)
24. Sclater, N.: Learning Analytics Explained. Routledge, New York (2017)
25. Campbell, J.P., DeBlois, P.B., Oblinger, D.G.: Academic analytics: a new tool for a new era. Educ. Rev. **42**, 40–57 (2007)
26. Bryman, A., Bell, E.: Business Research Methods. Oxford Univ. Press, Oxford (2011)
27. Myers, M.D., Newman, M.: The qualitative interview in IS research: examining the craft. Inf. Organ. **17**, 2–26 (2007)
28. Daniel, B.: Big Data and analytics in higher education: opportunities and challenges. Br. J. Educ. Technol. **46**, 904–920 (2015)

Digital Marketing and Artificial Intelligence

The Influence of Online Ratings and Reviews in Consumer Buying Behavior: A Systematic Literature Review

Saleh Kutabish[1], Ana Maria Soares[1,2] (iD), and Beatriz Casais[1,2(✉)] (iD)

[1] School of Economics and Management, University of Minho, Campus de Gualtar, 4710-057 Braga, Portugal
{amsoares,bcasais}@eeg.uminho.pt
[2] CICS.NOVA.Uminho, Campus de Gualtar, 4710-057 Braga, Portugal

Abstract. This paper presents a systematic literature review of the influence of online ratings and reviews in consumer buying behavior with the purpose of finding out trends, themes, directions, research problems, and potential future research avenues how ratings and reviews affect online consumer buying decision-making behavior. The only systematic literature review on online consumer reviews had presented the existing studies in relation to the communication model. The review found that no prior studies had focused on buying decision making. This study analyzes and discusses 63 papers published in the last three decades in international scientific journals indexed in Web of Science and Scopus grouped under four main themes: 1) quality of ratings and reviews; 2) sales and consumer behavior; 3) quality of products; and 4) ratings and reviews trustworthiness and credibility. A framework is proposed showing the five-stage model of the consumer buying decision-making process influenced by review ratings, aggregate ratings, review variance, rating volume, rating length, review ranking, top reviewers' reviews, average ratings, and review history. This influence is mediated by behavioral constructs. This study aims at contributing both to the understanding of online consumer buying decision making process and e-business literature expanding the knowledge on online ratings and reviews.

Keywords: rating · review · buying behavior · consumer · information search

1 Introduction

Consumers' search and use of information has changed immensely in the past years. In the digital environment, ratings and reviews (R&Rs) have become ubiquitous [10] as e-commerce websites allow consumers to share information about products they purchased. Reliance on consumer R&Rs for information search before purchasing is a growing trend.

This trend is in line with the growing engagement of consumers with brands through social media, co-creating value by generating content and electronic word-of-mouth, sharing experiences online. User generated content stimulate user participation and provide access to social knowledge and experiences to support online purchase [29]. Social commerce involves buyers acquiring information about products and services that interest them by perusing content generated by other buyers, in alignment with the principles of social learning theory. The social learning theory [7] is a significant theory of learning and development that highlights that humans can learn new behaviors and information by observation [29]. The elements of social commerce offer an ideal backdrop for shoppers to observe the behavior of others. Consumers can obtain social experiences and knowledge by engaging in online communities and forums, browsing through reviews and ratings posted by other users, or taking note of recommendations made on social networks [29].

Research on R&Rs and online consumer behavior has been growing in quantity and breath of topics. Searching the literature using generic keywords related to consumer online interaction such as: user-generated content, eWOM communication, online communities, virtual communities, etc. triggers massive number of published studies. Recently, Zheng [83] conducted a systematic literature review on online consumer reviews (OCRs). The study identifies and categorizes OCR dimensions based on social communication process theory. Zheng [83] review demonstrated the literature of past studies related to five categories based on the communication model, reviewer-related, review-related, recipient-bases, channel-based, and response-based studies. The review results in developing an integrated conceptual framework presenting the relationship between the five categories. Zheng [83] found that past research focused on consumer perceptions of online reviews, but less on investigating consumer decision making. However, there are no prior systematic literature reviews focusing specifically on published research addressing the impact of R&Rs in consumer buying decision making process.

The increasing importance of R&Rs for both business and individuals deserves the attention of scholars in the field, with a view to extend knowledge on the drivers of purchase behavior and emphasizes the importance of ratings and reviews in marketing. This study aims at analyzing the literature on online ratings and reviews and consumer buying behavior in order to expand knowledge on how R&Rs impact the different stages of the buying decision process and pave the way for further research on R&Rs in the context of consumer behavior and marketing. Therefore, this study will answer the following research questions: RQ1: How has the impact of R&Rs on consumer behavior been analyzed in extant research? RQ2: How do ratings and reviews affect consumer buying decision-making? This study aims at contributing to finding out trends, themes, directions, research problems, and potential future research directions.

This paper is structured as follows: we start by presenting the concepts of R&Rs. Secondly, we describe the methodology followed in this study. Subsequently we present and discuss the findings on R&Rs and buying decision-making. Then we suggest directions for future research. Finally, the conclusions of the study and theoretical and managerial implications are lined up.

2 Ratings and Reviews

Ratings and reviews (R&Rs) are important and enable shoppers to exchange feedback on goods and services and share their choices from their independent experience and point of view [67]. Ratings generally take the form of numerical values, typically ranging from one (indicating very poor quality) to five (indicating very high quality) [26], and are frequently accompanied by a brief textual description and a few images [15]. Reviews are product information and recommendations provided from a consumer perspective [41].

The use of R&Rs is trend intensified by the increase of social media popularity, which is causing online businesses to shift from e-commerce to social commerce [47, 78]. Social commerce is a fusion of e-commerce and social media [18], and it is revolutionizing the mode of consumer online communication from the traditional one-way communication to a more desirable two-way interaction [29] that enables consumers to interact with each other. In social commerce, consumers behave collaboratively [29] by sharing, recommending and advising each other. For example, virtual communities, defined as "A group of people who may or may not meet one another face to face, and who exchange words and ideas through the mediation of computer bulletin boards and networks" [43] p.262, can gather a rich amount of reviews and comments.

Technologies such as rating, review, and recommendation systems have become popular social shopping platforms' tools due to ease of use and simplicity in sharing buying experience and aggregating evaluations [4]. The adoption and use of these tools have earned social media platforms good reputation and transparency [35]. Opinions communicated and information exchanged in the form of rating and reviews represent a form of written Word of Mouth (WOM). According to Amblee et al. [4], electronic WOM (eWOM) should be considered by shoppers and e-tailers as a primary source of social shopping experience.

From a business standpoint, the incorporation of R&R features enables merchants to seamlessly integrate shopper feedback and community platforms into their websites. In the e-commerce ecosystem, product descriptions hold significant importance, and consumer reviews have emerged as complementary information to the product descriptions offered by the merchant [27]. In addition, from a consumer's perspective, user-generated content (UGC) provided by independent users and social media real shoppers, possesses a greater level of credibility and is more valuable in making purchasing decisions [36].

Hence, the importance of R&Rs is growing. Consumers increasingly rely on online reviews and often spend a considerable amount of time going through reviews to learn more about a product before making their purchase decision [21, 81]. Reviews play an important role in the buying decision process by providing an enhanced comprehension of a product or service.

Online R&R have a crucial function in reducing consumer uncertainty [60]. By examining the R&Rs posted by other buyers of a product, users can gain a better understanding of the quality of the product, thereby boosting their confidence in its characteristics and performance [15]. As a result, R&Rs facilitate informed decision-making by allowing consumers to learn about the quality and attributes of a product as shared by other customers. Hence, different facets of R&R studies have been studied: ratings and reviews quality [27, 75], reviews variance [49, 76], misleading between ratings and reviews and impact on product reputation [52], product average rating [50], ratings and reviews as an assessing tool for product quality and market value [23, 71], etc. The value of online reviews is consistent among most studies, but there are some diverging views regarding review credibility. Consumers face a trust-building challenge in most of their online purchases despite their level of concern regarding purchasing decisions. This explains why trust was a priority in many studies [2, 19, 39].

3   Method

This study comprises a systematic literature review centered on research related to the impact of R&Rs on consumer buying behavior. This study aims at mapping the extant body of knowledge on the topic by identifying research gaps, trends, and citation themes, with a view to propose a future research agenda. To conduct this study, we carried out a search for papers indexed in Web of Science (WoS) and Scopus, which are among the most comprehensive multidisciplinary databases of published research [55].

To focus the search on the main goal of this study, and aiming to answer the research questions, we considered four search terms – review*, rating*, consumer*, and buy* – to trace paper topics that were relevant for the review. The search was run on the following field tags: title, abstract, and keywords. The search was not limited to a specific period. The aim was to gather all relevant papers available in the databases regardless of their date of publication.

In WoS, a total of 99 papers were retrieved for the period 1996–2021 (Fig. 1). Subsequently, we used a number of inclusion and exclusion criteria to further refine the search. Firstly, only articles categorized in related areas to this study (Business, Management, Computer Science Information System, Computer Science Software Engineering, Information Science, and Communication) were included. All abstracts and conclusions were read, and irrelevant articles were excluded, leading to a total of 24 articles retrieved from WoS.

In Scopus, the initial search resulted in 109 papers, of which only 57 were articles. Refining the search to related areas (Computer Science, Business, Management, Social Science, Decision Science, Economics, Psychology, and Computer Engineering) resulted in 47 articles. There were some articles in languages other than English that have been excluded, leading to a total of 45 articles. Duplicated articles in both databases were also removed, yielding a final result of 49 articles, which were the object of our analysis.

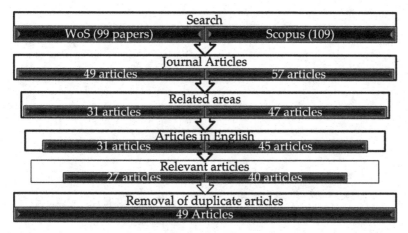

Fig. 1. Article selection process

4 Findings

In order to provide a roadmap of the literature, we conducted a content analysis of the papers. The analysis was divided into the following features: year of publication; journals and research areas; author provenance; number of citations; research methods and data collection techniques and main themes.

4.1 Year of Publication

There was no limited period selected for our study. The earliest paper in the set is dated from 2001. The collected papers were grouped into three time periods: 2001–2010 (4 papers), 2011–2020 (39 papers), and 2021 (6 papers). Therefore, almost 80% of studies were published in the past decade (2011–2020), which reflects the growing interest of scholars in shedding light on this specific area (Fig. 2).

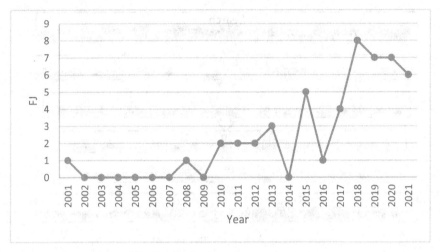

Fig. 2. Distribution of papers per year

4.2 Journals and Research Areas

The results regarding publication present 43 journals that published articles on the topic of R&Rs. Of those, 35 studies were published in different journals. Only 6 journals published more than one article: *Information System Research, International Journal of Advanced Science and Technology, International Journal of Electronic Commerce, International Journal of Innovation Technology and Exploring Engineering, International Journal of Mechanical and Technology, and Asia Pacific Journal of Marketing and Logistics*. Information system journals figure on top of the journal list, followed by management and marketing journals.

4.3 Author Provenance and Research Areas

Rating and reviews are published online; therefore, studies could not be classified based on countries where the studies were conducted, because the samples of review, surveys, and data were collected online. Therefore, we analyzed the academic affiliations of the authors. The studies were conducted by 120 authors from 24 different countries (Fig. 3). Most articles (35) were the result of more than one author contributing to the area, and only 10 articles were studies conducted by only one author. The majority of authors contributing to the area of study are located in India (31 authors). The USA comes second, with 21 authors; then comes China (13 authors), and Pakistan (11 authors). This result shows the global nature of research and widespread interest on the topic, including a growing interest in emerging countries.

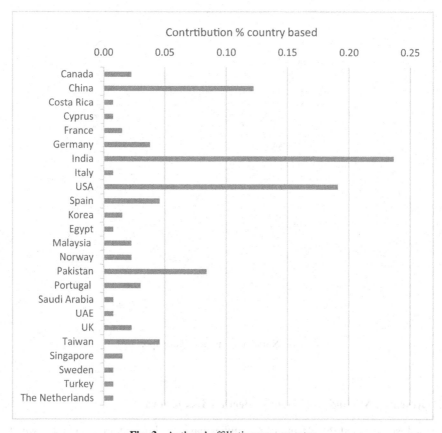

Fig. 3. Authors' affiliations per country

4.4 Citation Impact

The number of citations provides an indication of the impact of published papers. As per the citation report of WoS and Scopus, the total number of citations of the 45 articles is 1286. 33 articles were cited < 10 times, 6 articles were cited between 10–20 times, and 9 articles were cited > 20 times.

As shown in Fig. 4, the highest-impact papers (highly cited) are those published between 2008 and 2015. Five papers have made the highest contribution to the topic: with 109 times cited [24], 129 times [25], 132 times [70], 193 times [4], and 433 times [45]. Besides, 15 papers were not cited during the whole period. The most-cited articles were published between 2008 and 2017. These research papers investigated various topics, including the correlation between online ratings and the public's perception of physician quality, the influence of reviews and ratings on trust and purchase intention, the moderating function of online ratings on the reviewer's product rating, the impact of eWOM communication, and the exploration of how unique preferences of initial buyers can impact long-term consumer purchasing behavior and social welfare.

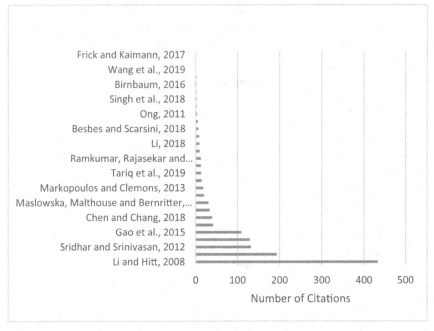

Fig. 4. Number of citations per paper

4.5   Research Methods and Data Collection Techniques

The analysis revealed that 45 out of 49 studies have used quantitative methods, which represents more than 91% of the total studies. Studying a specific phenomenon or behavior through the enormous amount of sales data, product descriptions, and R&Rs available online requires a method which can address a huge and varying volume of data. Surveys, online rating and reviews, and product descriptions are major sources of data for similar studies. Amazon.com was the most-used data source, probably because Amazon's data is known for having numerous attributes [71] and multiple public real-world dataset [81]. In addition, a few case studies (three) and two qualitative study were conducted (Table 1).

Table 1. Paper research method and data collection

Research Method	Data collection	Papers	References
Quantitative	Online survey	17	[5, 6, 8, 9, 17, 21, 28, 40, 43, 53, 56, 61, 68-70, 72, 82]
	Online survey + online reviews	2	[24, 46]
	Online survey + online review + observation	1	[35]
	Online data + observation	1	[12]
	Observation	2	[22, 84]
	Online reviews	14	[3, 4, 34, 37, 38, 45, 51, 58, 62, 65 74, 77, 79]
	Online reviews + product info	2	[44, 59]
	Online sales data	1	[50]
	Online ratings + Check-ins + citations	1	[48]
	Literature	2	[11, 49]
Qualitative	Case study	2	[1, 32]
Conceptual		3	[10, 25, 73]

Studies have used various mixed theories, models, concepts, and techniques. The variance shows that there is room for more studies to be conducted. The online data is numerous and unlimited, there is a huge number of products, reviews, ratings, sales data, processes, etc., which can be studied in several ways.

4.6 Main Themes

The articles were content-analyzed to identify the key research areas. We identified four research themes: quality of ratings and reviews (QR&Rs), consumer behavior and sales (CB&S), product quality (PQ), and trust and credibility (T&C). Therefore, the articles were organized into four groups (Table 2). However, there are some studies in which two or more areas were discussed due to the correlation between themes. Moreover, it is important to refer to the demonstration of the consumer buying behavior process and its structure. Research outlines a three-stage process that involves the following: recognizing the need, pre-purchase activities (such as information search and evaluation), the purchase itself, and post-purchase actions [16, 30, 31, 57].

Table 2. Main themes

Themes	Number of Studies	References	Description
Quality of Ratings and Reviews	21	[4, 8, 11, 12, 24, 28, 35, 37, 38, 44, 49], [50, 56, 58, 59, 61, 65, 70, 79, 84]	Usefulness of images in reviews of search products; forecast precision in recommendation schemes; forecast of rating; feature-based product recommendation; the moderating role of dispersed ratings on social media endorsement; improving doctor-patient communication; diversity of reviews and product quality assessment; ranking reviews in accordance to their rating aspects; reducing buyer uncertainty regarding taste-related product attributes; influence of reviews and ratings of products and services on opinions of buying and using; relationship between online ratings and population perceptions of physician quality; the moderating role of online ratings on reviewer online product rating; consumer reviews as a machine-processable structure using ontologies; effect of review inconsistency on purchase intention; complexities of online reviews

(continued)

Table 2. (*continued*)

Themes	Number of Studies	References	Description
Consumer behavior and sales	28	[1, 4, 5, 9, 17, 22, 24, 25, 28, 34, 35, 43, 45, 46, 48], [50, 53, 61, 62, 65, 68-70, 72, 73, 77, 80, 84]	Impact of R&Rs (valence, single vs aggregated on buyer decision-making process, usage patterns and post-purchase; attitude towards user-generated content (UGC) and R&Rs (positive and negative); perceived ease of use of UGC; luxury products;; impulse buying; intention to buy; trust; trial attitude formation; e-satisfaction; loyalty; differences between domestic and overseas consumers; self-claimed non-fully satisfied shopping experience and repurchase intention; recommendation process; effect on pricing in relation to proximity moderated by product rating, product popularity, and featured product website rankings; business-2-customer virtual communities (B2CVC); overrated products and returned purchase; top reviewer's review impact on sales; returning products impact on review; effect of eWOM communication; attributes of a product or service are relevant/impact consumer's rating

(*continued*)

Table 2. (*continued*)

Themes	Number of Studies	References	Description
Product Quality	8	[3, 10, 21, 22, 32, 51, 59, 84]	Influence of review on brand image and positioning; judging product consumption and competitiveness; ranking products through reviews; recovering the true quality of product and when social learning takes place; evaluating the market value of a new product using crowdsourcing; analyzing and calculating product score from reviews
Trust & Credibility	7	[5, 6, 8, 40, 65, 74, 84]	Detection of fake reviews; sentiments of customer reviews; dimensions of eWOM credibility regarding online purchasing activities; verifying sellers based on the experiences of friends; evaluation of peer-to-peer (P2P) platform markets

5 Discussion and Trends

In this section, we discuss the main findings and identify a number of trends in extant research. Our analysis suggests that the last decade shows an increase in studies on the topic and the past three years show a peak in the number of studies. This increase emphasizes the growing interest and importance of R&Rs and consumer buying. This may reflect the increase in the number of online stores, mobile shopping applications, and the development of online banking and financial services globally. Hence, we can expect a growing interest and awareness of the topic among companies and consumers. In addition, given the current world pandemic situation, e-commerce sales have further increasing [14]. Thus, online buying could be facilitated to ease the buying decision process and keep to level, which could further enhance the number of studies on this topic.

These results show the prevalence of the topic of R&Rs and consumer online buying in several fields, and enhance the significance of online activities of commercial, industrial, medical, agricultural, and technological sectors. It was interesting to note that only one consumer behavior journal has published an article on this topic, while electronic commerce journals have only published three papers during the whole period under study.

India, the USA, and China are the top three countries of affiliation of authors contributing to the topic, by order of importance. There could be several reasons to explain this fact. The main reason may be that these three countries come on the top list of the most populated countries (at the least for a decade). Highly populated countries are attractive target markets for many businesses and understanding online consumer behavior is essential, especially in a rapidly developing context.

The total number of citations for all papers is 1280. Figure 4 shows five papers which highly contribute to the topic, with a total of 996 citations (77.8%). The main focus theme of the three papers is CB&S: [45] was cited 433 times; [4] Amblee & Bui (2011), 193 times; and [25], 129 times. These three papers represent almost 60% of the total number of citations. This emphasizes the importance of CB&S studies in contributing to the main topic of R&R.

[70] and [24] were cited 193 times and 109 times, respectively. The two papers represent almost 23.6% of the total number of citations. The main focus of these papers is RRQ. [24] is the recent most-cited paper. This can be viewed as an important indicator of the growing interest in RRQ.

The majority of the studies have followed quantitative methodologies. Online surveys and online reviews were the most used method to collect data among all studies. The complexity of human behavior derives from rational and irrational thinking, cognitive and non-cognitive behavior, and emotions can trigger several different behaviors. Therefore, the massive information needed to study R&Rs and consumer behavior calls for a diversity of methodologies to collect and analyze data. In particular, experiment-based studies allow to control for relevant variables and can provide a rich database for wide analysis regarding this topic, as shown in [30, 31, 33]. Experiments allow for uncovering consumer patterns in gathering information and evaluation. However, there is a need for experiments focusing on the pre-purchase stage. Moreover, to understand consumer expressions and feelings, a qualitative approach would be adequate to study sentiments and emotional constructs.

The analysis shows that there are important interconnections among the identified themes (Table 3). This points out to the overlap between topics and the multidimensional nature and complexity of using R&Rs.

Consumer behavior and sales are affected by consumer trust and credibility on product/merchant. Trust on product and credibility of merchant are determined by consumer R&Rs and their level of satisfaction. Buyers are likely to share their experience and contribute by posting reviews and rating products. These R&Rs will shape the product's image on potential consumers' minds. Alternatively, R&Rs will impact their attention to buying, buying decision, and buying behavior.

In order to sum up the findings that emerged from our analysis and capture how R&Rs affect the different stages of the buying decision process, we developed a framework including three main dimensions: R&Rs relevant factors; mediators; and the buying decision process model stages [85], as shown in Fig. 5.

Table 3. Correlation of themes

	Consumer behavior and sales	Product quality	Trust & Credibility
Quality of Ratings and Reviews	the role of rating and review in mitigating consumer uncertainty; expected product quality which results in satisfaction or returning the product; the impact of positive ratings on sales; the impact of reviews on sales; the impact of reviews on consumer emotional and cognitive processes; review impact effect on consumer attitude alteration; single customer review and buying intentions; trustworthy review impact on skeptical recipient consumer; individual customer review and overall customer satisfaction; the impact of R&Rs on buying decision	single customer review and product-related attitudes; feature extraction; product quality ranking; semantic orientation; expected product quality; consumer services; quality perceptions; quality-of-care ratings	trust in consumers' reviews; trust in product reviews moderates single reviews effect and aggregate ratings; trust in product reviews moderates single reviews effect and aggregate ratings; trustworthiness estimation; credibility value estimation; trust in P2P platforms and review bias
Consumer behavior and sales		impact of customer review and additional signals of quality on buying behavior; the impact of product attributes on online purchase decision; the influence of product personality ratings on purchase intention; the impact of design constructs (credibility and features) on purchase intention	impact of trust on purchase intention; trustworthy reviews impact on skeptical recipient consumer

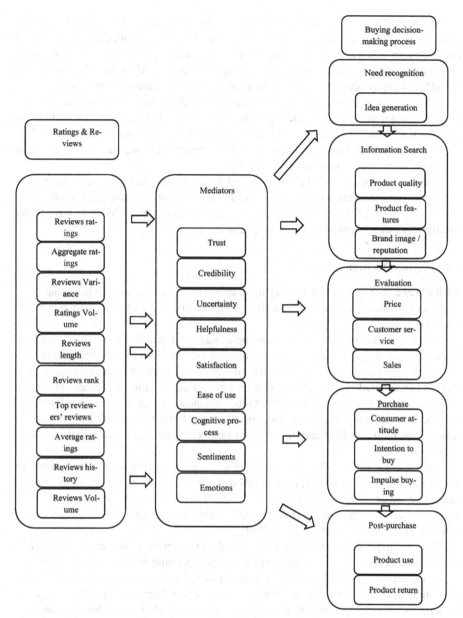

Fig. 5. Analysis map and framework

5.1 R&Rs Relevant Factors

We have identified a number of factors that have been pointed out as relevant to understand the impact of R&Rs: review ratings, aggregate ratings, review variance, rating volume, rating length, review ranking, top reviewers' reviews, average ratings, review history. According to Li et al. [42], the factors affecting online reviews are the number of reviews, where the average review rating is not directly controlled by merchants. In the same vein, Chen et al. [17] reported that the increase of rating volume after a certain number decreases the impact of rating on purchase intention. Moreover, Patra et al. [54] found that lengthy reviews may drop the recommendation/rating of a product.

The variance of consumer reviews creates a double-edged sword that can produce positive and negative effects. Heterogeneous consumer reviews are more useful to make strategic decisions [49]. Online consumers may disregard the primary product from their list of considerations due to the diversity of online reviews, fearing that it might not align with their preferences and requirements [76].

Consumer reviews could be more studied than ratings, because reviews offer more details on consumer experience, and therefore are more informative than ratings [65]. Hendrawan et al. [27] stated that readability value of a review is likely to have better quality score than a review with high usefulness value.

5.2 Buying Decision Process

R&Rs play a role throughout the buying decision process. Information in virtual communities and social forums can be a trigger for the first stage of need recognition and idea generation.

Moving to the second stage, consumers may start searching for information to learn more about products. The massive amount of online user-generated information derived from product reviews renders the mining of this information a challenging task. Reviews include additional information on product description, consumer opinion on products/sellers, etc. We should highlight that the quantity and diversity of information may be a distraction for readers and can affect the buying decision. This volume of information requires effort and time for consumers to analyze and make their purchase decisions.

Quality informative R&Rs are essential to ease the process of information search and evaluation. Vrânceanu [75] emphasizes the importance of online reviews as a tool to determine the quality or value of a product, as well as to enhance shopping intentions. In settings where users have access to a product's whole review history, they asymptotically learn the products' unknown qualities [10].

In regard to product evaluation, Rakesh et al. [58] propose a framework to efficiently rank different reviews in accordance with their aspects rating by calculating the review's aggregate rating. They used a ranked voting method to demonstrate the ranking of a large number of reviews by means of their aspects rating. Gangothri et al. [23] proposed a framework for rating calculation using customer feedback. On another note, Shaalan et al. [66] indicated that the average star rating of online reviews lacks a strong impact on product ranking, as the existing model of ranking aggregation largely overlooks the quality of opinions expressed in reviews. Nonetheless, ratings alone do not provide any contextual information that is crucial for evaluation purposes. Moreover, to obtain an accurate evaluation of products based on their R&Rs, aggregate ratings system and aggregate consumer feedbacks were used [23, 66, 81], regardless of some weakness in large-scale reviews. Consumer-generated product evaluation was found to increase buyer trust and support consumer decision-making [52], and it was found that ratings volume and reviews are important precursors of purchase intention [17]. In contrast, Vrânceanu [75] indicated that review quality does not influence product quality perception, value perception and shopping intentions. However, review ranking has a significant influence on those variables. The variety of online reviews, along with the diversity of aspects evaluated in reviews, can give the product a sense of uniqueness that enhances consumer purchase intention [76]. In this regard, Schuckert et al. [63] refer to online reviews as a strategic tool that has a significant role in online promotions, sales and brand reputation.

The credibility of consumer reviews may influence overall purchase expectations [84]. According to Ziegele et al. [84], individual customer reviews have an effect on potential buyers even when they do not reflect overall customer satisfaction. It is interesting to note that, according to Denker et al. [20], reviews rated as 'not credible' do not affect purchase decisions.

6 Direction for Future Research

A literature review paper aims at serving as platform for future research by identifying research gaps and identifying avenues for future research [55]. Investigation of future research would deliver rich outcomes in rapid developing countries, such as countries in Africa. Based on the previously discussed findings, we offer five main directions for further research:

6.1 Motivation to Provide R&Rs

Online reviews are a valuable source of product information which depends on consumers' motivations and willingness to provide content. More studies focusing on what leads consumers to provide feedback online, write reviews, and rate services and products are needed.

Future studies may study the relation between willingness to write a review and the value of the experience consumers get. The massive amount of online consumer reviews provides a valuable research opportunity to explore electronic word-of-mouth. Therefore, it is worthy to study the relation between the volume of reviews and willingness to write a review.

Some of the questions to be addressed are: How can companies incentivize consumer to provide R&Rs? How companies can maintain constant self-motivated star-rated reviews?

6.2 Understanding Review Quality

Reviews include rich additional information on product description, consumer opinion on product/seller, etc. Thus, categorizing these types of information by different items/dimensions that consumer need to evaluate, may make new users' tasks easier and faster. We should highlight that such an abundance of information may overwhelm consumers and delay buying decisions. According to Li et al. [42], the most utilized factors in studies on the effect of online product reviews were the number of reviews and the average review rating, which are not directly controlled by merchants. Average product rating does not show significant impact on consumer purchasing decision [66]. Therefore, further studies may investigate the impact of creating categories in reviews to make it easier for consumers to provide reviews.

Also, it is suggested for future studies to consider aggregate and average negative R&Rs as a variable affecting consumer decision-making and online behavior. Some studies referred to 'neutral reviews' posted by users. Neutral reviews may vary in nature. Some reviews may seem to be neutral to some users, but not to others. Therefore, it is essential to underline the effect of neutral reviews and give it more attention in future studies.

Implementing appropriate design and review policies will improve quality and validity of consumer reviews. Particularly, we highlight the following questions: What is the level/point of review saturation (when does a review cease to add value to the aggregate volume of reviews)? How does the use of hashtags in reviews' keywords contribute to the identification of trends regarding product features, quality, brand image, price, etc. and enhance the usefulness of reviews?

6.3 Understanding Consumer Preference and Use of R&Rs

Consumer decision-making style (maximizers vs satisficers) impacts the decision-making process [31]. While maximizers conduct an extensive search for all potential options and thoroughly analyzing the available information [64], satisficers demonstrate critical selectivity in their approach towards using and processing information [13]. Therefore, future research may consider buyer characteristics to better understand the usefulness of R&Rs. The usefulness of information gathered from reviews could be interpreted differently based on the consumer decision-making style.

Easy accessibility to reading and writing online reviews increases review heterogeneity in terms of nature, structure, language. Hence, since reviewers and readers may come from different cultures and world locations, understanding how culture affects both writing and reading reviews process is needed.

Finally, considering user demographic characteristics is recommended in future studies. Demographic characteristics can help to understand online consumer behavior in regard to R&Rs. In addition, it may help to identify consumers based on their demographics and alternatively display reviews to other consumers who share similar characteristics. Thus, main questions are: how do consumers perceive R&Rs across cultures? Does gender matter to understand the impact of R&Rs on consumer buying decision-making process? Does age impact the influence of R&Rs on the buying decision process?

6.4 Understanding the Impact of R&Rs Throughout the Buying Decision-Making Process

Relevant factors of R&Rs shows an impact of different stages of the buying decision-making process. The result of each stage plays a role in the next stage of the process. The type of information gathered in the "information search" stage will determine the aspect which will be evaluated in the "evaluating stage", and so on. Studying the impact of R&Rs factors on the buying decision-making process stages is essential to improve our understanding of consumer behavior. This could help prioritizing the relevant factors for each stage and increase of the efficiency of online marketing activities. Specific research questions here include: What type of R&R are sought in each phase of the decision buying behavior? Which platforms do consumers consider searching for R&Rs in each phase of the process?

6.5 R&Rs in Services

Out of 17 papers which collected data from online reviews, only 2 (11.7%) focused on services. Consumers purchasing online may check the return policy before purchasing on any platform. Consumers tend to return products in case of damage, default, wrong order delivery, etc. Tangible products can be returned to or replaced by the seller. Hence, consumers may not express their dissatisfaction or frustration by writing a negative review. This is not the case with services. Hence, service buyers require more information on the service from previous users who had the experience. Giving the service sector more attention, researchers will enrich consumer behavior and buying decision process studies; service reviews need further exploration. Therefore, some of the questions for further research are: What aspects in reviews are more relevant to service buyers? Are service consumers willing to write a review? Since some services need time to be evaluated, when do service buyers write a review?

7 Limitation

Main limitation of this study is the number of papers found/included in the initial search on the referred data bases. Aiming at pure studies on the topic of R&R in relation to consumer decision making behavior. Both topics R&R and consumer buying decision making process are extremely wide, especially from business perspective. Therefore, this study was keen to comprise studies that link both topics in relation.

8 Conclusions

This study aimed to analyze published research concerning online R&Rs to find out trends, themes, direction, research problems, and potential future research. The exploration of online R&R is crucial in aiding retailers and marketers to enhance and advance their online endeavors. This can lead to greater consumer engagement and participation by encouraging them to share their purchase experiences, ultimately influencing the purchasing decisions of other online consumers. It was concluded that different aspects of R&Rs, such as review ratings, aggregate ratings, review variance, rating volume, rating length, review ranking, top reviewer reviews, average rating, review history, moderated by behavioral constructs, have an impact on consumer buying decision-making process. For marketers and retailers who are investing in their online presence, it's important to gain a deep understanding of their customers' buying habits and behaviors, requirements, the difficulties they encounter. There is room for further studies to contribute to and develop an understanding of consumer buying behavior in this context. The objective of this research is to enhance the comprehension of consumer behavior, information systems, and e-business literature by expanding their knowledge base of online R&Rs and their different directions. This paper sheds light on existing studies and will enhance future research.

References

1. Ahluwalia, P., Hughes, J., Midha, V.: Drivers of e-retailer peak sales period price behavior: an empirical analysis. Int. J. Account. Inf. Manag. **21**(1), 72–90 (2013)
2. Aiken, K.D., Boush, D.M.: Trustmarks, objective-source ratings, and implied investments in advertising: investigating online trust and the context-specific nature of internet signals. J. Acad. Mark. Sci. **34**(3), 308–323 (2006)
3. Ajay Varma, V., Ramesh Krishna, T., Selvan, M.P.: Competitor identification by use the sentiment classification based on the user research. Int. J. Innov. Technol. Exploring Eng. **8**(9 Special Issue 2), 871–874 (2019)
4. Amblee, N., Bui, T.: Harnessing the influence of social proof in online shopping: the effect of electronic word of mouth on sales of digital microproducts. Int. J. Electron. Commer. **16**(2), 91–114 (2011)
5. Attar, R.W., Shanmugam, M., Hajli, N.: Investigating the antecedents of e-commerce satisfaction in social commerce context. British Food Journal, pp. 1–20 (2021)
6. Baharuddin, N.A., Yaacob, M.: Dimensions of EWOM credibility on the online purchasing activities among consumers through social media. Jurnal Komunikasi: Malaysian J. Commun. **36**(3), 335–352 (2020)
7. Bandura, A.: Social learning theory. General Learning Corporation, pp. 1–46 (1971)
8. Berg, L., Slettemeås, D., Kjørstad, I., Rosenberg, T.G.: Trust and the don't-want-to-complain bias in peer-to-peer platform markets. Int. J. Consum. Stud. **44**(3), 220–231 (2020)
9. Bernardino, S., Santos, J.F., Ribeiro, J.C., Freitas, A.: Determinants of the effective use of UGC (user-generated content) on hotel room bookings by portuguese travellers. Int. J. Online Market. **10**(2), 30–43 (2020)
10. Besbes, O., Scarsini, M.: On information distortions in online ratings. Oper. Res. **66**(3), 597–610 (2018)
11. Birnbaum, D.: Buyer beware: health choices information broadcast to the public. Int. J. Health Governance **21**(1), 35–40 (2016)
12. Byun, K., Ma, M., Kim, K., Kang, T.: Buying a new product with inconsistent product reviews from multiple sources: the role of information diagnosticity and advertising. J. Interactive Market. **55**, 81–103 (2021)
13. Chang, C.C.A., Burke, R.R.: Consumer choice of retail shopping aids. J. Retailing Consumer Services **14**(5), 339–346 (2007)
14. Chang, H.H., Meyerhoefer, C.D.: COVID-19 and the demand for online food shopping services: empirical evidence from Taiwan.American J. Agricultural Econ., pp 1–18 (2020)
15. Chen, A., Lu, Y., Gupta, S.: Enhancing the decision quality through learning from the social commerce components. J. Glob. Inf. Manag. **25**(1), 66–91 (2017)
16. Chen, C., Nguyen, B., Klaus, P.P., Wu, M., Chen, C., Klaus, P.P.: Exploring electronic word-of-Mouth (eWOM) in the consumer purchase decision-making process : the case of online holidays – evidence from United Kingdom (UK) consumers. J. Travel Tour. Mark. **32**(8), 953–970 (2015)
17. Chen, C.C., Chang, Y.C.: What drives purchase intention on Airbnb? perspectives of consumer reviews, information quality, and media richness. Telematics Inform. **35**(5), 1512–1523 (2018)
18. Chen, J., Shen, X.L.: Consumers' decisions in social commerce context: an empirical investigation. Decis. Support Syst. **79**, 55–64 (2015)
19. Cheung, M.Y., Luo, C., Sia, C.L., Chen, H.: How do people evaluate electronic word-of-mouth? informational and normative based determinants of perceived credibility of online consumer recommendations in China. PACIS 2007 - 11th Pacific Asia Conference on Information Systems: Managing Diversity in Digital Enterprises, pp. 69–81 (2007)

20. Denker, D., Gewald, H.: Influential factors for patients' online ratings of general practitioners. International Conference on Research and Innovation in Information Systems, ICRIIS, pp. 1–6 (2017)
21. Escoffier, N., Tournois, N., McKelvey, B.: Using crowdsourcing to increase new product's market value and positive comments for both the crowd involved and customers. Int. J. Innov. Manag. 22(2), 1–28 (2018)
22. Frick, B., Kaimann, D.: The impact of customer reviews and advertisement efforts on the performance of experience goods in electronic markets. Appl. Econ. Lett. 24(17), 1237–1240 (2017)
23. Gangothri, V., Saranya, S., Venkataraman, D.: Engender product ranking and recommendation using customer feedback. In: The International Conference on Soft Computing SystemsNew Delhi, pp. 851–859 (2016)
24. Gao, G.G., Greenwood B.N., Agarwal, R., McCullough, J.: Vocal Minority and Silent Majority: How Do Online Ratings Reflect Population Perceptions of Quality? 39(3), 565–589 (2015)
25. Hajli, M.: A research framework for social commerce adoption. Inf. Manag. Comput. Secur. 21(3), 144–154 (2013)
26. Hajli, N., Lin, X., Featherman, M., Wang, Y.: Social word of mouth how trust develops in the market. Int. J. Mark. Res. 56(5), 1–18 (2014)
27. Hendrawan, R.A., Suryani, E., Oktavia, R.: Evaluation of e-commerce product reviews based on structural, metadata, and readability characteristics. Procedia Comp. Sci. 124, 280–286 (2017)
28. Huang, G.H., Korfiatis, N.: Trying before buying: the moderating role of online reviews in trial attitude formation toward mobile applications. Int. J. Electron. Commer. 19(4), 77–111 (2015)
29. Huang, Z., Benyoucef, M.: User preferences of social features on social commerce websites: an empirical study. Technol. Forecast. Soc. Chang. 95, 57–72 (2015)
30. Karimi, S., Holland, C.P., Papamichail, K.N.: The impact of consumer archetypes on online purchase decision-making processes and outcomes: a behavioral process perspective. J. Business Res. 91, 71–82 (2018)
31. Karimi, S., Papamichail, K.N., Holland, C.P.: The effect of prior knowledge and decision-making style on the online purchase decision-making process: a typology of consumer shopping behaviour. Decis. Support Syst. 77, 137–147 (2015)
32. Kauffmann, E., Peral, J., Gil, D., Ferrández, A., Sellers, R., Mora, H.: Managing marketing decision-making with sentiment analysis: an evaluation of the main product features using text data mining. Sustainability (Switzerland) 11(15), 1–19 (2019)
33. Kazungu, I., et al.: A Purchase Decision-Making Process Model of Online Consumers and its Influential Factor a Cross Sector Analysis. Theses PhD, X, October, pp. 1–326 (2015)
34. Ke, D., Zhang, H., Yu, N., Tu, Y.: Who will stay with the brand after posting non-5/5 rating of purchase? An empirical study of online consumer repurchase behavior. Springer Berlin Heidelberg (2019)
35. Khalid, J., et al.: Significance of electronic word of mouth (e-WOM) in opinion formation. Int. J. Advanced Comput. Sci. Appl. 2, 537–544 (2020)
36. Kim, S., Park, H.: Effects of various characteristics of social commerce (s-commerce) on consumers' trust and trust performance. Int. J. Inf. Manage. 33(2), 318–332 (2013)
37. Koneru, A., Yamuna, S., Pavan, G., Divya, B.: FBP recommendation system through sentiment analysis. Int. J. Advanced Sci. Technol. 29(5), 896–907 (2019)
38. Krestel, R., Dokoohaki, N.: Diversifying customer review rankings. Neural Netw. 66, 36–45 (2015)
39. Lai, C.Y., Li, Y.M.: A social referral mechanism on e-marketplace. Lecture Notes in Bus. Inf. Process. 155 LNBIP, 97–108 (2013)

40. Lai, C.Y., Li, Y.M., Lin, L.F.: A social referral appraising mechanism for the e-marketplace. Inf. and Manage. **54**(3), 269–280 (2017)
41. Lee, J., Park, D.H., Han, I.: The effect of negative online consumer reviews on product attitude: an information processing view. Electron. Commer. Res. Appl. **7**(3), 341–352 (2008)
42. Li, C.-W., Chuang, H.-C., Li, S.-T.: Hedonic analysis for consumer electronics using online product reviews. In: Proceedings - 2016 5th IIAI International Congress on Advanced Applied Informatics, IIAI-AAI 2016, pp. 609–614 (2016)
43. Li, G., Elliot, S., Choi, C.: Electronic word-of-mouth in B2C virtual communities: an empirical study from CTrip.com. J. Global Academy of Marketing Sci. **20**(3), 262–268 (2010)
44. Li, X.: Impact of average rating on social media endorsement: the moderating role of rating dispersion and discount threshold. Inf. Syst. Res. **29**(3), 739–754 (2018)
45. Li, X., Hitt, L.M.: Self-selection and information role of online product reviews. Inf. Syst. Res. **19**(4), 456–474 (2008)
46. Li, X., Ma, B., Chu, H.: The impact of online reviews on product returns. Asia Pac. J. Mark. Logist. **33**(8), 1814–1828 (2021)
47. Lin, X., Li, Y., Wang, X.: Social commerce research: definition, research themes and the trends. Int. J. Inf. Manage. **37**(3), 190–201 (2017)
48. Luu, M.D., Lim, E.P.: Do Your Friends Make You Buy this Brand?: Modeling Social Recommendation with Topics and Brands. Springer US (2018). https://doi.org/10.1007/s10618-017-0535-9
49. Markopoulos, P.M., Clemons, E.K.: Reducing buyers' uncertainty about taste-related product attributes. J. Manag. Inf. Syst. **30**(2), 269–299 (2013)
50. Maslowska, E., Malthouse, E.C., Bernritter, S.F.: Too good to be true: the role of online reviews' features in probability to buy. Int. J. Advert. **36**(1), 142–163 (2017)
51. Mastan Rao, T., Mounika, N., Hema Chowdary, K., Sudhir, T.: A framework for generating rankings to E-commerce products based on reviews using NLP. Int. J. Mechanical Eng. Technol. **9**(1), 44–52 (2018)
52. Mudambi, S.M., Schuff, D., Zhang, Z.: Why aren't the stars aligned? an analysis of online review content and star ratings. In: Proceedings of the Annual Hawaii International Conference on System Sciences, pp. 3139–3147 (2014)
53. Ong, B.S.: Online shopper reviews: ramifications for promotion and website utility. J. Promot. Manag. **17**(3), 327–344 (2011)
54. Patra, G., Roy, D.: Assessing consumers' satisfaction through analyzing product review and rating. Pacific Bus. Rev. Int. **12**(1), 37–47 (2019)
55. Paul, J., Criado, A.R.: The art of writing literature review: what do we know and what do we need to know? International Business Review, p. 7 (2020)
56. Penumetsa, H.K., Mogalla, S.: Ml based naive bayes methodology for rate prediction using textual rating and find actual or movie rating based on mbnbr optimization. Int. J. Innovative Technol. Exploring Eng. **8**(10), 314–321 (2019)
57. Rad, A., Benyoucef, M.: A model for understanding social commerce. J. Inf. Syst. Applied Res. (JISAR) **4**(2), 63–73 (2011)
58. Rakesh, K., Sharan, A., Chandra, S.Y.: A framework for ranking reviews using ranked voting method. In: The Second International Conference on Computer and Communication Technologies New Delhi, pp. 263–272 (2016)
59. Ramkumar, V., Rajasekar, S., Swamynathan, S.: Scoring products from reviews through application of fuzzy techniques. Expert Syst. Appl. **37**(10), 6862–6867 (2010)
60. Safi, R., Yu, Y.: Online product review as an indicator of users' degree of innovativeness and product adoption time: a longitudinal analysis of text reviews. Eur. J. Inf. Syst. **26**(4), 414–431 (2017)
61. Sahoo, N., Dellarocas, C., Srinivasan, S.: The impact of online product reviews on product returns. Inf. Syst. Res. **29**(3), 723–738 (2018)

62. Sánchez-Pérez, M., Illescas-Manzano, M.D., Martínez-Puertas, S.: Online review ratings: an analysis of product attributes and competitive environment. J. Mark. Commun. **00**(00), 1–19 (2021)
63. Schuckert, M., Liu, X., Law, R.: Hospitality and tourism online reviews: recent trends and future directions. J. Travel Tour. Mark. **32**(5), 608–621 (2015)
64. Schwartz, B., Ward, A., Lyubomirsky, S., Monterosso, J., White, K., Lehman, D.R.: Maximizing versus satisficing: happiness is a matter of choice. J. Pers. Soc. Psychol. **83**(5), 1178–1197 (2002)
65. Şensoy, M., Yolum, P.: Automating User Reviews Using Ontologies: An Agent-Based Approach (2012)
66. Shaalan, Y., Zhang, X.: A time and opinion quality-weighted model for aggregating online reviews. In: Australasian Database Conference, pp. 269–282 (2016)
67. Shadkam, M., Hara, J.O.: Social commerce dimensions: the potential leverage for marketers. Journal of Internet Banking and Commerce, pp. 1–14 (2013)
68. Shin, D., Darpy, D.: Rating, review and reputation: how to unlock the hidden value of luxury consumers from digital commerce? J. Bus. Industrial Marketing **35**(10), 15531561 (2020)
69. Singh, P., Raveendra, P.V., Kumar, S.S., Namitha, H.N., Likith, R.: Customers' attitude towards online reviews on social media among youth in Bangalore. Int. J. Mechanical Eng. Technol. **9**(5), 841–848 (2018)
70. Sridhar, S., Srinivasan, R.: Social influence effects in online product ratings. J. Mark. **76**(5), 70–88 (2012)
71. Tama, V.O., Sibaroni, Y.: Labeling analysis in the classification of product review sentiments by using multinomial naive bayes algorithm. J. Physics: Conference Series **1192**(1), 1–11 (2019)
72. Tariq, A., Wang, C., Tanveer, Y., Akram, U., Akram, Z.: Organic food consumerism through social commerce in China. Asia Pac. J. Mark. Logist. **31**(1), 202–222 (2019)
73. Tomar, M., Pandey, A.K., Ahuja, V., Bansal, S.: How does e-marketing influence consumer's decision? a descriptive review. J. Advanced Res. Dynamical Control Syst. **11**(8 Special Issue), 2665–2680 (2019)
74. Viji, D., Asawa, N., Burreja, T.: Fake reviews of customer detection using machine learning models. Int. J. Advanced Sci. Technol. **29**(6), 86–94 (2020)
75. Vrânceanu, D.M.: The impact of online consumer reviews' quantity and rating on buying decisions: a perspective from Romanian market. In: The 11th International Management Conference, pp. 188–195 (2017)
76. Wang, F., Liu, X., Fang, E.: User reviews variance, critic reviews variance, and product sales: an exploration of customer breadth and depth effects. J. Retail. **91**(3), 372–389 (2015)
77. Wang, F., Yang, Y., Tso, G.K.F., Li, Y.: Analysis of launch strategy in cross-border e-Commerce market via topic modeling of consumer reviews. Electron. Commer. Res. **19**(4), 863–884 (2019)
78. Wang, Y., Yu, C.: International journal of information management social interaction-based consumer decision-making model in social commerce: the role of word of mouth and observational learning. Int. J. Inf. Manage. **37**(3), 179–189 (2017)
79. West, E. Pollution: Pedagogy for a post-truth society review pollution: pedagogy for a post -truth society. Media and Communication, **9**(3), 144–154 (2021)
80. Yang, J., Sarathy, R., Lee, J.K.: The effect of product review balance and volume on online shoppers' risk perception and purchase intention. Decis. Support Syst. **89**, 66–76 (2016)
81. Yang, R., Wang, D.: Hierarchical aggregation for reputation feedback of services networks. Math. Probl. Eng. **2020**, 1–12 (2020)
82. Yang, X., Zhang, X., Goh, S., Anderson, C.: Curvilinear effects of e-loyalty in China's online tourism industry. Nankai Business Rev. Int. **8**(2), 174–189 (2017)

83. Zheng, L.: The classification of online consumer reviews: a systematic literature review and integrative framework. J. Business Res. **135**, 226–251 (2021)
84. Ziegele, M., Weber, M.: Example, please! comparing the effects of single customer reviews and aggregate review scores on online shoppers' product evaluations. J. Consum. Behav. **14**(2), 103–114 (2015)
85. Zuschke, N.: An analysis of process-tracing research on consumer decision-making. J. Bus. Res. **2019**, 1–16 (2018)

The Impact of Technological Innovation on Employment: The Case of Morocco

Zineb Bachiri[✉] and Naima El Haoud

Scientific Engineering of Organisations Laboratory, University Hassan II- ENCG-C,
Casablanca, Morocco
Bachiri.zinb@gmail.com

Abstract. In digitization and automation context, Morocco, a middle-income country, quickly understood the importance of innovation for its growth, and implemented multiples strategies (digital Morocco, industrial acceleration plan, Morocco innovation initiative …) to catch up its technological delay and reduce disparities on innovation. However, while promoting innovation, we need to make enough attention to problems that can cause. Employment is one of the most worrying issues. Referring to Shumpeterian theories of creative destruction, and classical compensation via compensation mechanisms, the paper aims to determine short and long-term quantitative impacts of technological innovation on employment growth in Morocco, by investigates the relationships between the growth rates of patents, research and development (R&D), and employment. We deployed the vector error correction model (VECM) and found results consistent with theory. Results obtained show that in short term technological progress is responsible for job destruction. However, in the long-term effect remains positive and compensates destroyed jobs. We can conclude that employment growth in Morocco have strong relationship with technological innovation.

Keywords: employment growth · technological progress · innovation · patents

1 Introduction

The impact of technological progress on employment studies are paradoxical. Developing economies are profoundly transformed by dissemination of technological innovations (information and communication technologies, artificial intelligence, etc.) and yet little work in Morocco has been carried out and covers the consequences on jobs quantity. Developing economies are undergoing major structural change – driven by changes in demand, technologies, organizations and international production – yet the economic literature has not extensively addressed the issue of creation and destruction jobs due to innovation.

The potential negative impact of technological change on employment and job displacement are old and controversial issues in economic thought. Historically, these worries go back at least to ancient Greece, Aristotle (1965) imagined the situation in which "the shuttle will run automatically and the instrument will play automatically", therefore the craftsman will no longer need slaves, and the slave owner will not need slaves.

© The Author(s), under exclusive license to Springer Nature Switzerland AG 2023
R. Jallouli et al. (Eds.): ICDEc 2023, LNBIP 485, pp. 137–151, 2023.
https://doi.org/10.1007/978-3-031-42788-6_9

Keynes (1931) referred to possible "technological unemployment" as its name suggests is unemployment caused by the advent of rapid advances in technology and labor-saving machinery in 1930. In other words, the speed of technological progress exceeds human learning, leading to unemployment since workers cannot immediately find new jobs.

All the world is increasingly concerned; human jobs will be replaced by rapid technological progress. Graetz and Michaels (2015) find that industrial robots increase productivity and wages and reduce hours worked. Brynjolfsson and McAfee (2011) and (2014) refer to a growing gap between GDP and employment as "the great Decoupling", and their main message is that recent technological advances reduce employment. Similarly, for Autor et al. (2003), Acemoglu and Autor (2011) studies. Koch et al. (2019) find a net job creation in companies adopting robots. According to Su et al. (2022) there is no influence between technological innovation and employment. Faber (2018), Artuc et al. (2019) finds negative impacts of robot exposure for the specific case of Mexican employment.

In a digitization and automation context, Morocco, a middle-income country, quickly understood the importance of innovation for its growth, and implemented a range of strategies (digital Morocco, industrial acceleration plan, Morocco innovation initiative …) to catch up its technology delay and reduce disparities on innovation.

Although the link between employment and technological change, become a classic subject today, there's scarcity of studies in developing countries. The paper contributes to the literature by exploring for the first time in Morocco the impact of technological innovation on employment using two variables patents and research and development expenditure.

Given the scarcity of research on quantitative effects of technological innovation on employment in Morocco, this research will help promote the stability of Morocco's labor market, and the formulation of employment policies will also have an instructive significance. The paper aims to answer the following questions: What are the short and long-term quantitative effects of technological innovation on jobs in Morocco? Is there any compensation effect? The impact of technological innovation on employment in Morocco will vary depending on the short or long term.

To determine effects of technological shocks on employment, we have set the following variables in accordance with the literature: growth of employment, growth of research and development (R&D), growth of patents and labour compensation. Our data was collected from the World Bank databases, Penn world table 10.0 and the United Nations Educational, Scientific and Cultural Organization (UNESCO. In order to correctly exploit this data set, the vector error correction model (VECM) was used.

This paper is structured as follows. In Sect. 2 we illustrate the theoretical and empirical basis of relationship between innovation and employment dynamics and effects of technological innovation on employment growth. Following this, in Sect. 3 we present the results of impact of technological progress in short and long term on employment. Section 4 concludes.

2 Literature Review

2.1 Effects of Technological Innovation on Employment: Theoretical View

The relationship between innovation and employment dynamics is a key issue in economic theory. However, from theoretical and empirical point of view the analysis of this relationship is particularly complex. We will present the theoretical foundations by classifying the theories according to an equilibrium perspective (neoclassical analyses) and disequilibrium perspective (evolutionary, Keynesian, structural and regulationist theories). The main difference between the two points of view concerns the process of self-adjustment which begins as soon as the innovation is introduced. According to classical Adam Smith (1776) and Ricardo (1821), the introduction of innovation induces an increase in productivity and consequently in the growth rate. There is a causal effect between innovation and employment, via the increase in total output and the reduction in wages. Currents of disequilibrium consider that technological progress is a phenomenon and the effect of innovation on employment is not unequivocal.

Before industrial revolution, the working world and its vicissitudes did not really come to the attention of contemporary economists. In pre-classic times, mercantilists took seriously the potentially detrimental effect of machinery on employment. As noted by Freeman and Soete (1994), in France and England regulations have been implemented aims directly at controlling the use of machines in the production process (limiting the use of banners or sewing machines). Governments introduce industrial protectionism in order to avoid mass unemployment and social revolts.

With the advent of the laissez-faire principle, the interventionist mercantilist approaches were revisited. Indeed, the mechanization of labor induces a fall in prices and a long-term improvement, compensating for the initial labour displacement.

D. Ricardo (1772–1823) is one of the classical economists, the one who makes the most reference, directly or indirectly, to the consequences of technical progress on employment. Ricardo recognizes that mechanization will initially lead to a contraction of gross income and employment "the opinion of the working classes on machines which they believe to be fatal to their interests, is not based solely on error and prejudices, but on the firmest, clearest principles of political economy" Ricardo (1821). D. Ricardo considers that "the increase in the net income, evaluated in commodities, - a increase which necessarily entails the use of machinery - must lead to new savings". These savings manage to create a fund more considerable than the gross income destroyed due to machines discovery. Therefore, with each augmentation in capital, it will recruit more workers, so some of the people who lost his work will be reemployed.

Keynes opposes the classical theory that supply creates its own demand and that the market is always in equilibrium. In his work "General Theory of Employment, Interest and Money" Keynes considers that market does not have capacity to self-regulate, and that unemployment is only a temporary phenomenon resulting from "an overall demand shortfall and cannot be solved" in the labour market. Indeed, if wages fall in all companies, the impoverishment of employees will lead them to consume less, which will lead to a drop in production and unemployment, unlike the traditional current.

Schumpeterian theory marks a turning point in the analysis of the relationship between technical progress and employment. Schumpeter demonstrates the innovation role in economic dynamics. Innovation is conceptualized as a painful process, which creatively destroys old and paves way for new. Schumpeter (1912) supports thesis that economic evolution cannot come from a quantitative modification (such as the augmentation in population or capital) and shows that the determining factor leading to economic evolution is innovation. According to Schumpeter, unemployment arises as a consequence of technological innovation, the diffusion of which takes considerable time and affects different sectors asymmetrically. Consequently, the economic take-off it engenders occurs in a cyclical form, and these fluctuations constitute normal response of economy to the absorption of newness. Expansion phase is explained by the appearance of a cluster of new combinations allowing the rise in wages and interest rates as well as the fall in unemployment. The compensation mechanism is thus inscribed in the Schumpeterian vision.

The Schumpeterian heritage has been adopted by the neo-Schumpeterians. Nelson and Winter took up Schumpeter's ideas in their central work, "An evolutionary Theory of Economic Change" (Nelson and Winter, 1982). Nelson and Winter originated the developmental model of the economy emphasizing the function of innovation. Philippe Aghion and Peter Howitt (1992) gave birth to a new current of endogenous growth theory by modeling the intuitions of Joseph Schumpeter. According to Philippe Aghion and Peter Howit, innovations are likely to upset the entire economy, since each of them, by taking the place of the previous ones, raises companies productivity. The rate of economic growth therefore depends on the intensity of research in the economy, but also on the degree of competition between firms.

2.2   The Compensation Theory

The economic literature identifies six compensation mechanisms (Vivarelli, 1995, 2007; Simonetti et al. 2000).

- Compensation "via new machines"
     Stuart (1806–1873) explains how mechanization could lead to temporary unemployment, compensated in the long term by the growth of employment linked both to the sectors of machine production and to the compensation effect due to production growth linked to drop in prices. Sauvy (1980) recalls that the compensation mechanism "via new machines" is explained by three arguments. First, it takes workers to produce machines. Secondly, there is an extension of market and product consumption thus produced under more efficient conditions rises because there is a fall in prices. Thirdly, new activities appear to meet new needs.
- Compensation "via decrease in prices"
     Innovations reduce number of employees, and contribute to reducing the unit cost of production. In a competitive market, this effect results in lower prices. Decreasing prices stimulate new demand addressed to the innovating company or to other companies and thus an increase in production and new jobs are created. The increase in demand creates jobs in the long term.
- Compensation "via new investments"

The neoclassicals (Marshall, 1961) and Douglas (1930) specify that one of technological change consequences is reduction of costs. This decrease generates a drop in prices and subsequently an additional profit that can be accumulated by innovative entrepreneurs. These profits can be reinvested, so again, to increase production, therefore more employment.

- Compensation "via decrease in wages"

The direct innovation effect (destruction of jobs) can be offset by a wages adjustment in labour market. Wages reduction promotes an increase of employee's demand. Producers are ready to produce more at the same price given the fall in nominal wages.

- Compensation "via increase in income"

Pasinetti (1981) shows that increasing productivity implies decreasing production costs. Thus, consumers benefit from a lower price, which increases their real income. Consequently, an increase in consumption and therefore in production. This increase in demand promotes an increase in employment and that can compensate for the initial job losses due to innovations process.

- Compensation "via new products"

Katsoulakos (1984) judges, if process innovation reduces employment, product innovation has the opposite effect. New products create new demand, which leads companies to produce more and therefore to hire.

2.3 Previous Empirical Analysis of Technological Innovation Impact on Employment

The economic literature has long been interested in the links between technology, innovation and employment. As economic theory struggles to provide an unequivocal and definitive answer as to the effects of technologies on employment, many empirical studies show the effects of technological innovation on employment volume. Their results vary according to methodological choices: on the one hand technological progress variables (R&D expenditure, patents filed, investment in new equipment or software, introduction of product or process innovation) and another part (national economy, sectoral or companies).

To measure technical progress Chen and Puttitanun (2005), Furman et al. (2002) and Mancusi (2004) use patents as indicator for measuring innovation. Another measure of innovation appears in the literature the R&D expenditure. Saafi and Sboui (2012) use the number of patents, R&D expenditures and the value of imported technologies. Berman and Machin (2000) use computer at work and R&D expenditures to test the hypothesis of technological change bias.

At the macroeconomic level, Simonetti, Taylor and Vivarelli (2000) analyse, at the aggregate level, the role of patents in labor demand growth in United States, Italy, France and Japan between 1965 and 1993. Their first conclusion is that innovation process has a negative effect on employment in the short term. In the French case, this effect is offset by three mechanisms: lower prices, increased income and new machines. Product innovation have a positive effect.

Pak and Poissonier (2016) conduct a study at the macroeconomic level to test trade role, technology and consumption labour demand in France between 1983 and 2010. Their study at the aggregate level makes it possible to take into account and isolate the respective employment effects of the three factors in the overall economy. Indeed, this method only measures the effects on short-term employment and does not include the effects of long-term feedback.

James Bessen (2019) demonstrates that job growth was initially stimulated by automation due to the high elasticity of demand. Carbonero, Francesco & Ernst, Ekke-hard & Weber, Enzo (2020) provide evidence on the effects of robots on worldwide employment, they find that robots turn out to have a significantly negative impact on worldwide employment.

3   Methodology and Results

The estimation process in this study involves five steps. The first step is to examine the stationarity of the series, ensuring that all series are integrated of the same order. This stationarity step is essential because causality tests are very sensitive to the stationarity of the data series Stock and Watson (1989). This paper examines the stationarity of data series using the ADF unit root test as proposed by Dickey and Fuller (1979). The second step is to determine the optimal number of lags by the VAR procedure. The third step is to examine the presence of cointegration, or the long-run relationship between all variables in the model. For the cointegration test, we need to ensure that the data used are stationary. If one or more variables have different levels of integration, they cannot be cointegrated (Engle and Granger, 1987). In this paper, we have applied the Johansen cointegration test (Johansen, 1988) to verify the existence of cointegration between variables. Once the cointegration test has confirmed the existence of one or more cointegrating relationships between the variables in the model, the Vector Error Correction Model (VECM) will be applied for the Granger causality test in the fourth step. The VECM is the method that is only applicable if a long term relationship between the variables is present. The Granger causality of the VECM model confirms the long and short term causality directions. The ECT represents the error correction period that defines the effectiveness of the feedback or correction mechanism in stabilising the imbalance in the model. A single equation with a negative sign and statistical significance at the 1% level ensures the existence of cointegration and imbalance adjustment in the model (Narayan, 2005). However, if the cointegration test implies that there is more than one cointegrating equation, we test the significance of the error correction term (ECT). Similarly, we also use the chi-square test for all short-run coefficients to conclude the direction of the short-run causal relationship between the variables.

Finally, in the last step, the variance decomposition and impulse response function methods are adopted to describe the projected time scenarios of the dynamic relationship between the fourth variables based on the VECM model.

3.1 Methodology

3.1.1 Data and Variables

To determine effects of technological shocks on employment, we have set the following variables in accordance with literature: EMPLOI for employment growth, BREVETS for the number of patents, DEPENSERD for research and development expenditure and LABOURSH for the labour compensation.

We have used data from four statistical series of annual employment growth in Morocco between 1990 and 2016, research and development expenditure growth, patents growth, employment demand growth and labour compensation growth. Our data was collected from the World Bank databases, Penn world table 10.0 and the United Nations Educational, Scientific and Cultural Organization (UNESCO).

3.1.2 Stationarity and Variables Co-Integration

Most of economic variables are often non-stationary, so it is important to test stationarity before generalizing any relationship. We will start by testing the presence of unit roots through the augmented Dickey - Fuller (ADF) test. The test reveals that all variables are non-stationary. They all become stationary in first difference at the 5% significance level, see (Appendix 1). The co-integration relationship between the variables was tested by Johnsen's method (1988). The results, below the 5% level of significance, accept a single co-integration relationship at most, see (appendix 2). Assuming the existence of a co-integrating relationship, VECM model can be continued.

3.1.3 VECM Model

The paper used co-integration procedure and vector error correction model (VECM) to test the long-term equilibrium and the short-term relationship between the variables.

Our empirical study uses annual data series from 1990 to 2016 for Morocco obtained from the Indicators produced by the World Bank and High Commission for Planning. We transform all variables into logarithmic form in order to solve the problem of heteroskedasticity and induce stationarity in the variance-covariance matrix (Chang, 2010; Ahmad et al., 2016). Thus, the series can be interpreted in terms of growth after taking the first difference.

Furthermore, in order to explore the causal links between the variables, we develop the specified multiple regression equation. Meanwhile According to Granger's representation theorem, if the series are co-integrated with the employment rate as dependent variable, the dynamic relationship involving the variables could be examined within the framework of VECM as follows:

$$\Delta \ln\_TCEMPLOI_t = a_0 + \sum_{i=1}^{q} a_{1i} \Delta \ln\_tcemploi_{t-i} + \sum_{j=0}^{q} a_{2j} \Delta \ln\_brevet_{t-j}$$
$$+ \sum_{j=0}^{q} a_{3j} \Delta DEPRD_{t-j} + \sum_{j=0}^{q} a_{4j} \Delta LABOUSH_{t-j} + \theta ECT_{t-1} + e_t$$

$$(1)$$

With: Δ first difference operator;

a_0: Constant;

a_1...a_5: Short-term effects;

(e_(t)): Residual term which is assumed to be identical, independent and normally distributed.

Where " θ" is the error correction term, adjustment coefficient or restoring force. Based on this relationship, after estimation, the existence of a cointegrating relationship implies obtaining aθ^ negative and statistically significant (different from zero).

3.2 Results

3.2.1 Optimal Lag Choice and Results of the Johansen Cointegration Test

The results of the unit root test for all data sets in Appendix 1 confirm that we can use the Johansen cointegration test procedure to examine the cointegrating relationship between the variables. However, we first need to determine the optimal lag length for our equation models using the vector autoregression (VAR) specification.

Table 1 presents the results of the selection of the optimal lag length. It can be seen that the final prediction error (FPE) criterion and AIC suggest an optimal length of two lags.

Table 1. Selection of the optimal lag length

Endogenous variables: TC_EMPLOI LN_BREVETS LABOURSH DEPENSESRD
Exogenous variables: C
Sample: 1990 2016
Included observations: 25

Lag	LogL	LR	FPE	AIC	SC	HQ
0	150.3042	NA	9.71e-11	−11.70434	−11.50932	−11.65025
1	199.2107	78.25046	7.13e-12	−14.33686	−13.36176*	−14.06641*
2	217.5464	23.46968	**6.63e-12***	**−14.52371***	−12.76853	−14.03690

* indicates lag order selected by the criterion
LR: sequential modified LR test statistic (each test at 5% level)
FPE: Final prediction error
AIC: Akaike information criterion
SC: Schwarz information criterion
HQ: Hannan-Quinn information criterio

Based on these results, we selected two lags as the optimal lag length in our equation model and then applied the cointegration test to check whether the variables are cointegrated. We expected that there would be at least one cointegrating relationship among the variables in the model.

The key to the cointegration test lies in the choice of the appropriate form of the cointegration test and the order of lags. The Johansen cointegration test (Appendix 2) shows the Maximum Eigenvalue and Trace tests. The results, below the 5% significance level, accept at most a single cointegrating relationship. Assuming the existence of a cointegrating relationship, the VECM modelling can be continued.

Refer to appendix 2, we can see that the test performed suggests a cointegration equation (CE) in the specification of the vector error correction (VEC) at the 5% significance level. We therefore decide to apply the causality test to explore the causal relationships between the variables. As the optimal lag order of the VAR is 2, the lag order of the VECM should be 1 (due to first differentiation).

3.2.2 Granger Causality Test

First, long-term causality was checked by examining the coefficients of long-term equation. The Granger causality result based on the VECM shows that spending on research and development positively causes employment growth but not significantly. While patents positively and significantly cause employment growth in Morocco. See Table 2.

Table 2. Granger causality test result

VEC Granger Causality/Block Exogeneity Wald Tests
Sample: 1990 2016
Included comments: 25
Dependent variable: D(TC_EMPLOYMENT)

Excluded	Chi- sq	df	Prob
D(LN_PATENTS)	4.739876**	1	0.0295
D(LABORSH)	0.493651	1	0.4823
D(EXPENDITURERD)	19.29513***	1	0.0000
All	19.90533	3	0.0002

Source: Author (our estimates under EViews 10)
() Probabilities or p-value; *** significant at 1%; ** significant at 5%;* significant at 10%;

3.3 Variance Decomposition

The variance decomposition of employment forecast error reinforces our analysis. The variance decomposition refers to the decomposition of the mean squared error into the contributions of each variable.

Model's result variance decomposition show that an employment shock is mainly explained by research and development expenditure and patents. See Table 3.

According to this decomposition, we find that in short term 12% and 4% of employment variance forecast error are attributed respectively to patents and R&D expenditure. In the medium and long term, it turns out that the employment variation rate becomes more explained by R&D expenditure (46%), and less explained by patents (just 10.49%).

Variance decomposition results are in line with our expectations. Technological innovations clearly explain employment. Thus, there is a strong relationship between innovation and employment in Morocco.

Table 3. Variance decomposition of employment growth forecast errors

Period	SE	EMPLOYMENT	PATENTS	LABOURSH	EXPENSERD
1	0.019009	100.0000	0.000000	0.000000	0.000000
2	0.021058	83.16136	12.20071	0.043113	4.594814
3	0.028271	50.05133	8.582232	8.980434	32.38601
4	0.030189	44.18206	8.753697	9.007072	38.05717
5	0.031017	42.48500	10.85053	9.053592	37.61088
6	0.031994	39.94066	10.68772	9.940828	39.43079
7	0.033359	36.76489	10.22303	10.69475	42.31733
8	0.034450	34.50457	10.30620	11.09258	44.09665
9	0.035371	32.75636	10.51300	11.46559	45.26506
10	0.036346	31.02391	10.49210	11.89290	46.59110

3.4 Impulse Analysis

The impulse response functions have been presented in (Fig. 1) They indicate responses following a shock over a period of ten (10) years. (Fig. 1) provides line graphs of the impulse responses between employment growth and the determinants of technological innovation (patents and R&D expenditure. In our analysis, we distinguish between short-term and log-term shocks.

The impacts of patents on employment in Morocco

– **Short-term effects**

We find that in short term employment growth response to a patent shock is negative, and considerably significant. This result is fully consistent with previous empirical studies. From Fig. 1 below, it seems that in short term, any increase in patents will imply a significant decrease in employment. Product innovations contribute to destruction of many jobs at short term. It then turns out that technological progress is responsible for significant job destruction. Indeed, technological innovation will tend to replace man in several functions.

– **Long term effects**

Moreover, over the long term, the patent shock would become less significant and employment growth would be relatively stabilized. Indeed, in the medium and long term, the jobs destroyed will be compensated by new jobs.

It is more common for jobs destroyed in innovative sector (user sector of innovations process) to be replaced by jobs created in other sectors (sectors where innovations are produced). There will be "compensation" from one sector to another (Say, 1767–1832), we then see a compensation via "new machines".

Jobs compensation is also due to compensation mechanism via "decrease prices". Indeed, the decreasing prices stimulate a new demand addressed to innovating company or to other companies and therefore an increase in production and new jobs are created.

New products create new demand, which leads companies to produce more and therefore to hire. Historical facts can confirm this theoretical result. The results obtained are in accordance with the theory.

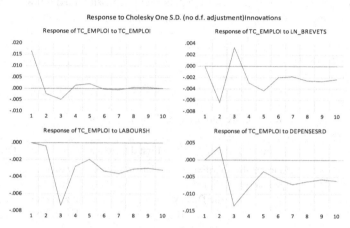

Fig. 1. Response of the dependent variable EMPLOI to the shocks produced over 10 years.

4 Conclusion

This research contributes to fill the gap in scarcity of research on quantitative effects of technological innovation on employment in Morocco. The paper contributes to the literature by exploring for the first time in Morocco the impact of technological innovation on employment using as variables patents growth, research and development expenditure, employment growth and compensation labour.

The aims of this paper is to analyze the short and long term quantitative effects of technological innovation on employment in Morocco. We deployed the vector error correction model (VECM) and found results consistent with compensation theory. Indeed, in the short term we have observed that technological progress causes job destruction due to the substitution of machines for men. In the long term, this effect is offset by job creation thanks to compensation mechanisms via new machines, via lower prices and via new products. We can conclude that employment growth in Morocco have strong relationship with innovation.

This study can help policymakers design policies and programs that support workers who have been displaced by technological innovation or are experiencing unemployment. This may include providing financial support, access to training programs, and other resources that help workers transition to new jobs or start their own businesses.

In conclusion, the main limit of this study is the problem of the databases which prevented us from introducing other variables into the model and from processing employment by sector of activity in order to better refine the analysis. Other limitations are also related to the period of the study, which ended in 2016. We hope to have better results with more data available. The forthcoming paper will deal with the qualitative effects of technological innovation on employment (Tables 4 and 5).

Appendix 1

Table 4. Result of the ADF stationarity test

Variables	Level		First difference		Order integration
	Statistical (probably)	Critical values of the Dickey Fuller test at the 5% threshold*	Statistics (prob)	Critical values of the Dickey Fuller test at the 5% threshold	
TC_EMPLOYMENT	−1.266783 (0.1831)	−1.95	−8.073584*** (0.00)	−1.95	I (1)
Ln_PATENTS	2.358464 (0.9940)	−1.95	−3.959745*** (0.0003)	−1.95	I (1)
ploughSH	−0.284461 (0.5736)	−1.95	−5.563363*** (0.00)	−1.95	I (1)
ExpensesRD	0.316466 (0.7695)	−1.95	−5.420427** (0.000)	−1.95	I (1)

Source: author (our estimates under EViews 10)
(.): Probabilities; *** stationary at 1%; ** stationary at 5%; * stationary at 10%

Appendix 2

Table 5. Result of the cointegration test

Sample (adjusted): 1992 2016
Included comments: 25 after adjustments
Trend assumption: Linear deterministic trend
Series: TC_EMPLOI LN_BREVETS LABOURSH DEPENSESRD
Lag interval (in first differences): 1 to 1
Unrestricted Cointegration Rank Test (Trace)

Hypothesized		Trace	0.05	
No. of CE(s)	Eigenvalue	Statistics	Critical Value	Prob.**
None *	0.778282	65.71790	47.85613	0.0005
At most 1	0.511775	28.05915	29.79707	0.0783
At most 2	0.319369	10.13469	15.49471	0.2705
At most 3	0.020441	0.516312	3.841465	0.4724

Trace test indicates 1 cointegrating eqn (s) at the 0.05 level
* denotes rejection of the hypothesis at the 0.05 level
** MacKinnon -Haug- Michelis (1999) p-values

Unrestricted Cointegration Rank Test (Maximum Eigenvalue)

Hypothesized		Max Eigen	0.05	
No. of CE(s)	Eigenvalue	Statistics	Critical Value	Prob.**
None *	0.778282	37.65875	27.58434	0.0018
At most 1	0.511775	17.92446	21.13162	0.1327
At most 2	0.319369	9.618381	14.26460	0.2382
At most 3	0.020441	0.516312	3.841465	0.4724

Max-eigenvalue test indicates 1 cointegrating eqn (s) at the 0.05 level

References

Aristotle, Politics, Commercial Press (1965)

Keynes, J.M.: Essays in Persuasion. Macmillan, London (1931)

Graetz, G., Michaels, G.: Robots at Work. CEP Discussion Paper No. 1335 (2015)

Brynjolfsson, E., McAfee, A.: Race Against The Machine. Digital Frontier Press, Lexington, MA (2011)

Autor, D.H., Levy, F., Murnane, R.J.: The skill content of recent technological change: an empirical exploration. Quart. J. Econ. **118**(4), 1279–1333 (2003)

Acemoglu , D., Autor, D.: Skills, tasks and technologies: implications for employment and earnings. In: Card, David and Orley Ashenfelter eds. Handbook of Labor Economics Vol. 4: Elsevier, Chap. 12, pp. 1043–1171 (2011)

Freeman, C., Soete, L.: Work for All or Mass Unemployment? Computerized Technical Change into the 21st Century. Pinterest Publisher, London and New York (1994)

Ricardo: Principles of Political Economy, volume 1, p.392

Keynes: General Theory of Employment, Interest and Money (1936)

In his Theory of Economic Evolution (published in 1912), Schumpeter speaks of "productive revolutions", p. 313

Aghion, P., Howitt, P.: A model of growth through creative destruction. Econometrica **60**(2), 323–51 (1992). JSTOR, https://doi.org/10.2307/2951599. Accessed 10 Jan 2023

Sauvy, A.: The machine and unemployment: technical progress and employment, Dunod , Collection l' Oeil Economique (1980)

Marshall, A.: The Principles of Economics. MacMillan, NY (1961)

Douglas, P.: Technological unemployment. American Federationist **37**(8), pp. 923-50 (1930)

Pasinetti, L.: Structural Change and Economic Growth. Cambridge University Press, Cambridge (1981)

Chen, Y., Puttitanun, T.: Intellectual property rights and innovation in developing countries. J. Dev. Econ. **78**, 474–493 (2005)

Furman, J.L., Porter, M.E., Stern, S.: The determinants of national innovative capacity. Res. Policy **31**, 899–933 (2002)

Mancusi, M.: International Spillovers and Absorvitive Capacity: A Cross-Country Cross-Sector Analysis Based on European Patents and Citations. University Bocconi, Institute of Economics Politica (2004)

Saafi, S., Sboui, F.: Consequences of the diffusion of technological innovations on industrial employment in Tunisia: an analysis on panel data. Econ. Rev. Ind. **137**(1), 85108 (2012)

Berman, E., Machin, S.: Skill-biased Technology Transfer, Evidence of Factor Biased Technological Change in Developing Countries. Working paper (2000)

Simonetti, R., Taylor, K., Vivarelli, M.: Modelling the employment impact innovation. In: The Employment Impact of Innovation: Evidence and Policy, pp. 26–43, Routledge, London (2000)

Feenstra, R.C., Inklaar, R., Timmer, M.P.: The next generation of the penn world table. American Econ. Rev. **105**(10), 3150–3182 (2015). www.ggdc.net/pwt

Pianta, M., Vivarelli, M. : The Employment Impact of Innovation: Evidence and Policy. Routledge (2003)

Piva, M., Vivarelli, M.: Innovation and employment: evidence from italian microdata. J. Econ. - Zeitschrift Für Nationalökonomie **86**(1), 65–83 (2005)

Mnif, S., Feki, C., Abdelkafi, I.: Effects of Technological Shock on Employment: Application of Structural Approach VECM. Journal of the Knowledge Economy (2016)

Calvino, F., Virgillito, M.E.: The innovation-employment nexus: a critical survey of theory and empirics. J. Econ. Surveys, **32**(1), 83–117 (2018)

Buerger, M., Broekel, T., Coad, A.: Regional dynamics of innovation: investigating the co-evolution of patents, research and development (R&D), and employment. Reg. Stud. **46**(5), 565–582 (2012)

Vivarelli, M.: Innovation, employment and skills in advanced and developing countries: a survey of economic literature. J. Econ. Issues **48**(1), 123–154 (2014)

Abramova, N., Grishchenko, N.: ICTs, labour productivity and employment: sustainability in industries in Russia. Procedia Manufact. **43**, 299–305 (2020)

Petit, P.: Employment and Technical Change. CEPREMAP (1993)

Bogliacino, F., Pianta, M.: Innovation and employment: a reinvestigation using revised Pavitt classes. Res. Policy **39**(6), 799–809 (2010)

Askenazy, P.: L'emploi face au changement technologique. Idées économiques et sociales, 2016/3 (N° 185), pp. 45–51. https://doi.org/10.3917/idee.185.0045

Piva, M., Vivarelli, M.: Technological Change and Employment: Were Ricardo and Marx Right? (2017)

Bogliacino, F., Vivarelli, M. : The job creation effect of R&D expenditures. Australian Economic Papers **51**(2), 96–113 (2012)

Coad, A., Rao, R.: The firm-level employment effects of innovations in high-tech US manufacturing industries. J. Evol. Econ. **21**(2), 255–283 (2011)

Ahmad, A., et al.: Carbon emissions, energy consumption and economic growth: an aggregate and disaggregate analysis of the Indian economy. Energy Policy **96**, 131–143 (2016)

Chang, C.C.: A multivariate causality test of carbon-dioxide emissions, energy consumption and economic growth in China. Appl. Energy **87**(11), 3533–3537 (2010)

Dickey, D.A., Fuller, W.A.: Distribution of the estimtors for autoregressive time series with a unit root. J. American Statistical Assoc. **74**(366), 427–431 (1979)

Engle, R.F., Granger, C.W.J.: Cointegration and error correction representation: estimation and testing. Econometrica **55**(2), 251–276 (1987)

Engle, R., Granger, C.: Long-Run Economic Relationships: Readings in Cointegration. Oxford University Press (1991)

Johansen, S.: Statistical analysis of cointegrating vectors. J. Econ. Dynamic Control **12**, 231–254 (1988)

Johansen, S.: Estimation and hypothesis testing of cointegration vectors in gaussian vector autoregressive models. Econometrica **59**, 1551–1580 (1991)

Narayan, P.K.: The saving and investment nexus for China: evidence from cointegration tests. Appl. Econ. **37**(17), 1979–1990 (2005)

Koch, M., Manuylov, I., Smolka, M.: Robots and firms. In: CESifo Working Paper No. 7608 (2019)

Su, C.W., Yuan, X., Umar, M., Lobonţ, O.R.: Does technological innovation bring destruction or creation to the labor market? Technol. Soc. **68**, 101905 (2022)

Faber, M.: Robots and Reshoring: Evidence from Mexican Local Labor Markets (2018)

Artuc, E., Christiaensen, L., Winkler, H.J.: Does Automation in Rich Countries Hurt Developing Ones? Evidence from the US and Mexico. The World Bank (2019)

Smith A.: "La richesse des nations", tome I, Flammarion, première édition 1771 (1991)

Bessen, J.E., Automation and Jobs: When Technology Boosts Employment. Boston Univ. School of Law, Law and Economics Research Paper No. 17–09 (2019)

Seamless Payment Through Artificial Intelligence in Food Retail: Factors Influencing Purchase Intent

Stephanie Jordan[(✉)] [ID], Maike Netscher[ID], Julia Leinweber[ID], Ceyda Kaplan[ID], and Alexander Kracklauer[ID]

Neu-Ulm University of Applied Sciences, Wileystrasse 1, 89231 Neu-Ulm, Germany
{stephanie.jordan,maike.netscher,Alexander.Kracklauer}@hnu.de

Abstract. This paper examines the impact of seamless payment considering the interventions of financial anxiety and convenience. The findings of the study are compared with the findings of Ghazwani et al. (2022) to examine the impact of cultural differences on the acceptance of cashierless shopping or seamless payment. The study used a convenience sample of 302 participants and applied a moderated mediation approach to the analysis. The results show that retailers must not only focus on technical innovations, but also consider cultural requirements. The Hofstede dimensions show a significant difference between German and Saudi Arabian cultures, highlighting the significant impact of culture on buying behavior. In addition, customers who perceive seamless payment as convenient have less financial anxiety, while purchase intention increases.

Keywords: Artificial Intelligence · Seamless Payment · Self-Checkout · Hofstede dimensions

1 Introduction

The COVID-19 pandemic has significantly accelerated the process of digitization and automation globally, with organizations implementing measures to minimize physical contact in an effort to curb the spread of the virus [3, 14]. The retail industry, particularly the food retail sector, has also undergone significant changes by increasing the use of self-checkout systems and card machines to minimize customer-cashier interactions involvement [24]. A more advanced system, known as seamless payment, further reduces human contact by incorporating artificial intelligence (AI) and cameras within stores, allowing customers to complete their purchases through mobile applications.

This study is a replication of "Artificial intelligence, financial anxiety and cashierless checkouts: a Saudi Arabian perspective" [16] and aims to investigate the potential for implementing this type of system in Germany, and specifically examines the role of cultural differences in shaping customer acceptance. The selection of Ghazwani et al. [16] as a reference model for this research is supported by multiple factors. Firstly, the study's emphasis on the factors that influence the adoption of cashierless shopping in retail stores aligns with the focus of this research on seamless payment. Secondly, the research design employed by Ghazwani et al. [16], which incorporated a large-scale survey of retail customers and structural equation model analysis, offers a validated framework for exploring the factors that affect the adoption of mobile payment systems.

Moreover, replicating and extending Ghazwani et al.'s [16] study can provide important practical and theoretical insights. Replication can allow for the testing of the generalizability of the study's findings, while extension can reveal how these factors interact with and influence each other in different contexts and among different populations. Additionally, it may be possible to identify new factors that have an impact on the adoption of mobile payment systems in retail. The Hofstede dimensions are used to compare and contrast the cultural differences between Germany and Saudi Arabia, with a focus on the dimensions of individualism and uncertainty avoidance. These dimensions are seen as having a significant impact on the use of seamless payment, with individualistic cultures placing a greater emphasis on transparency and communication from companies, and collectivistic cultures being more reliant on external factors such as the opinions of trusted individuals.

The remainder of the paper is structured as follows. In the second section, the theoretical background of AI and especially Self-Checkout Systems (SCSs) are outlined. The study utilizes a moderated mediation approach, which is explained in detail in the methodology section, to analyze the influence of convenience, financial anxiety, and cultural differences on purchase intentions. The study's results and conclusion in Sects. 4 and 5 offer insights into the challenges and opportunities associated with the implementation of seamless payment in Germany. The paper concludes with a discussion of the study's limitations and possible future extensions.

2   Theoretical Background

2.1   Artificial Intelligence

The advancement of AI is rapidly shaping various aspects of work and daily life. One crucial consideration is AI's potential to surpass human intelligence [21]. Artificial intelligence plays a critical role in the ongoing trend of digitization and digital transformation, which aims to harness the capabilities of digital technology. This trend can be seen as a continuation of the automation process, in which human tasks are increasingly performed by machines. The automation of work has been a significant cultural force since the industrial revolution, leading to the emergence of new occupations and the disappearance of traditional ones, requiring individuals and societies to adapt to the changing technological landscape [17]. For instance, the retail industry has been significantly impacted by the development of self-service technologies, which have altered both purchasing habits and the shopping experience [18].

2.2   Self-Checkout Systems (SCSs)

Self-Checkout Systems (SCSs) are technological interfaces that enable customers to complete a purchase independently of direct service employee involvement [24]. This technical change can lead to faster completion of the purchase process [4]. Efficiency, which is one of the three main factors determining service quality, plays a key role in assessing different forms of payment. Currently, there are two types of SCSs: fixed and automatic [4, 15]. Fixed SCSs are pre-installed cash desks where customers can independently scan their selected products, make payments via card or cash, and pack their purchases. Customers are then required to present their receipt to a scanner to exit the store [4, 25]. This process can occur without the assistance of a worker, but there is usually at least one person present to provide supervision, maintenance, and assistance to customers [25]. The duration of the purchase process for fixed SCSs depends on the number of products, but overall, customers can save time because they do not need to wait in a queue.

The concept of Just Walk Out technology refers to automatic self-checkout systems, which were first popularized by the cashierless retail store Amazon Go [28]. Artificial intelligence and cameras are strategically placed throughout the store, and customers are required to install an app and provide personal information such as bank details prior to shopping. The cameras and sensors track the products that customers pick up and add them to their virtual shopping cart, which is then displayed on their mobile device through the app. Once the customer has finished shopping, they can simply leave the store without any further action as the AI technology automatically deducts the products from their virtual shopping cart and charges their bank account [28, 29]. This seamless payment method offers the most efficient purchasing process for customers. This paper focuses on the concept of seamless payment because permanently installed self-checkout systems are now widespread in Germany, but the introduction of automated checkouts is only just emerging. Furthermore, Klaus and Tynan [22] for example, see seamless payment as one of the megatrends for retail.

Seamless payment systems in supermarkets aim to improve the customer experience by eliminating the need for cashier checkouts, reducing the need for packing and unpacking goods, and saving time. Additionally, these systems can provide cost savings for supermarket operators by reducing the need for cashier staff and associated personnel expenses. According to Ahrens [2], the average annual personnel costs per person employed in the food retail industry in Germany were approximately EUR 26,000 in 2020. Adopting seamless payment systems can also mitigate staffing shortages. However, using technology that reduces or eliminates the need for human interaction, such as that employed in seamless payment systems, can raise significant concerns related to privacy and data protection. Data collection and processing through camera surveillance must be secured by a corresponding legal basis and clearly defined according to the German General Data Protection Regulation (GDPR). Additionally, consumers may be dismissive of seamless payment's usability when encountering it for the first time. The perceived usability of the technology can also be an important factor in determining its adoption, and an individual's affinity for new technology and convenience orientation can play a critical role in the adoption of advanced analytics and other technological innovations.

2.3 Hofstede Dimensions: Germany versus Saudi Arabia

To ensure comparability between the results of this study and the original paper, the Hofstede dimensions are used as a framework to compare and contrast the cultural differences between Germany and Saudi Arabia. In Hofstede's dimensions, values are usually measured on a scale of 0 to 100, with higher values indicating a stronger presence of a particular cultural trait. Each dimension is independent of the others and scores are not comparable between dimensions.

Only the factors of the Hofstede dimensions that exhibit significant cultural differences between the two countries are discussed in the following sections. As such, the dimensions of Uncertainty Avoidance and Indulgence were not considered in this analysis.

The disparities observed in the results between our study and the original paper can be attributed to the dimensions of "Masculinity" and "Long-Term Orientation" according to Hofstede's cultural dimensions. Saudi Arabia is a collectivist society that focuses on the group rather than the individual. This culture is based on Islamic culture and its values of collectivism and group harmony, where individual ambition and success may not be as prominent. In addition, the role of women in Saudi Arabia is different than in Germany, with a stronger patriarchal structure, which could also play a role in the lower rating of the masculinity dimension. As previously mentioned, German society places a high value on performance and expects it at an early age. The priority is not on comfort, but on achieving high performance. Saving and investing are considered the norm, and money is only spent when necessary. Conversely, in Saudi Arabian culture, quality of life and comfort are markers of success, leading to a tendency toward spending money and less emphasis on saving for the future [19].

3 Hypotheses and Research Framework

Berry's [7] model of service convenience is one of the first frameworks to capture the significance of convenience in service experiences. The model argues that time and effort are linked to five types of convenience: Decision, Access, Transaction, Benefit, and Post-Benefit, which are the activities customers experience when buying or using a service. Time and effort are non-monetary costs that customers must ensure to obtain the service [1, 7]. These non-monetary costs can be perceived as the benefits of convenience (saving time and/or effort) or the burdens of inconvenience (wasting time and/or effort) [27]. Customer satisfaction is also strongly related to waiting time [10], and environmental factors such as parking, opening hours, and location [6]. The different weighting of these factors can increase or decrease customers' non-monetary costs. Because this paper replicates the study by Ghazwani et al. [16], the hypotheses in the first steps are strongly aligned with the original to check the extent to which the model and the hypotheses can be transferred to German retail.

H1: For consumers who perceive seamless payment as convenient, seamless payment (versus conventional) checkouts lead to higher purchase intent.

For those who do not consider seamless payment to be as convenient, however, the positive effect of such a checkout type is reduced.

Table 1. Cultural differences

Power Distance	Germany: 35	Saudi Arabia: 72
	Employee participation rights are extensive and must be taken into consideration by management. Direct communication is the norm and control is rejected	A hierarchical order is accepted by people – everyone has their place. Subordinates wait to be told what to do. An autocrat is the ideal leader
Individualism	Germany: 67	Saudi Arabia: 48
	Individualistic society. In small families, the relationship between parents and children is important. Communication is very direct. "Being honest, even if it hurts" – giving a fair chance to the other person to learn from their mistakes	Slightly collectivistic society. Long-term commitment to a group (family, extended family, etc.). Loyalty is of utmost importance. Taking responsibility for members of one's group. The relationship between employer and employee resembles a familial relationship
Masculinity	Germany: 66	Saudi Arabia: 43
	Masculine society. Performance is highly valued and expected early on. People live "to work." High self-esteem through tasks. Status symbols are proudly displayed: watches, cars, etc	Feminine society. Caring for others is important. Quality of life is the measure of success. It is not admirable to stand out from the crowd. Motivated by liking what one does
Long-Term Orientation	Germany: 83	Saudi Arabia: 27
	Pragmatic country. Truth depends on the situation, context, and time. Traditions are adapted to changed circumstances. Investing and saving are important. Persistence is important in achieving results	Important to find absolute truth. Normative in thinking. Great respect for tradition. Saving for the future is not as important. Focus on quick results

As new technologies revolutionize the retail industry, companies can improve operations and offer customers more functional benefits. However, customers must be willing and able to use these new technologies [24]. Financial anxiety is defined as the anxiety customers feel when interacting with financial transactions, including different types of checkouts. To use seamless payment, customers must register in advance and provide personal financial information. Companies that use seamless payment collect sensitive data, such as facial recognition and other customer information [11, 28, 29].

Hofstede's dimensions show that there are cultural differences between Germany and Saudi Arabia, but a commonality is discomfort with the unfamiliar [9, 19]. In Saudi Arabia, society is unwilling to accept change and is highly risk-averse, while in Germany, there is strong support for protecting privacy and strict laws that protect consumer data

[26]. Attitudes toward data privacy vary depending on personal knowledge of internet technologies and views on privacy in general. Despite concerns about data privacy, advanced technologies such as seamless payment offer many benefits that can lead to a more convenient shopping experience, potentially outweighing the fear of the unknown and financial anxiety. This forms the next hypothesis.

H2: For high-convenience consumers, seamless payment can lead to greater finan-cial anxiety, which enacts higher purchase intent. In contrast, the mediating effect of financial anxiety will be diminished for low-convenience consumers.

According to Hofstede's dimensions, cultural differences may prevent the hypotheses from being directly transferred to Germany. Saudi Arabia is considered a collectivist culture where individuals prefer to be in groups and value communication. This may lead to a greater emphasis on service from cashiers when shopping. The emphasis on communication while shopping has implications for customer convenience. In contrast, Germany is considered an individualized and performance-oriented culture where people prefer efficiency and practicality, which may lead to a greater emphasis on performance during the shopping experience. Long-term orientation has a differential impact on customers' financial anxiety, as investment and frugality are culturally different (Table 1). The different emphasis of cultures on convenience and financial anxiety will affect the model of moderate mediation.

4   Research Design

4.1   Data Collection and Questionnaire Rationale

In this study, a quantitative research approach was applied using an online survey developed with Lighthouse (Sawtooth). The survey was conducted from November 14–28, 2022 in Germany, as a convenience sample and distributed via WhatsApp, email, and social media to participants aged 18 and older, with a focus on the target group aged 18 to 35. The survey sampling method used in this study involved recruiting participants through the authors' social media platforms. Specifically, the authors distributed the survey through their personal social media accounts, which may have influenced the age distribution of the participants. The sample population included individuals aged between 18 to 35 years, with 18–25-year-olds comprising the initial cohort of participants followed by 73 respondents aged between 26 to 35 years. This age distribution may be partially explained by the authors' social media following, which may have a higher proportion of younger individuals within the 18 to 25-year-old age range. It is important to note that this sampling approach has potential limitations and may not be representative of the wider population. Nonetheless, the findings of this study provide valuable insights into the attitudes and behaviors of the surveyed age groups. Consumers in this age group are the main users of mobile payment apps such as payback in the German market according to Dommick et al. [13]. The survey was anonymous and the sample size was 630 respondents, of which 302 completed the questionnaire in full.

The questionnaire was divided into five sections: 1. Including attribution to seamless payment or traditional payment; 2. Convenience rating; 3. Financial anxiety; 4. Purchase intention; and 5. Demographic data. In the first section, participants were shown a video depicting either the seamless payment or conventional payment process. The videos were filmed in the showroom of the company Wanzl GmbH & Co. KGaA to ensure accuracy and avoid potential misunderstandings. No merchant brand names are shown on the videos, only the application of the payment process. The questions from the paper were translated into German to reflect the way the study was conducted in the German market. The study aimed to determine the correlations between the variables and the payment processes and to draw a holistic picture of the German market.

4.2 Moderated Mediation Design

In this study, a moderated mediation approach was employed to examine the impact of seamless payment on purchase intention, considering the effects of financial anxiety and convenience in the German food retail (Model 7, 10,000 bootstrap samples, Hayes, 2017). The independent variables were identified as forms of conventional payment and seamless payment, the dependent variable was defined as purchase intention, the moderator variable was identified as convenience, and the mediator variable was identified as financial anxiety. The moderated mediation design allows for an examination of the direct causal effect of the predictor on the criterion [5], which is mediated by the mediator, and further moderated by the strength or intensity of the moderator [23]. The hypotheses and paths are illustrated in Fig. 1.

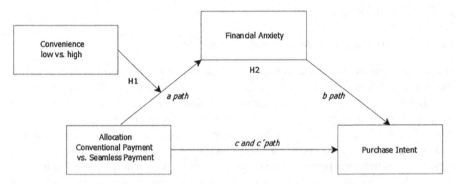

Fig. 1. Own representation of the concept of moderated mediation and hypotheses

5 Findings

5.1 Demographic Data

The sample of the study consisted of 302 participants, with 143 assigned to the conventional payment group and 159 assigned to the seamless payment group. The sample was largely composed of young adults, with the majority (n = 139) falling within the age range of 18–25 years followed by 73 participants in the age range of 26–35 years. This may be attributed to the distribution of the survey primarily through the authors' social media, which likely reflects the age distribution of their followers. The participants in the survey were well-educated, with 38.7% holding academic degrees and another 43.4% having college or university admission (Table 2).

Table 2. Demographic data

		Frequency	Percent
Allocation	Conventional Payment	143	47.4
	Seamless Payment	159	52.6
Gender	Male	119	39.4
	Female	180	59.6
	Divers	3	1.0
Age	18–25	139	46,0
	26–35	73	24,2
	36–45	27	8,9
	46–59	30	9,9
	Over 60	33	10,6
Qualification	Lower secondary school	4	1,3
	Secondary school	50	16,6
	A-levels	131	43,4
	Diploma	13	4,3
	Bachelor's	57	18,9
	Master's	34	11,3
	Doctor	13	4,3

5.2 Cronbach's Alpha

To determine the internal consistency of the questionnaire, Cronbach's alpha was calculated for convenience (7 items), financial anxiety (5 items), and purchase intent (4 items) (Table 3).

Evaluated by the modified interpretation according to Blanz [8], the internal consistency of the questionnaire is interpreted as falling between acceptable and excellent.

5.3 Moderated Mediation Analysis

To ensure the validity of the moderated mediation analysis, the linearity of the variables was tested beforehand. After visual inspection of the scatter plot with LOESS smoothing, it was determined that the relationship between the variables was approximately

Table 3. Cronbach's alpha of internal consistency

Variable	Cronbach's Alpha	Number of Items
Convenience	0,793	7
Financial Anxiety	0,780	5
Purchase Intent	0,916	4

linear. Additionally, by visualizing the Q-Q plots of all variables, it was determined that the values were normally distributed. Therefore, the necessary precondition for the moderated mediation design was met.

The evaluation using SPSS (Table 4) did not reveal any significant moderated mediation, as the index of moderated mediation was not significantly different from 0 and the bootstrapping confidence interval intersected 0 (MMI = 0.032, SE = 0.056, CI 95% = -0.076, 0.147).

Table 4. Results of the moderated mediation design (seamless payment) with SPSS

Outcome Variable	Path		Effect	SE	p-value	CI 95%
Financial Anxiety	A path		−0,083	0,149	0,576	−0,376−0,210
	Interaction effect					
		Low convenience	0,182	0,199	0,361	−0,209−0,573
		High convenience	0,012	0,197	0,952	−0,376−0,399
Purchase Intent	Direct effect (c path)		0,070	0,144	0,630	−0,214−0,354
	Direct effect (b path)		-0,386	0,060	0,000	−0,505−0,267
	Indirect effect (Moderator)					
		Low convenience	−0,070	0,076		−0,232−0,070
		High convenience	−0,005	0,076		−0,156−0,148
Moderated mediation model			Index		SE	Ci
			0,032		0,056	−0,076−0,147

To more thoroughly assess the individual characteristics of the model, an examination was conducted to determine whether there was a moderation effect due to the variable convenience and a mediation effect due to the variable financial anxiety.

A moderation analysis (Model 1, 10,000 bootstrapping samples, Hayes, 2017) was conducted to investigate the extent to which the interaction between the convenience variable and the seamless payment variable significantly predicted the purchase intent variable. The model was found to be significant ($F (3, 298) = 36.876$, $p < 0.001$) with a variance resolution of 31.5%.

However, the results of the moderation analysis suggest that convenience does not significantly moderate the effect of seamless payment on purchase intent ($\Delta R^2 = 2\%$, $F (1, 298) = 0.468$, $p = 0.494$, CI 95% -0.192, 0.416). The interaction term explains only an additional 2% of the variance. Therefore, it is concluded that no moderation effect is present.

A mediation analysis (Model 4, 10,000 bootstrapping samples, Hayes, 2017) was conducted to investigate the extent to which the allocation to seamless payment predicts purchase intent, and whether the direct path is mediated by financial anxiety. No total effect of seamless payment on purchase intent (c path) was found ($\beta = 0.123$, $p = 0.424$). After including the mediator in the model, the allocation to seamless payment did not significantly predict the mediator (a path) ($\beta = -0.138$, $p = 0.330$). However, the mediator significantly predicted purchase intent (b path) ($\beta = -0.386$, $p < 0.001$). The relationship between seamless payment and purchase intent has no direct effect even after the inclusion of the mediator (c' path) and is not significant ($\beta = 0.070$, $p = 0.632$). It is therefore concluded that no mediation is present ($\beta = 0.053$, CI 95% -0.056, 0.161).

Based on these statistical results, hypotheses H1 and H2 are rejected. As pointed out in Sect. 4.2, the cultural variances between the German market and the context of Ghazwani et al.'s [16] study make it inappropriate to directly apply their model and findings.

5.4 Adapted Moderated Mediation Analysis

Consistent with the theoretical assumptions outlined in Sects. 2.3 and 4.2, the moderated mediation model has been adjusted to suit the German market. Specifically, the roles of the variables convenience and financial anxiety have been exchanged as mediator and moderator, respectively, in the moderated mediation design of the subsequent research. In the adapted model, convenience acts as the mediator, while financial anxiety serves as the moderator. The decision to exchange these variables is primarily driven by the cultural differences in orientation towards individualism and long-termism.

Hypotheses 1 and 2 are modified to the adapted moderated mediation design as follows.

H1a: Low Financial Anxiety leads to higher Convenience for customers with Seamless Payment.

H2a: High moderated Convenience leads to higher Purchase Intention among customers with Seamless Payment.

Figure 3 shows the adapted moderated mediation design and the adapted hypotheses (Fig. 2).

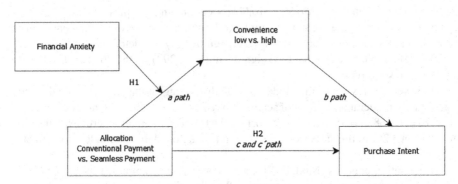

Fig. 2. Adjusted own representation of adapted moderated mediation and hypotheses

In the evaluation of the adapted model (Table 5), a moderated mediation could be established (MMI −0.169, SE 0.066, CI 95% −0.296, −0.039).

The a path has a high goodness of fit with R = 0.543 (corrected R^2 = 0.295) [12]. According to the Johnson–Neyman method, the a-path is significant up to a value of financial anxiety of 0.475 (β = 0.233, p = 0.05). This suggests that the strength of financial anxiety only has a significant effect on convenience when the value is low. That includes 65,563% of the values.

The effect of seamless payment and conventional payment on purchase intent for different levels of financial anxiety and convenience are illustrated in Fig. 3. The simple slopes for a specific value of financial anxiety and convenience are depicted in comparison to seamless payment and conventional payment. These slopes can be determined with the equations y = 7.170.51x for seamless payment and y = 6.090.28x for conventional payment.

Table 5. Results of the adapted moderated mediation design (Seamless Payment) with SPSS

Outcome Variable	Path		Effect	SE	p-value	CI 95%
Convenience	A path		−0,227	0,092	0,014	−0,408−0,046
	Interaction effect					
		Low financial anxiety	0,620	0,133	< 0,001	0,3590,882
		High financial anxiety	0,062	0,167	0,710	−0,2670,392
Purchase Intent	Direct effect (c path)		−0,170	0,132	0,198	−0,4300,089
	Direct effect (b path)		0,742	0,073	< 0,001	0,5990,885
	Indirect effect (Moderator)					
		Low financial anxiety	0,460	0,102		0,2660,663
		High financial anxiety	0,046	0,121		−0,1830,291
Moderated mediation model			Index		SE	Ci
			−0,169		0,066	−0,296−0,039

Stephanie Jordan, Maike Netscher, Julia Leinweber,
Ceyda Kaplan, Prof. Dr. Alexander Kracklauer

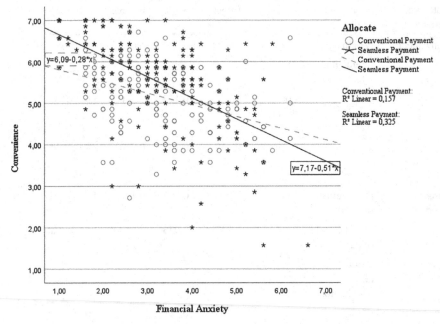

Fig. 3. Interaction effect of a path represented by simple slope

H1a is accepted. Convenience decreases with increasing financial anxiety. Conversely, convenience increases with decreasing financial anxiety (Fig. 3).

The b path can be interpreted as a simple regression and is significant ($p < 0.001$, CI 95% 2.000, 299.000). With an $R = 0.559$ (corrected $R^2 = 0.313$), the model has a high goodness of fit [12]. As a result, purchase intent increases mediated by higher convenience are moderated by low financial anxiety.

Using the bootstrapping intervals for the moderated a path (CI 95% −0.399, −0.053) and b path (CI 95% 0.599, 0.881), the results of the hypothesis test could be confirmed as significant.

In light of the non-significance of the direct effect of the predictor (seamless payment) on the criterion (c path: $\beta = -0.170$, $p = 0.198$, CI 95% −0.4300.089), it can be concluded that there is full moderated mediation. This suggests that seamless payment has a significant indirect effect (c' path) on purchase intent when financial anxiety is low ($\beta = 0.460$, CI 95% 0.2660.663), thereby increasing convenience. Therefore, hypothesis H2a is accepted.

Despite this, the moderated mediation index (MMI −0.169, SE 0.066, CI 95% −0.296, −0.039) is negative. This suggests that customers from the seamless payment group have an increased purchase intent due to lower financial anxiety and increased convenience, but in contrast to the conventional payment group (MMI 0.169, SE 0.066, CI 95% 0.041, 0.298), the purchase intent is lower.

6   Conclusion

The primary objective of this study was to identify the factors influencing the acceptance of seamless payment in the German market and to test whether the results and methods of Ghazwani et al. [16] can be transferred to the German market. While Ghazwani et al. [16] conducted their study in Saudi Arabia, this study was conducted in Germany, which could have contributed to differences in factors influencing the adoption of seamless payment systems. In addition, other contextual factors, such as differences in the retail environment or in the penetration of mobile payment systems, could have influenced the results.

In addition, cultural differences could also contribute to the observed differences. While our study did not empirically examine cultural differences, we highlighted the potential impact of cultural differences on the adoption of seamless payment systems and discussed the relevant Hofstede dimensions. The results of the study indicate that food retailers in Germany must not only integrate smart applications to remain competitive but also take into account cultural demands.

Hofstede dimensions reveal clear differences between Saudi Arabian and German cultures, particularly in long-term orientation and individualism. These differences are particularly evident in how convenience and financial concerns are weighed in relation to seamless payment.

In this study, it became clear that the model used by Ghazwani et al. [16] is not directly transferable to the German market. The adapted moderated mediation design shows a significant influence of convenience as a mediator and financial anxiety as a moderator on purchase intention in Germany. These results suggest that German food retailers should focus on offering low-threshold access to seamless payment stores and reducing financial anxiety through education and targeted customer outreach.

7   Limitations

Although this study provided important insights into the adoption of seamless payments, its generalizability has some limitations. The study relied on a limited number of participants. Due to the random sampling method used, the results cannot be generalized to the entire population, but they do reflect the reality of current app usage in German grocery stores. Future research could gain better insight into the acceptance of seamless payment in Germany based on a larger sample and a questionnaire specifically designed for the German market and could as well address the influence of cultural differences and other contextual factors and examining the factors that might explain differences in different cultural and contextual settings. Furthermore, from a research perspective, it is necessary to develop application-oriented recommendations for action that would facilitate an expansion of app use, which is necessary for the use of seamless payment.

One limitation pertains to the measurement of cultural dimensions as extensive questions were not included to measure these dimensions. In this research, the possible influence of cultural factors has been discussed. These factors were not empirically pretested in our study. This is a limitation of our study, as cultural differences may contribute to differences in the adoption of seamless payment systems in different countries. Although a diverse sample of participants was recruited, unaccounted cultural variations may exist. Future research may overcome these limitations by adopting more comprehensive measures of cultural dimensions and recruiting larger and more diverse samples. The Hofstede dimensions used in this paper to understand the interpretation of cultural differences are intended as an overview. It should be noted that cultures are complex and diverse and should not be generalized. Therefore, this integration should be understood as a starting point for further research in the area of seamless payment acceptance in cross-country and cross-cultural contexts. In addition, it is important to keep in mind that these dimensions are based on research conducted primarily in the 1970s and 1980s, and may not fully capture the complexity and diversity of modern cultures [20]. It should be noted that the study is not based on separate research examining the impact of technology use on purchase intention. Separating the studies of technology acceptance from those of the influence of financial anxiety and convenience can be the subject of further research.

References

1. Aagja, J.P., Mammen, T., Saraswat, A.: Validating service convenience scale and profiling customers: a study in the Indian retail context. Vikalpa **36**(4), 25–50 (2011). https://doi.org/10.1177/0256090920110403
2. Ahrens, S.: Personalkosten im Lebensmitteleinzelhandel in Europa nach Ländern 2020 (2022). Accessed 09 Jan 2023. https://de-statista-com.ezproxy.hnu.de/statistik/daten/studie/472118/umfrage/personalkosten-im-lebensmitteleinzelhandel-in-europa-nach-laendern/
3. Al-Turjman, F., Artificial Intelligence and Machine Learning for COVID-19. Vol. 924. Studies in Computational Intelligence. Springer International Publishing, Cham (2021). https://doi.org/10.1007/978-3-030-60188-1
4. Andriulo, S., Elia, V., Gnoni, M.G.: Mobile self-checkout systems in the FMCG retail sector: a comparison analysis. Int. J. RF Technol. **6**(4), 207–224 (2015). https://doi.org/10.3233/RFT-150067
5. Baltes-Götz, B.: Mediator- Und Moderatoranalyse Mit SPSS Und PROCESS. Universität Trier. (Rev. 201216) (2020)
6. Bell, S.J.: Image and consumer attraction to intraurban retail areas: an environmental psychology approach. J. Retail. Consum. Serv. **6**(2), 67–78 (1999). https://doi.org/10.1016/S0969-6989(98)00015-0
7. Berry, L.L., Seiders, K., Grewal, D.: Understanding service convenience. J. Mark. **66**(3), 1–17 (2002). https://doi.org/10.1509/jmkg.66.3.1.18505
8. Blanz, M.: Forschungsmethoden und Statistik für die Soziale Arbeit: Grundlagen und Anwendungen. 1st ed. Stuttgart: Kohlhammer Verlag (2015). https://ebookcentral.proquest.com/lib/kxp/detail.action?docID=2002189
9. Brosdahl, D.J., Almousa, M.: Risk Perception and Internet Shopping: Comparing United States and Saudi Arabian Consumers (n.d.)
10. Carmon, Z., Shanthikumar, J.G., Carmon, T.F.: A psychological perspective on service segmentation models: the significance of accounting for consumers' perceptions of waiting and service. Manage. Sci. **41**(11), 1806–1815 (1995). https://doi.org/10.1287/mnsc.41.11.1806
11. Celik, H.: Customer online shopping anxiety within the unified theory of acceptance and use technology (UTAUT) framework. Edited by Ian Phau. Asia Pacific Journal of Marketing and Logistics **28**(2) (2016). https://doi.org/10.1108/APJML-05-2015-0077

12. Cohen, J.: Statistical Power Analysis for the Behavioral Sciences. 2nd ed. Hoboken: Taylor and Francis (1988). https://ebookcentral.proquest.com/lib/kxp/detail.action?docID=1192162
13. Dommick, D., Reichhart, P.: Payback – Der heilige Gral oder wie Smartphones den Handel revolutionieren. In: Hierl, L. (eds) Mobile Payment. Edition Bankmagazin. Springer Gabler, Wiesbaden (2017). https://doi.org/10.1007/978-3-658-14118-9_16
14. European Commission. Joint Research Centre. 2020. Artificial Intelligence and Digital Transformation: Early Lessons from the COVID 19 Crisis. LU: Publications Office. https://data.europa.eu/doi/https://doi.org/10.2760/166278
15. Fejes, A.: Digital Transformation in Grocery Retail. Germany. Hofstede Insights (blog). Accessed 21 Dec. 2022 (n.d.). https://www.hofstede-insights.com/country/germany/
16. Ghazwani, S., van Esch, P., Cui, Y., Gala, P.: Artificial intelligence, financial anxiety and cashier-less checkouts: a Saudi Arabian perspective. Int. J. Bank Marketing **40**(6), 1200-1216 (2022). https://doi.org/10.1108/IJBM-09-2021-0444
17. Gethmann, C.F., et al.: Künstliche Intelligenz in der Forschung. Neue Möglichkeiten und Herausforderungen für die Wissenschaft. 1. Aufl. 2022. Berlin, Heidelberg: Springer Berlin Heidelberg (Ethics of Science and Technology Assessment, 48) (2022)
18. Giroux, M., Kim, J., Lee, J.C., Park, J.: Artificial intelligence and declined guilt: retailing morality comparison between human and AI. J. Bus. Ethics: JBE **178**(4), 1027–1041 (2022). https://doi.org/10.1007/s10551-022-05056-7
19. Hofstede Insights (Hg.). Country comparison. Accessed 21 December 2022 (2022). https://www.hofstede-insights.com/country-comparison/germany,saudi-arabia/
20. Jones, M.: Hofstede - Culturally questionable?. Oxford Business & Economics Conference. Oxford, UK, pp. 24–26 (2007)
21. Kitzmann, A.: Künstliche Intelligenz. Wie verändert sich unsere Zukunft? Wiesbaden: Springer Fachmedien Wiesbaden; Imprint Springer (Springer eBook Collection) (2022)
22. Phil, K., Tynan, C.: The future of luxury management – 5 megatrends that are here to stay: guidance for researchers and managers. J. Mark. Manag. **38**(13–14), 1271–1277 (2022). https://doi.org/10.1080/0267257X.2022.2148908
23. Ledermann, T., Bodenmann, G.: Moderator- und mediatoreffekte bei dyadischen daten. Zeitschrift für Sozialpsychologie **37**(1), 27–40 (2006). https://doi.org/10.1024/0044-3514.37.1.27
24. Meuter, M.L., Ostrom, A.L., Roundtree, R.I., Bitner, M.J.: Self-service technologies: understanding customer satisfaction with technology-based service encounters. J. Mark. **64**(3), 50–64 (2000). https://doi.org/10.1509/jmkg.64.3.50.18024
25. Schliewe, J., Kerstin, P.: a cross-cultural comparison of factors influencing self-scan checkout use. J. Bus. Econ. Res. (JBER) **8**(10). https://doi.org/10.19030/jber.v8i10.772
26. Schomakers, E.-M., Lidynia, C., Müllmann, D., Ziefle, M.: Internet users' perceptions of information sensitivity – insights from Germany. Int. J. Inf. Manage. **46**(June), 142–150 (2019). https://doi.org/10.1016/j.ijinfomgt.2018.11.018
27. Srivastava, M., Kaul, D.: Social interaction, convenience and customer satisfaction: the mediating effect of customer experience. J. Retail. Consum. Serv. **21**(6), 1028–1037 (2014). https://doi.org/10.1016/j.jretconser.2014.04.007
28. Wankhede, K., Wukkadada, B., Nadar, V.: Just walk-out technology and its challenges: a case of amazon go. Int. Conference on Inventive Res. Computing Appl. (ICIRCA) **2018**, 254–257 (2018). https://doi.org/10.1109/ICIRCA.2018.8597403
29. Zhang, Y., Xiao, Z., Yang, J., Wraith, K., Mosca, P.: A Hybrid Solution for Smart Supermarkets Based on Actuator Networks. 2019 7th International Conference on Information, Communication and Networks (ICICN), pp. 82–86 (2019). https://doi.org/10.1109/ICICN.2019.8834962

E-Finance and Digital Assets

Is Bitcoin's Environmental Risk Inflated? Elasticity and Fossil Fuels

Thabo J. Gopane[(✉)] [iD]

Department of Finance and Investment Management, University of Johannesburg,
Johannesburg, South Africa
tjgopane@uj.ac.za

Abstract. Whereas prior studies quantify absolute measures and correlational tests in Bitcoin's greenhouse gas (GHG) emissions, the elasticity behaviour of Bitcoin's pollution is yet to be understood. To inquire whether Bitcoin's environmental risk is inflated, the study borrows the economics method of time series decomposition and accepts carbon dioxide (CO_2) emission as a proxy for environmental pollution. The empirical objective of the study is to quantify the elasticity of GHG emissions with respect to Bitcoin electricity usage in total and disaggregated by fossil fuels. The results show that total electricity has an elasticity of less than one, while natural gas and oil have an elasticity of greater than one for both short and long runs. Also, all fossil fuels have an elasticity coefficient greater than one in the long run. The results reveal that assessing the Bitcoin environmental impact in aggregated electricity data is not a good idea. Another revelation is that even though coal energy is a higher pollutant, CO_2 emissions are less responsive to Bitcoin's coal usage than oil and natural gas. These results need to be digested with caution due to the data limitation problem that leads to using average shares to desegregate total electricity time series. The outcome of this study should empower environmental activists, policymakers, and sustainable investment investors with practical information.

Keywords: Bitcoin · Carbon dioxide · Cryptocurrency · Elasticity · Electricity consumption · Greenhouse gas emissions · Fossil fuels

1 Introduction

Globally the issue of environmental impact is critical but a historically contested terrain. For instance, "drops in emissions often provoke claims from climate sceptics that worries over global warming are exaggerated, while increases in emissions lead to concerns among environmental groups that not enough is being done to address the issue" [5, p.58]. Over the years, financial market participants have, by and large, responded positively toward sustainable investment mobilisations. This global receptiveness is indicated in the increasing adoption of Environment, Social, and Governance (ESG) compliant investment products

R. Jallouli et al. (Eds.): ICDEc 2023, LNBIP 485, pp. 171–184, 2023.
https://doi.org/10.1007/978-3-031-42788-6_11

and the mushrooming ESG monitoring indices in the world's financial markets. In contrast, Bitcoin, as a firstborn and dominant cryptocurrency, has attracted criticism that it is an "environmental disaster" [40, p.384]. The claim is based on the fact that Bitcoin mining (or production) consumes excessive electricity, often sourced from fossil fuels known to be sources of greenhouse gas (GHG) emissions. GHG emissions raise a socio-economic problem because they trap (or house) heat in the atmosphere and then emit it back to the earth with harmful consequences. The heat-trapping occurrence of GHG is known as the greenhouse effect. The greenhouse effect is part of a more concerning problem with its causal relationship with global warming or climate change. The prominent members of GHG are sulfuric hexafluoride (SF_6), nitrogen dioxide (N_2O), Methane (CH_4), and carbon dioxide (CO_2). The scope of the current study is confined to the latter because it is known to be the more problematic of the four gases.

Before elaborating on the contribution of the current study, it is important to lay the background by answering preliminary questions. What is Bitcoin, and why does it consume excessive electricity leading to environmental notoriety? Bitcoin is the first successful and dominant cryptocurrency. It was introduced in 2009 by pseudonymous programmer(s). Bitcoin was designed to be a digital currency that works autonomously in person-to-person online transactions free of trusted third parties like central banks, commercial banks, or foreign exchange agencies. The financial literature has questioned Bitcoin's identity and subjected it to diverse definitions such as money, speculative assets, digital gold, and the like. Nevertheless, Bitcoin is still used as currency, among others.

The first transaction of Bitcoin occurred on 12th January 2009, but its actual activity took off from a minuscule starter of $0.09 in July 2010. Since then, Bitcoin has experienced volatile fluctuations characterised by several rallies, crashes, and an all-time high price of just under $69 000 in 2021 [13,14]. Currently, the market entry has increased to 800 cryptocurrencies and still counting while others experience fail-exit quietly. The cryptocurrency industry is valued at USD 897 billion. As a leading cryptocurrency, Bitcoin has always maintained a dominant market share, currently standing at 36% and a price of USD16 811. Table 1 gives a picture of Bitcoin's legal status around the world. The table shows that Bitcoin's legal operation varies from the absolute ban, implicit ban, and co-existence with other financial instruments, to full adoption as a legal tender in at least two countries, El Salvador on 5 June 2021 and Central African Republic on 28 April 2022 [21]. It appears that this adoption is out of need rather than experimentation since both countries do not have their own currency but each have adopted a foreign currency. El Salvador uses USD, while the Central African Republic co-uses XAF (Central African CFA Franc) with five other countries within the region: Cameroon, Chad, the Republic of the Congo, Equatorial Guinea, and Gabon. The XAF is pegged to the Euro and backed by France's Treasury under specified conditions.

Besides the mixed biographical sketch painted above, Bitcoin has earned itself a favourable profile within a short space of time. First, before its birth, prior developers launched several cryptocurrencies like eCash, eGold, Hashcash, B-money, and Bit-Gold. Although they planted beneficial innovation seeds, they

Table 1. Cryptocurrency's legal status in different countries

Adopted	Legal	Implicit ban	Absolute ban
El Salvador	Denmark	Bahrain	Algeria
CAR	France	Burundi	Bangladesh
	Germany	Cameroon	China
	Iceland	CAR	Egypt
	Japan	Gabon	Iraq
	Mexico	Georgia	Morocco
	Spain	Guyana	Nepal
	United Kingdom	Kuwait	Qatar
		Lesotho	Tunisia
			Libya
			Macao
			Maldives
			Vietnam
			Zimbabwe

Source: LOC [23] Kshetri [21]. CAR = Central African Republic.

failed to sustain existence (see review by Subramanian and Chino [37]). Second, not only has Bitcoin maintained business continuity since its inception, its technology-oriented business plan appears viable in the future thus far. Third, Bitcoin has reasonably tested blockchain technology which has promising industry applications like smart contracts, decentralised notary, digital identity, digital academic certificate, and central bank digital currency, among others. Besides this positive outlook, Bitcoin has some disappointing drawbacks, including its convenience for money laundering activities and environmental pollution. The latter is the focus of the current study.

The heavy electricity usage in Bitcoin is due to its inherent technical design. In order to produce or validate Bitcoin currency, an army of decentralised computers (called nodes) operated by individuals or pools (known as miners) have to solve a complex computer algorithm called proof of work (PoW). Bitcoin money supply has a built-in control to limit the flooding of the market. This is achieved by maintaining a production rate of one block per 10 min by adjusting the system complexity (called difficulty). The mining difficulty is re-scaled after every 2016 block, approximately every two weeks. Each computer node must go through many rounds of guessing (or hashing) to solve a mathematical puzzle. The first computer that finds the correct solution is rewarded with Bitcoin units and the rest stop. The process continues for the subsequent production cycles. This intensive and competitive hashing process has to be sustained with high electricity consumption, leading to notable environmental impact because fossil fuel is a significant Bitcoin's energy source.

The previous literature that researched the problem of Bitcoin and the cryptocurrency environmental problem predominantly came from the fields of mathematics, engineering, and natural sciences and less from financial economics [40]. These past studies have profitably helped to compute the absolute electricity usage and correlational association of electricity usage with environmental impact. There is also a need to enrich knowledge from the perspective of economic science. In this regard, the current paper investigates the elasticity of environmental degradation (proxied with CO_2) with respect to electricity resource usage of Bitcoin mining. This investigation is essential for several reasons. First, the method of time series decomposition into the short-term cycle and the long-term trend is standard application in the economics of environmental impact ([6] but it is yet to be applied productively in the Bitcoin case. Second, the recent events sparked a public and investor reassessment, which needs a corresponding relevant update in empirical research. These events include market shocks arising from the collapse of the cryptocurrency exchange, FTX, and the resultant legal predicament for its management. Also, the widely publicised criticism of Bitcoin's environmental impact by the well-known business person and chief executive officer of Tesla corporation, [25] generates questionable environmental anxiety. Recently New York state in the U.S has reacted to the ensuing bad publicity of environmental impact by announcing a two-year ban on new permits for 'fossil fuel'- based cryptocurrency mining operations [10]. Though this appears inconsistent with the fact that 77% of the U.S's electricity consumption comes from fossil fuels [1].

The rest of this paper is organised as follows: Sect. 2 describes the Bitcoin network, Sect. 3 provides a literature review, Sect. 4 explains the methodological details of the study, Sect. 5 presents the empirical results as well as a discussion, and Sect. 6 concludes the study.

2   Description of the Bitcoin Network

Bitcoin is a decentralised virtual cryptocurrency, and it is a person-to-person money system that does not utilise an intermediary like a banking institution or central bank service. These digital transactions are nameless and use computer addresses (or keys). The Bitcoin money system has metric (or unit code), usually symbolised as XBT, B, or BTC. Bitcoin's operation software (blockchain) is implemented as a permissionless network. The following attributes characterise Bitcoin operation:

Design and Integrity: Bitcoin is a family of cryptocurrencies, and it uses a digital signature and a cryptographic hash function to ensure authentication, non-repudiation, and integrity. All this is intended to protect the Bitcoin network against multiple-spending or counterfeiting.

Maximum Coin Capacity: The Bitcoin system is designed to allow a maximum of 21 million coins, which is expected to be realised in 2140. At the time of writing, the number of BTC in circulation is 18.9 million, and 2.1 million are to be mined still.

Blockchain: Bitcoin transactions are recorded chronologically and maintained in a blockchain cryptographic ledger. The blocks are generated at the rate of one per 10 min to safeguard against flooding the Bitcoin market with excess coins.

Bitcoin Mining Reward: The greatest incentive for miners is the Bitcoin Block Reward. When miners successfully execute and validate a transaction algorithm, they are rewarded with BTC. The reward amount is designed to reduce by half for every 210,000 blocks. This happens approximately every four years, starting from 50 BTC in 2009, decreasing to 25 BTC in November 2011, reducing to 12.5 BTC in July 2016, and now 6.25 BTC since May 2020. The reward is expected to equal zero in 2140.

Technology Improvement: The mining of bitcoin or similar cryptocurrencies is done through relevant computer hardware and bitcoin software. Due to the high demand for computing power to solve the Bitcoin algorithm, over the years, the miners have upgraded from different computer capabilities starting from central processing unit (CPU) to graphic processing unit (GPU), field-programmable gate array (FPGA), and now application specific integrated circuit (ASIC) which is built specifically for cryptocurrency mining.

Bitcoin Mining Farms: Fig. 1 illustrates the interior and exterior of the industrial Bitcoin mining farm and the typical privately owned coal-operated electricity generation plant. Not all Bitcoin farms own private power-generating plants.

Fig. 1. Illustration of Bitcoin mining rig (left panel) and mining farm (right panel)

3   Literature Review

The question arises: Is a coal-powered electricity plant dedicated to Bitcoin mining a welcome industrial competitiveness or a depressing environmental threat? This critical issue is the centre of the current study. Whereas sustainable investing has recently regained momentum, the history of environmental impact assessment has a long history in economic growth [30–32] and in the broadly encompassing debate of ESG [27,35]. In fact, the rate of investor mobilisation to adopt sustainable investment has a corresponding research deepening in sub-themes of climate finance [11], green finance [24], green mutual funds [4]; green bonds [42], and green cryptocurrency [34]. Arguably, the latter is the least green asset, especially Bitcoin, which is the focus of the current study.

Empirical questions on the greenness of Bitcoin (or lack of it) straddle the literature streams that explain the Bitcoin network, blockchain [15], electronic waste (e-waste) meaning the disposable of old Bitcoin mining machines [8,39], Bitcoin electricity consumption [22], and Bitcoin's environmental impact [41]. The current study proceeds to use electricity data computed by other researchers [3] and focuses on the impact of its usage (especially fossil fuel) on GHG emissions.

Past research (see review by Wendl et al. [41]) concurs that Bitcoin, due to its brute-force hashing and PoW algorithm architecture, is an electricity-intensive operation with pollution burdens but disagrees with the extent of increasing anxiety of environmental damage. One set of researchers (for example, [12,29,33]) appears to associate with the media screams that "Bitcoin ...is a dirty currency" [25, p.1] alluding that its carbon footprint is excessive, and an environmental crisis. Another set of literature [18,20,26] that happens to align with the sentiment of the Bitcoin community is that Bitcoin's pollution estimates are prone to mistakes, erroneous assumptions, and often misleadingly overstated. The disagreement centres mainly on how Bitcoin electricity consumption is computed to quantify the resultant GHG emissions. The exact quantity of Bitcoin's electricity usage by its miners is unknown. Therefore, researchers approximate this information through a combination of operational assumptions and production variables including hash rate, miners' rewards, difficulty changes, equipment efficiency, and the like (details listed in Koomey et al. [19]).

A good example of the cited disagreements is highlighted in Mora et al. [29, p.931]'s projection that "Bitcoin ...could alone produce enough CO_2 emissions to push global warming above 2 °C within less than three decades." After a comprehensive rebuttal, [26, p.654] argue that this projection is "...fundamentally flawed and should not be taken seriously by the public, researchers or policymakers." In view of the above, it is evident that more careful research is needed in this area. In this regard, the current study is privileged to benefit from the improved and refined online databases by early researchers [3,38].

The strength of prior studies manifests in the careful design and deepening of the quantitative methods of electricity measures and often showing the resultant correlational relationship [28] between Bitcoin's resource usage and its impact on the environment. The current study differs from the said studies by applying lessons from economics and using time series decomposition to evaluate the elasticity of Bitcoin GHG emissions with respect to their resource usage for aggregate growth rates, short-term cycles, and long term-trends.

4 Methodology

4.1 Econometric Models

The econometric design applied in this paper is a modified model used by Cohen et al. [5]. Unlike their configuration, in the current study Eq. (4) includes a polynomial trend in Eq. (4) to combat possibilities of spurious regression behaviour. The intuition with this model (Eqs. 1 to 4), is to distinguish environmental impact that is associated with short-term cycles and long-term trends.

$$\text{H-P filter: } \min_{\tau} \sum_{t=1}^{T}(z_t - z_t^{\tau}) + \lambda \sum_{t=1}^{T}[(z_t^{\tau} - z_{t-1}^{\tau}) - (z_{t-1}^{\tau} - z_{t-2}^{\tau})]^2 \qquad (1)$$

$$\Delta y_t = \alpha + \beta \Delta x_t + \epsilon_t \qquad (2)$$

$$y_t^c = \alpha^c + \beta^c x_t^c + \epsilon_t^c \qquad (3)$$

$$y_t^{\tau} = \alpha^{\tau} + \beta^{\tau} x_t^{\tau} + \delta^{\tau} q_t + \epsilon_t^{\tau} \qquad (4)$$

Table 2 lists and defines all the variables and parameters used in Eqs. 1 to 4.

Table 2. Variable Definitions

z_t	$\in (y_t, x_t)$
x	$\in$ (Total electricity, Coal energy, Oil energy, Gas energy)
y	Carbon dioxide (CO_2)
t	Time
c	Cycle
τ	Trend
λ	Smoothing parameter
α	Intercept
β	Elasticity
ϵ	Error term
δ	Coefficients of control variables
q	Control variables, including trend

Source: Own compilation

In Eqs. 1 to 4, the superscripts c, and τ indicate cycle, and trend respectively while the subscript t is the index of time in months ($t = 1, 2, 3, \ldots T$). We use the last three equations to compute the elasticity (β) of CO_2 (y_t) with respect to (x_t) which represents, in turn, total electricity, coal energy, natural gas energy, and oil energy. This computation is repeated three times for original series in growth rates (Eq. 2), short term cycle (Eq. 3), and long-term trend (Eq. 4). In order to decompose the time series (z_t) into trend (z_t^τ) and cycle ($z_t - z_t^\tau$) we minimize Eq. (1), the Hodrick-Prescott filter by Hodrick and Prescott [16]. This filter is is widely applied in economics and econometrics. We set the smoothing parameter (λ) at 14400 as it is normally the practice for monthly time series. The variable, q for control variables, includes a polynomial trend to exclude the potential spurious behaviour in Eq. (4).

4.2   Data Characteristics

This empirical study uses monthly data for the entire Bitcoin network. CO_2 and electricity consumption data are sourced from Cambridge Centre for Alternative Finance [3]. CO_2 is expressed in million tonnes of carbon dioxide equivalent abbreviated, $MtCO_2e$. This means that CO_2 emissions are standardised on their equivalent of 100-year global warming potential (GWP100). Electricity consumption is measured in tera-watt hours (TWh). CCAF [3] publishes monthly shares of electricity by source from coal, oil, and natural gas. We use the monthly averages of these shares to evaluate electricity consumption by source. The details of data gathering assumptions for CO_2 and electricity time series are explained by CCAF [3]. Figure 2 (Panel A) shows the sources of electricity in the Bitcoin industry are nuclear, wind, hydro, solar, and other renewables, as well as natural gas, oil, and coal. In the graph it is evident that fossil fuel (gas, oil, and coal) are the main sources of electricity for Bitcoin mining. Figure 2 (Panel B) shows the relative sizes of the leading GHG, fluorinated gases (3%), nitrous oxide (7%), methane (11%), and CO_2 has a very dominant share of 79%.

5   Empirical Results and Discussion

5.1   Interpretation of Elasticity Results

The results show Bitcoin's carbon emissions in the context of growth rates and short-term cycles (in Table 3), as well as a long-term trend (in Table 4). These results were computed using Eqs. 2 to 4. The econometric equations were estimated with robust time series regressions and the significant F-test provides further assurance of model reliability. The variable of interest is elasticity in the first row in Table 3 (for Panel A and B) and Table 4. Based on elasticity interpretation principles, if the elasticity coefficient is greater than one but positive, this means that for every one percent increase in electricity usage, Bitcoin's carbon emission increases by more than one percent. All the elasticity coefficients in Tables 3 and 4 are positive and statistically significant. This means

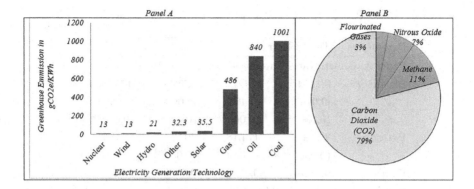

Fig. 2. Life cycle GHG Emissions according to Electricity (Panel A), and the relative sizes of greenhouse gas emissions. The graph shows the median of life cycle GHG emissions assuming one-time upstream, ongoing combustion, ongoing non-combustion, and one-time downstream. Source: Own graphics, data from CCAF [3] and EPA [9]

that electricity usage affects carbon emissions positively. When comparing the total elasticity with its separate sources, it is clear that the elasticity of carbon emission is mainly greater than unity for fossil fuels, especially for the long-term trend. This suggests that in the long run Bitcoin's pollution impact is greater than short term effects. The pattern of results also indicate the importance of disaggregating total electricity numbers into energy sources and then into cycles and trends.

5.2   Discussion of Results

Although prior research [2,3,7,17,36] have covered much ground to reliably answer the question: what is the Bitcoin carbon footprint? Meaning what is the extent of environmental pollution of Bitcoin via GHG emission measures? This set of literature differ but complimentary to the current study. Prior studies tend to produce absolute measure that enables comparison with other GHG emitters (like country, or other industries). The current study is designed to answer the question: If Bitcoin electricity consumption increases by one percent, how much will CO_2 increase by? That is, elasticity of CO_2 with respect to electricity usage. The results are complimentary (prior and current studies) in that in both approaches Bitcoin footprint is measured, and it is shown to be significant. The current study is similar in context but differs in method to the stream of literature that use correlational analysis to explain the impact of Bitcoin pollution, like the application of Vector Error Correction Model, or VECM [40]. The latter model is able to show pollution effect in the short-run and long-run by examining error correction components and cointegration relationship. However, the VECM analysis is different to the current paper's approach of decomposing time series into cycles (short-run) and trends (long-term). All models, including the current analysis, concur that Bitcoin mining poses an environmental risk.

Table 3. Bitcoin's Elasticity of Carbon Emissions

Parameters	Total Electr	Oil	Gas	Coal
Panel A: Growth rates Carbon emissions (Eq. 2)				
Elasticity	0.3774	6.421	0.7848	0.7936
	[0.0136]	[0.4865	[0.0936]	[0.0390
	(0.000***)	(0.000***)	(0.000***)	(0.000***)
F-Test	35.18	174.18	70.28	393.67
	(0.000***)	(0.000***)	(0.000***)	(0.000***)
R_sq	0.1866	0.5423	0.3235	0.7281
Panel B: Cyclical Carbon Emissions (Eq. 3)				
Elasticity	0.3833	8.4609	1.283	0.8287
	0.0119961	0.53726	0.114864	0.035857
	(0.000***)	(0.000***)	(0.000***)	(0.000***)
F-Test	1020.74	248.01	124.76	534.18
	(0.000***)	(0.000***)	(0.000***)	(0.000***)
R_sq	0.8734	0.6263	0.4574	0.783
Observations	150	150	150	150

Numbers in square brackets and brace brackets are standard errors, and probabilities, respectively.

Table 4. Trend-based Elasticity of Carbon Emissions for Bitcoin

Parameters	Total Electr	Oil	Gas	Coal
Elasticity	0.339	10.5364	1.5212	1.0742
	[0.0043]	[0.3389]	[0.0201]	[0.0046]
	(0.000***)	(0.000***)	(0.000***)	(0.000***)
Trend	2.2267	5.5834	0.9379	0.9641
	[0.8556]	[1.1145]	[0.4809]	[0.2093]
	(0.000***)	(0.000***)	(0.000***)	(0.000***)
Trend sq	−1.0312	−4.9068	−1.3475	0.1815
	[0.5331]	[0.6850]	[0.2995]	[0.0199]
	(0.000***)	(0.000***)	(0.000***)	(0.000***)
Trend tube	0.0756	0.9835	0.3449	0.1815
	[0.0815]	[0.1042]	[0.0461]	[0.0199]
	(0.000***)	(0.000***)	(0.000***)	(0.000***)
F-Test	65169.23	6445.01	22842.48	9100
	(0.000***)	(0.000***)	(0.000***)	(0.000***)
R_sq	0.9977	0.9776	92	0.9
Observations	150	150	150	150

Numbers in square brackets and brace brackets are standard errors, and probabilities, respectively.

The moral of the story is that GHG emissions contribute to climate change which has "the potential to impact the health and well-being of nearly every person on the planet" [11, p.16]. For this reason, there is global collaboration and standing protocols like United Nation's SDGs and Paris Climate Accords to monitor greenhouse effect. Due to its architecture of PoW algorithm and brute-force hashing to mine and validate its cryptocurrency; the Bitcoin operation is electricity intensive and include fossil fuels. Accordingly, Bitcoin is accused of excessive carbon footprint or being a significant source of pollution. The environmental activism-friendly research [12,29,33] tend to generate fears that Bitcoin, alone, may cause countries to fail to achieve their GHG control targets. A balanced comprehensive rebuttal [26] shows that the fear-generating results are inflated due to imprecise empirical design which is consistent with the conclusion of the current study. The current study has shown that, although CO_2 is a higher pollutant than other GHG's, CO_2 emission has lower response rate to Bitcoin's electricity usage compared to other fossil fuels.

6   Conclusion

Environmental degradation is one of the global concerns and priority watch list of the twenty-first century, which is highlighted in the sustainable development goals (SDG) 13, 14, and 15 of the United Nations, as well as the increasing topicality of Environment, Social, and Governance (ESG) investing. Accordingly, observers worry that the environmental impact of cryptocurrency is excessive, but proponents believe the matter is exaggerated.

The previous literature on Bitcoin's environmental impact majored in quantifying the problematic magnitudes of electricity consumption in Bitcoin mining operations. The current study uses one of these refined databases to answer the question: what is the CO_2 emission response to a one per cent increase in total Bitcoin's electricity consumption, and disaggregated electricity usage from fossil fuels (natural gas, oil, and coal)? The analysis is based on decomposed times series into cycles (short-term), and trends (long-term). The results show that all fossil fuels have a strong long-term effect with elasticity coefficients of greater than one. This means that if Bitcoin increases its fossil fuel consumption by one percent this will lead to a long-run CO_2 emission of greater than one percent. Unlike coal, natural gas and oil have elasticity greater than one for both cycle and trend time series, meaning that they have higher pollution effect. Elasticity coefficient from aggregated total elasticity series shows an elasticity coefficient of less than one. This will mean that an increase in one percent of total consumption is associated with less than one percent increase in CO_2 emissions. Clearly this is incomplete measure since it hides the bigger impact in the disaggregated assessment of separate energy sources. Therefore, the conclusion of the study is that while some fossil fuels have both short and long run pollution effects in Bitcoin operation, they are all sources of higher environmental impact in the long run. It is also insightful to note that while coal is relatively the highest pollutant, the results show that it is not as environmentally impactful as oil and natural gas. This study provides useful empirical information for policy makers and environment-sensitive investors. The application of the study says policy measures that are designed to alleviate the problem of Bitcoin pollution should have a long-term perspective and not short run. In terms of academic studies, the results provide an important lesson that it is necessary to examine environmental impact in short and long runs. Also, that there is value in time series decomposition. The current study used the Hodrick-Prescott filter. Future studies may apply alternative decomposition methods to see if the results are confirmatory.

References

1. American Geosciences Institute: What are the major sources and users of energy in the United States? (2017)
2. de Vries, A.: Online Live Dashboard and Database for Bitcoin Electricity Consumption
3. Cambridge Centre for Alternative Finance: Bitcoin Electricity Consumption Index. Cambridge Digital Assets Programme, the Cambridge Centre for Alternative Finance. Judge Business School, University of Cambridge (2023)
4. Chang, C., Nelson, W., Doug Witte, H.: Do green mutual funds perform well? Manag. Res. Rev. **35**(8), 693–708 (2012). https://doi.org/10.1108/01409171211247695
5. Cohen, G., Jalles, J., Loungani, P., Marto, R.: The long-run decoupling of emissions and output: evidence from the largest emitters. Energy Policy **118**, 58–68 (2018). https://doi.org/10.1016/j.enpol.2018.03.028
6. Cribari-Neto, F.: On time series econometrics. Q. Rev. Econ. Finance **36**, 37–60 (1996). https://doi.org/10.1016/S1062-9769(96)90007-1
7. de Vries, A., Gallersdörfer, U., Klaaßen, L., Stoll, C.: Revisiting Bitcoin's carbon footprint. Joule **6**(3), 498–502 (2022). https://doi.org/10.1016/j.joule.2022.02.005
8. de Vries, A., Stoll, C.: Bitcoin's growing e-waste problem. Resour. Conserv. Recycl. **175**, 105901 (2021). https://doi.org/10.1016/j.resconrec.2021.105901
9. EPA: Greenhouse gas inventory data explorer. United states environmental protection agency
10. Ferré-Sadurní, L., Ashford, G.: New York enacts 2-Year ban on some crypto-mining operations (2022)
11. Giglio, S., Kelly, B., Stroebel, J.: Climate finance. Annu. Rev. Financ. Econ. **13**, 15–36 (2021). https://doi.org/10.1146/annurev-financial-102620-103311
12. Goodkind, A., Berrens, B., R.P.: Cryptodamages: monetary value estimates of the air pollution and human health impacts of cryptocurrency mining. Energy Res. Soc. Sci. **59**(101281), 1–9 (2020). https://doi.org/10.1016/j.erss.2019.101281
13. Gopane, T.J.: Volatility behaviour of bitcoin as a digital asset: evidence of shock transmission dynamics from the south African financial markets. J. Telecommun. Digit. Econ. **10**(2), 195–213 (2022). https://doi.org/10.3316/informit.587286953523524
14. Gopane, T.J.: An assessment of inter-market volatility and shock dynamics of bitcoin as a digital asset. In: Jallouli, R., Bach Tobji, M.A., Mcheick, H., Piho, G. (eds.) ICDEc 2021. LNBIP, vol. 431, pp. 104–117. Springer, Cham (2021). https://doi.org/10.1007/978-3-030-92909-1_7

15. Gopane, T.: Blockchain technology and smart universities. In: Proceedings of 4th International Conference on the Internet, Cyber Security and Information Systems 2019, vol. 12, pp. 72–84 (2019). https://doi.org/10.29007/rkv5
16. Hodrick, R.J., Prescott, E.C.: Postwar U.S. business cycles: an empirical investigation. J. Money Credit Bank, **29**(1), 1–16 (1997)
17. Köhler, S., Pizzol, M.: Life cycle assessment of bitcoin mining. Environ. Sci. Technol. **53**(23), 13598–13606 (2019). https://doi.org/10.1021/acs.est.9b05687
18. Koomey, J.: Estimating bitcoin electricity use: a beginner's guide, coin center report (2019)
19. Koomey, J., Schmidt, Z., Hummel, H., Weyant, J.: Inside the black box: understanding key drivers of global emission scenarios. Environ. Model. Softw. **111**, 268–281 (2019). https://doi.org/10.1016/j.envsoft.2018.08.019
20. Krause, M., Tolaymat, T.: Quantification of energy and carbon costs for mining cryptocurrencies. Natl. Sustain. **1**(11), 711–718 (2018). https://doi.org/10.1038/s41893-018-0152-7
21. Kshetri, N.: Bitcoin's adoption as legal tender: a tale of two developing countries. IT Prof. **24**(5), 12–15 (2022). https://doi.org/10.1109/MITP.2022.3205528
22. Küfeoğlu, S., Özkuran, M.: Bitcoin mining: a global review of energy and power demand. Energy Res. Soc. Sci. **58**, 101273 (2019). https://doi.org/10.1016/j.erss.2019.101273
23. Law Library of Congress: Regulation of cryptocurrency around the world: November 2021 update, the law library of congress, global legal research directorate (2021)
24. Malhotra, G., Thakur, K.: Evolution of green finance: a bibliometric approach. Gedrag Organisatie Rev. **33**(2), 583–594 (2020)
25. Martin, K., Nauman, B.: Bitcoin's growing energy problem: 'it's a dirty currency'. Financial Times Newspaper (2021)
26. Masanet, E., Shehabi, A., Lei, N., Vranken, H., Koomey, J., Malmodin, J.: Implausible projections overestimate near-term Bitcoin CO2 emissions. Nat. Clim. Change **9**, 653–654 (2019). https://doi.org/10.1038/s41558-019-0535-4
27. Matos, P.: ESG and Responsible Institutional Investing around the World: A Critical Review. CFA Institute Research Foundation, New York (2020)
28. Mohsin, M., Naseem, S., Zia-ur-Rehman, M., Baig, S.A., Salamat, S.: The crypto-trade volume, GDP, energy use, and environmental degradation sustainability: an analysis of the top 20 crypto-trader countries. Int. J. Financial Econ. **28**(1), 651–667 (2020). https://doi.org/10.1002/ijfe.2442
29. Mora, C., et al.: Bitcoin emissions alone could push global warming above 2°C. Nat. Clim. Change **8**, 931–933 (2018). https://doi.org/10.1038/s41558-018-0321-8
30. Nordhaus, W.: Economic growth and climate: the carbon dioxide problem. Am. Econ. Rev. **67**(1), 341–46 (1977)
31. Nordhaus, W.: To slow or not to slow: the economics of the greenhouse effect. Econ. J. **101**(407), 920–37 (1991)
32. Nordhaus, W.: An optimal transition path for controlling greenhouse gases. Science **258**(5086), 1315–1319 (1992)
33. O'Dwyer, K., Malone, D.: Bitcoin mining and its energy footprint. In: 25th IET Irish Signals & Systems Conference and China-Ireland International Conference on Information and Communications Technologies (2014). https://doi.org/10.1049/cp.2014.0699
34. Oğhan, V.: Environmental policies for green cryptocurrency mining. In: Akkaya, S., Ergüder, B. (eds.) Handbook of Research on Challenges in Public Economics in the Era of Globalization, USA, Hershey, pp. 217–227 (2022). https://doi.org/10.4018/978-1-7998-9083-6.ch013

35. Pástor, L., Stambaugh, R., Taylor, L.: Sustainable investing in equilibrium. J. Financ. Econ. **142**(2), 550–71 (2021). https://doi.org/10.1016/j.jfineco.2020.12.011

36. Stoll, C., Klaaßen, L., Gallersdörfer, U.: The carbon footprint of bitcoin. Joule **3**(7), 1647–1661 (2019). https://doi.org/10.1016/j.joule.2019.05.012

37. Subramanian, R., Chino, T.: The state of cryptocurrencies, their issues and policy interactions. J. Int. Technol. Inf. Manag. **24**(3), 24–40 (2015)

38. Vries, A.: Digiconomist. Online live dashboard and database for bitcoin electricity consumption (2023)

39. de Vries, A.: Renewable energy will not solve bitcoin's sustainability problem. Joule **3**(4), 893–898 (2019). https://doi.org/10.1016/j.joule.2019.02.007

40. Wang, Y., Lucey, B., Vigne, S., Yarovaya, L.: An index of cryptocurrency environmental attention (ICEA. China Finance Rev. Int. **12**(3), 378–414 (2022). https://doi.org/10.1108/CFRI-09-2021-0191

41. Wendl, M., Doan, M., Sassen, R.: Environmental impact of cryptocurrencies using proof of work and proof of stake consensus algorithms: a systematic review. J. Environ. Manag. **326**, 16530 (2023). https://doi.org/10.1016/j.jenvman.2022.116530

42. Zerbib, O.: The effect of pro-environmental preferences on bond prices: Evidence from green bonds. J. Bank. Finance **98**, 39–60 (2019). https://doi.org/10.1016/j.jbankfin.2018.10.012

The Initial Coin Offering: Is It a Profitable Tool for Investment?

Hicham Sadok[(✉)]

Mohammed V University in Rabat., Rabat, Morocco
h.sadok@um5r.ac.ma

Abstract. Initial Coin Offerings (ICOs) have established themselves since 2017 as an attractive alternative for financing innovative companies. However, these new modes of financing from the world of blockchain technology have a very volatile return on investment (ROI) in the short term, and very ambivalent in the medium and long term: 90% of ICOs issued since 2017 have failed. This article attempts to shed some light on the question of the ROI of ICOs. The analysis of some databases of the most significant platforms for ICOs reveals that the highest ROIs reached on average 3100% at their peak and 30% on average over the period 2017- 2022. The results of the analysis suggest that given the level of risk of ICOs, they do not represent a good financial asset over a long period; on the other hand, they would be a good lever for speculation and possibly a good financial strategy to boost the financial performance of a diversified portfolio.

Keywords: Initial coin offering · Return on investment · Blockchain · Financial regulation · financial risk

1 Introduction

Since the creation of blockchain technology, new means of payment have appeared such as crypto-currencies (e.g. Bitcoin), accompanied by fundraising methods with underlying crypto- currencies (e.g. Initial Coin Offerings or ICO). An ICO can be defined as an open call by a company or an ongoing project for funding to raise funds through a blockchain, where crypto- assets are issued. The ICO fundraising mechanism resembles in some aspects more traditional funding channels (public offering, venture capital, crowdfunding), but nevertheless has its own characteristics [1]. The important step when issuing ICOs is the white paper, which is similar to a prospectus. The latter is a document providing details of a company's project proposal to obtain funding. The white paper summarizes the team involved, the project envisaged, the investors sought and the funds required, all including an evaluation of the project for potential investors. Regarding the price of ICOs when issuing tokens, a "pre-ICO price" is determined beforehand by the management team, while the post-ICO price is set afterwards by transactions on the market and by network participants. However, this liquidity is not guaranteed: only some of the tokens are traded on an exchange platform, and even if the token is listed, any bearer will not be able to find counterparty. By analyzing 1,009 tokens created since 2015,

R. Jallouli et al. (Eds.): ICDEc 2023, LNBIP 485, pp. 185–194, 2023.
https://doi.org/10.1007/978-3-031-42788-6_12

Amsden and Schweizer [2] observe that only 42% of tokens are listed on a secondary market after their ICO. In addition, this liquidity injection, while the project is still in the development stage, generates high volatility in token prices, which are determined by supply and demand based on limited information, which represents a risk factor for both token holders and project developers [3].

In this regard, the research developed around ICOs as a financing and investment method has grown in recent years [4–7].It therefore seems interesting to make a contribution to this literature by answering the following research question: Have the ICOs issued in recent years proved profitable for investors?

This problem raises two intrinsically linked questions in the field of technological finance [8]. The first relates to the search for a return on investment adequate to the risk backed by each type of project; the second concerns the control of the risks associated with this technological financing, a question that is all the more relevant with regard to the blockchain, the innovative technology on which the ICOs are based.

To provide some answers to this question, our article is structured as follows. The first part introduces an inventory and a brief review of the literature dealing with ICOs. The second point presents the risks associated with ICOs and the supervision of market regulators. The third part will deal with the method and the results obtained from certain platforms on the ROI of ICOs, to end with a conclusion and discussion.

2   ICOs: Specificities, Inventories and Literature Review

As a new funding vehicle, ICOs have been studied by the field of technology finance or by entrepreneurial finance [2, 9–11]. These studies cover the areas of token valuation, the nature of the projects, the amount raised by ICOs and their liquidity, as well as the risks incurred by investors and which mainly relate to the high volatility of crypto-assets and the possibility of fraud [12]. Overall, current research asks questions about operation, risk and regulation rather than providing answers about their relevance.

Thus, it also emerges from this literature review that the phenomenon of fundraising by ICO is recent and the amounts are relatively small compared to other means of financing: in total, the amounts raised by ICO would represent $22.9 billion, mainly in2017 and 2018 ($6.8 billion and $15.7 billion respectively). The number of projects increased significantly in 2017 (more than 800 projects, including 521 for the fourth quarter alone), then in 2018 (1,114) before falling sharply from the third quarter as shown in the graph below. This graph reveals that ICOs may have accounted for up to 6.3% of total global equity financing (IPO and venture capital) in the first quarter of 2018, all sectors combined, compared to an average of 1.6% in 2017 over four quarters (Graph 1).

However, and from the database on ICOs "Icobench", it turns out that between 2019 and 2020 the number of IPOs increased by 36% (1,415 IPOs are registered in 2020 compared to 1,040 in 2019) with a total amount raised, which increased by 66% and amounted to$331 billion. Additionally, alternative methods of financing in cryptocurrencies follow the same evolution. From 2017until the end of 2020, around 4,000 ICOs have been counted for a total amount raised of 11.5 billion dollars with a concentration in 2018/2019.

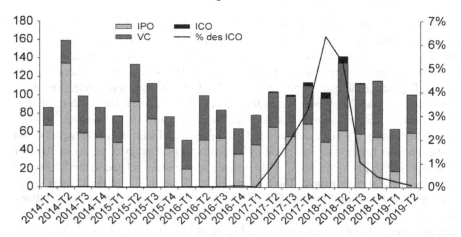

Source: AMF. The data comes from ICOdata and Coindesk

Graph 1. Amounts raised by ICO compared to equity financings in the world(in billions of dollars). Source: AMF. The data comes from ICOdata and Coindesk

Regarding the geographical distribution of fundraising, according to data from ICObench at the end of 2019, corroborated by data from ICOwatchlist, ten countries represent 59% of global fundraising. The prevalence of the United States is clear (12% of successful projects, $7.5 billion raised) and Singapore (12% of successful projects, $2.3 billion). In Europe, Switzerland and the United Kingdom are preferred countries for ICOs (respectively 6% and 9% of projects, $1.9 billion and $1.5 billion raised), as well as Estonia (6% projects, $910 million raised).The British Virgin Islands ($2.4 billion raised) and the Cayman Islands ($1.1 billion raised) are in the top ten countries in terms of amounts raised by ICO. The location of the ICO is also partly due to the legal environment of the country, since there is an overrepresentation of small countries whose regulation or absence of regulation is favourable to ICOs.

In terms of application sectors, ICO projects have evolved as the industry has matured: if the first period was dominated by data management, trading or new blockchain protocols, we have since observed the end of 2017 the appearance of projects aiming for a broader application of blockchain technology in the fields of health, energy, retail, as well as in the use of smart contracts to replace certain business processes (e.g. transactions and means of payment or legal agreements) [13].

To better understand the motivations and characteristics of the issuance of ICOs, the Financial Markets Authority in France (AMF) has launched questionnaire in 2018 with 83 French ICO project leaders to collect data on the terms of the ICO, on a voluntary and declarative basis, with a response rate by 43%.Project leaders cite as a criterion for choosing this method of financing the possibility of appealing to a committed community of investors on their platform (58%). The second reason cited is nevertheless that of the absence of capital dilution (28%); they are also 11% to cite the benefit of their independence vis-à-vis other stakeholders or intermediaries. Some project leaders choose the ICO route because of the access to international investors (22%), media exposure (17%), the simplicity and speed of fundraising allowed by ICOs (8%), or the possibility of having access to large amounts (8%).In addition, the vast majority of these token issues (89%) would have utility characteristics, i.e. conferring rights of use or payment that do not comply with the services rendered by the issuing companies (utility tokens).Regarding the use of the funds raised, which are relatively modest (between 200,000 Euros and 20 million Euros),the majority is used to ensure the development of the project: 25% on average for software development, 25% for salaries, 16% for project marketing, 7% for overheads and 5%for legal and administrative aspects. Part of the amounts is generally set aside by the issuers (19% on average, up to 70% for certain projects). The other funds could be used for expenses related to the ICO or the development of their platform. The issuance of ICOs which aim to raise larger funds, ranging from 1 Million Euros to 180 (21.8 million on average, 11.5 million median), are dedicated to financing projects related to software development, connected objects, data management and the energy sector. Unlike ICOs which target small fundraisers, most future project leaders have already had access to funding for amounts ranging from 30,000 Euros to 22 million Euros: 24% have benefited from love money or funds from business angels, 52% to have already completed a private equity round and 23% to have benefited from public subsidies. This indicates that the ICO mechanism would not only be a means of raising funds for companies that do not have access to traditional financing methods, but on the contrary would insert a new stage in a more traditional financing process.

Regarding the distribution of tokens, a significant part of them belongs to external investors, via sale or presale (37% and 5% respectively), but also to managers and employees of the structure (10% on average). Between 6% and 80% of tokens are kept by issuers (25% on average). The other tokens (20% on average) can be, depending on the ICO, used for future sales rounds or used to remunerate investors in the future.

While ICOs generally only accepted investments in crypto-assets, some ICO projects target a wider audience, accepting investments in crypto-assets, but also in euros and dollars or other international currencies. Nevertheless, for all the ICOs observed, the management of the exchange risk between traditional currencies and crypto-assets seems difficult, given the volatility of the latter. Some projects display fixed exchange rates between their token and traditional currencies, requiring the subscriber to bear the exchange risk. Conversely, some projects outsource this exchange risk management to a specialist. Other projects instead plan to manage it themselves by using their cash strategically.

3   ICO: Risks and Regulations

Investing in corporate finance through ICO instruments presents several risks. For Dimitropoulos [14, 15], there are significant risks and challenges when investing in ICOs. He described these fundraisers as a "Wild West" which sparkles "attractive projects" to attract uninformed investors»: the financed projects being mainly at the idea stage, the probability that they will not succeed is high. Information asymmetry is also a major risk. By analyzing disclosure documents from over 1,000 ICOs, Zetzsche et al. [16] observe that in 31% of cases, they provide no information on the project leaders and that they do not provide any information on the budget forecast in 25% of cases.

The possibilities of turning around for the consumer seem low when the authors observe that only 33% of the documents contain elements on the applicable legislation and 45% basic information such as the address of the issuer [17]. In addition, some ICOs have turned out to be frauds, for various reasons (poor budget management, disappearance of managers and/or employees, Ponzi scheme, etc.). DeadCoins draws up a list of more than 1,700 fraudulent ICOs, the amounts of which have been lost, however, remain difficult to estimate. The most documented cases concern the American company PlexCorps, which raised $15 million; the Vietnamese company Modern Tech, which supposedly raised $660 million via two ICOs, and the English company BitConnect, which supposedly raised $700,000.

Landau & Genais [18] highlights the risk of concealing the origin of funds and money laundering. Indeed, by design, crypto-asset transactions involve a high degree of anonymity. Therefore, preventative measures such as know-your-customer requirements are an indispensable part of fundraising. The European Union recently amended the Directive on the prevention of the use of the financial system for the purpose of money laundering or terrorist financing (EU Directive 2018/843), to include the trading of crypto assets as entities subject to money laundering requirements.

The investor may also be subject to a risk of dilution or lack of price transparency, the project holder being able to carry out pre-sales or carry out new issues of tokens after the public sale, reducing the individual value of the tokens. Finally, due to the newness of the technology, the technological, operational or cyber-attack risk remains significant. At this point, the majority of international regulators do not consider ICOs to pose a threat to financial stability, given the relatively small volumes and limited linkages between digital and traditional financial markets [19].

However, the diversity of approaches is significant depending on the regulators: some have chosen to ban ICOs on their territory permanently (China, Vietnam, Algeria, Morocco) or temporarily (South Korea); others have adopted a regulatory framework to attract virtuous projects (Malta, Gibraltar). Most offer a case-by-case approach, due to the remaining division on the qualification of tokens, such as Switzerland, Canada, Brazil or Germany. Despite this relatively common approach, differences remain. US regulations, for example, apply case law from the US Supreme Court to determine whether a crypto-asset constitutes a financial instrument within the meaning of US law. The latter establishes that a token will qualify as a financial instrument if it meets three cumulative conditions, namely: (1) be an investment, (2) carried out as part of a common project, which is reasonably likely to generate profits and (3) the latter must be generated by the efforts of third-party entrepreneurs or managers, and not by the investors [20]. This approach adopted by the United States in terms of applicable law leads to considering most crypto-assets as financial instruments [21].

Nevertheless, since ICO projects are by definition cross-border, investors may be exposed to risks related to the heterogeneity of regulatory regimes and investors may resort to regulatory arbitrage. This is why consistency and international cooperation in the regulation of ICOs seem essential: this can involve sharing requirements in terms of transparency and risk management of ICOs [22], by setting up international standards [23], as well as through international cooperation in the fight against fraud.

However, and in the absence of a regulatory framework at the international level and in most countries, the protection of Investors is therefore not sufficiently guaranteed. So how can investors' growing interest in ICOs be explained?

4   The ROI of ICOs

According to some authors [24], the main advantages claimed when funding ICOs, including speed of launch, few compliance requirements and low costs, are very attractive advantages for start-ups and small and medium-sized businesses that cannot afford the costs and time required by the demands of other traditional funding sources. Knowing that technology companies and those operating in the blockchain sphere must act quickly, these advantages during financing are of paramount importance. Other claimed benefits of ICO funding are the efficiency and reliability of blockchain transactions, where funds can be collected from around the world and quickly transferred after verification. Thus, companies using blockchains for ICOs can raise significant funds in a very short time and without geographical restrictions.

However, the main explanation for the enthusiasm of investors for ICOs lies in the possible return on investment. From an investor's perspective, some ICOs offer investors "anonymity" and potentially large returns. Indeed, according to Momtaz [25], projects have a strong incentive to reward short-term investors by underestimating the sale price of their token in order to generate liquidity in the secondary market and signal the growth potential of their project. Moreover, from a very large sample of ICOs during the period following the launch of the projects, Benedetti and Kostovetsky [26] observe that the average return on investment of an investor is 179%. This return has been estimated for successful ICOs whose tokens are traded on a secondary market. Even taking into account the negative returns of delisted or failed ICO tokens, the return for an average investor is 82%.

Finally, ICO can be an asset when it comes to diversifying the assets of a portfolio. Indeed, the most important crypto-assets (Bitcoin, Ethereum, Ripple, etc.) have very little correlated returns with each other [22], and are also not correlated with other asset classes such as equities, customary macroeconomic factors, other currencies or commodities [27].

Thus, and to verify the return on investment, measured by the investment gain minus the investment cost, all divided by the investment cost, we randomly selected from the CoinMarketCap database 10 ICOs issued since the end June 2019 to assess their rate of return on investment (ROI) as of December 31, 2022. It follows that from the 10 randomly chosen initial coin offerings we calculated their return on investment and ranked in order in the table below (Table 1).

A first reading of this table makes it easy to deduce that at least the first 6 ICOs have a significantly higher ROI than any other type of investment, taking into account the period studied and without taking into account the level of risk incurred. Nevertheless, such an analysis deserves to be extended according to a more rigorous methodology on the 4000 ICOs listed, and continued over time in order to observe the returns generated beyond the period.

Thus, and to conduct a more in-depth study on this issue, we used another "cryptorank" database which includes 1648 ICOs in order to gauge their rate of return on

Table 1. Top 10 randomly chosen ICO with their ROI

Ranking	ICO	% ROI
1	NXT	11547,519
2	Spectercoin	676,227
3	IOTA	522,900
4	Ethereum	442,869
5	Neo (Formerly Antshares)	378,453
6	Stratis	302,900
7	Lisk	50,952
8	QTUM	34,383
9	DigixDAO	17,011
10	Ark	9,190

Source: The data comes from CoinMarketCap database

investment (ROI). This database aggregates data on the sale price of the ICO, the start date of the ICO, and what interest us in this study are the current return on investment (ROI), as well as the ROI at all-time high (ATH) (Graph 2).

ICOs - Return of Investment
Year-to-year comparison

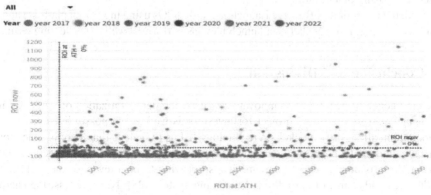

Source: cryptorank.io

Graph 2. Source: cryptorank.io

In the chart above, ICOs launched in different years are represented by distinct colors. The chart shows the investment returns of each cryptocurrency during its all-time high (ATH) as well as when the chart was created (01/09/2023). The horizontal axis shows how much back the token/coin has made in the logarithmic scale. The black line indicates a ROI of 0% when launching the ICO. The farther the points are to the right of the black line, the better the ROI. The analysis of this database allows in the first place deducing 2 observations:

First, at their ATH, the ROI of these ICOs was very high on average. Almost all of these ICOs have delivered an ROI of several hundred to one thousand percent for the period observed; Then, if we focus on the outliers of this graph. Returns on investment from the highest ICOs were in the tens of thousands percent at their peak. This can give an overview of the level of volatility of the investment in these financial assets. Specifically, when we note that on average, the returns on investment were 3,100% for their respective ATH. However, their current average ROI is only 30%.

Going through the individual years, it turns out that the returns on investment from ICOs vary significantly from year to year. The average ROI at ATH compared to the average ROI of each ICO is highly volatile and largely depends on the year of issuance. Thus, it can be observed that in general, investing in ICOs from 2017 to 2021 and reselling them to their respective ATHs generates returns of several thousand percent. On the other hand, ICOs Issued in 2022 generated a lower return on investment. It also appears that the ICOs issued in 2020 have surpassed the ICOs launched in other years.

Thus, the analysis of the graph shows that on average, the long-term holders of ICOs have achieved negative ROIs. The ICOs issued in 2021 and 2022, on the other hand, display the worst ROIs recorded in this database.

However, some elements during the analysis of this database attract attention and deserve more attention during more in-depth studies concerning the performance of these financial assets: First, there is a negative correlation between the total amount collected and performance of ICOs;

Returns on investment from ICOs that have used the Binance Launchpad far exceed other ICOs using other platforms;

With the exception of Binance Launchpad, only ICOs using the Huobi platform and, to a lesser extent, DAO Maker as a launch pad has performed well over the long term.

5 Conclusion and Discussion

The emergence of new types of innovative issuers, the democratization of a new form of engagement in a business project for investors as well as the possibilities of disintermediation allowed by blockchain technology led us to believe that there is space for this new fundraising process alongside the usual funding channels. Beyond its financial innovation, this new mode of financing is also proving to be a lever for the inclusion of those excluded from the traditional financing system [28]. Nevertheless, the sharp drop in projects and amounts raised since the end of 2019 suggests that this method of financing must continue to be structured and benefit from the supervision of international regulators in order to continue to be acclaimed by investors.

Regarding the return on investment of ICOs issued from 2017 until the end of 2022, it turned out that the results are mixed. The analysis made on the cryptorank database reveals some interesting elements that deserve other much more in-depth studies. The results obtained first confirm that 90% of ICO issues fail during their first years for various reasons related mainly to the risk of the project. This point confirms what has already been raised previously in the literature review. The second interesting point concerns the very high volatility of investing in ICOs. We found that on average the ROI was 3,100% for their ATH and current average ROI is 30%. This observation may explain the interest of investors for ICOs who rely on the speculative aspect of an ICO for the diversification of their portfolio. However, two major risks arise. On the one hand, the risk of the secondary market which is not yet organized and which remains confidential for the moment [29]. On the other hand, since ICOs are only carried out in cryptocurrency, there is a very significant exchange risk.

References

1. Lipusch, N.: Initial Coin Offerings – A Paradigm Shift in Funding Disruptive Innovation (2018). https://papers.ssrn.com/abstract=3148181. https://doi.org/10.2139/ssrn.3148181
2. Amsden, R., Schweizer, D.: Are blockchain crowdsales the new "gold rush"? success-determinants of initial coin offerings. SSRN J. (2018). https://doi.org/10.2139/ssrn.3163849
3. Kaal, W.A., Dell'Erba, M.: Initial Coin Offerings: Emerging Practices, Risk Factors, and Red Flags (2017). https://papers.ssrn.com/abstract=3067615. https://doi.org/10.2139/ssrn.3067615
4. Alshater, M.M., Joshipura, M., Khoury, R.E., Nasrallah, N.: Initial coin offerings: ahybrid empirical review. Small Bus Econ. 118 (2023). https://doi.org/10.1007/s11187-022-00726-2
5. Bellavitis, C., Fisch, C., Wiklund, J.: A comprehensive review of the global development of initial coin offerings (ICOs) and their regulation. J. Bus. Ventur. Insights 15, e00213 (2021). https://doi.org/10.1016/j.jbvi.2020.e00213
6. Li, J., Mann, W.: Initial coin offerings: current research and future directions. In: Rau, R., Wardrop, R., Zingales, L. (eds.) The Palgrave Handbook of Technological Finance, pp. 369–393. Springer International Publishing, Cham (2021). https://doi.org/10.1007/978-3-030-65117-6_15
7. Moxotó, A.C., Melo, M.P.A., Soukiazis, E.: Initial Coin Offering (ICO): A Systematic Review of the Literature, pp. 4177–4186 (2021). https://doi.org/10.24251/HICSS.2021.507
8. Sadok, H., Sakka, F., El Maknouzi, M.E.: Artificial intelligence and bank credit analysis: a review. Cogent Economics & Finance 10, 1 (2022). https://doi.org/10.1080/23322039.2021.2023262
9. Ackermann, E., Bock, C., Bürger, R.: Democratising entrepreneurial finance: the impact of crowdfunding and initial coin offerings (ICOs). FGF Studies in Small Business and Entrepreneurship, pp. 277–308 (2020)
10. Adhami, S., Giudici, G., Martinazzi, S.: Why do businesses go crypto? an empirical analysis of initial coin offerings. J. Econ. Bus. 100, 64–75 (2018). https://doi.org/10.1016/j.jeconbus.2018.04.001
11. Huang, W., Meoli, M., Vismara, S.: The geography of initial coin offerings. Small Bus. Econ. 55, 77–102 (2020). https://doi.org/10.1007/s11187-019-00135-y
12. Sadok, H., El Maknouzi, M.E.H.: The regulation of virtual currencies in comparative perspective: new private money or niche technological innovation? J. Money Laundering Control 24(4), 712–724 (2021). https://doi.org/10.1108/JMLC-09-2020-0101
13. Howell, S.T., Niessner, M., Yermack, D.: Initial Coin Offerings: Financing Growth with Cryptocurrency Token Sales (2018). https://ecgi.global/sites/default/files/working_papers/documents/finalhowellniessneryermack.pdf
14. Dimitropoulos, G.: The Law of Blockchain (2020)

15. El Maknouzi, M.E., Sadok, H.: Regulation of virtual currencies in the United Arab Emirates: accounting for the emerging public/private distinction. Dev. Studies Res. **8**(1), 346–355 (2021). https://doi.org/10.1080/21665095.2021.1980413
16. Zetzsche, D.A., Buckley, R.P., Arner, D.W., FFhr, L.: The ICO gold rush: it's a scam, it's a bubble, it's a super challenge for regulators. SSRN J. (2017). https://doi.org/10.2139/ssrn.3072298
17. El Alami, A., Sadok, H., Elhaoud, N.: Cloud computing & the organizational performance different approach of assessment. In: 2015 International Conference on Cloud Technologies and Applications (CloudTech), Marrakech, Morocco, pp. 1–5 (2015). https://doi.org/10.1109/CloudTech.2015.7337007
18. Landauean, P., Genais, A.: Les crypto-monnaies. Ministère de l'Economie et des Finances (2018)
19. Financial Stability Board: Crypto-Asset Markets: Potential Channels for Future Financial Stability Implications (2018)
20. Benkhayat, A., Manouar, A., Sadok, H.: Firm business strategy and IT strategy alignment:a proposal of a new model. In: 2015 Xth International Scientific and Technical Conference "Computer Sciences and Information Technologies" (CSIT), Lviv, Ukraine, pp. 172-178 (2015). https://doi.org/10.1109/STC-CSIT.2015.7325460.
21. Hinman, W.: Digital Asset Transactions: When Howey Met Gary (Plastic), https://www.sec.gov/news/speech/speech-hinman-061418. Accessed 14 Jan 2023
22. International Monetary Fund: Global Financial Stability Report April 2018: A Bumpy Road Ahead (2018)
23. Demertzis, M., Wolff, G.B.: The Economic Potential and Risks of Crypto Assets: is a Regulatory Framework Needed? (2018)
24. Deng, H., Huang, R.H., Wu, Q.: The Regulation of Initial Coin Offerings in China: Problems, Prognoses and Prospects (2018). https://papers.ssrn.com/abstract=3245875
25. Momtaz,P.P.: Initial Coin Offerings. SSRN J. (2018). https://doi.org/10.2139/ssrn.3166709
26. Benedetti, H.E., Kostovetsky, L.: Digital tulips? returns to investors in initial coinofferings. SSRN J. (2018). https://doi.org/10.2139/ssrn.3182169
27. Liu, Y., Tsyvinski, A.: Risks and Returns of Cryptocurrency (2018)
28. Sadok, H.: How can inclusive growth be enabled from financial technology? Int. J. Business Performance Manage. **22**(2–3) (2021). https://doi.org/10.1504/IJBPM.2021.116410
29. Mahboub, H., Sadok, H.: Implementing enterprise digital transformation: a contribution to conceptual framework design. Nankai Bus. Review Int. **14**(1), 35–50 (2023). https://doi.org/10.1108/NBRI-06-2022-0067

Does Digital Financial Inclusion Affect Economic Growth? New Insights from MENA Region

Amal Ben Abdallah, Hamdi Becha, Maha Kalai, and Kamel Helali[✉]

Faculty of Economics and Management of Sfax, University of Sfax, Airport Road Km 4.5, B.P.
1088-3018 Sfax, Tunisia
kamel.helali@fsegs.usf.tn

Abstract. Digital financial services have been a key driver of finance inclusion in recent years more specially from 2014 in Africa and continue to accelerate since the onset of the coronavirus disease pandemic in China. Although these terms have attracted growing attention from academics and policy makers, the effect of digital financial inclusion on economic growth has not been studied sufficiently. Therefore, this research examines the association between traditional financial services, digital financial inclusion and economic growth on a set of 14 of the Middle East and North Africa (MENA) countries over the period 2000–2021. Using the PMG-ARDL and GMM-System approaches, to capture both short- and long-term relationships concurrently by STATA 17 and Winrats 9.0, we find that the exogenous component of digital financial inclusion is positively correlated with GDP per capita, concluding that digital financial inclusion was better than traditional financial services. Empirical estimates of internet users and mobile subscriptions are key determinants of digital financial inclusion in this region. The results of this research will then be used to inform policy recommendations in areas related to the digitization of financial services to promote finance inclusion.

JEL Classification: C33 · C36 · G10 · G20 · O30

Keywords: FinTech · digital finance inclusion · finance inclusion · Covid-19 · MENA region

1 Introduction

The coronavirus disease (Covid-19) pandemic has changed the way most people conduct financial transactions, including using digital-based payment systems and using mobile banking firstly in Asia. This is because the use of digital-based payment systems can help break the chain of transmission of Covid-19 (Allam, 2020). In addition, the recent war in Ukraine has left many people from their homes, offices and families. This sad situation will force more people to access their banks, wealth management accounts, insurance companies and more digitally. It can be argued that Financial Technology (FinTech) (technological innovation in the financial sector) community has a chance.

© The Author(s), under exclusive license to Springer Nature Switzerland AG 2023
R. Jallouli et al. (Eds.): ICDEc 2023, LNBIP 485, pp. 195–221, 2023.
https://doi.org/10.1007/978-3-031-42788-6_13

In fact, months after the World Health Organization (WHO) declared a pandemic, leading companies and multilateral institutions began documenting how pandemic restrictions have accelerated digital momentum. Back in 2020, the international consulting firm McKinsey declared: "The post-COVID-19 recovery will be digital". More precisely, the pandemic itself is digital, as increased internet and mobile phone usage has been accompanied by increased infection rates[1].

The prolonged pandemic lockdown has prompted millions of men and women to change the way they pay for groceries or utility bills. They have moved from physical cash payments – considered unsafe in the context of the pandemic due to distance and hygiene measures – to digital payments directly from accounts (by direct transfer, using credit or debit cards, or mobile currency account).

This acceleration in digitization was the most important subject in recent years and noticed by IMF (2019) report. In his working papers, the authors affirmed that Digital Financial Services (DFS), enabled by FinTech, have become a key of financial inclusion in Emerging Markets and Developing Economies (EMDE) (IMF, 2021). It can help overcome often cited barriers to accessing traditional financial services, such as cost, geographic barriers, and information asymmetries (Khera et al., 2022). In addition, the Global Finance Index report (2021) provides a wealth of data on account ownership, usage and financial resilience on a global scale. An analysis of the data reveals two trends that are particularly interesting, given the impact they have already had and their prospects for the future. These are the growth in digital payments recorded against the backdrop of the pandemic, and the relationship between the adoption of digital payments and the use of other financial services[2].

It is very observable that this rise of DFS reflected in the proportion of adult users in developing countries who are using FinTech payments for the first time, as provided by the Global Financial Index (2021) database. Indeed, this phenomenon has been studied empirically for the case of countries (Jack and Suri, 2011, 2014; Tarazi and Breloff, 2010) and regions (Khera et al., 2021 & 2022; Al-Smadi, 2022; Kammoun et al., 2020; Sy et al., 2019; Loukoianova et al., 2019; Blancher, 2019) to provide subjective evidence of how FinTech can improve access to financial services.

In this paper has two main contributions. First, the aim of this research is to investigate the impact of traditional financial services on the economic growth, also, the impact of digital financial inclusion on economic growth across 14 countries of the MENA region by using Pooled Mean Group Auto-Regressive Distributed Lag method (PMG-ARDL) and the Generalized Method of Moment-System estimation (GMM-system) during the period 2000–2021, and second, we examine the main drivers of digital financial inclusion and give some policy implications. We use the digital financial inclusion model developed by Khera et al. (2021). Our objective is to show that digital financial inclusion is more important than traditional financial service uses, but unfortunately, access is limited in certain countries. So, we will therefore find a response to the major follow question: Does digital financial inclusion will improve more economic growth than traditional financial service in the future?

---

[1] Visit the siteweb: https://www.findevgateway.org/fr/blog/2022/07/global-findex.

[2] Visit the siteweb: https://www.worldbank.org/publication/globalfindex.

More precisely, this research focuses on comparison between non-digital and digital economic growth, that is important to acknowledge that non-digital economic growth still plays a significant role in many economies, especially in developing countries.

One justification for studying both non-digital and digital economic growth is that they are not mutually exclusive. In fact, they are often complementary and can work together to drive economic growth. For example, non-digital sectors such as agriculture and manufacturing can benefit from the adoption of digital technologies, such as precision agriculture and Industry 4.0 manufacturing techniques, which can improve productivity and efficiency.

Another reason to study both non-digital and digital economic growth is that they can have different impacts on different segments of the population. Digital economic growth can create new job opportunities in high-tech industries, while non-digital economic growth can create jobs in traditional industries that may be more accessible to those with lower levels of education and skills.

Overall, it is important to study both non-digital and digital economic growth to understand how they can work together to drive economic development, and how different segments of the population can benefit from these different types of growth.

The choice of this country among others is justified by several reasons. First, it is having a low rate of adult account ownership, high financial depth, and a high loan concentration ratio, which limits the amount of financing available to start-ups and small businesses (Emara and El Said, 2021). Second, Demirguc-Kunt et al. (2015) presented that 14% of adults have a bank account compared with an average of 54% in other developing regions. Financial inclusion's gender and youth gap are also bigger in the MENA region than in other developing areas (Lyons and Kass-Hanna, 2021). Finally, governments and policy makers in this region need to intervene and adopt strategies to enhance financial inclusion, thus achieving monetary stability and fostering economic growth (Emara and El Said, 2021; Al-Smadi, 2022).

There is a wealth of literature demonstrating the beneficial effects of financial development on economic expansion (Levine, 2005). According to several recent studies, traditional financial inclusion is positively correlated with both national poverty reduction and economic growth (Beck, Demirguc-Kunt and Levine, 2007). By examining the nexus between traditional financial services, digital financial inclusion and economic growth, our paper adds to this body of literature.

The remainder of this paper has been organized as follows: Sect. 2 presents a review of the literature that has previously verified the nature of the link between financial inclusion, digital financial and economic growth. Then, in Sect. 3, we expose the theoretical framework of the model. The empirical results are presented in Sect. 4. Finally, Sect. 5 is devoted to drawing our main conclusions and suggesting some relevant recommendations.

2 Theoretical Background

This section complements the existing literature on financial development by theoretically and empirically examining the relationship between, for one hand, financial inclusion and economic growth, the digital financial inclusion and economic growth for another hand.

2.1 Financial Inclusion and Economic Growth

By definition, the financial inclusion, "implying better access to and more intensive use of financial services" (Guérineau and Jacolin, 2014), is a multifaceted concept can be discussed within two broad areas which are financial development (financial depth and liquidity) and financial inclusion (financial access) (Lenka, 2022).

However, the basis for understanding the relationship between the financial sector and economic growth can be found firstly in the work of Schumpeter (1911), Shaw (1973) and Mckinnon (1973). Indeed, these fundamental theories state that the financial sector is one of the most important foundations for explaining patterns of economic growth. In allocating the scarce resources available in an economy, the financial sector plays an important role in providing affordable financial services, thereby promoting economic growth (Chen et al., 2021; Ifediora et al., 2022). Furthermore, Fabya (2011) added that the financial sector's ability to provide borrowers with a variety of high quality, low-risk financial instruments will ultimately accelerate economic growth.

Generally, the focus of financial development is the integration of financial markets, institutions, and foreign capital flows to reduce information, enforcement, and transaction costs (Ibrahim and Alagidede, 2018). The most objective of their research is to link the financially underserved to transparent, affordable, and reliable financial services to the benefits of mostly the poor (Sarma, 2015; Siddik et al., 2018).

Another role, the financial development has four economically beneficial functions, namely: (a) reduce risk; (b) mobilize savings; (c) reduce transaction and information costs; and (d) promote specialization (Levine, 2005). Other studies have found that greater financial inclusion has positive effects on growth and reductions in poverty and inequality, we can cite the work of Sahay and Čihák (2020) find that higher financial inclusion in payments is associated with reduced inequality, especially for those at the bottom of the income distribution and when women's financial inclusion is high. Regarding the effect on growth, Sahay et al. (2015) find that for countries with low financial inclusion (25th percentile), increasing financial inclusion to the 75th percentile leads to an average increase in GDP growth rate of 2–3 percentage points. As well, Demirgüç-Kunt et al. (2015) discuss the benefits of financial inclusion in reducing poverty and inequality.

Empirically, the literature is rich in explanations of the link between financial inclusion and economic growth. Several studies report a positive relationship (Inoue and Hamori, 2016 & 2019; Kim et al., 2018a, 2018b; Thomas et al., 2017; Sethi and Acharya (2018); Singh and Stakic, 2021; Huang et al., 2021).

Precisely, Inoue and Hamori (2016) draw our attention to examining the impact of financial access on economic growth in 37 sub-Saharan African nations for the period 2004–2012. The study used the panel dynamic GMM estimator, and the findings revealed a link between real GDP per capita and the quantity of commercial bank branches. Additionally, financial deepening significantly and favorably impacted sub-Saharan Africa's economic growth.

In a major advance, Kim et al. (2018a, 2018b) used dynamic panel estimates, panel vector autoregressive (VAR) technique, impulse-response functions (IRF), and panel Granger causality tests to examine the association between financial inclusion and economic growth in 55 Organization of Islamic Cooperation (OIC) nations. Dynamic panel estimations' findings demonstrated that financial inclusion has a beneficial impact on economic growth.

In the same vein, Thomas et al. (2017) looked into the connection between financial accessibility and economic growth in eight South Asian nations from 2007 to 2015. The results of using the GMM estimators demonstrated that rising financial accessibility resulted in rising income. Furthermore, economic growth in low-income nations was more affected by rising financial access indices than it was in middle-income countries.

In addition, Sethi and Acharya (2018) used the following panel data models: country-fixed effect, random effect, and time fixed effect regressions, panel cointegration, and panel causality tests to examine the effect of financial inclusion on economic growth for 31 developed and developing countries from 2004 to 2010. The findings showed a long-term, positive correlation between financial inclusion and economic growth across the chosen nations, as well as a causal association that worked both ways. The study found that financial inclusion had an impact on economic growth and suggested that, over time, policies that promote financial inclusion will lead to better rates of economic growth.

In all eight South Asian Association for Regional Cooperation (SAARC) nations, Singh and Stakic (2021) looked studied the relationship between the financial inclusion index and economic growth from 2004 to 2017. The Pedroni (2004) panel co-integration test, Fully Modified Ordinary Least Square (FMOLS), and Dynamic Ordinary Least Square (DOLS) methodologies were all used in the study. Financial inclusion and economic growth in the SAARC countries have a long-term association, according to the Pedroni panel co-integration test. The financial inclusion index and a few chosen control variables support economic growth, according to the FMOLS and DOLS coefficients. The Granger causality test also supported the existence of a bi-directional causal relationship between financial inclusion and economic growth.

Similar to this topic, Huang et al. (2021) compared the old and new EU (27) nations between 1995 and 2015 to assess the relationship between financial inclusion and economic progress. The study revealed that financial inclusion is crucial for economic growth and employed FMOLS and panel autoregressive distributed lag (ARDL) models to support its findings. In contrast to high-income and established EU countries, it is more significant for low-income and new EU countries.

More recent evidence like Ifediora et al. (2022), during the period from 2012 to 2018, they used panel data from 22 Sub-Saharan African (SSA) nations to examine the effect of financial inclusion on economic growth. The system Generalized Method of Moments (GMM) is used in the study. We found that the availability dimension of financial inclusion, the penetration dimension of financial inclusion, and the composite financial inclusion (all indicators taken together) have a significant and positive impact on economic growth while the usage dimension of financial inclusion has a small but positive impact on economic growth. Additionally, bank branches and ATMs have a favorable and considerable impact on economic growth, while deposit accounts, outstanding loans, and outstanding deposits have a less significant but nonetheless negative impact.

Using the generalized technique of moments and the Dumitrescu-causality Hurlin's (2012) test, Adekoun and Aga (2021) evaluate the relationship between financial inclusion and economic growth in Sub-Saharan African (SSA) nations over the years 2004–2017. A main component analysis was used to create a composite financial inclusion index based on the multidimensionality of the financial inclusion metrics. The findings demonstrate that financial inclusion significantly boosts economic growth in SSA nations. According to other research, there is a short-term causal relationship between economic growth and financial inclusion. To increase equitable growth across the continent, policymakers should place a strong emphasis on initiatives that promote access to high-quality, reasonably priced financial services and products.

Recent evidence, Azimi (2022) uses a large number of panels categorized by income and geographical levels from 2002 to 2020 to examine the effects of financial inclusion on economic growth from a global viewpoint. A long-term association between economic growth, financial inclusion, and the control variables in the complete panel, income-level, and regional economies is supported by the panel cointegration test results. Additionally, analyze the effects of financial inclusion and the control predictors on economic growth using GMM-System estimators. The findings unmistakably show that financial inclusion greatly boosts economic growth across all panels, suggesting that financial inclusion is a useful instrument for promoting rapid global economic growth.

2.2 Digital Finance and Economic Growth

In cross-country studies of financial development and economic growth nexus, leading to two main growth models, like, exogenous growth model and endogenous growth model. However, the exogenous growth models emphasize the importance of labor productivity (Domar, 1946) and exogenous technological progress (Solow, 1956) as key factors explaining global growth differences. On the other hand, the exogenous growth models have been criticized for failing to recognize efficiencies such as macroeconomic conditions, appropriate regulatory frameworks, and institutions that convert savings into investment (Chirwa and Odhiambo, 2018; Levine et al., 2000; Levine, 1999). Indeed, the endogenous growth model is interested in innovation capital, intellectual capital and human capital to explain differences in economic growth between countries and time (Inoue and Hamori, 2019). This new theory of economic growth assumes that technological progress occurs through innovation; in the form of new products, processes and markets, many of which are determined by economic activity (Ifediora et al., 2022).

These researches are restricted to determining the causal relationship between economic growth and financial development. There is little evidence of a causal link between financial inclusion, and particularly digital financial inclusion, and economic outcomes. The purpose of this study is to close this evidence gap by presenting the data on how the use of digital financial affects economic growth.

However, the digital financial inclusion is the fourth stage of the financial revolution after developing microcredit, microfinance, and financial inclusion (Wang and He, 2020). Compared to financial inclusion, digital financial inclusion places more importance on technology to broaden the accessibility to formal financial services. Furthermore, in the last decade, Financial Technology (FinTech), also known as digital finance, has developed and grown popular in bringing innovative financial services and products to people via mobile phones, personal computers, the internet, and cards (Manyika et al., 2016) which has introduced innovative means of interaction and communication between borrowers and lenders.

Until now, the digital financial services are revolutionizing the payment, savings, and lending environments, especially in the context of financial inclusion (Ozili, 2018). The FinTech growth may successfully reduce transaction costs and ease information asymmetry within the financial system due to more customer testing, information sharing and risk assessment that are made easier. It therefore boosts entrepreneurship (Honglei, 2021; Yin et al., 2019), increases household income (Zhang et al., 2020), increases household consumption (Li et al., 2020), encourages international trade (Fernández-Olit et al., 2020), improves financial development (Fu et al., 2020; Meifang et al., 2018) with these proxies widely documented to contribute to economic growth (Appiah-Otoo and Song, 2022; Peia and Roszbach, 2015; Hook and Singh, 2014).

According to Gomber et al. (2017), the digital financial services includes innovative financial products, finance related software and a great way of interaction and communication with the customers and such services are provided by FinTech and other finance related service providers. It can transform people from cash-based to cashless transactions where they need a mobile phone which is owned by almost 50% of people in the developing countries (World Bank, 2013). Most of the countries of the world are turning to this service. According to Pénicaud and Katakam (2019), more than 80 countries in the world are launching digital financial services through mobile phones as it brings welfare to the people (CGAP, 2015).

In a major advance, Nizam et al. (2020) analyzed the relationship between economic growth and financial inclusion in industrialized and developing countries. The level of financial inclusion was measured for each country using a new financial inclusion index. The authors examined the role of financial inclusion in economic development using a cross-sectional threshold regression approach. The results of the research show that financial inclusion and economic growth have substantial non-monotonic links. This study should encourage economists and the financial sector to improve financial inclusion to promote sustainable economic growth.

Thus, not only can digital financial inclusion be thought to promote economic growth, but also the nature and level of these inclusions can shape the relationship between financial development and economic growth. Therefore, we can formulate our research hypothesis as follows:

Hypothesis 1: Digital financial inclusion positively affects economic growth in MENA countries.

In fact, digital financial inclusion can refer to the use of digital technologies, such as mobile banking and e-wallets, to provide access to financial services to individuals and small businesses who are excluded from traditional financial systems. The impact of digital financial inclusion on economic growth in MENA (Middle East and North Africa) countries can be dependent on various factors, including the level of internet and mobile phone penetration, the regulatory environment, and the level of financial literacy.

While it is possible that digital financial inclusion can have a positive impact on economic growth, it is important to consider potential challenges, such as cybersecurity risks and the potential for exclusion of vulnerable populations who lack access to digital technologies.

Ultimately, the hypothesis would need to be tested using rigorous research methods and data analysis to determine the relationship between digital financial inclusion and economic growth in MENA countries.

3 Data and Methodology

3.1 Data Description and Model Specification

Using an annual panel time-series data for 14 emerging economies of the MENA region namely Tunisia, Algeria, Morocco, Egypt, Iran, Syria, Lebanon, Iraq, Libya, Saudi Arabia, Kuwait, the UAE, Jordan, and Oman, with datasets collected from the International Monetary Fund's (IMF) Financial Access Survey (FAS), the International Union of Telecommunication (IUT), and the World Development Indicators (WDI) databases for the period 2000–2021, this study investigates how digital financial inclusion uses can be increasing economic growth. The considered periodicity is based on data availability of the indicators of digital financial inclusion by developed by Khera et al. (2021).

Consistent with previous literature discussed in Sect. 2, we use the Cobb–Douglas production function to analyze firstly the impact of traditional financial services and other control variables, on economic growth (Eq. 1) and the impact of digital financial inclusion and other control variables on economic growth (Eq. 2). Our model is presented and investigated according to Al-Smadi (2022), Khera et al. (2022), Khera et al. (2021), Andiansyah (2021), Shen et al. (2021), and Sahay et al. (2020). So, the two estimated models are specified and written symbolically as follows:

$$LnGDPC_{it} = \beta_0 + \beta_1 LnPOP_{it} + \beta_2 LnGFCF_{it} + \beta_3 LnFDI_{it} + \beta_4 LnTrade_{it} + \beta_5 LnCPI_{it} + \beta_6 LnATM_{it} \\ + \beta_7 LnCR_{it} + \varepsilon_{1it} \tag{1}$$

$$LnGDPC_{it} = \beta_0 + \beta_1 LnPOP_{it} + \beta_2 LnGFCF_{it} + \beta_3 LnFDI_{it} + \beta_4 LnTrade_{it} + \beta_5 LnCPI_{it} + \beta_6 LnIU_{it} \\ + \beta_7 LnMS_{it} + \varepsilon_{2it} \tag{2}$$

where $LnGDPC_{it}$ represents the logarithm of the real GDP per capita rate, $LnGFCF_{it}$ is the stock of physical capital measured by gross fixed capital formation (% of GDP) in logarithm; $LnPOP_{it}$ represents the logarithm of the Labor force, $LnFDI_{it}$ expresses the logarithm of foreign direct investment (% of GDP), $LnTrade_{it}$ represents the logarithm of trade openness, $LnCPI_{it}$ is the logarithm of the Consumer Price Index (base = 100), $LnATM_{it}$ is the logarithm of the Automated Teller Machine per 100,000 adults, $LnMS_{it}$ represents the logarithm of the Mobile Subscription per 100,000 adults $LnIU_{it}$ is the logarithm of the Internet Users (% of population), $LnCR_{it}$ represents the logarithm of Domestic Credit to private sector (% of GDP), and the ε_{1it} and ε_{2it} are the associated error term assumed as in the usual fashion to be serially uncorrelated with zero mean and constant variance. The parameters of the model measure the sensitivity of the variables to the economic growth. We summarize all these variables in Table 1.

Table 1. Variable definitions

Variables	Definition	Source
LnGDPC	Gross Domestic Product per capita	WDI
LnPOP	Labor force, total	WDI
LnGFCF	Gross fixed capital formation (% of GDP)	WDI
LnFDI	Foreign direct investment, net inflow (% of GDP)	WDI
LnTrade	Sum of exportations and importations (% of GDP)	WDI
LnCPI	Consumer Price Index (2010 = 100)	WDI
LnATM	Automated Teller Machine (per 100,000 adults)	FAS
LnMS	Mobile Subscription (per 100,000 adults)	ITU
LnIU	Internet Users (% of population)	ITU
LnCR	Domestic credit to private sector (% of GDP)	WDI

3.2 Research Method

To validate the two-proposed hypotheses of this study, we apply two approaches: the GMM System method (GMM-System) and the Pooled Mean Group Auto-Regressive Distributed Lag method (PMG-ARDL). Several reasons motivate us to use these methods: (i) the number of years (T = 22) is superior than the number of countries (N = 14) (Roodman, 2009; Baltagi, 2005; Bond, 2002); (ii) it produces more efficient estimates by reducing the finite sample bias compared to the difference GMM (D-GMM) estimation method, (Baltagi, 2005); (iii) it also resolves the potential bias associated with the possible correlation between "country-fixed effects" and the error term. This avoids a problem of correlation between this term and the explanatory variables; (iv) it permits resolving the potential issue of endogeneity of the independent variables with the dependent variable, especially since in our specifications, the explanatory variables are of macroeconomic and institutional nature, hence the risk of reverse causality with economic growth. For example, previous studies suggest that two-ways causation may exist between, for example, traditional financial services and economic growth (e.g., Kammoun et al., 2020; Song et al., 2022), digital financial inclusion and economic growth (e.g., Al-Smadi, 2022; Khera et al., 2022). Moreover, omitted variable bias may be another cause of endogeneity. For this reason, GMM-System is suggested to address this issue and ensure the reliability of our estimate. A two-step GMM-System is used because it addresses concerns of heteroscedasticity.

The Pooled Mean Group-Autoregressive Distributed Lag (PMG-ARDL) model, which Pesaran et al. (1999) recommended for analysis, was used in this investigation. The pooling and averaging of the coefficient over the cross-sectional units is related to it. In order to determine the ideal lag duration for each variable, this model estimates (n + 1)^k number of regressions. k is the number of variables in the estimation, and n is the total number of lags that were employed. Choosing an adequate lag using measures like the Schwarz Bayesian criterion (SBC) and the Akaike information criterion (AIC).

The following short-term model was estimated if there was proof of cointegration among the variables:

$$\Delta LnGDPC_{it} = b_{01} + b_{11}LnGDPC_{it-1} + b_{21}LnPOP_{it-1} + b_{31}LnGFCF_{it-1} + b_{41}LnFDI_{it-1} + b_{51}LnTrade_{it-1}$$
$$+ b_{61}LnCPI_{it-1} + b_{71}LnATM_{it-1} + b_{81}LnCR_{it-1} + \sum_{j=1}^{p} a_{11j}\Delta LnGDPC_{it-j} + \sum_{j=0}^{q} a_{21j}\Delta LnPOP_{it-j}$$
$$+ \sum_{j=0}^{q} a_{31j}\Delta LnGFCF_{it-j} + \sum_{j=0}^{q} a_{41j}\Delta LnFDI_{it-j} + \sum_{j=0}^{q} a_{51j}\Delta LnTrade_{it-j} + \sum_{j=0}^{q} a_{61j}\Delta LnCPI_{it-j}$$
$$+ \sum_{j=0}^{q} a_{71j}\Delta LnATM_{it-j} + \sum_{j=0}^{q} a_{81j}\Delta LnCR_{it-j} + u_{1it} \tag{3}$$

$$\Delta LnGDPC_{it} = b_{02} + b_{12}LnGDPC_{it-1} + b_{22}LnPOP_{it-1} + b_{32}LnGFCF_{it-1} + b_{42}LnFDI_{it-1} + b_{52}LnTrade_{it-1}$$
$$+ b_{62}LnCPI_{it-1} + b_{72}LnIU_{it-1} + b_{82}LnMS_{it-1} + \sum_{j=1}^{p} a_{12j}\Delta LnGDPC_{it-j} + \sum_{j=0}^{q} a_{22j}\Delta LnPOP_{it-j}$$
$$+ \sum_{j=0}^{q} a_{32j}\Delta LnGFCF_{it-j} + \sum_{j=0}^{q} a_{52j}\Delta LnFDI_{it-j} + \sum_{j=0}^{q} a_{52j}\Delta LnTrade_{it-j} + \sum_{j=0}^{q} a_{62j}\Delta LnCPI_{it-j}$$
$$+ \sum_{j=0}^{q} a_{72j}\Delta LnIU_{it-j} + \sum_{j=0}^{q} a_{82j}\Delta LnMS_{it-j} + u_{2it} \tag{4}$$

The short run dynamics' ARDL specification can be obtained by building an error correction model with the following structures:

$$\Delta LnGDPC_{it} = \beta_{01} + \delta_1 ECT_{1it} + \sum_{j=1}^{p} \beta_{11j}\Delta LnGDPC_{it-j} + \sum_{j=0}^{q_1} \beta_{21j}\Delta LnPOP_{it-j}$$
$$+ \sum_{j=0}^{q_2} a_{31j}\Delta LnGFCF_{it-j} + \sum_{j=0}^{q_3} \beta_{41j}\Delta LnFDI_{it-j} + \sum_{j=0}^{q_4} \beta_{51j}\Delta LnTrade_{it-j}$$
$$+ \sum_{j=0}^{q_4} \beta_{61j}\Delta LnCPI_{it-j} + \sum_{j=0}^{q_4} \beta_{71j}\Delta LnATM_{it-j} + \sum_{j=0}^{q_4} \beta_{81j}\Delta LnCR_{it-j} + v_{1it} \tag{5}$$

$$\Delta LnGDPC_{it} = \beta_{02} + \delta_2 ECT_{2it} + \sum_{j=1}^{p} \beta_{12j}\Delta LnGDPC_{it-j} + \sum_{j=0}^{q_1} \beta_{22j}\Delta LnPOP_{it-j}$$
$$+ \sum_{j=0}^{q_2} a_{32j}\Delta LnGFCF_{it-j} + \sum_{j=0}^{q_3} \beta_{42j}\Delta LnFDI_{it-j} + \sum_{j=0}^{q_4} \beta_{52j}\Delta LnTrade_{it-j}$$
$$+ \sum_{j=0}^{q_4} \beta_{62j}\Delta LnCPI_{it-j} + \sum_{j=0}^{q_4} \beta_{72j}\Delta LnIU_{it-j} + \sum_{j=0}^{q_4} \beta_{82j}\Delta LnMS_{it-j} + v_{2it} \tag{6}$$

In order to check for a cointegration relationship between the study variables, the Autoregressive Distributed Lag (ARDL) approach was used to achieve the paper's goal.

When compared to previous single cointegration processes like Engle and Granger (1987) and Johansen and Juselius (1990), this strategy was thought to be a better econometric model in the existing literature.

3.3 Variables Description

Before addressing the economic and empirical analysis of the co-integration relationship between the variables, it is necessary to begin with a descriptive analysis of the main variables used. To highlight our objective, in a first step, we present the descriptive statistics of the various variables transformed into logarithm in Table 2. Moreover, it should be pointed out that, based on the results, all the series show the presence of a serial autocorrelation problem so the added value of the Born and Breitung (2016) test is less than 5% for 2 lags.

Table 2. Summary of the variables statistics in logarithm

Designations	LnGDPC	LnPOP	LnGFCF	LnFDI	LnTrade	LnCPI	LnATM	LnCR	LnIU	LnMS
Mean	8.813	15.450	3.032	0.133	4.340	4.622	2.652	3.611	2.946	3.932
SD	1.032	1.004	0.395	1.891	0.358	0.451	1.273	0.957	1.447	1.437
Maximum	6.555	17.248	3.763	3.158	5.152	6.937	4.518	4.846	4.605	5.400
Minimum	6.556	13.600	1.071	-6.907	3.409	2.900	-1.283	-0.059	-2.364	-2.577
Median	8.476	15.538	3.084	.439	4.381	4.609	3.075	3.969	3.309	4.394
Kurtosis	2.343	1.881	7.198	8.080	2.686	8.742	2.936	5.108	4.536	8.413
Skewness	0.300	0.107	−1.629	−2.041	−0.093	0.696	−0.780	−1.420	−1.282	2.216
Coefficient of variation	0.117	0.0650	0.130	14.227	0.082	0.097	0.480	0.265	0.491	0.365
Jarque-Bera (JB) test	10.120	16.650	362.60	545	1.713	448.100	31.330	160.700	114.700	628.400
JB Probability	0.006	0.000	0.000	0.000	0.425	0.000	0.000	0.000	0.000	0.000
Born-Breitung (BB) test	28.620	14.910	15.200	4.460	22.860	6.140	10.400	11.500	37.950	14.230
BB p-value	0.000	0.001	0.001	0.108	0.000	0.046	0.006	0.003	0.000	0.001
Observations	308	308	308	308	308	308	308	308	308	308

Notes: JB represents the Jarque and Bera (1987) statistic; BB represents the Born and Breitung (2016) statistic

To describe their link in the following subsection, we will attempt in what follows to proceed to a statistical description of the various variables. First, we will interpret the main descriptive statistics of the different variables presented in Table 2. Indeed, after visualizing the data, we see that most of them are asymmetric left-spread and have the leptokurtic shape. In addition, we reject the hypothesis of the normality of the series through the test of Jarque and Bera (1987) except that the variable LnTrade accept the hypothesis of the normality. Referring to the data autocorrelation test of panel Born and Breitung (2016), it is quite clear that all the variables have serial autocorrelation problems.

3.4 Study of Stationary: The Unit Root Test with Rupture

One of the central problems of panel unit root testing concerns the form of heterogeneity of the model used to test the unit root. Indeed, and in general, the simplest form of heterogeneity is that of assuming the presence of variables specific to each individual. We are of course talking about modelling with individual effects (defined in a fixed or random way), which reflects heterogeneity only on average but which retains the hypothesis of homogeneity of the other parameters of the model and in particular of the autoregressive root. In particular, this modelling is the one that will be used for the first unit root tests by Levin and Lin (1992). But very quickly, this whole conception of heterogeneity restricted solely to individual effects or to deterministic tendencies became implausible in the case of macroeconomic applications. On the other hand, and because of the various disturbances observed in the various series, it is wise to look for a dynamic relationship between the different variables. For all these reasons, we tested the presence of a unit root by means of the tests of Levin et al. (2002), Im et al. (2003) and Hadri (2000) in level and in first difference in the Table 3.

According to this table, all cycles failed all three-unit root tests (LLC, IPS, and Hadri). Obviously, the tests of LLC and IPS remains the most appropriate since all the series reveal the presence of unit roots in level (rejection H_0). Instead, this same series accepts the hypothesis of the stationarity of the first-order differential. We can therefore consider that all the series are integrated of order 1 (I(1)). The same the same result was found by using the test of Karavias and Tzavalis (2014). According to the Table 4 bellow, the results present that all variables are stationary in first difference while giving the dates of rupture caused by economic, financial and health shocks.

Table 3. The unit root tests without Break

Variables	In level				In first difference			
	LLC	IPS	Hadri	Decision	LLC	IPS	Hadri	Decision
LnGDPC	-2.845^{***}	0.409	30.807	NS	-4.915^{***}	-5.601^{***}	-0.706^{***}	S
LnPOP	-4.099^{***}	-0.385	45.816	NS	-3.432^{***}	-3.611^{***}	9.610	S
LnGFCF	-0.629	0.938	19.460	NS	-4.534^{***}	-7.795^{***}	-0.757^{***}	S
LnFDI	-2.820^{***}	-4.194^{***}	20.142	NS	-8.131^{***}	-10.944^{***}	-2.393^{***}	S
LnTRADE	-2.973^{***}	-1.008	20.132	NS	-7.100^{***}	-8.153^{***}	-0.601^{***}	S
LnCPI	0.729	7.589	44.648	NS	-2.459^{***}	-3.646^{***}	10.972	S
LnATM	-3.814^{***}	-0.300	45.237	NS	-2.655^{***}	-5.164^{***}	2.261	S
LnCR	-3.559^{***}	0.945	40.459	NS	-8.846^{***}	-6.184^{***}	0.141^{***}	S
LnIU	-9.506^{***}	-6.566^{***}	42.249	NS	-16.373^{***}	-5.885^{***}	12.016	S
LnMS	-10.151^{***}	-9.049^{***}	32.700	NS	-3.164^{***}	-5.050^{***}	22.148	S

Notes: *, **, *** significant at 10%, 5%, 1%. S denotes stationary; NS denotes non-stationary; LLC refers to the test Levin et al. (2002); IPS refers to the test Im et al. (2003).

Table 4. The unit root test with Break

Variables	In level	In first difference
LnGDPC	-5.202^{***} (2012)	-26.749^{***} (2020)
LnPOP	-12.897^{***} (2020)	-7.532^{***} (2001)
LnGFCF	-10.502^{***} (2020)	-35.707^{***} (2020)
LnFDI	-11.798^{***} (2013)	-31.527^{***} (2020)
LnTrade	-8.282^{***} (2001)	-22.391^{***} (2001)
LnCPI	-11.779^{***} (2020)	-13.092^{***} (2020)
LnATM	-12.826^{***} (2001)	-22.348^{***} (2020)
LnCR	-5.825^{***} (2001)	-19.943^{***} (2001)
LnIU	-19.113^{***} (2020)	-20.228^{***} (2020)
LnMS	-16.721^{***} (2020)	-15.952^{***} (2020)

Note: *** significance at 1%.

4   Results and Discussion

Since most variables are stationary in the first difference, it is important to study whether there is a cointegration relationship between them. To do this, we proceed directly to the cointegration tests between the different variables of the two macroeconomic models. In order to empirically analyze the long-term relationships and short-term dynamic interactions between the variables, we apply the PMG-ARDL and the GMM-sys models.

4.1   Cointegration and Dependence Tests on Panel Data

It is important to emphasize the fact that the presence of a cointegrating relationship allow to increase the acceptability of the estimated results for policy making. Therefore, it is essential to confirm the possibility of a cointegrating relationship between the series before testing the models. Thus, we perform Kao (1999), Pedroni (2004) and Westerlund (2007). According to these tests (see Table 5), we can affirm that there is a cointegrating relationship for all the variables of our models.

Table 5. Cointegration tests

	M_1		M_2	
Tests	Value (p-value)	Decision	Value (p-value)	Decision
Kao (1999)	1.109 (0.134)	No Cointegration	0.199 (0.421)	No Cointegration
Pedroni (2004)	-1.838 (0.033)	Cointegration	0.033 (0.062)	Cointegration
Westerlund (2007)	1.398 (0.081)	Cointegration	2.167 (0.015)	Cointegration

For many researchers, cross-sectional dependence may exist within and across coun-tries and regional economies following the globalization of the world economy (Bilgili et al., 2017; Dong et al., 2018a, 2018b; Shahbaz et al., 2017a, 2017b; Shahbaz et al., 2018). In addition, the results of unit root and panel cointegration tests are likely to have substantial size distortions if cross-sectional dependence is ignored (Atasoy, 2017; O'Connell, 1998).

Table 6. Cross-dependence test

Tests	M_1	M_2	Decision
Friedman (1937)	30.606 (0.003)	25.904 (0.017)	Dependence
Breusch-Pagan (1980)	133.5 (0.002)	115.71 (0.041)	Dependence
Frees (1995 & 2004)	2.729 (0.000)	2.601 (0.000)	Dependence
Pesaran et al. (2008)	2.406 (0.016)	2.742 (0.006)	Dependence

Therefore, to test for cross-sectional dependence, the Lagrange tests proposed by (Breusch and Pagan, 1980; Frees, 1995; Friedman, 1937; Pesaran et al., 2008) are used. These tests were essential to discover the frequent occurrence of shocks in the cross-sectional aspect of the longitudinal data set. The results of Table 6 denotes a collapse to reject the null hypothesis of cross-sectional independence.

4.2 PMG-ARDL Results

With regard to Eq. 5 and Eq. 6 above, Table 7 shows the short-term estimation, the recall power of the ECM model as well as the series of diagnoses relating to the validity of the two models at the time of the ARDL approach.

With regards to the results of the short-term in M_1 shown by ARDL(1,1,0,1,0,3,3,1) with unrestricted constant and unrestricted trend, the error correction term ECT_{it-1}, is statistically significant and negative, and this proves the presence of a cointegrating relationship between the variables of the short-term model. In particular, the estimated value of ECT_{it-1} is equal to −0.760, which means that the speed of adjustment of the long-term equilibrium in response to the imbalance caused by the short- term shocks of the previous period is trimmed to 76%. In other words, this coefficient associated with the strength of the recall allows us to conclude that the shocks on economic growth in the MENA region are adjusted to 76%, which entails that the imbalance between the desired level and the actual level of economic growth is resolved by 76%. This implies that a shock to economic growth is fully absorbed after 1 year 3 months and 24 days. While, the second panel (M_2) clarifies the effects of the variables of digital financial inclusion on GDPC. Indeed, the most appropriate model is represented by an ARDL(2,1,0,0,0,0,5,1) with unrestricted constant and without trend In the short term, we see the positive and significant effect of all variables on economic growth but the CPI variable has the inverse impact. In addition, the result of the error correction model is statistically significant and negative, either 34%, which proves that there is an integration relationship between the

Table 7. Short-term ARDL estimation

Variables	M_1	M_2
	ARDL(1,1,0,1,0,3,3,1)	ARDL(2,1,0,0,0,0,5,1)
Constant	1.671 (0.003)	-8.632^* (1.890)
$LnGDPC_{it-1}$	$-0.449^{***}(-5.011)$	$-0.497^{***}(4.998)$
$LnPOP_{it-1}$	$0.326^{**}(2.615)$	0.241^* (1.810)
$LnGFCF_{it-1}$	$0.161^{**}(2.150)$	$0.101^{**}(2.085)$
$LnTrade_{it-1}$	$0.112^{**}(2.608)$	$0.098^{**}(2.006)$
$LnCPI_{it-1}$	$-0.129 (-0.627)$	$-0.410 (-0.208)$
$LnFDI_{it-1}$	0.411^{**} (2.338)	$0.315^{**}(2.108)$
$LnATM_{it-1}$	$0.247^{***}(4.118)$	-
$LnCR_{it-1}$	$0.061^{**}(2.274)$	-
$LnIU_{it-1}$	-	$0.262^{**}(2.520)$
$LnMS_{it-1}$	-	0.482^* (1.686)
$\Delta LnGDPC_{it-1}$	$0.272^{***}(4.835)$	$0.148^{**}(2.290)$
$\Delta LnGDPC_{it-2}$	-	$0.202^{***}(3.191)$
$\Delta LnPOP_{it}$	$-0.0004 (-1.848)$	$-0.0002 (0.735)$
$\Delta LnPOP_{it-1}$	$-0.0004 (-1.610)$	$-0.0001 (-0.522)$
$\Delta LnGFCF_{it}$	$-0.596^{***}(-2.925)$	$-0.558^{***}(2.581)$
$\Delta LnTrade_{it}$	$0.356^{***}(4.249)$	$0.423^{***}(4.590)$
$\Delta LnTrade_{it-1}$	$-0.274^{***}(7.293)$	-
$\Delta LnCPI_{it}$	$-2.724 (-0.948)$	$-0.262 (-0.855)$
$\Delta LnFDI_{it}$	0.388 (0.931)	0.521 (1.082)
$\Delta LnFDI_{it-1}$	0.387 (0.976)	-
$\Delta LnFDI_{it-2}$	0.386 (0.963)	-
$\Delta LnFDI_{it-3}$	0.574 (1.549)	-
$\Delta LnATM_{it}$	0.346 (1.280)	-
$\Delta LnATM_{it-1}$	$-0.044 (-0.162)$	-
$\Delta LnATM_{it-2}$	$-1.039^{***}(-3.546)$	-
$\Delta LnATM_{it-3}$	$-0.627^*(-1.940)$	-
$\Delta LnCR_{it}$	$-0.409^{***}(-2.824)$	-
$\Delta LnCR_{it-1}$	0.173 (1.158)	-
$\Delta LnIU_{it}$	-	$-0.197 (-0.912)$
$\Delta LnIU_{it-1}$	-	$-0.201 (-0.906)$

(continued)

Table 7. (*continued*)

Variables	M_1	M_2
	ARDL(1,1,0,1,0,3,3,1)	ARDL(2,1,0,0,0,0,5,1)
$\Delta LnIU_{it-2}$	-	$-0.845\ (-0.361)$
$\Delta LnIU_{it-3}$	-	$-0.290\ (-1.178)$
$\Delta LnIU_{it-4}$	-	$0.384\ (1.466)$
$\Delta LnIU_{it-5}$	-	$0.575^{*}\ (1.910)$
$\Delta LnMS_{it}$	-	$0.126\ (1.627)$
$\Delta LnMS_{it-1}$	-	$-0.715\ (-0.986)$
Trend	$-0.589^{***}(-2.606)$	-
ECT_{it-1}	$-0.760^{***}(-5.716)$	$-0.342^{**}(-2.141)$
ARCH Test	2.934 [0.710]	6.829 [0.233]
LM test	4.876 [0.090]	1.115 [0.291]
Ramsey RESET test	2.624 [0.106]	2.346 |0.126]

Notes: *, ** and *** significant at 10%, 5% and 1%, respectively. LM test = the Lagrange Multiplier test (Breusch–Godfrey serial correlation). ARCH = the autoregressive conditional heteroscedasticity test. RESET = Ramsey Regression Equation Specification Error Test. (ECT_{it-1}) is the error correction term that shows the speed of adjustment towards long-term equilibrium (this term must be significantly negative in order to guarantee the existence of the long-term relationship). t_statistic in parentheses. P-value in square brackets.

variables of the model. This implies that a shock to economic growth is fully absorbed after almost 3 years.

Likewise, the diagnostic tests results are illustrated above. It was validated that the error terms of the short-run model are free of heteroscedasticity, and have neither serial correlation nor a specification error. The results used to shorten the determination of long-term estimates are shown in Table 8 for the M_1 and M_2.

This table above presents the long-term ARDL estimation of the first model. Thus, the results prove that the variables $LnPOP_{it}$, $LnGFCF_{it}$, $LnTrade_{it}$, $LnFDI_{it}$, $LnATM_{it}$ and $LnCR_{it}$ has a positive and significant effect on $LnGDPC_{it}$. In other words, any increase of 1% of these variables increase GDP per capital by 0.72%, 0.35%, 0.25%, 0.91%,0.55% and 0.13%, respectively.

In fact, financial inclusion as a driver of the economic growth in the long-term (Ali et al., 2021). Moreover, Sahay et al. (2015) argued that better access of corporations and households to different banking services, along with increasing women users of these facilities, has a robust positive impact on economic development. Also, financial inclusion promotes economic development through value creation of small businesses with progressive spillover effects on human development indicators such as health, decrease in inequality, education and reduction in poverty (Agnello et al., 2012; Park and Mercado, 2015; Nanda and Kaur, 2016).

Table 8. Long-term ARDL estimation

Variables	M1		M2	
	Coefficient	t-statistic	Coefficient	t-statistic
Constant	3.720	0.003	-17.366^*	-1.950
$LnPOP_{it}$	0.724^{**}	2.263	0.486^*	1.707
$LnGFCF_{it}$	0.358^{**}	2.150	0.203^{***}	2.085
$LnTrade_{it}$	0.249^{***}	3.135	0.197^{**}	2.262
$LnCPI_{it}$	-0.287	-0.635	-0.824	-0.209
$LnFDI_{it}$	0.915^{***}	2.419	0.634^{**}	2.107
$LnATM_{it}$	0.551^{***}	4.434	-	-
$LnCR_{it}$	0.136^{***}	2.290	-	-
$LnIU_{it}$	-	-	0.527^{**}	2.504
$LnMS_{it}$	-	-	0.970^*	1.669

Note: *, ** and *** significant at 10%, 5% and 1%, respectively.

The second model explains the effect of digital financial inclusion on GDPC. The results of this research show that all coefficient of variables has a positive and significant impact on economic growth except CPI variable have a negative and non-significant effect. In fact, the coefficients of internet users and mobile subscription have a positive and significant effects on economic growth. That is mean that these two variables considered a driver of digital financial inclusion and consequently economic growth (Khera et al., 2021; Al-Smadi, 2022).

4.3 GMM-System Results

After the estimation of the two-model (M_1 and M_2), we can conclude that there are some limitations to using the ARDL model. However, The ARDL approach assumes that there is a co- integration relationship between the variables, and if this assumption is not met, the results of the model may not be reliable. Indeed, the ARDL model is commonly used to model the cointegration relationship between variables, while the GMM-System is often used to model dynamic relationships between variables. Both approaches are well-suited for analyzing long-term relationships in data.

This implication we allow to use the GMM-System method of Arellano and Bover (1995) and Blundell and Bond (1998). In fact, the results used GMM-System to the determination of long-term estimates are shown in Table 9 for the two-models. According to the table below, our consequences of the M_1 and M_2 presents the positive and significant effects of $LnGFCF_{it}$, $LnTrade_{it}$, $LnFDI_{it}$, $LnATM_{it}$, $LnCR_{it}$, $LnIU_{it}$ and $LnMS_{it}$ on economic growth, and the negative and non-significant effect of the CPI variable on economic growth. These results are the same as the estimate by the ARDL model. For $LnPOP_{it}$, its impact is negative in the first model and positive in the second model.

The results of the diagnostic tests of the GMM-System method presented in Table 9 above. In fact, the Arellano and Bond (1991) test for serial autocorrelation of order 1 and

212 A. Ben Abdallah et al.

2 are insignificant, which confirms the conditions of application of the GMM estimator. Moreover, the Hansen (1982) test shows that the instruments are over-identified.

Table 9. Two-step GMM-System estimation

Variables	M_1	M_2
$LnGDPC_{it-1}$	0.841 (0.000)	0.904 (0.000)
$LnPOP_{it}$	−0.081 (0.124)	0.067 (0.007)
$LnGFCF_{it}$	0.115 (0.012)	0.193 (0.042)
$LnTrade_{it}$	0.211 (0.040)	0.099 (0.050)
$LnCPI_{it}$	−0.066 (0.292)	−0.093 (0.202)
$LnFDI_{it}$	0.122 (0.000)	0.019 (0.020)
$LnATM_{it}$	0.116 (0.083)	-
$LnCR_{it}$	0.142 (0.042)	-
$LnIU_{it}$	-	0.217 (0.001)
$LnMS_{it}$	-	0.031 (0.027)
Constant	2.544 (0.094)	3.031 (0.057)
Hansen test	6.03 (1.000)	5.09 (1.000)
AR(1) test	−1.27 (0.204)	−1.40 (0.160)
AR(2) test	1.06 (0.291)	0.89 (0.376)

Note: values in brackets represent the p-values

Furthermore, our findings of both approaches reveals that the development of human capital has a significant and positive effect on economic growth. This positive relationship is due to the capacity benefits associated with funding initiatives designed to build the force of citizens to include in the mainstream economy. Indeed, the results also reveal a positive and significant relationship between economic growth and foreign and domestic investment in the MENA region, an indication of the importance of capital commitment to activities, which promote finance inclusion and real capital accumulation. Therefore, the need for investment increase across economic sectors in the region and consequently economic growth and development.

The MENA region has seen significant growth in digital financial inclusion in recent years, with many initiatives aimed at increasing access to financial services for individuals and small businesses. Here are some statistics illustrating this trend: It is estimated that by 2020, mobile banking penetration in the MENA region will reach around 50%. The number of mobile wallet users in the MENA region is estimated to exceed 100 million in 2020, a significant increase from a few years ago. According to the World Bank (2021), the number of people in the MENA region who have access to formal financial services has increased from the covid-19 pandemic, reaching around 65% in 2020. The use of digital payment methods such as mobile payments and e-wallets is growing rapidly in the MENA region, with more and more merchants accepting these payment methods.

According to the results reported in Table 10 using the causality test of Dumitrescu and Hurlin (2012), there is bidirectional causality between ATM and GDP per capita, CR and GDP per capita, IU and GDP per capita and MS and GDP per capita. In fact, ATM induces a statistically significant positive effect on economic growth.

The ATMs can contribute to economic growth by improving the efficiency and convenience of banking services, which in turn can stimulate economic activity. ATMs can facilitate and streamline the financial activities of businesses and individuals by providing 24/7 access to cash and allowing customers to make deposits and withdrawals without a physical bank branch. This can reduce transaction costs, increase productivity and promote economic growth. On the other hand, economic growth can also encourage the adoption and expansion of ATMs. Increased economic activity is often accompanied by increased demand for banking services, and banks can meet this demand by investing in new ATM infrastructure. In addition, economic growth can also provide the financial resources to develop and maintain ATMs and technical innovations to improve their security and ease of use.

The Credit can be a key driver of economic growth because it provides individuals and businesses with the money they need to invest, grow and innovate. By borrowing money, businesses can invest in new equipment, hire additional labor and develop new products or services. It helps increase productivity, boost output and create economic growth. Similarly, individuals can use loans to finance education, housing or business, which can also stimulate economic activity. On the other hand, economic growth can also stimulate demand for credit as businesses and individuals attempt to take advantage of new opportunities and expand their operations. As economic activity increases, banks and other financial institutions may respond by increasing the supply of credit, which can further stimulate economic growth.

The Internet users can foster economic growth by providing access to new markets and expanding trade and commerce opportunities. With the help of the Internet, businesses can reach customers in new and distant locations, remove barriers to market entry, and expand their customer base. This can increase competition, innovation and growth throughout the economy. In addition, the Internet can also facilitate the exchange of information and ideas, increasing collaboration and information sharing, which can increase innovation and productivity. On the other hand, economic growth can also encourage Internet adoption and expansion. As an economy grows, the demand for connections and access to information often increases, which can lead to investments in Internet infrastructure and the development of new technologies. This, in turn, can increase the use of the Internet as more people access it and more businesses use it to expand their operations.

The Mobile phone subscriptions can stimulate economic growth by providing access to new markets and expanding trade and commerce opportunities. With mobile phones, businesses can reach customers in new and remote locations, eliminate barriers to market entry and expand their customer base. This can increase competition, innovation and growth throughout the economy. Mobile phones can also facilitate financial transactions such as mobile banking and mobile money transfers, which can help increase financial

inclusion and spur economic growth. On the other hand, economic growth can also
encourage the adoption and expansion of cell phone subscriptions. As economies grow,
the demand for connectivity and access to information often increases, which can spur
investment in mobile infrastructure and the development of new technologies. This, in
turn, can lead to an increase in the use of cell phones as more and more people acquire
them and businesses use them to expand their operations.

The results of this research is online with the findings of Jima and Makoni (2023).
In addition, this effect is justified not only by ATM but also by the MS in the form of IU
and CR.

Table 10. Causality test

H₀: no causality		W-bar	Z-bar	Z-bar tilde	Z-bar p-value	Z-bar tilde p-value	Causality
ATM	→ GDPC	4.494	9.244	7.190	0.000	0.000	Yes
GDPC	→ ATM	3.634	6.970	5.356	0.000	0.000	Yes
CR	→ GDPC	2.990	5.264	3.980	0.000	0.000	Yes
GDPC	→ CR	2.996	5.280	3.993	0.000	0.000	Yes
IU	→ GDPC	3.469	6.531	5.002	0.000	0.000	Yes
GDPC	→ IU	1.995	2.634	1.858	0.008	0.063	Yes
MS	→ GDPC	3.442	6.460	4.944	0.000	0.000	Yes
GDPC	→ MS	3.996	7.927	6.127	0.000	0.000	Yes

The growth of digital financial services in the MENA region is driven by several
factors, including increased use of smartphones and the internet, government initiatives
to promote financial inclusion, and efforts by financial institutions to provide digital
financial services to underserved populations. These statistics highlight the significant
progress the MENA region has made in increasing digital financial inclusion, but much
remains to be done to ensure that all individuals and businesses in the region have access
to the financial services they need to succeed.

After conducting our analysis, we can assert that our research hypothesis, which
posits that Digital financial inclusion positively affects economic growth in MENA
countries, has been verified. In particular, we discovered proof that supports the existence
of a favorable and stable correlation between digital financial inclusion and economic
growth in MENA countries.

Digital financial inclusion, which refers to providing individuals and businesses with
access to affordable and convenient financial services through digital channels, has the
potential to positively impact economic growth in the Middle East and North Africa
(MENA) region.

One of the main benefits of digital financial inclusion is that it can help to increase
financial access and usage, particularly among those who are underserved or excluded
from traditional financial services. This can lead to increased savings, investment, and
entrepreneurship, which can contribute to economic growth.

In addition, digital financial inclusion can improve financial stability and efficiency by reducing transaction costs, enhancing transparency and accountability, and promoting financial sector development. These factors can attract more investment and contribute to overall economic growth.

Furthermore, digital financial inclusion can also lead to greater financial literacy and empowerment, which can help individuals and businesses make better financial decisions and improve their economic outcomes.

However, it is important to note that the impact of digital financial inclusion on economic growth may depend on a range of factors, including the regulatory environment, infrastructure, and the availability of digital payment systems. Governments and financial institutions in the MENA region must work together to create an enabling environment that fosters digital financial inclusion and supports sustainable economic growth.

5 Conclusion and Policy Implications

This research aims to analyze the effects of traditional and digital financial inclusion on economic growth for 14 MENA countries between 2000 and 2021 using PMG-ARDL and GMM- sys. The results indicate that digital financial inclusion has a significant effect on economic growth in this region, compared to traditional financial inclusion. In the path to digitalization, MENA countries need to engage in a process of digital financial inclusion to promote economic growth.

Thus, the need for widespread digital infrastructure, and the need to ensure that digital financial services are accessible and affordable for all segments of the population and so digital financial inclusion is a key driver of economic growth in the MENA region, and policymakers can play a critical role in promoting digital financial inclusion by addressing challenges and fostering a supportive environment for digital financial services.

Digital financial services require a robust and reliable digital infrastructure, including access to the internet, mobile phones, and other digital devices. Thus, policymakers can incentivize the development of digital infrastructure, such as through tax incentives for companies that invest in digital infrastructure, to increase access to digital financial services.

Also, financial literacy and education are critical to promoting digital financial inclusion by supporting financial education initiatives, such as providing educational resources and tools, to help people understand the benefits and risks of digital financial services. Moreover, to ensure that digital financial services are accessible, secure, and affordable for all, policymakers can establish regulations and standards for digital financial service providers regarding data protection, cybersecurity, and consumer protection.

Additionally, competition among digital financial service providers can drive innovation and increase access to digital financial services by creating a level playing field for digital financial service providers and removing barriers to entry for new entrants and digital financial inclusion can help to increase digital financial inclusion by bringing together the expertise and resources of government, the private sector, and civil society.

Policymakers can encourage public-private partnerships by providing funding, technical support, and other resources to support digital financial inclusion initiatives.

The work carried out finally has the ambition to lead to new results which are distinguish, in part, from those obtained in other regions of the world.

References

Adedokun, M.W., Ağa, M.: Financial inclusion: a pathway to economic growth in Sub-Saharan African economies. Int. J. Financ. Econ. **28**, 2712–2728 (2021). https://doi.org/10.1002/ijfe.2559

Agnello, L., Mallick, S.K., Sousa, R.M.: Financial reforms and income inequality. Econ. Lett. **116**(3), 583–587 (2012). https://doi.org/10.1016/j.econlet.2012.06.005

Ali, M., Hashmi, S.H., Nazir, M.R., Bilal, A., Nazir, M.I.: Does financial inclusion enhance economic growth? Empirical evidence from the IsDB member countries. Int. J. Financ. Econ. **26**(4), 5235–5258 (2021). https://doi.org/10.1002/ijfe.2063

Allam, A.: Three Essays on Financial Inclusion. Bangor University, United Kingdom (2020)

Al-Smadi, M.O.: Examining the relationship between digital finance and financial inclusion: evidence from MENA countries. Borsa Istanbul Rev. **23**, 464–472 (2022). https://doi.org/10.1016/j.bir.2022.11.016

Andiansyah, F.: The influence of financial inclusion and macroeconomic on foreign direct investment (FDI) flows in the organization of Islamic cooperation (OIC) countries. Optimum: Jurnal Ekonomi dan Pembangunan **11**(1), 71 (2021). https://doi.org/10.12928/optimum.v11i1.4017

Arellano, M., Bover, O.: Another look at the instrumental variable estimation of error-components models. J. Econometrics **68**(1), 29–51 (1995). https://doi.org/10.1016/0304-4076(94)01642-D. http://hdl.handle.net/RePEc:eee:econom:v:68:y:1995:i:1:p:29-51

Arellano, M., Bond, S.: Some tests of specification for panel data: Monte Carlo evidence and an application to employment equations. Rev. Econ. Stud. **58**(2), 277 (1991). https://doi.org/10.2307/2297968

Atasoy, B.S.: Testing the environmental Kuznets curve hypothesis across the US: evidence from panel mean group estimators. Renew. Sustain. Energy Rev. **77**, 731–747 (2017). https://doi.org/10.1016/j.rser.2017.04.050

Azimi, M.N.: New insights into the impact of financial inclusion on economic growth: a global perspective. PLoS ONE **17**(11), 1–25 (2022). https://doi.org/10.1371/journal.pone.0277730

Baltagi, B.H.: Econometric Analysis of Panel Data, 3rd edn. Wiley, New York (2005)

Beck, T., Demirgüç-Kunt, A., Levine, R.: Finance, inequality and the poor. J. Econ. Growth **12**, 27–49 (2007). https://doi.org/10.1007/s10887-007-9010-6

Bilgili, F., Koçak, E., Bulut, Ü., Kuloğlu, A.: The impact of urbanization on energy intensity: panel data evidence considering cross-sectional dependence and heterogeneity. Energy **133**, 242–256 (2017). https://doi.org/10.1016/j.energy.2017.05.121

Blancher, N.: Financial inclusion of small and medium-sized enterprises in the Middle East and Central Asia. IMF Departmental Paper no. 19/02, International Monetary Fund (IMF) (2019)

Blundell, R., Bond, S.: Initial conditions and moment restrictions in dynamic panel data models. J. Econometrics **87**(1), 115–143 (1998). https://doi.org/10.1016/S0304-4076(98)00009-8. http://hdl.handle.net/RePEc:eee:econom:v:87:y:1998:i:1:p:115-143

Bond, S.R.: Dynamic panel data models: a guide to micro data methods and practice. Port. Econ. J. **1**, 141–162 (2002). https://doi.org/10.1007/s10258-002-0009-9

Born, B., Breitung, J.: Testing for serial correlation in fixed-effects panel data models. Economet. Rev. **35**(7), 1290–1316 (2016). https://doi.org/10.1080/07474938.2014.976524

Breusch, T.S., Pagan, A.R.: The Lagrange multiplier test and its applications to model specification in econometrics. Rev. Econ. Stud. **47**(1), 239–253 (1980). https://doi.org/10.2307/2297111

CGAP: What is Digital Financial Inclusion and Why Does it Matter? http://www.cgap.org/blog/what-digital-financialinclusion-and-why-does-it-matter (2015). 10 Mar 2015

Chen, Y., Kumara, E.K., Sivakumar, V.: Investigation of finance industry on risk awareness model and digital economic growth. Ann. Oper. Res. **326**, 15 (2021). https://doi.org/10.1007/s10479-021-04287-7

Chirwa, T.G., Odhiambo, N.M.: Exogenous and endogenous growth models: a critical review. Comp. Econ. Res. Central Eastern Europe **21**(4), 63–84 (2018). https://doi.org/10.2478/cer-2018-0027

Demirgüç-Kunt, A., Klapper, L., Singer, D., Van Oudheusden, P.: The global findex database 2014: Measuring financial inclusion around the world. World Bank Policy Research Working Paper No 7255 (2015)

Domar, E.D.: Capital expansion, rate of growth, and employment. Econometrica J. Econometric Soc. **14**(2), 137–147 (1946). https://doi.org/10.2307/1905364

Dong, K., Hochman, G., Timilsina, G.R.: Are driving forces of CO_2 emissions different across countries? Insights from identity and econometric analyses (Policy Research Working Paper No. 8477). World Bank, Washington, DC (2018a)

Dong, K., Hochman, G., Zhang, Y., Sun, R., Li, H., Liao, H.: CO_2 emissions, economic and population growth, and renewable energy: empirical evidence across regions. Energy Econ. **75**, 180–192 (2018b). https://doi.org/10.1016/j.eneco.2018.08.017

Dumitrescu, E.I., Hurlin, C.: Testing for granger non-causality in heterogeneous panels. Econ. Model. **29**(4), 1450–1460 (2012). https://doi.org/10.1016/j.econmod.2012.02.014

Emara, N., El Said, A.: Financial inclusion and economic growth: the role of governance in selected MENA countries. Int. Rev. Econ. Financ. **75**, 34–54 (2021). https://doi.org/10.1016/j.iref.2021.03.014

Engle, R.F., Granger, C.W.J.: Co-integration and error correction: representation, estimation, and testing. Econometrica **55**(2), 251 (1987). https://doi.org/10.2307/1913236. http://hdl.handle.net/RePEc:ecm:emetrp:v:55:y:1987:i:2:p:251-76

Fabya: Analysis of the influence of financial sector developments on economic growth in Indonesia. Sci. J. Fac. Econ. Manag. (2011). Bogor Agricultural Institute, Indonesia

Fernández-Olit, B., Martín Martín, J.M., González, E.P.: Systematized literature review on financial inclusion and exclusion in developed countries. Int. J. Bank Market. **38**(3), 600–626 (2020). https://doi.org/10.1108/IJBM-06-2019-0203

Frees, E.W.: Longitudinal and Panel Data: Analysis and Applications in the Social Sciences. Cambridge University Press, Cambridge (2004)

Frees, E.W.: Assessing cross-sectional correlation in panel data. J. Econometrics **69**(2), 393–414 (1995)

Friedman, M.: The use of ranks to avoid the assumption of normality implicit in the analysis of variance. J. Am. Stat. Assoc. **32**(200), 675–701 (1937)

Fu, J., Liu, Y., Chen, R., Yu, X., Tang, W.: Trade openness, internet finance development and banking sector development in China. Econ. Model. **91**, 670–678 (2020). https://doi.org/10.1016/j.econmod.2019.12.008

Global Finance Index report: Financial Inclusion, Digital Payment and Resilience in the Age of Covid-19. World Bank, Washington, DC (2021)

Gomber, P., Koch, J.A., Siering, M.: Digital Finance and FinTech: current research and future research directions. J. Bus. Econ. **67**(5), 537–580 (2017). https://doi.org/10.1007/s11573-017-0852-x

Guérineau, S., Jacolin, L.: L'inclusion financière en Afrique subsaharienne: faits stylisés et déterminants. Revue d'économie financière **4**, 57–80 (2014). http://hdl.handle.net/RePEc:hal:journl:halshs-01167301

Hadri, K.: Testing for stationarity in heterogeneous panel data. Econometrics J. **3**(2), 148–161 (2000). https://doi.org/10.1111/1368-423X.00043. https://EconPapers.repec.org/RePEc:ect:emjrnl:v:3:y:2000:i:2:p:148-161

Honglei, G.: Internet finance innovation and entrepreneurship based on classification algorithm. In: Sugumaran, V., Xu, Z., Zhou, H. (eds.) MMIA 2020. AISC, vol. 1234, pp. 729–733. Springer, Cham (2021). https://doi.org/10.1007/978-3-030-51556-0_111

Huang, R., Kale, S., Paramati, S.R., Taghizadeh-Hesary, F.: The nexus between financial inclusion and economic development: Comparison of old and new EU member countries. Econ. Anal. Policy **69**, 1–15 (2021). https://doi.org/10.1016/j.eap.2020.10.007

Ibrahim, M., Alagidede, P.: Effect of financial development on economic growth in sub-Saharan Africa. J. Policy Model. **40**(6), 1104–1125 (2018). https://doi.org/10.1016/j.jpolmod.2018.08.001

Ifediora, C., et al.: Financial inclusion and its impact on economic growth: empirical evidence from sub-Saharan Africa. Cogent. Econ. Financ. **10**(1), 2060551 (2022). https://doi.org/10.1080/23322039.2022.2060551

Im, K.S., Pesaran, M.H., Shin, Y.: Testing for unit roots in heterogeneous panels. J. Econometrics **115**(1), 53–74 (2003). https://EconPapers.repec.org/RePEc:eee:econom:v:115:y:2003:i:1:p:53-74

Inoue, T., Hamori, S.: Financial access and economic growth: evidence from Sub-Saharan Africa. Emerg. Mark. Financ. Trade **52**(3), 743–753 (2016). https://doi.org/10.1080/1540496X.2016.1116282

Inoue, T., Hamori, S.: Financial Inclusion, Remittance Inflows, and Poverty Reduction in Developing Countries: Evidence from Empirical Analyses. WORLD SCIENTIFIC (2019) https://EconPapers.repec.org/RePEc:wsi:wsbook:11231

International Monetary Fund: Fintech: The Experience so Far. IMF Policy, Washington, D.C. (2019)

International Monetary Fund: Is Digital Financial Inclusion Unlocking Growth? IMF Policy, Washington, D.C. (2021)

Jack, W., Suri, T.: Mobile money: The economics of M-PESA, NBER Working Paper, No. 16721, http://hdl.handle.net/RePEc:nbr:nberwo:16721 (2011)

Jack, W., Suri, T.: Risk sharing and transactions costs: evidence from Kenya's mobile money revolution. Am. Econ. Rev. **104**(1), 183–223 (2014). https://EconPapers.repec.org/RePEc:aea:aecrev:v:104:y:2014:i:1:p:183-223

Jarque, C.M., Bera, A.K.: A test for normality of observations and regression residuals. Int. Stat. Rev./Revue Internationale de Statistique **55**(2), 163 (1987). https://doi.org/10.2307/1403192

Jima, M.D., Makoni, P.L.: Causality between financial inclusion, financial stability and economic growth in Sub-Saharan Africa. Sustainability **15**(2), 1152 (2023). https://doi.org/10.3390/su15021152

Johansen, S., Juselius, K.: Maximum likelihood estimation and inference on cointegration–with applications to the demand for money. Oxford Bull. Econ. Stat. **52**(2), 169–210 (1990). https://EconPapers.repec.org/RePEc:bla:obuest:v:52:y:1990:i:2:p:169-210

Kammoun, S., Loukil, S., Loukil, Y.B.R.: The impact of FinTech on economic performance and financial stability in MENA Zone. In: Naifar, N. (ed.) Impact of Financial Technology (FinTech) on Islamic Finance and Financial Stability, pp. 253–277. IGI Global (2020). https://doi.org/10.4018/978-1-7998-0039-2.ch013

Kao, C.: Spurious regression and residual-based tests for cointegration in panel data. J. Econometrics **90**(1), 1–44 (1999). https://EconPapers.repec.org/RePEc:eee:econom:v:90:y:1999:i:1:p:1-44

Karavias, Y., Tzavalis, E.: Testing for unit roots in short panels allowing for a structural break. Comput. Stat. Data Anal. **76**, 391–407 (2014). https://doi.org/10.1016/j.csda.2012.10.014

Khera, P., Ng, M.S.Y., Ogawa, M.S., Sahay, M.R.: Is Digital Financial Inclusion Unlocking Growth? International Monetary Fund (2021)

Khera, P., Ng, S., Ogawa, S., Sahay, R.: Measuring digital financial inclusion in emerging market and developing economies: a new index. Asian Econ. Policy Rev. **17**(2), 213–230 (2022). https://doi.org/10.1111/aepr.12377

Kim, D.-W., Yu, J.-S., Hassan, M.K.: Financial inclusion and economic growth in OIC countries. Res. Int. Bus. Financ. **43**(1), 1–14 (2018a). https://doi.org/10.1016/j.ribaf.2017.07.178

Kim, M., Zoo, H., Lee, H., Kang, J.: Mobile financial services, financial inclusion, and development: a systematic review of academic literature. Electron. J. Inform. Sys. Dev. Countries **84**(5), e12044 (2018b). https://doi.org/10.1002/isd2.12044

Lenka, S.K.: Relationship between financial inclusion and financial development in India: is there any link? J. Public Aff. **22**, e2722 (2022). https://doi.org/10.1002/pa.2722

Levin, A., Lin, C.F.: Unit Root Test in Panel Data: Asymptotic and Finite Sample Properties, University of California at San Diego, Discussion Paper No. 92–93 (1992). https://EconPapers.repec.org/RePEc:eee:econom:v:108:y:2002:i:1:p:1-24

Levin, A., Lin, C.F., Chu, C.S.J.: Unit root tests in panel data: asymptotic and finite-sample properties. J. Econometrics **108**(1), 1–24 (2002). https://EconPapers.repec.org/RePEc:eee:econom:v:108:y:2002:i:1:p:1-24

Levine, R.: Law, finance, and economic growth. J. Financ. Intermediation **8**(1–2), 8–35 (1999). https://EconPapers.repec.org/RePEc:eee:jfinin:v:8:y:1999:i:1-2:p:8-35

Levine, R.: Finance and growth: theory and evidence. Handbook Econ. Growth **1**, 865–934 (2005). http://hdl.handle.net/RePEc:eee:grochp:1-12

Levine, R., Loayza, N., Beck, T.: Financial intermediation and growth: causality and causes. J. Monetary Econ. **46**(1), 31–77 (2000). http://hdl.handle.net/RePEc:eee:moneco:v:46:y:2000:i:1:p:31-77

Li, J., Wu, Y., Xiao, J.J.: The impact of digital finance on household consumption: evidence from China. Econ. Model. **86**, 317–326 (2020). https://doi.org/10.1016/j.econmod.2019.09.027

Loukoianova, E., Davidovic, S., Sullivan, C., Tourpe, H.: Strategy for fintech applications in the Pacific Island countries. IMF Departmental Paper no. 19/14, International Monetary Fund (IMF) (2019)

Lyons, A.C., Kass-Hanna, J.: Financial inclusion, financial literacy and economically vulnerable populations in the Middle East and North Africa. Emerg. Mark. Financ. Trade **57**(9), 2699–2738 (2021). https://doi.org/10.1080/1540496X.2019.1598370

Manyika, J., Lund, S., Bughin, J.: Digital Globalization: The New Era Global Flows. McKinsey Global Institute (2016)

McKinnon, R.I.: Money and Capital in Economic Development. The Brookings Institution, Washington, D.C. (1973)

Meifang, Y., He, D., Xianrong, Z., Xiaobo, X.: Impact of payment technology innovations on the traditional financial industry: a focus on China. Technol. Forecast. Soc. Chang. **135**, 199–207 (2018). https://doi.org/10.1016/j.techfore.2017.12.023

Nanda, K., Kaur, M.: Financial inclusion and human development: a cross-country evidence. Manag. Labour Stud. **41**(2), 127–153 (2016). https://doi.org/10.1177/0258042X16658734

Nizam, R., Karim, Z.A., Rahman, A.A., Sarmidi, T.: Financial inclusiveness and economic growth: new evidence using a threshold regression analysis. Econ. Res.-Ekonomska istraživanja **33**(1), 1465–1484 (2020). https://doi.org/10.1080/1331677X.2020.1748508

O'Connell, P.G.: The overvaluation of purchasing power parity. J. Int. Econ. **44**, 1–19 (1998). https://EconPapers.repec.org/RePEc:eee:inecon:v:44:y:1998:i:1:p:1-19

Ozili, P.K.: Impact of digital finance on financial inclusion and stability. Borsa Istanbul Rev. **18**(4), 329–340 (2018). https://EconPapers.repec.org/RePEc:bor:bistre:v:18:y:2018:i:4:p:329-340

Park, C.Y., Mercado, R.: Financial Inclusion, Poverty, and Income Inequality in Developing Asia (No. 426). Asian Development Bank (2015). http://hdl.handle.net/RePEc:ris:adbewp:0426

Pedroni, P.: Panel cointegration: asymptotic and finite sample properties of pooled time series tests with an application to the PPP hypothesis. Econometric Theory **20**(3), 597–625 (2004). https://EconPapers.repec.org/RePEc:wil:wileco:2004-15

Peia, O., Roszbach, K.: Finance and growth: time series evidence on causality. J. Financ. Stab. **19**, 105–118 (2015). https://doi.org/10.1016/j.jfs.2014.11.005

Pénicaud, C., Katakam, A.: State of the industry 2013: mobile financial services for the unbanked. Gates Open Res. **3**, 14–29 (2019). https://doi.org/10.2139/ssrn.2524220

Pesaran, M.H., Ullah, A., Yamagata, T.: A bias-adjusted LM test of error cross-section independence. Econometrics J. **11**(1), 105–127 (2008). https://EconPapers.repec.org/RePEc:ect:emj rnl:v:11:y:2008:i:1:p:105-127

Pesaran, M.H., Shin, Y., Smith, R.P.: Pooled mean group estimation of dynamic heterogeneous panels. J. Am. Stat. Assoc. **94**(446), 621–634 (1999). https://doi.org/10.2307/2670182

Roodman, D.: A note on the theme of too many instruments. Oxford Bull. Econ. Stat. **71**(1), 135–158 (2009). https://doi.org/10.1111/j.1468-0084.2008.00542.x

Sahay, R., et al.: The Promise of Fintech: Financial Inclusion in the Post COVID-19 Era. IMF Departmental Paper No. 20/09. International Monetary Fund, Washington, D.C. (2020)

Sahay, R., et al.: Financial inclusion: Can it meet multiple macroeconomic goals? IMF Staff Discussion Note. International Monetary Fund (2015)

Sahay, R., Čihák, M.: https://ideas.repec.org/p/imf/imfsdn/2020-001.html. Finance and Inequality, https://ideas.repec.org/s/imf/imfsdn.html. IMF Staff Discussion Notes 2020/001, International Monetary Fund (2020)

Sarma, M.: Measuring financial inclusion. Econ. Bull. **35**(1), 604–611 (2015). http://hdl.handle. net/RePEc:ebl:ecbull:eb-14-00854

Schumpeter, J.A.: The Theory of Economic Development. Harvard University Press, Cambridge (1911)

Sethi, D., Acharya, D.: Financial inclusion and economic growth linkage: some cross country evidence. J. Financ. Econ. Policy **10**(3), 369–385 (2018). https://doi.org/10.1108/JFEP-11-2016-0073

Shahbaz, M., Shahzad, S.J.H., Mahalik, M.K., Sadorsky, P.: How strong is the causal relationship between globalization and energy consumption in developed economies? A country-specific time-series and panel analysis. Appl. Econ. **50**, 1479–1494 (2018). https://doi.org/10.1080/000 36846.2017.1366640

Shahbaz, M., Nasreen, S., Ahmed, K., Hammoudeh, S.: Trade openness–carbon emissions nexus: the importance of turning points of trade openness for country panels. Energy Econ. **61**, 221–232 (2017a). https://doi.org/10.1016/j.eneco.2016.11.008

Shahbaz, M., Sarwar, S., Chen, W., Malik, M.N.: Dynamics of electricity consumption, oil price and economic growth: global perspective. Energy Policy **108**, 256–270 (2017b). https://doi.org/10.1016/j.enpol.2017.06.006

Shaw, E.S.: Financial Deepening in Economic Development. New York, Oxford University Press (1973). https://doi.org/10.2307/2978421

Shen, Y., Hu, W., Hueng, C.J.: Digital financial inclusion and economic growth: a cross-country study. Procedia Comput. Sci. **187**, 218–223 (2021). https://doi.org/10.3390/su14074340

Siddik, M., Alam, N., Kabiraj, S.: Does financial inclusion induce financial stability? Evidence from cross-country analysis. Australas. Account. Bus. Financ. J. **12**(1), 34–46 (2018). https://doi.org/10.14453/aabfj.v12i1.3

Singh, D., Stakic, N.: Financial inclusion and economic growth nexus: evidence from SAARC countries. South Asia Res. **41**(2), 238–258 (2021). https://doi.org/10.1177/0262728020964605

Solow, R.M.: A contribution to the theory of economic growth. Q. J. Econ. **70**(1), 65–94 (1956). https://EconPapers.repec.org/RePEc:oup:qjecon:v:70:y:1956:i:1:p:65-94

Song, J., Geng, L., Fahad, S., Liu, L.: Fiscal decentralization and economic growth revisited: an empirical analysis of poverty governance. Environ. Sci. Pollut. Res. **29**(19), 28020–28030 (2022). https://doi.org/10.1007/s11356-021-18470-7

Song, N., Appiah-Otoo, I.: The impact of fintech on economic growth: evidence from China. Sustainability **14**(10), 6211 (2022). https://doi.org/10.3390/su14106211

Sy, A.N., Maino, R., Massara, A., Perez-Saiz, H., Sharma, P.: Fintech in Sub-Saharan African countries: A game changer? IMF Departmental Paper no. 19/04, International Monetary Fund (IMF). http://hdl.handle.net/RePEc:imf:imfdps:2019/004 (2019)

Tarazi, M., Breloff, P.: Nonbank e-money issuers: regulatory approaches to protecting customer funds. Focus Note **63**, 1–10 (2010)

Thomas, A.E., M. Bhasi, Chandramouli, R.:. Financial accessibility and economic growth. Evidence from SAARC countries. In: Contemplations on New Paradigms in Finance, pp. 32–52. Directorate of Public Relations and Publications, CUSAT, Kochi (2017). https://doi.org/10.1177/0262728020964605

Wang, X., He, G.: Digital financial inclusion and farmers' vulnerability to poverty: evidence from rural China. Sustainability **12**(4), 1668 (2020). https://doi.org/10.3390/su12041668

Westerlund, J.: Testing for error correction in panel data. Oxford Bull. Econ. Stat. **69**(6), 709–748 (2007). https://doi.org/10.1111/j.1468-0084.2007.00477.x

World Bank: Global financial development report 2014: Financial inclusion, vol. 2. World Bank Publications (2013)

World Bank: The State of Economic Inclusion Report 2021: The Potential to Scale. World Bank, Washington (2021)

Yin, X., Xu, X., Chen, Q., Peng, J.: The sustainable development of financial inclusion: how can monetary policy and economic fundamental interact with it effectively? Sustainability **11**(9), 2524 (2019). https://doi.org/10.3390/su11092524

Zhang, D., Hu, M., Ji, Q.: Financial markets under the global pandemic of COVID-19. Financ. Res. Lett. **36**, 101528 (2020). https://doi.org/10.1016/j.frl.2020.101528

Antecedents and Outcomes of Brand Hate: A Case of Anti-brand Community

Latifa Mednini[1]([✉]) [iD] and Imen Charfi Ben Hmida[2] [iD]

[1] Deeptech & Nanoscience, 63 rue de Tolbiac, 75013 Paris, France
Latifamednini@yahoo.com
[2] The Institute of Higher Commercial Studies of Sfax, Sfax, Tunisia

Abstract. This study aims to explore the antecedents and outcomes of brand hate, especially in the case of the anti-brand community. Brand hate is an emerging concept in brand-consumer relationships. Qualitative research has been conducted on brand hate from both the consumer and brand perspectives. A netnographic study has been applied to understand the antecedents and consequences of brand hate from the consumer perspective. This study specifically aims to examine the phenomenon of brand hate in the context of air travel. Moreover, a retrospective interview has been conducted with the brand manager from the brand perspective. As a first result, our qualitative studies reveal that negative past experiences, brand unfairness, corporate social irresponsibility, and poor management of the company workforce are antecedents of brand hate. As a second result, the outcomes explored in our research were brand avoidance, negative word-of-mouth, brand retaliation, anti-brand community creation, and consumer distrust. The paper provides a deeper understanding of the feeling of hate from both the customer and brand perspectives. Furthermore, this work enables brand managers to investigate brand hate in the context of an anti-brand community.

Keywords: Brand hate · Anti-brand community · Consumer emotions · Consumer- brand relationship

1 Introduction

Every company aspires to have a positive relationship with its customers. However, some brands have failed to keep their customers satisfied. In 2012, United Airlines lost 180 million dollars because of one passenger's dissatisfaction. This incident has taught several companies that consumer emotions toward a brand can be devastating and should not be ignored. Hate is one of the most powerful emotions [25].

With the development of the internet, brand hate has gained attention. Scholars have investigated several antecedents of brand hate, such as negative past experiences [1, 46], ideological incompatibility [1, 2, 45], brand embarrassment [19], corporate so- cial irresponsibility [1, 24]; offensive advertising [33]. Additionally, several academics have discussed the negative consequences of brand hate, such as brand avoidance (18), Negative word of mouth [18, 25], and brand retaliation [25]. However, hate becomes more

© The Author(s), under exclusive license to Springer Nature Switzerland AG 2023
R. Jallouli et al. (Eds.): ICDEc 2023, LNBIP 485, pp. 222–234, 2023.
https://doi.org/10.1007/978-3-031-42788-6_14

visible with the presence of an anti-brand community. The anti-brand community is one of the spaces that gathers all consumers who have negative feelings toward a specific brand. To the best of our knowledge, few researchers have studied brand hate in negative communities (Rodrigues et al., 2021). The work of Rodrigues et al. (2021) was conducted on two anti-brand communities in the technology sector. However, other sectors such as the airline industry were not mentioned. Our paper will discuss the feeling of hate in this context. The research question is: What are the antecedents and outcomes of hate regarding a brand in the case of an anti-brand community? Therefore, our research provides a response to the call for more studies on negative brand relationships by focusing on brand hate and presents a taxonomy of the antecedents and consequences of this concept. The first contribution of our paper is to provide a more comprehensive understanding of the antecedents and consequences of this negative feeling from two perspectives, namely, from the consumer and brand's point of view. The second contribution is to raise awareness among brand managers, allowing companies to implement appropriate management strategies.

The rest of the paper is organized as follows: We begin by examining relevant literature on brand hate, anti-brand community, antecedents, and outcomes. After that, we will discuss the methodology used to achieve our research goals. Following that, we will present the findings. Finally, we will address the theoretical and practical implications of our results and offer diverse recommendations for future research.

2 Literature Review

2.1 Brand Hate

Hate is a destructive emotion that can ruin a relationship between two individuals. Due to culture and religion, people are often hesitant to express their feelings of hate towards others (Ben-Ze'ev, 2001), an emotion [32, 42, 43], or a motivation [41]. This emotion has negative consequences such as avoidance or retreat [32], separation [41], destruction or diminution [37].

Hate is not limited to people; it can also affect objects. In marketing literature, Romani et al. (2012) explored hate as a secondary emotion of detestation for the first time. The researchers proposed six factors: dislike, sadness, dissatisfaction, anger, inquisitiveness, and embarrassment. The study concluded that these factors play a significant role in consumer-brand relationships. According to Stenberg's theory, Kucuk (2019b) defined the concept as follows: "consumers' detachment from a brand and its associations as a result of consumers' intense and deeply held negative emotions such as disgust, anger, contempt, devaluation, and diminution..." (p. 19). Kucuk (2019b) identified several emotions that make up the main concept, including contempt, disgust, anger, devaluation, and diminution. Another point of view is Zarantonello et al.'s (2016) identification of hate as a collection of negative emotions, examining its components such as anger, contempt, disgust, fear, disappointment, shame, and dehumanization. However, some academics have overlooked these feelings in their own definitions [8, 9, 18, 24].

2.2 Anti-brand Community

With the proliferation of the internet, customers now have a greater voice and can redefine the relationship between consumers and businesses [25]. The virtual community has become a platform for customers to express negative emotions towards brands, such as hate. Complaints about product or service failures are now easier to broadcast than ever before. Kucuk (2007) was the first academic to suggest the concept of the anti-brand community, which he defined as "groupings of people who have negative feelings towards a brand and self-select to join together to voice their antipathy to the brand" [referring to Dessart et al. (2020)]. The primary goals of these communities are to diminish the brand value and seek vengeance [Grégoire et al., 2009; Cooper et al., 2019]. Anti-brand communities can serve as a valuable source of knowledge for businesses seeking to gain a better understanding of brand hate [23].

2.3 Antecedents of Brand Hate

Negative Past Experience. Some companies fail to provide good service or products to their consumers, and such failures cannot be recovered within the consumer's tolerance period, resulting in dissatisfaction that can turn into hate [25]. Bad experiences can be influenced by a multitude of factors, including product failures, disappointing offerings, or other negative associations. Expectations are compared to actual performance after using the products and services, and consumers discover whether their level of expectations was satisfied at this stage or not (Halstead, 1989; Oliver, 1980). Consumers are content when their expectations are met during the consumption process; but if expectations are not met, dissatisfaction reigns supreme, resulting in a negative experience [34].

Kucuk (2019a) found that 37% of customers identified service failure as the second most common reason for brand hate. In the context of luxury brands, Bryson et al. (2013) found that consumer dissatisfaction is the strongest predictor of brand hate. In their study, Zarantonello et al. (2016) identified "expectation violation" as a crucial factor leading to hate. In contrast, Abid and Khattak (2017) used "unmet expectations" as a synonym for negative experience. According to several studies, negative experience is one of the motivators of brand hate, among other antecedents [16, 18].

Price Unfairness. The monetary value refers to the transaction between the seller and the customer (McMahon-Beattie, 2002). The difference between the value obtained and the value sacrificed during the purchase of a product is known as product monetary value perception [41, 44]. The lack of fairness in this evaluation is considered an unjust act [4]. According to Adam's (1965) theory of equity, price unfairness is the customer's perception of a difference between the price and the quality offered by other competitors [22]. Nowadays, with the development of the Internet, customers can easily discover what other customers are paying online through various means such as chat, blogs, Facebook, and Instagram.

Some companies offer products or services at high prices, which can lead customers to stop using the brand if they feel that the quality of the offering is not commensurate with the price. Ali et al. (2020) have coined the term "Perceived Price Unfairness (PPUN)" to describe this phenomenon, which reinforces consumer dissatisfaction and can ultimately lead to brand hate.

Corporate Social Irresponsibility. Corporate social responsibility is an important factor in determining brand perception among consumers. Companies that act irresponsibly with their customers are likely to generate anger, which can eventually turn into hate. Kucuk's (2019) study found that 29% of customers confirmed that corporate social irresponsibility is a source of consumer hate regarding the brand. Kucuk (2018) further stated that customers may dislike a brand if there is a low level of corporate social responsibility and a high level of product and service failure, leading to consumer dissatisfaction and rage. However, Bryson et al. (2013) found that consumer perceptions of corporate social performance are not seen as a significant antecedent of brand hate.

2.4 Outcomes of Brand Hate

Brand Avoidance. Brand avoidance is the act of consumers avoiding a brand without having purchased it in the past. It is a form of anti-consumption that occurs when consumers reject certain brands because they may bring undesired meanings to their lives [2, 45]. In fact, brand avoidance is a phenomenon in which customers choose freely to detach themselves from or reject a brand after a negative experience. Previous studies have shown that brand avoidance is a result of brand hate [12, 18]. According to Banerjee and Goel (2020), brand hate can also have a significant impact on political brand avoidance.

Negative EWOM. Negative brand relationships, particularly brand hate, are believed to drive negative word of mouth (WOM) and impact avoidance activity [46]. Consumers who have a bad purchase experience often use negative WOM to alert others about the failure of a brand [18, 25]. Negative WOM can be categorized into two types: "private complaining," which involves talking negatively about a brand to friends or family, and "public complaining," which involves making online posts on blogs, websites, or social media. Previous studies have shown that brand hate has a significant effect on both private and public complaining. Additionally, bad feelings toward a brand can lead consumers to speak poorly about the company both offline and online, and ultimately refuse to make a repeat purchase.

Brand Retaliation. Retaliation refers to actions taken by consumers to restore a sense of fairness after a negative experience with a brand, rather than to damage the brand itself, based on the equity theory (Kahr et al., 2016). Hegner et al. (2017) confirmed that brand hate can lead to direct "punishment" behavior towards the brand, such as complaining to the company's employees, stealing from the brand, or harming its property [18]. According to Zhang et al. (2020), the severity of the failure experienced by the consumer influences their negative feelings towards the brand, which in turn affects their intention to retaliate. Noor et al. (2021) found that a consumer's attitude towards offensive advertising has a favorable impact on their level of brand hate and their likelihood of retaliating. Overall, negative consumer-brand relationships often result in brand retaliation, which is mostly based on brand hate and arises when customers harbor negative feelings towards a specific brand (Noor et al., 2021) [36].

3 Methodology

In the methodology part, we opted for the triangulation of data by trying to collate the results via 2 qualitative studies, namely in-depth interviews and netnography, in order to aspire to a better robustness of our results. This study specifically aims to examine the phenomenon of brand hate in the context of air travel.

3.1 Study 1

In this research, we aim to understand the antecedents of hate and the negative consequences of this issue in the relationship between customers and brands. The netnography approach is useful in obtaining information on sensitive subjects, such as the ones presented in our study. In fact, customers can express their feelings honestly through an anti-brand community, which is difficult to attain using traditional quantitative methods. To obtain rich data, we used Facebook, which offers a high level of interactivity and many communicators and heterogeneous participants [28]. In Tunisain case, and according to "Digital Discovery Tunisia" statistics from 2022, there were 7,737,8001[1] "Facebook" accounts.

As per "Digital Discovery Tunisia" statistics from 2022, where there were 7,737,811 Facebook accounts in Tunisia. Drawing on Kozinets (2002), the netnography method is composed of five steps. First, we started with the entry step, with the goal of understanding the antecedents and outcomes of brand hate in the anti-brand community. Therefore, we selected three negative communities that align with Bernard's (2004) guidelines and meet our research objectives in terms of the volume of traffic, number of participants, and descriptive richness of data as shown in Appendix 2. To understand consumer behavior and rituals, we logged into Facebook and participated in the selected communities. Second, following Bernard (2004), the netnography process is categorized by non-participating and participating observation. In the non-participating observation, we acquired 150 comments from the three communities. In the participating observation, we started an online discussion group and invited individuals to join the discussion. Using the focus group technique, we reached out to 36 passengers from multiple nationalities and from three anti-brand communities. However, only 10 members signed up for the focus group. Considering the low response rate, we decided to invite 16 additional passengers to participate in individual interviews. The characteristics of our sample are detailed in Appendix 1. In the third step, we used open coding (inductive coding applied on first reading) to ensure data analysis and interpretation, following the guidelines of Decrop and Degroote (2015, p. 7). We then used the software "Nvivo 11" to classify the themes in a theme grid and extract the necessary themes from the verbatim of each participant. In the fourth step, we obtained permission from members to post their messages and comments. Finally, as noted by Bernard (2004), this step allowed us to obtain additional and more specific elements on the meanings of consumers.

---

[1] https://www.digital-discovery.tn/.

3.2 Findings 1

Antecedent of Brand Hate. He results indicate the following percentage: negative experience (22.22%), price unfairness (30.33%), corporate social irresponsibility (14.12%), and poor workforce management (33.33%).

Most passengers have negative experiences with brand selected. We quote the next verbatim" This was my first trip with this company. It was a terrible experience. The cancellation of flights necessitates notifying passengers, as well as delays, which resulted in my spending two days at the airport. Respectful statement" (Female, 29). Similarly, to the literature, negative past experiences have significant impact on brand hate [1, 18, 46]. Moreover, members noted that some brands are so expensive when we compare their quality. We revealed the next verbatim" At the very least, one may understand why their tickets are so expensive! They have done it by themselves to remunerate the 7800 employees, which is deplorable..." (Female, 50). Confirmed with Ali et al. (2020), dissatisfaction and complaint behavior may be influenced by perceived brand price unfairness [7, 21, 37]. The results indicate the following percentages: negative past experience (22.22%), price unfairness (30.33%), corporate social irresponsibility (14.12%), and poor workforce management (33.33%). Most passengers reported having negative experiences with the selected brand. One participant stated, "This was my first trip with this company. It was a terrible experience. The cancellation of flights necessitates notifying passengers, as well as delays, which resulted in my spending two days at the airport. Respectful statement" (Female, 29). Similarly, to the literature, negative past experiences have a significant impact on brand hate (Kucuk, 2018; Abbasi et al., 2022).

In addition, participants noted instances of price unfairness and corporate social irresponsibility by Tunisair. One participant reported, "Due to a lack of professionalism on the side of Tunisair, I canceled my flight on June 22nd, and despite numerous phone calls and emails, I have yet to receive compensation" (Female, 30). Kucuk (2018) and Abbasi et al. (2022) have demonstrated that extreme anger and brand hate are basic consumer reactions to corporate social irresponsible brands. In such cases, the company's excellent complaint handling is critical in resolving consumer misunderstandings and recovering consumer trust and satisfaction. Furthermore, participants mentioned that poor workforce management is an antecedent that can lead customers to hate a brand. One participant stated, "Customer dissatisfaction on all levels: absolute overcharging, impolite and unpleasant staff, expensive equipment fees, systematic delays, no interaction with customers, flight cancellations and reports without indication" (Female, 37). Effective planning and management of work-in-progress within businesses, which includes recruiting, developing, and dispatching employees to the right places at the right time, is crucial in achieving organizational and individual goals (Henderson et al., 2007).

Consequences of Brand Hate. Our netnography study demonstrated that 12.22% of members have avoided the brand, while 30.33% of passengers have applied negative WOM to promote a negative impression of the brand. Similarly, 12.22% of customers have disclosed instances of brand retaliation, consumer distrust (35.23%), and anti-brand community creation (10%).

Some passengers avoid the brand and encourage other customers to do the same, as illustrated in the following verbatim: "TUNISAIR is the most rotten company, they are not professional, they never think of their passengers, their delays have become unbearable...my parents slept yesterday at the airport, they are old, and they spent 4 pm on the floor...there were other old people with them. It was the 10 pm flight to the medina...it gives zero respect to these people, it is not given reasons for the delay. I have never taken this company and I will never take it, and I will advise everyone not to take it" (Male, 34). Consumers who are triggered by brand hate engage in brand avoidance by moving to a rival or refusing to consume the brand [18]. Due to the general negative effects of intimacy and hate, individuals avoid them by switching to other [34].

In addition, our netnography study found that most Tunisair passengers resorted to negative eWOM in the virtual community to express their hate for the brand. One member stated, "Avoid flying with Tunisian airlines and instead fly with other airlines that provide better prices and services..." (Male, 42). Previous research has confirmed that negative WOM reinforces brand hate [18]. On the other hand, some passengers were more active in their expression of dissatisfaction and participated in anti-branding activities. One member reported, "This airline company does not adhere to international agreements, does not reimburse travel expenses for long-term delays, and does not communicate with attorneys or judges. For the time being, the situation is such that we will file an EXECUTION against the company" (Male, 55). Zhang et al. (2020) found that failure severity increases negative feelings (brand hate), which in turn affects consumer retaliation intention.

Additionally, our study is the first to investigate the creation of an anti-brand community because of brand hate. Certain passengers chose to form an anti-brand group to express their dissatisfaction with the brand and inform other customers. The creator of one such community stated, "I created this community for many reasons... Since every time I take a Tunisair flight there is a problem, I could name hundreds. I specify that I travel a lot and that I take many other companies and it is the worst" (Male, 42). Our findings shed light on the creation of an anti-brand community as an outcome of brand hate. These communities can fulfill the brand hater's desire for brand-related knowledge that has been re-conditioned and modified to convey a humorous meaning and consumers' personal opinions [10].

3.3 Study 2

To gain a broader perspective on brand hate, we conducted a retrospective interview with a marketing manager of *"Tunisair"*. Our main objective is to understand brand hate from the airline company part.

The interview is used to get a greater understanding of participants' opinions, values, and motives [15]. The Thiétart (2007) noticed that the interview is a "technique intended to collect, in the perspective of their analysis, discursive data reflecting in particular the conscious or unconscious mental universe of individuals' (p.274). We prepared our guide interview that included three topics: Brand hate, Antecedents, and outcomes. The participant spanned a median about one hour. To examine the results of our qualitative research, the interview was recorded and transcribed. We used Nvivo 11 software to analyze manager interview. The data analysis procedure followed Wolcott's (1994) guidelines, which included the three major phases of description (which relied heavily on verbatim quotes from respondents), analysis (which identified key factors, themes, and relation- ships), and interpretation (which made sense of meanings in the perspective).

3.4 Findings 2

The objective of the semi structured interview was to understand the awareness of brand managers about antecedents and consequences of brand hate.

The interviewee demonstrated that the media display a role to destroy the brand image. In this perspective, the brand manager noted that:" The reasons for this are false information spread through the media and social media, which frequently distribute videos or articles about another company and claim it is Tunisair... for customers, the degree of satisfaction depends on the customer personality" (Male, 50). According to the literature, Ali et al. (2020) discovered that customers who do not see a match between their own personality and that of the brand, and that this mismatch leads to neg- ative feeling. The participant was aware about severity and hate emotion. The manager demonstrated that: "It's possible to have a negative impact on businesses, particularly service businesses that rely on consumer trust...Also, the financial side will result in addi- tional charges on one hand, and on the other hand, it will harm our brand image" (Male, 50). Similar to Molm et al. (2000), customer trust is considered a principal element of enduring long-term relationships with a company.

In order to investigate brand hate in the case of the anti-brand community. We asked interviewees about anti-Tunisair communities. His response was as follows:" It is a series of blunders that have the goal of creating a sense of distrust in our national company…If you do a search on these pages, you'll find that the creators of the page are paid by private companies competing with Tunisian Airlines. I had an experience with someone who always talks about "Tunisian Airlines" and how bad their service is, and when I asked him where he had problems, he said he'd never been on an airplane" (Male, 50). Consistent with Kucuk (2019), a true hater, a troll, a review farm, or a competitor-affiliated source such as a paid-blogger can all be examples of customer hater.

4 Discussion

4.1 Theoretical and Managerial Implication

For scholars, the study of brand hate has several theoretical implications. The primary notion behind analyzing brand hate is that it can have significant financial costs for both businesses and customers when customers lose trust and switch to a different brand. Thus, our study provides an opportunity for authors to better understand the concept of brand hate, as detailed in appendix 3. It is important to note that hate towards a brand may not always be directed at the brand itself, but rather towards its employees. We have identified poor workforce management as a precursor to brand hate. Additionally, our research has investigated the creation of anti-brand communities and brand distrust as consequences of brand hate. Many businesses have overlooked the anti-brand community, which can influence customers to boycott a brand to avoid negatively affecting other customers. Following the footsteps of Kucuk (2019a) regarding the management of brand hate, this study has placed a new milestone by extending the current qualitative work into exploratory research in digital context. Our study contributes to the literature on anti-brand communities and the antecedents for hate towards a brand. Thus, the present work enriches the literature on anti-brand movements, anti-consumption, the brand-consumer relationship, and customer complaints, providing a comprehensive understanding of the causes behind consumer hate for academics.

For managerial implications, our study enables companies to understand the mechanisms of brand hate in anti-brand communities, as well as the primary factors that may cause brand hate and its consequences. In the past, negative feelings disappeared and forged because there was no effective way to communicate and express hate toward brands. With the advancement of the Internet, particularly, the brand's virtual community has made it easier for angry customers to express their dissatisfaction and seek solutions to their complaints. We revealed that the anti-brand community is a good place to detect hate and also listen, engage and negotiate with haters [30]. Companies must have a fully working customer support center to address any issues that customers may have with their products or services. The current research noticed that brand hate antecedents and outcomes may differ from one country culture to another. In fact, customers may be in each country due to cultural differences, such as fashion trends, attitudes toward certain materials or styles, or even political or historical factors.

To address brand haters, companies can analyze the comments and posts of consumers in anti-brand communities to understand the causes of their dissatisfaction and develop effective management strategies. It is important to recognize that hate may not be directed towards the brand itself, but towards its employees, and companies must have a thorough understanding of the underlying causes of consumer hate. Additionally, our study highlights the importance of corporate social responsibility in satisfying consumer desires and reducing negative sentiment towards a brand. As an example, we encourage companies to engage in cause-related marketing. Partner with nonprofit organizations or social causes that resonate with the target audience, and donate a portion of sales to support those causes. Furthermore, our research indicates that hate can sometimes arise from employees who work for competitors, suggesting the need for marketers to implement listening technologies to differentiate between genuine complaints and malicious intent. In fact, we advise marketers to activate monitor social media and review sites for feedback. Set up alerts and dashboards that allow managers to quickly identify and respond to negative feedback, as well as track sentiment over time.

5 Limitations of the Study and Future Research

The current research has some limitations. The first of this study's limitations is inherent in its qualitative methodology. In fact, our research has led to a netnographic study that aims to investigate the phenomenon of brand hate. In this perspective, Komis et al. (2013) point out that qualitative research is part of a non-positivist epistemological paradigm. These data are recorded observations or interactions that are complicated and contextual, and they cannot be reduced or transformed into numbers immediately [27]. This allows us to proceed to a quantitative approach, which allows us to confirm the findings. The second limitation consists of longitudinal research. A longitudinal and comprehensive study will be required to track the evolution of this dissatisfaction among members and, as a result, to provide management strategies (Fournier and Lee, 2009). Third, the current investigation has not confirmed the source of customer hate. Occasionally, the customer is dissatisfied with the company's employees rather than the company itself. A future research path aims to pinpoint the different sources. Fourth, the current study investigated the antecedent and consequences of brand hate without considering the degree of hate. According to Kucuk (2019), this feeling might range from mild to severe. As a result, it will be interesting to discuss how to measure the intensity of customer hate.

Appendix 1. Sample Characteristics

Age			Gender		
	Number	Frequency%		Number	Frequency %
Between 20 and 25	1	3.85%	Female	7	26.92%
Between 26 and 30	9	34.62%	Male	19	73.07%
More than 30	16	61.53%			
Profession					
Student	7	26.92%			
Employee	19	73.07%			

Appendix 2. Anti-Brand Community Characteristics

Anti-brand community	Number of memberships	Period
"Boycottons Tunisair et ses tarifs indécents"	4000 participants	September 2021 to September 2022
"Scandale Tunisair"	6900 participants	September 2021 to September 2022
"Réclamations Tunisiar"	845 participants	September 2021 to December 2022

Appendix 3. Theoretical Model

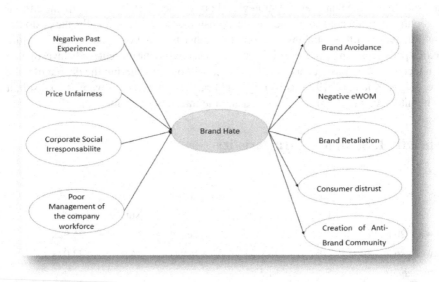

References

1. Abbasi, A.Z., Fayyaz, M.S., Ting, D.H., Munir, M., Bashir, S., Zhang, C.: The moderating role of complaint handling on brand hate in the cancel culture. Asia-Pacific Journal of Business Administration (2022)
2. Abid, R., Khattak, A.: Brand avoidance motivators stimulate to brand equity in the mediating role of brand hate: a case of smartphone industry of Pakistan. J. Account. Market. 6(3), 250 (2017)
3. Ahmed, S., Hashim, S.: The moderating effect of brand recovery on brand hate and desire for reconciliation: a PLS-MGA approach. Int. J. Bus. Soc. 19(3), 833–850 (2018)
4. Ali, S., Attiq, S., Talib, N.: Antecedents of brand hate: mediating role of customer dissatisfaction and moderating role of narcissism. Pakistan J. Commer. Soc. Sci. (PJCSS) 14(3), 603–628 (2020)
5. Banerjee, S., Goel, P.: Party brand hate in political market: antecedents and consequences. Asian J. Polit. Sci. 28(2), 97–121 (2020)
6. Bernard, Y.: La netnographie: une nouvelle méthode d'enquête qualitative basée sur les communautés virtuelles de consommation. Décisions Marketing 36, 49–62 (2004)
7. Bozkurt, S., Gligor, D.: Customers' behavioral responses to unfavorable pricing errors: the role of perceived deception, dissatisfaction and price consciousness. J. Consum. Mark. 36(6), 760–771 (2019)
8. Bryson, D., Atwal, G., Hultén, P.: Towards the conceptualisation of the antecedents of extreme negative affect towards luxury brands. J. Cetacean Res. Manag. 16(4), 393–405 (2013)
9. Bryson, D., Atwal, G.: Brand hate: the case of Starbucks in France. British Food Journal 121(1), 172–182 (2018)

10. Dessart, L., Veloutsou, C., Morgan-Thomas, A.: Brand negativity: a relational perspective on anti-brand community participation. European J. Market. **54**(7), 1761–1785 (2020). https://doi.org/10.1108/EJM-06-2018-0423
11. Evrard, Y., Pras, B., Roux, E.: Market: fondements et méthodes des recherches en marketing. Dunod, Paris (2009)
12. Fahmi, T.M., Zaki, H.S.: Drivers and outcomes of brand hate in the tourism sector. J. Fac. Tourism Hotels-Univ. Sadat City **2**(2), 130–150 (2018)
13. Farhat, Z., Chaney, D.: Introducing destination brand hate: an exploratory study. Curr. Issue Tour. **24**(17), 2472–2488 (2021)
14. Fetscherin, M.: The five types of brand hate: how they affect consumer behavior. J. Bus. Res. **101**, 116–127 (2019)
15. Giannelloni, J.-L., Vernette, E.: Etudes de marché Vuibert, 2ème édition. Paris (2001)
16. Hashim, S., Kasana, S.: Antecedents of brand hate in the fast food industry. Spanish J. Market. - ESIC **23**(2), 227–248 (2019)
17. Halstead, D.: Expectations and disconfirmation beliefs as predictors of consumer satisfaction, repurchase intention, and complaining behavior: an empirical study. J. Consum. Satisfaction Dissatisfaction Complaining Behav. **2**(1), 17–21 (1989)
18. Hegner, S.M., Fetscherin, M., van Delzen, M.: Determinants and outcomes of brand hate. J. Prod. Brand Manag. **26**(1), 13–25 (2017)
19. Husnain, M., Syed, F., Hussain, K., Zhang, Q., Usman, M., Javed, M.: Explaining the mechanism of brand hate: a mixed-method investigation using moderated mediation in emerging markets. Kybernetes (2022)
20. Jmour, A., Hmida, I.C.B.: Not always a co-creation: exploratory study of reasons, emotions and practices of the value co-destruction in virtual communities. In: Jallouli, R., Zaïane, O.R., Tobji, M.A.B., Tabbane, R.S., Nijholt, A. (eds.) Digital Economy. Emerging Technologies and Business Innovation: Second International Conference, ICDEc 2017, Sidi Bou Said, Tunisia, May 4–6, 2017, Proceedings, pp. 41–54. Springer International Publishing, Cham (2017). https://doi.org/10.1007/978-3-319-62737-3_4
21. Katyal, K., Kanetkar, V., Patro, S.: What is a fair fare? Exploring the differences between perceived price fairness and perceived price unfairness. J. Revenue Pricing Manag. **18**(2), 133–146 (2019)
22. Kaura, V., Prasad, C.S.D., Sharma, S.: Service quality, service convenience, price and fairness, customer loyalty, and the mediating role of customer satisfaction. Int. J. Bank Market. **33**(4), 404–422 (2015). https://doi.org/10.1108/IJBM-04-2014-0048
23. Kucuk, S.U., Krishnamurthy, S.: An analysis of consumer power on the Internet. Technovation **27**(1–2), 47–56 (2007)
24. Kucuk, S.U.: Macro-level antecedents of consumer brand hate. J. Consumer Market. **35**(5), 555–564 (2018)
25. Kucuk, S.U.: Brand Hate Navigating Consumer Negativity in the Digital World. Palgrave Macmillan, Cham (2019)
26. Kucuk, S.U.: Consumer brand hate: Steam rolling whatever I see. Psychol. Mark. **36**(5), 431–443 (2019)
27. Komis, V., Depover, C., Karsenti, T. : L'usage des outils informatiques en analyse des données qualitatives (2013)
28. Kozinets, R.V.: The field behind the screen: using netnography for marketing research in online communities. J. Mark. Res. **39**(1), 61–72 (2002)
29. McMahon-Beattie, U., Yeoman, I., Palmer, A., Mudie, P.: Customer perceptions of pricing and the maintenance of trust. J. Revenue Pricing Manag. **1**(1), 25–34 (2002)
30. Mednini, L., Turki, M.D.: What leads customer to create and participate in anti-brand community: a netnographic approach. In: Tobji, M.A.B., Jallouli, R., Strat, V.A., Soares, A.M.,

Davidescu, A.A. (eds.) Digital Economy. Emerging Technologies and Business Innovation: 7th International Conference on Digital Economy, ICDEc 2022, Bucharest, Romania, May 9–11, 2022, Proceedings, pp. 159–169. Springer International Publishing, Cham (2022). https://doi.org/10.1007/978-3-031-17037-9_11

31. Molm, L.D., Takahashi, N., Peterson, G.: Risk and trust in social exchange: an experimental test of a classical proposition. Am. J. Sociol. **105**(5), 1396–1427 (2000)

32. Neufeldt, V., Guralnik, D.B.: Webster's New World College dictionary. McMillian, New York (1997)

33. Noor, U., Mansoor, M., Rabbani, S.: Brand hate and retaliation in Muslim consumers: does offensive advertising matter? J. Islamic Market. (2021)

34. Oliver, R.L.: A cognitive model of the antecedents and consequences of satisfaction decisions. J. Mark. Res. **17**(4), 460–469 (1980)

35. Park, C.W., Eisingerich, A.B., Park, J.W.: Attachment–aversion (AA) model of customer-brand relationships. J. Consum. Psychol. **23**(2), 229–248 (2013)

36. Pinto, O., Brandão, A.: Antecedents and consequences of brand hate: empirical evidence from the telecommunication industry. Eur. J. Manag. Bus. Econ. **30**, 18–35 (2020). https://doi.org/10.1108/EJMBE-04-2020-0084

37. Rempel, J.K., Burris, C.T.: Let me count the ways: an integrative theory of love and hate. Pers. Relat. **12**(2), 297–313 (2005)

38. Riquelme, I.P., Román, S., Cuestas, P.J., Iacobucci, D.: The dark side of good reputation and loyalty in online retailing: when trust leads to retaliation through price unfairness. J. Interact. Mark. **47**, 35–52 (2019)

39. Robison, J., Curry, L., Gruman, C., Porter, M., Henderson, C.R., Jr., Pillemer, K.: Partners in caregiving in a special care environment: cooperative communication between staff and families on dementia units. Gerontologist **47**(4), 504–515 (2007)

40. Romani, S., Grappi, S., Dalli, D.: Emotions that drive consumers away from brands: measuring negative emotions toward brands and their behavioral effects. Int. J. Res. Mark. **29**(1), 55–67 (2012)

41. Sahut, J.M., Hikkerova, L., Pupion, P.C.: Perceived unfairness of prices resulting from yield management practices in hotels. J. Bus. Res. **69**(11), 4901–4906 (2016)

42. Schoenewolf, G.: The Art of Hating. J. Aronson (1991)

43. Schoenewolf, G.: Hate .The Encyclopedia of Human Behavior. Academic Press, New York (1994)

44. Suri, R., Monroe, K.B.: The effects of time constraints on consumers' judgments of prices and products. J. Consum. Res. **30**(1), 92–104 (2003)

45. Thompson, C.J., Rindfleisch, A., Arsel, Z.: Emotional branding and the strategic value of the doppelgänger brand image. J. Mark. **70**, 50–64 (2006)

46. Valenzuela, C., Castellucci, L., Mena, M.T., Bianchi, C.: Consumer brand hate: the role of ambivalence. Int. Rev. Retail Distrib. Consum. Res. **32**(1), 100–125 (2022)

47. Zarantonello, L., Romani, S., Grappi, S., Bagozzi, R.P.: Brand hate. J. Prod. Brand Manag. **25**(1), 11–25 (2016)

48. Zhang, C., Laroche, M.: Brand hate: a multidimensional construct. J. Prod. Brand Manag. **30**(3), 392–414 (2020)

Digital Marketing and Data Analytics

A Systematic Literature Review on CRM Critical Success Factors
The Transversal Role of Data Analytics Capabilities

Roula Jabado[1]([⊠]) [iD] and Rim Jallouli[2] [iD]

[1] School of Business, Lebanese International University, Beirut, Lebanon
roula.jabado@liu.edu.lb
[2] University of Manouba, ESEN, LIGUE, Manouba, Tunisia
rimjallouli@esen-manouba.org

Abstract. The evolution of digital technologies and connectivity has led to a massive increase in data generation by organizations, reassessing the effectiveness of the traditional approaches to customer relationship management (CRM) systems. Businesses need to adopt more advanced approaches to CRM systems, that would leverage big data analytics, machine learning tools, and artificial intelligence, to provide a more personalized and seamless customer experience. Several previous research attempted to integrate Data Analytics Capabilities DAC dimension as a new CSF for modern CRM implementation. However, they are still in the exploratory phase, mainly using qualitative methodologies that focused on one or more critical success factors separately. This paper aims to (1) extend theory further through a systematic literature review (SLR) that explores the relationship linking 'People', 'Process', 'Technology' and 'Data Analytics Capabilities'; (2) shed the light on the transversal role of DAC with other CSFs for CRM systems to ensure intrinsic and extrinsic performance. Findings are consolidated in a novel theoretical framework showing the transversal role of 'Data Analytics Capabilities' as key factors in ensuring the CRM system's effective marketing decisions, customer satisfaction and business profitability. Moreover, this paper provides essential material to empirically test the framework on hand through future quantitative research.

Keywords: Critical Success Factors · Customer Relationship Management · Data Analytics Capabilities · Systematic Literature Review

1 Introduction

Hargreaves et al. (2018) define Customer Relationship Management (CRM) as *"a tool and strategy for managing customers' interaction using technology to automate business processes"*. CRM has emerged as one of the fastest-growing business management technology solutions in recent years, making it a critical tool for businesses seeking sustainability (Gil-Gomez et al., 2020). This led to a significant increase in data generation by organizations, as businesses collect data from various sources such as social media, customer interactions, online transactions, and sensor data from Internet of Things

© The Author(s), under exclusive license to Springer Nature Switzerland AG 2023
R. Jallouli et al. (Eds.): ICDEc 2023, LNBIP 485, pp. 237–262, 2023.
https://doi.org/10.1007/978-3-031-42788-6_15

(IoT) devices (Lokuge et al., 2020). CRM systems capture vast amounts of customer data, including customer contact information, purchase history, website behavior, social media activity, and more. This data provides valuable marketing insights, enabling businesses to make data-driven decisions and improve their overall performance (Chatterjee et al., 2020).

The past few years have witnessed significant advancements in computing and e-commerce technologies, including the widespread adoption of artificial intelligence (AI) based technologies such as cloud computing, big data analytics, data mining and machine learning (Singh & Anuradha, 2022; Bach Tobji et al., 2018; 2020). These technological advancements have transformed the way businesses interact with customers and manage their marketing decisions (Jallouli & Kaabi, 2022). One critical aspect of CRM is the ability to analyze the vast amount of data generated by the system to gain insights into customer behavior, preferences, and needs (Hamida et al., 2022).

The challenge of analyzing CRM data lies in the limitations of traditional data analysis tools. Indeed, traditional tools are not designed to handle the volume and complexity of CRM data (Lokuge et al., 2020). These tools also lack the ability to perform advanced analytics such as predictive modeling and machine learning, which are critical for gaining insights into customer behavior and preferences (De Mauro et al., 2022). Previous research has emphasized on the importance of data mining tools and techniques used in the context of CRM functional solutions (Chapman, 2019; Mahafzah et al., 2020). Data analytics were yet to be effectively used to form responses to real time shifts in customers' actions and behavior (Mahafzah et al., 2020; Maulana & Napitpulu, 2022). It requires sophisticated data collection, storage, and analysis techniques by specialized skills and expertise to manage the massive amounts of data generated by CRM systems (De Mauro et al., 2022). Furthermore, the data must be analyzed using advanced data analytics tools and capabilities to interpret the data correctly for the improvement of business operations (Chapman, 2019; Mikalef & Krogstie, 2020; Shahbaz et al., 2020; Akter et al., 2020; Song & Liang, 2021, Jabado & Jallouli, 2021, Benslama & Jallouli, 2022).

Data analytics capabilities (DAC) came as a response to the identified gap: it would help, through data mining tools and techniques, transforming this wealth of information collected through CRM systems into effective marketing decisions that would boost businesses' overall performance (Gupta & Chandra, 2020; Kaabi & Jallouli, 2019).

To bridge this gap, businesses need to integrate DAC as a critical success factor for CRM systems, and this by investing in advanced data analysis tools, hiring specialized professionals, and developing a data-driven culture that values and prioritizes data analysis (Wang et Dong, 2022).

According to Shahbaz et al. (2020), the integration of Big Data Analytics (BDA) with CRM capabilities has the potential to significantly enhance perceived sales performance and dynamic capabilities within organizations, enabling them to respond quickly to changes in customer needs and preferences, leading to increased agility and adaptability in the market. Moreover, previous studies have acknowledged the importance of Data Analytics Capabilities (DAC) as one of the key success factors for E-commerce technologies in general, and more specifically for CRM systems (Chapman, 2019; Akter et al., 2020; Mikalef & Krogstie, 2020; Shahbaz et al., 2020; Song & Liang, 2021). However, previous research presented theoretical frameworks integrating DAC with other critical success factors for CRM systems that focused mainly on the operational function of CRM and have mainly examined its Information Systems (IS) dimension. Thus, there is a need for further exploration of the collaborative and analytical functions of CRM, specifically in the context of new technologies and data analysis related to marketing decisions.

The purpose of this study is to: (1) build on existing research by conducting literature review investigating the critical success factors of CRM systems; (2) highlight the transversal role of DAC in ensuring effective performance of CRM systems in organizations; (3) conduct a Systematic literature review (SLR) of variables related to DAC as a key success factor of CRM systems in the domains of marketing, management, and information systems. (4) propose a novel theoretical framework, for future quantitative research, highlighting the transversal role of DAC with other identified CSFs for CRM implementation in firms.

The first part of this paper will go through the existing literature review about CRM: Definitions, approaches, CSFs and outcomes. Based on previous research, six core elements were identified as a baseline that will guide the SLR, namely: technology, people, process, DAC, intrinsic outcomes and net benefits.

Then, the second part will discuss the methodology adopted: The study opted for a SLR approach. This part includes the research sources, keywords, inclusion, and exclusion criteria along with data extraction techniques.

Furthermore, the third part will present the findings of the SLR: This involves a detailed description of the six main concepts, while emphasizing on the major transversal role of DAC for the implementation of CRM in firms. Subsequently, a theoretical framework is proposed for empirical validation in future quantitative research and includes the sub-dimensions and measurement scales identified as relevant for the empirical studies of successful CRM implementation.

Finally, the last part of this research will include the main conclusions and recommendations for future research.

2 CRM Approaches, Critical Success Factors (CSFs) and Outcomes

CRM systems are important for any organization seeking sustainability and survival on the long run (Gil-Gomez et al., 2020).

2.1 CRM Approaches

CRM approach is comprehensive in nature, and it integrates technology and business features. CRM also challenges organizations to handle broader issues such as social responsibility, sustainability, and human-resource practices that go beyond profit maximization (Gil-Gomez et al., 2020; Guerola-Navarro et al., 2020; Meyliana et al., 2016).

Furthermore, CRM architecture includes three major areas: operational CRM, collaborative CRM, and analytical CRM (Almohaimmeed, 2021; Hasan, 2021; Silva et al., 2021; Teo et al., 2006). Any interaction between customers and points of sales is managed by operational CRM. A collaborative CRM method, on the other hand, allows for the integration and synchronized sharing of all customer interaction data throughout a company, with the goal of increasing customer satisfaction, loyalty, and retention. Finally, analytical CRM entails the study and assessment of all data gathered through business intelligence services (Chalmeta, 2006).

2.2 A Traditional Approach to CSFs for CRM: the People, Process, and Technology (PPT) Framework

One of the most common definitions for 'success factor' related to 'CRM' is for Pan et al. (2007): *"the success factors could be defined as the generic ingredient that has to be the essential part of any successful CRM implementation"*. CRM systems play a major role for the success or failure of modern enterprises, as they help establish long-term relationships between organizations and customers. Iriarte and Bayona (2020) indicate that there is no clear definition of CSFs for CRM systems: existing literature offers a *"vast and overlapped list of factors"*. Moreover, a holistic approach is necessary due to fast technological changes. Different methods have been applied to establish CSFs in previous research studies, and each organization has its own critical arguments for validating CSFs. The implementation and linkage of these factors into existing management processes are crucial for a successful CRM implementation (Da Silva & Rahimi, 2007; Mendoza et al. 2007; King & Burgess, 2008; Pan et al., 2007; Shatat and Udin, 2013).

Previous research emphasize that the success of implementing information technology relies on the dimensions of people, process, and technology (Ali & Alshawi, 2003; Almotairi, 2009; Arab et al., 2010; Askool & Nakata, 2010; Chen & Popovich, 2003; Mendoza et al., 2007). Indeed, the CRM implementation model proposed by Chen & Popovich (2003) integrates people, process, and technology within a customer-driven, technology-integrated, and cross-functional organization. Additionally, Payne & Frow (2004; 2005) argue that CRM implementation is a strategic approach that integrates people, process, and technology to understand customers, increase stakeholder value, and build profitable and long-lasting customer relationships (Almotairi, 2009). Therefore, a closer look at each dimension was necessary:

Technology. The importance of technology in managing and establishing long-term customer relationships is highlighted by Kumar & Mokha (2022), who note that CRM systems and data mining technology are crucial for the sustainability and profitability of companies. A centralized CRM system accessible to all stakeholders can optimize CRM efficiency and decision-making process (Ayyagari, 2019).

People. The human element is also important, as people must be able to effectively use the available technology (Song & Liang, 2021). The use of automated systems is necessary as humans struggle to analyze vast amounts of consumer data in a fast and accurate manner (Chatterjee & Chaudhuri, 2022). As well, new data mining technology requires firms to upgrade people's technical capabilities to use the available CRM system effectively (Song & Liang, 2021), firms should also consider environmental transformations that affect people's commitment, including changes in the social environment, which can influence all stakeholders' internal and external commitment (Kumar, 2018).

Process. CRM processes are efficient when technology is aligned with a company's strategy and supports management in developing new services and products (Tsou, 2022). A customer-centric approach is also required to improve the workflow and collaboration between the front and back offices and enhance customer relationship efficiency (Hargreaves et al., 2018; Rahimi, 2022).Nowadays, businesses are facing a challenge in analyzing massive, varied, and volatile consumer data collected from e-commerce platforms. Therefore, a dependable holistic data architecture is required to accurately process consumer insights for future marketing decisions (Harvard Business Review Analytical Services, 2018).

2.3   A Novel Approach to CSFs for CRM: The Transversal Role of Data Analytics Capabilities with the PPT Framework

Businesses use CRM systems to access important customer data for effective marketing strategies (Dixit, 2022), but the main challenge lies in using the data effectively and selecting the appropriate data analytics techniques (Chapman, 2019). Learning new skills is necessary to analyze larger amounts of customer data (Robert et al., 2014), and companies should carefully analyze the data analytics tools to integrate into CRM systems (Gončarovs, 2017). Based on the Harvard Business Review Analytical Services (2018) survey on real-time analytics, CRM-based DAC can be divided into three correlated sectors with the goal of improving consumer experience, decisions and strategies: (1) capability to unify customer data platforms collected in-stores or via online mediums, (2) proactive analytics capability by incorporating customers' awareness and marketing tasks with the help of Artificial Intelligence (AI), (3) contextual analytics capability by incorporating "real time insights" of customers' online and in-store experiences for enhanced Marketing strategies.

The complexity and scale of data mining techniques may act as a repelling agent to new technology adoption, and strategic process integration may be time-consuming and costly. Consequently, CRM and data analytics tools are valuable direct marketing techniques that can help discover focused and potential customers who are responding to new product offerings and provide a higher return on investment (Al-Alawi et al., 2020).

However, the traditional approach to CRM systems that focus on the PPT framework as CSFs is not designed to handle the vast amounts of data generated today, which is often stored in multiple databases and data warehouses, making it challenging to access and analyze. The use of a modern approach that includes advanced data analysis tools and capabilities can bridge this gap, enabling businesses to gain insights into customer behavior, preferences, and needs.

2.4   Intrinsic and Extrinsic Outcomes of Successful CRM Implementation

CRM systems are effective not just in terms of their operational capabilities, but also in terms of their cultural and innovative capabilities combined with CRM and Data Analytics. Results could be intrinsic, improving the effectiveness of marketing decisions, or extrinsic, thus increasing business net benefits (Chapman, 2019; Dixit, 2022). The integration of DAC with CRM capabilities has the potential to significantly enhance perceived sales performance and dynamic capabilities within organizations, leading to increased agility and adaptability in the market (Shahbaz et al, 2020). By investing in advanced data analysis tools, hiring specialized professionals, and developing a data-driven culture, businesses can shift from a product-centric to a customer-centric approach (Gončarovs & Grabis, 2017; Maulana & Nalitupulu, 2022), leading to improved customer satisfaction and loyalty (Maulana & Nalitupulu, 2022). For example, clustering techniques positively influence supply chain management and E-commerce competitive strategies (Benslama & Jallouli, 2020). Thus, data analytics capabilities must be continually updated to keep up with market changes, technology skills and expertise, as well as customers' expectations (Kumar, 2018, 2021).

2.5   The Theoretical Framework for CSFs of CRM Systems Integrating DAC

Based on the previously discussed available literature, this study proposes a theoretical framework (as shown in Fig. 1 that includes the identified CSFs for CRM implementation, while highlighting the transversal role of DAC, the intrinsic and extrinsic outcomes. The framework will be used to summarize the findings of the literature review (SLR).

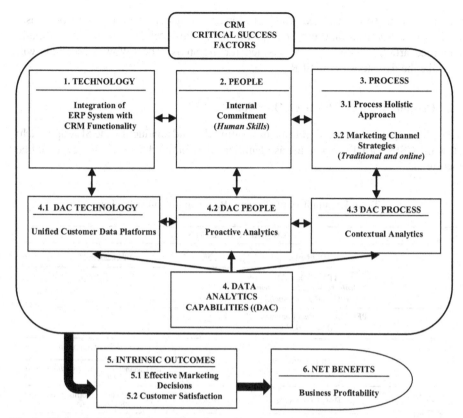

Fig. 1. Theoretical framework of CSFs dimensions for CRM implementation integrating DAC (based on previous literature)

3 Methodology: A Systematic Literature Review (SLR)

The literature review identified the 'CRM critical success factors' for improved 'marketing decisions' as an 'intrinsic outcome' and 'net Benefit' as an extrinsic outcome. Results were presented in Fig. 1 through a 'Theoretical Framework for Successful CRM Implementation'. The reliability and validity of the framework are yet to be verified. Therefore, a SLR approach was conducted to ensure the proper operationalization of the variables for the proposed framework. It aims to make a synthesis of previous research dealing with main concepts involved in the framework of CSFs of CRM systems integrating DAC dimension. Based on Weerakkody et al. (2013) and Taha et al. (2013), this SLR follows 5 steps: (1) defining research question that was stated in the introduction, (2) determining research sources, (3) accomplishing the finding process by using keywords, (4) extracting data, and (5) analyzing the findings to answer research questions.

The review of the available literature started in August 2020 and ended in March 2021. A search across various databases over a 20-year period from 2000 to 2020 resulted in 237 articles. To ensure precision, control, and detailed bibliographic records, the

SCOPUS database was utilized. The inclusion and exclusion criteria were meticulously applied to extract relevant and high-quality data. Ultimately, out of the 237 initially identified articles, only 42 were retained for the study. The following sections will describe the five steps of the SLR.

3.1 Defining the SLR Research Question

The following question highlights the motivations behind conducting the SLR approach: How the CSFs for CRM systems, as identified through the theoretical review could be measured?

Table 1. Summary of Concepts Based on Literature Review

CONCEPTUAL LEVELS			
#	Dimension	N#	Sub-Dimension
1	TECHNOLOGY *'Integration of ERP System with CRM Functionality'*		–
2	PEOPLE *'Internal Commitment'* *(Human skills)*		–
3	PROCESS	3.1	Process Holistic Approach
		3.2	Marketing Channel Strategies *(traditional and online)*
4 (DATA ANALYTICS CAPABILITIES)	DAC - *Technology*	4.1	Unified Customers data platforms *(Online and offline channels)*
	DAC - *People*	4.2	Proactive Analytics Capabilities
	DAC - *Process*	4.3	Contextual Analytics
5	INTRINSIC OUTCOMES	5.1	Effective Marketing Decisions
		5.2	Customer Satisfaction
6	EXTRINSIC OUTCOMES *'Net Benefits' (Business Profitability)*		–

The literature review identifies the conceptual levels that are presented in Table 1, including six dimensions with their sub-dimensions.

This step of providing the related variables for a successful CRM implementation in firms is essential. Therefore, the SLR applied in the fields of marketing, management and information systems is adopted to capture the main variables that contribute to answering this question.

3.2 SLR Research Sources

Once the SLR research question was defined, it was crucial to conduct the SLR through reliable sources such as digital libraries and databases. The 42 retained articles related CSFs of CRM systems were identified and SCOPUS indexing was utilized as one of the most extensive databases containing abstracts and citations for peer-reviewed literature. The six sources that constituted the SLR are classified in Fig. 2:

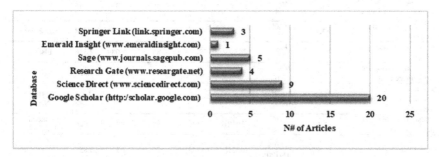

Fig. 2. Classification of articles by database

The retained articles' publication date range between 2007 and 2020. A main emphasis is placed on the most recent articles published in 2018, 2019, 2020 to ensure the collection of the most recent data regarding CSFs of CRM systems and DAC (as shown in **Fig. 3**).

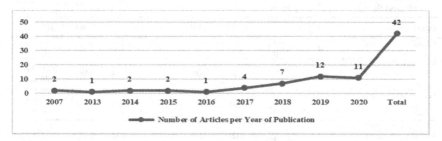

Fig. 3. Classification of articles by year of publication

This SLR uses Scopus for the selection of retained papers.

Due to the vast amount of data available in the literature the retained articles focused on the main disciplines related to the study on hand to ensure that specific information is collected: Marketing (11 articles), Information Systems Management (23 articles), and Business and Management (8 articles). For example, studies related to medicine are very rich with CSFs of CRM systems' information. Nevertheless, they were not retained due to the irrelevance of the results for the study on hand.

Details of the Scopus report for 2021 related to selected papers are summarized in Table 2:

Table 2. Scopus Report: CiteScore, SNIP and SJR Values

Source title	SCOPUS CiteScore	Highest percentile	2018-21 Citations	2018-21 Documents	% Cited (citations / documents)	SNIP	SJR	Publisher
Applied Computing and Informatics	24.3	99.0% 4/747	1678	69	87	3.512	1.589	Emerald Publishing
Journal of Management Information Systems	13.9	97.0% 3/120	2316	167	76	3.54	4.365	Taylor & Francis
Technological Forecasting and Social Change	13.7	97.0% 12/423	25247	1843	85	3.097	2.336	Elsevier
Information and Management	13.1	97.0% 4/120	5151	392	83	3.092	2.558	Elsevier
Journal of Business Research	11.2	94.0% 12/195	30303	2707	85	3.089	2.316	Elsevier
Information Processing and Management	11	97.0% 2/62	7899	718	86	3.01	1.854	Elsevier
Business and Information Systems Engineering	8.9	88.0% 40/353	1349	151	84	2.239	1.279	Springer Nature
Industrial Management and Data Systems	7.3	92.0% 5/57	3018	412	84	1.411	1.006	Emerald Publishing
PLoS ONE	5.6	87.0% 15/120	365216	65549	75	1.368	0.852	Public Library of Science
Journal of Open Innovation: Technology, Market, and Complexity	5.1	95.0% 12/260	3066	603	81	1.414	0.588	MDPI
Sustainability	5	86.0% 99/747	181699	36485	73	1.31	0.664	MDPI
Information (Switzerland)	4.2	64.0% 125/353	7540	1807	70	1.133	0.624	MDPI
Journal of Relationship Marketing	3.9	60.0% 77/195	232	59	75	1.179	0.591	Taylor & Francis
Entrepreneurial Business and Economics Review	3.7	90.0% 60/608	703	191	80	0.83	0.473	Cracow University of Economics
Complexity	3.5	79.0% 25/120	15481	4404	62	0.766	0.463	Hindawi
Journal of Marketing Analytics	3.4	79.0% 39/189	251	74	62	1.41	0.535	Springer Nature
International Journal of Business Information Systems	1.8	41.0% 78/132	560	309	50	0.787	0.381	Inderscience Publishers
Lecture Notes in Business Information Processing	1.8	44.0% 235/423	4586	2546	53	0.469	0.303	Springer Nature
EAI/Springer Innovations in Communication and Computing	1.3	25.0% 267/359	1421	1108	38	0.303	0.178	Springer Nature
International Journal of Modern Education and Computer Science	1.1	36.0% 900/1406 Education	72	68	41	0.866	0.374	Modern Education and Computer Science Press
Journal of Applied Business Research	1	35.0% 253/394	285	280	43	0.362	0.166	Western Academic Publishers
Journal of Applied Business Research	copus	20.0% 335/423	76	87	30	0.363	0.136	Western Academic Publishers
Journal of Physics: Conference Series	0.8	18.0% 195/240	74925	96702	30	0.395	0.21	IOP Publishing Ltd

(continued)

Table 2. (*continued*)

Source title	SCOPUS CiteScore	Highest percentile	2018-21 Citations	2018-21 Documents	% Cited (citations / documents)	SNIP	SJR	Publisher
Journal of Global Business and Technology	0.4	11.0% 173/195	9	24	29	0.456	0.11	Global Business and Technology Association
Journal of Xi'an University of Architecture & Technology	0.4	39.0% 90/149	193	487	25	0.368	0.172	Science Press
International Journal of Simulation: Systems, Science and Technology	N/A	N/A	N/A	N/A	N/A	0.291	N/A	*Discontinued*
Asian Social Science	N/A	N/A	N/A	N/A	N/A	N/A	N/A	*Discontinued*
International Journal of Scientific and Technology Research	N/A	N/A	N/A	N/A	N/A	0.421	N/A	*Discontinued*

3.3 The Use of Keywords in the SLR Finding Process

The use of keywords was applied to find papers that are connected to the study on hand. Popular Boolean operators such as "AND, OR, NOT" were used in the library databases to focus the search on the related topics of interest for each author. Thus, the keywords applied are: 'big data analytics', 'critical success factors', 'CSFs' "customer relationship management', 'CRM', 'data analytics capabilities', 'CRM analytics', 'literature review', 'marketing', 'measurement scales', and 'metrics'.

3.4 Data Extraction through the SLR

In order to manage the large volume of available articles, a set of criteria was employed to determine which papers would be included in the research. The following considerations were taken into account:

- The publication year of the article (between 2000 and 2020).
- Articles from reliable journals and conference proceedings with SCOPUS impact.
- Articles with a focus on the disciplines of Marketing, Management Information Systems, Business and Management.
- Relevant abstracts, keywords, and results.

Exclusion criteria were also used to ensure the quality and relevance of the selected articles. Specifically, articles were excluded if:

- The abstracts were irrelevant.
- The measurement scales used were outdated.
- Duplicates of the same article through a different source.
- The results were not relevant, or the articles did not fall within the relevant disciplines.

Additionally, books, theses, and unpublished works were also excluded.

3.5   Findings and Discussion: Main Concepts and Measurement Scales of CSFs for CRM Systems Integrating DAC

Based on the findings from the available literature, there is a large number of CSFs scattered throughout the applied literature. Inspired by the mapping process applied by Meyliana et al. (2016), and to facilitate comprehension, all CSFs have been categorized and mapped according to the six dimensions previously identified through the LR, as summarized in Table 1: Technology, People, Process, Data Analytics Capabilities (DAC), Intrinsic Outcomes, and Net Benefits. This mapping was informed by the research of Farhan et al. (2018), Khlif and Jallouli (2014), Meyliana et al. (2016), and Mikalef et al. (2020) that investigated the CSFs for CRM systems and the effect of DAC on CRM systems. The SLR resulted in the identification of 24 variables that measure the relevant dimensions of the theoretical framework on hand. A more detailed presentation of the mapped CSFs is illustrated as follows:

Technology Dimension – Integration of ERP System with CRM Functionality. The available literature highlighted the importance of unified data platforms by integrating the ERP system with CRM functionality, such as the Omni-channels and suppliers' portal (Chen & Popovich, 2003; Chen et al, 2016; 2020; Krasnikov et al., 2009; Kitchens et al., 2018; Mendoza et al., 2007). It provides organizations with the necessary tools to stay competitive in today's market. By leveraging the insights gained from this integration, businesses can improve customer service, better track their customer relationships, and optimize their operations. The SLR results have identified the following sub-dimensions and measurement scales for 'Technology' dimension, as shown in Table 3:

Table 3. "Technology" dimension of CRM successful implementation: dimensions, sub-dimensions, and measurement scales (SLR results)

#	CONCEPTUAL LEVELS			VARIABLES		Sources	Description
	Dimension	N#	Sub-Dimension Title	N#	Retained Variables from SLR Results		
1	TECHNOLOGY 'Integration of ERP System with CRM Functionality'	–		1.1.1	System Quality	Guimaraes, Staples and McKeen (2007), DeLone and McLean (2003).	System Quality measures the desired characteristics of an e-commerce system (Usability, availability, reliability, adaptability, and response time).
				1.1.2	Knowledge Stock	Kulkarni et al. (2006); Pitt et al. (1995)	The degree of relevance, comprehensiveness, reliability, and accuracy of the codified knowledge in the IT system.

The SLR results focus on the importance of the system's quality and knowledge stock in the implementation of CRM and its impact on organizational performance. It also highlights their impact on organizational performance (Chen & Popovich, 2003; Chen et al, 2016; 2020; Krasnikov et al., 2009; Kitchens et al., 2018; Mendoza et al., 2007). System quality is critical for successful CRM implementation as it ensures that the CRM system meets users' needs and expectations, leading to improved efficiency, effectiveness, customer satisfaction, and loyalty (Rana et al., 2021). The knowledge stock of an organization is also essential in effective CRM implementation, including both tacit and explicit knowledge (Chen et al., 2020). Investing in employee training and development and creating a culture of knowledge-sharing and continuous learning can improve knowledge stock (Mehdiabadi et al., 2022).Integrating CRM and ERP systems is vital for modern business operations (Chen et al., 2016; 2020), but requires experienced personnel, specialized software, and consideration of costs related to implementation and maintenance (Mehdiabadi et al., 2022).

People Dimension – Internal Commitment 'HUMAN SKILLS' The available literature highlighted the importance of 'Internal Commitment' in term of 'Human Skills' as a major sub-dimension for 'People': it would help organizations manage customer interactions effectively (Chen & Popovich, 2003; Mendoza et al., 2007; Kumar, 2018). The SLR results have identified the following sub-dimensions and measurement scales for 'People' dimension, as shown in Table 4:

Table 4. "People" dimension of CRM successful Implementation: dimensions, sub-dimensions and measurement scales (SLR results)

CONCEPTUAL LEVELS				VARIABLES		
#	Dimension	N#	Sub-Dimension Title	N#	Retained Variables from SLR Results	Sources	Description
2	PEOPLE *'Internal Commitment' (Human skills)*		–	2.1.1	Customer interaction management capability	Jayachandran et al. (2005); Feng and Wang (2008); Feng and Wang (2012); Alshura (2018)	Refers to the skills that firms use to identify, acquire and retain profitable customers (e.g., customer identification, customer acquisition and customer retention).
				2.1.2	Customer Orientation	Feng and Wang (2012); Jayachandran et al. (2005); Deshpande´ et al. (1993); Day and Van den Bulte (2002)	Reflects the values, behavioral norms, the shared mental modes that enables a firm to put customers' interest first
				2.1.3	Customers' Involvement	NIkzad et al, (2015); Farhan et al. (2018)	Refers to the state of mind that motivates a consumer to make a purchase, or the importance a consumer places on a product or service. The engagement level between employees and customers can have an influence in the decision-making process.

The success of CRM is not only measured by technology factors, it is essential to consider several key human factors, including employee commitment, customer interaction management capability (CIMC), customer orientation, and customer involvement.According to Hamida et al. (2021), employee commitment can be fostered by providing training and development opportunities, recognizing and rewarding contributions to CRM, and establishing a culture of customer service. Firms with high CIMC, as highlighted by Shahbaz et al. (2020), can better understand customer needs and preferences, leading to increased customer satisfaction and loyalty. Improving CIMC can be achieved by investing in technology, process improvements, and employee training. Customer orientation, as emphasized by Hamida et al. (2022) and Kumar et al. (2021), is critical for tailoring products and services to customer needs and preferences. Technologies such AI, IoT and Blockchain have contributed to automate personalization of products and services in order to influence customer behaviors (Khemiri & Jallouli, 2022). Furthermore, organizations can develop a customer-oriented culture by prioritizing customer needs, involving them in product development, offering incentives for participation and continuously gathering feedback to improve satisfaction. Lastly, customer involvement, as noted by Shokouhyar et al. (2021), has a positive impact on customer satisfaction and loyalty.

Process Dimension – 'Process Holistic Approach and Marketing Channel Strategies'. Concerning the 'Process' dimension, two sub-dimensions were identified in literature (Aljawarneh et al., 2020; Rund, 2018): (1) Process holistic approach and (2) Marketing channel strategies for traditional stores and online shopping. The SLR results have identified the following sub-dimensions and measurement scales, as shown in Table 5. "Process" dimension of CRM successful implementation: dimensions, sub-dimensions and measurement scales (SLR results):The SLR results highlight the importance of organizational structures, effective CRM processes, sales automation, customer win-back capabilities, and marketing automation as essential factors of the 'process' dimension that contribute to the measurement of CRM success (Khanh et al., 2021; Alalwan et al., 2019; Eriksson et al., 2021; Onyike & Orga, 2022; Chatterjee et al., 2019; Singh et al., 2021).A customer-centric organizational structure that promotes collaboration and decision-making positively impacts CRM success (Khanh et al., 2021), and effective CRM processes lead to improved customer satisfaction, loyalty, and organizational performance (Alalwan et al., 2019). Sales automation and marketing automation are also critical components for process' efficiency (Chatterjee et al. 2019; Eriksson et al., 2021), and require investments in technology and employee training for output maximization. Lastly, having customer win-back capabilities through feedback systems, surveys, and data analytics positively affects customer satisfaction and loyalty (Singh et al., 2021).

Data Analytics Capabilities Dimension The available literature revealed 3 sub-dimensions for DAC: (1) Unified customers' data platforms, (2) Proactive analytics capabilities and (3) Contextual analytics (Robert et al., 2014; Payne et al., 2017; Harvard Business Review Analytical Services, 2018; Chapman, 2019). The identified sub-dimensions and measurement scales, through the SLR results, are shown in Table 6:The SLR results identify seven DAC measurement scales for a successful CRM implementation. They are grouped into three sub-dimensions for the purpose of highlighting the transversal role of DAC with technology, people and process.

Unified Customers' Data Platforms: The Transversal Role of DAC with Technology. To improve customer experience, organizations need to adopt Knowledge Management Systems (KMS) and advanced analytics. KMS helps in capturing, storing, and sharing knowledge, while advanced analytics uses statistical methods, algorithms, and machine

Table 5. "Process" dimension of CRM successful implementation: dimensions, sub-dimensions and measurement scales (SLR results)

CONCEPTUAL LEVELS				VARIABLES		
#	Dimension	N#	Sub-Dimension Title	N#	Retained Variables from SLR Results	Sources	Description
				3.1.1	Organizational Structure	Rahimi et al (2001); Esteves et al (2001), Daniel et al (2002); Ahearne et al (2012); Fidler et al (2012); Almotairi (2008)	How the organization is structured and different departments communicate together.
		3.1	Process Holistic Approach	3.1.2	Customer-centric organizational system	Srivastava et al. (1999); Day (2003); Boulding et al. (2005); Jayachandran et al. (2005)	Refers to the effectiveness of CRM activities that depends on how CRM is integrated with the firm's existing processes and structures
3	PROCESS			3.1.3	Sales Automation	Kotelu et al. (2012) ; Kim et al. (2007)	Sales automation is the mechanization of manual, time-consuming sales tasks using software, artificial intelligence (AI), and other digital tools.
		3.2	Marketing Channel Strategies (traditional and online)	3.2.1	Customer win-back capabilities	Jayachandran et al. (2005); Reichheld and Sasser (1999); Feng and Wang (2008); Feng and Wang (2012); Alshura (2018)	The skills firms use to re-establish the relationship with lost or inactive but profitable customers since loss of those customers will have a huge negative impact on firm performance in the long run.
				3.2.2	Marketing Automation	Kotelu et al. (2012) ; Kim et al. (2007)	Marketing automation is technology that manages marketing processes and multifunctional campaigns, across multiple channels, automatically.

learning to analyze data and identify patterns (Chaithanapat & Rakthin, 2020).For effective integration of CRM with KMS, organizations need to focus on their IT and big data analytics capabilities. According to Mikalef et al. (2020), successful integration requires investment in technology, data management, and analytics capabili ties. Additionally, Suoniemi et al. (2021) emphasized the importance of DAC, which enhance an organization's ability to adopt new technologies and processes to achieve its goals. These steps will help organizations effectively integrate strategic and operational CRM, leading to an exceptional customer experience and reinforcing the transversal role of DAC with technology (Chaithanapat & Rakthin, 2020; Mikalef et al., 2020; Suoniemi et al., 2021).

Table 6. "Data Analytics Capabilities" dimension of CRM successful implementation: dimensions, sub-dimensions and measurement scales (SLR results)

		CONCEPTUAL LEVELS		VARIABLES			
	#	Dimension	N#	Sub-Dimension Title	N#	Retained Variables from SLR Results	Sources	Description

DATA ANALYTICS CAPABILITIES	#	Dimension	N#	Sub-Dimension Title	N#	Retained Variables from SLR Results	Sources	Description
	4	DAC (Technology)	4.1	Unified Customers Data Platforms (online and offline channels)	4.1.1	Knowledge Management Systems	Kulkarni et al. (2006); Pitt et al. (1995)	The degree of availability, accessibility, ease of use, stability, and responsive time provided by the IT infrastructure.
					4.1.2	Advanced analytics	Akter et al. (2017); Raguseo et al, (2018)	The extent to which the employees of the organizations perceive that DAC will provide the information regarding customers by using advanced and latest tools of analyzing data.
					4.1.3	IT Capability	Gold et al. (2001); Tanriverdi (2005)	The degree of sharing existing information, finding information sources, creating data, and executing IT-based tasks within a firm
		DAC (People)	4.2	Proactive Analytics Capabilities	4.2.1	Big Data Analytics Capabilities (Human Skills and Intangible)	Gupta and George (2016); Kiron et al. (2014); Wamba et al. (2017)	Big Data Analytics Capability (BDAC) is defined as the ability of the firm to capture and analyze data toward the generation of insights, by effectively deploying its data, technology, and talent through firm-wide processes, roles and structures.
					4.2.2	Improved relation knowledge	Akter et al. (2016) ; Jiang et al. (2003); Kim et al. (2012)	The degree to which the organization's employees perceive that outcomes provided by DAC will improve their knowledge regarding the improvement of relations with the Customers.
		DAC (Process)	4.3	Contextual Analytics	4.3.1	Big Data Analytics Capability (Data and Technology)	Reinartz et al. (2004); Gupta and George (2016); Kiron et al. (2014); Wamba et al. (2017)	Big Data Analytics Capability (BDAC) is defined as the ability of the firm to capture and analyze data toward the generation of insights, by effectively deploying its data, technology, and talent through firm-wide processes, roles and structures.
					4.3.2	Customer relationship upgrading capabilities	Jayachandran et al. (2005); Feng and Wang (2008); Feng and Wang (2012); Alshura (2018)	Refers to the skills that firms use for up-selling (sell more expensive items, upgrades) and cross-selling (sell additional products or service) to existing customers based on scientific customer data analysis.

Proactive Analytics Capabilities: The Transversal Role of DAC with 'PEOPLE'. According to Chatterjee et al. (2022), the ability to effectively analyze and interpret large volumes of data extracted from CRM systems depends on an organization's big data analytics capabilities, which involve both human skills and technology. Furthermore, Al-Suraihi et al. (2020) explain that improved relation knowledge is vital for an organization's ability to leverage data to gain a deeper understanding of customer needs, preferences, and behaviors. Therefore, CRM success depends on the organizations' human capability in using data analytics to segment customers, personalize marketing and sales activities, and enhance the overall customer experience.

Contextual Analytics: The Transversal Role of DAC with 'PROCESS'. Big Data Analytics Capability (Data and Technology) and customer relationship upgrading capabilities are important factors for measuring CRM success (Kumar & Mokha, 2021; Shahbaz et al., 2021). Organizations can enhance customer relationships over time by utilizing data analytics to identify opportunities for personalized services, loyalty programs, and improved customer experiences (Shahbaz et al., 2021).Moreover, Cao et al. (2021) stressed the importance of contextual analytics in marketing analytics and its favorable impact on various aspects of organizational performance, including marketing planning, implementation, brand management, customer relationship management, and product development management. Thus, the transversal role of DAC with an organization's process can be enhanced by prioritizing these key factors for better customer-centric capabilities and organizational performance.

Intrinsic Outcomes Dimension – 'Effective Marketing Decisions and Customer Satisfaction'. The available literature highlighted two sub-dimensions for 'Intrinsic Outcomes' (Krishna & Schwarz, 2014; MacInnis & Folkes, 2017; Parker et al., 2016; Stone & O'Shea, 2019): (1) Effective marketing decisions and (2) Customer satisfaction. The SLR results are summarized in Table 7 and list the identified sub-dimensions and measurement scales.This section explores the relationship between CRM intrinsic outcomes and the identified key success factors. A successful implementation of CRM systems can lead to better marketing capabilities, such as lead generation, customer segmentation, and campaign management (Cao et al., 2021). Dynamic capabilities, such as the ability to adapt to changing customer needs, are essential for organizations seeking to achieve CRM intrinsic outcomes (Chatterjee et al., 2022). Perceived customer services, including responsiveness, empathy, and reliability, are positively related to customer satisfaction and loyalty (Kumar & Mokha, 2021). Personalization can enhance customer experiences and improve customer loyalty (Wang & Dong, 2022). Improving customer interactions can increase customer satisfaction and loyalty (Kumar & Mokha, 2021). Over-all, investing in CRM systems, developing dynamic capabilities, improving customer services, providing personalized experiences, and increasing customer satisfaction and loyalty can lead to better business performance and a competitive advantage in today's market.

Table 7. "Intrinsic Outcomes" dimension of CRM successful implementation: dimensions, subdimensions and measurement scales (SLR results)

CONCEPTUAL LEVELS				VARIABLES	Sources	Description
#	Dimension	N#	Sub-Dimension Title	N#	Retained Variables from SLR Results		
5	INTRINSIC OUTCOMES	5.1	Effective Marketing Decisions	5.1.1	Marketing Capabilities	Spanos and Lioukas (2001); Wilden and Gudergan (2015); Morgan et al. (2004); Day and Van den Bulte (2002); Day (200)3	Marketing capabilities are defined as the ability of the firm to serve certain customers based on the collective knowledge, skills, and resources related to market needs. (Example: brand management capabilities, customer-relating capabilities)
				5.1.2	Dynamic Capabilities	Teece (2007); Teece et al. (1997); Hunt and Morgan (1995)	Dynamic capabilities are defined as the capacity of the firm to (a) sense and shape opportunities and threats, (b) seize opportunities, and (c) maintain competitiveness through enhancing, combining, protecting, and, when necessary, reconfiguring the business enterprise's intangible and tangible assets.
				5.1.3	Better Customer Services (Perceived)	Doll and Torkzadeh (1998), Trivellas and Santouridis (2013)	The degree to which the employees perceive the information as an output provided by DAC would help provide better services to customers
				5.1.4	Personalization	Parasuraman et al. (2005) ; Xu et al. (2009)	The degree to which the organization's employees perceive that DAC will provide customized information as an output regarding the customers
		5.2	Customer Satisfaction	5.2.1	Customer Satisfaction & Loyalty	Roh and al (2005); Anderson et al. (2004); Oliver (1999); Kotler (1997); Fornell (1992)	Satisfaction is "a person's feeling of pleasure or disappointed resulting from comparing a product's perceived performance (or outcome) in relation to his or her expectations". Loyalty is "a deeply held psychological commitment to rebuy or repatronize a preferred product/service consistently in the future, thereby causing repetitive same-brand or same brand-set purchasing, despite situational influences and marketing efforts having the potential to cause switching behavior".

Net Benefits Dimension. The available literature highlighted 'business profitability' as a major sub-dimension of 'Extrinsic Outcomes', also referred to as 'Net Benefits' (Delone & McLean, 2003; Petter et al., 2013; Shahbaz et al., 2020). The SLR results have identified two measurement scales (as shown in Table 8).

Table 8. "Net Benefits" dimension of CRM successful implementation: dimensions, sub-dimensions and measurement scales (SLR results)

	CONCEPTUAL LEVELS				VARIABLES	Sources	Description
#	Dimension	N#	Sub-Dimension Title	N#	Retained Variables from SLR Results		
6	EXTRINSIC OUTCOMES 'Net Benefits' (Business Profitability)		–	6.1.1	Perceived Sales Performance	Behrman et al. (1982); Hunter et al. (2006); Ryals (2005); Shahbaz (2020)	Perceived sales value refers to employees" evaluation about analytical and operational sales processes in a firm.
				6.1.2	Competitive Performance	Barney (1991, 2001); Peteraf (1993); Rai and Tang (2010); Roh and al. (2005), Ngobo and Ramaroson (2005)	Competitive performance is defined as the degree to which a firm attains its objectives in relation to its main competitors

SLR results show that the net benefits of CRM have been explored in the literature, highlighting its ability to measure the firm performance and customer satisfaction (Rana et al., 2021). Perceived sales performance and competitive performance are critical components in understanding the net benefits of CRM. Sawal et al. (2022) found that perceived sales performance leads to higher levels of customer satisfaction, resulting in improved competitive advantage. Implementing a CRM system can result in various net benefits for an organization, including increased efficiency, improved customer satisfaction and loyalty, better customer insights, optimized processes, and increased revenue (Gil-Gomez et al., 2020).

3.6 Enriched Theoretical Framework: Measurement Scales for CRM Successful implementation

Based on the findings through the SLR, **Fig. 4** presents an enriched theoretical framework that synthesizes all dimensions of CSFs for CRM successful implementation. It includes the main dimensions, sub-dimensions along with the relevant variables that measure a successful CRM implementation. Moreover, it highlights the transversal role of DAC with technology, people and process; along with the intrinsic outcomes and net benefits.

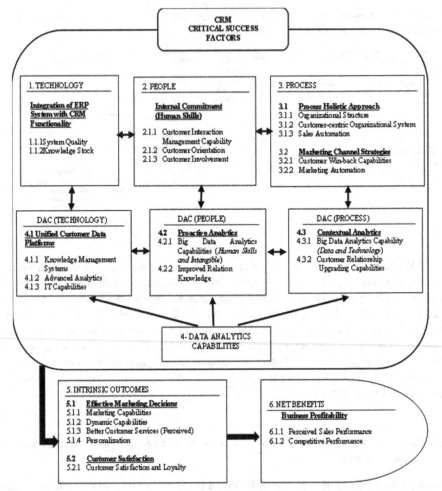

Fig. 4. Enriched theoretical framework of Critical Success Factors for CRM implementation (SLR results).

4   Conclusion, Implications and Recommendations for the Future

An effective implementation of CRM systems helps companies in achieving a sustainable competitive advantage towards a greater business profitability (Dixit, 2022). Businesses should stay up to date with frequent changes in market trends and new E-commerce tools and techniques. Previous related studies have acknowledged the growing role of DAC for successful CRM implementation, leading companies towards a new set of skills that are yet to be measured. The objective of this study is to providing companies with measurement scales for testing the integration of DAC dimension with other CSFs of CRM systems. Hence, this paper uses the SLR approach in an attempt to identify the available CSFs dimensions, sub-dimensions and measurement scales for successful CRM implementation, while integrating the DAC dimension.

The SLR results have identified six dimensions for CSFs that contribute to the success of CRM systems: (1) technology, where CRM functions should become an integral part of the enterprise resources' planning (ERP) system (2) people, highlighting the importance of internal commitment in organizations (3) process, with an emphasis on the holistic approach and online/in-store marketing strategies (4) DAC "as a transversal and integrative dimension that provides added value to other CSFs" (5) intrinsic outcomes in terms of effective marketing strategies and customer satisfaction, and (6) net benefits for both firms and customers.

The SLR results were illustrated in an enriched theoretical framework, as shown in Fig. 4, including of the key CSFs for CRM systems. These results are expected to contribute to extending research further. Indeed, the current study facilitates the quantitative empirical validation of the theoretical framework on hand in different contexts and fields.

Finally, the SLR results were limited to literature of peer-reviewed journals. Future studies can benefit from additional sources such as other databases, books and conferences' proceedings that can provide a more complete analysis .

References

A harvard business review: analytical services: In: Real-Time Analytics: The Key to Unlocking Customer Insights & Driving the Customer Experience I SAS. Retrieved 10 April 2023 (2018). https://www.sas.com/en/whitepapers/real-time-analytics-109676.html

Al-Alawi, A., Alalawi, E.: Customer relationship management: the application of data mining techniques in the telecommunications sector. J. Xi'an Univ. Archit. Technol. **XII**(IV), 3836-3876 (2020) https://doi.org/10.37896/jxat12.04/1125

Al-Alawi, R., Oliver, G., Donaldson, J.F.: Systematic review: predictors of students' success in baccalaureate nursing programs. Nurse Educ. Practice **48**, 102865 (2020). https://doi.org/10.1016/j.nepr.2020.102865

Al-Suraihi, W.A., Al-Suraihi, A.H.A., Ibrahim, I., Al-Tahitah, A., Abdulrab, M.: The effect of customer relationship management on consumer behavior: a case of retail industry in Malaysia. Int. J. Manag. Human Sci. (IJMHS) **4**, 32-40 (2020). https://ejournal.lucp.net/index.php/ijmhs/article/view/1139

Alalwan, A.A., Baabdullah, A.M., Rana, N.P., Dwivedi, Y.K., Kizgin, H.: Examining the influence of mobile store features on user e-satisfaction: extending utaut2 with personalization, responsiveness, and perceived security and privacy. In: Pappas, I.O., Mikalef, P., Dwivedi, Y.K., Jaccheri, L., Krogstie, J., Mäntymäki, M. (eds.) I3E 2019. LNCS, vol. 11701, pp. 50–61. Springer, Cham (2019). https://doi.org/10.1007/978-3-030-29374-1_5

Ali, M., Alshawi, S.: Investigating the impact of cross-cultural on CRM implementation: a comparative study. Brunel Univ. Res. Arch. **89**, 391–403 (2003). http://bura.brunel.ac.uk/handle/2438/1876

Aljawarneh, N.M., Sokiyna, M., Obeidat, A.M., Alomari, K.A.K., Alradaideh, A.T., Alomari, Z.S.: The role of CRM fog computing on innovation and customer service quality: an empirical study. Market. Manag. Innov. **2**, 286–297 (2020). https://doi.org/10.21272/mmi.2020.2-21

Almohaimmeed, B.: The impact of analytical CRM on strategic CRM, operational CRM and customer satisfaction: empirical study on commercial banks. Uncertain Supply Chain Manag. **9**(3), 711–718 (2021). https://doi.org/10.5267/j.uscm.2021.4.007

Almotairi: A framework for successful CRM implementation [Citeseer]. In: European and Mediterranean Conference on Information Systems, pp. 1–12 (2009). https://citeseerx.ist.psu.edu/document?repid=rep1&type=pdf&doi=6a945dc46e900fe9e444ba1ca72a5e9d8236ed49

Arab, P., Rofouei, M.K., Khani, H., Gupta, V.K., Vafaei, Z.: Multi-walled carbon nanotubes-ionic liquid-carbon paste electrode as a super selectivity sensor: application to potentiometric monitoring of mercury ion(II). J. Hazardous Mater. **183**(1–3), 402–409 (2010). https://doi.org/10.1016/j.jhazmat.2010.07.039

Askool, S., Nakata, K.: A conceptual model for acceptance of social CRM systems based on a scoping study. AI & Soc. **26**(3), 205–220 (2010). https://doi.org/10.1007/s00146-010-0311-5

Ayyagari, M.R.: A Framework for analytical CRM assessments challenges and recommendations. Int. J. Bus. Soc. Sci. **10**(6), 5–13 (2019). https://doi.org/10.30845/ijbss.v10n6p2

Bach Tobji, M.A., Jallouli, R., Koubaa, Y., Nijholt, A. (eds.): Digital Economy. Emerging Technologies and Business Innovation. In: Lecture Notes in Business Information Processing (2018). https://doi.org/10.1007/978-3-319-97749-2

Benslama, T., Jallouli, R.: Clustering of social media data and marketing decisions. In: Tobji, M.A.B., Jallouli, R., Samet, A., Touzani, M., Strat, V.A., Pocatilu, P. (eds.) ICDEc 2020. LNBIP, vol. 395, pp. 53–65. Springer, Cham (2020). https://doi.org/10.1007/978-3-030-646 42-4_5

Benslama, T., Jallouli, R.: Social media data analytics for marketing strategies: the path from data to value. J. Telecommun. Dig. Econ. **10**(2), 96–110 (2022). https://doi.org/10.18080/jtde.v10 n2.523

Boulding, W., Staelin, R., Ehret, M., Johnston, W.J.: A Customer relationship management roadmap: What is known, potential pitfalls, and Where to go. J. Mark. **69**(4), 155–166 (2005). https://doi.org/10.1509/jmkg.2005.69.4.155

Cao, G., Tian, N., Blankson, C.: Big data, marketing analytics, and firm marketing capabilities. J. Comput. Inform. Syst. **62**(3), 442–451 (2021). https://doi.org/10.1080/08874417.2020.184 2270

Chaithanapat, P., Rakthin, S.: Customer knowledge management in SMEs: review and research agenda. Knowl. Process Manag. **28**(1), 71–89 (2020). https://doi.org/10.1002/kpm.1653

Chalmeta, R.: Methodology for customer relationship management. J. Syst. Softw. **79**(7), 1015–1024 (2006). https://doi.org/10.1016/j.jss.2005.10.018

Chapman, C.: Commentary: mind your text in marketing practice. J. Market. **84**(1), 26–31 (2019). https://doi.org/10.1177/0022242919886882

Chatterjee, S., Chaudhuri, R.: Adoption of artificial intelligence integrated customer relationship management in organizations for sustainability. In: Vrontis, D., Thrassou, A., Weber, Y., Riad Shams, S.M., Tsoukatos, E., Efthymiou, L. (eds.) Business Under Crisis, vol. III. PSCBRIAEAB, pp. 137–156. Springer, Cham (2022). https://doi.org/10.1007/978-3-030-765 83-5_6

Chatterjee, S., Chaudhuri, R., Vrontis, D.: Big data analytics in strategic sales performance: mediating role of CRM capability and moderating role of leadership support. EuroMed J. Bus. **17**(3), 295–311 (2022). https://doi.org/10.1108/EMJB-07-2021-0105

Chatterjee, S., Chaudhuri, R., Vrontis, D., Thrassou, A., Ghosh, S.K.: ICT-enabled CRM system adoption: a dual Indian qualitative case study and conceptual framework development. J. Asia Bus. Stud. **15**(2), 257–277 (2020). https://doi.org/10.1108/JABS-05-2020-0198

Chatterjee, S., Ghosh, S.K., Chaudhuri, R., Nguyen, B.: Are CRM systems ready for AI integration?: a conceptual framework of organizational readiness for effective AI-CRM integration. Bottom Line **32**(2), 144–157 (2019). https://doi.org/10.1108/BL-02-2019-0069

Chen, I.J., Popovich, K.: Understanding customer relationship management (CRM): people, process and technology. Bus. Process Manag. J. **9**(5), 672–688 (2003). https://doi.org/10.1108/14637150310496758

Chen, R.R., Ou, C.X., Wang, W., Peng, Z., Davison, R.M.: Moving beyond the direct impact of using CRM systems on frontline employees' service performance: the mediating role of adaptive behaviour. Inf. Syst. J. **30**(3), 458–491 (2020). https://doi.org/10.1111/isj.12265

Da Silva, R.V., Rahimi, I.D.: A critical success factor model for CRM Implementation. Int. J. Electron. Customer Relat. Manag. **1**(1), 3 (2007). https://doi.org/10.1504/IJECRM.2007. 014422

De Mauro, A., Sestino, A., Bacconi, A.: Machine learning and artificial intelligence use in marketing: a general taxonomy. Ital. J. Mark. **2022**(4), 439–457 (2022). https://doi.org/10.1007/ s43039-022-00057-w

Dixit, S.: Artifical intelligence and CRM. In: Advances in Marketing, Customer Relationship Management, and E-Services, pp. 92–114 (2022). https://doi.org/10.4018/978-1-7998-7959-6.ch006

Eriksson, D., Hilletofth, P., Tate, W., Gothager, M.: Critical manufacturing prerequisites for successful reshoring. Operat. Supply Chain Manag.: an Int. J. **14**, 249–260 (2021). https://doi.org/ 10.31387/oscm0450300

Farhan, M.S., Abed, A.H., Ellatif, M.A.: A systematic review for the determination and classification of the CRM critical success factors supporting with their metrics. Future Comput. Inform. J. **3**(2), 398–416 (2018). https://doi.org/10.1016/j.fcij.2018.11.003

Gil-Gomez, H., Guerola-Navarro, V., Oltra-Badenes, R., Lozano-Quilis, J.A.: Customer relationship management: digital transformation and sustainable business model innovation. Econ. Res.-Ekonomska Istraživanja **33**(1), 2733–2750 (2020). https://doi.org/10.1080/1331677X. 2019.1676283

Gončarovs, P.: Data analytics in CRM processes: a literature review. Inform. Technol. Manag. Sci. **20**(1), 103–108 (2017). https://doi.org/10.1515/itms-2017-0018

Guerola-Navarro, V., Oltra-Badenes, R., Gil-Gomez, H., Gil-Gomez, J.A.: Research model for measuring the impact of customer relationship management (CRM) on performance indicators. Econ. Res.-Ekonomska Istraživanja **34**(1), 2669–2691 (2020). https://doi.org/10.1080/ 1331677X.2020.1836992

Gupta, M.K., Chandra, P.: A comprehensive survey of data mining. Int. J. Inf. Technol. **12**(4), 1243–1257 (2020). https://doi.org/10.1007/s41870-020-00427-7

Hamida, A., Alshehhia, A., Abdullaha, A., Mohamed, E.: Key success factors for customer relationship management (CRM) PRojects within SMEs. Emirati J. Bus. Econ. Soc.; Stud. **1**(2), 73–85 (2022). https://doi.org/10.54878/ejbess.176

Hargreaves, I., Roth, D., Karim, M.R., Nayebi, M., Ruhe, G.: Effective customer relationship management at ATB financial: a case study on industry-academia collaboration in data analytics. In: Moshirpour, M., Far, B., Alhajj, R. (eds.) Highlighting the Importance of Big Data Management and Analysis for Various Applications. SBD, vol. 27, pp. 45–59. Springer, Cham (2018). https://doi.org/10.1007/978-3-319-60255-4_4

Hasan, A.A.T.: Sustainable Customer Relationship Management (sus-CRM) in Customer Loyalty Perspective: An Empirical Study on Restaurant Industries in Bangladesh. Global Media J. (2021). https://doi.org/10.35841/1550-7521.21.19.258

Iriarte, C., Bayona, S.: IT projects success factors: a literature review. Int. J. Inform. Syst. Project Manag. **8**(2), 49–78 (2021). https://aisel.aisnet.org/ijispm/vol8/iss2/4

Jabado, R., Jallouli, R.: An enriched framework for CRM Success factors outlining data analytics capabilities' dimension. In: Alareeni, B., Hamdan, A., Elgedawy, I. (eds.) ICBT 2020. LNNS, vol. 194, pp. 102–130. Springer, Cham (2021). https://doi.org/10.1007/978-3-030-69221-6_9

Jallouli, R., Kaabi, S.: Mapping top strategic e-commerce technologies in the digital marketing literature. J. Telecommun. Dig. Econ. **10**(3), 149–164 (2022). https://doi.org/10.18080/jtde. v10n3.554

Jiang, H., Zhang, Y.: Research on customer relationship management in software industry based on multi-agent. In: Advances in Social Science, Education and HumanitiesResearch (2015). https://doi.org/10.2991/emcs-15.2015.168

Kaabi, Safa, Jallouli, Rim: Overview of e-commerce technologies, data analysis capabilities and marketing knowledge. In: Jallouli, R., Bach Tobji, M.A., Bélisle, D., Mellouli, S., Abdallah, F., Osman, I. (eds.) ICDEc 2019. LNBIP, vol. 358, pp. 183–193. Springer, Cham (2019). https://doi.org/10.1007/978-3-030-30874-2_14

Khanh, C.N.T., Phong, L.T., Cao, K.D.: The impact of organizational factors on E-CRM success implementation. VINE J. Inform. Knowl. Manag. Syst. 52(4), 612–629 (2021). https://doi.org/10.1108/VJIKMS-05-2020-0096

Khemiri, M., Jallouli, R.: Technology-enabled personalization for mobile banking services: literature review and theoretical framework. J. Telecommun. Dig. Econ. 10(2), 173–194 (2022). https://doi.org/10.18080/jtde.v10n2.545

Khlif, H., Jallouli, R.: The success factors of CRM systems: an explanatory analysis. Managing Interconnected World: Pioneering Bus. Technol. Excellence 10(2), 242–258 (2014). https://www.researchgate.net/profile/Emeka-Obioha/publication/264644998_Implementing_Ethics_and_Prevention_of_Corruption_at_Management_and_Leadership_Levels_of_Organisations/links/53ea0c970cf2dc24b3cb02d3/Implementing-Ethics-and-Prevention-of-Corruption-at-Management-and-Leadership-Levels-of-Organisations.pdf#page=259

King, S.F., Burgess, T.F.: Understanding success and failure in customer relationship management. Ind. Market. Manag. 37(4), 421–431 (2008). https://doi.org/10.1016/j.indmarman.2007.02.005

Kitchens, B., Dobolyi, D., Li, J., Abbasi, A.: Advanced customer analytics: strategic value through integration of relationship-oriented big data. J. Manag. Inf. Syst. 35(2), 540–574 (2018). https://doi.org/10.1080/07421222.2018.1451957

Kumar, A., Soni, A., Sahastrabuddhe, K.: Implications on customer satisfaction and loyalty in CRM. Zenodo (2021). https://doi.org/10.5281/zenodo.6612755

Kumar, P., Mokha, A.K.: Relationship between E-CRM, customer experience, customer satisfaction and customer loyalty in banking industry: a review of literature. Res. Rev. Int. J. Multi. 6(2), 127–137 (2021). https://doi.org/10.31305/rrijm.2021.v06.i02.022

Kumar, P., Mokha, A.K.: Electronic customer relationship management (E-CRM) and customer loyalty: the mediating role of customer satisfaction in the banking industry. Int. J. E-Bus. Res. 18(1), 1–22 (2022). https://doi.org/10.4018/IJEBR.293292

Kumar, V.: Transformative marketing: the next 20 years. J. Market. 82(4), 1–12 (2018). https://doi.org/10.1509/jm.82.41

Lokuge, S., Sedera, D., Ariyachandra, T., Kumar, S., Ravi, V.: The next wave of CRM innovation: implications for research, teaching, and practice. Commu. Assoc. Inform. Syst. 46, 560–583 (2020). https://doi.org/10.17705/1CAIS.04623

Mahafzah, A., Mohammad Aljawarneh, N., Abdel Kader Alomari, K., Altahat, S., Saleh Alomari, Z.: Impact of customer relationship management on food and beverage services quality: the mediating role of employees satisfaction. Humanit. Soc. Sci. Rev. 8(2), 222–230 (2020). https://doi.org/10.18510/hssr.2020.8226

Maulana, A., Napitupulu, T.A.: Lost won opportunity prediction in sales pipeline B2b CRM using machine learning. J. Theor. Appl. Inform. Technol. 100(10), 1817-3195 (2022) http://www.jatit.org/volumes/Vol100No10/31Vol100No10.pdf

Mehdiabadi, A., Shahabi, V., Shamsinejad, S., Amiri, M., Spulbar, C., Birau, R.: Investigating industry 5.0 and its impact on the banking industry: requirements, approaches and communications. Appl. Sci. 12(10), 5126 (2022). https://doi.org/10.3390/app12105126

Mendoza, L.E., Marius, A., Pérez, M., Grimán, A.C.: Critical success factors for a customer relationship management strategy. Inform. Softw. Technol. 49(8), 913–945 (2007). https://doi.org/10.1016/j.infsof.2006.10.003

Meyliana, N., Hidayanto, A.N., Budiardjo, E.K.: The critical success factors for customer relationship management implementation: a systematic literature review. Int. J. Bus. Inform. Syst. **23**(2), 131–174 (2016). https://doi.org/10.1504/ijbis.2016.078904

Mikalef, P., Krogstie, J.: Examining the interplay between big data analytics and contextual factors in driving process innovation capabilities. Eur. J. Inform. Syst. **29**(3), 260–287 (2020). https://doi.org/10.1080/0960085X.2020.1740618

Mikalef, P., Krogstie, J., Pappas, I.O., Pavlou, P.: Exploring the relationship between big data analytics capability and competitive performance: the mediating roles of dynamic and operational capabilities. Inform. Manag. **57**(2), 103169 (2020). https://doi.org/10.1016/j.im.2019.05.004

Onyike, J.U., Orga, C.C.: Customer Relationship Management Strategy and Organizational Performance of Cadbury Nigeria Plc, Lagos State. Zenodo (2022). https://doi.org/10.5281/zenodo.7295911

Pan, Z., Ryu, H., Baik, J.: A case study: crm adoption success factor analysis and six sigma DMAIC application. In: 5th ACIS International Conference on Software Engineering Research, Management & Applications (SERA 2007) (2007). https://doi.org/10.1109/sera.2007.6

Payne, A., Frow, P.: The role of multichannel integration in customer relationship management. Ind. Market. Manag. **33**(6), 527–538 (2004). https://doi.org/10.1016/j.indmarman.2004.02.002

Payne, A., Frow, P.: A strategic framework for customer relationship management. J. Market. **69**(4), 167–176 (2018). https://doi.org/10.1509/jmkg.2005.69.4.167

Petter, S., DeLone, W., McLean, E.R.: Information systems success: the quest for the independent variables. J. Manag. Inform. Syst. **29**(4), 7–62 (2013). https://doi.org/10.2753/MIS0742-1222290401

Rahimi, R.:. Customer Relationship Management (CRM). Encyclopedia Tourism Manag. Market., 734–736 (2022). https://doi.org/10.4337/9781800377486.customer.relationship.management. ISBN: 9781800377479, eISBN: 9781800377486

Rana, N.P., Chatterjee, S., Dwivedi, Y.K., Akter, S.: Understanding dark side of artificial intelligence (AI) integrated business analytics: assessing firm's operational inefficiency and competitiveness. Eur. J. Inf. Syst. **31**(3), 364–387 (2021). https://doi.org/10.1080/0960085x.2021.1955628

Sawal, A.B., Ahmad, M., Muralitharan, M.A., Loganathan, V., Jhanjhi, N.Z.: Machine intelligence in customer relationship management in small and large companies. In: Ahmad, M., Zaman, N. (eds.) Empowering Sustainable Industrial 4.0 Systems With Machine Intelligence, pp. 132–153. IGI Global (2022). https://doi.org/10.4018/978-1-7998-9201-4.ch007

Shahbaz, M., Gao, C., Zhai, L., Shahzad, F., Abbas, A., Zahid, R.: Investigating the impact of big data analytics on perceived sales performance: the mediating role of customer relationship management capabilities. Complexity **2020**, 1–17 (2020). https://doi.org/10.1155/2020/5186870

Shahbaz, M., Gao, C., Zhai, L., Shahzad, F., Luqman, A., Zahid, R.: Impact of big data analytics on sales performance in pharmaceutical organizations: the role of customer relationship management capabilities. PLOS ONE **16**(4), e0250229 (2021). https://doi.org/10.1371/journal.pone.0250229

Shatat, A.S., Udin, Z.M.: Factors affecting ERP system effectiveness in post-implementation stage within Malaysian manufacturing companies. Int. J. Bus. Inform. Syst. **14**(3), 348 (2013). https://doi.org/10.1504/ijbis.2013.056722

Shokouhyar, S., Shokoohyar, S., Raja, N., Gupta, V.: Promoting fashion customer relationship management dimensions based on customer tendency to outfit matching: mining customer orientation and buying behaviour. Int. J. Appl. Dec. Sci. **14**(1), 1 (2021). https://doi.org/10.1504/ijads.2021.112932

Silva, E.C., Pedron, C.D., Picoto, W.N.: Customer relationship management and innovation capability: a multiple case study. Int. J. Bus. Innov. Res. **26**(2), 240 (2021). https://doi.org/10.1504/ijbir.2021.118443

Singh, A., Dode, N., Barve, R.: Automation in Marketing: A Survey (2021). https://doi.org/10.20944/preprints202105.0074.v1

Singh, B., Anuradha, L.S.: E-CRM practices and customer satisfaction in insurance sector. SAARJ J. Bank. Insur. Res. 11(4), 16–23 (2022). https://doi.org/10.5958/2319-1422.2022.00010.8

Song, D., Liang, C.: Application research of data mining technology in customer relationship management. In: 2021 4th International Conference on Advanced Electronic Materials, Computers and Software Engineering (AEMCSE) (2021). https://doi.org/10.1109/aemcse51986.2021.00244

Suoniemi, S., Terho, H., Zablah, A., Olkkonen, R., Straub, D.W.: The impact of firm-level and project-level IT capabilities on crm system quality and organizational productivity. J. Bus. Res. 127, 108–122 (2021). https://doi.org/10.1016/j.jbusres.2021.01.007

Teo, Thompson S.H.., Devadoss, Paul, Pan, Shan L.: Towards a holistic perspective of customer relationship management (CRM) implementation: a case study of the housing and development board, Singapore. Dec. Support Syst. 42(3), 1613–1627 (2006). https://doi.org/10.1016/j.dss.2006.01.007

Tsou, H.T.: Linking customization capability with crm technology adoption and strategic alignment. Serv. Sci. 14(1), 60–75 (2022). https://doi.org/10.1287/serv.2021.0286

Wang, Z., Dong, F.: Experience of pro-poor tourism (PPT) in China: a sustainable livelihood perspective. Sustainability 14(21), 14399 (2022). https://doi.org/10.3390/su142114399

Consumer Experience and Augmented Reality Wine Label Application

Amalia Triantafillidou⬿, Michalis Vrigkas⬿, Alexandros Kleftodimos⬿,
Anastasia Yannacopoulou⬿, Maria Matsiola⬿, Stefanos Gkoutzios,
and Georgios Lappas$^{(\boxtimes)}$⬿

Department of Communication and Digital Media, University of Western Macedonia, 52100
Kastoria, Greece
glappas@uowm.gr

Abstract. Augmented reality (AR) applications are regarded as effective experiential marketing practices that can help companies promote their products/services in an interactive manner and deliver exceptional consumer experiences. The purpose of the present study is to evaluate a wine-label AR mobile application by examining its impact on consumer experience dimensions, satisfaction, and re-usage intentions towards the application, as well as attitude and purchase intentions towards the wine product. Moreover, to test the effect of product-consumption related factors (consumption frequency, amount of spending, wine expertise, and attention to wine labels) and technology-related factors (consumers' familiarity with smartphone applications, number of AR applications used in smartphone, and extent of information search for wine-related information through smartphones) on the experiential dimensions of entertainment, flow, escapism, and education. Towards this end, a wine AR label application was developed and evaluated using a quantitative survey. In total, 306 respondents answered a self-administered questionnaire after interacting with the application. Results indicate that the AR application induced the entertainment and educational dimensions of consumer experience. The AR experience was also able to increase respondents' satisfaction with the application and in turn help them form positive attitudes and purchase intentions for the wine. Moreover, the present study revealed that respondents' expertise for wine, attention to wine label, familiarity with smartphone applications, and information search for wine-related information through smartphones are important factors that have an impact on the experience lived by consumers when using the AR label application.

Keywords: Augmented reality · wine labels · consumer experience · flow · entertainment · escapism · education · evaluation · antecedents · Digital Marketing · Digital Transformation

1 Introduction

Augmented reality (AR) technologies have been used as a viable marketing strategy for promoting in an innovative way products and services and are characterized as effective alternative means for delivering valuable experiences to consumers [1]. AR technologies

© The Author(s), under exclusive license to Springer Nature Switzerland AG 2023
R. Jallouli et al. (Eds.): ICDEc 2023, LNBIP 485, pp. 263–273, 2023.
https://doi.org/10.1007/978-3-031-42788-6_16

can support marketing and promotional activities of companies and in turn foster the relationships of consumers with the brands [2]. Marketers are utilizing these technologies to provide augmented and immersive content for a product/service using a physical background [3]. These applications can be used across the customer journey affecting pre-consumption (attitude formation), consumption (core experiences and emotions) and post-consumption experiences (satisfaction and re-purchase intentions [4].

AR technologies can offer exceptional experiences to consumers since they aim at enhancing consumers' interactions with the product/service [5]. Herein, consumer experience is a multidimensional construct [6] that encapsulates various dimensions such as hedonism-entertainment, flow, escapism, learning, challenge, socialization, and communitas [7]. AR applications used for marketing purposes can enhance consumers cognitive, emotional, esthetic, and social experience with the product/service [8] and can also lead users to a state of flow where consumers are absorbed and immersed in an activity such as using their mobile phones to scan a product and interact with augmented reality information [9]. Thus, special attention is paid to AR applications for mobile phones and to the integration of AR technology in e-commerce stores [10]. Today, consumers can easily download relevant applications on their mobile phones, discovering more information about the products of their interest. However, AR technologies adoption remains limited by commercial enterprises, although the market is growing over the years. Some studies show that companies consider these technologies complicated, expensive, and less efficient, thus remaining reluctant to adopt them [11].

Research interest in AR ads has increased in recent years regarding advertising effectiveness in this new technological environment. Studies show that through AR technology, consumers meet better the quality characteristics of the products they buy online, thus reducing the likelihood of being dissatisfied with a purchase [12, 13]. At the same time, consumers consider AR ads more enjoyable, innovative, attractive, more informative, and less intrusive/annoying compared to traditional ads [14, 15]. In this way, AR ads have positive effects on brand recall, positive attitudes toward the brand and advertise products, and intention to purchase the advertised products [4].

Consumers' experience from an AR product-related application can have a varying impact on consumers depending on a number of factors. Until now the majority of studies that test the antecedents of consumers' evaluation of AR product-related applications have mainly utilized the TAM framework [16]. The present study enhances the literature on antecedents of consumers' experience from AR mobile applications by examining the impact of consumers' product consumption and technology related factors on four experience dimensions namely, entertainment, flow, escapism, and education. Thus, the aim of the study is three-fold. First, to evaluate a wine-label AR mobile application by examining its impact on consumer experience dimensions, satisfaction and re-usage intentions towards the application, as well as attitude and purchase intentions towards the wine product. Second, to test the effect of product consumption-related factors (consumption frequency, amount of spending, wine expertise, and attention to wine labels) on the four experiential dimensions. Third, to decipher the impact of technology-related factors such as consumers' familiarity with smartphone applications, number of AR applications used in smartphone, and extent of information search for wine-related information through smartphones on the experiential dimensions of entertainment, flow, escapism, and education.

2 Augmented Reality Wine Label Application

Wine companies nowadays are increasingly utilizing AR technologies to promote their products. With the help of augmented-reality technology, wineries are able to provide rich digital content to their customers through videos, 2D/3D animations, photos, and text to enhance their experience [17]. Specifically, consumers can download an AR application on their smartphones and then scan the label to interact with the product.

To test the objectives of the present study, an AR wine label application was developed using Unity 2018.4.31f1 and Vuforia Engine 10.2 platforms. The underlying application was implemented for Android mobile devices.

Upon launch of the wine "live" label application to the user mobile device, users are prompt to target their mobile camera to the front bottle label. Once the camera recognizes the target image, the AR application generates the augmented multimedia content which is then shown on the users' smartphone. Specifically, the AR content of the application includes:

- Videos of the winery's production procedures such as harvesting and crushing grapes, fermenting, maturing, and bottling.
- Interactive and 360° videos of the infrastructure of the winery.
- Videos and animation narratives about wine products.
- Information about the wine ingredients and calories in text format and short animated clips.

The user can interact with the AR content by selecting the proper action from the application menu and the corresponding information pops up. Furthermore, once the user presses the info button that is located on the bottom right side of the application, a 2D animation character appears on the screen providing additional information in both text and audio form such as wine ingredients, calories, and storage temperature.

Furthermore, one important feature of the wine "live" label application is the way the front image label interacts with the user. Once the image target is recognized by the AR application, a virtual augmented front image label appears to open as a "virtual door". This feature reveals hidden information to the user in the form of a short intro animation video. The intro video plays for a few seconds and the "virtual door" automatically closes so the user can navigate freely inside the application. Also, a short 3D animation appears to the screen that depicts vine branches that progressively start to grow around the bottle. Figure 1 shows some indicative screenshots of the wine "live" label application.

A help section is also displayed at the bottom left of the screen of the mobile device that explains how to use the application or provides additional information about it. The video menu that surrounds the target image label also contains important information about the application. The user may select a video which is then displayed in full screen. After watching the previous video, the user can switch to the next one by pressing the "Next" button.

In addition, an assessment of the user's knowledge of the wine label is carried out through a short quiz game incorporated into the "live" label application. Users are asked

Fig. 1. Indicative screenshots of the AR wine label application

questions about the wine product via a small multiple-choice survey during this phase. While choosing between four possible answers, the user is provided with feedback regarding his/her success or failure. Finally, following the completion of all questions, a summary of correct and incorrect answers is displayed to the user.

3 Method

To evaluate the AR application and test the study's objectives, a survey was conducted with a self-administered questionnaire through a convenience sampling approach. More specifically, the questionnaires were delivered during the Hotelia exhibition in Thessaloniki, Greece (November 18–20, 2023) that was directed to professionals in the field of hotel equipment, as well as catering and coffee services. Seven university students approached attendees of the exhibition and asked them to participate in the survey. Participants that agreed to take part in the survey, were first shown the application by scanning the label of the wine bottle. Then, they completed the questionnaire. In total, 325 questionnaires were completed. However, only 306 were used in subsequent analysis due to incomplete data.

The questionnaire was comprised of five sections. The first section included questions about the wine consumption frequency, consumer's wine expertise, money spending on wine, attention to wine labels, and factors affecting the choice of wine. The second section asked participants to indicate their level of familiarity with new technologies (e.g., smartphones, smartphone applications), the number of AR applications used in their smartphones, and the degree to which they search information about wines through their smartphones. The third section included questions about the application's experience. Specifically, the experience was measured through four dimensions and 12 items, namely: entertainment, flow, escapism, and knowledge. The items that comprised each dimension were derived from the consumption experience scale of [7]. All items were rated on a five-point likert scale ranging from 1: strongly disagree to 5: strongly agree. The fourth section asked participants to evaluate their satisfaction with the application and re-usage intentions concerning the AR application (Kim, Kang, Song, and Lee, 2020). Moreover, the questionnaire included questions about respondents' attitude towards the wine and their intentions to consume the wine in the future (Graham and Wilder, 2020). Satisfaction and re-usage intentions items were measured using five-point scale ranging from 1: not at all to 5: very much. The last section of the questionnaire was comprised of the demographic characteristics of the sample (gender, age, income).

4 Results

4.1 Sample

In total 306 respondents participated in the survey. Table 1 shows the demographic characteristics of the sample. Most of them were males (52.3%) and had a bachelor's degree. 28.1% of respondents aged between 18 to 25 years old and 27.1% between 26 to 35 years old. Moreover, most respondents had a monthly income ranging from 801 to 1500 euros (45.2%).

Table 1. Demographic Characteristics of the Sample

Gender	Percent	Age	Percent
Males	52.3%	18–25	28.1%
Females	46.1%	26–35	27.1%
Other	1.6%	36–45	15.4%
		46–55	19.3%
		56–65	8.8%
		66 +	1.3%
Education		**Monthly Income**	
Primary Education	0.3%	Up to 800 euros	27.2%
Secondary Education	18.5%	801–1500 euros	45.2%
Bachelor	52.8%	1501–2000 euros	12.0%
Master	27.1%	More than 2001 euros	15.3%
Ph D	1.3%		

Regarding respondents' wine consumption, 26.5% were characterized by low consumption levels (up to 1 time per month), 42.2% by medium consumption (2 to 3 times a month), and 31.4% by high consumption levels. Moreover, 27.1% of the respondents were low wine product spenders (up to 20 euro), 59.8% were moderate spenders (21 to 40 euros), and 13.1% were characterized as high spenders (more than 41 euros).

Figure 2 shows the mean scores of the factors that affect respondents when making decisions about wine purchases. Based on the findings, respondents rated as the most important factors when choosing wine, the grape variety (M = 3.78), the color of the wine (M = 3.70), and the brand name (M = 3.67). Regarding respondents' expertise in wine, the majority of them were characterized by low (68.6%) and moderate experience (24.5%).

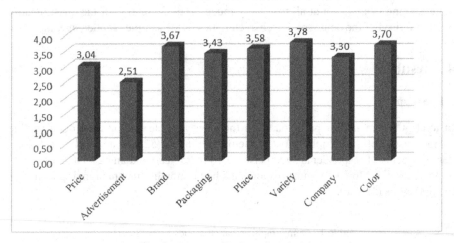

Fig. 2. Factors affecting wine choice

In addition, 75.8% of respondents evaluated themselves as high in familiarity with using applications on their smartphones, and 59.5% of the sample had more than one application on their smartphones. Moreover, 57.7% of respondents indicated that they do not search frequently via their smartphones for information about wine, 22.6% of them search in a moderate frequency, and 19.6% of the sample search extensively through their smartphone for wine related information.

4.2 Experience with AR Application

Next, four scales were created by summing the items that comprised each of the four experience dimensions and substracting them with the number of items. All scales exhibited satisfactory internal reliability as the value of Cronbach's alpha exhibited the 0.70 threshold (entertainment: 0.884, flow: 0.844, escapism: 0.860, educational experience: 0.817). Figure 3 shows the mean scores for each experience dimension concerning the AR wine label application. Based on the results, respondents rated the AR experience as highly educational (M = 3.82) and entertaining experience (M = 3.68). Flow was experienced in a moderate level by participants (M = 3.37) while escapism was experienced to a lesser extent (M = 2.80).

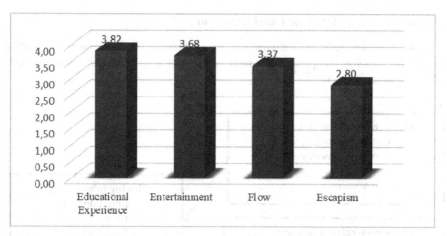

Fig. 3. Mean scores of experience dimensions with AR application

4.3 Satisfaction, Attitude, and Re-Usage Intentions

Again, four new scales were developed regarding respondents' satisfaction with the application and their re-usage intentions as well as their attitudes towards the wine and their intentions to buy the wine in the future. All scales had Cronbach's values above the 0.70 cut off criterion (satisfaction with application: 0.893, application re-usage intentions: 0.897, wine attitude: 0.744, intentions to buy the wine: 0.879). Figure 4 shows the mean scores of the four scales.

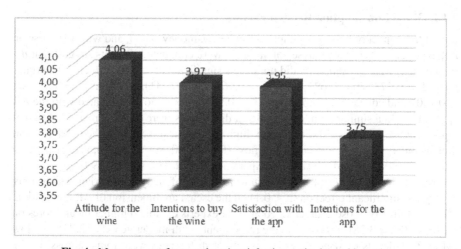

Fig. 4. Mean scores of respondents' satisfaction, attitude, and intentions

As Fig. 4 illustrates, participants showed a positive attitude for the wine (M = 4.06) and high intentions to buy the wine (M = 3.97). Moreover, they were highly satisfied with the application (M = 3.95) and exhibited moderate to high intentions to re-use the application (M = 3.75).

4.4   Antecedents of AR Wine Label Experience

To test whether certain factors shown in Fig. 5 have an impact on the the four experiential dimensions, Pearson rho product moment correlation tests and analyses of variance (ANOVA) were conducted.

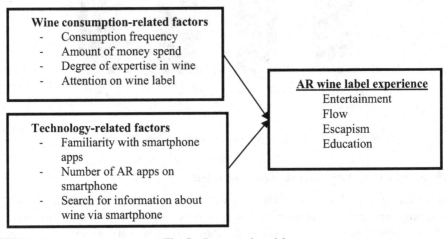

Fig. 5. Conceptual model

4.4.1   Wine Consumption Related Factors

To test the impact of wine consumption frequency, money spend, and wine expertise on AR experience one-way analyses of variance were conducted. Results suggest that *the frequency of wine consumption* did not have a significant ($p < 0.05$) effect on entertainment ($F = 0.478$, sig $= 0.621$), flow ($F = 0.061$, sig $= 0.941$), escapism ($F = 0.289$, sig $= 0.750$), and educational experience ($F = 0.571$, sig $= 0.561$) associated with the AR application. In a similar vein, no significant differences were found across the different types of wine spenders (low, moderate, high) in the mean scores of the entertainment dimension ($F = 1.495$, sig $= 0.226$), flow ($F = 0.850$, sig $= 0.428$), escapism ($F = 2.290$, sig $= 0.103$), and educational experience ($F = 1.212$, sig $= 0.299$).

Regarding, the degree of *expertise in wine*, results of analysis of variance show only a marginal significant effect on ($p < 0.1$) on the escapism dimension of AR application. More specifically, those characterized as wine experts exhibited higher mean scores on escapism ($M = 3.28$) compared to the respondents with moderate ($M = 2.85$), and low ($M = 2.72$) levels of wine expertise. No other differences were found across for the experience dimensions of entertainment ($F = 1.411$, sig $= 0.246$), flow ($F = 1.438$, sig $= 0.239$), and education ($F = 1.699$, sig $= 0.185$).

To examine the interaction between *wine label reading frequency* and the four-experience dimension, Pearson's correlation coefficient was calculated. Based on the results wine label reading frequency was marginally correlated ($p < 0.1$) with the entertainment dimension ($r = 0.109$, sig $= 0.056$) and significantly correlated at the 0.05 level with the educational dimension of the AR experience (r = 0.121, sig = 0.034). These correlations were low in strength. No significant correlations were found between wine label reading frequency, flow (r = 0.079, sig = 0.168) and escapism (r = 0.040, sig = 0.489).

4.4.2   Technology-Related Factors

Analysis of variance was conducted to test whether respondents' familiarity with smartphone applications and the number of smartphone applications had an impact on the four experience dimensions. Based on the findings, significant differences were found across *familiarity* segments in the mean scores of the escapism dimension (F = 3.075, sig = 0.391). Specifically, respondents with low familiarity (M = 3.14) experience higher levels of escapism by the AR application compared to respondents with moderate (M = 3.02) and high (M = 2.71) levels of familiarity with smartphone applications. No other differences were found between the familiarity levels in the mean scores of entertainment (F = 0.797, sig = 0.452), flow (F = 1.007, sig = 0.366), and educational experience (F = 0.941, sig = 0.391).

No significant differences were found in the mean scores of entertainment (F = 0.919, sig = 0.400), flow (F = 1.469, sig = 0.232), escapism (F = 0.957, sig = 0.385), and educational experience (F = 0.707, sig = 0.494) based on the *number of AR applications* that respondents use in their smartphones. Next, Pearson rho was calculated to test the relationship between the *extent of smartphone information search for wine issues* and the four dimensions. Results indicate that low positive and significant (p < 0.05) correlations were found between the extent of information search through smartphones for wine-related issues and the dimensions of entertainment (r = 0.142, sig = 0.013), flow (r = 0.199, sig = 0.001), escapism (r = 0.148, sig = 0.009), and education (r = 0.196, sig = 0.001).

4.5   Conclusions

The purpose of the present study was to examine the impact of Augmented Reality smartphone applications embedded in wine labels on consumers' experience and their subsequent perceptions and intentions. Moreover, this paper aims to test the effect of a number of wine consumption and technology-related factors on consumers' experience with the AR application.

Findings indicate that the AR wine label application induced the entertainment and educational dimensions of consumer experience while feelings of flow and escapism were triggered by the AR application to a lesser extent to respondents. Thus, positive feelings and new knowledge can be generated through wine AR label applications. The AR experience was also able to increase respondents' satisfaction with the application and in turn enable them to form positive attitudes and purchase intentions for the wine. Hence, AR wine label applications can have a positive effect on consumers' perceptions and behavioral intentions towards the wine product, thus making them an effective marketing tool for the wine industry.

Moreover, the present study revealed that respondents' expertise for wine, wine label reading frequency, familiarity with smartphone applications, and information search for wine issues through smartphones are important factors that have an impact on the experience lived by consumers when using the AR label application. More specifically, consumers' who are self-perceived as wine experts felt higher feelings of escapism compared to non-experts. Thus, wine experts were able to escape from reality through the AR application. Escapism was also related to respondents who were not familiar with smartphone applications. Moreover, respondents who pay attention to wine labels were more inclined to feel positive emotions and gain knowledge about the wine product compared to the other consumers. In addition, all experience dimensions were positively influenced by the extent to which respondents search wine information through their smartphones. Thus, a holistic experience is lived for consumers who active seekers of wine information through their smartphones.

Important practical implications could be derived from the findings of the present study. First, an AR application in the labels of wine bottles is an effective experiential marketing practice. Moreover, wine marketers can introduce this type of application to consumers that are regarded as wine experts and like to search for wine related information through their smartphones. In addition, these applications could target to consumers with low familiarity in smartphone applications.

Future research could test the moderating effect of several variables on the relationships found. For example, fruitful findings could be derived by testing the moderating effect of wine expertise on the antecedents of AR application experience. Moreover, the study's findings could be confirmed by using structural equation model to test the causal effect of the examined variables on users' experience.

Acknowledgements. This work has been co-funded by the European Union and Greek national funds through the operational program competitiveness, entrepreneurship, and innovation, under the call research-create-innovate (project code: T2EDK-03856). All statements of fact, opinion or conclusions contained herein are those of the authors and should not be construed as representing the official views or policies of the sponsors.

References

1. Chylinski, M., Heller, J., Hilken, T., Keeling, D.I., Mahr, D., de Ruyter, K.: Augmented reality marketing: a technology-enabled approach to situated customer experience. Australas. Market. J. (AMJ) **28**(4), 374–384 (2020)
2. Rejeb, A., Rejeb, K., Treiblmaier, H.: How augmented reality impacts retail marketing: a state-of-the-art review from a consumer perspective. J. Strateg. Market. **31**(3), 718–748 (2021)
3. Hsu, S.H.Y., Tsou, H.-T., Chen, J.-S.: "Yes, we do. Why not use augmented reality?" customer responses to experiential presentations of AR-based applications. J. Retail. Consum. Serv. **62**, 102649 (2021). https://doi.org/10.1016/j.jretconser.2021.102649
4. Wedel, M., Bigné, E., Zhang, J.: Virtual and augmented reality: advancing research in consumer marketing. Int. J. Res. Mark. **37**(3), 443–465 (2020)
5. Vaidyanathan, N., Henningsson, S.: Designing augmented reality services for enhanced customer experiences in retail. J. Serv. Manag. **34**(1), 78–99 (2022)
6. Gentile, C., Spiller, N., Noci, G.: How to sustain the customer experience: An overview of experience components that co-create value with the customer. Eur. Manag. J. **25**(5), 395–410 (2007)

7. Triantafillidou, A., Siomkos, G.: Consumption experience outcomes: satisfaction, nostalgia intensity, word-of-mouth communication and behavioural intentions. J. Consum. Mark. 31(6/7), 526–540 (2014)
8. Flavián, C., Ibáñez-Sánchez, S., Orús, C.: The impact of virtual, augmented and mixed reality technologies on the customer experience. J. Bus. Res. 100, 547–560 (2019)
9. Barhorst, J.B., McLean, G., Shah, E., Mack, R.: Blending the real world and the virtual world: exploring the role of flow in augmented reality experiences. J. Bus. Res. 122, 423–436 (2021)
10. Haile, T.T., Kang, M.: Mobile augmented reality in electronic commerce: investigating user perception and purchase intent amongst educated young adults. Sustain Sci. 12(21), 9185 (2020). https://doi.org/10.3390/su12219185
11. Wafa, S.N., Hashim, E.: Adoption of mobile augmented reality advertisements by brands in Malaysia. Procedia Soc. Behav. Sci. 219, 762–768 (2016). https://doi.org/10.1016/j.sbspro.2016.05.077
12. Hopp, T., Gangadharbatla, H.: Novelty effects in augmented reality advertising environments: the influence of exposure time and self-efficacy. J. Curr. Issues Res. 37(2), 113–130 (2016). https://doi.org/10.1080/10641734.2016.1171179
13. Rambli, D.R.A., Irshad, S.: UX design evaluation of mobile augmented reality marketing products and services for Asia pacific region. In: APCHIUX pp. 42–45. Melbourne, Australia (2015). https://doi.org/10.1145/2846439.2846450
14. Yang, S., Carlson, J.R., Chen, S.: How augmented reality affects advertising effectiveness: the mediating effects of curiosity and attention toward the ad. J. Retail. Consum. Serv. 54, 102020 (2020). https://doi.org/10.1016/j.jretconser.2019.102020
15. Yaoyuneyong, G., Foster, J., Johnson, E., Johnson, D.: Augmented reality marketing: consumer preferences and attitudes toward hypermedia print ads. J. Interact. Advert. 16(1), 16–30 (2016). https://doi.org/10.1080/15252019.2015.1125316
16. Alam, S.S., Susmit, S., Lin, C.Y., Masukujjaman, M., Ho, Y.H.: Factors affecting augmented reality adoption in the retail industry. J. Open Innov.: Technol. Market Complexity 7(2), 142 (2021)
17. Vrigkas, M., Lappas, G., Kleftodimos, A., Triantafillidou, A.: Augmented reality for wine industry: past, present, and future. In: SHS Web of Conferences, vol. 102, p. 04006. EDP Sciences (2021)

Portuguese Digital Agencies and Their Clients' Social Networks

Liliana Simões Ribeiro[1,2](✉) 🆔 and Melissa Paço Farinha[3]

[1] School of Accounting and Administration, University of Aveiro, Rua Associação Humanitária
Bombeiros Voluntários de Aveiro, 3810-500 Aveiro, Portugal
`lilianasimoesribeiro@ua.pt`
[2] NECE-Research Center in Business Sciences, University of Beira Interior, Covilhã, Portugal
[3] University Europeia, Quinta do Bom Nome, Estr. da Correia 53, 1500-210 Lisboa, Portugal

Abstract. Currently, with the percentage of active users on social networks increasing, it becomes almost mandatory for brands to have a communication strategy using social networks. Digital agencies come to fill the need for brands to communicate with their customers through these channels, but it is possible to see that not all social networks are used by digital agencies for this strategy. The present investigation focuses on understanding the factors that lead Portuguese digital agencies to adopt a certain social network as a communication tool for their clients. Was followed a qualitative methodology, using semi-structured interviews with digital agencies in Portugal. It was possible to verify that digital agencies in Portugal do not look for specific characteristics in social networks, but rather functionalities such as the possibility of integrating third-party applications. This investigation was the first to study the relationship between Portuguese Digital Agencies and Social Networks, a topic that until then had no references. In this way, for future investigations, this study leaves many paths to explore to expand knowledge on the subject.

Keywords: Digital marketing · Social networks · Digital Agencies

1 Introduction

Currently social networks are one of the most used forms of social communication on the Internet, where individuals or groups of individuals interact with each other [1]. As technology advances, the variety of social networks has increased as well as the number of users. According to data from the Datareportal report 2023 [2], the percentage of active users of social media in Portugal is 8.05 million people, which is equivalent to 78,5% of the Portuguese population. In this way we can say that most Portuguese consumers are present in social networks, leading to the emergence of brands in these digital platforms.

To address the need for communication with the consumer, taking into account the constant change and emergence of new social networks, digital agencies are increasingly specializing in delivering value to their customers. But not all social networks are currently being the target of the work of Portuguese digital agencies which led the researchers to ask why and to try to understand how Portuguese digital agencies determine the potential of a social network as a communication tool.

Also less is known about the way, in a reality, Portugal, where most companies are small and medium enterprises 99,9% [3], agencies are working and how are the relationships with their clients.

The overall objective of this research is to understand the factors that lead digital agencies in Portugal to adopt a particular social network. To achieve this goal, five specific objectives have been set. First to identify the social networks most used by Portuguese digital agencies, second to understand what was the path of these in the adoption of social networks, thirdly understand what the main characteristics sought by Portuguese digital agencies in a social network, fourthly realize that potential emerging networks may be used by agencies and why, and, finally, in fifth place, identify the functionalities sought by Portuguese digital agencies in new social networks.

2 Literature Review

2.1 Digital Marketing and Social Media

With the constant advance of technologies, the world has become increasingly digitized, being difficult to talk about marketing without considering the digital component [4]. Considering the popularization of the Internet, digital marketing emerged as a response to strengthen the relationship between customers and companies [5]. The definition of the term digital marketing has evolved over time, according to the American Marketing Association [6], digital marketing is "the use of digital or social channels to promote a brand or reach consumers. This kind of marketing can be executed on the internet, social media, search engines, mobile devices and other channels. It requires new ways of marketing to consumers and understanding the impact of their behaviour".

Despite the undeniable advantages that digital marketing offers, from the point of view of Ryan and Jones [7], before start is necessary to formulate a strategy, not only to make informed decisions, but also to ensure that all resources are focused on the elements, tools and channels of digital marketing that are most relevant to the business. For Chaffey and Chadwick [8] the interaction and integration between online and offline is a key part of developing a strategy. According to these authors there are some factors that characterize an effective digital marketing strategy, such as being aligned with the company's business and overall marketing strategy; defined clear objectives; consistency with the types of customers of the various channels; defining a differentiated value proposition; the use of tools both online and in the offline; an adequate monitoring of the customer's purchasing process, as well as manage their life cycle.

Specifically in relation to marketing means, for many years they were based on traditional media such as television, newspapers, radio, and mail, today, most current marketing campaigns use digital channels. Social media is now fundamental in this context. According to Ryan and Jones [7] the oncept of social media is based on a general term that presupposes web-based software and services that allow users to share, discuss, communicate, and participate as a form of social interaction. Completing this thought, Filo et al. [9], define social media as new technologies that facilitate interactivity and co-creation in the development and sharing of user content between organizations and individuals.

In 2010, Kaplan and Haenlein [10], due to the so comprehensive definition of social media, distinguished them into six groups: Blogs, Social networking sites (e.g. Facebook), Virtual social worlds (e.g., Second Life. The now popularized metaverse); Collaborative projects (sites that allow the creation of content by all users as a form of information and knowledge, such as Wikipedia), Content communities: sites that allow the sharing of content between users, such as Youtube and Virtual game worlds (platforms that allow the user to appear with various avatars and characters and interact with other users such as World of Warcraft). This classification was obtained based on two dimensions, social presence and degree of self-revelation. Of social presence, the authors presuppose a concept of media richness that varies between low, medium and high, and is related to the effectiveness and power of the social communication of each group, and, of a degree of self-revelation that differs between low and high, the authors refer to the ability to reveal more sentimental aspects by the author that allow a closer connection with the user.

Meanwhile, Chaffey and Chadwick [8] considered ten types of social presence, these being Social Networks (social platforms of interaction for consumer audiences, companies or for both. Example of Facebook, LinkedIn, and Twitter respectively), Social Publishing and news (newspapers and magazines with possibility of participation with comments on articles, blogs and communities), Social commenting in blogs (explore the blog as a form of social communication strategy), Social niche communities (communities and independent forums), Social customer service (customer support sites and forums), Social knowledge (sites and forums for answers and knowledge. Example of Yahoo), Social bookmarking (lucky game sites online), Social Streaming (streaming sites of photos, videos and podcasting. Example of.

Youtube), Social search (search engines with ability to tag, comment and vote on search results), Social commerce (reviews and product ratings and sharing coupons on details).

From the combination of the concepts of marketing and social media, arises the concept of social media marketing that for Tuten and Solomon [11], is summarized in the use of technologies and channels as a way of exchanging value offers between individuals and organizations. In this order of thought, Dwivedi et al. [12] had a parallel approach to the concept, arguing that social media marketing consists of frequent dialogue between stakeholders with the aim of promoting some promotional information. Finally, in a more complete aspect, Chaffey and Chadwick [8] consider that social media marketing is an important area of digital marketing that stimulates communication with customers through the most diverse digital media, from website, social networks and blogs. This communication, according to the authors, may be related to products, promotions or customer services allowing you to learn more about your customers and consequently generate more value around the brand. As a way of presenting the use of marketing on social media, Charlesworth [13] recreated a four-dimensional matrix, adapted from Zhu and Chen's [14] social media matrix. This matrix allows to have an insight of the marketing practiced in the media based on two important characteristics of social media:

the nature of the connection (focused on the profile and focused on the content) and the level of personalization of the message (standard message and personalized message).

In terms of the nature of the connection, Zhu and Chen [14] define the "profile-focused" connection as centered on individual people, where the nature of the information is related to the person and the main objective is for users to create interactions based on the interest, they have for the user behind the social network profile. On the opposite side we have the connections "focused on content", which the authors define as totally related to the content posted on social networks, being the interactions, discussions and comments generated only because the user likes the content of the profile. In terms of message customization level, according to the authors, the "custom message" is defined as a malicious message for a specific person or a small audience, and the "standard message" is a general message directed at all interested audiences.

As a way of trying to understand the connection between social media and human needs, Zhu and Chen [14] conducted a study where they proved that there are four common activities in the media that contribute to a sense of relationship and need satisfied in the human being. These activities are to communicate about personally relevant subjects, participate in shared activities, feel understood and appreciated, and finally participate in fun activities. Realizing then the relationship between social media and the human being, what will be the benefits and risks associated with marketing in digital channels? For [1] there are five great benefits such as ease and immediacy in customer contact, the variety of tools and ease in managing the brand's reputation, allows you to find the target audience more specifically and accurately, has low cost and easy-to-use tools, as well as allows to increase the notoriety and stimulates the promotion of the brand and products. As risks this author refers to the need for time for continued management and the results may not be visible instantly, a misinterpreted error or comment can go viral and affect the reputation of the brand, there is no complete control over WOM, a bad strategy lead to spending time and resources and the audience may ignore it.

In 2014, Dahnil et al. [15] conducted a study that aimed to understand the factors that influenced SMEs to adopt marketing on social media. The authors reviewed all academic literature related to the topic including studies on the barriers of SMEs in adopting technology, and the emerging concept of marketing on social media and factors related to its adoption. With this study it was possible to conclude that regarding the barriers of SMEs in adopting technology, many of the problems go through: limited capacity of resources, lack of capital, associated risk, lack of people, existence of complex procedures and customer service. In terms of factors that lead to the adoption of marketing on social media, the authors reveal that there are five main factors, namely end users(the insufficiency or lack of technical knowledge on the part of technology users in SMEs can be one of the major barriers to adopting marketing on social media); organizational characteristics (the fact that team heads in organizations are aware of technologies and comfortable in using them combined with the existence of experiences and innovations positively influences adoption); technology itself (the costs of technologies, their credibility and associated problems such as language and spam, can be determining factors that influence adoption); management (leaders who are well informed about the technologies can positively influence team leaders to consider using them); and the business environment (many

SMEs see technology as a tool to maintain competitiveness by positively influencing its adoption).

Almost in the same and with similar conclusions, in 2015, Siamagka et al. [16] conducted a study with the objective of understanding the potential of social media as a marketing tool, focusing on the factors that determine its adoption in B2B organizations. The variables that are part of this study were the perception of utility, the perception of ease of use, organizational innovation, barriers to technology such as compatibility, privacy and security, image, that is, the perception of the organization's employees about the image they pass when using a specific technology. The results of this study reveal that utility perception and organizational innovation are the main factors that lead B2B organizations to adopt social media. The most insignificant factor for this adoption is the perception of ease of use. This study also allowed us to conclude that utility perception is negatively affected by perceived barriers and positively affected by the image.

2.2 Social Media Networks

It is important to realize that the concepts of social media and social networks do not represent the same because, despite being related, they are two distinct concepts. As mentioned, previous, social networks are types of digital presence within social media. For Miller [17], these are a large part of the internet that welcomes a community, facilitates communication between users and allows the sharing of experiences and opinions. Similarly, [1] define social networks as one of the most used forms of social communication on the Internet, where individuals or groups of individuals interact with each other, sharing content from text, images, videos, links, among other media.

But what drives people to use social networks? For these authors there are nine main reasons: socializing among users, having access to news and news by the minute, keeping in touch with friends and family, planning events, sharing content, using apps and games, meeting new people, increasing business awareness or because everyone uses it. According to datareportal world statistics [18] in the top five reasons to use social networks are in descending order: be aware of news (37%), consume interesting content and entertainment (35%), fill free time (34%), socialize, and keep in touch with friends (33%) and finally share photos and videos with other users (28%). In this way makes perfect sense and it becomes very important the presence of brands on social networks, both to engage with consumers, as well as to have access to specific analyses because consumers are online [7] With the characteristics of social networks, it is easy to find, talk and convert the market, being essential to have three components when marketing on social networks: advertising, building brand presence and Word of mouth (WOM) [1].

Over the years there were many social networks that appeared, some stayed, others disappeared. There is a huge variety distinguished through their purpose and functionality. There are social networks more focused on people in general like Friendster, Hi5 and Facebook and others focused more on the professional area like Linkedin. On the other hand, we have social networks focused on sharing photos and videos such as MySpace, Youtube and Flickr, social networks more inclined to news like Reddit, Digg and Delicious and finally, we also have social networks in the form of microblog like Twitter [19]. According to data from the Datareportal [18] report, there are 4.20 billion active social media users, which is equivalent to about 54% of the world's population. In the case of Portugal, this percentage is 77%, which means that more than 3/4 of the Portuguese population are active users of social networks. With regard to age and gender, there is a greater focus on social media consumption between 18–34 years and male incidence. In Portugal, according to Marktest's studies of 27 October 2020, it was possible to find that there are no differences between the two genders in the profile of users of social networks, however in terms of age the results show that younger people (15–24 years old) spend about more than an hour a day on social networks than older ones.

According to Marktest [20] in terms of social networks where Portuguese users have an account, Facebook leads with 92%, followed by Whatsapp with about 80%, in 3rd place is Instagram with about 73%, 4th Facebook Messenger with almost 72% and finally in 5th place Youtube with 53%. For the most widely used social networks, Facebook retains 1st place for older audiences, however, for the youngest audience of 15–25 years of age, Instagram is in the lead with 57% for Facebook's 16%.

On the adoption of different social networks by brands, one study on the engagement behaviour on social media in luxury brand sector [21] identify trends and the amount of time the platform exist and the consequence reliability of it to the general audience, as the main factors that could explain brand's first choice to adopt a certain social network, because of the perception to be a safer option.

2.3 Agencies

Over the years with the interconnection of communication with technological innovation, new social behaviors and new forms of relationship between people and companies took place. With the emergence of digital media, particularly social networks, brands, and companies have seen these platforms as a new way to connect with their online audience. In view of this new market need, the first communication agencies with digital-targeted services that were later expanding and diversifying into differentiated segments began to emerge [5].

According to the article of the blog Media on target [22], over these years, with the emergence of new technologies, marketing strategies and ways of making advertising, the market of agencies in the sector of communication, advertising and marketing has increased and has been divided into different models. Currently, considering the objectives of the agencies, these can be divided into 14 types: Advertising Agencies, Communication Agencies, Full Service Agencies, In-house agencies, Public relations agencies, Digital Marketing Agencies, also called digital agencies, Content agencies, Design Agencies, Social Media Agencies, Web development agencies, Live marketing agencies, Branding agencies, Endomarketing agencies, Out-Of-Home agencies.

More specifically about Digital Agencies, these are responsible for everything that involves a company's digital marketing strategy, from the creative, technical, and analytical. They offer services for website development, Google Ads campaign management, social networks, SEO and others [22]. According to Sant'Anna [23], digital agencies are companies specialized in delivering services related to the entire digital environment with the aim of increasing brand awareness among online consumers. Ryan and Jones [7] share the same view, reinforcing that agency specializing in digital marketing offer marketing and creative advertising services by creating targeted online campaigns and strategies. According to Santos et al. [24] the Internet is a means that undergoes numerous modifications and the emergence of new platforms adapted to each reality is constant, forcing agencies to innovate and adapt information to meet the needs of customers. Conde et al. [5] shares the same idea, saying that in view of this constant evolution, agencies face new challenges in relation to relationships with the target audience of brands, proving to be an opportunity to adjust to the new demands of the market.

3 Research Methodology

The results of this investigation were obtained through qualitative data collected through semi-structured interviews. The qualitative methodology is advantageous for small samples chosen based on a set of predefined criteria. This methodology allows direct contact between the researcher and the study participants for data collection, allowing the exploration of emerging issues. When there are no investigations related to the area of study, the investigation refers to the type of exploratory descriptive study to characterize and describe the object of study and thus increase knowledge [25]. This investigation fits into the situation identified by the authors. Exploratory, therefore, this study aims to explore the relationship between Portuguese digital agencies and social networks, an area of which there is a gap in terms of scientific knowledge in Portugal. Descriptive, analysis, registration, and interpretation of the opinion of the agencies is made without interference from the interviewer's opinion. Regarding the research method, this is qualitative because the object of study will be interpreted in terms of its meaning through textual data and is also observational because an analysis of the opinions of the sample of this investigation is made based on a semi-structured interview.

In this research, the Universe of study are the digital agencies in Portugal, so, in the impossibility of studying the entire population due to factors such as time, the sample was reduced to nine Portuguese digital agencies. This sample was randomly chosen by searching the Google search engine by the keyword "digital agencies in Portugal". Initially it was planned to conduct twelve interviews, but with its course and as the arrival at the ninth interview it was already possible to trace a pattern in the results obtained, according to the saturation principle, it was decided to finish the interviews and the sample was reduced to nine Portuguese digital agencies. According to Thiry-Cherques [26], data collection is given as saturated when no new information is extracted, making it unnecessary to continue adding new elements, without compromising the understanding of the phenomenon investigated. This criterion allows you to establish the validity of a dataset. For sampling methods, given that this research will be to fill a knowledge gap about social networks within portuguese digital agencies, the sampling technique used in this study is non-probabilistic by judgment [27]. The sample was selected because it has two previously defined characteristics: to be a 100% Portuguese digital agency and provide services related to social networks. Within each agency, the criteria applied to the interviewee focused on, having a position of leadership or management within the company, having knowledge of the history of the social networks used in the agency and thirdly that has decision-making power within the organization. With the knowledge of the professionals of the nine Portuguese digital agencies it was possible to collect relevant data and information to answer the research question and achieve the objectives proposed in this study.

In this study, the data collection technique chosen was the semi-structured interview because it is the most effective way to collect the opinion of the various agencies. In the case of the present study the interviews were conducted by guidelines, and a structured script with open and closed questions was created for this purpose. According to Júnior and Júnior [28], the interviews by guidelines present a certain degree of structuring based on points of interest explored by the researcher during the interview. In this type of interview, the interviewer asks few direct questions, letting the interviewee speak freely, while reporting to the marked agendas.

The nine Portuguese digital agencies were all first contacted via email and due to the lack of response were contacted by telephone for the appointment of the interview. Considering the pandemic and the distance of some agencies, the nine interviews were conducted online via Google Meet, through a link created to the situation. All interviewees were informed about the guarantee of confidentiality, privacy, and anonymity in the treatment of information, and all accepted the full recording of the audio of the interview for transcription purposes. All interviews were transcribed in full using the recording so that no information was lost. The script created for this purpose was structured with 26 questions divided into 4 parts: data on respondents, information about the agency and its customers, history of social networks of the agency and opportunity regarding new social networks. The various open and closed questions allow the interviewee to reveal details related to the theme of the interview that are social networks. The questions chosen for the interviews were duly chosen to address the research question and the proposed objectives.

4 Presentation and Analysis of Results

From June 1st to 29, 2021, nine interviews were conducted, with an approximate duration of 22 min, to nine digital agencies spread throughout Portugal. The interviewed subjects are identified from A1 to A9 in order to preserve their true names and the agencies where they work for ethical reasons, in order to enable the publication of the results of this investigation.

71% of the interviewees are male and 22% female, where the average age is around 42 years and the youngest person interviewed was 32 years old and the oldest person 66 years old. In terms of position at the agency, 89% of respondents are General Directors/CEO and 11% are members of the agency. Regarding the number of years of work in the organization on average, the interviewees have 12 years of work, with a minimum of 5 years and a maximum of 32 years. About years of experience in social media management on average the sample has 11 years of experience with a minimum of 5 years and a maximum of 17 years of experience.

Data on the agencies interviewed and their clients where we can observe that 2 agencies are from the North, 1 in central Portugal, 3 in the Lisbon Metropolitan Area, 1 in Alentejo and 2 in the Algarve. The 9 branches are 100% Portuguese with an average age of 12 years where the youngest agency is 5 years old and the oldest agency has 32 years of existence. Most of the agencies interviewed are considered micro-enterprises and other small enterprises. Regarding the target sectors of the agencies, all stated that they do not have a main target sector, assuming to work with all sectors. The A4 interviewee assumed:

We have clients from various areas, that is, we do not have a specific target sector, we have some clients of real estate, credit and the financial information part. But we both have clients who have a goldsmith's shop and we have from a computer agency. A little bit of everything. (A4, 2021) In terms of business model most of the agencies interviewed are Business-to-Business (B2B) and the rest are Business-to-Consumer (B2C). All of them provide services that involve Social Networks, and in addition to this, the 4 most provided services are SEO, website development and design work. More than half of the agencies interviewed (56%) say their main types of customers are small businesses, 22% claim to be big brands and the remaining 22% of agencies claim to be a mix of startups, small businesses, and big brands. The 4 main sectors where the agencies' clients are inserted are Fashion and Beauty (67%), the Hospitality and Catering sector (44%), Health (44%) and the Services sector (44%).

The portfolio of social networks that the agencies have as a tool for customers, go through Facebook, Instagram, LinkedIn, Twittter, Pinterest, Youtube, Tiktok and Clubhouse. Of the 3 most used by the agencies are Facebook, Instagram and LinkedIn with 100% agreement of the sample. "We use Facebook, Instagram and LinkedIn more. Twitter in Portugal does not have the necessary footprint for our type of customers. It is used more at the institutional and political level. But yes who has an international aspect, Twitter is important. We focus more on Facebook, Instagram and LinkedIn, I say this actively, we have accounts in all of them, but actively with a strategy and the creation of linked content." (A6, 2021) The A7 interviewee completes saying that he uses more the "Facebook, Instagram and LinkedIn. Which are the most prevalent in Europe. (2021)".

Regarding the route of agencies through the world of social networks, each had its own route, but in agreement with the majority the 1st social network used was Facebook, then in 2nd place is Instagram, in 3rd place LinkedIn, moving to 4th place is Twitter and Pinterest on an equal footing and last in 5th place Tiktok and Clubhouse, these being the last social networks where the agencies entered. The factor that led to this transition between social networks was trends with 100% agreement of the sample. "Something we are always aware of is market trends and digital trends and this is a determining factor for our activity. Digital Marketing is an activity that is constantly updating and varies a lot and we are very attentive to trends and adapt our business and suggest to our customers in the face of these market trends" (A9, 2021) The A6 full interviewee say that: "It is to follow trends, we are in the area, we follow trends and if it is social networks will always appear new, then it has to do with doing a job well done it is necessary to have a dedicated effort for this and also internal capacity to be able to meet this need. Therefore, social networks are appearing, we always analyze their trends and what kind of content we can make there, the effort that this entails and the result that can come (A6, 2021). As regards the question of whether there was any social network that the agencies stopped using, the answers were almost equally distributed between no and yes. On the one hand, we have opinions like that of the interviewee A1 who says that "in professional terms I did not stop using anything, I consider the hypotheses all, like or do not like, think good or not, if the target audience is on the social network we have to be there" (2021) and on the other hand we have the opposite opinion as that of the A6 interviewee who says that: "We have accounts open on all networks, now use is a little different from having open accounts. We actually have on Pinterest, but we do not use, does not add value, Twitter is another equal network we also think that for now never added value. So eventually had an initial maintenance effort, but then we stopped using it." (A6, 2021). Regarding the reasons that led agencies to stop using some social networks, the A6 interviewee clarifies "We came to use Pinterest and Twitter in customers, but we did not get results from it, so we stopped using" (2021), and the A8 interviewee completes with another reason "Google Plus, it was also a social network that we used with some customers, but then we stopped using because it ceased to exist" (2021). Making clear the two main reasons for this abandonment: the lack of results and the disappearance of certain social networks.

The question of the possibility of agencies betting on new emerging social networks could be seen as an almost perfect division between no and yes. On the one hand, we have opinions like that of the interviewee A2 who says: "I am very sincere, I think not, at this stage no, from the point of view that fortunately we do not need. I haven't quite figured out what targets Tiktok can achieve, although we all think it's a younger audience, but there hasn't been a request yet. That is, I think we can do something in Tiktok when customers start ordering Tiktok, it's a bit out there. "(A2, 2021) On the other hand, we have the opposite opinion as that of the A8 interviewee who states that he intends to bet on:

"Tiktok and Clubhouse, none more. Poparazzi we know, but no." (A8, 2021) Of the 4 agencies that said they wanted to bet on new social networks, 2 said they wanted to bet on TikTok, 1 agency talked about betting on the Clubhouse and another says that it would be willing to bet on both TikTok and Clubhouse. Regarding the characteristics sought in a new social network, most agencies, do not look for any specific characteristics as the interviewee A1 concludes: "I do not see things that way, I do not look for anything on the social network, I look for what the social network has to give to my clients, I start to go there. I work with a social network at a professional level, I don't care if the social network is good, if it's bad, if it's easy to move, has this or that feature. I always ask and put my strategy, how can this benefit the client, always, and I go there. So, if it can benefit the customer, if the customer makes sales or earns in his image or somehow gets to benefit from the use of the social network, then I use it in what the tool allows, but there are things that I like in some social networks, there are things that I like more and less." (A1, 2021) With regard to tools or features that would look for in a new social network the answers are varied. Interviewee A3 states that they would look for the ability of the social network to offer advertising: "It would always be the advertising part, understand how it works, how events are created, pixels, how they become sales, if it only generates awareness, etc." (2021). From another perspective we have the A6 interviewee who states that he would look for the possibility of the social network integrating third-party applications: "It is important that these platforms make api calls available and then be integrated into these platforms of automation of publications and also the analysis of metrics and results. It is very important in agencies because when working multiple accounts, it is a clear difference between a day or a few hours. So there this, resource optimization and the result is also always different and in a way it is also important that the third platforms update themselves and be able to have these integrations." (A6, 2021). Still in this approach the interviewee A5 has a contrary opinion, stating that he seeks a complete network without needing to integrate third-party applications. For the

284   L. S. Ribeiro and M. P. Farinha

agencies interviewed, the advantages of betting on new social networks are to be aware of the current/Innovation/Technology (89%), new markets (22%), more supply (33%) and more billing (11%). On the other hand, the advantages that agencies see in customers who bet on new social networks are reaching more audiences/new customers/more points of communication (78%), notoriety/brand image/visibility (56%) and being aware of the current (11%).

5 Discussion of Results

Regarding the specific objectives, with the results obtained it was possible to identify that the social networks most used by Portuguese digital agencies are Facebook, Instagram and LinkedIn which coincides, in the case of Facebook in 1st place and Instagram in 3rd place, with applications where the Portuguese most have account according to the data of Marktest (2020, October 27).

With regard to the path of Portuguese digital agencies in the adoption of social networks it was possible to realize that the first social network used by the agencies was Facebook, then in 2nd place is Instagram, in 3rd place LinkedIn, moving to 4th place is Twitter and Pinterest on an equal footing and last in 5th place TikTok and Clubhouse. With this result, it was also possible to understand that this transition between social networks is fuelled by the trend factor, not going according to the timeline of the appearance of social networks, which goes in line with Iryna et al. study [21]. The results obtained in this investigation also indicate that most Portuguese digital agencies do not have a checklist of features that they would look for in a new social network, agencies choose to observe what the network has to offer and then decide whether to bet considering the objective of the social network and whether it makes sense for the client portfolio that the agency has.

When it comes to tools or features sought in a new social network, most agencies ask for the possibility of integrating third-party applications to facilitate work within the agency. From this research it was also possible to identify that the potential emerging networks that may be used by Portuguese digital agencies are Tiktok and Clubhouse because they are social networks that are currently trending in Portugal. Crossing the results obtained from this investigation with the conclusions drawn from the study by Siamagka et al. [16] previously mentioned, it is possible to notice that there is a similarity between the factors that lead B2B organizations to adopt social media and Portuguese digital agencies to adopt social networks. In the study of these authors, it was revealed that "perception of use" and "organizational innovation" are the main factors that lead to this adoption. Looking at the results of interviews with Portuguese digital agencies, it is possible to see that most agencies claim to benefit from the adoption of new social networks for their portfolio of services not only in terms of current but also notoriety and, in terms of innovation, are entirely open to new social networks that may arise.

Another conclusion that is based on the study of these authors is the insignificance of the factor "perception of ease of use" in the adoption of social media. Comparing with the results of the interviews it is visible that if it is necessary to adopt a new social network the agencies do not look at their difficulty of use, if the client wants to be present in the social network, the agencies move forward with their use without looking at the means. Finally, the last conclusion drawn from the study by Siamagka et al. [16] is that "perception of use" is negatively affected by "barriers" and positively affected by "image". By crossing the answers of the interviews it is possible to understand that barriers such as the lack of results can lead Portuguese digital agencies to abandon social networks and, in terms of image, if an agency works with Facebook (social network where the Portuguese have more account, according to data from Marktest, 2020, October 27), will only add value to the factor "perception of use".

6 Conclusions

The general objective of this work was to understand the factors that lead Portuguese digital agencies to adopt a certain social network as a tool for their customers. With the empirical study carried out it was possible to realize that most Portuguese digital agencies do not look for specific characteristics in a social network but look for features such as the possibility of integrating third-party applications.

As limitations of this study, we can mention the scarcity of resources on the subject, not allowing comparison with more studies related to the area. Another limitation is the impossibility of ensuring that the opinion of the 9 Portuguese digital agencies interviewed convey the overall opinion of all digital agencies in Portugal.

For future investigations, a comparative study between countries is recommended to deepen the knowledge about the relationship between digital agencies and social networks, as it is an area that is still little explored. It would be an interesting topic because each country is different and the perception about the use of social networks also differs which would certainly lead to relevant conclusions about the differences and patterns between countries. In addition to comparing with other countries, it would also be relevant to respond to the following hypotheses that emerged from the conclusions of this study. H1: Agencies that structure the characteristics they seek in a social network, achieve their objectives and strategies more quickly H2: The portfolio of social networks that agencies work is a determining factor to be chosen by customers.

References

1. Jones, A., Malczyk, A., Beneke, J.: Internet marketing: a highly practical guide to every aspect of internet marketing. GetSmarter (2011)
2. DataReportal – Global Digital Insights, "Local Country Headlines Report," retrieved January 2023 (2023). https://datareportal.com/reports/digital-2023-local-country-headlines
3. Pordata. Empresas: total e por dimensão (2021). https://www.pordata.pt/Portugal/Empresas+total+e+por+dimens%c3%a3o-2857
4. Nguyen, D.T.T., Nguyen, P.V., Bui, V.T.T., Nguyen, A.T.H.: Factors affecting application of e-marketing at proprietorships and the impact of e-marketing use on proprietorships' marketing success. Int. J. Econ. Res. 12(1), 47–60 (2015)
5. Conde, I., Cirino, F., Vieira, M., Chiari, M.: Agências de Comunicação na Amazônia Digital: Adequação e Desafios. Universidade da Amazônia, Belém, PA, Intercom – Sociedade Brasileira de Estudos Interdisciplinares da Comunicação, XIV Congresso de Ciências da Comunicação na Região Norte (2015)
6. AMA. Digital Marketing definition (2021). https://www.ama.org/topics/digital-marketing/

7. Ryan, D., Jones, C.: Understanding digital marketing: marketing strategies for engaging the digital generation. Kogan Page, London; Philadelphia (2009)
8. Chaffey, D.: Digital marketing strategy, implementation and practice sixth edition. J. Chem. Inf. Model. (2016)
9. Filo, K., Lock, D., Karg, A.: Sport and social media research: a review. Sport Manage. Rev. 18(2), 166–18 (2015)
10. Kaplan, A.M., Haenlein, M.: Users of the world, unite! The challenges and opportunities of Social Media. Business Horizons (2010). https://doi.org/10.1016/j.bushor.2009.09.003
11. Tuten, T.L., Solomon, M.R.: "Social Media Marketing," 2nd Edition, Sage (2015)
12. Dwivedi, Y.K., Kapoor, K.K., Chen, H.: Social media marketing and advertising. Mark. Rev. 15(3), 289–309 (2015)
13. Charlesworth, A.: "Digital Marketing," in Digital Marketing (2018). https://doi.org/10.4324/9781315175737
14. Zhu, Y., Chen, H.: Social media and human need satisfaction: implications for social media marketing. Bus. Horiz. 58, 335–345 (2015)
15. Dahnil, M.I., Marzuki, K.M., Langgat, J., Fabeil, N.F.: Factors influencing SMEs adoption of social media marketing. Procedia. Soc. Behav. Sci. 148, 119–126 (2014). https://doi.org/10.1016/j.sbspro.2014.07.025
16. Siamagka, N.-T., Christodoulides, G., Michaelidou, N., Valvi, A.: Determinants of social media adoption by B2B organizations. Ind. Mark. Manage. 51, 89–99 (2015). https://doi.org/10.1016/j.indmarman.2015.05.005
17. Miller, M.: The Ultimate Web Marketing Guide (2010)
18. DataReportal – Global Digital Insights, "Digital 2021: Global Overview Report," Retrieved 3 February 2021 (2021). https://datareportal.com/reports/digital-2021-global-overview-report
19. Kietzmann, J.H., Hermkens, K., McCarthy, I.P., Silvestre, B.S.: Social media? Get serious! Understanding the functional building blocks of social media. Bus. Horiz. 54, 241–251 (2011). https://doi.org/10.1016/j.bushor.2011.01.005
20. Marktest. (2020, Outubro 27). Quem usa e o que faz nas redes sociais? Marktest Grupo. Retrieved 3 February 2021 (2021). https://www.marktest.com/wap/a/n/id~26c7.aspx
21. Iryna, P., Véronique, Guilloux., Anca, C.M.: Exploring social media engagement behaviors in the context of luxury brands. J. Advertising 47(1), 55–69 (2018). https://doi.org/10.1080/00913367.2017.1405756
22. Gondim (2019, Outubro 9). Quais são os tipos de agência na comunicação? https://blog.midianoalvo.com.br/tipos-de-agencia/
23. Sant'Anna, A.: Propaganda: teoria, técnica e prática. (8°ed). Thomson Learning, São Paulo, Brasil (2009)
24. Santos, E.S., Oliveira, P.S., Santana Presller, N.G., de Oliveira, I.C.G. Agências Digitais: a implementação online na Amazônia. Temática 14(3) (2018)
25. Haro, F., et al.: Investigação em ciências sociais: guia prático do estudante. Lisboa: Pactor (2016)
26. Thiry-Cherques, H.R.: Saturação em pesquisa qualitativa: estimativa empírica de dimensionamento. Revista PMKT São Paulo 3(2), 20–27 (2009)
27. Sousa, M., Baptista, C.: "Como fazer investigação, dissertações, teses e relatórios" (4.ª ed.). Lisboa: Pactor. 52–86 (2011)
28. Júnior, Á.F.B., Júnior N.F.: A utilização da técnica de entrevista em trabalhos científicos. Evidência: olhares e pesquisa em saberes educacionais 04, 129–148 (2011)

Extracting Business Activities for Digital Transformation in the SET Healthcare Sector Using Verb Phrases Analysis

Sompong Promsa-ad and Nichnan Kittiphattanabawon[✉]

School of Informatics, Walailak University, 222 Thasala District, Nakhonsithammarat 80161, Thailand
knichcha@wu.ac.th

Abstract. Without standardized roadmap, firms in the healthcare sectors have found it challenging to adopt digital transformation. This study, based on signaling theory, alleviated the issue by applying automated information extraction to retrieve such demanding knowledge from firms' information disclosure while avoiding a tedious and time-consuming task of manually extracting information from huge text documents. The main objectives of this study were 1) to extract evolving business activities relating to digital healthcare transformation and 2) to identify whether extracted business activities align with a particular digital maturity model. The samples were firms listed in the healthcare sector of the Stock Exchange of Thailand. The data was obtained from firms' annual reports covered period 2017–2021. To extract business activities, this study employed phrase extraction technique based on words' parts of speech tagging. The extracted phrases then were filtered using custom-made dictionary. The findings indicated that while investing in key infrastructure and leveraging digital technology to improve business processes made up the majority of a company's early period business activities, later timeframe business activities were more focused on value generation activities and new business models creation. The changes of activities in different periods also suggested that some business activities might require prerequisite activities. Assigning extracted business activities into relevant dimensions of the specific maturity model further proved that the extracted business activities adhere to the elements of chosen digital maturity model. The elements carried out by firms expressed the nature of the sector as well as how highly they prioritize digital transformation.

Keywords: Healthcare · Digital Transformation · Business Activities · Information Extraction

1 Introduction

Almost every industry has witnessed a fundamental transformation in how businesses operate because of the advent of digital technology. Healthcare is one sector where digital disruption is becoming mainstream. Companies in this sector are under pressure to embrace digital transformation to improve consumer value. The COVID-19 pandemic, in which virtual visits were deemed a more effective infection prevention tool than traditional face-to-face medical practices, has also spurred the implementation of digital healthcare [1].

Digital transformation is defined as the use of digital technologies to enhance business operations, customer relationships, and business models [2]. Possible applications of using digital technology in the healthcare sector include maintaining and managing electronic healthcare data with blockchain technology [3], analyzing big data to enable early detection and prevention of disease [4], connecting via online channels to consult with physicians [5], adding a revenue channel by providing telehealth [6], etc.

Most digital initiatives, 70 percent or more, were reported as not having the desired outcomes [7]. Additionally, some businesses are finding it difficult to determine where to begin to create new development prospects or to confirm that existing transformative programs are on the correct track [8]. The high failure rate of digital transformation may be attributed to several reasons, including its complexity. The transformation is considered a continuing process consisting of three consecutive phases: digitization, digitalization, and digital transformation. Each phase has its own set of key elements, and when the first two incremental phases are in place, firms can now move to the most pervasive phase, digital transformation [9]. Implementing certain elements usually leads to a profound change in several firms' business activities [10].

Firms' digital journeys may also follow a certain path referred to as a "digital maturity model," which consists of two components: maturity levels and dimensions. To create a roadmap for future growth, both components indicate what tasks must be completed as well as what level firms currently belong to. Currently, there are at least eighteen digital maturity models available, suggesting that the lack of a standard guideline for digital transformation is a critical problem for practitioners [11]. The same issue is also evident in the healthcare sector. There is still a lack of consensus over which factors should be assessed. Additionally, the stages of digital maturity have largely been ignored [12].

According to signaling theory, it is possible to gain more understanding on the digital transformation practices by learning from firm's voluntary disclosure. Companies tend to disclose the market with more and better information as they want to signal their future prospects to investors. As a result, firms are able to attract more capital at cheaper costs [13]. One of the most important channels that publicly listed firms provide information to potential investors is often through their annual reports. However, it is a tedious and time-consuming task to manually extract such information from huge amounts of text data. Weighing upon these concerns, this article raises two research questions 1) what are the main business activities of digital healthcare transformation and how do they change over time? and 2) Does the digital transformation of firms in the healthcare sector adhere to a specific roadmap? Our objectives were to extract evolving business activities relating to digital transformation and to identify whether extracted business activities follow a digital maturity model. Examining the problem from the perspective of business activities will provide academics as well as practitioners a less abstract way of depicting required dimensions for digital transformation and indicators that can be used to measure them.

This article is structured as follows. The key literature is summarized in the next section, which is then followed by the research methodology, presentation of the results, discussion, and conclusion.

2 Literature Review

2.1 Digital Healthcare Transformation

Digital technology has fundamentally changed how businesses operate across almost all sectors, including healthcare. An adoption of digital healthcare is also accelerated by COVID-19 pandemic, in which digital technologies have been applied in many different contexts in order to curb the spread of coronavirus. For instance, internet-based medical material support and scheduling platform was established to track the manufacturing capacity, output, inventory, and transportation of various materials [14]. Digital healthcare transformation can take many different forms. It includes collecting and analyzing personal healthcare data for preventing possible disease [15], creating virtual environment for digital education like simulated medical and surgical education [16], providing a wide range of healthcare services in form of telemedicine [6], etc.

There are challenges in implementing digital technologies in the healthcare sector. Data fragmentation is one of the common issues caused by the enormous variety and amount of medical data, which makes data collection difficult [14]. Collecting and analyzing customer' health data also raise privacy issues [17]. Security is another problem that is growing up since there are more entry points for attackers to perform illegal actions due to the vast number of connected devices [18].

2.2 Business Activities

Business activities cover all the economic activities performed by a company to meet its primary objective of making profit [19]. In this study, we attempted to find potential business activities that represent firms' digital transformation rather than categorizing firms according to the performed business activities. Common business activities include "launch new product", "provide after sale services", "advertise through social media", "invest in new plant", etc.

Business activity plays an important role in adding value to inputs and turning them into desirable products in the eyes of end customers. Based on sectors of industry perspectives, all productions may be divided into three broad types of business activity: primary sector, secondary sector, and tertiary sector. Primary sector relates with any activities concerning an exploitation or extraction of natural resources. Its output can be viewed as raw materials that will be processed by companies in the secondary sector. For the third sector, key business activities are those conducted by firms that provide services to consumers and other businesses [20].

The business value chain framework makes it clear how business activity contributes to resource value added and user appealing. The concept is defined as a series of actions taken in order to create a finished product, from its idea to its delivery to a consumer. Value chain consists of four supporting activities and five primary activities [21]. With the rise of digital technology, it is worth noting that some activities once performed by humans may be replaced by machine. For bank's housing loan review service, for instance, activities like checking submitted documents and determining loan amounts can be executed by artificial intelligence service system [22].

2.3 Digital Maturity Model

Digital transformation is assumed to follow some particular roadmap referred to as digital maturity model. The model is described as a point of reference to direct businesses' improvement efforts and an indicator of the level of maturity or key phases of specific dimensions of a company in the process of achieving digital transformation [23]. Currently, there are several digital maturity models available. As a result, businesses undergoing digital transformation are unsure of whether the model they have chosen was built in the most comprehensive and systematic way [11].

The problem is also one of the most debated issues in healthcare sector. Based on the survey conducted by [12], most healthcare digital maturity models are inadequate, and the dimensions to be assessed are unclear. The decomposition of digital maturity into stages has also been neglected. The same study suggests that the comprehensive model should consist of 7 dimensions: strategy; information technology capability; interoperability; governance and management; patient-centered care; people, skills, and behavior; and data analytics. According to [24], the health sector may also need domain-specific models because the delivery of healthcare services differs greatly from offering traditional services or from manufacturing sector activities.

2.4 Information Extraction

Information extraction from text, such as from business news, firm disclosures, and social media, is an efficient method for discovering knowledge concealed in economic text [25]. Its main task is to locate a predetermined set of concepts in a given domain while rejecting other irrelevant data [26]. There are several tasks of information extraction. One of the most popular applications of information extraction technology is Named Entity Recognition (NER). The method is used to identify various kinds of proper names, including those of people and companies, as well as occasionally unique kinds of entities, including dates and times, which may be quickly recognized using surface-level textual patterns [25].

Automate key phrase extraction is another useful method to identify the key phrases that classify a text's subject or domain in unstructured text [27]. Despite its ease of use, the technique is considered to be an effective one for obtaining crucial information from unstructured data. One technique for phrase extraction is phrase extraction based on parts of speech (POS) tags [28]. The term "part of speech" refers to the category of words that are determined by the many functions that they may serve. Nouns, verbs, adjectives, adverbs, etc. are typical examples of POS. Currently, there are natural language processing (NLP) algorithms that can identify word types in text, making information extraction based on text POS convenient [29].

3   Research Methodology

3.1   Population and Sample

The Stock Exchange of Thailand (SET), which lists twenty-three companies in the healthcare sector, served as the study's population. To be included as samples, firms must provide their English version's annual reports and those reports should be easily converted into text forms. Unfortunately, there were only nine firms that fit the requirements. Then, we chose five firms that, taken individually, may be representative of big, medium-sized, and small businesses. From 2017 to 2021, these companies made their English annual reports available for public access. The websites of the Securities and Exchange Commission and the websites of the respective organizations provided annual reports. In total, this study used twenty-five reports.

Table 1.   Characteristics of firms in the samples

Company	Age	# Hospital	Total asset (Mill. THB)	Market Cap (Mill. THB)
BDMS	52	53	128,453.62	365,516.04
BH	46	2	20,856.80	112,036.58
PRINC	21	12	17,415.35	18,052.62
VIH	34	4	3,639.28	6,391.45
THG	45	12	23,798.73	31,628.23

Source: Firms' website and www.set.or.th

According Table 1, the names of the companies were represented by the corresponding stock market tickers. Age was the number of years from founding date to year-end 2021. The hospital column displayed the total number of hospitals operating within the company's network. Market capitalization and total assets were used to measure a firm's size. Note that all numbers were as of year-end 2021.

3.2   Data Preparation

The data used in this study were obtained from the annual reports of the firms in the samples. Texts from the nature of business and market and competition sections were used, as firms usually revealed their digital transformation practices in these parts of the reports. The annual reports in PDF format were converted into textual forms. In order to get meaningful and interpretable phrases, original text patterns were preserved as much as possible. Therefore, only stop-words removal was performed in the step of text preprocessing.

To obtain only business activities relating to digital transformation, extracted phrases were filtered using domain-specific keywords. Therefore, a dictionary of digital transformation in the healthcare sector was constructed. It began with collecting relevant key terms from relevant sources, including three online dictionaries and four published

research articles, as detailed in Table 2. After removing redundant words, the final
dictionary consisted of 2,216 key terms.

Table 2. List of sources used for constructing dictionary of healthcare digital transformation

Source	#Category	# Key terms
Techopedia [30]	11	547
Techterms [31]	7	1,544
Digital health terminology guide [32]	9	127
The Effects of Digital Transformation on Firm Performance: Evidence from China's Manufacturing Sector [33]	3	49
Impact of the Digital Transformation of Small- and Medium-Sized Listed Companies on Performance: Based on a Cost-Benefit Analysis Framework [34]	3	21
Digital Maturity and Corporate Performance: The Case of the Baltic States [35]	6	49
A literature review of digital transformation in healthcare [36]	4	26
Total		2,363

3.3 Extracting Business Activities

As this study aimed to extract business activities, natural language processing techniques
were utilized to extract information from raw texts. Specifically, the Python syntax library
was used to detect word types in text referred to as words' parts of speech. Then, relevant
phrases based on these words' functions were extracted, containing contents indicating
firms' digital transformation-related business activities. In this study, several patterns
from English's sentences, verb phrases, and noun phrases were extracted. In English,
the parts of a sentence involve the subject, verb, object, complement, and adverbial.
They can be arranged to form various sentence structures [37].

Under these structures, verb complementation is required to follow verbs of different types to fully convey their meaning. The objects or complements can be noun
phrases, adjectives, prepositional phrases, or whole clauses [38]. In this study, 25 verb
patterns proposed by [39] were employed. Although Hornby's verb patterns have been
critiqued for their complexity and have been simplified by later language experts, they
are nonetheless valuable, particularly for the issue at hand, as the extent of a pattern's
coverage is more important than how interesting and simple it is to understand (Fig. 1).

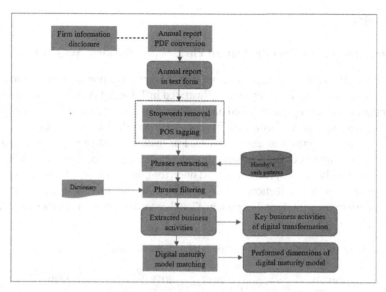

Fig. 1. Proposed framework

For simplicity, we excluded the objects of the verb that are in the form of a that-clause or dependent clause. For each remaining verb pattern, at least three different sub-patterns were created in order to minimize any deviations. In addition, we supplemented nouns in the patterns with varying forms of noun phrases as suggested in [40], and [41]. Then we extracted these verb patterns with difference type of subjects including noun, pronoun, and proper noun. We also extracted these verb patterns with subject omitted. With some experiments, we found that the extraction using noun phrases can deliver the relevant outputs. Thus, we included them in the extraction process.

3.4 Matching Business Activities with Digital Maturity Model

After the filtering stage, not all extracted phrases were interpretable. Therefore, ambiguous phrases without a clear meaning were omitted. The remaining phrases were ones that could indicate digital transformation-related business activities. Most of business activities were directly deduced from extracted phrases whereas some were slightly rewritten. Then, these activities were linked to the digital maturity model proposed by [12]. We chose this model because it is the most recent and comprehensive model that was synthesized from key existing maturity models. In this stage, each business activities has been assigned into relevant dimension year on year to see whether the obtained business activities aligned with dimensions perceived as necessary ingredients for digital transformation journey and how they changed over the course of the study period.

4 Results

4.1 Descriptive Statistics of Extracted Phrases and Business Activities

Based on specified phrase patterns and our digital transformation dictionary, the results of the information extraction stage were illustrated in Table 3. For each firm, we showed the number of extracted phrases based on specified patterns, and the number of extracted phrases containing desired keywords. Phrases with specified keywords then were subsequently translated into business activities. For instance, one of the phrases that was extracted was "impress customers with digital experiences direct". As this phrase also had pre-specified keywords, it was counted once for both extracted phrases and phrases with keywords. To make it more understandable, the phrase was then rewritten into "impress customers with digital experience" and recorded once for business activities.

Table 3. Descriptive statistics of extracted phrases and business activities

Firms	Count	2017	2018	2019	2020	2021
BDMS	Extracted phrases	1,148	840	1,121	1,881	2,088
	Phrases with keywords	233	155	192	294	306
	Business activities	20	18	26	38	23
BH	Extracted phrases	313	343	612	591	879
	Phrases with keywords	36	42	89	67	169
	Business activities	2	9	6	2	18
PRINC	Extracted phrases	1,511	1,863	1,266	1,455	1,039
	Phrases with keywords	279	348	192	219	102
	Business activities	12	20	20	22	11
VIH	Extracted phrases	835	840	904	996	1,053
	Phrases with keywords	72	78	85	97	108
	Business activities	6	7	8	8	9
THG	Extracted phrases	687	587	683	835	1,587
	Phrases with keywords	99	103	123	132	201
	Business activities	6	6	9	11	12

According to Table 3, all of the sample firms conducted activities related to digital transformation. Among these companies, the top two firms that had the greatest number of extracted business activities are BDMS and PRINC. They also had similar business activity patterns in that their peak years coincided with the global pandemic of the COVID-19 in 2020. Although having the fewest activities overall, BH was the only company that showed a drastically increased in the most recent time. The activities carried out by VIH and THG gradually increased during the study period.

4.2   Characteristics of Obtained Business Activities

In total, there were 306 obtained business activities. Example of extracted business activities of all firms in year 2021 were illustrated in Fig. 2. Selected samples of business activities occurred in each period were also depicted in Fig. 3 in order to show how these activities evolve from the early study period to the later time frame. According to Fig. 3, the majority of the business's activities in the early period entailed utilizing digital technologies to improve business processes and investing on key infrastructures. Example of key activities of this period included "communicate via digital media & online channel", "sell via internet", "employ electronic medical record", etc.

Fig. 2. Example of business activities of all sample firms in year 2021

Business activities during the later time frame, on the other hand, indicated the shift to ones that oriented toward firms' value creation. Specifically, the unique activities observed in the later period included "impress customers with digital experiences", "develop mobile application", "recruit startups", "offer digital loyalty card", "consult physician via online treatment system", "launch virtual hospital application", etc. These actions reflect the new business model, which enables companies to add value or develop new revenue streams. Emerging activities in the recent period also indicated the rising trends of artificial intelligence, open innovation, and cybersecurity.

The finding also indicated the relationship between obtained business activities and firms' characteristics. Specifically, the top two firms with the most extracted business activities were also the top two businesses with the greatest number of hospitals in their network. Moreover, the firms with the highest number of extracted business activities were the biggest firm regardless of which metric used. The type of activity a firm engaged in may also have been influenced by its size as the larger firms tended to pursue the more genuine digital transformation. Particularly, the largest firm made use of digital technologies to improve businesses' operations on a larger scale. For instance, it employed digital technology to improve business processes as illustrated by phrases like "train clinical skill with simulation network system", "employ healthy bot", "conduct virtual meeting", "convert analog data into electronic book", etc. It also brought technologies to create new business model as shown in phrases like "consult physician via online treatment system". On the contrary, one small company limited its business activities at the digitalization stage as its main business activities were illustrated in phrases like "employ digital marketing" and "use computer system in inventory management".

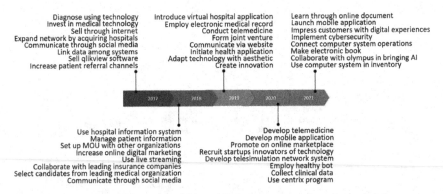

Fig. 3. Evolving business activities of digital transformation of sampled firms

4.3   Relation Between Obtained Business Activities and Digital Maturity Model

In the final experiment, we linked firms' obtained business activities with dimensions required in digital maturity model proposed by [12]. Using the model's description and indicators, we classified each company's business activities into the appropriate dimensions year on year. For example, "develop telesimulation network system" was assigned to the information technology capability dimension. It should be noted that some activities could show many dimensions. For instance, the phrase "offer digital loyalty card" suggested the use of data as well as patient-driven treatment.

The evolution of dimensions of each firm was shown in Fig. 4. The list of dimensions for a particular firm displayed in each period were all dimensions accumulated from the beginning up to that point. In the last period, the missing dimensions were marked in the bold letters. The results showed that every company in the sample had performed elements considered to be important for digital transformation. In the second timeframe of the study period, PRINC was the company that fully implemented those aspects first, followed by BDMS and BH a year later. VIH, the smallest firms in the sample, had the most missing key elements. It should be noted that while building IT capability was common for all businesses, some important elements particularly those that were related to business human resources and data usage tended to be employed more recently.

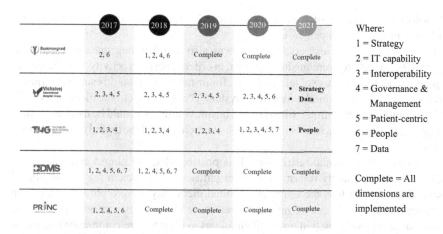

Fig. 4. The evolution of dimensions required in digital maturity model for each firm

5 Conclusion and Discussion

The focus of this study was to extract evolving business activities relating to digital healthcare transformation and to identify the alignment between extracted business activities and a particular digital maturity model. Using phrase extraction technique based on words' parts of speech, the findings indicated that all samples' companies engaged in digital transformation-related activities during the study period. While investing in key infrastructure and leveraging technology to improve business processes made up the majority of a company's early activities, later activities were more focused on new business models. The results also showed that the larger firms conducted a greater variety of business activities covering all three stages of the digital journey.

The results further proved that the extracted business activities adhere to the dimensions specified in the chosen digital maturity model. According to Fig. 4, extracted business activities can be classified into any dimensions of the chosen digital maturity model. However, some firms had not implemented all necessary elements for digital transformation. Additionally, some aspects have been implemented more recently than others especially the development of human resources and the utilization of data for improved decision-making.

By looking from the perspective of business activities, we gained a clearer picture of the transformation of digital healthcare. First, in line with other industries, larger healthcare companies engaged more in digital transformation than smaller ones, both in terms of depth and coverage. Second, the business activities relating to IT capabilities, interoperability, governance & management, and patient-driven care dimensions were conducted by all companies regardless of firms' characteristics. The existence of a governance and management element was not surprising given that healthcare procedures involve a variety of risks that have the potential to cause catastrophic injury or even death to patients [42]. Giving top priority to the business activities about the interoperability element was also anticipated provided that their operations involve several key stakeholders and systems such as patients, pharmaceutical firms, clinical organizations, regulators, insurance companies, etc. [43].

Third, from time series perspective, it was also worth noting that some business activities might require prerequisite activities. In order to perform activity "launch virtual hospital application" or "use of telemedicine, for instance, firm should establish required activities like "launch hospital information system", "employ electronic medical record", or "launch mobile application". In this sense, business activities could be used as a tool to evaluate the dynamics of a necessary dimension at each stage of the digital transformation process.

This research had some restrictions. It is possible that our phrase extraction approach may not adequately return all relevant phrases. The problem may be attributed to several factors, such as the usage of a limited dictionary or verb phrase patterns. In our future works, therefore, we intend to seek more effective extraction approach and its evaluation method which in turn will enable us to obtain more comprehensive list of business activities. Another drawback was the lack of clarity around the business activity patterns that lead to effective digital transformation and may be used as a roadmap for the process. Therefore, a promising field of research was to relate business activity patterns of organizations to their firm financial performance.

References

1. Rha, J.S., Lee, H.H.: Research trends in digital transformation in the service sector: a review based on network text analysis. Serv. Bus. 1–22 (2022)
2. Kraus, S., Durst, S., Ferreira, J.J., Veiga, P., Kailer, N., Weinmann, A.: Digital transformation in business and management research: an overview of the current status quo. Int. J. Inf. Manage. **63**, 102466 (2022)
3. Arumugam, S.K., Sharma, A.M.: Blockchain: opportunities in the healthcare sector and its uses in COVID-19. In: Lessons from COVID-19, pp. 61–94. Academic Press (2022)
4. Rehman, A., Naz, S., Razzak, I.: Leveraging big data analytics in healthcare enhancement: trends, challenges and opportunities. Multimedia Syst. **28**(4), 1339–1371 (2022)
5. Čavoški, S., Vujović, V., Devrnja, V., Ferenc, B., Lukić, F.: Digital transformation in healthcare healthcare on demand. In: 2022 21st International Symposium INFOTEH-JAHORINA (INFOTEH), pp. 1–6. IEEE (2022)
6. Velayati, F., Ayatollahi, H., Hemmat, M., Dehghan, R.: Telehealth business models and their components: systematic review. J. Med. Internet Res. **24**(3), e33128 (2022)
7. Tabrizi, B., Lam, E., Girard, K., Irvin, V.: Digital transformation is not about technology. Harv. Bus. Rev. **13**(March), 1–6 (2019)
8. Digital transformation academy.: Thailand 2021 Digital Transformation Readiness (2021)
9. Verhoef, P.C., et al.: Digital transformation: a multidisciplinary reflection and research agenda. J. Bus. Res. **122**, 889–901 (2021)
10. Stalmachova, K., Chinoracky, R., Strenitzerova, M.: Changes in business models caused by digital transformation and the COVID-19 pandemic and possibilities of their measurement—case study. Sustainability **14**(1), 127 (2021)
11. Gökalp, E., Martinez, V.: Digital transformation maturity assessment: development of the digital transformation capability maturity model. Int. J. Prod. Res. 1–21 (2021)
12. Duncan, R., Eden, R., Woods, L., Wong, I., Sullivan, C.: Synthesizing dimensions of digital maturity in hospitals: systematic review. J. Med. Internet Res. **24**(3), e32994 (2022)

13. Salvi, A., Vitolla, F., Rubino, M., Giakoumelou, A., Raimo, N.: Online information on digitalisation processes and its impact on firm value. J. Bus. Res. **124**, 437–444 (2021)
14. Wang, Q., Su, M., Zhang, M., Li, R.: Integrating digital technologies and public health to fight Covid-19 pandemic: key technologies, applications, challenges and outlook of digital healthcare. Int. J. Environ. Res. Public Health **18**(11), 6053 (2021)
15. Lepore, D., et al.: Interdisciplinary research unlocking innovative solutions in healthcare. Technovation, 102511 (2022)
16. Tan, T.F., et al.: Metaverse and virtual health care in ophthalmology: opportunities and challenges. Asia-Pacific J. Ophthalmol. **11**(3), 237–246 (2022)
17. Cummins, N., Schuller, B.W.: Five crucial challenges in digital health. Front. Digital Health **2**, 536203 (2020)
18. Siriwardhana, Y., Gür, G., Ylianttila, M., Liyanage, M.: The role of 5G for digital healthcare against COVID-19 pandemic: opportunities and challenges. Ict Express **7**(2), 244–252 (2021)
19. Business activities: definition and 3 main types., https://www.investopedia.com/terms/b/bus iness-activities.asp, last accessed 2023/01/20
20. Stimpson, P., Smith, A.: Business Management for the IB Diploma Coursebook. Cambridge University Press (2015)
21. Ricciotti, F.: From value chain to value network: a systematic literature review. Manage. Rev. Quart. **70**(2), 191–212 (2019). https://doi.org/10.1007/s11301-019-00164-7
22. Takeuchi, H., Ichitsuka, A., Iino, T., Ishikawa, S., Saito, K.: Assessment method for identifying business activities to be replaced by AI technologies. Procedia Comput. Sci. **192**, 1601–1610 (2021)
23. Zapata, M.L., Berrah, L., Tabourot, L.: Is a digital transformation framework enough for manufacturing smart products? The case of Small and Medium Enterprises. Procedia Manuf. **42**, 70–75 (2020)
24. Burmann, A., Meister, S.: Practical application of maturity models in healthcare: findings from multiple digitalization case studies. In: HEALTHINF, pp. 100–110 (2021)
25. Hobbs, J.R., Riloff, E.: Information Extraction. Handb. Nat. Lang. Process. **15**, 16 (2010)
26. Piskorski, J., Yangarber, R.: Information extraction: past, present and future. In: Multi-source, Multilingual Information Extraction and Summarization. Springer, Berlin, Heidelberg, 23–49 (2013). https://doi.org/10.1007/978-3-642-28569-1_2
27. Martinez-Rodriguez, J.L., Hogan, A., Lopez-Arevalo, I.: Information extraction meets the semantic web: a survey. Seman. Web **11**(2), 255–335 (2020)
28. Sarkar, D.: Text Analytics with Python. Apress, New York, NY, USA (2016)
29. Kochmar, E.: Getting Started with Natural Language Processing. USA. Manning publications, NY (2022)
30. Techopedia (2023). https://www.techopedia.com/. Accessed 01 Jan 2023
31. Techterms (2023). https://techterms.com/. Accessed 04 Jan 2023
32. Digital health terminology guide (2023). http://sil-asia.org/digital-health-terminology-guide/. Accessed 06 Jan 2023
33. Guo, L., Xu, L.: The effects of digital transformation on firm performance: evidence from China's manufacturing sector. Sustainability **13**(22), 12844 (2021)
34. Teng, X., Wu, Z., Yang, F.: Research article impact of the digital transformation of small-and medium-sized listed companies on performance: based on a cost-benefit analysis framework (2022)
35. Eremina, Y., Lace, N., Bistrova, J.: Digital maturity and corporate performance: the case of the Baltic states. J. Open Innov.: Technol. Market Complex. **5**(3), 54 (2019)
36. Ivančić, L., Glavan, L.M., Vukšić, V. B.: A literature review of digital transformation in healthcare. In: 2020 43rd International Convention on Information, Communication and Electronic Technology (MIPRO), pp. 1351–1355. IEEE (2020)

37. John, E.: Oxford Practice Grammar: With answers John Eastwood (2002)

38. Carter, R., McCarthy, M.: Cambridge English Grammar. Cambridge, Cambridge (2006)

39. Hornby, A.S.: Guide to Patterns and Usage in English (1995)

40. What is a noun phrase in English? (2023). https://grammar.collinsdictionary.com/easy-learning/what-is-a-noun-phrase-in-english. Accessed 7 Jan 2023

41. Noun phrases (2023). https://learnenglish.britishcouncil.org/grammar/english-grammar-reference/noun-phrases. Accessed 7 Jan 2023

42. Benjamin, K., Potts, H.W.: Digital transformation in government: Lessons for digital health? Digital Health **4**, 2055207618759168 (2018)

43. Hermes, S., Riasanow, T., Clemons, E.K., Böhm, M., Krcmar, H.: The digital transformation of the healthcare industry: exploring the rise of emerging platform ecosystems and their influence on the role of patients. Bus. Res. **13**, 1033–1069 (2020)

Digital Economy

Stock Market Activity and Financing Decisions in the Technology Industry: Does Upstream-Downstream Innovation Matter?

Tanyarandzwa Gandanhamo📵 and Thabo J. Gopane⁽⊠⁾📵

Department of Finance and Investment Management, University of Johannesburg, Johannesburg, South Africa
{ashleyg,tjgopane}@uj.ac.za

Abstract. Although technological innovation's impact on society is well-known, the stylized facts of financing decisions in the technology sector are yet to be established. The present paper contributes towards bridging this knowledge gap. The study investigates the combined effect of stock market activity and vertical integration of upstream-downstream innovation on financing decisions of the technology industry. The study applies an econometrics-validated random effects model and a carefully screened panel dataset of 11 stock exchange-listed firms over twenty years. The study results are enlightening for this emerging market technology sector of South Africa. First, variation in vertical integration affects changes in leverage. Second, stock market activity affects leverage, but upstream-downstream innovation does matter. This study's outcomes will benefit innovation industrialists, policymakers, and technology-oriented investors interested in emerging markets.

Keywords: Capital structure · Debt · Equity · Financing decisions · Innovation · Leverage · Technology

1 Introduction

The financing decisions of a firm generally manifest through the resultant capital structure. The phrases *firm financing* and *capital structure* typically mean the same thing and will be used interchangeably in this paper. For a business to exist and operate, it may be financed through loans (commonly known as debt, D) or listing on the stock market (equity financing, E). Other financing instruments exist, but D and E are considered representative enough in the literature. Therefore, a firm's capital structure is defined as proportions of debt and equity known as the debt-equity ratio, $\left(\frac{D}{D+E}\right)$ or leverage.

Capital structure is one of the critical areas in corporate finance (Dao & Ta, 2020) because of its significant influence on financial stability and business profitability. The literature on capital structure has historically worried about the question: what is the optimal capital structure of a firm, and how is it determined? In response, pioneering academic research proposed several answers which were further refined over time, including irrelevance theory (Modigliani & Miller, 1958, 1963), trade-off theory (Kraus & Litzen-berger, 1973), agency theory (Jensen & Meckling, 1976), and pecking order theory (Myers, 1984) to mention the main ones. The literature assumed static capital struc-ture for a long time, but this has since adapted to the reality of changing business and economic environment. Consequently, a dynamic capital structure emerged. Studies of dynamic capital structure tend to ask whether firms rebalance (Welch, 2004) their capi-tal structures over time, and if so, what is the speed of adjustment (Fischer et al., 1989; Flannery & Rangan, 2006; Ozkan, 2001). Whether static or dynamic, empirical studies are by and large structured in a similar manner, to investigate the determinants of capital structure, and this is evident in literature reviews (Harris & Raviv, 1991; Iqbal et al., 2012; Kumar et al., 2017; Miglo, 2011).

While the typical research of capital structure determinants focuses on a firm's finan-cial characteristics, another stream of literature examines capital structure by questioning the role of prevailing business environments. Such business factors include non-financial stakeholders (Istaitieh & Rodríguez-Fernández, 2006), suppliers-customer characteris-tics (Kalea & Shahrurb, 2007), supplier chain management (Son & Kim, 2022), and corporate strategy (Barton & Gordon, 1988; Cappa et al., 2020; Kochhar & Hitt, 1998). The current study contributes to the latter sub-group, and it warrants a close interroga-tion because research on the "impact of corporate strategy decisions on capital structure" often culminates in "mixed and inconclusive results" (Cappa et al., 2020, p.379).

The current study asks whether integration (upstream-downstream) in the technology industry affects firm financing decisions. In this regard, the present study is closest to the literature dimension examining the business environment, especially corporate strategy but differs in one important respect. The similarity is that vertical integration or industry structure is a common consideration in both the present study and the aforesaid literature stream. The distinguishing factor is that business environment studies of capital structure evolve around the renowned issue of *relationship-specific investment*. This is the idea that the value of the investment is maximised within a continued relationship more than without. For example, the relationship may "involve an upstream supplier who makes investments to customize her product for the needs of the downstream purchaser" (Strieborny, 2016, p.1488). In contrast, the present inquiry zooms into whether there is a common effect of equity activity and upstream-downstream innovation in financing decisions of the technology industry.

The current study adds value to the literature in several ways. First, we correct the imbalance in the literature. A recent systematic review (Bajaj et al., 2021, p.173) of capital structure studies found that most studies tend to stack firms from different industries into the same *sample* "... whereas the focus on a particular industrial sector was meagre." Second, since the dynamics of technology sectors in "emerging and developing markets" differ from developed economies (Kedzior et al., 2020) it is crucial to spread the knowledge horizon to enrich future stylised facts that emerge from global research. Third, and more importantly, the technology transfer or innovation upstream and downstream has the potential to have different financing decisions since they effectively have different business models even though they are operating within the same industry. In our view, the above factors necessitate the current research initiative.

The rest of the paper is organised as follows: Sect. 2 lays the background of the study by explaining the technology sector, innovation, and the South African experience. Section 3 introduces the econometric model, empirical design, model validation procedures, and data characteristics. Section 4 presents and interprets the results. Section 5 discusses the results, while Sect. 6 concludes the study.

2 Technology, Innovation, and the South African Experience

The technology sector is involved in inter- and intra-industry innovation, diffusion, and digitalisation (Gopane, 2020; Rasiah & Gopane, 2004). Business activities of technology firms include manufacturing electronics, building computer hardware, producing computer software, and marketing end-user products and services in information technology and data analytics, among others. Technological advancement continues to introduce innovation in business operations and improve the quality of life for ordinary citizens. For example, the convergence of mobile, Internet technologies, and the Internet of Things is causing a significant socioeconomic change in many economies, including South Africa. For instance, there is growing evidence that broadband directly promotes economic performance, including job creation, the expansion of educational opportunities, improved public service delivery, and rural development, among others. However, to optimise beneficiation, all these technological innovations require critical mass in modern computerised hardware and software capabilities such as broadband networks and infrastructure (Roller & Waverman, 2001).

It is now accepted wisdom (Khalil & Kenny, 2008) that investments in information technology, telecommunications, and mobile telecommunications significantly influence economic growth or gross domestic product (GDP) in developed and developing nations. In this regard, the information communication technology (ICT) sector has played an important role in South Africa since the fourth industrial revolution (4IR) commenced. Private and public sector organisations that promote the ICT sector in South Africa include the Department of Communications and Digital Technologies (DCDT), State Information Technology Agency, Computer Society South Africa, Tech Central, Fitch Connect, Internet Service Providers Association (ISPA), Information Technology Association (ITA), and the South African Communications Forum (SACF). As a reflection of some of its value-add, the ICT sector has drastically decreased transaction costs and boosted productivity over time, providing instant connectivity in terms of voice, data, and visuals leading to enhanced efficiency, accuracy, and transparency in business processes. Further, the ICT sector has facilitated the increase in software and hardware by providing access to previously unavailable goods and services. Also, the ICT sector has expanded the outlook of different markets and business operations through technology diffusion and equipping the workforce with critical technical vocational skills.

In their study, Rosin et al. (2020) concur that firms that have adopted digital technologies have improved value and maximised growth. Further, business decisions and actions can be streamlined when companies, for instance, digitalise information-intensive procedures to replace manual stages. Digitalisation promotes cost-effectiveness by helping businesses automate data collection, performance analysis, supply-chain management, and business expansion (Ladeira et al., 2019). The value of technological progress and digitalisation in domestic and global economies is indisputable. A dedicated dimension of combative research that seeks to understand the intricacies of capital structure in the technology industry is missing, particularly in the emerging market of South Africa. The current study contributes towards this goal.

3 Methodology

3.1 Econometric Model

The panel data specification's random effects model (REM) is appropriate for this study. We follow the usual modeling selection process to arrive at the appropriate version of the panel data model, the REM specification. First, the panel data setup is ideal for ameliorating data constraints in which we have 11 firms that satisfy the selection criteria over 20 years (2000 to 2019). Therefore, pooling the data allows us to maximise the sample size to 220 (=11 x 20). Second, we use the Chow Test (Chow, 1960), and Hausman test (Hausman, 1978) to guide the decision against pooled ordinary least square (POLS) and fixed effects model (FEM), respectively, in favour of REM presented in Eq. (1). Although we use a different econometric model, the empirical framework is similar to Welch (2004)

$$\Delta Lev_{it} = \alpha + \beta_1(\Delta Equity)_{it} + \beta_2 Intgrate_{it} + \beta_3 Upward_{it} + \beta_4 Down_{it} + \delta Contrl_{it} + \varepsilon_{it} \tag{1}$$

where,

$$ADR_t = \frac{D_t}{D_t + E_t} \tag{2}$$

$$IDR_t = \frac{D_t}{D_t + E_t(1 + r_{t+1})} \tag{3}$$

$$r_t = Ln(P_t) - Ln(P_{t-1}) \tag{4}$$

$$\Delta Lev_t = (ADR_{t+1} - ADR_t) = \frac{D_{t+1}}{D_{t+1} + E_{t+1}} - \frac{D_t}{D_t + E_t} \tag{5}$$

$$(\Delta Equity)_t = \frac{D_t}{D_t + E_t(1 + r_{t+1})} - \frac{D_t}{D_t + E_t} \tag{6}$$

$$Intgrte = \frac{Sales - Purchases}{Sales} \tag{7}$$

In the equations above, the subscript i is an index of firms ($i = 1, 2, 3 \ldots 11$), and t is time in years ($t = 1, 2, 3 \ldots 20$). The dependent variable, leverage (ΔLev_{it}), is computed from Eq. (5), and it is the change in actual debt-equity ratio (ADR, see Eq. (2). In debt-equity ratio, D is proxied with the firm's total debt, and E is the product of the firm's market price and the total number of issued shares. The first covariate, $\Delta Equity$, , is the change in equity which manifests in the implied debt ratio (IDR, see Eq. 3) being a debt ratio net of variation in equity, as per Eq. (6). The variable, r, is the return on equity calculated from Eq. (4). The variable, *Integrate*, measures the degree of integration (Cappa et al., 2020), and it is computed from Eq. (7). This valued-added variable is bound between 0 and 1. The variable uses the intuition that as the cost of purchases decreases, this indicates reliance on internal inputs for the firm's operations. That is vertical integration. The variables, *Upward* and *Down* are dummy variables for upstream and downstream integration, respectively. The last variable, *Contrl*, , represents a list of control variables namely, firm's number of years in existence (age), a measure of firm size (size), book-to-market ratio (bkratio), and a proxy for market risk (risk). These variables have been used in the literature in one form or another (see review, Kumar et al., 2017)The parameters, β_1, β_2, β_3, β_4, δ are estimated in the model while ε is the regression error term, and it is assumed to follow a normal distribution.

3.2 Study Objective and Analytical Approach

We have some indication from previous studies (Welch, 2004) that changes in equity affect capital structure which we set out to confirm in the current study. Next, we extend this result by inquiring whether these changes differ according to the upstream and downstream integration in the technology industry. Applying econometrics rationale, we can measure these joint effects with two sets of three-way interaction of the variables $\Delta Equity$, *Intgrte*, and *Hdware*. In the second three-way interaction, we substitute hardware with software. So, to proceed with the analysis, in Eq. (1), we recall that the variables, upward, and downward are equivalent to ($\Delta Equity \times Intgrte \times Hdware$), and ($\Delta Equity \times Intgrte \times Sware$), respectively. With this in mind, we take the partial derivatives of Eq. (1) and report the answer in Eq. (8). We disregard subscripts for clarity.

$$\frac{\partial(\Delta Lev)}{\partial(\Delta Equity)} = \beta_1 + \beta_3(Intgrte \times Hdware) + \beta_4(Intgrte \times Sware) \qquad (8)$$

Equation (8) says that the slope (β_1) of leverage (ΔLev) with respect to change in equity ($\Delta Equity$), is affected by integration (*Intgrte*), a dummy for upstream (upward) proxied by hardware firms (*Hware*), and a dummy for downstream proxied by software firms (*Sware*). We quantify Eq. (8) for numerical analysis with regression results from Eq. (1). The numerical solution will inform us whether changes in equity affect leverage differently for upstream and downstream innovation.

3.3 Data Characteristics

This study is based on technology firms listed on Johannesburg Stock Exchange (JSE) in South Africa. The dataset is obtained from financial statements sourced from the Iress online database (Iress, n.d). The study uses annual data from 2000 to 2019. The database lists 63 technology firms which we subject to a relevant selection criterion. Firms with unique capital structures, such as parastatals, banking, and insurance companies, are excluded. All the firms that have insufficient data are excluded. The total firms that satisfied the selection process resulted in a balanced panel of 11 firms over 20 year-period which aggregates to 220 observations. Due to the necessary screening and data constraints, sample sizes of this magnitude are common in the literature. For instance, Choua et al. (2021) estimated a panel data model with 14 firms over 11 years (1999 to 2009), resulting in 140 observations.

3.4 Model Validation

It is essential to conduct and report the outcome of model validation before interpreting the results. First, we have the assurance that pre-modelling validation is satisfactory after conducting the REM panel data specification test (Hausman, 1978). Second, in Table 2 (Appendix), we note the absence of multicollinearity among the model covariates. Third, the post-estimation validation corroborates pre-estimation tests. All covariates are individually significant, and the overall model fit is adequate, judging by the statistical significance of the F-test. Fourth, the inspection of normality in Fig. 2 shows that residuals reasonably satisfy the assumption of normal distribution for error terms in Eq. (1). Lastly, in order to control for the potential problem of heteroscedasticity and serial correlation, we apply White's (1980) robust cluster standard errors in REM estimation. Overall, the model validation is satisfactory, allowing for a reliable results interpretation.

4 Empirical Results

The results of the study are presented in Table 1. Our empirical objective is to examine whether changes in equity affect leverage differently in upstream and downstream technology firms. In this regard, Table 1 shows that the variables of interest, ΔEquity, Integrate, Down, Upward, and Down are positive and significant, indicating that changes in equity affect leverage differently for upstream and downstream firms. Also, judging by the coefficient magnitudes, it is evident that changes in equity for the upstream firms affect leverage more than the downstream firms. In Eq. (8), if we substitute for the variable, *Integrate* with its average, 0.4713 and use the values of coefficients $(\beta_1, \beta_3, \beta_4)$ from Table 1, we find that the change in leverage with respect to change in equity is 0.31 for the upstream firms (hardware), and 0.18 for the downstream firms. Thus far, the results may be construed as saying changes in equity do affect leverage in the technology sector. It does so more in the upstream firms (with an intensity of 30%) compared to downstream firms (with an intensity of around 20%) on average.

To have a graphical view of the above interpretation, we repeat the calculations for Eq. (8), but this time rather than use average, we compute for a range of values for *Integrate* between 0 and unity when *hardware* = 1 and for *software* = 0. We reverse the values of the dummy variables and then repeat the computations. The results are plotted in Fig. 1. The vertical axis shows the linear predictions for leverage changes while the horizontal axis labels the proxies for integration which is value-added calculated in Eq. (7). The dots are a scatter plot of changes in *leverage* against *integration*. The straight lines are the focus of this interpretation and are a graphical representation of Eq. (8). The upper straight line says that the change in leverage with respect to changes in equity as integration varies from 0 to 1 has a steeper slope for upstream firms and a gentle slope for downstream firms. This means that changes in equity affect leverage more in the upstream firms of technology innovation than downstream.

Table 1. Results of Panel Data Model (from Eq. 2)

Variable	Short Name	Coefficient	Std Error	Prob
Intercept	Intercept	0.3180	0.2245	0.1871
Change in Equity	ΔEquity	0.1439	0.0306	0.0008***
Integration	Integrate	0.1583	0.0475	0.0076**
Integration upstream	Upward	0.3444	0.0768	0.0012***
Integration downstream	Down	0.0702	0.0260	0.0222**
Log of firm age	Logage	−0.1654	0.0712	0.0426**
Size	Logsales	0.0127	0.0049	0.0283**
Book-to-market ratio	bkratio	0.9608	0.4859	0.0762*
Market risk	Risk	−0.0114	0.0035	0.0091***
Observations	220			
R-Squared	0.1939			
F-Statistic	6.3448			0.0000***

Legend: Statistical significance, ***1%, **5%, *10%

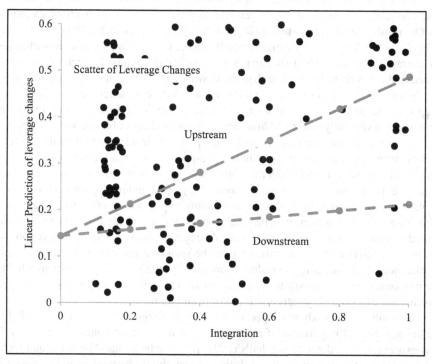

Fig. 1. Linear predictions of leverage changes in response to equity changes are affected by integration upstream and downstream in the technology industry. Integration is proxied by the value-added ratio in Eq. (7), while proxies for upstream and downstream are dummies for hardware and software firms. **Source:** Authors' own graphics.

In Table 1, the rest of the regression output relates to control variables namely, firm age, sales (proxy for size), book-to-market ratio, and market risk which are all statistically significant with economically intuitive signs. Firm age and market risk are each negatively correlated with changes in leverage. The negative sign on firm age or number of years in existence is consistent with the pecking order theory (Myers, 1984) that old and established firms prefer to utilise internal funding as a priority rather than use debt financing. This finding is similar to that of (Huynh & Petrunia, 2010). Book to market ratio is positive as expected because it is a proxy for profitability indicating that profitable firms can take on more debt. This result is similar to the finding of (Flannery & Rangan, 2006). The negative association between leverage and market risk reflects the intuition that banks are less likely to approve debt for high-risk firms (Barton & Gordon, 1988). In tandem with the study of Al-Najjar & Hussainey (2011), these results reflect the idea that high-risk firms imply high risk of default in debt financing. The positive sign on firm size is in line with the rationale that large firms are more entrenched with a lower likelihood of debt default so that they can acquire more debt successfully (Rajan & Zingales, 1995).

5 Discussion of Results

This study aims to confirm whether changes in equity affect leverage and whether such changes differ in upstream firms compared to downstream firms in the technology industry. Our results confirm prior studies (Baker & Wurgler, 2002; Welch, 2004) that changes in equity affect leverage. Further, the results reveal that the impact of equity changes on leverage differ according to the mapping of vertical integration for technology firms, affecting the upstream firms more than the downstream firms. That is, leverage is positively correlated with vertical integration. These results contradict the related study of (Cappa et al., 2020), who found a negative association. They interpret their results as implying that vertically integrated firms are more entrenched, stable and with reasonable control over their value chains. As such, they prefer their adequate internal resources to debt financing. This reasoning is intuitive especially for non-technology industries which seems to be consistent with the aggregated sample of the listed firms that (Cappa et al., 2020) examined. On the contrary, technology firms' unique capital structure environment is characterized by the limited availability of physical assets. Technology firms are known to be endowed more with intangible assets such as intellectual property and skilled human resource capital. Since vertical integration is known to increase economic power, we conjecture that integration should be seen as capacitating technology firms to take more debt financing as needed. Consequently, the given explanation highlights the uniqueness of technology firms in capital structure matters and explains why the positive association with integration is possible and intuitive.

The results of this study are important for several reasons. First, this study highlights the uniqueness and importance of technology considerations in financing decisions. It is consistent with Lederer & Singhal's (1994, p.333) advice that "financing and technology choice is long-term strategic decisions that should be made jointly." Second, the literature on the relationship between capital structure and product markets (Miao, 2005, p.2621) makes an important observation that, "there is substantial inter- and intra-industry variation in leverage." Through their empirical inquiry, Aghion et al. (2004, p.284) investigated the inter-industry difference relating to technology firms and concluded that: "Our results suggest that the financial behavior of more innovative firms ... differs from the financial behavior of less innovative firms". The current study completes the picture and confirms that there is variation in the intra-industry behaviour of the technology sector's financing decisions. Therefore, this study concludes that upstream and downstream innovation matters in the technology industry's financing decisions. Regarding capital structure studies, the above insight makes the wisdom of aggregating technology firms with other industries into one sample questionable.

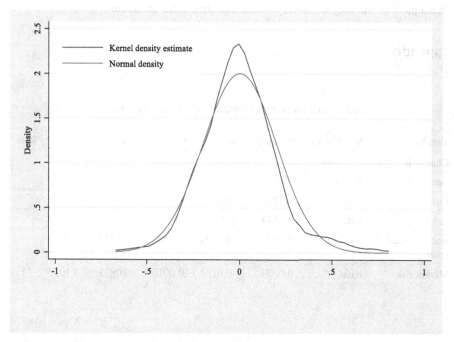

Fig. 2. Kernel Density estimate for the model residuals. The normal density graph shows the true shape of the normal distribution, while the Kernel density graph shows a reasonable estimation of the true graph. Source: Authors' own graphics.

6 Conclusion

This study has examined the question of whether upstream-downstream innovation matters in financing decisions of the technology industry. In particular, the investigation has empirically confirmed that changes in equity affect capital structure and has extended these results to show that the effect of equity changes affects leverage differently in the upstream and downstream firms of the technology industry. The literature has already demonstrated that "equity financing is the optimal strategy for innovating firms, which can use their financial structure as a signalling device to attract outside investors" (Santarelli, 1991, p.279). The discovery from the current study is important because it reveals that the mentioned equity signalling is likely to vary based on the degree of vertical integration upstream and downstream in the technology industry. Although the sample size in the current study satisfies econometric analysis, a re-examination with generous data availability is desirable. Further, the present study looked at two polar relationships of upstream and downstream innovation. Further study is recommended to evaluate the same problem under vertical integration within different phases of product development, such as new product design, manufacturing process, inventory management, and distribution chains. Overall, the observations from prior studies, coupled with wisdom emerging from the current study, allow us to conclude that the financing decisions of technology firms vary within and from other industries.

Appendix

Table 2: Cross-correlation matrix of explanatory variables

Variable	Short Name	ΔEquity	Intgrte	Age	Sales	BkRatio	Risk
Change in equity	ΔEquity	1					
Integration	Intgrte	-0.2396	1				
Firm age	Age	0.2708	-0.3848	1			
Sales	Sales	0.0334	0.3466	-0.1251	1		
Book-to-market ratio	Bkratio	0.1996	-0.3394	0.1589	-0.0743	1	
Market risk	Risk	0.0009	-0.0194	0.0010	-0.0873	-0.1026	1

References

Aghion, P., Bond, S., Klemm, A., Marinescu, I.: Technology and financial structure: are innovative firms different? J. Eur. Econ. Assoc. 2(2–3), 277–288 (2004). https://doi.org/10.1162/154247604323067989

Al-Najjar, B., Hussainey, K.: Revisiting the capital-structure puzzle: UK evidence. J. Risk Finance 12(4), 329–338 (2011)

Bajaj, Y., Kashiramka, S., Singh, S.: Application of capital structure theories: a systematic review. J. Adv. Manage. Res. 18(2), 173–199 (2021). https://doi.org/10.1108/JAMR-01-2020-0017

Baker, M., Wurgler, J.: Market timing and capital structure. J. Finance 57(1), 1–32 (2002). https://doi.org/10.1111/1540-6261.00414

Barton, S.L., Gordon, P.J.: Corporate strategy and capital structure. Strateg. Manag. J. 9(6), 623–632 (1988). https://doi.org/10.1002/smj.4250090608Berger

Cappa, F., Cetrini, G., Oriani, R.: The impact of corporate strategy on capital structure: evidence from Italian listed firms. Quart. Rev. Econ. Finance 76, 379–385 (2020). https://doi.org/10.1016/j.qref.2019.09.005

Choua, C.C., Linb, W.T., CLeec, C., Taod, X., Qiane, Z.: The impacts of information technology and E-commerce on operational performances: a two-stage dynamic partial adjustment approach. J. Industr. Prod. Eng. **38**(4), 291–322 (2021).https://doi.org/10.1080/21681015.2021. 1887381

Chow, G.C.: Tests of equality between sets of coefficients in two linear regressions. Econometrica: J. Econometric Soc. **28**(3), 591–605 (1960)

Dao, B.T.T., Ta, T.D.N.: A meta-analysis: capital structure and firm performance. J. Econ. Dev. **22**(1), 111–129 (2020). https://doi.org/10.1108/JED-12-2019-0072

Fischer, E.O., Heinkel, R., Zechner, J.: Dynamic capital structure choice: Theory and tests. J. Finance **44**(1), 19–40 (1989). https://doi.org/10.1111/j.1540-6261.1989.tb02402.x

Gopane, T.J.: Digitalisation, productivity, and measurability of digital economy: evidence from BRICS. In: Bach Tobji, M.A., Jallouli, R., Samet, A., Touzani, M., Strat, V.A., Pocatilu, P. (eds.) Digital Economy. Emerging Technologies and Business Innovation. ICDEc 2020. Lecture Notes in Business Information Processing, vol. 395. Springer, Cham (2020). https://doi.org/ 10.1007/978-3-030-64642-4_3

Flannery, M.J., Rangan, K.P.: Partial adjustment toward target capital structures. J. Financ. Econ. **79**(3), 469–506 (2006)

Harris, M., Raviv, A.: The theory of capital structure. J. Finance **46**(1), 297–355 (1991)

Hausman, J.A.: Specification tests in econometrics. Econometrica : J. Econometric Soc. **46**(6), 1251–1271 (1978)

Huynh, K.P., Petrunia, R.J.: Age effects, leverage and firm growth. J. Econ. Dyn. Control **34**(5), 1003–1013 (2010)

Iqbal, J., Muhammad, S., Muneer, S., Jahanzeb, A.: A critical review of capital structure theories. Inf. Manag. Bus. Rev. **4**(11), 553–557 (2012)

Iress. (n.d). McGregor-BFA Online Financial Database. Verfügbar unter: http://research.mcgreg orbfa.com/Default.aspx

Istaitieh, A., Rodríguez-Fernández, J.M.: Factor-product markets and firm's capital structure: a literature review. Rev. Financ. Econ. **15**(1), 49–75 (2006). https://doi.org/10.1016/j.rfe.2005. 02.001

Jensen, M.C., Meckling, W.H.: Theory of the firm: managerial behaviour, agency costs and ownership structure. J. Financ. Econ. **3**(4), 305–360 (1976). https://doi.org/10.1016/0304-405 X(76)90026-X

Kalea, J.R., Shahrurb, H.: Corporate capital structure and the characteristics of suppliers and customers. J. Financ. Econ. **83**, 321–365 (2007)

Kedzior, M., Grabinska, B., Grabinski, K., Kedzior, D.: Capital structure choices in technology firms: empirical results from Polish listed companies. J. Risk Financ. Manage. **13**(9), 221 (2020). https://doi.org/10.3390/jrfm13090221

Khalil, M., Kenny, C.: The next decade of ICT development: access, applications, and the forces of convergence. Inf. Technol. Int. Dev. **4**(3), 1–6 (2008)

Kochhar, R., Hitt, M.A.: Linking corporate strategy to capital structure: diversification strategy, type and source of financing. Strateg. Manag. J. **19**(6), 601–610 (1998)

Kraus, A., Litzenberger, R.H.: A state-preference model of optimal financial leverage. J. Financ. **28**(4), 911–922 (1973). https://doi.org/10.1111/j.1540-6261.1973.tb01415.x

Kumar, S., Colombage, S., Rao, P.: Research on capital structure determinants: a review and future directions. Int. J. Manag. Finance **13**(2), 106–132 (2017). https://doi.org/10.1108/IJMF-09-2014-0135

Ladeira, M.J.M., Ferreira, F.A.F., Ferreira, J.J.M.: Exploring the determinants of digital entrepreneurship using fuzzy cognitive maps. Int. Entrepreneurship Manage. J. **15**(4), 1077–1101 (2019). https://doi.org/10.1007/s11365-019-00574-9

Lederer, P.J., Singhal, V.R.: The effect of financing decisions on the choice of manufacturing technologies. Int. J. Flex. Manuf. Syst. **6**(4), 333–360 (1994). https://doi.org/10.1007/BF0132 4800

Miao, J.: Optimal capital structure and industry dynamics. J. Finance **60**(6), 2621–2659. American Finance Association, Wiley (2005)

Miglo, A.: Trade-off, pecking order, signaling, and market timing models. (H.K. Baker & G.S. Martin, eds.) (pp. 171–191). Wiley and Sons (2011). https://doi.org/10.2139/ssrn.1629304

Modigliani, F., Miller, M.H.: The cost of capital, corporation finance and the theory of investment. Ame. Econ. Rev. **48**(3), 261–297 (1958)

Modigliani, F., Miller, M.H.: Corporate income taxes and the cost of capital: a correction. Am. Econ. Rev. **53**(3), 433–443 (1963)

Myers, S.C.: The capital structure puzzle. J. Finance **39**(3), 574–592 (1984). https://doi.org/10. 1111/j.1540-6261.1984.tb03646.x

Ozkan, A.: Determinants of capital structure and adjustment to long-run target: evidence from UK company panel data. J. Bus. Financ. Acc. **28**(1–2), 175–198 (2001). https://doi.org/10.1111/ 1468-5957.00370

Rasiah, R., Gopane, T.: Technology, local sourcing and economic performance in South Africa (pp. 50–71) (2004). https://doi.org/10.4337/9781845423551.00009

Rajan, R.G., Zingales, L.: What do we know about capital structure? Some evidence from international data. J. Finance **50**(5), 1421–1460 (1995). https://doi.org/10.2307/2329322Ramas wamy

Roller, L.H., Waverman, L.: Telecommunications infrastructure and economic development: a simultaneous approach. Am. Econ. Rev. **91**(4), 909–923 (2001)

Rosin, A.F., Proksch, D., Stubner, S., Pinkwart, A.: Digital new ventures: assessing the benefits of digitalization in entrepreneurship. J. Small Bus. Strateg. **30**(2), 59–71 (2020)

Santarelli, E.: Asset specificity, R&D financing, and the signalling properties of the firm's financial structure. Econ. Innov. New Technol. **1**(4), 279–294 (1991). https://doi.org/10.1080/104385 99100000008

Son, I., Kim, S.: Supply chain management strategy and capital structure of global information and communications (2022). https://doi.org/10.3390/su14031844

Strieborny, M.K.M.: Investment in relationship-specific assets: does finance matter? Rev. Finance **20**(4), 1487–1515 (2016). https://doi.org/10.1093/rof/rfv049

Welch, I.: Capital structure and stock returns. J. Polit. Econ. **112**(1), 106–131 (2004). https://doi.org/10.1086/379933

White, H.: A heteroskedasticity-consistent covariance matrix estimator and a direct test for heteroskedasticity. Econometrica: J. Econometric Soc. **48**(4), 817–838 (1980). https://doi.org/10. 2307/1912934

The Symmetric and Asymmetric Effects of Digitalization on Economic Growth in African Countries: Evidence from Linear and Non-Linear ARDL Models

Hamdi Becha, Maha Kalai, Saifeddine Houidi, and Kamel Helali[✉]

Faculty of Economics and Management of Sfax, University of Sfax, Aerodrome Road Km 4.5, B.P. 1088-3018 Sfax, Tunisia
kamel.helali@fsegs.usf.tn

Abstract. This study tries to answer whether the relationship between digitalization, measured by information and communication technologies (ICT) imports and economic growth, is symmetric or asymmetric by applying Pooled Mean Group Autoregressive Distributed Lag (PMG-ARDL) and Pooled Mean Group Non-linear Autoregressive Distributed Lag (PMG-NARDL) models in 45 African countries from 2000 to 2021. Using the PMG-ARDL model, the results reveal that the ICT imports have a significant and positive impact on economic growth evaluated at 0.13%. On the other hand, the results of PMG-NARDL model show that a positive shock of ICT imports affects economic growth significantly and positively by 0.15%. However, a negative shock of this variable does not affect economic growth significantly. The results also prove that eight countries in the sample have an asymmetric ICT-Growth link which confirms the asymmetry of the relationship. Thus, digitalization is important to ensure sustainable and self-reliant economic growth. Therefore, African countries need to focus on improving their ICT infrastructure in various economic sectors and achieve better efficiency and productivity.

Keywords: Economic Growth · ICT imports · PMG-ARDL · PMG-NARDL · Africa

JEL Classification: O11 · O55 · C22 · C24 · L63 · L96

1 Introduction

Digital is not just part of the economy – it has become the economy (Anderson and Wladawsky-Berger, 2016). The digital economy can be defined as an 'economic activity that results from billions of everyday online connections between people, businesses, devices, data and processes' (Deloitte, 2012). In addition, it includes all industries that work with communications and networks compatible with the Internet protocol, regardless of their sector of activity and relies on enhanced network connectivity and interoperability of digital platforms across all sectors of the economy and society to deliver convergent services (UNDP, 2017). Furthermore, digital economy is defined as one that "can

© The Author(s), under exclusive license to Springer Nature Switzerland AG 2023
R. Jallouli et al. (Eds.): ICDEc 2023, LNBIP 485, pp. 315–345, 2023.
https://doi.org/10.1007/978-3-031-42788-6_20

provide a high quality of information and communication technologies (ICT) infrastructure and harness the power of ICTs to benefit consumers, businesses and governments" (World Bank, 2016).

In fact, the digital economy as a phenomenon introduced by Tapscott (1996) marks the beginning of a new era, not only in terms of economic relations, but rather in terms of human communication infrastructure in general which makes a clear distinction between the Fourth Industrial Revolution, which carries forward a revolution of the mind and therefore of a worldview driven by advanced technology and a rapidly developing information economy, and the First, Second and Third Industrial Revolutions which depend on tools or means of production (Safronchuck and Sargeeva, 2019).

Ben Youssef et al. (2021) report that digital technologies, including the Internet, smartphones and other applications, enable one to gather, store, treat and share information and play a transformational role in the worldwide economy. In this regard, they have enormously facilitated the creation of new entrepreneurship processes, jobs, products, market channels and marketing strategies.

In the world, internet usage has passed the 50% mark (51.4% globally at the end of 2019) and 75% of the total global population has an active mobile broadband subscription and the Fixed broadband subscription had increased to just over 15% and over 57% of households have home internet access. In addition, with the high demand for data from bandwidth-intensive services, average international bandwidth grew at a compound annual growth rate (CAGR) of 36% between 2017 and 2020, compared to 26% between 2017 and 2019 (ITU, 2021).

However, urban areas of the world are covered by mobile broadband networks and there are still many gaps in rural areas and the gender gap remains a reality as women still benefit less than men from internet use which shows the existence of a digital divide due to the unequal distribution of technology and internet access among different groups of people, leading to disparities in education, employment and social and economic opportunities. As most countries in the world grapple with the consequences of the COVID-19 pandemic, the role of ICT and digital services and the digital infrastructure has become critical in promoting economic and social activity and mitigating the effects of the pandemic (ITU, 2021).

The use of ICT in recent decades has transformed the world into a genuine information community. In fact, landlines, mobile phones, internet and broadband networks have enabled individuals, businesses and governments to access information and knowledge in greater quantity, volume and speed. ICT infrastructure plays an important role to promote growth and the emergence of digital economies by reducing transaction costs and enriching market information (Prahalad, 2006; Christensen et al., 2008; Vu, 2011), improving the dissemination of knowledge and the quality of decision-making (Andrianaivo and Kpodar, 2011) and productivity (Palvia et al., 2018; Andrianaivo and Kpodar, 2011; Lehr and Lichtenberg, 1999).

The deployment of ICT infrastructure influences revenue generation through taxation on goods and services, income, value added tax, social amenities, public infrastructure, and service revenue related to ICT, which also contributes to GDP. In addition, cell phone penetration, fixed and mobile broadband can increase connectivity that positively affects financial depth and inclusion, resulting in economic growth (Shamim, 2007; Andrianaivo and Kpodar, 2011).

Moreover, through optical fiber cables, satellite communications, wireless applications and e-commerce, ICT technologies can reduce costs and management issues in their supply chain (Steinmueller, 2001), which directly affects the manufacturing sector implicitly or explicitly by generating various positive Spillovers and leads to large expenditures while generating new jobs (Datta and Agarwal, 2004) and therefore increases growth (Nadiri et al., 2018; Kolko, 2012; Bose and Haque, 2005).

With regard to Africa, the continent became the world's third-fastest growing region after its post- 2000 economic enhancement (UNDP, 2017) and this growth was largely attributable to the increase in domestic investment in the services sector largely influenced by better ICT usage and efficiencies (Asongu and Le Roux, 2017; Baro and Endouware, 2013). More particularly in rural African regions, the usage of ICT services has contributed to the positive transformation of lives and livelihoods evidenced by job-creation, increased income, cost minimization, reduction in uncertainty and risk, and familial bonding, to mention a few (Baro and Endouware, 2013; Batuo, 2015; World Bank, 2017).

Thus, Africa can use ICT to "leapfrog" development stages particularly through mobile subscriptions, which directly allows to create new jobs, promote e-commerce, improve human capital development, promote information diffusion, and network externalities (Adeleye and Eboagu, 2019) and indirectly accelerates growth by promoting economic freedom, social and political stability, network externalities, and productive efficiency (Thompson and Garbacz, 2011). According to Tan et al. (2018), technology leapfrogging is defined as the implementation of a new and up-to-date technology in an application area in which at least the previous version of that technology has not been deployed (Davison et al., 2000), is one of the most cost efficient and effective ways for developing countries to attain an advanced state of ICT development and connectivity (Liu et al., 2015).

For his part, Niebel (2018) stated that if the leapfrogging hypothesis is confirmed, the influence of ICT on economic growth should be greater in developing and emerging economies as compared to developed economies. However, the success of the leapfrogging impact depends on the absorptive capacity or the ability of workers as well as their managers to implement the new technology of these developing countries (Henry et al., 2009; Keller, 2004).

Between 2017 and 2020, the region witnessed continued, albeit slow growth in most areas of ICT infrastructure, access and use in Africa where 88.4% of the population lives within reach of a mobile cellular signal, 77% of the population is now within reach of a 3G signal, and 44.3% is within reach of a long-term evolution (LTE) mobile broadband signal. In addition, the percentage of individuals using the Internet increased from 24.8% in 2017 to 28.6% by the end of 2019, with households that have Internet access at home increasing by 0.1 percentage points from 14.2% in 2017 to 14.3% by the end of 2019. Furthermore, both fixed and mobile broadband markets have shown some growth between 2017 and 2020, with active mobile broadband subscriptions outpacing fixed broadband subscriptions (ITU, 2021).

.Internet access in Africa is expensive, limited and dependent on mobile technology provided and maintained by private sector companies in the most profitable urban areas. However, many African countries still depend on 3G communication networks which are slow, expensive and inefficient, while the availability of faster 4G networks is very limited except for South Africa where the authorities are still in the process of licensing 5G networks, which will be faster than previous generations and capable of transmitting more information like Big Data and will reduce communication costs (Viviers et al., 2021). In January 2022, the 5G network was installed in Nigeria and in this sense presents a structural challenge for the economies and industries of sub-Saharan Africa. This technology is invested by telecom operators who are trying to expand their service offering.

Statistically, the number of broadband connections in Africa passed the 400 million in 2018 mark (nearly twenty times 2010 levels), the regional average broadband penetration-including 3G and 4G connections-is only 25% in 2018. Mobile broadband coverage in Africa is still at 70% of the population. Even in North Africa, there is ample room for growth with 4G networks covering only about 60% of the population. Additional challenges, such as the lack of access to reliable and affordable electricity, make accelerating Africa's digital transformation journey even more difficult (Gallegos et al., 2020).

The impact of ICT on economic growth has been an important research topic in these recent years. ICT have the potential to accelerate economic growth by improving business efficiency and productivity, promoting innovation, increasing competitiveness, creating new jobs and increasing consumer demand. However, despite numerous studies on this topic, there is still a lack of research that fully reflects the impact of ICT on economic growth, mainly due to the dynamics of ICT sub-sectors in developing countries. It is important to note that the COVID-19 pandemic has accelerated the adoption of ICTs in many economic sectors, which has significantly affected business operations and communication with consumers. This rapid development makes it even more important to understand the impact of ICT on economic growth in order to better understand how businesses can use these technologies to improve their performance and competitiveness.

With the outbreak of the COVID-19 pandemic and despite all the economic and social devastation it has caused, this crisis presents African countries with an opportunity to innovate and to go to the digitalization. Indeed, ICT activities are spreading across the continent and young Africans are responding with digital technology to the challenges posed by this crisis. In addition, African countries are accelerating digitalization through market consolidation and regional cooperation and creating significant new opportunities through the promotion of local industry, the formalization of small businesses and the upgrading of urban infrastructure.

Through the use of digital technology, African countries have benefited from the opportunity to shift away from dependence on natural resources to diversify their economies, helping to alleviate the financial constraints faced by entrepreneurs, including the need for funding start-ups. For example, Nigeria and Kenya have become financial technology (FinTech) epicenters on the continent. Both countries are using low-cost and affordable technologies to engage consumers with innovative tools, including digital loans (M-Shwari in Kenya) as well as savings and investment platforms (PiggyVest and Cowrywise in Nigeria) (World Bank, 2021a, 2021b).

Moreover, the intensity of the use of digital technologies was higher in financial services as well as in large and formal enterprises particularly notable for e-commerce. For example, the African platform "Jumia" saw an increase of more than 50%, from 3.1 million to 4.7 million, in transaction volume in the first six months of 2020, compared to the same period in 2019 (World Bank, 2021a, 2021b).

Furthermore, the COVID-19 crisis reinforced the potential of digitalization through accelerating the productive transformation of the African economy and proliferated the number of vibrant start-up ecosystems especially with the mobile payments' revolution which has reached 300 million of mobile payment accounts in Africa. Indeed, these digital ecosystems have already begun to transform labor markets through the creation of direct and indirect jobs, modernize the banking sector, develop financial services for underserved populations, and foster innovative business models (OECD, 2021).

Within this strategy, African authorities have used many digital solutions to combat the COVID-19 pandemic at the local, national, regional and continental levels. For instance, Ministries of Education in 27 African countries were able to set up effective E-learning platforms for students as early as May 2020 (UNESCO, 2020).

In summary, and based on the panoply of work and issues cited above, digital technologies will offer the potential to diversify African economies away from natural resources, helping to alleviate the financial constraints faced by entrepreneurs, particularly the capital requirements for start-ups. To this end, this paper seeks to answer the following main question: How can digitalization improve economic growth in African countries in the presence of several financial and social barriers?

For this purpose, this study contributes the effect of ICT (as measured by ICT imports) on economic growth (measured by GDP Growth) using a balanced panel dataset covering 45 African countries for the period between 2000 and 2021. In addition, it highlights the symmetrical and asymmetrical effects of digitalization on growth. Therefore, to study this relationship, we use two econometric models, namely the ARDL model proposed by Pesaran et al. (2001) and the nonlinear ARDL model proposed by Shin et al. (2014).

Hence, in order to achieve all the objectives described above, this article consists of five sections apart from the introduction. Section 2 deals with the theoretical and empirical literature reviews as well as development hypothesis. Section 3 represents the methodologies applied in the empirical assessment. Section 4 shows the empirical results. Finally, Sect. 5 contains the conclusion and policy implications of the study.

2 Literature Review and Hypothesis Development

2.1 Theoretical Framework

Technological change is generally revolutionary in nature, which means that it is disruptive, continuous and sometimes abrupt, bringing about profound and long-term changes in the socio- economic status quo and constituting the main engine for the growth and development of savings (Landes, 2003) and represents a key factor in the economic growth (Fagerberg and Verspagen, 2002).

In theory, Veblen (1915) is the first author who examined the role of technological change in economic development and the process of catching up. He argued that due to technology transfers between different countries, poor countries inevitably have to embark on a path of sustainable growth and catch up with developed economies. Moreover, the neo-Schumpeterian approach (Schumpeter, 1934; Pyka and Andersen 2012) and neoclassical growth which explains the technological change by the Solow (1956) residual, have established an important positive relationship between ICT and economic growth.

Therefore, according to the neo-Schumpeterian and exogenous theories, ICT is an important input into the economic supply in the form of capital and leads to improvements in the production process by deepening capital and promoting technology and the quality of the workforce. Therefore, ICTs create value added at the firm level and at the sectoral level and thus improve the total factor productivity and economic growth of a country (Quah, 2002; Aghaei and Rezagholizadeh, 2017).

In contrast, the endogenous theory provides an explanation of technological progress which represents an endogenous factor that has a role in sustaining long-term economic growth. This theory models the generation and distribution of ideas and information as a key driver of economic growth (Lucas, 1988; Romer, 1990; Aghion and Howitt, 1998). Therefore, the dissemination of information at lower cost can facilitate the adoption of new technologies designed by others, which again promotes economic growth (Nelson and Phelps, 1966; Benhabib and Spiegel, 2005).

The rapid growth in the ICT sector is bringing digital opportunities to many countries, yet the general impact of increased ICT spending on a nation's development is difficult to assess. The term ICT was born in the era of the Internet revolution, and encompasses telecommunications, computer networks, the Internet, radio and television (ITU, 2007). Moreover, ICT tools, such as the Internet, significantly lower the cost of obtaining information and therefore represent an important driver for economic development (Li, 2011).

Moreover, ICTs are used by people to seek information and to communicate it to those who appreciate its value. This becomes knowledge which is of great value to human development – the technology serves as a channel to disseminate the knowledge (UNDP, 2003) and represents a means of disseminating information through a combination of complementary technologies (UNDP, 2003; ITU, 2007). As a result, ICT use has led to enormous changes in economic systems, as well as in social structure and organizations, and the economic sectors have recently started to include a larger share of ICT (Schumpeter, 1942; Nelson, 1959; Griliches, 1991; Brynjolfsson and McAfee, 2014).

2.2 Empirical Literature

In the empirical side, the impact of ICT on economic growth has been the subject of extensive research in recent years. Tripathi and Inani (2016) examined the short- and long-term relationships between GDP per capita and Internet use for 42 sub-Saharan African countries for the period 1998 to 2014 using ARDL model. The results reveal that GDP per capita and Internet usage are cointegrated, and that there is a two-way causality between these variables which plays a positive and significant role in the economic growth of Sub-Saharan African countries. Similarly, the increase in GDP per capita is also responsible for the increase in internet usage.

Using the GMM technique, Albiman and Sulong (2016) examined the long-term impact of ICTs on economic growth over the period 1990 and 2014 in 45 countries in the Sub-Saharan Africa (SSA) region. The authors found that the mobile phone and the Internet triggered economic growth, but for the analysis of the non-linear effect, the massive penetration of ICT seems to slow down economic growth with a threshold penetration rate of 4.5% for mobile phone and internet, and 5% for landline before economic growth is triggered. Furthermore, the authors found that except for financial development, human capital, quality of institutions and domestic investment are the main transmission channels of ICT use in the economy that promote growth.

Further, Niebel (2018) analyzed the impact of ICT on economic growth in 59 developing, emerging and developed countries over the period 1995–2010. The results confirm that the relationship between ICT capital and GDP growth is positive. Furthermore, the estimated elasticity of ICT output is greater than the share of ICT factor compensation, suggesting excessive returns to ICT capital. The regressions for the sub-samples of developing, emerging and developed countries do not reveal statistically significant differences in the elasticity of ICT production between these three groups of countries. Thus, the results indicate that developing and emerging countries do not derive more benefits from ICT investments than developed economies.

Based on a sample of 54 African countries, Adeleye and Ebaogu (2019) assessed the impact of Information and Communication Technology (ICT) on economic growth in Africa between 2005 and 2015 which is further divided into five sub-regions using pooled ordinary least squares, random and fixed effects and the System-GMM method and three ICT indicators (Internet users, mobile subscribers and landline telephone subscribers). The authors reveal that the development of ICT positively and significantly affects economic growth and that the production elasticities of the three ICT indicators are significantly different. Furthermore, the leapfrogging hypothesis is valid and mobile subscription has the highest elasticity of production across specifications and has the greatest potential to enable Africa to "leapfrog" traditional development stages. Moreover, the regressions for the sub-samples show statistically significant differences in the elasticity of production of ICT indicators.

Using GMM method, Asongu et al. (2020) studied the improvement of ICT on value addition in all sectors of 25 sub-Saharan African countries using data for the period 1980–2014 and the GMM method. Their results show that improving mobile phone and Internet penetration has net negative effects on the value added of the agricultural and manufacturing sectors and has extremely positive net effects on the value added of the services sector. In addition, ICT improvement in agriculture and manufacturing sectors is expected to exceed certain value-added thresholds of 114.375 mobile phone penetrations per 100 people for value added in the agriculture sector and 22.625 internet penetrations per 100 people for value added in the manufacturing sector.

In a recent study, Abdulqadir and Asongu (2021) studied the asymmetric effect of Internet access on economic growth in 42 countries in Sub-Saharan Africa (SSA) over the period 2008–2018 through the application of the PSTR model. The results revealed a significant threshold effect of Internet access equal to 3.55%. Furthermore, the short-term linear effect of Internet access on economic growth while controlling for the effects of credit to the private sector and trade openness are negative.

More recently, Kouam and Asongu (2022) examined the non-linear relationship between fixed broadband and economic growth for 33 African countries for the period 2010 to 2020 by the PSTR regression. The authors showed that the proportion of the population with access to electricity above and below which the relationship between fixed broadband and economic growth changes sign is around 60% and below this thresh-old, each 1% increase in fixed broadband subscriptions induces a decline in economic growth of around 2.58%. Above this threshold, economic growth would increase by 2.43% when fixed broadband subscriptions increase by 1%. These results are robust by the sensitivity analysis and the estimation by GMM method.

2.3 Hypothesis Development Relying ICT to Economic Growth

The relationship between ICT and economic growth is characterized by its complexity and multidimensionality. In fact, ICT technologies leads to timely and extensive informa-tion transfer and contributes to economic growth by increasing firm productivity (Dutta, 2001; Consoli, 2012; Bartel et al., 2007; Brynjolfsson and Hitt, 2000 & 2003), by increas-ing the capacity for innovation and the competitiveness of firms (Mehmood and Siddiqui, 2013; Tranos, 2012; Ongori and Migiro, 2010; Yoo and Kwak, 2004) and by reducing the costs associated with compilations, conversions, transmissions and data systemati-zations (Brynjolfsson and Hitt, 2000). Nevertheless, the relationship between ICT and economic growth can be affected by external factors such as literacy, telecommunica-tions infrastructure, and government policies. Thus, with inadequate telecommunications infrastructure, ICT adoption may be limited and impede economic growth.

In Africa, the use of mobile phones has increased and some barriers have been over-come. As a result, they have become an important means of communication and access to information. In addition, mobile banking, payment applications, and money trans-fer services have grown rapidly in Africa, providing innovative solutions for banks and businesses in areas where traditional banking services are underdeveloped. According to the Mobile Money Regulatory Index scores, Sub-Saharan African countries with a few exceptions have broadly enacted enabling regulatory frameworks based on their higher country index scores ranging between 70 and 100, which is an indication of more enabling regulation for widespread mobile money adoption (GSMA, 2019). In brief, ICT in Africa offer challenges, but also great opportunities to promote economic growth and social development on the continent.

However, ICT adoption in Africa remains relatively low compared to other regions of the world, mainly due to poor telecommunications infrastructure in some parts of the continent. The high cost and poor quality of the Internet and lack of access to electricity also hinder ICT adoption in many parts of Africa. In addition, the use of ICT in Africa is often limited to specific activities such as communication, access to information, and entertainment, rather than more productive activities such as innovation and business processes. As a result, ICT are still largely underutilized for their potential to promote economic growth and social development. For all these reasons, our work attempts to verify the following research hypothesis (H1): The relationship between ICT and economic growth is asymmetric.

Regarding the hypothesis that the relationship between ICT and economic growth is asymmetric, it is possible that some factors may affect the relationship differently in different contexts. For example, the availability of infrastructure and human capital in Africa, as well as the level of competition in the market, may influence how much ICT can contribute to economic growth. Additionally, the way in which ICT is used can also affect its impact on economic growth.

3 Empirical Methodology

3.1 Sample Data and Variables Descriptions

The study aims to explore the relationship between the import of information and communication technologies and economic growth for a Panel of 45 Sub-Saharan African countries, namely, Algeria, Angola, Benin, Botswana, Burkina Faso, Burundi, Cameroon, Cape Verde, Central African Republic, Comoros, Congo, DR Congo, Egypt, Eswatini, Ethiopia, Gabon, Gambia, Ghana, Guinea, Guinea-Bissau, Ivory Coast, Kenya, Lesotho, Libya, Madagascar, Malawi, Mali, Mauritania, Mauritius, Morocco, Mozambique, Namibia, Niger, Nigeria, Rwanda, Senegal, Sierra Leone, South Africa, Sudan, Tanzania, Togo, Tunisia, Uganda, Zambia and Zimbabwe between the period from 2000 to 2021 and all the variables considered for this study are extracted from the World Bank. Thus, with reference to Abdelkafi et al. (2022), we will consider the following specification:

$$GDPG_{it} = \beta_0 + \beta_1 Activity_{it} + \beta_2 GFCF_{it} + \beta_3 Trade_{it} + \beta_4 FDI_{it} + \beta_5 ICT\_IMP_{it} + \varepsilon_{it}$$

The coefficients of β_1, β_2, β_3, β_4, β_5 express the long-run relationship between variables, and ε_{it} denoted for error correction term in the equation. The variables used in this study are presented as follows:

- GDPG (endogenous variable): indicates the growth rate of GDP in percentage. In fact, economic growth is the sustained increase over one or more long periods of a dimensional indicator for a nation, the net aggregate product in real terms (Perroux, 1961). The concept of economic growth is important for achieving economic and social development, which is a major national objective (Dahmani et al., 2022). In theory, economic growth is explained neither by the increase in the active population nor by that of fixed capital, but rather by a residual that he attributes to the efficiency of the factors of production (Solow, 1956). In contrast, according to endogenous growth theories, economic growth is a self-sustaining phenomenon, due to increasing returns and positive externalities of certain factors of production such as human capital, infrastructure, knowledge, technical progress, etc. (Romer, 1986 & 1990; Lucas, 1988; Barro, 1990; Aghion and Howitt, 1992).
- Activity: it represents the ratio of the labor force to the working age population (15 years and over). This variable represents a key of the production factor in developing countries for which technical skills and education are acquired to improve labor productivity while achieving a high level of growth (Adeleye and Eboagu, 2019).

- GFCF (percentage of GDP): this variable is represented as the investment rate which is measured by the ratio of gross fixed capital formation as a percentage of GDP. It includes the net increase in physical assets over the measurement period that does not take into account the consumption (depreciation) of fixed capital and does not include land purchases. This indicator captures the absorption capacity to produce, which in turn affects economic growth.
- Trade (percentage of GDP): the ratio of the sum of exports and imports divided by GDP. This variable shows the extent of integration between countries on the continent and with the rest of the world and it is expected that increased trade will have a positive impact on growth (Adeleye and Ebaogu, 2019).
- FDI (percentage of GDP): refers to total foreign direct investment, net inflows (percentage of GDP). This variable corresponds to investments in a subsidiary located in a country other than the head office of the investing company which transfers various production resources such as capital, equipment, raw materials, knowledge, and capacity organization. In addition, the investing company controls the subsidiary created by direct investment, owning a certain percentage of the capital and influences the decision-making process and the selection criteria for technology, raw materials, etc. (Apostolopoulos et al., 2020). Using the PMG-ARDL model for 22 sub-Saharan African countries from 1988 to 2019, Ayenew (2022) examined the short- and long-term effects of foreign direct investment on economic growth and showed that in the long-term, foreign direct investment has a favorable and significant effect, but it is statistically insignificant in the short term. Therefore, foreign direct investment boosts long-term economic growth and Sub-Saharan African countries should focus on attracting kind of investment.
- ICT_IMP (percentage of total goods imports): any country can import ICT goods from other countries. In particular, developing countries, including African nations, are the largest importers of these technologies. These ICT goods imports are part of the total goods imports for each African country. ICT goods Imports including telecommunications, audio, video, computers and related equipment, electronic components and other ICT goods, namely software (World Bank Definition). This variable was included in a model built by Naanaa and Sellaouti (2017) to study the effect of technology diffusion on economic growth in the Tunisian manufacturing sector. Their results show that ICT imports have a positive effect on TFP growth, which shows that ICTs are essential for growth and necessary not only to develop a country's productive capacity in all sectors of the economy, but also to connect a country to the global economy and ensure competitiveness.

Moreover, Sassi and Goaied (2013) examined the relationship between ICT (using ICT goods imports in percentage of total goods imports) and economic growth by using GMM-System method between 1960 and 2009. Their results reveal a positive and significant direct effect of ICT proxies on economic growth. This implies that MENA countries need to reinforce their ICT policies and improve using of new Information and Communication Technology. In our study, African countries are nations that import technologies, as well as the MENA region and 5 North African countries belong African continent. Therefore, we have the possibility to use this variable in the estimation of the model.

The distribution of ICT imports across the 45 selected African countries appears to be highly heterogeneous, with no clear pattern of distribution. In some cases, the distribution is skewed to the right, while in others it is skewed to the left. This suggests that these countries have not yet achieved significant growth in terms of ICT imports compared to developed countries.

There could be a variety of reasons for this, including limited infrastructure for ICT development, lack of access to capital, inadequate education and training programs, political instability, and other socio-economic factors. It is important for these countries to prioritize the development of ICT infrastructure and skills in order to compete in the global economy and benefit from the opportunities provided by digital technologies.

3.2 Technique Estimations

In the analysis between economic variables, it is important to emphasize the importance of econometric modelling because it allows for the analysis of the effect of the independent variables on the dependent variable while controlling for the effects of other explanatory variables. Both Autoregressive Distributed Lag (ARDL) model of Pesaran et al. (2001) and Non-linear Autoregressive Distributed Lag (NARDL) model of Shin et al. (2014) are econometric methods frequently used to analyze short- and long-term relationships between economic variables, taking into account lagged effects and linear or non-linear relationships. These models are particularly useful in macroeconomic analysis and are widely used in empirical research. Indeed, this subsection describes in detail the ARDL and NARDL models and their applications in econometric analysis.

We begin with the presentation of the methodology of the ARDL approach. This technique was proposed by Pesaran et al. (2001) in order to overcome the limitations related to the methods of Engle and Granger (1987) and Johansen (1991). This model has the advantage that it is applicable for pure cointegration regressors I(0), pure I(1) or mixed. It therefore avoids the potential biases associated with unit root and cointegration tests.

Moreover, this approach is better suited for samples of smaller sizes in contrast to the cointegration technique of Johansen (1988) which requires a large sample to give an unbiased result. This ARDL approach requires a simple reduced form of the equation but in other techniques, a system of equations is necessary. In addition, it allows for the use of different delays for recorders as opposed to cointegration VAR models where mixed delays for variables are not allowed (Pesaran et al., 2001). The ARDL short-term equation will be as follows:

$$\Delta GDPG_{it} = \delta_0 + \delta_1 GDPG_{it-1} + \delta_2 Activity_{it-1} + \delta_3 GFCF_{it-1} + \delta_4 Trade_{it-1} + \delta_5 FDI_{it-1}$$
$$+ \delta_6 ICT\_IMP_{it-1} + \sum_{i=1}^{p} \alpha_{1i} \Delta GDPG_{it-i} + \sum_{i=0}^{q_1} \alpha_{2i} \Delta Activity_{it-i} + \sum_{i=0}^{q_2} \alpha_{3i} \Delta GFCF_{it-i}$$
$$+ \sum_{i=0}^{q_3} \alpha_{4i} \Delta Trade_{it-i} + \sum_{i=0}^{q_4} \alpha_{5i} \Delta FDI_{it-i} + \sum_{i=0}^{q_5} \alpha_{6i} \Delta ICT\_IMP_{it-i} + \varepsilon_{it}$$

Alternatively, an error-corrected dynamic model (ECM) may be drawn, whose error correction term ρ must be negative and significant in order to give an indication of the adjustment speed, the time required variables to return to long-term equilibrium. Thus, the ECM model can be represented by the following equation:

$$\Delta GDPG_{it} = \rho_0 + \rho\hat{\varepsilon}_{it-1} + \sum_{i=1}^{p}\alpha_{1i}\Delta GDPG_{it-i} + \sum_{i=0}^{q_1}\alpha_{2i}\Delta Activity_{it-i} + \sum_{i=0}^{q_2}\alpha_{3i}\Delta GCF_{it-i}$$

$$+ \sum_{i=0}^{q_3}\alpha_{4i}\Delta Trade_{it-i} + \sum_{i=0}^{q_4}\alpha_{5i}\Delta FDI_{it-i} + \sum_{i=0}^{q_5}\alpha_{6i}\Delta ICT\_IMP_{it-i} + \mu_{it}$$

where $\hat{\varepsilon}_{it-1}$ is the lagged residual term of the short-term equation above.

For the asymmetric NARDL model, this model has significant advantages over existing methodological approaches as it offers joint modeling of cointegrating asymmetries and dynamics and efficiently detecting cointegrating relationships in small samples. In addition, this model does not require the integration of recorders of the same order, which makes it possible to include the chronological processes I(0) and I(1) (but not I(2)) in the equilibrium relation long term. This version commonly known as asymmetric panel investigation incorporates positive and negative shocks of the explanatory variables in the equation. In other words, positive and negative shocks might not produce the same sign in coefficients of both positive and negative shock. Thus, the NARDL model of Shin et al. (2014) takes into account the asymmetry by decomposing ICT_IMP_t into its positive ($ICT\_IMP_t^+$) and negative ($ICT\_IMP_t^-$) parts as follows:

$$ICT\_IMP_t^+ = \sum_{i=1}^{t}\Delta ICT\_IMP_i^+ = \sum_{i=1}^{t}\max(\Delta ICT\_IMP, 0)$$

$$ICT\_IMP_t^- = \sum_{i=1}^{t}\Delta ICT\_IMP_i^- = \sum_{i=1}^{t}\min(\Delta ICT\_IMP, 0)$$

Then the asymmetric long-term equilibrium relationship can be given by:

$$GDPG_{it} = \beta_0 + \beta_1 Activity_{it} + \beta_2 GFCF_{it} + \beta_3 Trade_{it} + \beta_4 FDI_{it} + \beta_5^+ ICT\_IMP_{it}^+$$

$$+ \beta_5^- ICt\_IMP_{it}^- + u_t$$

where β_5^+ and β_5^- are long-term asymmetric coefficients corresponding to positive and negative changes in $ICT\_IMP_{it}^+$ and $ICT\_IMP_{it}^-$, respectively. According to Shin et al. (2014), the long-term asymmetric relationship associated with the linear ARDL model (Pesaran et al., 2001) results in the following NARDL model:

$$\Delta GDPG_{it} = \delta_0 + \delta_1 GDPG_{it-1} + \delta_2 Activity_{it-1} + \delta_3 GFCF_{it-1} + \delta_4 Trade_{it-1} + \delta_5 FDI_{it-1}$$

$$+ \delta_6^+ ICT\_IMP_{it-1}^+ + \delta_6^- ICt\_IMP_{it-1}^- + \sum_{i=1}^{p}\alpha_{1i}\Delta GDPG_{it-i} + \sum_{i=0}^{q_1}\alpha_{2i}\Delta Activity_{it-i}$$

$$+ \sum_{i=0}^{q_2}\alpha_{3i}\Delta GFCF_{it-i} + \sum_{i=0}^{q_3}\alpha_{4i}\Delta Trade_{it-i} + \sum_{i=0}^{q_4}\alpha_{5i}\Delta FDI_{it-1}$$

$$+ \sum_{i=0}^{q_5}\alpha_{6i}^+ \Delta ICT\_IMP_{it-i}^+ + \sum_{i=0}^{q_6}\alpha_{6i}^- \Delta ICT\_IMP_{it-i}^- + v_{it}$$

In addition, it is possible to derive a dynamic error correction (ECM) model whose error correction term ρ is negative and significant because it indicates the adjustment speed, that is, the time required variables to return to long-term equilibrium. Thus, the ECM model can be represented by the following equation:

$$\Delta GDPG_{it} = \rho_0 + \rho \hat{v}_{it-1} + \sum_{i=1}^{p} \alpha_{1i} \Delta GDPG_{it-i} + \sum_{i=0}^{q_1} \alpha_{2i} \Delta Activity_{it-i} + \sum_{i=0}^{q_2} \alpha_{3i} \Delta GFCF_{it-i}$$

$$+ \sum_{i=0}^{q_3} \alpha_{4i} \Delta Trade_{it-i} + \sum_{i=0}^{q_4} \alpha_{5i} \Delta FDI_{it-i} + \sum_{i=0}^{q_5} \alpha_{6i}^{+} \Delta ICT\_IMP_{it-i}^{+}$$

$$+ \sum_{i=0}^{q_6} \alpha_{6i}^{-} \Delta ICT\_IMP_{it-1}^{-} + \varphi_{it}$$

The next step is to examine long- and short-term symmetries using standard Wald tests. In particular, the positive and negative coefficients are $\Theta^{+} = -\delta_6^{+}/\delta_1$ and $\Theta^{-} = -\delta_6^{-}/\delta_1$ and the null and alternative hypothesis of this test is:

$$\begin{cases} H_0 : \theta^{+} = \theta^{-} \\ H_1 : \theta^{+} \neq \theta^{-} \end{cases}$$

Then, the asymmetric cumulative dynamic multiplier effects of m_h^{+} and m_h^{-} per change unit ICT_IMP^{+} and ICT_IMP^{-} are obtained using the NARDL model. In particular, the above-mentioned multiplier effects are given by:

$$m_h^{+} = \sum_{i=0}^{h} \frac{\partial GDPG_{t+j}}{\partial ICT\_IMP_t^{+}} \quad \text{and} \quad m_h^{-} = \sum_{i=0}^{h} \frac{\partial GDPG_{t+j}}{\partial ICt\_IMP_t^{-}} \quad \text{which } h \to \infty; m_h^{+} \to \theta^{+} \quad \text{and} \quad m_h^{-} \to \theta^{-}$$

From the estimated multipliers, it is possible to determine both the trajectory of the old towards the new equilibrium after a positive or negative shock and the equivalent duration of the temporary imbalances.

4 Empirical Results and Discussions

We begin firstly by the descriptive analysis of the variables. In fact, the Panel considered in this study includes 45 African countries, namely, Algeria, Angola, Benin, Botswana, Burkina Faso, Burundi, Cameroon, Cape Verde, Central African Republic, Comoros, Congo, DR Congo, Egypt, Eswatini, Ethiopia, Gabon, Gambia, Ghana, Guinea, Guinea-Bissau, Ivory Coast, Kenya, Lesotho, Libya, Madagascar, Malawi, Mali, Mauritania, Mauritius, Morocco, Mozambique, Namibia, Niger, Nigeria, Rwanda, Senegal, Sierra Leone, South Africa, Sudan, Tanzania, Togo, Tunisia, Uganda, Zambia and Zimbabwe between 2000 and 2021, that is to say 22 observations per country.

4.1 Univariate Analysis of the Variables

According to the Table 1, GDP growth rates differ according to the economic conditions of the countries in the sample. This variable has an overall average of 3.929, a median of 4.260 and a standard deviation of 5.729. In addition, the minimum and maximum of this variable are respectively −50.339 and 86.827 with positive Skewness and Kurtosis. For the ICT_IMP variable, the trend at the country level is characterized by volatility for most countries, these variables experienced upward and downward trends between 2000 and 2021. In addition, it has an overall mean of 3.871, a median of 3.582 and a standard deviation of 2.003. In addition, the minimum and maximum distribution is between 0.006 and 12.774 with positive Skewness and Kurtosis. The two series was characterized by non-normality and no autocorrelation.

Table 1. Overall descriptive analysis of variables

Designation	GDPG	Activity	GFCF	Trade	FDI	ICT_IMP
Observations	990	990	990	990	990	990
Mean	3.929	64.604	21.923	66.336	3.415	3.871
Median	4.260	65.237	20.68	58.964	2.175	3.582
Standard Error	5.729	13.092	8.963	29.654	5.040	2.003
Minimum	−50.339	39.874	1.097	0.785	−12.675	0.006
Maximum	86.827	88.35	81.021	175.798	47.273	12.774
Skewness	1.508	−0.047	1.193	0.960	3.705	1.133
Kurtosis	59.884	1.820	7.004	3.979	23.878	4.814
Jarque-Bera (JB) statistics	1.3e + 05	57.75	896.2	191.5	2.0e + 04	347.5
JB Probability	0.000	2.9e−13	3.e−195	2.6e−42	0.000	3.5e−76
Born-Breitung (BB) statistics	5.18	52.48	33.75	34.44	8.50	57.76
BB Probability	0.075	0.000	0.000	0.000	0.014	0.000
Coefficient of Variation	1.458	0.202	0.409	0.447	1.476	0.517

Note: BB refers to Born and Breitung (2016) serial autocorrelation test; JB refers to Jarque and Bera (1987) normality test

We begin firstly by testing the cross-section dependence test which is important before examining the relationship between ICT and economic growth. This test allows us to test the null hypothesis of cross-sectional independence. De Hoyos and Sarafidis (2006) highlight the necessity and the importance of the cross-sectional dependence test in dynamic panel data. Specifically, Sarafidis and Robertson (2006) point out that the absence of cross-sectional dependence in the data can lead to inconsistency in all estimation procedures. In other words, ignoring Cross-Dependence tests in panel data can lead to biased outcomes since some unit-root, Cointegration, and long-run estimation techniques (Can and Ahmed, 2023).

In 1937, Friedman proposed a cross-section dependence test based on averaging Spearman's rank correlation coefficient to assess the robustness of an analysis. This test was improved upon by Frees in 1995, who introduced a new test procedure based on the summation of the squared rank order of correlations on the residual (Shahzad et al., 2023). Pesaran (2004, 2006, 2015) and Pesaran et al. (2008) have emphasized the importance of testing for cross-sectional dependence in panel data analyses. They argue that cross-sectional dependence may arise from unobserved differences between individual units or exogenous shocks that affect multiple units simultaneously. Therefore, it is essential to account for cross-sectional dependence to obtain unbiased estimates and accurate inferences in panel data analysis.

Table 2. Cross-section Dependence tests

Tests	Value	Probability	Decision
Friedman (1937)	140.534	0.000	Dependence
Breusch-Pagan (1980)	1653	0.000	Dependence
Frees (2004)	1.094	0.000	Dependence
Pesaran (2004)	21.75	0.000	Dependence
Pesaran (2006)	18.395	0.000	Dependence
Pesaran et al. (2008)	18.19	0.000	Dependence
Pesaran (2015)	22.427	0.000	Dependence

According to this table, the p-values associated with different cross-dependence tests are below 1%, suggesting that the augmentation with current and lagged cross-sectional averages adequately account for cross-sectional dependence (see Table 2). This requires the use of second-generation panel unit root tests techniques to obtain robust and reliable empirical estimates and policy suggestions (Akadiri et al., 2020). There are several second-generation unit root tests that can be applied to panel data analysis such as Pesaran (2003) and Pesaran (2007). These tests have been developed to asymptotically eliminate the problem of dependence between series and have the property of being robust. Thus, to control the order of integration, second generation panel root tests have been performed.

The results of second-generation panel unit root tests presented in Table 3 below established a mixed order of integration, which is implying that variables GDPG, FDI are stationary in level while the variables Activity, GFCF, Trade and ICT_IMP are stationary in first difference in Pesaran (2003) test while variables GDPG, FDI and ICT_IMP are stationary in level while the variables Activity, GFCF, Trade and are stationary in first difference in Pesaran (2007).

In addition, we will use the unit root test with break of Karavias and Tzavalis (2014) to confirm the possibility of the application of a non-linear model. According to Table 4 of the unit root with break test above, we can conclude that the series are stationary in level or in first difference and that there is no integrated variable of order [I(2)]. The mixed order of variables integration allows investigating long-run relationship by applying NARDL model proposed by Shin et al. (2014). Thus, after applying cross-sectional dependence test and second-generation unit root tests, it is necessary to verify the existence of a cointegration relationship between the variables of the model.

Based on the results of Table 5, which presents the various Cointegration tests such as the Kao (1999), Pedroni (2004), Westerlund (2007) and Persyn and Westerlund (2008)

Table 3. Second-generation unit root tests

Pesaran (2003) test						
Variables	GDPG	Activity	GFCF	Trade	FDI	ICT_IMP
Panel A: In level						
Constant	-2.757***	-1.128	-1.547	-1.555	-2.106***	-2.220***
Trend	-3.188***	-0.921	-2.249	-2.608**	-2.564**	-2.484
Decision	S	NS	NS	NS	S	NS
Panel B: In first difference						
Constant	-4.600***	-3.222***	-3.193***	-3.174***	-3.467***	-3.706***
Trend	-4.519***	-3.837***	-3.314***	-3.156***	-3.416***	-3.759***
Decision	S	S	S	S	S	S
Pesaran (2007) test						
Variables	GDPG	Activity	GFCF	Trade	FDI	ICT_IMP
Panel A: In level						
Constant	-3.828***	-1.159	-1.758	-1.723	-2.985***	-2.784***
Trend	-4.179***	-0.906	-2.249	-2.683**	-3.522***	-3.130***
Decision	S	NS	NS	NS	S	S
Panel B: In first difference						
Constant	-5.610***	-3.103***	-4.257***	-4.200***	-5.320***	-5.432***
Trend	-5.619***	-3.544***	-4.403***	-4.228***	-5.396***	-5.541***
Decision	S	S	S	S	S	S

Notes: *, **, *** represent significance at 10%, 5%, 1%, respectively. S denotes stationary; NS denotes non-stationary.

Table 4. Un it root test with break

Variables	In level	In first difference
GDPG	−44.290*** (2001)	−59.288*** (2019)
Activity	−10.219*** (2001)	−34.752*** (2001)
GFCF	−11.069*** (2020)	−38.379*** (2019)
Trade	−7.466*** (2010)	−40.590*** (2001)
FDI	−17.724*** (2020)	−53.338*** (2019)
ICT_IMP	−19.201*** (2020)	−47.781*** (2001)

Notes: Value between brackets represents break date. *** represents significance at 1%.

Table 5. Cointegration tests

Tests	Statistics	Probability	Decision
Kao (1999)	−10.939	0.000	Cointegration
Pedroni (2004)	−15.582	0.000	Cointegration
Westerlund (2007)	−4.047	0.000	Cointegration
Persyn and Westerlund (2008)			
G_t	−3.077	0.002	Cointegration
G_a	−1.302	1.000	No Cointegration
P_t	−16.504	0.493	No Cointegration
P_a	−0.968	1.000	No Cointegration

tests, all tests have a probability below the 5% threshold. Therefore, we can say that there is at least one cointegration relationship for all the variables in our model. However, the three statistics of Persyn and Westerlund (2008), G_a, P_t and P_a suggest the acceptance of the null hypothesis of no cointegration between variable models. Nevertheless, G_t statistics show the rejection of the null hypothesis of no cointegration. In total, there is at least one cointegration relationship between the variables of the model.

4.2 PMG-ARDL Results

The next step after examining the Cointegration test consists of the estimation of the models considered to analyze the relationship between ICT and Economic Growth. We begin firstly by analyzing this relationship using Pooled Mean Group ARDL (PMG-ARDL). The model results are presented below in Table 6.

In the short-term model results, the error correction term, ECT_{it-1}, is statistically significant and negative, proving that there is a cointegration relationship between the short-term model variables. More precisely, the estimated value ECT_{it-1} is equal to −0.818, implying that the adjustment speed of the long-term equilibrium in response to the imbalance caused by the short-term shocks of the previous period is adjusted to 81.8%. In other words, this coefficient combined with the strength of the recall allows us to conclude that the shocks on economic growth in the African region are corrected to 81.8%, This means that we manage to settle 81.8% of the imbalance between the desired level and the effective level of economic growth and that a shock on economic growth is fully absorbed after 1 year 2 months and 20 days. In addition, the constant is highly significant, indicating that there are no variables omitted in our estimated model.

In the long-term estimation, an increase of 1% increase in activity rate leads to a 0.15% increase in economic growth. In Africa, the activity rate is high and the labor force has increased massively between 2000 and 2021, which positively affects labor productivity and therefore economic growth is increasing. In addition, youth and the increasing level of qualifications of the African population are another factor accelerating the continent's digital transformation especially where the number of Africans aged between 15 and 29. From 2010 to 2020, the number of students in upper secondary education rose from 47 million to 77 million. This increase is particularly notable in North Africa, where 47% of young people have at least a level of education corresponding to upper secondary education. It is also a very important factor in the positive impact of labor force participation in economic growth (OECD, 2021).

However, Gross Fixed Capital Formation represents a negative and significant effect. Indeed, any increase of 1% of this variable leads to a decrease of 0.038% in economic growth. This is due to two main factors which are tax pressure and corruption. Within the framework of the Ramsey (1928) Standard Optimal Growth Model, Cass (1965) and Koopmans (1965) demonstrated that capital taxation has strong negative effects on capital accumulation and leads to a lower level of capital and production (Djankov et al., 2010). Moreover, Chamley (1986) and Judd (1985) showed that any positive tax rate on capital will distort the intertemporal allocation of resources between consumption and saving, discourage saving and leading to less capital accumulation. In addition, corruption and bad governance negatively affect investment and thus economic growth which can records low rates (De Paulo et al., 2022).

Trade has a positive and significant effect on economic growth. Indeed, any 1% increase of openness leads to a 0.023% increase in economic growth. Among the factors contributing to this positive effect, African countries have created zones of integration between themselves and have helped countries to facilitate multilateral exports and imports, which has benefited the whole region. In addition, long-term growth gains can be achieved through improvements in factor productivity that can occur through various channels such as technology diffusion and innovation (Kim and Lin, 2009).

The variable FDI represents a positive and significant effect on economic growth. Indeed, any 1% increase in economic growth leads to a 0.3% increase in the long term. In fact, any net inflow of FDI to African countries helps multinational firms to settle in this region due to incentives from tax regulations and therefore facilitates the inflow of capital. Indeed, FDI inflows generate positive externalities more than domestic investment for the host countries and thus contribute to the improvement of trade openness, job creation and therefore economic growth (Borensztein et al., 1998; Kalai and Zghidi, 2019; Ben Abdallah, 2023).

Table 6. Pooled Mean Group ARDL model estimation

Variables	Coefficient	Standard Error	t-statistic	Probability
Short-term estimation: dependent variable $\Delta GDPG_{it}$: ARDL (1,0,0,1,0,0)				
Constant	−6.053	0.458	−12.48	0.000
$Activity_{it-1}$	2.214	0.473	4.68	0.000
$GFCF_{it-1}$	0.181	0.077	2.34	0.019
$Trade_{it-1}$	−0.036	0.050	−0.73	0.467
FDI_{it-1}	0.155	0.140	1.10	0.269
ICT_IMP_{it-1}	−0.385	0.242	−1.59	0.112
ECT_{it-1}	−0.818	0.048	−16.98	0.000
Long-term estimation: dependent variable $GDPG_{it}$				
$Activity_{it}$	0.149	0.040	3.69	0.000
$GFCF_{it}$	−0.038	0.019	−2.04	0.041
$Trade_{it}$	0.023	0.009	2.28	0.010
FDI_{it}	0.298	0.049	6.07	0.000
ICT_IMP_{it}	0.129	0.059	2.19	0.029
Hausman test (1)	3.16 (0.675)			
Hausman test (2)	3.01 (0.698)			
Observations	990			

For ICT_IMP, any 1% increase in economic growth leads to a 0.13% increase in the long-term. In Africa, the expansion of ICT imports has been a major driver of growth and production as it is strongly linked to African industries, agriculture and financial sectors. The adoption of these technologies, particularly in developing countries, transforms their economies initially based on natural resources into a digital economy and allows them to accentuate their productivity gains and embark on a trajectory to the benefits of new technologies.

Therefore, ICT imports can affect the economy, production and industrial production through direct and indirect channels. The direct channel refers to the industrial or manufacturing sector that purchases infrastructure services needed or used as inputs in the production process although indirect channels exist at various levels by increasing profits through well-functioning infrastructure, improving access of productive resources to local, national, regional and international markets and attracting foreign direct investment, good education and better health outcomes that serve sectors.

4.3 PMG-NARDL Results

In the NARDL model, like the ARDL, the PMG is the right estimator for this model in presence of high dependence, because its Hausman probability is greater than 5% and therefore it is more favored than the other two MG and DFE estimators. In the short-term model results, the error correction term, ECT_{it-1}, is statistically significant and negative, proving that there is a cointegration relationship between the short-term model variables. More precisely, the estimated value ECT_{it-1} is equal to -0.809, implying that the adjustment speed of the long-term equilibrium in response to the imbalance caused by the short-term shocks of the previous period is adjusted to 80.9%. In other words, this coefficient combined with the strength of the recall allows us to conclude that shocks to economic growth in the African region are corrected to 80.9%. This means that a shock on economic growth is fully absorbed after 1 year 2 months and 25 days. In addition, the constant is highly significant, indicating that there are no variables omitted in our estimated model (see Table 7).

Table 7. Pooled Mean Group NARDL model estimation

Variables	Coefficient	Standard Error	t-statistic	Probability
Short-term estimation: dependent variable $\Delta GDPG_{it}$: ARDL (1,0,0,1,0,0,0)				
Constant	-4.114	0.378	-10.89	0.000
$Activity_{it-1}$	2.063	0.410	5.04	0.000
$GFCF_{it-1}$	0.180	0.083	2.17	0.030
$Trade_{it-1}$	-0.023	0.049	-0.47	0.641
FDI_{it-1}	0.458	0.189	2.42	0.016
$ICT\_IMP\_pos_{it-1}$	-0.479	0.381	-1.26	0.209
$ICT\_IMP\_neg_{it-1}$	-0.545	0.471	-1.16	0.248
ECT_{it-1}	-0.809	0.047	-17.11	0.000
Long-term estimation: dependent variable $GDPG_{it}$				
$Activity_{it}$	0.120	0.039	3.13	0.002
$GFCF_{it}$	-0.042	0.019	-2.04	0.028
$Trade_{it}$	0.015	0.009	1.74	0.082
FDI_{it}	0.317	0.048	6.61	0.000
$ICT\_IMP\_pos_{it}$	0.150	0.069	2.18	0.029
$ICT\_IMP\_neg_{it}$	0.114	0.071	1.60	0.109
Hausman test (1)	2.77 (0.838)			
Hausman test (2)	6.29 (0.392)			
Observations	990			

In long-term analysis, the activity rate represents a positive and significant effect on economic growth. Indeed, every 1% increase in economic growth leads to an increase of 0.12% in the long-term. In Africa, economic growth in the region has been high and the labor market has been influenced by the availability and demand for labor of enterprises by the increase of IT contractors and turning to working from home, remote work and virtual collaboration. In addition, a young and growing population is generally considered to provide a "demographic dividend" to GDP growth and GDP per capita growth through labor supply (AfDB, OECD and UNDP, 2016).

Moreover, boosting human capital in African countries is crucial to enable broader participation of all segments of the population in the digital economy that will entail supporting a critical mass of inventors and entrepreneurs in developing and scaling digital technologies to boost the productivity of low-skilled workers and should complement increased investments in early childhood education and health care service delivery and therefore develop resilience to possible future pandemics (Choi et al., 2020). In addition, research and development activities play an important role in creating knowledge and promoting learning and absorptive capacity and consequently positively affect the efficiency of workers and promote economic growth (Aghion and Howitt, 1998; Griffith et al., 2004).

Nevertheless, Gross Fixed Capital Formation represents a negative and significant effect on economic growth. Indeed, any 1% increase in economic growth leads to a decrease of 0.042% in the long term. This is justified by the low national savings rate as a reason for the low level of investment in African countries, which leads to a scarcity of capital invested in the continent and therefore in economic growth. The assumption that financial liberalization in the form of an appropriate rate of return on real cash balances is a means of promoting economic growth. This hypothesis states that a low or negative interest rate will discourage saving, which reduces the amount of lending funds given by banks to investors and consequently reduces economic growth (McKinnon, 1973; Shaw, 1973). Therefore, the banks in terms of a financial intermediary can no longer mobilize their main function which is the granting of loans.

In this model, Trade represents a positive and significant effect on long-term economic growth. Indeed, every 1% increase in economic growth leads to an increase of 0.015% in the long-term. This positive effect has been justified by the creation of African integration zones to help countries facilitate trade between them, which has a positive effect on the entire region. Moreover, the countries of the African region have put in place well-targeted structural trade policies, which encourage the national companies of each country to increase its production and export it to other countries to acquire more foreign exchange and increase its Total Factor Productivity and hence economic growth. Thus, trade openness increases the productivity, efficiency and innovation capacity of domestic producers and allows domestic producers to benefit from high quality intermediate products and to exploit the ideas generated by imports of innovative products, including ICT (Huchet-Bourdon et al., 2018).

In addition, the FDI variable represents a positive and significant effect on economic growth. Indeed, any 1% increase in economic growth leads to an increase of 0.32% in the long term. In this case, any net inflow of FDI to African countries helps multinational firms to settle in this region due to the incentives of regulations concerning these firms to encourage the creation of wealth jobs and thus economic growth. Furthermore, these flows promote economic development through structural transformation and rapid economic growth in developing host countries (Ozawa, 1992; Ozturk, 2007) and are recognized as providers of technology, management expertise, financing and connection to the global market, as well as increased job opportunities (Aitken and Harrison, 1999; Caves, 1982; Haddad and Harrison, 1993; Helleiner, 1989; Ozawa, 1992).

ICT_IMP$^+$ represents a positive and significant effect on economic growth. Indeed, an increase of a positive shock of this variable of 1% leads to an increase of 0.15% of long-term economic growth. In Africa, investment has shifted to the sector for greater impacts on economic growth and efforts have focused on harnessing the benefits of using ICTs. This can reduce the increase in costs attributable to the use of communication technology facilities and therefore policy measures need to be put in place to strengthen the ICT infrastructure in order to reduce the cost and develop the productivity of the sectors. However, ICT_IMP$^-$ represents a positive but an insignificant effect on economic growth. This implies that a negative shock on ICT imports no longer has an influence on growth because in the region. It is true that there is a greater digitalization but it has been concentrated and used in productive economic sectors that increase the productivity and therefore economic growth and not used for non-productive activities.

After conducting our analysis, we can say that our research hypothesis, postulating an asymmetry in the relationship between ICT and economic growth within African countries, has been confirmed. Indeed, although ICT can play an important role in promoting economic growth and development, its influence on economic growth in African countries has been limited due to several factors such digital divide. In many African countries, access to ICT infrastructure, such as high-speed internet and mobile networks, remains limited, especially in rural areas. This limits the potential for ICT to contribute to economic growth by reducing transaction costs, increasing market efficiency, and enabling innovation and productivity gains.

Also, African Countries suffered to the lack of skilled human capital, which is essential for leveraging the benefits of ICT sector, which limits their ability to develop and implement advanced ICT solutions and this shortage is partly due to inadequate investment in education and training programs in ICT- related fields. Moreover, African countries are also vulnerable to external shocks, such as changes in global commodity prices and geopolitical instability, which can adversely affect their economic growth. These shocks can also have a negative impact on ICT investment and adoption, which can further limit the potential for ICT to contribute to economic growth.

5   Conclusion and Policy Implications

The purpose of this article is to show the nature of the relationship between the import of Information and Communication Technologies and Economic Growth through an empirical methodology of the PMG-ARDL and PMG-NARDL models. Indeed, the results, using the PMG- ARDL model, show that an increase of ICT imports by 1% have a significant and positive impact on economic growth by 0.13%. From the PMG-NARDL model, the results show that a positive shock of 1% increases of ICT imports has a positive and a significant impact on economic growth of 0.15%. However, a negative shock of this variable has no significant impact on growth economic. The results also prove that eight countries in the sample have an asymmetric ICT-Growth link which confirms the asymmetry of the relationship in some countries. From these results, digitalization is important to ensure sustainable and self-reliant economic growth, and African countries need to focus on improving their ICT infrastructure in various economic sectors to achieve a greater efficiency and productivity.

The digitalization increases the competitiveness of manufacturing in Africa and so African countries need to pursue a range of different active industrial policies to strengthen the manufacturing sectors. These policies include developing and building ICT backbone infrastructure including optical fiber and submarine cables, developing appropriate technical skills, securing better funding for digitization by attracting investment in the sector and complementing them through the use of public funds, taxes and incentives, business capacity building, development of national innovation systems and related ICT infrastructure and facilitating the integration of digital service providers in global value chains Banga and te Velde (2018, 2020).

Moreover, digital economy allows countries to benefit from the opportunities offered by prioritizing investments in R&D, science and technology and implementing projects to encourage innovation and positively affect economic sectors. In addition, ICTs help companies to create new jobs in different economic sectors and generate revenue for the state coffers through the mechanism of direct and indirect tax regimes, taxes on the sale of ICT goods and services, taxes on the income of employees of ICT companies and corporate taxes (Ojo, 2020).

In addition, Africa needs to remove barriers to digital technology adoption and innovation to enable small and medium enterprises to grow and compete in the digital age when accelerated coordination at continental and regional level is essential to complement national strategies. In particular, the adaptation of the African Continental Free Trade Area (AfCFTA) to the digital age requires greater cooperation to improve communication infrastructure, roaming services, data regulations as well as security, and only 28 African countries have comprehensive personal data protection legislation, while only 11 countries have adopted substantive legal rules to combat cybercrime (OECD, 2021). Thus, using digitalization to reduce non-tariff barriers to international trade is expected to boost intra- African trade in manufactured goods and the full implementation of the African Continental Free Trade Area should itself have significant positive impacts on the industrialization of the continent (ECA and Union, 2017).

Also, policymakers in African countries should develop a specific policy approach for the co- development of digital technology infrastructure and economic prosperity in these countries by applying adequate actions to benefit from the positive role of digitalization in stimulating sustainable economic growth by strengthening human capital and adopting sound government policies in all sectors of the economy and structural policies to facilitate trade and financial openness between these countries. Furthermore, African governments should strengthen and expand social protection systems to help workers manage risks in the formal and informal economy in a changing world of work which affects both to mobilize revenue from domestic sources and to improve the efficiency of current social expenditures (Choi et al., 2020).

Moreover, E-government policies have to be based on the achievement of more efficient and effective government, allowing greater public access to information, and offering consumer-oriented services. As well, E-administration solutions need to be developed in order to meet the needs of the customers. In order for the state to benefit from the resources offered by the internet and digitalization, efforts should be focused on the adaptation and customization of existing technologies (Ben Youssef, 2021).

In Africa, industries are moving into the digital age, offering an opportunity for sustainable growth and this continent with the emergence of the Fourth Industrial Revolution has a renewed and unique opportunity to address the problem of unemployment on its territory. This will be achieved by adopting education models that act as catalysts for innovation and enhance the needs of the next generation for digital transformation in the fourth industrial revolution. Thus, African governments have made the decision to invest in education and develop retraining programs that provide technological complements, rather than replacing the workforce with strong collaboration and alignment between government, universities, science councils, business, and the labor sector (Enaifoghe, 2021).

While African governments may face different sets of policy choices, there is a surplus of policy opportunities readily available to government in a variety of sectors, from health to education to more regionalized models of manufacturing and forward-looking development of technology-enhanced service delivery. Governments may be able to manage the effect of the digitization of the economy through technological advancement and adaptation, while focusing primarily on traditional development pathways, unambiguously on the manufacturing sector (Enaifoghe, 2021).

References

Abdelkafi, I., Ben Romdhane, Y., Mefteh, H.: Economic issue and technological resilience of pre- and post-COVID-19. Arab Gulf J. Sci. Res. **40**, 330–346 (2022). https://doi.org/10.1108/AGJSR-06-2022-0084

Abdulqadir, I.A., Asongu, S.A.:. The asymmetric effect of internet access on economic growth in subSaharan Africa: Insight from a dynamic panel threshold regression. European Xtramile Centre of African Studies, WP/21/014 (2021)

Adeleye, N., Eboagu, C.: Evaluation of ICT development and economic growth in Africa. NETNOMICS **20**(1), 31–53 (2019). https://doi.org/10.1007/s11066-019-09131-6

AfDB, OECD and UNDP: African Economic Outlook: Sustainable Cities and Structural Transformation. AfDB,Abidjan (2016). https://doi.org/10.1787/19991029

Aghaei, M., Rezagholizadeh, M.: The impact of information and communication technology (ICT) on economic growth in the OIC Countries. Econ. Env. Stud. **17**(42), 257–278 (2017). https://doi.org/10.25167/ees.2017.42.7

Aghion, P., Howitt, P.: A model of growth through creative destruction. Econometrica **60**(2), 323 (1992). https://doi.org/10.2307/2951599

Aghion, P., Howitt, P.: Endogenous Growth Theory. MIT Press, Cambridge (1998)

Aitken, B.J., Harrison, A.E.: Do domestic firms benefit from direct foreign investment? Evidence from Venezuela. Am. Econ. Rev. **89**(3), 605–618 (1999). https://doi.org/10.1257/aer.89.3.605

Akadiri, A.C., Gungor, H., Akadiri, S.S., Bamidele-Sadiq, M.: Is the causal relation between foreign direct investment, trade, and economic growth complement or substitute? The case of African countries. J. Public Affairs **20**(2), e2023 (2019). https://doi.org/10.1002/pa.2023

Albiman, M.M., Sulong, Z.: The role of ICT use to the economic growth in Sub Saharan African region (SSA). J. Sci. Technol. Policy Manag. **7**(3), 306–329 (2016). https://doi.org/10.1108/JSTPM-06-2016-0010

Anderson, L., Wladawsky-Berger, I.: The 4 things it takes to succeed in the digital economy, Harvard Business Review (2016)

Andrianaivo, M., Kpodar, K.R.: ICT, financial inclusion, and growth: Evidence from African countries. IMF Working Papers (2011). https://doi.org/10.5089/9781455227068.001

Apostolopoulos, N., Dermatis, Z., Liargovas, P.: Foreign direct investment and growth causality in the EU countries and in the transition economies. In: Nikas, C. (ed.) Economic Growth in the European Union: Analyzing SME and Investment Policies, pp. 113–124. Springer International Publishing, Cham (2020). https://doi.org/10.1007/978-3-030-48210-7_9

Asongu, S.A., Le Roux, S.: Enhancing ICT for inclusive human development in Sub-Saharan Africa. Technol. Forecast. Soc. Chang. **118**, 44–54 (2017). https://doi.org/10.1016/j.techfore.2017.01.026

Asongu, S.A., Rahman, M., Nnanna, J., Haffar, M.: Enhancing information technology for value added across economic sectors in Sub-Saharan Africa. Technol. Forecast. Soc. Chang. **161**, 120301 (2020). https://doi.org/10.1016/j.techfore.2020.120301

Ayenew, B.B.: The effect of foreign direct investment on the economic growth of Sub-Saharan African countries: an empirical approach. Cogent Econ. & Financ. **10**(1), 2038862 (2022). https://doi.org/10.1080/23322039.2022.2038862

Banga, K., te Velde, D.W.: Digitalisation and the Future of Manufacturing in Africa, SET report, Overseas Development Institute, London (2018)

Banga, K., te Velde, D.W.: Covid-19 and disruption of the digital economy; evidence from low and middle-income countries. Digital Pathways at Oxford Paper Series (2020)

Baro, E.E., Endouware, B.E.C.: The effects of mobile phone on the socio-economic life of the rural dwellers in the Niger Delta region of Nigeria. Inf. Technol. Dev. **19**(3), 249–263 (2013). https://doi.org/10.1080/02681102.2012.755895

Barro, R.J.: Government spending in a simple model of endogeneous growth. J. Polit. Econ. **98**(5), 103–125 (1990). https://doi.org/10.1086/261726

Bartel, A., Ichniowski, C., Shaw, K.: How does information technology affect productivity? Plant-level comparisons of product innovation, process improvement, and worker skills. Q. J. Econ. **122**(4), 1721–1758 (2007). https://doi.org/10.1162/qjec.2007.122.4.1721

Batuo, E.M.: Role of telecommunications infrastructure in the regional economic growth of Africa. J. Dev. Areas **49**(1), 1–19 (2015). https://doi.org/10.1353/jda.2015.0005

Ben Abdallah, A.: The relationship between trade openness, foreign direct investment inflows, and economic growth in middle east and north of Africa region: autoregressive distributed lag model vs. vector error correction model. J. Knowl. Econ. (2023). https://doi.org/10.1007/s13132-023-01099-x

Ben Youssef, A.: Digital Transformation in Tunisia: Under Which Conditions Could the Digital Economy Benefit Everyone?. Economic Research Forum, Working Paper No. 1512 (2021)

Ben Youssef, A., Boubaker, S., Dedajc, B., Carabregu-Vokshic, M.: Digitalization of the economy and entrepreneurship intention. Technol. Forecast. Soc. Chang. **164**(5), 1–14 (2021). https://doi.org/10.1016/j.techfore.2020.120043

Benhabib, J., Spiegel, M.M.: Human Capital and Technology Diffusion, pp. 935–966. Elsevier (2005). https://doi.org/10.1016/S1574-0684(05)01013-0

Borensztein, E., De Gregorio, J., Lee, J.W.: How does foreign direct investment affect economic growth? J. Int. Econ. **45**(1), 115–135 (1998). https://doi.org/10.1016/S0022-1996(97)00033-0

Born, B., Breitung, J.: Testing for serial correlation in fixed-effects panel data models. Economet. Rev. **35**(7), 1290–1316 (2016). https://doi.org/10.1080/07474938.2014.976524

Bose, N., Haque, M.E.: Causality between public investment in transport and communication and economic growth. J. Econ. Dev. **30**(1), 95–106 (2005). https://doi.org/10.2139/ssrn.764465

Breusch, T.S., Pagan, A.R.: The Lagrange multiplier test and its applications to model specification in econometrics. Rev. Econ. Stud. **47**(1), 239–253 (1980). https://doi.org/10.2307/2297111

Brynjolfsson, E., McAfee, A.: The second machine age: Work, progress, and prosperity in a time of brilliant technologies. WW Norton & Company (2014)

Brynjolfsson, E., Hitt, L.M.: Beyond computation: information technology, organizational transformation and business performance. J. Econ. Perspect. **14**(4), 23–48 (2000). https://doi.org/10.1257/jep.14.4.23

Brynjolfsson, E., Hitt, L.M.: Computing productivity: firm-level evidence. Rev. Econ. Stat. **85**(4), 793–808 (2003). https://doi.org/10.1162/003465303772815736

Can, M., Ahmed, Z.: Towards sustainable development in the European Union countries: does economic complexity affect renewable and non-renewable energy consumption? Sustain. Dev. **31**(1), 439–451 (2023). https://doi.org/10.1002/sd.2402

Cass, D.: Optimum growth in an aggregative model of capital accumulation. The Rev. Econ. Stud. **32**(3), 233 (1965). https://doi.org/10.2307/2295827

Caves, R.E.: Multinational Enterprise and Economic Analysis. Cambridge University Press, Cambridge (1982)

Chamley, C.: Optimal taxation of capital income in general equilibrium with infinite lives. Econometrica **54**(3), 607–622 (1986). https://doi.org/10.2307/1911310

Choi, J., Mark, A.D., Usman, Z.: The Future of Work in Africa: Harnessing the Potential of Digital Technologies for All. Africa Development Forum. Washington, DC (2020). http://hdl.handle.net/10986/32124

Christensen, C.M., Grossman, J.H., Hwang, J.: The Innovator's Prescription: A Disruptive Solution for Health Care. McGraw-Hill, New York (2008)

Consoli, D.: Literature analysis on determinant factors and the impact of ICT in SMEs. Procedia Soc. Behav. Sci. **62**, 93–97 (2012). https://doi.org/10.1016/j.sbspro.2012.09.016

Dahmani, M., Mabrouki, M., Ben Youssef, A.: ICT, trade openness and economic growth in Tunisia: what is going wrong? Econ. Chang. Restruct. **55**(4), 2317–2336 (2022). https://doi.org/10.1007/s10644-022-09388-2

Datta, A., Agarwal, S.: Telecommunications and economic growth: a panel data approach. Appl. Econ. **36**(15), 1649–1654 (2004). https://doi.org/10.1080/0003684042000218552

Davison, R., Vogel, D., Harris, R., Jones, N.: Technology leapfrogging in developing countries - an inevitable luxury? Electron. J. Inform. Syst. Dev. Countries **1**(1), 1–10 (2000). https://doi.org/10.1002/j.1681-4835.2000.tb00005.x

De Hoyos, R.E., Sarafidis, V.: Testing for cross-sectional dependence in panel-data models. Stand. Genomic Sci. **6**(4), 482–496 (2006)

Deloitte: e-Transform Africa: Agriculture Sector Study: Sector Assessment and opportunities for ICT, Deloitte Consulting New York (2012)

Djankov, S., Ganser, T., McLiesh, C., Ramalho, R., Shleifer, A.: The effect of corporate taxes on investment and entrepreneurship. Am. Econ. J. Macroecon. **2**(3), 31–64 (2010). https://doi.org/10.1257/mac.2.3.31

Dutta, A.: Telecommunications and economic activity: an analysis of Granger causality. J. Manag. Inf. Syst. **17**(4), 71–95 (2001). https://doi.org/10.1080/07421222.2001.11045658

ECA, U., Union, A.: Assessing regional integration in Africa VIII: bringing the Continental Free Trade Area about, Economic Commission for Africa: United States of America (2017). https://policycommons.net/artifacts/7503/assessing-regional-integration-in-africa-viii/4460/

Enaifoghe, A.: Digitalisation of African economies in the fourth industrial revolution: opportunities for growth and industrialisation. African J. Dev. Stud. **11**(2), 31–53 (2021). https://doi.org/10.31920/2634-3649/2021/v11n2a2

Engle, R.F., Granger, C.W.J.: Co-integration and error correction: representation, estimation, and testing. Econometrica **55**(2), 251 (1987). https://www.jstor.org/stable/1913236

Fagerberg, J., Verspagen, B.: Technology-gaps, innovation-diffusion and transformation: an evolutionary interpretation. Res. Policy **31**(8–9), 1291–1304 (2002). https://doi.org/10.1016/S0048-7333(02)00064-1

Frees, E.W.: Assessing cross-sectional correlation in panel data. Journal of econometrics **69**(2), 393–414 (1995). https://doi.org/10.1016/0304-4076(94)01658-M

Frees, E.W.: Longitudinal and Panel Data: Analysis and Applications in the Social Sciences. Cambridge University Press, Cambridge (2004). https://doi.org/10.1017/CBO9780511790928

Friedman, M.: The use of ranks to avoid the assumption of normality implicit in the analysis of variance. J. Am. Stat. Assoc. **32**(200), 675–701 (1937). https://doi.org/10.1080/01621459.1937.10503522

Gallegos, D., et al.: Connecting Africa Through Broadband: A Strategy for Doubling Connectivity by 2021 and Reaching Universal Access by 2030. World Bank, Washington DC (2020)

Griffith, R., Redding, S., Reenen, J.V.: Mapping the two faces of R&D: productivity growth in a panel of OECD industries. Rev. Econ. Stat. **86**(4), 883–895 (2004). https://doi.org/10.1162/0034653043125194

Griliches, Z.: The Search for R&D Spillovers. NBER Working Paper No. 3768. National Bureau of Economic Research, Cambridge, MA (1991). https://doi.org/10.3386/w3768

GSMA: Mobile Money Metrics-Regulatory Index. https://www.gsma.com/mobilemoneymetrics/#regulatoryindex?y=2019 (2019). Accessed on 20 Jan 2021

Haddad, M., Harrison, A.: Are there positive spillovers from direct foreign investment?: evidence from panel data for Morocco. J. Dev. Econ. **42**(1), 51–74 (1993). https://doi.org/10.1016/0304-3878(93)90072-U

Helleiner, G.K.: Transnational corporations and direct foreign investment. Handb. Dev. Econ. **2**, 1441–1480 (1989). https://doi.org/10.1016/S1573-4471(89)02014-0

Henry, M., Kneller, R., Milner, C.: Trade, technology transfer and national efficiency in developing countries. Eur. Econ. Rev. **53**(2), 237–254 (2009). https://doi.org/10.1016/j.euroecorev.2008.05.001

Huchet-Bourdon, M., Le Mouël, C., Vijil, M.: The relationship between trade openness and economic growth: some new insights on the openness measurement issue. World Econ. **41**(1), 59–76 (2018). https://doi.org/10.1111/twec.12586

International Telecommunication Union: Measuring the Information Society: ICT Opportunity Index and World Telecommunication/ICT Indicators. International Telecommunication Union (2007)

International Telecommunication Union: Digital trends in Africa 2021 Information and communication technology trends and developments in the Africa region 2017–2020 (2021). http://handle.itu.int/11.1002/pub/81836c3c-en

Jarque, C.M., Bera, A.K.: A test for normality of observations and regression residuals. Int. Stat. Rev. **55**, 163–172 (1987). https://doi.org/10.2307/1403192

Johansen, S.: Statistical analysis of cointegration vectors. J. Econ. Dyn. Control **12**(2–3), 231–254 (1988). https://doi.org/10.1016/0165-1889(88)90041-3

Johansen, S.: Estimation and hypothesis testing of cointegration vectors in gaussian vector autoregressive models. Econometrica **59**(6), 1551 (1991). https://doi.org/10.2307/2938278

Judd, K.L.: Redistributive taxation in a simple perfect foresight model. J. Public Econ. **28**(1), 59–83 (1985). https://doi.org/10.1016/0047-2727(85)90020-9

Kalai, M., Zghidi, N.: Foreign direct investment, trade, and economic growth in MENA countries: empirical analysis using ARDL bounds testing approach. J. Knowl. Econ. **10**(1), 397–421 (2019). https://doi.org/10.1007/s13132-017-0460-6

Kao, C.: Spurious regression and residual-based tests for cointegration in panel data. Journal of econometrics **90**(1), 1–44 (1999). https://doi.org/10.1016/S0304-4076(98)00023-2

Karavias, Y., Tzavalis, E.: Testing for unit roots in short panels allowing for a structural break. Comput. Stat. Data Anal. **76**, 391–407 (2014). https://doi.org/10.1016/j.csda.2012.10.014

Keller, W.: International technology diffusion. J. Econ. Lit. **42**(3), 752–782 (2004). https://www.jstor.org/stable/3217250

Kim, D.H., Lin, S.C.: Trade and growth at different stages of economic development. J. Dev. Stud. **45**(8), 1211–1224 (2009). https://doi.org/10.1080/00220380902862937

Kolko, J.: Broadband and local growth. J. Urban Econ. **71**(1), 100–113 (2012). https://doi.org/10. 1016/j.jue.2011.07.004

Koopmans, T.: On the concept of optimal economic growth. In Study Week on the Econometric Approach to Development Planning, 7–13 Oct. Pontifical Academy of Science, Rome (1965). https://cowles.yale.edu/sites/default/files/files/pub/d01/d0163.pdf

Kouam, J.C., Asongu, S.: The non-linear effects of fixed broadband on economic growth in Africa. Journal of Economic Studies (2022). https://doi.org/10.1108/JES-03-2022-0159

Landes, D.S.: The Unbound Prometheus: Technological Change and Industrial Development in Western Europe from 1750 to the present. Cambridge University Press (2003)

Lehr, B., Lichtenberg, F.: Information technology and its impact on productivity: firm-level evidence from government and private data sources, 1977–1993. Can. J. Econ. **32**(2), 335–362 (1999). https://doi.org/10.2307/136426

Li, R.Y.M.: Internet boost the economic growth of Mainland China? Discovering knowledge from our World Wide Web. Global Bus. Manag. Res.: An In. J. **3**(3/4), 345–355 (2011). https://ssrn.com/abstract=2287867

Liu, S.Q., Sang, S.X., Liu, H.H., Zhu, Q.P.: Growth characteristics and genetic types of pores and fractures in a high-rank coal reservoir of the southern Qinshui basin. Ore Geol. Rev. **64**, 140–151 (2015). https://doi.org/10.1016/j.oregeorev.2014.06.018

Lucas, R.E.: On the mechanics of economic development. J. Monet. Econ. **22**(1), 3–42 (1988). https://doi.org/10.1016/0304-3932(88)90168-7

McKinnon, R.I.: Money and Capital in Economic Development. The Brookings Institution, Washington, D.C. (1973)

Mehmood, B., Siddiqui, W.: What causes what? panel cointegration approach on investment in telecommunication and economic growth: case of Asian countries. Rom. Econ. J. **16**(47), 3–16 (2013)

Naanaa, I.D., Sellaouti, F.: Technological diffusion and growth: case of the Tunisian manufacturing sector. J. Knowl. Econ. **8**(1), 369–383 (2017). https://doi.org/10.1007/s13132-015-0270-7

Nadiri, M.I., Nandi, B., Akoz, K.K.: Impact of modern communication infrastructure on productivity, production structure and factor demands of US industries: Impact revisited. Telecommun. Policy **42**(6), 433–451 (2018). https://doi.org/10.1016/j.telpol.2018.03.008

Nelson, R.R.: The simple economics of basic scientific research. J. Polit. Econ. **67**(3), 297–306 (1959). https://doi.org/10.1086/258177

Nelson, R., Phelps, E.S.: Investment in humans, technological diffusion, and economic growth. Am. Econ. Rev. **56**(1/2), 69–75 (1966). https://www.jstor.org/stable/1821269

Niebel, T.: ICT and economic growth–Comparing developing, emerging and developed countries. World Dev. **104**, 197–211 (2018). https://doi.org/10.1016/j.worlddev.2017.11.024

OECD: Dynamiques du développement en Afrique 2021: Transformation digitale et qualité de l'emploi. OECD, Paris (2021)

Ojo, T.: Political Economy of ICT4D and Africa. In: Servaes, J. (ed.) Handbook of Communication for Development and Social Change, pp. 1243–1255. Springer Singapore, Singapore (2020). https://doi.org/10.1007/978-981-15-2014-3_64

Ongori, H., Migiro, S.O.: Information and communication technologies adoption in SMEs: literature review. JCE **2**(1), 93–104 (2010). https://doi.org/10.1108/17561391011019041

Ozawa, T.: Foreign direct investment and economic development. Transnational Corporations **1**(1), 27–54 (1992)

Ozturk, I.: Foreign direct investment-growth nexus: a review of the recent literature. Int. J. Appl. Econometrics Quantitative Stud. **4**(2), 79–98 (2007). http://www.usc.es/economet/reviews/ija eqs424.pdf

Palvia, P., Baqir, N., Nemati, H.: ICT for socio-economic development: a citizens' perspective. Inform. Manag. **55**(2), 160–176 (2018). https://doi.org/10.1016/j.im.2017.05.003

Paulo, L.D.D., Lima, R.C.D.A., Tigre, R.: Corruption and economic growth in Latin America and the Caribbean. Rev. Dev. Econ. **26**(2), 756–773 (2022). https://doi.org/10.1111/rode.12859

Pedroni, P.: Panel cointegration: asymptotic and finite sample properties of pooled time series tests with an application to the PPP hypothesis. Economet. Theor. **20**(3), 597–625 (2004). https://doi.org/10.1017/S0266466604203073

Perroux, F.: L'économie du XX siècle, 3 éd. 1969. PUF, Paris (1961)

Persyn, D., Westerlund, J.: Error-correction–based cointegration tests for panel data. Stand. Genomic Sci. **8**(2), 232–241 (2008). https://doi.org/10.1177/1536867X0800800205

Pesaran, M.H.: General diagnostic tests for cross section dependence in panels. Cambridge Working Papers in Economics No. 435, University of Cambridge, and CESifo Working Paper Series No. 1229 (2004). https://doi.org/10.17863/CAM.5113

Pesaran, M.H., Shin, Y., Smith, R.J.: Bounds testing approaches to the analysis of level relationships. J. Appl. Economet. **16**(1), 289–326 (2001). https://doi.org/10.1002/jae.616

Pesaran, M.H.:. Estimation and inference in large heterogeneous panels with cross section dependence. SSRN385123 (2003). https://doi.org/10.2139/ssrn.385123

Pesaran, M.H.: Estimation and inference in large heterogeneous panels with cross section dependence. Econometrica **74**(4), 967–1012 (2006). https://doi.org/10.1111/j.1468-0262.2006.00692.x

Pesaran, M.H.: A simple panel unit root test in the presence of cross-section dependence. J. Appl. Economet. **22**(2), 265–312 (2007). https://doi.org/10.1002/jae.951

Pesaran, M.H.: Testing weak cross-sectional dependence in large panels. Economet. Rev. **34**(6–10), 1089–1117 (2015). https://doi.org/10.1080/07474938.2014.956623

Pesaran, M.H., Ullah, A., Yamagata, T.: A bias-adjusted LM test of error cross section independence. Economet. J. **11**(1), 105–127 (2008). https://doi.org/10.1111/j.1368-423X.2007.00227.x

Prahalad, C.K.: The Fortune at the Bottom of the Pyramid: Eradicating Poverty Through Profits. Wharton School Publishing, Upper Saddle River (2006)

Pyka, A., Andersen, E.S.: Introduction: long-term economic development–demand, finance, organization, policy and innovation in a Schumpeterian perspective. J. Evol. Econ. **22**(4), 621–625 (2012). https://doi.org/10.1007/s00191-012-0279-z

Quah, D.: Technology dissemination and economic growth: Some lessons for the new economy (2002)

Ramsey, F.P.: A mathematical theory of saving. Econ. J. **38**(152), 543–559 (1928). https://doi.org/10.2307/2224098

Romer, P.M.: Increasing returns and Long Run Growth. J. Polit. Econ. **94**(5), 1002–1037 (1986). https://www.jstor.org/stable/2677818

Romer, P.M.: Endogenous technological change. J. Polit. Econ. **98**(5), 71–102 (1990). https://www.jstor.org/stable/2937632

Safronchuk, M.V., Sergeeva, M.V.: The concept of economic growth through digital economy perspective. In: Popkova, E.G., Sergi, B.S. (eds.) ISC 2019. LNNS, vol. 198, pp. 1264–1271. Springer, Cham (2021). https://doi.org/10.1007/978-3-030-69415-9_138

Sarafidis, V., Robertson, D.: On the impact of cross section dependence in short dynamic panel estimation. University of Cambridge (2006)

Sassi, S., Goaied, M.: Financial development, ICT diffusion and economic growth: lessons from MENA region. Telecommun. Policy **37**(4–5), 252–261 (2013). https://doi.org/10.1016/j.telpol.2012.12.004

Schumpeter, J.A.: The theory of economic development: an inquiry into profits, capital, credit, interest and the business cycle. Harvard University Press (1934)

Schumpeter, J.A.: Capitalism, Socialism and Democracy. Harper & Row (1942)

Shahzad, U., Elheddad, M., Swart, J., Ghosh, S., Dogan, B.: The role of biomass energy consumption and economic complexity on environmental sustainability in G7 economies. Bus. Strateg. Environ. **32**(1), 781–801 (2023). https://doi.org/10.1002/bse.3175

Shamim, F.: The ICT environment, financial sector and economic growth: a cross-country analysis. J. Econ. Stud. **34**(4), 352–370 (2007). https://doi.org/10.1108/01443580710817452

Shaw, E.S.: Financial Deepening in Economic Development. Oxford University Press, New York (1973)

Shin, Y., Byungchul, Y., Greenwood-Nimmo, M.: Modelling asymmetric cointegration and dynamic multipliers in a nonlinear ARDL framework. In: Sickles, R.C., Horrace, W.C. (eds.) Festschrift in Honor of Peter Schmidt: Econometric Methods and Applications, pp. 281–314. Springer New York, New York, NY (2014). https://doi.org/10.1007/978-1-4899-8008-3_9

Solow, R.M.: A contribution to the theory of economic growth. Q. J. Econ. **70**(1), 65–94 (1956). https://doi.org/10.2307/1884513

Steinmueller, W.E.: ICTs and the possibilities for leapfrogging by developing countries. Int. Labour Rev. **140**(2), 193–210 (2001). https://doi.org/10.1111/j.1564-913X.2001.tb00220.x

Tan, B., Ng, E., Jiang, J.: The process of technology leapfrogging: case analysis of the national ICT infrastructure development journey of Azerbaijan. Int. J. Inf. Manage. **38**(1), 311–316 (2018). https://doi.org/10.1016/j.ijinfomgt.2017.10.008

Tapscott, D.: The Digital Economy: Promise and Peril in the Age of Networked Intelligence. McGraw-Hill, New York, NY (1996). https://doi.org/10.5860/choice.33-5199

Thompson, J.H., Garbacz, C.: Economic impacts of mobile versus fixed broadband. Telecommun. Policy **35**(11), 999–1009 (2011)

Tranos, E.: The causal effect of the internet infrastructure on the economic development of European city regions. Spat. Econ. Anal. **7**(3), 319–337 (2012). https://doi.org/10.1080/17421772.2012.694140

Tripathi, M., Inani, S.K.: Does internet affect economic growth in sub-Saharan Africa? Econ. Bull. **36**(4), 1993–2002 (2016)

UNCTAD. UNDP: Human Development Index Reveals Development Crises, Human Development Reports (2003)

UNDP:. Income inequality trends in Sub-Saharan Africa: divergence, determinants and consequences. (2017)

UNESCO: National learning platforms and tools. United Nations Educational, Scientific and Cultural Organization (2020)

Veblen, T.: Imperial Germany and the Industrial Revolution. The University of Michigan Press, New York (1915). https://doi.org/10.4324/9780429337727

Viviers, W., Parry, A., van Rensburg, S.J.: Africa's digital future: From theory to action. In: The Future of International Trade and Development, vol. 1. AOSIS, Cape Town (2021). https://doi.org/10.4102/aosis.2021.BK199

Vu, K.M.: ICT as a source of economic growth in the information age: empirical evidence from the 1996–2005 period. Telecommun. Policy **35**(4), 357–372 (2011). https://doi.org/10.1016/j.telpol.2011.02.008

Westerlund, J.: Testing for error correction in panel data. Oxford Bull. Econ. Stat. **69**(6), 709–748 (2007). https://doi.org/10.1111/j.1468-0084.2007.00477.x

World Bank: World development report 2016: Digital dividends. World Bank Publications, Washington, DC (2016). https://doi.org/10.1596/978-1-4648-0671-1

World Bank:. Leapfrogging: The Key to Africa's Development? from Constraints to Investment Opportunities. Washington, DC (2017). http://hdl.handle.net/10986/28440

World Bank: Africa's Pulse: An Analysis of Issues Shaping Africa's Economic Future. Washington, DC (2021a). http://hdl.handle.net/10986/36332

World Bank: Africa's Pulse: Charting the Course for Economic Recovery. Washington, DC (2021b). http://hdl.handle.net/10986/35342

Yoo, S.H., Kwak, S.J.: Information technology and economic development in Korea: a causality study. Int. J. Technol. Manage. **27**(1), 57–67 (2004). https://doi.org/10.1504/IJTM.2004.003881

Online Session

Societal Complexity Problem of E Learning Adoption in a Post Covid Context: A Tunisian University Case

Sana Essaber[ID], Ibticem Ben Zammel[ID], and Sana Tebessi[(✉)] [ID]

Higher Institute of Accountancy and Business Administration, Manouba University, La Manouba, Tunisia
sanaessaber@gmail.com, ibticembenzammel@gmail.com, sana.tebessi@iscae.uma.tn

Abstract. The COVID-19 crisis has raised significant concerns for the entire education community: policymakers, educators, and learners. School and university closures around the world have disrupted the learning and lives of a generation of students. Despite efforts to maintain educational provision through distance and online learning, unprecedented 'institutional' de- schooling has partly taken place, with an impact on learning. How to prevent this risk and mitigate its impact on learning inequalities and lifelong learning trajectories has become a major policy issue. This research aims to provide a conceptual framework for e-learning by adopting a complex societal approach that illustrates the profound changes brought about by the adoption of this education mode in society. From a theoretical foundation and based on our empirical explorations on one of the University of Manouba (UMA) institutions that chose to pursue this E-learning approach, this research identified the economic and social factors of E-learning analyzed through the complex societal approach developed by DeTombe (2008) in order to propose a redefinition of this mode of education. We show in this research how the different learning acquired as a result of the COVID-19 crisis constitutes a real societal issue and leads not only to a transformation of learning techniques but also to profound societal mutations in the different groups affected by this change process.

Keywords: Societal complexity approach · Impact · Crisis · Transformation · Developing Countries · Post COVID

1 Introduction

The E-learning experience following the COVID-19 crisis in Tunisia has started with an official ministerial initiative to implement a hybrid mode of teaching via learning platforms. The efforts of the State were directed towards supporting the technological infrastructure of universities and providing free connection to the moodle platform for students. Thus, the crisis has allowed the different actors of higher education (teachers, ministry, universities, students, and unions) to become aware of the relevance of E-learning as a complementary learning mode.

R. Jallouli et al. (Eds.): ICDEc 2023, LNBIP 485, pp. 349–359, 2023.
https://doi.org/10.1007/978-3-031-42788-6_21

Most university institutions are trying to develop relevant mechanisms in order to deliver knowledge in an equitable manner and eliminate the geographical, linguistic and social barriers.

It is worth to be reminded that Tunisia has been committed to E-learning since 2002 with the launch of the Tunisian Virtual University (UVT). This commitment has been realized by the decision to increase the distance courses to 20% of the volume of the classroom program in universities in 2011. The field has been prepared by training students in the use of Information and Communication Technologies (ICTs). Tunisia ranks 5th among the African countries in the use of ICTs according to the NRI (Network Readiness Index) of the World Economic Forum, and it benefits from a fairly developed infrastructure. The digital sector in Tunisia contributes to 4.3% of the Tunisian GDP (INS, 2021). Moreover, 17.2% of students in Tunisia are enrolled in ICT courses. The Internet access rate is estimated at 64% in 2020 for a number of subscribers amounting to 7.55 million.

For all these reasons, several Tunisian institutions have opted for the perpetuation of E-learning in view of its advantages, thus taking advantage of the State support in the framework of its digitalization strategy (e-government project).

However, the sudden shift to e-learning induced by the Covid-19 crisis has disrupted the educational system in the Tunisian universities and prompted a reconsideration of the active teaching pedagogy, the technological and administrative infrastructure, and the valorization of the active learner's role in the learning process.

Based on an exploratory study analyzed through the complex societal approach developed by DeTombe (2008), we will show how the various learning approaches acquired as a result of the covid 19 crisis constitute a real challenge for society and lead not only to a transformation of learning techniques but also to profound societal mutations in the different groups affected by this change.

For the rest of the study, we proceed as follows. Part 2 is a review of the factors contributing to the effectiveness of E-learning and it emphasizes the complex societal aspect of this learning. Part 3 describes the methodology adopted in the study, while the results and interpretation of the complex societal process related to the adoption of E-learning are detailed in Part 4. Finally, we conclude in the fifth and last part.

2 Factors of E-learning Efficiency: Towards a Complex Societal Approach

The e-learning is considered as a privileged learning mode drawing on technological innovations covering all learning formulas, assisted by computer, designed to be used on internet, intranet or extranet (Sousa and Rocha, 2019; Al-Fraihat et al., 2020, Dick et al., 2020, Wijekumar, 2021).

The choice of using this learning mode at the level of the Tunisian universities is explained by the acquired advantages in terms of saving time and effort. It is assimilated to a particular teaching mode based on the availability of students of teaching content via an electronic medium. Therefore, it allows a permanent learning, customized to the student's needs, independent of spatial and temporal constraints (Sousa and Rocha, 2019).

The Equity, essentially opportunity equity, is one of the major concerns of the political authorities. It is an integral part of the notion of quality in higher education. In this paper, we identify three key factors in the implementation and sustainability of e- learning:

2.1 Frustration Related to the Structural Transformation of the Teaching Method

E-learning is one of the new emerging technologies replacing or complementing the traditional pedagogical approaches. This practice is distinguished by certain particularities insofar as it implements new pedagogical approaches (Ben Zammel et al., 2016; Dick et al., 2020).

Subjected to technological and social pressures, following the COVID crisis, public universities have not ceased to be adaptive in order to respond to the request of the Ministry of University Education to ensure pedagogical continuity. They have embarked on E-learning project crisis concretized by the evolution of platforms, technological tools of teaching modes and students belonging to Z generation.

However, the implementation of e-learning project crisis has led to a profound change in learning methods, generating resistance on the part of the involved actors (Dick et al., 2020). Indeed, the requirement to go beyond the universities and its actors in the covid context has resulted in a change in learning pedagogies and provoked a change management approach.

The learning process is seen as a collaborative relationship that supports knowledge construction, rather than as a simple process of transmitting knowledge. Knowledge is a collaborative construction: the learner must be placed in a context that allows him or her to construct knowledge, and the teacher must change roles and help students to acquire knowledge (Dick et al., 2020). The adoption of such approach to learning is legitimized by the idea that knowledge can only be obtained if the learner takes an active part in the learning process (Ben Zammel and Najar, 2021).

2.2 The Technological Infrastructure

Unlike traditional teaching, e-learning efficiency is mainly determined by the technological aspect (Sousa and Rocha, 2019, Ben Zammel et al., 2018). Indeed, many studies have shown that technology in different forms has positive effects on learning (Parasuraman et al., 2005; Al-Fraihat et al., 2020).

Lack of funds is one of the main obstacles to the development of distance education in public universities. This new education method is hindered by the lack of resources, accessibility of technological infrastructure and the importance of social factors mainly in the developing countries (Al-Fraihat et al., 2020).

Experience shows that the technological challenges can cause frustration and dropout (Parasuraman et al., 2005; Al-Fraihat et al., 2020, Malik et Al-Toubi, 2018). Hence, characterized by the physical separation of the teacher and the student during the teachings, e-learning can be considered as a source of de-motivation.

2.3   Change Management for a Sustainable E- Learning Experience

The efficiency of e-learning depends on the change management of the adopted pedagogical approach, but also remains among the involved actors.

University teachers are particularly at the center of this change. This transformation goes from the simple introduction of some tools (platform, EAD, meetings, trainings, etc.) to the redesign of the whole teaching process.

Similarly, the student is invited to actively participate in the learning process. In this way, the motivation to learn or teach emerges as an essential condition for learning. Effectively managing this change depends on several elements such as:

The first factor is Individual efficiency, it is reflected in the beliefs and convictions of people in their abilities to achieve behaviours through the use of technologies (Artino, 2007, Wijekumar, 2021). It means an individual's belief in his or her ability to successfully perform a given task which plays an important role in motivation to learn. Training is essential to support these changes by developing new skills needed to perform their jobs.

Also, the beliefs of the individual in relation to the achievement of a behaviour are strongly influenced by the opinion of people or reference groups (Wijekumar, 2021), Hislop, 2013). This means that when teachers encourage the use of e-learning, students will therefore perceive its usefulness.

On the other hand, learning alone at a distance can lead to student demotivation. For this reason, it is recommended to encourage social interaction through knowledge sharing. Thus, the integration of e-learning as a teaching mode based on technologies evokes a socialization process revealing the interaction between technology and its users. Indeed, e-learning technologies promote resources sharing in the form of texts, images, videos allowing an interactive communication through different tools such as wikis, forums, chat and peer-to-peer activities (Sousa and Rocha, 2019, Wijekumar, 2021).

3   Methodology

Realizing that there was no specific analysis that directly addresses complex societal problems related to E-learning adoption, we have first used the methodological approach of storytelling which for us constituted an empirical asset, then we defined the thematic content analysis based on a post-covid context on which storytelling has been conducted, and finally we assessed the economic and social factors of E-learning and explained how its adoption constitutes a real complex societal problem.

3.1   Storytelling as an Empirical Research Methodology

In this research, we have mobilized the methodological approach of storytelling, which is a method used to investigate the organizational practices and discourses. This method has become increasingly popular with the rise of new technologies, digital storytelling and new management practices, leading us to storytelling management. The diversity of the actors and objects involved in our study and the nature of the available data, have led us to adopt this methodology for data qualitative analysis. The storytelling analysis method best fits our research since it constitutes a way of accessing deep realities by exploring the "conveyed symbolism" (Chautard and Collin-Lachaud, 2019, P.33). This methodological approach aims at exploring the experiences and reality, which presents itself to us as an empirical asset, in order to organize and transmit the experiences of e-learning in knowledge perspective to others. Indeed, our research aims to explore how the university institutions have evolved by introducing e-learning in periods of crisis and pushes us to question the collective and organizational dynamics that have influenced individuals and markets by putting their transformations into stories.

3.2 The Study Context

Our analysis based on storytelling has been conducted over the selected qualitative materials in the context of a case study (Yin, 2003, Chautard and Collin-Lachaud, 2019) in this particular case of the Higher Institute of Accounting and Business Administration (ISCAE), University of Manouba (UMA) and has proceeded to a triangulation of data collection tools (Yin, 2003). It should be highlighted that two phases of data collection have been conducted: A first phase taking place during the adoption E-learning during the covid-19 crisis and a second phase of collection conducted during the implementation of hybrid E-learning in the same institution. For this purpose, we have resorted to documents shared by the institution (emails, reports, minutes, etc.). Furthermore, our status as intervening researcher has allowed us to participate in the different meetings organized with the different project actors. In this same way, we have followed and have witnessed the E-learning experience in this institution as a participant (crisis E-learning) and coordinator (hybrid E-learning). Finally, twelve semi-structured interviews have been conducted with the teachers who participated in crisis E- learning and a focus group has been conducted with the teachers who have adopted the hybrid mode as their preferred teaching mode post-covid.

4 Results and Discussion: Towards a Societal Transformation in Adopting E-Learning Approach

The results of a thematic content analysis based on a post-covid allow us to assess the economic and social factors of E-learning and to show that its adoption constitutes a real complex societal problem (DeTombe, 2008), and leads us to a renewal of the definition of E-learning that includes the complex societal aspect.

4.1 The E-learning Approach: A Process of Societal Transformation

We have mobilized DeTombe's approach (2008, 2013, 2015) to prove the existence of a complex societal problem related to the institutionalization of E-learning as a teaching mode in the Tunisian university after the Covid period.

According to DeTombes (2015); "When a person or group of people becomes aware of a complex social problem they can address the problem in more detail through reading, discussion, and observation. This process transforms the vague concept of awareness. The problem into a clearer problem .The problem can be a challenge or a threat, a challenge in terms of obtaining new and interesting opportunities; a threat because it causes or will harm a certain group of people. By thinking about the problem, they can decide whether the problem should be dealt with politically or non-politically."

A more precise definition of a complex social problem is given by DeTombes (2013): "A complex social problem is a real problem that has a large and often different impact on different social groups. The problem often affects all levels of society, micro, meso and macro. Often the problem seems to "go away". The problem is dynamic; it changes during its development. The future development of the problem is uncertain. Awareness of the problem and putting it on the political agenda is often difficult. It is difficult to understand and deal with the problem. Only changes are possible, not "solutions". The problem contains information, power and emotional components. The problem consists of many phenomena that are intricately intertwined. Information is often missing; the information is incomplete, uncertain or contradictory. The problem is multidisciplinary and requires theories from different fields to explain what is happening. There are many parties. Each party has a different vision, a different definition, and different goals and desires. Often the parties have different "solutions" to the problem. Different parties have different influence on the problem. A problem often creates a lot of emotion in society."

In short, social complexity theory focuses on the entire spectrum of the problem-handling process, from problem awareness (step 1) to assessing the dynamics of the problem (step 2), focusing on the problem; how difficult it is (step 3), identifying different and interrelated interventions (step 4), assessing the interdisciplinary nature of the problem (step 5), identifying many parties (step 6), and concluding that the problem often generates many emotions in society (step 7), (see Fig. 1).

Step 1: The Problem Has Different Impacts on Different Groups of Society and is a Real Problem in Life

The content analysis identified the impact and importance of adopting e-learning on the different involved actors. The results emphasize the consideration of this practice especially in times of covid 19 crisis at the time of the confinement "distance courses are the unique means to stay in touch with our students" (teacher 3, crisis e- learning), "it is essential to ensure a pedagogical continuity to succeed in the academic year" (teacher 1, crisis e-learning). Furthermore, during the post- covid period, this teaching mode has given students a certain flexibility to organize their time and allow them to continue their university studies regardless of social and geographical constraints: "e-learning allows students who are far from the institution or who work to access a master's degree and to continue their studies without worrying about problems related to class attendance" (Head of the Virtual Department, hybrid e-learning). This not only saves time for the student, but also financial savings related to travel, accommodation, etc. This learning mode thus contributes to reducing social inequalities by allowing everyone access to quality education, as targeted in ODD 4[1]. From a structural point of view, it allows, among other things, to solve the problems related to the lack of classrooms "hybrid teaching has made it possible to overcome the problem of classrooms and to arrange a

---

[1] ODD 4: Quality education: Ensuring equitable access to quality education for all and promoting lifelong learning opportunities.

better schedule for students" (minutes of the scientific council) as well as that related to the costs of teaching which weigh heavily on the state budget. Therefore, focusing only on the education quality without considering the socio-economic elements can hinder its implementation and can generate various problems and conflicts.

Step 2: The Problem is Dynamic
The unions reject the use of E-learning, explaining that it reduces the equality of opportunities for access to education because of the unequal allocation of financial and technological resources to students. *"To implement E learning, it is necessary to give the means to poor students to be able to adopt it and especially not to accuse them of being lazy wrongly, because they have no money to equip themselves"* (Teacher unionist, crisis e- learning). They specify that Tunisian universities suffer from a recurrent shortage of computer hardware and software which makes the adoption of this teaching mode precarious. Challenges of confidentiality, data security, Internet connection speed, virus attacks hinder any attempt of digitalization. We can see that generalizing E- Learning to at all education levels would be difficult, unless we take into account these dynamic constraints to succeed in driving change related to E-Learning adoption, operation and sustainability.

Step 3: It is Difficult to Handle the Problem
E-learning is a solution, but because of its inadequate implementation, it can lead to societal problems. During the crisis education, the adopted approach was related to a desire for educational continuity that did not respect the proper method of E-learning. It is a sharing of unscripted course resources (pdf, video...) accompanied by online meetings. We have noted several criticisms in the teachers' observations about the ethics of its adoption *"It is a disappointment to see some colleagues who are happy to finish their course with a PDF file of which thousands are available on the internet and a chat of which hundreds of forums are accessible and people from all over the world can answer questions"* (Teacher 2, crisis E-learning).

Several actions have been recently implemented as a project of awareness, support and monitoring has been implemented for the benefit of teachers since April 2020, mandatory training and technical sessions, the use of a unique platform namely the platform designed by the virtual university of Tunis UVT in order to avoid all the loopholes related to data security, administrative control (compliance with the charter) and design a pilot project for master students to adopt the hybrid mode (small number of students and equipped with the necessary tools and resources).

Step 4: The Problem Consists of Many Interlinked Elements
As we have indicated, the E-learning project involves several actors: the learner, the tutor, the administration, the university, the E-learning unit, and the union. The diversity of these actors does not make the problem of adopting and sustaining E- learning easy, since it involves several complicated and interrelated elements.

On the part of the E-learning unit, colleagues need to undergo training: *"colleagues need to launch the courses; however we can't start without training"* (obs 1 post covid). The administration plays a role in adjusting schedules and fixing the timetables established for this purpose in order to satisfy the teachers and the students.

"there are teachers who have in the timetable in the same day both courses for the Masters' Degree and courses for the Licenses Degree (which does not benefit from the hybrid mode) and therefore when they come to teach they will have off hours because at the time of the E learning course, they will not teach but they will have to wait for the face-to-face course for license students" (Teacher 7; hybrid E- learning).

Step 5: The Problem is Interdisciplinary and Requires Background Theories from Many Fields to Understand What is Going on
In order to properly initiate E-learning and move towards the digitalization of higher education in the country, all the participants must be committed to this revolutionary approach from the political, economic, social, technological and legal (PESTEL) perspective.

Several data that take into consideration the social aspect of E-learning are necessary to carry out the learning digitalization project which is among the priorities of the e-government project of Tunisia. This strategic orientation will enable us to meet the expectations of the new generation (generation Z) and to guarantee knowledge transfer (access to information) but above all the new approach to education (transparency, equity) by promoting digital inclusion and improving the individuals' life quality (disabled people, economically disadvantaged people). In order to respond to the ecological issues, E-learning offers several advantages: zero waste, minimizing transport and therefore polluting emissions, reducing energy costs, etc.

It is the role of the university to establish a regulatory framework and an adequate technological infrastructure for E-learning planning. The university has also established an *EAD unit* that accompanies and coordinates the various activities related to this system.

Step 6: Numerous Parties Are Implicated and Each Has a Different Influence on the Solution
We can say that several parties are involved in E- learning and each one differently impacts its implementation and sustainability. The importance of the actors' role and their interdisciplinarity (students, tutors, unions, and administration), have an impact in the outcome and each has a different influence. As we have highlighted, following the covid crisis, the University of Manouba (UMA) has decided to organize hybrid courses, alternating face- to-face and e-learning, which concerns only the master's students, responding to the financial constraint and the availability of students' equipment revealed in this research. This decision is supported by connectivity difficulties, computer equipment purchase, and timetables programming on the part of the administration, accentuated by the refusal of union representatives to accept this learning mode (the principle of equal opportunity). In addition, several teachers offered to provide distance learning courses. These teachers were optimistic about using this teaching method because it enables them to use different techniques of teaching tools offered by the platform improving the learning level *"having the possibility to put video capsules and that's where it would be interesting. Especially for subjects like finance or math where*

we record ourselves and make video sequences with slides and send them as a capsule to the students".

Step 7: The Problem Frequently Leads to Much Emotion in the Society

E-learning is an efficient solution to avoid infrastructure expenses for the State and a solution for students who cannot travel for different reasons (disability, high cost of studies, etc.) and makes possible equal opportunities between learners. This education mode can contribute to fight against school dropout and women marginalization, especially in rural areas. This paradigm change is certainly a source of deep emotion in society. The students were enthusiastic, motivated, involved, focused and attentive. They repeatedly intervened either to ask questions or to give illustrative examples. *"I truly believe that the basic ingredient for success in E-learning is empathy and caring on our part, and motivation and overcoming the fear of the unknown (E-learning) on the part of the students. This is certainly not to minimize the logistical problems and lack of resources among some of our students, but I can see that the university is doing what it has to do to help them."*

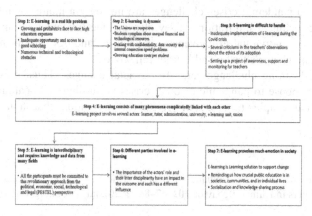

Fig. 1. Is e-learning approach a complex process of societal transformations?

5 Conclusion

E-learning has shown its importance especially during the COVID crisis as an unavoidable solution to any kind of crisis, not only health crisis.

Social science knowledge is an indispensable part of the global scientific, policy and social mobilization effort required. It can also perform the role of being a co-designer of relevant and effective solution strategies to succeed the generalization of e- learning, namely in the developing countries. Adopting some new educational policies for SDG4 that may lead to co-benefits between education quality and other sustainable development goals, have gained increasing attention in recent years. Initially, our analysis reveals a paradigm shift in society with respect to the adoption of e-learning.

Positive effects of technology on learning would be noticed (Sousa and Rocha, 2019). The effectiveness of teaching has become essentially technology- determined (Sousa and Rocha, 2019) and the availability of technological resources is a major condition for e-learning implementation. Thus, the availability of a technology platform is needed to use web-based technologies, the basis for e-learning. That's why giving learners a practice session on the computer in advance of the training would be helpful in improving attitudes, especially feelings of self- efficiency (Ho, 2009; Ho and Kuo, 2010; Ho et al., 2010).

E-learning creates new challenges for the global society. Adopting this new approach of learning is a complex process of societal transformations that should be studied as such. The contribution of the social sciences is crucial to the understanding of these change processes. The growing body of knowledge on E learning techniques, its determinants and consequences is not matched by an equivalent understanding of the societal changes it poses.

Despite the growing scientific evidence, the consequences of e-learning and its efficiency remain contested by different groups in society and are associated with different perceptions of uncertainty, risks and urgency.

Responses to pandemic crises challenges are not only a matter of infrastructural adjustments or technical innovations. They also include fundamental changes in our way of educating, individual effectiveness of using technology, group influence and social image, knowledge sharing and learner reflexivity.

As such, e-learning challenges are also societal changes. Thus, it is fair to say that effective response to pandemic or other crises perturbing classical approaches to education involve complex processes of societal transformations that should be studied.

References

Al-Fraihat, D., Joy, M., Ra'ed M., Sinclair, J.: Evaluating E-learning systems success: An empirical study. Computers in Human Behavior **102**, 67–86 (2020). https://doi.org/10.1016/j.chb.2019.08.004

Artino, A.R.: Motivational beliefs and perceptions of instructional quality: predicting satisfaction with online training. J. Comp. Assi. Learn. **24**, 260–270 (2007). https://doi.org/10.1111/j.1365-2729.2007.00258.x

Ben Zammel, I., Chichti, F., Gharbi, J.: Comment favoriser le transfert d'apprentissage dans l'organisation par le biais de l'utilisation du e-learning? Réflexion à partir du contexte tunisien. @GRH, 20, 81–101 (2016). https://doi.org/10.3917/grh.163.0081

Ben Zammel, I., Najar, T., Belghith, A.: Determinants of e-learning effectiveness: the case of Tunisian virtual school of post office. Digital Economy. Emerging Technologies and Business Innovation: Third International Conference, ICDEc 2018, Brest, France, May 3–5, 2018, Proceedings 3. Springer International Publishing (2018). https://doi.org/10.1007/978-3-319-97749-2_13

Ben Zammel, I., Najar T.: Towards a conceptual framework of reflexivity and practices in knowledge management. Management Decision **59**(13), 2809–2826 (2021). 12, https://doi.org/10.1108/VJIKMS-09-2021-0191

Chautard, T., Collin-Lachaud, I.: Introducing the storytelling analysis methodology in marketing: principles, contributions and implementation. Rech. Appl. Mark. **34**(3), 27–46 (2019). https://doi.org/10.1177/205157071984122

DeTombe, D.J.: Towards sustainable development: a complex process. Int. J. Environ. Sustain. Develop. **7**(1), 49–62 (2008). https://doi.org/10.1504/IJESD.2008.017896

DeTombe, D.: Editorial: special issue on methodology of societal complexity, J. Transformation Soc. Change 5.3, pp.193–195 (2008). https://doi.org/10.1386/jots5.3.235/1

DeTombe, D.: How to handle societal complexity. In: Kyamakya, K., et al. (eds) Selected Topics in Nonlinear Dynamics SCI 483, pp. 227–244. Springer Verlag (2013). https://doi.org/10.1007/978-3-642-37781-5_13

DeTombe, D.: Handling Societal Complexity: A Study of the Theory and the Methodology of Societal Complexity and the COMPRAM Methodology. Springer Verlag, Heidelberg (2015). ISBN/EAN 978-3-662-43916-6

DeTombe, D.: Societal problems more complex than presumed: The Compram methodology. J. Syst. Sci. Syst. Eng. **6**, 303–320 (2017). https://doi.org/10.1007/s11518-017-5334-8

Dick, G., Akbulut, A.Y., Matta, V.: Teaching and learning transformation in the time of the Coronavirus crisis. J. Info. Technol. Case and Appl. Res. **22**(4), 243–255 (2020). https://doi.org/10.1080/15228053.2020.1861420

Hislop, D.: Knowledge management in organizations: A critical introduction. Oxford University Press (2013)

Malik, H., Al-Toubi, S.: Knowledge management in the public sector. In: Syed, J., Murray, P., Hislop, D., Mouzughi, Y. (eds) The Palgrave Handbook of Knowledge Management, pp. 515–538. Palgrave Macmillan, Cham, (2018). https://doi.org/10.1007/978-3-319-71434-9_1

Parasuraman, A., Zeithaml, V.A., Malhotra, A.: E-S-QUAL: a multiple-item scale for assessing electronic service quality. J. Ser. Res. **7**(3), 213–233 (2005). https://doi.org/10.1177/1094670 5042711

Sousa, M.J., Rocha, A.: Digital learning: developing skills for digital transformation of organizations. Futu. Genera. Comp. Sys. **91**, 327–334 (2019). https://doi.org/10.1016/j.future.2018.08.048

Yin, R.K.: Case study research: design and methods. Sage, Thousand Oaks, CA (2003)

Wijekumar, K.: Influence of emotions on digital learning. Education Tech. Research Dev. **69**(1), 55–57 (2021). https://doi.org/10.1007/s11423-021-09957-8

Promoting the Relationship Between E-Governance and Good Governance Through Public Trust: The Case of Tunisian Government Institution

Kaouther Korbi[1][(✉)] and Amel Boussaidi[2]

[1] The Higher Institute of Accounting and Business Administration (I.S.C.A.E), The Accounting, Financial and Economic Modeling Research Laboratory (MOCFINE), University of Manouba, Manouba, Tunisia
kaouther.korbi@iscae.uma.tn

[2] The Higher Institute of Accounting and Business Administration (I.S.C.A.E), Interdisciplinary Laboratory of University-Company Management (LIGUE), University of Manouba, Manouba, Tunisia

Abstract. E-governance is accepted as an effective tool for the achievement of good governance in developed countries and developing countries such as Tunisia. Several authors have shown the positive effect of e-governance on good governance, nevertheless, few writings have shown the mediating role of public trust in strengthening this relationship. Drawing upon stakeholder theory we developed and tested a model on how public trust allows the strengthening of the relationship between e-governance and good governance. We hypothesized a positive relationship on each side of the triangular configuration through mixed research methods (qualitative and quantitative). We use a structural equation model to test the hypotheses with 217 observations from questionnaire survey data collected at a government institution in Tunisia. The results of this research indicate that e-governance positively influences good governance, and public trust acts positively and significantly on the relationship between e-governance and good governance. Especially, the study offers theoretical insights into the role of public trust as a mediator in the relationship between e-governance and good governance. In addition to the theoretical implications, the results of this study also provide important insight for policymakers in general and in Tunisia particularly.

Keywords: E-governance · good governance · public trust

1 Introduction

The use of Information and Communication Technologies (ICTs) in the delivery of public services seems to be one of the main reforms of public administration and is becoming one of the primary objectives of governments. This reform constitutes "a real opportunity to strengthen the effectiveness and efficiency of public services" (Boulesnane et al., 2019, p17), which influences and facilitates good governance and ensures user satisfaction with

R. Jallouli et al. (Eds.): ICDEc 2023, LNBIP 485, pp. 360–387, 2023.
https://doi.org/10.1007/978-3-031-42788-6_22

the services provided online. For Heeks (2001a, 2001b, p1), the use of ICT simplifies the administrative process and facilitates performance more effectively and efficiently is guaranteed by e-governance. This one is the use of Information and Communication Technologies (ICTs) in government in ways that either: (1) alter governance structures or processes in ways that are not feasible without ICT and/or (2) create new governance structures or processes that were heretofore not possible without ICT and/or (3) reify heretofore theoretical ideas or issues in normative governance (Bannister and Connolly, 2012).

Olamide Samson (2022, p3) sees e-governance as "a new coordination process based on the advancement of Information and Communication Technologies (ICTs) towards Governance. It means using ICTs as servants to the master of good governance. ICTs are no longer seen as an end in themselves and they are seen to work only as part of a wider systemic 'package'. Overall, then, e-Governance is the ICT-enabled route to achieving good governance (Kalsi et al., 2009). However, to ensure good governance, public trust is a sine qua non. This is becoming increasingly evident in a framework marked by the decline in public trust in local governments, the evolution of ICT, and the importance of its influence on society and governments. In this sense, Doullah and Uddin, (2020) show through their study that e-governance and trust foster each other's: e-governance promotes trust, and vice-versa. Other ways, the promotion of e-government can be a way to increase the citizen trust in government and improve citizen evaluations of government. The study shows that e-government initiatives can enhance public trust by improving interactions and responsiveness and encouraging participatory mechanisms. E-Governance serves as an effective tool for restoring public trust which helps to improve transparency, effectiveness, and efficiency, and foster participation in decision-making. These indicators reflect the principles of good governance which present a form of public administration reforms, as proven by Polat and Alkan, (2020, p1). According to these authors, "good governance acts in the public administration according to a consensual, transparent, accountable and efficient management approach".

Thus, the successful implementation of an e-governance system can positively impact the public trust and therefore strengthen good governance, reduce corruption, and improve service delivery. Governments should then focus on implementing an e-governance system that will build public trust to ensure the strengthening of good governance within government institutions. In terms of e-governance, several authors have shown the positive effect of e-governance on good governance (Hartanto et al., 2021; Bala and Verma, 2018; Kals and Kiran, 2015; Saxena, 2005a, 2005b; Sarfaraz, 2007a, 2007b; Zhang, 2006a, 2006b; Barthwal, 2003; Sapru, 2014, and Alaaraj et al. 2016). However, few writings have shown the mediating role of public trust in strengthening this relationship.

Based on these reflections, we suggest in this article study the role of e-governance in strengthening good governance through public trust by referring to the stakeholder theory.

Consequently, this study aims to explore the strengthening effect of public trust in this relationship. It consists in contributing to research work linking good governance practices and e-governance. Through both theoretical and empirical studies in the context of Tunisian government institutions, we will try to identify and analyze the intermediate effect of public trust in the e-governance/good governance relationship. The study offers theoretical insights into the role of the public trust as a mediator in the relationship between e-governance and good governance. Moreover, to our knowledge, this is a unique study in the field of governance that deals with this issue. Indeed, in the literature, few works combine these different concepts in a single theoretical framework. On the practical level, the particularity of this research consists of the empirical study carried out in the framework of Tunisian government institutions. The specificity of the Tunisian context is essential, especially concerning the change that the country is undergoing in the context of a post-revolutionary democratic transition.

The remainder of the paper is structured as follows: Sect. 2 presents a synthesis of the literature concerning the basic concepts of our research, namely e-governance, good governance, and public trust, and the theory mobilized, Sect. 3 describe the context of our research, Sect. 4 develops the causal links between the three concepts, Sect. 5 presents the research methodology, Sect. 6 analyses and interprets the results of our research, both quantitative and qualitative, Sect. 7 discusses the research findings and contributions and finally a conclusion, limits of the research and future work are presented.

2 Literature Review

In this section we will first try to study, through a review of the literature, the basic concepts of our research, namely: E-governance, good governance, and public trust and to develop the theory mobilized in this theoretical framework.

2.1 The Basic Concepts of the Research

In the literature there is often confusion regarding the use of concepts associated with e-governance, namely "e-administration" and "e-government". However, these concepts are different,e-administration or digital administration, "refers to one of many mechanisms that transform paper processes in a traditional office into electronic processes, in order to create a paperless office" (Pólkowski and Radu, 2014, p 20).As for e-government, it refers to "the set of roles and activities of the administration that relies on the use of Information and Communication Technologies (ICTs)" (Brown, 2005, p2). E-government therefore, implies the automation or computerization of existing non-computerized procedures.

Regarding e-governance, it refers to the use of Information and Communication Technologies by the public sector, e-governance seeks to improve service delivery, encourage citizen participation in decision-making, and make government more accountable, transparent, and effective (Palvia and Sharma, 2007). In the same vein, Khan (2018, p137) defines "e-governance as a new form of administrative management through the practical use of communication methods such as the Internet or other virtual spaces". Accordingly, e-governance refers to the way of directing, managing, and administering the practices of a government online, allowing it, through the use of ICTs, to improve transparency, define responsibilities, provide information quickly to all, make the administration efficient, and improve services. This is confirmed by Palvia and Sharma in 2007 (p3), "the application of e-governance has become an important mechanism in the public administration system to enhance citizen participation in decision making, monitor and evaluate government projects, ensure accountability and transparency of the government as well as the transfer of information from one sector to another and of course, ensure the effectiveness and efficiency of this system", hence the notion of good governance. This is "recognized as a process where yesterday's 'best practices' become today's standard practices" (O'Connell and Ward, 2020, p1).

As for good governance, there is no single definition. The idea of good governance has been introduced and widely used by the World Bank since the early 1990s, where we find the most common definition: "how power is exercised in the management of a country's economic and social resources for development. According to Herasymiuk et al. (2020, p547) "good governance implies the participation of citizens in public administration". Also, for Sitompul et al. (2020, p245), "good governance is a regulatory principle of governance that allows for effective public services, a reliable judicial system, and its responsibility is accountable to the public". However, for Jameel et al. (2019a, 2019b, p 301) "good governance is not only a procedure but also a structure that directs socio-economic and political relations and it ensures characteristics or elements such as participation, transparency, accountability and voice, responsiveness and rule of law". So, we can note that good governance is a way of exercising power, managing an organization's resources, and involving citizens and public servants in decision making which requires transparency of information, responsibility, and accountability. The most cited definition has come from the United Nations itself, which deems it to have eight major characteristics. According to this definition, good governance is participatory, consensus oriented, accountable, transparent, responsive, effective and efficient, equitable and inclusive, and follows the rule of law (UNDP, 2016). Furthermore, it seeks to ensure that corruption is minimized, the views of minorities are taken into account, and that the voices of the most vulnerable in society are heard in decision-making. It is also responsive both to the present and future needs of society. (UNESC for Asia and Pacific).

In this article, we refer to six dimensions: accountability, transparency, efficiency, reactivity, the primacy of law, and participation. We note that accountability means the responsibility perceived by organizations or government departments toward the mutual arrangement between stakeholders or between bodies of equal standing to provide public services (Almquist et al., 2013).

As far as public trust is concerned, it is at the origin of the reforms of Public institutions in a New Public Management perspective as well as in a new governance and Post-New Public Management perspective, this is confirmed by Eun and Pupion (2019, p 23). It is a source of major change in the relationship between the institution and users but also between government institutions and its various stakeholders, especially in times of crisis. In the literature, public trust has been defined in different ways. According to Poppo et al. (2010, p126), "public trust is the extent to which a group of stakeholders, has a collective trust orientation towards an organization". Trust is built through legitimate institutions. Trust in government " is also necessary for the fair and effective functioning of democratic public institutions, it is one of the key factors that determine the competitiveness of government...Public trust in government is important because it reflects the quality of the relationship that exists between citizens and their government." (Beshi and

Kaur, 2020, p340). Thus, we can conclude that public trust in government helps shape the sustainability and quality of the relationship of citizens with their government and will therefore allow for the legitimacy of institutions. Based on previous research such as McEvily and Tortoriello (2011), McKnight et al. (2002), and Mayer et al. (1995) about trust organizational, we can conceptualize public trust as a composite of three dimensions (Grimmelikhuijsen and Kneis, 2017, p6): 1) competence or ability: " the extent to which a citizen sees a government organization as capable, effective, competent, and professional", 2) benevolence: "the extent to which a citizen sees a government organization as concerned with the public welfare and motivated to act in the public interest," and 3) integrity: "the extent to which a citizen perceives a government organization as sincere, truthful, and delivering on its promises".

2.2 Theory Mobilized

Given that the objective of our research is to study the strengthening of good governance through the use of e-governance, Stakeholder Theory seems to be the most mobilized theory because as a theory of organizations, it contributes to the foundation of a relational model of the organization/individuals.Several researches show that the Stakeholder Theory allows the realization of the principles of Good Governance on the one hand, and forms a theoretical foundation for e-governance on the other hand. In this respect, we note the work of Pesqueux (2020, p9), Freitas Langrafe et al (2020, p4), Franklin (2020, p2) and Panday and Chowdhury, 2020, p5).As for the relationship of the Stakeholder theory with e-governance, Flak and Rose (2005, p644), note that this theory seems to be the most appropriate as a theoretical foundation for e-governance for three raisons: 1) government can be conceptualized as the management of the relationships and interests of society's stakeholders which explains why all democratic political models are committed to balancing the legitimate competing interests of society, 2) e-Governance focuses on the management of successful technological innovation in a complex stakeholder environment. Stakeholder theory may be able to provide a theoretical basis for tools and techniques that help in the realization of these tasks and 3) government agencies are faced with "increasing demands to run government like a business" and normally optimize their budgets in relation to their various customers (or stakeholders) rather than maximizing their profits in relation to shareholders. Stakeholder theory therefore represents a type of organizational theory better suited to the governmental context than conventional profit-maximizing management theories.

Before studying the existing relations between the three basic concepts previously defined we consider in what follows the study of the context of our research.

3 The E-Governance and the Good Governance in the Tunisian Context

Since the 1990s, the government has initiated a program to upgrade the Tunisian administration and has established a communicating administration through several management systems such as the Management System of Administrative Affairs of State Personnel (INSAF), the Budget Decision Support System (ADEB), the Information System of

Automatic Customs Clearance (SINDA).... These actions were carried out following an awareness of the need to establish good governance based on democracy.

However, after the revolution, the Tunisian government began a series of efforts to improve the quality of governance, advance administrative reforms, fight against corruption, increase social inclusion and reduce regional disparities. Or, In the development of electronic and open government and as part of an overall strategy of reform and modernization of the administration a program "Smart Gov 2020" has also been implemented. The mission of this program is based on four major axes: (according to the portal of the Tunisian government): 1) "Centering" the administration and public services around the needs of its users, 2) "integrate" the administration via interoperability and mutualization of infrastructure and state systems and electronic data exchange and 3) "open" the administration via a framework of transparency, 4) citizen participation and co-creation of value. All this through "Digital Ownership" by securing the digital transformation of the administration, the generalization of digital use, and the establishment of digital trust within the administration and with its users.

In addition, according to Gueldich (2017), In Africa, Tunisia ranks fourth after South Africa (65), Mauritius (75), and Seychelles (85) and first in North Africa ahead of Morocco (101), Egypt (103) and Algeria (112) (according to the report Tunisia Tribune, E-Governance, October 2022). The development of ICT will thus have an impact on most of the mandatory and optional competencies in the administration. To ensure good governance, the Tunisian government is called upon to develop strategies and invest more in digital transformation projects.

After the presentation of the context of our research, we will attempt in what follows to study the direct effect of e-governance on good governance and the indirect effect of this relationship through the mediating variable of public trust. This will allow us to see the reinforcing role of the latter and the important role played by the three dimensions in the relationship between e-governance and good governance. For more precision, we note that one-way e-governance is included in the current study's design. We are interested in the service provided by the government to citizens and the trust that people bestow on a government.

4 The Conceptual Framework: Causal and Mediating Links

4.1 The E-Governance/Public Trust Relationship

E-governance also enhances process-based Trust by improving people's interactions and perceptions of responsiveness (Alaaraj and Ibrahim, 2014, p96).In this sense, Hong (2013) showed that e-governance could increase process-based trust by improving citizen interactions and perceptions of responsiveness" and that e-governance has been proposed as a way to increase citizen trust in government and improve citizen evaluations of government. At this point in the evidence of our research problem, it is widely accepted that e-governance has the potential to improve the transparency, availability, accessibility, and responsiveness of government. The significant and positive impact of Internet use on external political trust and effectiveness has also been raised by Jameel et al. (2019a, 2019b, p 4). Through the Information Technology revolution, we could help the government get closer to the people, a result that could increase the citizens' trust in the government (Gordon et al., 2019, p460). E-governance can thus provide a way for citizens to express their anger or opinion. This confirmation allows us to test the expected relationship between e-governance and public trust, hence the 1st hypothesis of our research:

H1: E-governance is positively related to public trust.

4.2 Relationship Between Public Trust and Good Governance

Godé-Sanchez, (2003, p10) sees that "the production of Public Trust can be considered a new tool of public management; it plays a fundamental role in the governance of public actions". Indeed, a higher level of Public Trust in government institutions leads to good governance and effective execution of public policies (Hasan, 2018). Beshi and Kaur (2020, p342) also consider that Public Trust is a key element of good governance and can be enhanced by strong policies that promote the safety and security of people and can be an outcome of good governance. We note that the trust that people bestow on a government and its officials, state institutions, and executives, differs significantly from the interpersonal trust because of the multi-faceted nature and complexities of the system (Newton 2001:201–204). Political trust is founded on good governance that is based on the existence of ethical codes and accountability mechanisms in all spheres of human life. Such an understanding implies that citizens expect good and ethical governance at all levels of society. This reality pinpoints the fact that politicians and public administrators are obligated and expected to adhere to the principles of accountability, transparency, and integrity, which are the cornerstones of anti-corruption measures such as detection, prevention, and deterrence (Woods and Mantzaris 2012:121; Gisselquist 2012a, 2012b:10).

In this framework, several works have also proven the existence of positive relationships between governance principles and public trust. We mention as an example, the positive relationship between participation, transparency, and public trust demonstrated by Alaaraj and Hassan (2016).Thus, when the principles of good governance are applied and practiced by the government, the government provides quality service to the public, gives appropriate information about the service, etc., which in turn increases the trust of citizens in the government (Yousaf et al., 2016, p202). Consequently, a positive relationship between participation transparency and public trust has been demonstrated by Alaaraj and Hassan (2016). Through the exploration of causal relationships between expected good governance, corruption, and citizen trust that affected citizen actions, Pillay (2017a, 2017b) showed that corruption in all its forms leads to citizen distrust and actions in a wide variety of societal terrains and locations such as the two regions Brazil and South Africa. The positive effect of e-governance has also been demonstrated by Heeks (2001a, 2001b). This author studied the effect of new information and communication technologies and how they can make a significant contribution to the achievement of good governance goals. The paper elaborates on information systems (IS) and claimed E-governance is the ICT-enabled route to achieving good governance. Saxena (2005a, 2005b) argued that e-governance initiatives in most countries promise a more citizen-centric government and reduce operational costs. Unfortunately, most of these initiatives have not been able to achieve the benefits claimed. e-governance requires the initiative to be effectiveness-driven and not merely efficiency-driven. This will require the initiative to be led by good governance. We can therefore consider public trust as a precondition for and an outcome of good governance. Governments can therefore improve public trust by making the processes of their institutions more efficient, transparent, and accountable. It turns out, therefore, that public trust and good governance are positively interrelated. Hasan, (2018, p4) argues that a higher level of public trust in public organizations establishes good governance and effective execution of public policies. Therefore, to promote good governance in any democratic government, public trust is considered one of the essential elements, which allows us to propose the 2nd hypothesis:

H2: Public trust has a positive influence on good governance.

4.3 Relationship Between E-Governance and Good Governance

E-governance is not intended only for hosting or exploring high-tech tools, it primarily attempts to bring out a revolution in approach and work culture to assimilate government processes and functions to assist the nation's progress (Al-Hossienie and Barua, 2018; Sadashivam, 2010). E-governance is not intended only for hosting or exploring high-tech tools, it primarily attempts to bring out a revolution in approach and work culture to assimilate government processes and functions to assist the nation's progress (Al-Hossienie and Barua, 2018; Sadashivam, 2010). The emergence of e-governance has been one of the most prominent expansions of the web. Global shifts towards increased deployment of Information Technology. Today, the development of any nation depends on the use of e-governance and its permeation (Qian, 2011; Dawes, 2008; Ndou, 2004; West, 2004). Many states are in transition for development and emphasize their ICT capacity in development work, including the concept of e-governance. However, technical aspects are just one side of the issue. E-governance can and should be a tool for good governance -not just governance. Transitioning to e-services, public or private, should not be an end in itself but a way to make a needed and desired service more accessible, efficient, and attractive. Thus, Olamide Samson, (2022, p1) expresses that e-governance is an important tool to improve transparency and accountability in public service delivery. He adds in the same article that "e-governance aims to build services based on citizen choice; make government more accessible; facilitate social inclusion; provide information responsibly; use government resources efficiently; reduce public expenditure; provide online services; and involve citizens in the process of good governance". This means that any e-governance application must have common goals such as transparency, accountability, efficiency, equity, speed, mobile site services, public-private partnership, and cost savings. Vaidya (2020, p4) states that "e-governance has been implemented by developed as well as developing countries to be a catalyst for speeding up processes, providing a higher level of service to citizens and businesses, increasing transparency and accountability while reducing costs."Therefore, through e-governance, government services are accessible to citizens in a convenient, efficient, and transparent manner. In the same vein, Saikia and Gogoi, 2020, p1) adds that the use of Information and Communication Technologies ICTs in e-governance. These reflections consolidate Wong et al. (2007, p928) ideas: "the concept of e-governance is incorporated into public administration to ensure the realization of the principles of good governance as well as its strengthening at four different levels:1) transforming the business of government, 2) increasing participation, openness, transparency, and communication, 3) transforming the interactions between government and its internal and external customers, classified as government-citizen (G2C), government-business (G2B), government-internal business (G2E), government-other-government (G2G) and citizen-citizen (C2C) and, 4) transforming society through the emergence of electronic societies, which include networks of relationships such as citizen-to-citizen and non-governmental organization (NGO) relationships."

Based on the work of Olamide Samson, (2022, p1), Bindu et al., 2019, p1), Vaidya, (2020, p4), Saikia and Gogoi, 2020, p1), and Wong (2007, p928), we will try in the following table to present the role of e-governance in the strengthening of good governance in the public sector (see Table 1):

Table 1. Promoting good governance through e-governance

Good governance Principles	Role of e-governance in strengthening good governance
Accountability and transparency	- Ubiquitous access to timely, complete, relevant, high-quality, and reliable information about government operations - Active disclosure of governance information leads to accountability and transparency
Participation	- Enable all stakeholders to participate in policy development and implementation, e-participation, and e-feedback
Reactivity	- Enabling services to be provided to citizens responsively - Creating a government-citizen platform
Effectiveness and Efficiency	- Speed up the service delivery process by eliminating unwanted delays and resource dissipation
Equity	Ensure in-depth equity and fairness in the delivery of public services - Citizens enjoy the benefits of e-services, e-administration regardless of social level, race, religion and gender
Consensus building	- Create a relationship between government and the public for access and exchange of information - This type of connection results in a consensus between "who governs" and "who is governed" - Contribute to the development of an atmosphere of invisible electronic dialogue between the government and the citizen

According to Giri, et al (2018, p3), e-governance is increasingly being promoted as a means for governments to strengthen good governance. Hence the third hypothesis of our research:

H3: e-governance is positively linked to good governance.

E-governance, therefore, plays an important role in achieving good governance in government institutions. It allows the principles of good governance to be achieved and even contributes to the strengthening of good governance. At this level, an important question arises: can this reinforcement be accentuated and even consolidated if there is "public trust confidence" in the existing relationship between e-governance and good governance? To answer this question, it is necessary to present the relationship between public trust, good governance, and e-governance.

4.4 The Role of Public Trust in Promoting the E-Governance/Good Governance Relationship

Moti, (2009, p16) states that "trust is an essential ingredient in building a competent state that strives to promote and maintain what can be called a culture of trust. A culture of trust is one in which citizens feel that they have a more or less equal and potential chance to make a difference in decision-making. This is where good governance comes in as an indispensable consequence of a culture of trust. Janssen, Rana, Slade, and Dwivedi, (2018, p650), suggest that the dimensions of public trust namely benevolence, integrity and competence are relevant to e-governance, and they also add in the same context (on page 662), "Although e-governance has the potential to improve transparency, responsiveness, and government responsibility, electronic services will only be adopted if citizens find them trustworthy". This means as already proven in the theory, that e-governance acts positively on the achievement of good governance and this will be more confirmed when there is trust in the government and the use of the internet.

Similarly, Giri, (2019, p270) expresses that good governance services from e-governance lead to the success of Government to Citizen (G2C), Government to Business (G2B), Government to Employee (G2E), and Government to Government (G2G) applications that would integrate all levels of government functions and the public trust granted by ICT applications lead to better delivery of public services. He also adds that the adoption of a technology-based administration could make service delivery easy and quick and foster persistent trust. Furthermore, Praveena, (2020, p8) adds that "public trust contributes to the perception of the relationship between the Public Administration and its citizens. E-governance initiatives should be more citizen-centric. The process design of these initiatives must ensure that citizens are comfortable using these applications. This can lead to improved trust and promotion of transparency in services, making it more effective in service relationships."Dwivedi et al, (2020, p7) also prove that governments can also play a vital role in accelerating the ICT infrastructure, especially in developing countries, which enables the digital transformation of businesses, including facilitating employees to work from home and online education… This has a positive effect on public trust which will strengthen good governance. Thus, we can confirm that e-governance, good governance, and public trust seem to be interdependent. We have tried to show theoretically the existing relationship between the three concepts. To empirically demonstrate the importance of these relationships and to specify the direct and indirect relationships between these variables, the mediating effect of public trust is highlighted. This relationship is weakly studied in the literature, as some researchers have examined the mediating role of good governance between e-governance and public trust such as Alaaraj et al. (2016) in an Arab context (Lebanon). In our research, we will study the mediating role of public trust in the relationship between e-governance and good governance. Therefore, this research presents the theoretical model that conceptualizes public trust as the mechanism by which e-governance influences good governance.

4.5   The Conceptual Model of the Research

The conceptual model we will try to develop for this research study is based on a conceptual and theoretical analysis presented in the literature review. The model presents e-governance as a means to achieve good governance through public trust. To summarize the relationships between the variables in our model, we present the following diagram (see Fig. 1):

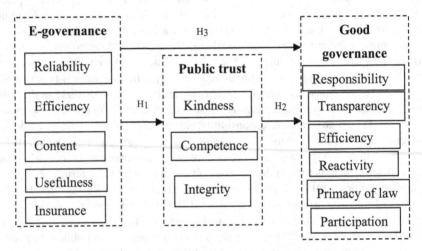

Fig. 1. Conceptual Model

Therefore, the public trust allows the relationship between e-governance and good governance to be reinforced. This relationship will be verified empirically in the following parts of our article.

5   Research Methodology

5.1   Epistemological Positioning and Target Population

In the framework of our research, our problem is explanatory and causal in the fact that we want to explain the role of e-governance in the reinforcement of good governance via public trust. We, therefore, adopt a positivist position adapted to be able to present an objective view of the existing relationship between the concepts.

To answer our research problem and to verify it in the Tunisian field, we selected a population of the Tunisian public sector that uses Information and Communication Technologies (ICT) in the provision of services and that has a direct impact on the achievement of good governance in government institutions. In our population, our unit of analysis is composed of the state officials who have a direct impact on the realization of good governance, namely the administrators of the Ministry of Higher Education and Scientific Research who are the providers of administrative services (administrative managers in the rectorates and all the university institutions as well as administrative agents). We have constituted our sample according to the criterion of homogeneity of the public sector concerning our problem as already mentioned (Law No. 83–112 of December 12, 1983, on the general status of state personnel, local authorities, and public establishments of an administrative nature).

The Tunisian higher education sector has made considerable efforts to install new methods of distance learning within universities that include new ways of learning. With the abrupt shift to e-learning, without prior pedagogical and technical preparation, accelerated experimentation of new learning practices is imposed in Tunisian universities which have been challenged to adjust to this new context.

All efforts have been directed towards supporting the digital infrastructure of the sector by doubling the number of servers made available to universities, a task that was entrusted to the Virtual University of Tunis (UVT), with an increase in the speed of internet flow in academic institutions, the Ministry of Higher Education and Scientific Research has coordinated with the Ministry of Finance to invest in this process. All these measures have not only overcome the difficulties associated with the spread of Covid-19 in Tunisia, but they have also enabled the Tunisian University to be in tune with modern technological changes, on the way to strengthening the process of "intelligent university" in the country.

5.2   Data Collection and Analysis Procedures

According to Thiétart and Coll (1999, P101): "It is possible to associate the qualitative and the quantitative using triangulation, the idea is to attack a formalized problem from two complementary angles". We have opted for a qualitative approach to be able to examine managers' conception of e-governance and its impact on the realization of the principles of good governance in the Tunisian government institution and, to find out whether these institution values their human capital and integrates it into its good governance process by seeking to ensure public trust.

To collect the data we conducted individual semi-directive interviews with state employees located at the top of the hierarchical pyramid in the Tunisian university rectorates and the universities. We conducted semi-structured interviews with the general secretaries of the universities and the managers of the rectorates. We were able to conduct ten interviews with appointments (administrative managers, deputy directors, administrative agents, university teachers, students, and their representatives).

Our questionnaire is composed of closed-ended questions to study the behaviors of people interviewed by confronting them with our hypotheses. This questionnaire was appropriated from published articles in the literature namely the article by Gupta et al (2008) and the article by Amuche (2019). A five-point Likert scale was used to measure the variables in the study.

To measure the dependent variable of good governance, we referred to the measurement scales used by Jameel et al. (2019a, 2019b, p307), these authors adapted the measures of good governance using thirty items from Salminen and Ikola-Norrbacka

(2010) revealing sufficient reliability ($\alpha > 0.70$). We mobilize this measurement scale because it is used in an Arab context similar to the Tunisian context (Lebanon and Jordan). We use six items: responsibility, transparency, efficiency, reactivity, the primacy of law, and participation. For the independent variable e-governance, we used the measurement scales proposed by the EGOSQ tool with five variables adopted by Welch and Hinnant (2003) with adequate reliability ($\alpha > 0.70$), reliability, efficiency, content, usefulness, and, insurance. To assess the mediating variable, the public trust, we used three items from the study by Salminen and Ikola-Norrbacka (2010) reported in the article by Jameel et al. (2019a, 2019b, p307), Cronbach's alpha for public trust was 0.93, indicating good reliability ($\alpha > 0.70$), kindness, competence, and integrity.

Regarding the method of qualitative data analysis, we opted for a grid according to which we prepared the questions of our interview guide. It seems to be the most appropriate to obtain, on the one hand, the managers' conception of the role of e-governance in the strengthening of good governance through public trust, and on the other hand, to obtain new avenues of research, not provided by the theoretical analysis phase (see Table 2).

Table 2. Descriptive coding of verbatims

Theme number	Identification of themes
1	Confidence in online services
2	Definition of e-governance
3	Definition of good governance
4	Definition of public trust
5	E-governance and public trust relationship
6	Relationship between e-governance and good governance
7	Relationship between good governance and public trust
8	The role of public trust in strengthening good governance through e-governance

For our questionnaire, we developed a pre-test based on a population of twenty people. The feedback from the respondents consisted mainly in translating the questions into Arabic to understand the items. For this reason, we proceeded in a second phase to the translation in Arabic of the questions presented in the questionnaire. Two hundred and seventeen (217) interviewed replied to our questionnaire... In our research, we opted for the modeling by the structural equation of partial least squares by the PLS approach. The importance of this method lies in its ability to simultaneously test the existence of causal relationships between several latent variables including the mediating variable. It is of great interest to test the structural model of our research because according to Sosik et al (2009, p. 17): "The method PLS works better in practice because the field data used in modeling are never perfect, and are often highly correlated. Selecting the best linear combination to predict the dependent variables, provides more meaningful structural coefficients.

In our analysis, our estimation and validation procedure consists of two parts: first, the validation of the measurement model, and second, the validation of the structural model. In this context, we used the SmartPLS version 3 software for data processing and hypothesis testing. The following figure shows our research model with its indicators as presented by the PLS method (see Fig. 2):

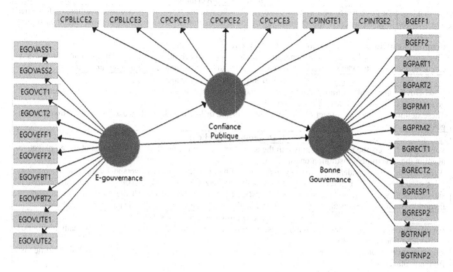

Fig. 2. Research model presented in Smart PLS 3

6   Analysis and Interpretation of Results

6.1   Results of the Qualitative Study

In the following, we will show the results according to the themes presented in the thematic grid (see Table 3):

So, from the above, we can conclude that managers who present at the top of the hierarchical pyramid see that the practice of e-governance has a direct effect on the achievement of good governance. Similarly, public trust has a significant effect on the relationship between e-governance and good governance in the Tunisian government institution, which allows us to conclude that public trust allows the strengthening of good governance. Therefore, the managers' conception of the relevance of the existing relationship between e-governance and good governance through Trust is quite obvious and will have a direct effect on the behavior of other stakeholders. Indeed, this conception will be transmitted to the administrative agents who present the service requesting party and consequently to the service providers. We note that this qualitative research is preliminary to our quantitative study. Its interest consists in determining the position of managers regarding the introduction of e-governance and good governance in the government institution and seeing their conception of the relationship between the three concepts.

Table 3. Results of the qualitative analysis

1- Trust in online services
All respondents express confidence in the services offered online, which can be reflected in the confidence of other stakeholders in these services. In the Tunisian government institution, all stakeholders have confidence in the use of ICT in the provision of online services.
2- Definition of e-governance
For managers, e-governance is a system of service delivery using ICTs in government institutions; for other interviewees, e-governance is the digitization of the administration, it is e-administration, and it is digital bureaucracy. Confirmation of the confusion examined in the literature review. This confusion is reflected in the conception of the other stakeholders, namely administrators, university teachers, and students, who see, according to the pre-test, that e-governance is digital administration.
3- Definition of good governance
Good Governance is about transparency, effectiveness, efficiency, and timeliness. For others respondents, good governance is the management of human resources. These definitions have an impact on the conception of the different stakeholders about the definition of good governance in a government institution.
4- Definition of public trust
Public trust reflects the trust of the public in the administration on the one hand and the trust of the employee or agent in the government institution on the other. According to the respondents, this is only guaranteed if there is the security of personal data online if there are rules established by the government that allows the organization of work in both directions: the citizen is satisfied with the quality of the service requested and the administrator has all the opportunities to work in favorable conditions, this is also linked to the availability of information at any time and to all stakeholders.
5- E-governance/public trust relationship
E-governance is directly related to public trust because according to the respondents and as already mentioned in the definition of public trust: E-governance ensures the personal data of stakeholders, and facilitates access to information at any time and from any place 24/7. E-governance acts directly and significantly on public trust.
6- Relationship between e-governance and good governance
For managers, e-governance is essential to achieve good governance as e-governance ensures speed, efficiency, quality of service, control, and organization of work. E-governance has a direct effect on good governance because it ensures the realization of the principles of good governance.
7- Relationship between good governance and public trust
Public trust ensures the participation of the different stakeholders in the decision-making process. It also ensures accountability of those stakeholders, with everyone being responsible for their decisions and work. Public trust affects good governance and ensures the realization of the principles of good governance.
8- Role of public trust in strengthening good governance through e-governance
E-governance ensures the speed of online service delivery which consequently ensures the realization of the principles of good governance. E-governance shares the same principles of good governance, namely transparency, efficiency, and security, which guarantees the trust of stakeholders in the government institution. This is confirmed in the literature review where Praveena (2020, p8) expresses that "e-governance initiatives should be more focused on needs of citizens. The process design of these initiatives must ensure that citizens are comfortable using these applications. This can lead to improved trust and the promotion of transparency in services, making it more effective in service relationships. Trust plays an important role in strengthening good governance through e-governance.

6.2   Results of the Quantitative Study

The validation approach according to Hair et al (2017, p125) consist of two parts namely: first, the validation of the measurement model, and second, the validation of the structural model.

Validation of the Measurement Model

This validation refers to the identification and estimation of latent variables from the indicators. This first part of the validation of our quantitative analysis is made up of two parts which are respectively convergent validity and discriminant validity.

-*Convergent Validity*

Our basic model contains 32 items. After measuring the convergent validity by applying the PLS approach, we found that 11 items have values lower than 0.7, which leads us to delete them and retain just 18 items. Therefore, we can present the items retained for each variable in the following three tables (see Tables 4, 5 and 6):

Table 4. Convergent validity measures for e-governance (source: Smart PLS 3)

E-governance

	Reliability	Efficiency	Content	Usefulness	Insurance
EGOVFBT 2	0.759	-	-	-	-
EGOVEFF1	-	0.716	-	-	-
EGOVEFF2	-	0.743	-	-	-
EGOVCT1	-	-	0.800	-	-
EGOVCT2	-	-	0.709	-	-
EGOVUTE1	-	-	-	0.708	-
EGOVUTE2	-	-	-	0.759	-
EGOVASS2	-	-	-	-	0.722

This is summarized in the following figure (see Fig. 3):

We propose in the following to present the reliability of the measurement scales which is evaluated by the two indicators as already indicated: the Composite Reliability (CR) which must be greater than 0.7, which shows that the measurement model is of good quality (or Cronbach's Alpha which must be greater than 0.6) and the Average Variance Extracted (AVE) which must be greater than 0.5, which indicates that the latent variable shares at least 50% of its variance with its measurement indicators (see Table 7):

Analysis of this table shows that the three variables have Composite Reliability (CR) > 0.7 and Composite Reliability (CR) above the thresholds for E-Governance and Good Governance > 0.5, while for Public Confidence it is < 0.5:

- AVE for e-governance = 0.521
- AVE of good governance = 0.511
- The value of both variables > 0.50 this indicates that on average, the variable explains more than half of the variance of its indicators.

Table 5. Convergent Validity Measures of good governance (source: Smart PLS 3)

	Participation	Primacy of the law	Reactivity	Responsibility	Transparency
Good governance					
BGPART1	0.704	-	-	-	-
BGPART2	0.702	-	-	-	-
BGPM1	-	0.827	-	-	-
BGPM2	-	0.757	-	-	-
BGRECT1	-	-	0.739	-	-
BGRECT2	-	-	0.790	-	-
BGRESP1	-	-	-	0.722	-
BGTRNP2	-	-	-	-	0.7.00

Table 6. Convergent Validity Measures of public trust (Source: Smart PLS 3)

	Integrity
Public trust	
CPINGTE1	0.802
CPINGTE2	0.794

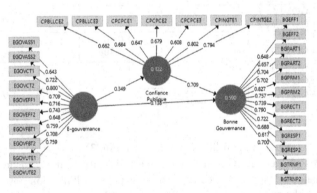

Fig. 3. Estimation of the model items by the PLS approach (Source: Smart PLS 3)

- AVE of public trust = 0.490
- The value of Public trust < 0.5 which indicates that on average, there is more variance left in the error of the items than in the variance explained by the variable and this is what explains the removal of the eight items from the variable.

Table 7. The correlation of CF, AVE and cronbach's alpha (Source: Smart PLS 3)

Matrix	Cronbach's Alpha	Composite Reliability (CR)	Average variance extracted (AVE)
E-Governance	0.898	0.916	0.521
Public Trust	0.824	0.869	0.490
Good Governance	0.912	0.926	0.511

Discriminant Validity

"This is the extent to which such a variable is truly distinct from other variables by empirical standards. Thus, establishing discriminant validity implies that a variable is unique and captures phenomena not represented by other variables in the model" (Hair et al., 2017, p138).

We present in the following table, the correlation of the variables in our research (see Table 8):

Table 8. The HTMT Index: Correlation of variables (Source: Smart PLS)

	Good governance	Public trust	E-governance
Good governance			
Public trust	0.862		
E-governance	0.408	0.403	

To assess the discriminant validity, the PLS approach allows us to use the HTMT index. In our research, we find a strong correlation between the variables given that the HTMT indices found are < 0.9.

In conclusion, the results reveal a good quality measure: the measures are reliable and show an acceptable convergent validity. It is therefore possible to conclude that the scale has discriminant validity. After having verified the quality of our measurement model, we will proceed to the test of the structural model.

Structural validity of the model

To validate the structural model according to the PLS method, we can group the results of the different indices obtained from Smart PLS in the following table (see Table 9):

Table 9. The validation indices of the structural model

	R2	F2	Q2	GOF
Good governance	0.598	0.041	0.290	0.55

As shown in the table above, the value of the coefficient of determination exceeds the minimum threshold presented in the literature (Croutsche, 2002), which is set at 0.1 ($R2 > 0.1$),

=> Good Governance is 60% explained by e-governance.

Similarly, for the predictive validity of our model, the redundancy coefficient is positive: $Q2 = 0.290 > 0$.

The goodness of fit of our search model in the PLS model is tested by the GOF index which must be greater than 0.36 to be satisfactory, it is calculated according to Hair et al (2017, p235) by: $\sqrt{(R2 \times AVE)}$.

The R2 index for the good governance variable is 0.598 and the average AVE index of the model variables is 0.507. Our model, therefore, has a GOF index of 0.550.

=>Our model presents a satisfactory quality of fit.

For the structural validation of our model, we will try to verify the hypotheses of our research. The validation of the hypotheses depends on the importance and significance of the structural relations. To do this, thanks to the calculation by the method of Bootstrapping and the PLS Algorithm of the software Smart PLS, we will be able to test the hypotheses of our model. We present the results obtained through the PLS software by the Bootstrapping method in the table (see Table 10):

Table 10. Results of hypothesis validation tests (total effect): T-Student and Path coefficient (source: Smart PLS)

Hypothesis	Relationship	Original sample (O)	Sample average (M)	Standard deviation (STDEV)	T-Value (O/STDEV)	P-Value	Decision
H2	Public trust->good governance	0.709	0.710	0.065	10.971	0.000	Checked
H3	E-governance->good governance	0.138	0.141	0.068	2.031	0.043	Checked
H1	E-governance->public trust	0.349	0.358	0.068	5.134	0.000	Checked

By examining the results obtained, we find that the p-values that measure the relationships between the variables must have an error rate of (-) 5%, and this is the case for the three hypotheses: H1, H2 and H3 which are significant at the 5% threshold. The same is true for the T-Student values, which must exceed 1.96 for the three relationships, so we can confirm the three hypotheses:

– Therefore, the analysis of the results showed us that public trust has a positive effect on good governance ($T = 10.971$) (Hypothesis 2).
– E-governance also has a positive effect on good governance ($T = 2.031$) (Hypothesis 3).
– E-governance has a positive effect on public trust with ($T = 5.134$) (Hypothesis 1).

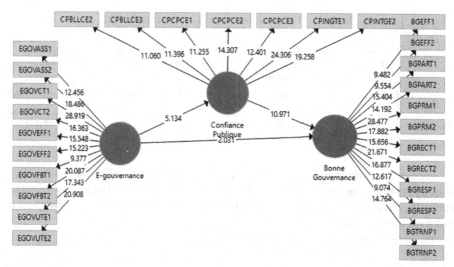

Fig. 4. Measurement model and structural model after the application of the Bootstrapping method (source: Smart PLS)

To verify the existence of a mediating effect of the public trust variable on the link between the independent variable e-governance and the dependent variable good governance, we use the approach proposed by Preacher and Hayes (2008) in two steps to assert the existence of mediation:

1. Bootstrapping the indirect effect: the relationship between the independent variable and the dependent variable via the mediating variable must be significant the p-value tends to zero and the T-value (T-student) > 1.96. This is confirmed by the following figure (see Fig. 4):

   The results obtained lead us to conclude that the relationship between e-governance and good governance via the public trust is significant: T = 4.42 and p-value = 0000.

2. Estimation by bootstrapping of the 95% confidence interval (Lower and upper level): The only condition for the existence of a significant indirect effect is a bootstrap test with a confidence interval that excludes zero. Therefore, we need a model for the mediation calculation in Excel to determine the limits of the 95% confidence interval. To derive these results, we refer to the work of Preacher and Hayes (2008, p880). To do this, we present the model for the mediation calculation based on Table 11 which shows the total effects:

For the analysis of the above table, we must first give an identification of the different table cells:

To verify the existence of mediation, we need to examine the result of the 95% confidence interval in Table 12.

According to the research of Preacher and Hayes (2008, p881), the mediation effect seems to be significant since the confidence interval excludes zero [0.124; 0.371].

Table 11. The mediation calculation (Source excel)

	E-governance->public trust	Public trust->good Governance	Automatic calculation	Standard deviation	Automatic calculation	Bootstrapped Confidence Interval	
	Path a	**Path b**	**indirect effect**	**SE**	**T-Value**	**95%LL**	**95%UL**
Mediation	0,349	0,709	0,247	0,063	3,928	0,124	0,371

We can therefore conclude that there is a mediation effect of public trust in the relationship between e-governance and good governance and therefore we can conclude that public trust acts positively and significantly on the relationship between e-governance and good governance.

We summarize our results in the following table:

Table 12. Testing the research hypotheses

The number of the hypothesis	The meaning of the research hypothesis	Confirmation of Hypotheses
H1	E-governance is positively linked to public trust	**Confirmed**
H2	Public trust has a significant and positive influence on good governance	**Confirmed**
H3	E-governance is positively linked to good governance	**Confirmed**

7   Discussion of the Results and Contributions of the Research

The interviews with the managers of the university administrations reveal that the relationships between the variables of our research, namely e-governance, public trust, and good governance, are quite relevant. Furthermore, e-governance affects strengthening good governance via public trust, there is also a significant relationship between e-governance, good governance, and public trust. Similarly, our empirical study of a qualitative nature confirms our choice of organizational theory namely the stakeholder theory seen that according to managers, e-governance allows the participation of stakeholders in decision-making, this is confirmed in the literature review by Dicarlo, 2020, p10): "it is necessary to take into consideration the needs of all stakeholders", also for Damak Ayadi and Pesqueux (2003, p7): "Stakeholders are partners in decision making" and "The theory is interested in managerial decision making". The results of our qualitative study are confirmed by our quantitative study.

The purpose of this study was to highlight the links between e-governance and good governance on the one hand and to show the mediating effect of public trust on the strengthening of good governance through e-governance on the other hand. The results of our research confirm the reliability and validity of the conceptual model of our research and demonstrate that in the Tunisian government institution e-governance is positively linked to public trust and that the latter positively influence good governance. In the same vein, we note the existence of a relationship between good governance and e-governance via public trust. Hence, we can conclude that e-governance is necessary for the achievement of good governance through public trust. This shows the indirect effect of e-governance on good governance through public trust in the Tunisian government institution.

Our research presents both theoretical and empirical contributions. At the theoretical level, our results present a confirmatory dimension to the literature. E-governance increases the effectiveness and efficiency of services provided online to the public because it facilitates the transfer of information between departments in a simple manner. It allows for the rapid processing of administrative tasks and procedures on time. Within the government, institution e-governance improves productivity because administrative agents work faster through the automation of tasks. It allows the realization of the principles of good governance, which makes it possible to sensitize government policymakers to give more importance to ICT in the public sector. Thus, Tunisian government policymakers need to prioritize ICT in their development strategies, especially since service seekers want the facilitation of services and a faster flow of information while ensuring the security of personal data, which will increase their trust in the government. This is equivalent to the research of Olamide Samson, (2022, p1) who expresses that e-governance is an important tool to improve transparency and accountability in public service delivery. Similarly, the work of (Çakir, 2019), Subramanian, (2012), and Bolbull, (2018) shows that e-governance acts positively on good governance.

For the public trust, also we confirm the work of Jameel et al. (2019a, 2019b) who asserts the existing relationship between good governance and public trust. We also confirm the work of Janssen et al, (2018) who suggest that the dimensions of public trust namely benevolence, integrity, and competence are relevant to e-governance, and that e-governance has the potential to improve transparency, responsiveness, and accountability of government, e-services will only be adopted if citizens find them trustworthy.

Empirically, we have provided results on a little-studied field, namely e-governance for good governance through public trust in the Tunisian context. We have dealt with a problem verified in Asian countries such as India, China, and Bangladesh and in some Middle Eastern countries such as Lebanon and Jordan. The structural approach is little used in management research and more precisely in the theme of "good governance". We have found that e-governance helps to achieve good governance and that public trust helps to strengthen good governance.

8 Conclusion

We started with the following observations: the government institution suffers from rigid bureaucracy, too much waste of paper, the long circuit of information passage, and the lack of speed in the treatment of the service applicants. We also started with research conducted and validated in Asian countries and the Middle East. We wanted to verify this research on the Tunisian field.

Our research problem is thus presented as follows: Does Public Trust allow the strengthening of the relationship between e-governance and good governance?

Our research comes to enrich the works dealing with the theme of governance, trying to bring a new vision of the concept of "good governance" of government institutions and this by verifying the existing relationship between e-governance and good governance. Jameel et al. (2019a, 2019b, 2014, 2015) verified the mediation relations of e-governance between public trust and good governance in Lebanon and Jordan. Bhuiyan (2011) also showed that the modernization of government institutions is provided by e-governance in Bangladesh.

Bringing together the efforts in our literature review as well as our empirical research, we find originality in verifying the effect of public trust in the existing relationship between e-governance and good governance in the Tunisian field. The mobilization of the Stakeholder Theory helped us to understand the behavior and the conception of the different stakeholders towards the introduction of e-governance and good governance in the government institution. The definition we have chosen for good governance is that of Jameel et al. (2019a, 2019b, p 301): "good governance is not only a procedure but also a structure that directs socio-economic and political relations and ensures characteristics or elements such as participation, transparency, accountability and voice, responsiveness, and rule of law". For e-governance, we have retained the definition of Palvia and Sharma, (2007, p3): "e-governance is the use of Information and Communication Technologies by the public sector to improve service delivery, encourage citizen participation in decision-making, and make government more accountable, transparent, and effective". Similarly for public trust, we have retained Poppo's et al. definition, (2010, p126) "public trust is the extent to which a group of stakeholders, has a collective trust orientation towards an organization. Trust is built through legitimate institutions.

The confirmation of the hypotheses of our research consolidates the objectives that we have set, namely: 1) demonstrate that there is a positive interaction between e-governance and good governance and, 2) demonstrate that public trust has a positive and significant effect on the relationship between e-governance and good governance and enables the strengthening of good governance.

Thus, the contributions of our research can be seen as follows: 1) E-governance is essential for public administration reform, 2) it ensures the realization of the principles of good governance and 3) public trust is an essential element in strengthening good governance.

Our research enriches previous research by proposing a model that has not, to our knowledge, been the subject of previous research and that measures the mediating effect of public trust between e-governance and good governance. It also enriches previous research from an empirical point of view, as, to our knowledge, all previous research has conducted quantitative research using SPSS software, whereas we conducted pre-liminary qualitative research to determine the position of managers regarding the idea of introducing e-governance and good governance in the government institution and to see their conception towards the relationship between the three concepts. Then a quantitative study was conducted through a questionnaire to generalize our first results using structural modeling by the SmartPLS-3 software.

However, our research has limitations that relate to the small size of the sample on the one hand and the other hand, to the health situation in the world and in Tunisia, which has hindered us to move to expand our sample. Another limitation could relate to the lack of Tunisian research on our problem.

Finally, this study opens the way to new avenues of research by making links with the findings of our research and the new concepts that we identified during the semi-structured interviews: broaden the target population by looking at other ministries in Tunisia, test the relationship between e-governance and good governance by considering moderating variables such as: "Resistance to change", "gender"... And, test the relationship between e-governance and good governance by considering mediating variables such as: "human capital"...

References

Alaaraj, H., Ibrahim, F.: Does practicing good governance enhance the public trust towards the Lebanese government. Int. J. Sci. Res. Publ. 4(10), 1–4 (2014)

Alaaraj, H., Hassan, S.: Does good governance mediate relationship between e-government and public trust in Lebanon? Int. Rev. Manag. Mark. 6(3), 500–509 (2016)

Amuche, O.M.: Electronic governance and service delivery in selected ministries in Ebonyi State, Nigeria. J. Contemp. Res. Soc. Sci. 1(1), 11–37 (2019)

Al-Hossienie, C.A., Barua, S.K.: Applications of e-governance towards the establishment of digital Bangladesh: prospects and challenges. Journal of E-Governance 36(3), 152–162. In: Singh, M., Sahu, G.P.: (2018) Study of e-governance implementation: a literature review using classification approach. International Journal of Electronic Governance 10(3), 237–260 (2013)

Almquist, R., Grossi, G., Van Helden, G.J., Reichard, C.: Public sector governance and accountability. Crit. Perspect. Account. 24(7–8), 479–487 (2013)

Arfaoui, R.: Pandémie covid-19: Défis et réponses de l'enseignement supérieur en Tunisie. Higher Education Reform Expert (2018–2021) Bureau National Erasmus+ Tunisie. https://www.era smusplus.tn/doc/Impact-Corona-virus-sur-les-etablissements-Rafiaa-Arfaoui-2021.pdf

Bakkour, D.: Un essai de définition du concept de gouvernance. Laboratoire montpelliérain d'Economie Théorique et Appliquée, n 2013–05 (2013)

Bannister, F., Connolly, R.: Defining e-governance. E-Service Journal, Vol. 8, No. 2, pp.3–25 (2012). In: Singh, M., Sahu, G.P.: Study of e-governance implementation: A literature review using classification approach. International Journal of Electronic Governance 10(3), 237 (2018)

Bala, M.D., Verma, D.: A critical review of digital marketing. Int. J. Manage. IT Eng. 8(10), 321–339 (2018)

Barthwal, C.P.: E-governance for good governance. Indian J. Political Sci. 64, No. 3/4 (July-December, 2003), pp. 285–308 (24 pages) (2003)

Belwal, R., Al-zoubi, K.: Public centric e-governance in Jordan. J. Inf. Commun. Ethics Soc. 6(4), 317–333 (2008)

Beshi, T.D., Kaur, R.: Public trust in local government: explaining the role of good governance practices. Public Organ. Rev. 20(2), 337–350 (2020)

Bhuiyan, S.H.: Modernizing Bangladesh public administration through e-governance: benefits and challenges. Gov. Inf. Q. 28(1), 54–65 (2011)

Bindu, N., Sankar, C.P., Kumar, K.S.: Research collaboration and knowledge sharing in e-governance. Econ. Transforming Gov.: People, Process Policy **13**(1), 2–33 (2019)

Boulesnane, S., Benaissa, M., Bouzidi, L., Chappoz, Y.: L'intégration des TIC dans les services publics : le cas des projets numériques des Métropoles. Gestion 2000 **36**(5), 17–39 (2020)

Brown, D.: Le gouvernement électronique et l'administration publique. Revue Internationale des Sciences Administratives **71**(2), 251–266 (2005)

Çakir, C.: E-governance comparatively in the united states (USA) and Russia. Academic Studies in Social Human and Administrative Science (2) (2019)

Croutsche, J.J.: Etude des relations de causalité : utilisation des modèles d'équations structurelles. La revue des sciences de gestion **198**, 81–97 (2002)

Damak-AyadI, S., Pesqueux, Y.: La théorie des parties prenantes en perspective (2003)

Dalton, R.J.: Democratic Challenges, Democratic Choices: The Erosion of Political Support in Advanced Industrial Democracies. Oxford University Press, Oxford (2004). https://doi.org/10. 1093/acprof:oso/9780199268436.001.0001

Dawes, S.S.: The evolution and continuing challenges of e-governance. Public Adm. Rev. **68**, S86–S102 (2008)

Freitas Langrafe, De T., Barakat, S.R., Stocker, F., Boaventura, J.M.G.: A stakeholder theory approach to creating value in higher education institutions. The Bottom Line **33**(4), pp. 297–313. Emerald Publishing Limited 0888–045X (2020). https://doi.org/10.1108/BL-03-2020-0021

Dicarlo, E.: The real entity theory and the primary interest of the firm: equilibrium theory, stakeholder theory and common good theory. Chapter in book: Accountability, Ethics and Sustainability of Organizations, pp. 3–21 (2020)

Doullah, S.U., Uddin, N.: Public trust building through electronic governance: an analysis on electronic services in Bangladesh. Technium Social Sciences Journal **7**, 28–35, May 2020 ISSN: 2668–7798 (2020). www.techniumscience.com

Dwivedi, Y.K., et al.: Impact of covid-19 pandemic on information management research and practice: transforming education, work and life. Int. J. Inf. Manage. **55**, 102211 (2020)

Eun, J., Pupion, P.C.: Le management public entre confiance et défiance. Management international/International Management/Gestiòn Internacional **23**, Numéro 3, 74–88 (2019)

Flak, L.S., Rose, J.: Stakeholder governance: adapting stakeholder theory to e-government. Commun Assoc Inf Syst **16**(1), 31 (2005)

Franklin, A.L.: Introduction to Stakeholder Engagement. Stakeholder Engagement. E.book (2020)

Giri, S.: Obstacles of civil service in public service delivery in nepal: e-governance for good governance. Int. J. Comput. Sci. Mob. Comput. **8**(3), 269–274 (2019)

Giri, S., Shakya, S., Pande, R.: NE-Governance implementation: challenges of effective service delivery in civil service of Nepal. Glob. J. Comput. Sci. Technol. **18**(3), Version 1.0 (2018)

Godé-Sanchez, C.: Confiance et gouvernance de l'action publique: réflexions à partir de l'Espace du Partage Aubagnais. Revue Economique et Sociale **4**, 255–266 (2003)

Gisselquist, R.M.: Good governance as a concept, and why this matters for development policy, Working Paper No. 2012a/30, UNU-WIDER, Helsinki, March (2012a)

Gueldich, H.: L'open-Gov et l'e-Participation en Tunisie: un nouveau défi pour la bonne gouvernance, in Mélanges Mohamed Saleh Ben Aissa, CPU (2017)

Gordon, S., Garen, J., Clark, J.R.: The growth of government, trust in government, and evidence on their co evolution. J. Econ. Finance **43**(3), 456–480 (2019)

Gisselquist, R.M.: Good Governance as a Concept, and Why This Matters for Development Policy. WIDER Working Paper No.30 (2012b)

Grimmelikhuijsen, S., Knies, E.: Validating a scale for citizen trust in government organizations. Int. Rev. Adm. Sci. **83**(3), 1–19 (2017)

Gupta, B., Dasgupta, S., Gupta, A.: Adoption of ICT in a government organization in a developing country: an empirical study. J. Strateg. Inf. Syst. **17**(2), 140–154 (2008)

Hair, J.F., Matthews, L.M., Matthews, R.L., Sarstedt, M.: PLS-SEM or CB-SEM: updated guidelines on which method to use. Int. J. Multivar. Data Anal. **1**(2), 107–123 (2017)

Hasan, A.R.: Governance and Trust. Global Encyclopedia of Public Administration, Public Policy, and Governance. E.book, Springer, Cham (2018)

Heeks, R.: Understanding e-governance for development, i-government. The i-Government working paper series, no. 11, University of Manchester (2001a). <http://www.seed.manchester.ac.uk/medialibrary/IDPM/working_papers/igov/igov_wp11.pdf

Heeks, R.: I-Government. In: Heeks, R.: 11th Part, Understanding E-Governance for Development. Institute for Development Policy and Management, Manchester, 1–27 (2001b)

Herasymiuk, K., Martselyak, O.V., Kirichenko, Y.N., Zhmur, N.V., Shmalenko, I.: Principles of integrity and good governance in public administration. Int. J. Manag. **11**(4), 545–555 (2020)

Hong, H.: Government websites and social media's influence on government-public relationships. Public Relat. Rev. **39**(4), 346–356 (2013)

Hartanto, D., Dalle, J., Akrim, A., Anisah, H.U.: Digital policy, regulation and governance **23**(6), 598-616 (2021)

Jameel, A., Asif, M., Hussain, A.: Good governance and public trust: assessing the mediating effect of e-government in Pakistan. LexLocalis **17**(2), 299–320 (2019)

Jameel, A., Asif, M., Hussain, A., Hwang, J., Sahito, N., Bukhari, M.H.: Assessing the moderating effect of corruption on the e-government and trust relationship: an evidence of an emerging economy. Sustainability **11**(23), 6540 (2019)

Janssen, M., Ranan, P., Slade, E.L., Dwivedi, Y.K.: Trustworthiness of digital government services: deriving a comprehensive theory through interpretive structural modelling. Public Manag. Rev. **20**(5), 647–671 (2018)

Kalsi, N.S., Kiran, R.: E-governance success factors: an analysis of e-governance initiatives of ten major states of India. Int. J. Pub. Sect. Manage. **26**(4), 320–336 (2013)

Khan, H.A.: The challenges of e-governance in public administration. In: Globalization and the Challenges of Public Administration, pp. 135–160. Palgrave Macmillan, Cham (2018)

Kalsi, N., Kiran, R., Vaidya, S.C.: Effective e-governance for good governance in India. Int. Rev. Bus. Res. Pap. **5**(1), 212–229 (2009)

Kals, N.S., Kiran, R.A.: Strategic framework for good governance through e-governance optimization: a case study of Punjab in India. Program Electron. Libr. Inf. Syst. **49**(2), 170–204 (2015)

Mayer, R.C., Davis, J.H., Schoorman, F.D.: An integrative model of organizational trust. Acad. Manag. Rev. **20**(3), 709–734 (1995)

Mcevily, B., Tortoriello, M.: Measuring trust in organizational research: review and recommendations. J. Trust Res. **1**(1), 23–63 (2011)

Mcknight, D.H., Choudhury, V., Kacmar, C.: The impact of initial consumer trust on intentions to transact with a web site: a trust building model. J. Strateg. Inf. Syst. **11**(3–4), 297–323 (2002)

Moti, U.: Building trust in government for good governance: implications for the transformation agenda. Nigerian Tribune **17** (2009)

Muhammad, M.I., Abu Momtaz, S.A.: Understanding e-governance: a theoretical approach. J. Asian Aff. **29**(4), 29–46 (2007)

Newton, K.: Trust, social capital, civil society, and democracy. Int. Polit. Sci. Rev. **22**(2), 201–214 (2001)

Nyman-Metcalf, K., Repytskyi, T.: Exporting good governance via e-governance: Estonian e-governance support to eastern partnership countries. Political and Legal Perspectives of the EU Eastern Partnership Policy 81–100 (2016)

Ndou, V.: E-government for developing countries: opportunities and challenges. Electron. J. Inf. Syst. Dev. Ctries. **18**(1), 1–24 (2004)

Nehemia, M., Iyamu, T., Shaanika, I.: A Comparative Analysis of E-Governance and IT Governance. Open Innovations (OI) pp. 288–296 (2019)

O'Connell, M., Ward, A.M.: Corporate Governance, Measurement of. Encyclopedia of Sustainable Management, vol. 55, p. 1. Springer Nature (2020)

Palvia, S.C.J., Sharma, S.S.: E-government and e-governance: definitions/domain framework and status around the world. In: International Conference on E-governance No. 5 (2007)

Panday, P.K., Chowdhury, S.: Responsiveness of local government officials: insights and lessons from participatory planning and budgeting. Asia Pac. J. Publ. Adm. **42**, 1–20 (2020)

Pesqueux, Y.: La théorie des parties prenantes, une théorie aisément idéologisable (2020)

Pillay, P.: Public trust and good governance: a comparative study of Brazil and South African. J. Publ. Aff. **9**(8), 31–47 (2017)

Polat, Z.A., Alkan, M.: The role of government in land registry and cadastre service in Turkey: towards a government 3.0 perspective. Land Use Policy **92**, 104500 (2020)

Pólkowski, Z., Radu, A.M.: Theoretical, technical and practical aspects of e-administration. Zeszyty Naukowe Dolnośląskiej Wyższej Szkoły Przedsiębiorczości I Techniki W Polkowicach. Studia Z naukspołecznych (7), 185–210 (2014)

Poppo, L., Schepker, D.J.: Repairing public trust in organizations. Corp. Reputation Rev. **13**(2), 124–141 (2010)

Praveena, A.L.: A study on service quality aspects in e-governance efficiency. Int. J. New Innovations Eng. Tech. **14**(2), 7–13 (2020)

Preacher, K.J., Hayes, A.F.: Asymptotic and resampling strategies for assessing and comparing indirect effects in multiple mediator models. Behav. Res. Methods **40**(3), 879–891 (2008)

Pillay, P.: Public trust and good governance a comparative study of Brazil and South Africa. Afr. J. Public Aff. **9**, 8 (2017)

Qian, M.: Is voting with your feet an effective mutual fund governance mechanism? J. Corp. Finan. **17**(1), 45–61 (2011)

Saikia, N., Gogoi, N.: ICT and e-governance: an overview of the challenges of e-governance in Assam. JCR **7**(19), 6733–6738 (2020)

Salminen, A., Ikola-Norrbacka, R.: Trust, good governance and unethical actions in finnish public administration. Int. J. Public Sect. Manage. **35**, 647–668 (2010)

Samson, O.: E-Governance and bureaucratic corruption in Nigeria. Int. J. Publ. Policy Adm. **3**(1), 1–37 (2022). https://carijournals.org/journals/index.php/IJPPA/article/view/817

Sarfaraz, H.: E-Governance: a case for good governance in Pakistan. (2007a). Available at SSRN 1415689

Saxena, A.: E-governance and good governance: the indian context. Indian J. Polit. Sci. **66**, 313–328 (2005)

Sitompul, F., Lumbanraja, P., TarmizI, H.B.: Effect of good governance application against public satisfaction with excellent service as an intervening variable in the medan tembungsub-district office. Int. J. Res. Rev. **7**(1), 244–252 (2020)

Sosik, J., Kahai, S., Piovoso, M.: Silver bullet or voodoo statistics? a primer for using the partial least squares data analytic technique in group and organization research. Group Org. Manag. **34**(1), 5–36 (2009)

Singh, M., Sahu, G.P.: Study of e-governance implementation: a literature review using classification approach. Int. J. Electron. Gov. **10**(3), 237–260 (2018)

Saikia, N., Gogoi, N.N.: Effectiveness of ICT in E-Governance: The Assam Experience

Salam, M.A.: E-governance for good governance through public service delivery. A Dissertation, MAGD, Institute of Governance Studies, BRAC University, Dhaka SAXENA ET HEEKS (2013)

Sarfaraz, H.: E-Governance: a case for good governance in Pakistan (2007b). papers.ssrn.com/sol3/Delivery.cfm/SSRN_ID1415689_code634203

Saxena, K.B.C.: Towards excellence in e-governance. Int. J. Public Sect. Manag. **18**, 498–513 (2005)

Sadashivam, T.: A new paradigm in governance: is it true for e-governance?. Journal of the Knowledge Economy 1(4), 303–317 (2010). In: Singh, M., Sahu, G. P.: Study of e-governance implementation: a literature review using classification approach. International Journal of Electronic Governance 10(3), 237–260 (2018)

Subramanian, C.: E-governance: a key to good governance in India. Int. J. Recent Sci. Res. 3(5), 305–308 (2012)

Sapru, R.K.: Public Policy: Formulation Implementation and Evaluation. Sterling Publishing Pvt. Ltd., New Delhi (2014)

Thietart, R.A.: Méthodes de recherche en management. Dunod, Paris (2014)

Thietart, R.-A., et al.: Méthodes de recherche en management. 2eme édition, Dunod, Paris (1999)

Tolbert, C.J., Mossberger, K.: The effects of e-government on trust and confidence in government. Public Adm. Rev. 66(3), 354–369 (2006)

Vaidya, M.: E-governance initiatives in Chandigarh (India): an analytical study. Int. J. Electron. Gov. 12(1), 4–25 (2020)

Welch, E.W., Hinnant, C.: Internet use, transparency, and interactivity effects on trust in government. In: 36th Annual Hawaii International Conference on System Sciences. Proceedings of the (pp. 7-pp). IEEE (2003) January

West, D.M.: Global e-government. Center for Public Policy, Brown University, Providence, RI (2004)

Wong, K., Fearon, C., Philip, G.: Understanding egovernment and egovernance stakeholders partnerships and CSR. Int. J. Qual. Reliab. Manage. 24, 927–943 (2007)

Woods, D., Mantzaris, E.: Anti-corruption guide, ACCERUS, University of Stellenbosch (2012). In: Pillay, P.: Public Trust and Good Governance A Comparative Study of Brazil and South Africa. African Journal of Public Affairs, Vol. 9, number 8 September (2017)

Yousaf, M., Ihsan, F., Ellahi, A.: Exploring the impact of good governance on citizens' trust in Pakistan. Government Information Quarterly 33(1), 200–209 (2016). In: Pillay, P.: Public Trust and Good Governance: A Comparative Study of Brazil and South African Journal of Public Affairs, 9, number 8, September (2017)

Zhang, J.: Good governance through e-governance? Assessing China's e-government strategy. J. E-gouvernement 2(4), 39–71 (2006)

Frank Zhang, X.: Information uncertainty and analyst forecast behavior. Contemp. Acc. Res. 23(2), 565–590 (2006)

World Bank. Collaborative Governance, World Bank website, http://www.worldbank.org

United Nations Development Programme UNDP, Good Governance and Sustainable Human Development. http://mirror.undp.org/magnet/policy/chapter1.htm

United Nations Economic and Social Commission for Asia and the Pacific, "What is good governance?" Available from http://www.unescap.org/sites/default/files/good-governance.pdf

Plan National Stratégique Tunisie Digitale (2020). https://www.mtc.gov.tn/index.php?id=14

Le portail du gouvernement Tunisien. http://fr.tunisie.gov.tn/101-pr%C3%A9sentation-g%C3%A9n%C3%A9rale-de-l-e-strat%C3%A9gie.htm

Le rapport Tunisie Tribune (E-Gouvernance) october (2022). https://www.aa.com.tr/fr/afrique/e-gouvernance-la-tunisie-occupe-la-88ème-place-sur-193-pays/2716176#:~:text=La%

E-Government Survey. The Future of Digital Government. (2022). https://desapublications.un.org/sites/default/files/publications/2022-09/Web%20version%20E-Government%202022.pdf

Le plan stratégique national. Tunisie numérique (2020). http://fr.tunisie.gov.tn/101-pr%C3%A9sentation-g%C3%A9n%C3%A9rale-de-l-e-strat%C3%A9gie.htm

Fake News Detection in the Tunisian Social Web

Yosr Haddad and Hadhemi Achour[✉]

Université de Tunis, ISGT, LR99ES04 BESTMOD, 2000 Le Bardo, Tunisia
`haddadyosr@outlook.fr`, `hadhemi_achour@yahoo.fr`

Abstract. In recent years the growth of social media use all over the world, has had a big impact on the proliferation of misleading information and fake news on the social web. The possibility of sharing any content that is given to users, has emphasized this issue and made the automatic detection of fake news a crucial need. In this work, we focus on the Tunisian social web and address the issue of automatically detecting fake news in the Tunisian social media platforms. We propose a hybrid detection approach, combining content-based and social-based features, and using an RNN-based model. For implementing the proposed approach, we conduct an exploratory study of several variants of RNNs, which are Simple LSTM, Bi-LSTM, Deep LSTM and Deep Bi-LSTM combination. The obtained results are also compared with experiments we conducted, using an SVM-based model.

Keywords: Fake News Detection · Tunisian Social Web · Deep Learning · Recurrent Neural Network · LSTM · Machine Learning · SVM · Natural Language Processing · Text Mining

1 Introduction

Fake news (FN) is not a new phenomenon and already has a long history dating back to the 18th century [1], but it is clear that it has taken on greatly increasing importance over the past few years. The term Fake News, being very widely used in the 2016 US presidential elections, was selected as the international word of that year.

As simple and self-explanatory as it may seem, there has been no universal definition for Fake News which is indeed, usually connected to several related terms and concepts such as maliciously false news, false news, satire news, disinformation, misinformation, rumor [2]. Still according to Zhou and Zafarani [2], Fake News can be defined broadly, as false news focusing on the news authenticity regardless it's intention, or can have a narrower definition that considers Fake News as news that are intentionally false, intended to mislead readers.

Over the last few years, the interest around the Fake News phenomenon has considerably increased. This is mainly due to the massive use of the Internet and more precisely the social networks. These applications are allowing users, to freely share and spread any content. However, as user's intentions aren't monitored, this liberty has made these sites, growingly, a source of misinformation and fake news [3]. Troude-Chastened in

R. Jallouli et al. (Eds.): ICDEc 2023, LNBIP 485, pp. 388–397, 2023.
https://doi.org/10.1007/978-3-031-42788-6_23

[4], distinguishes between three web source categories issuing fake news: satire websites whose objective is humor; conspiratorial sites which sometimes take the form of clickbait sites, aiming to generate advertising revenue; and Fake News Websites which disseminate rumors and hoaxes of all kinds.

Since humans are considered as "poor lie detectors" [5] and considering the big amount of news, generated on the web and spread over social networks, the automatic Fake News detection has become a crucial need and an inspiring research field. Many analysis and detection approaches have been proposed for Fake News, including among others, fact-checking and various classification techniques.

In this work, we are mainly concerned with the case of the Tunisian social web. According to the latest stats given in [6], the number of social media users in Tunisia, reached 8.2 million in January 2021, which corresponds to 69% of the Tunisian population, among which 68.8% are active Facebook users. As a result, social networks and Facebook in particular, have become a very popular source of news information for Tunisian people. However, this has also led to the proliferation of fake accounts, fake pages and fake news on the Tunisian social web. In particular, political false information spreads very quickly and increasingly, becomes a means of discrediting opponents, spreading unfounded rumors or diverting information. As a result, some initiatives are beginning to emerge to fight against fake news on the Tunisian social web. They essentially consist of the emergence of a few fact-checking platforms, among which we can cite "Birrasmi.tn"[1], "BN Check"[2], "Tunisia Checknews"[3], etc. However, there is no to date, a vigorous study about the audience perception of fact-checking in the Tunisian context [7] and actions token against Fake News in the Tunisian Social web, remain still limited.

As for the automatic detection of Fake News and to our knowledge, there is not yet published works tackling the case of Tunisian social media, especially since the specificities of the latter make the FN automatic detection, a quite complex and challenging task. Indeed, the user-generated and shared content over the social media in Tunisia is informal, multilingual, may use both the Latin and the Arabic script for writing Arabic and dialectal content, and often, include code-switching [8].

We propose in this work, a deep learning-based approach for detecting Fake news on the Tunisian social web, using Recurrent Neural Network (RNN) models. It takes into consideration the Tunisian social web content specificities and explores different features combinations: content-based features (news title and text) and social-based features (users' comments and reactions). For implementing the proposed approach, we conducted an exploratory study of several variants of RNNs, which are Simple Long Short-Term Memory Network (LSTM), Bi-LSTM, Deep LSTM and Deep Bi-LSTM combination. The obtained results are also compared with experiments we conducted, using an SVM-based model.

The work carried out is described in this paper, which is organized as follows: in Sect. 2, we provide a brief literature review, related to the issue of the automatic FN detection, focusing in particular, on the related work dealing with the Arabic language.

---

[1] http://birrasmi.tn/ (accessed on 29 April 2022)

[2] http://ar.businessnews.com.tn/bncheck (accessed on 29 April 2022)

[3] http://tunisiachecknews.com/ (accessed on 29 April 2022)

Section 3 is dedicated to describing the proposed hybrid approach for the automatic fake news detection. The conducted experiments and the obtained results are presented and discussed in Sect. 4. Finally, our work is summarized in the conclusion section and future work is presented.

2 Related Work

The automatic detection of fake news has aroused the interest of many researchers in the few last years. The study presented in [9] shows indeed, a significant upward trend in the number of publications dealing with rumors detection from 2015, as well as a surge in the number of publications on the detection of fake news from 2017. A study of the literature allows us to distinguish three main approaches, adopted in research work when dealing with FN detection, which are content-based approaches, social-based approaches and hybrid approaches combining content and social features.

Content-based FN detection approaches mainly rely on the news content features [9, 10]. They consider linguistic and visual information extracted from the news content such as text, images, or videos. Some studies investigated in combining textual and non-textual content features [11]. However, in most of studies, it is above all the textual characteristics that have been the most investigated, by exploiting NLP techniques and tools for analyzing the textual content, at different language levels: lexical, syntactic, semantic and discourse levels [2]. In [4], FN detection models were built by combining different sets of features, such as N-grams, punctuation, psycholinguistic features, readability and syntax, and experiments were conducted using a linear SVM classifier. Linguistic features have also been frequently considered such as, in [12] that experimented with an SVM model, using linguistic features related to Absurdity, Humor, Grammar, Negative Affect, and Punctuation.

Social-based FN detection approaches, also referred to as context-based approaches in [9, 10], or network-based approaches in [13], mainly rely on extracted information around the news, such as the news source, its propagation, the features of users producing or sharing the news, other social media users' interactions with the news, etc. We can cite in this respect, the work in [14] which showed that differences in the way messages propagate on twitter, can be helpful in analyzing the news credibility. In [2], a classification of Facebook posts as hoaxes or non-hoaxes was proposed. The classification was based on users' reactions to the news, using Logistic Regression and Boolean Label Crowdsourcing as classification techniques. Authors in [15] consider the news propagation network on social media and investigate in particular, news hierarchical propagation network for FN detection. They show that the propagation network features from structural, temporal, and linguistic perspectives, can be exploited to detect fake news. A model for early detecting fake news, through classifying news propagation paths, was proposed in [16], in which, a news propagation path is modeled as a multivariate time series, and a time series classifier incorporating RNN and CNN networks, is used.

Several works have combined both content-based and Social-based features, in order to improve the performance of FN detection. Authors in [17] show indeed, that RNN and CNN models, trained on tweet content and social network interactions, outperform lexical models. We can also mention the work in [18], which considered a combination of content signals, using a logistical Regression model, and social signals, using Harmonic Boolean Label Crowdsourcing. In [19], a model called CSI is proposed. It uses an RNN model and combines characteristics of the news text, the user activity on the news and the source users promoting it.

It should be noted that with regard to Arabic FN detection, recent works are beginning to emerge, but remain still relatively few in number. Among these works, we can cite [20], who collected a corpus from Youtube, for detecting rumors. They focused in particular, on proven fake news concerning the death of three Arab celebrities. Machine learning classifiers (SVM, Decision Trees and Multinomial Naïve Bayes) were then proposed for detecting rumors. In order to detect check-worthy tweets on a given topic, [21] have experimented with traditional ML classifiers (SVM, Logistic Regression and Random Forest) using both social and content-based features, and with a multilingual BERT (mBERT) pre-trained language model. They showed that the used mBERT model achieved better performance. These models were trained on a dataset including three topics, each having 500 annotated Arabic tweets and were was tested on a dataset including twelve topics with 500 Arabic tweets. Authors in [22], addressed the problem of detecting fake news surrounding COVID-19 in Arabic tweets. They manually annotated a dataset of tweets that were collected using trending hashtags related to COVID-19 from January to August 2020. This dataset was used to train a set of machine learning classifiers (Naïve Bayes, LR, SVM, MLP, RF and XGB). Authors in [23] presented a manually-annotated Arabic dataset for misinformation detection, called ArCOV19-Rumors and which covers tweets spreading claims related to COVID-19, during the period from January to April 2020. It contains 138 COVID-19 verified claims and 9.4K labeled tweets, related to these claims with their propagation networks. Results on detecting the veracity of tweets, were also presented, using a set of classification models (Bi-GCN, RNN+CNN, AraBERT, MARBERT), applied on a dataset of 1108 tweets.

As we can see, the lack of Arabic FN datasets remains a difficulty to overcome and most of the examined works were confronted with a stage of building a dataset in order to be able to propose an approach of Arabic FN detection. Regarding the case of Tunisian social media in particular, we can notice that no work addressing the automatic FN detection has yet been published to date. In this work, we propose a first exploratory study that addresses this issue, considering the case of the Tunisian social web and its specificities.

3 Fake News Detection proposed Approach

In this work, we consider the FN detection task as a binary classification aiming to predict whether a given posted news is fake or not. We propose a hybrid classification approach that combines content-based and social-based features. This approach takes into consideration the Tunisian social web specificities and explores different features combinations:

- *Content-based features.* We mainly consider two textual contents characterizing a news item, namely its title and its body;

- *Social-based features.* In our approach, we propose to consider two social signals categories: first, users' comments on social media about posted news as they may carry user's behaviors and opinions about the news and may thus, be a very informative source about its veracity. Second, we propose to take into account the users' reactions to the news post and to investigate their effectiveness in predicting the veracity of the news. As a matter of fact, reactions allow users to express their behavior easily, and this facility of reacting may make this type of information more available than comments. In our case, we consider the six types of reactions provided by Facebook which are: *"like"*, *"love"*, *"haha"*, *"wow"*, *"sad"*, *"angry"*.

In order to implement our approach, we proceeded to build a corpus of fake news in Arabic, extracted from Tunisian pages on Facebook. This corpus is described in the next sub-section. Using the collected data, we propose a deep learning FN detection model, based on Recurrent Neural Networks known to show good performance with textual inputs. In particular, we propose to adopt LSTM networks for the binary classification of Fake news. For this purpose, we conduct an exploratory study of several variants of this model: simple LSTM, Bi-LSTM, Deep LSTM, as well as the combination Deep Bi-LSTM. As our Fake News corpus has a limited size, we propose in our exploratory study of the LSTM-based approach, a comparison with a traditional machine learning model. For this purpose, we proposed a model based on SVMs and compared the obtained results.

3.1 Dataset Construction

As no Tunisian fake news dataset is available, we proceeded to build a dataset, which we collected from Facebook, using the tool Facepager[4] (a tool for fetching public data from social networks). The first step in our data collection was to select the pages from where, posts containing fake and true news will be extracted. We resorted to the pages of Mosaique FM and Jawhara FM radios as truthworthy. As for the pages that we considered to be sources of Fake News, we have identified them, from the fact checking platforms (cited in Sect. 1), which indicate the source page that posted a news checked as fake. We mainly collected a set of fake news (after we verified they were fake) from these Facebook pages:

"ضحك بالدموع"(*"Laugh to tears"*), "المظلية الاخبارية"(*"El Mdhilla News"*), "Capital News", "Asslema Tunisie" (*"Hello Tunisia"*), " تونسة حول العالم " (*"Tunisians around the world"*).

Posts we collected are related to different domains such as social subjects, sports, politics and news about covid-19 pandemic. The obtained dataset contains 350 fake news and 350 legitimate news. It provides for each posted news:

- its textual title content,
- its textual body,
- the textual comments related to the post,
- the total number of users' reactions,
- the number of *"like"* reactions,

---

[4] https://github.com/strohne/facepager.

- the number of "love" reactions,
- the number of "*haha*" reactions,
- the number of "*wow*" reactions,
- the number of "*sad*" reactions,
- the number of "*angry*" reactions,

The collected news are written in MSA (Modern Standard Arabic), however, users' comments are written in Arabic, French or in the Tunisian dialect. As mentioned in Sect. 3, some of them are multilingual and may contain code-switching.

3.2 Classification models

As mentioned above, we implemented the proposed approach combining both content-based and social-based features, using various variants of LSTM neural networks for the FN binary classification. The experimented classification models are:

- LSTM model. Long Short-Term Memory networks [24] are a special kind of Recurrent Neural Networks, characterized by their ability to learn long-term dependencies, by remembering information for long periods. The standard LSTM architecture consists of a cell and three gates also called "controllers": an Input gate that decides whether the input should modify the cell value; a Forget gate that decides whether to reset the cell content and an Output gate that decides whether the contents of the cell should influence the neuron output. These three gates constitute sorts of valves using a sigmoid function.
- Bi-LSTM model. Bidirectional LSTM is an extension of the LSTM model, where two LSTM models are trained and combined, so that the input sequence information is learned in both directions: forward and backwards. The outputs from both these two LSTM layers can be combined in several ways (such as average, sum, multiplication, concatenation).
- Deep LSTM model. A deep (or Stacked) LSTM network [25], is an extension of the original LSTM model. Indeed, instead of having a single hidden LSTM layer, it has multiple hidden layers, each containing multiple memory cells. The addition of layers makes the model deeper and puts on additional levels of abstraction of input observations over time.
- Deep Bi-LSTM model. It is an LSTM variant that is based on a multiple Bi-LSTM hidden layers.
- SVM model. Support Vector Machines [26] basic idea is to find a hyperplane separating the data to be classified, so as to group the data belonging to each class in the same side of this hyperplane. This hyperplane must maximize the margin separating it from the nearest data samples, called support vectors. SVMs are known to be well suited for textual data classification [27, 28]. [28] points out, the independency of their learning capacity from the feature space dimensionality, which make them suitable for text classification, generally characterized by a high dimensional input space.

3.3 Text Representation

The various LSTM-based models we have implemented, incorporate a word embeddings layer, which is their first hidden layer. It encodes the input words as real-valued vectors in a high dimensional space. Word embeddings are learned from the training textual dataset, based on their surrounding words in the text. Being part of the model, this embedding layer is learned jointly with the proposed model.

As for the SVM-based model, we simply used a TF-IDF (Term Frequency-Inverse Document Frequency) vectorization of the textual data.

4   Experiments and Results

For all the conducted experiments, we used the dataset we collected from Facebook as described in 4.1. In order to evaluate the effectiveness of the proposed models with different features combinations, we have randomly dedicated 80% of the dataset samples for the training process and 20% for testing the models. We propose in Table 1, the results obtained with several textual feature combinations as input, before adding the users' reactions, while Table 2 shows the obtained results after adding reactions. Results given in Tables 1 and 2 represent the accuracy of the implemented classification models.

Table 1. Results without considering users' reactions.

Textual Features	LSTM	Bi-LSTM	Deep LSTM	Deep Bi-LSTM	SVM
Post title	0.4928	0.4428	0.4642	0.4428	0.8357
Post text	**0.7785**	0.7285	**0.7571**	0.8071	**0.9**
Post title + text	0.7357	**0.7357**	0.7285	**0.8357**	**0.9**
Users' comments	0.6214	0.5714	0.6	0.5571	0.6142
All features	0.7642	0.5928	0.4357	0.6142	0.8142

Table 2. Results of experiments considering users' reactions.

Textual Features	LSTM	Bi-LSTM	Deep LSTM	Deep Bi-LSTM	SVM
Post title	0.5285	0.5642	0.4928	0.4714	0.8175
Post text	0.7785	**0.8**	0.7785	0.8357	**0.9197**
Post title + text	0.8	0.75	**0.8428**	**0.85**	0.9136
Users' comments	0.6285	0.6142	0.6357	0.6428	0.6715
All features	**0.8142**	0.7785	0.5714	0.80	0.8905

Considering results given in Tables 1 and 2, we can observe the relevance of the content-based features, since the best results were always obtained when considering the textual post body or the textual post body jointly with the title. We can indeed see that, for all the implemented models, adding the user's comments to the input features, did not improve results and instead, has degraded them, except for the experiment conducted with the LSTM model, where combining all textual features and adding users' reactions have led to an improved accuracy (reaching 0.8142, as shown in Table 2).

Similarly, considering only users' comments has led to an accuracy not exceeding 0.6715 (obtained with the SVM model in Table 2), remaining significantly lower than that obtained by models considering the textual body and title content, which confirms the relevance of content-based features. The relatively limited performance of textual social-based features (users' comments) can be explained by the complex nature of the written user-generated comments, which are frequently multilingual and informal, since they do not follow any specific spelling rules. These comments may be written in French, Arabic, or in the Tunisian dialect and sometimes in English. Arabic comments can be written both in the Latin and the Arabic script and may include code-switching. These characteristics specific to the Tunisian social web complicate the classification task and affect the quality of learning, especially since the dataset used in our case, remains of limited size.

However, taking into consideration the second type of social-based features which are the users' reactions, within the proposed models, has clearly improved the accuracy of all of them. The non textual social-based features, which are the nature and the percentage of each type of reaction, seem thus to be efficient features in detecting fake news on Tunisian Facebook pages. As shown in Table 2, best results obtained when considering these features vary between an accuracy that ranges from 0.8 to 0.9197.

As for the proposed deep learning models, we can observe from Tables 1 and 2, that the Deep Bi-LSTM model outperformed the three other variants of LSTM-based models, reaching an accuracy of 0,8357 when considering only content-based features (post title and body), and 0,85 when adding users' reactions. This therefore, confirms the performance improvement we were expecting by stacking two Bi-LSTM layers in order to learn more abstract features.

However, in our experiments, the proposed deep learning models did not outperform the SVM-based machine learning model which resulted in an accuracy reaching 0.9 when considering only content-based features, and 0,9197 when adding users' reactions. This can be explained by the limited size of our training corpus, as deep learning algorithms need large datasets to be more effective.

5   Conclusion

In this work, we proposed a first exploratory study that tackles the issue of automatically detecting fake news the Tunisian Social web, which represents a challenging task due to the Tunisian social web specificities, such as multilingualism and code-witching. To our knowledge, it is the first work dealing with the automatic FN detection considering the Tunisian context, in particular. The main contributions of this work are:

- the elaboration of a real word dataset, containing posts that we collected from public Tunisian Facebook pages. This dataset could be a starting point for other future works aiming to its enrichment and its use in automatic FN detection works, dealing with the Tunisian context.

- A study and evaluation of a hybrid approach combining a set of content-based and social-based features. In this context, multiple variants of LSTM networks have been explored: Bi-LSTM, deep LSTM and Deep Bi-LSTM, and an SVM-based machine learning was also investigated.

The results of this study showed that an accuracy of over 91% can be achieved with an SVM model, and an accuracy of 85% is reached using a Deep Bi-LSTM model. They also allowed us to measure the relevance of various content-based and social-based features.

We consider this work as starting point for future more elaborated investigations. We plan indeed as a first step, to work on collecting more data, in order to expand and enrich our Tunisian FN corpus. Then, we plan to explore other deep learning techniques, such as BERT embeddings and classifiers. As we obtained good results with the SVM model, we also propose to investigate deep hybrid learning-based approaches that combine deep learning with machine learning classifiers.

References

1. Allcott, H., Matthew, G.: Social media and fake news in the 2016 election. J. Econo. Perspect. **31**(2), 211–236 (2017)
2. Zhou, X., Zafarani, R.: Fake news: A survey of research, detection methods, and opportunities. arXiv preprint arXiv:1812.00315 (2018)
3. Tacchini, E., Ballarin, G., Della Vedova, M.L., Moret, S., De Alfaro, L.: Some like it hoax: Automated fake news detection in social networks. arXiv preprint arXiv:1704.07506 (2017)
4. Troude-Chastened, P.: Fake news et post-vérité. De l'extension de la propagande au Royaume-Uni, aux États-Unis et en France. Quaderni **96**, 87-101 (2018)
5. Shu, K., Sliva, A., Wang, S., Tang, J., Liu, H.: Fake news detection on social media. ACM SIGKDD Explorations Newsl **19**(1), 22–36 (2017)
6. Kemp, S.: Digital 2021: Tunisia. DataReportal. Retrieved from. Accessed in 2022-03-15
7. Zamit, F., Kooli, A., Toumi, I.: An examination of Tunisian fact-checking resources in the context of COVID-19. JCOM **19**(07), A04 (2020)
8. Jerbi, M.A., Achour, H., Souissi, E.: Sentiment Analysis of Code-Switched Tunisian Dialect: Exploring RNN-Based Techniques. In: Smaïli, K. (ed.) Arabic Language Processing: From Theory to Practice. ICALP 2019. Communications in Computer and Information Science, vol. 1108. Springer, Cham (2019)
9. Bondielli, A., Marcelloni, F.: A Survey on fake news and rumour detection techniques. Inf. Sci. **497**, 38–55 (2019)
10. Shu, K., Sliva, A., Wang, S., Tang, J., Liu, H.: Fake news detection on social media: a data mining perspective. ACM SIGKDD Explor. Newslett. **19**(1), 22–36 (2017)
11. Parikh, S.B., Atrey, P.K.: Media-rich fake news detection: a survey. In: Proceedings of the IEEE Conference on Multimedia Information Processing and Retrieval (MIPR'18). IEEE, pp. 436-441 (2018)
12. Rubin, V., Conroy, N., Chen, Y., Cornwell, S.: Fake news or truth? Using satirical cues to detect potentially misleading news. In: Proceedings of the NAACL-CADD Second Workshop on Computational Approaches to Deception Detection, pp. 7–17. San Diego, California, USA (2016)
13. Qazvinian, V., Rosengren, E., Radev, D.R., Mei, Q.: Rumor has it: Identifying misinformation in microblogs. In: Proceedings of the Conference on Empirical Methods in Natural Language Processing (EMNLP), pp. 1589–1599. Association for Computational Linguistics, Edinburgh, Scotland, UK (2011)

14. Castillo, C., Mendoza, M., Poblete, B.: Information credibility on twitter. In: Proceedings of the Twentieth International Conference on World Wide Web, pp. 675–684. ACM, Hyderabad, India (2011)
15. Shu, K., Mahudeswaran, D., Wang, S., Liu, H.: Hierarchical propagation networks for fake news detection: Investigation and exploitation. arXiv:1903.09196 (2019)
16. Liu, Y., Frang, Y., Wu, B.: Early detection of fake news on social media through propagation path classification with recurrent and convolutional networks. Association for the Advancement of Artificial Intelligence (2018)
17. Volkova, S., Shaffer, K., Jang, J.Y., Hodas, N.: Separating facts from fiction: linguistic models to classify suspicious and trusted news posts on twitter. In: Proceedings of the Fifty Fifth Annual Meeting of the Association for Computational Linguistics (Volume 2: Short Papers), 2, pp. 647–653 (2017)
18. Della Vedova, M.L., Tacchini, E., Moret, S., Ballarin, G., DiPierro, M., de Alfaro, L.: Automatic Online Fake News Detection Combining Content and Social Signals. The 22nd Conference of Open Innovations Association (FRUCT) (2018)
19. Ruchansky, N., Seo, S., Liu, Y.: CSI: a hybrid deep model for fake news detection. In: Proceedings of the 26th ACM International Conference on Information and Knowledge Management (CIKM) (2017)
20. Alkhair, M., Meftouh, K., Smaïli, K., Othman, N.: An Arabic Corpus of Fake News: Collection, Analysis and Classification. In: Smaïli, K. (ed.) Arabic Language Processing: From Theory to Practice. ICALP 2019. Communications in Computer and Information Science, vol 1108. Springer, Cham (2019)
21. Hasanain, M., Elsayed, T.: bigIR at CheckThat! 2020: Multilingual BERT for Ranking Arabic Tweets by Check-worthiness (2020)
22. Mahlous, A.R., Al-Laith, A.: Fake news detection in arabic tweets during the COVID-19 pandemic. Int. J. Adva. Comp. Sci. Appl. **12**(6) (2021)
23. Haouari, F., Hasanain, M., Suwaileh, R., Elsayed, T.: Arcov19-rumors: Arabic covid-19 twitter dataset for misinformation detection. In: Proceedings of the Sixth Arabic Natural Language Processing Workshop, WANLP 2021 (2021)
24. Hochreiter, S., Schmidhuber, J.: Long short-term memory. Neural Comput. **9**(8), 1735-80 (1997 Nov 15)
25. Lundberg, S., Lee, S.: Advances in Neural Information Processing Systems 30, pp. 4768–4777. Curran Associates, Inc. (2017)
26. Cortes, C., Vapnik, V.: Support-Vector Networks. In: Machine Learning (1995)
27. Vinot, R., Grabar, N., Valette, M.: Application d'algorithmes de classification automatique pour la détection des contenus racistes sur l'Internet. In: Proceedings of the 10th annual conference on Natural Language Processing TALN, Batz-sur-Mer (2003)
28. Joachims, T.: Text categorization with support vector machines: In: Proceedings of the 10th European Conference on Machine Learning, Chemnitz (1998)

The Role of Innovation in Mediating the Relationship Between Organisational Culture and Financial Performance

Arem Say[1]([✉]) [iD], Adel Necib[1], and Anis Jarboui[2]

[1] Higher Institute of Business Administration, GafsaUniversity, Gafsa, Tunisia
arem2say@yahoo.fr, aremsaai2020@gmail.com
[2] Faculty of Economics and Management, Sfax, Tunisia

Abstract. This study examines the dimensions of innovation and industry and tests the relationship between corporate culture and organisational performance. A survey was conducted among 70 companies listed on the Tunis BVMT stock exchange. The data are analysed using principal component analysis and the relationships are tested using linear regression. This result shows the importance of the implementation of an innovation system. They show a positive impact on company performance and competitive advantage.

Keywords: Innovation · BVMT · Corporate culture · financial performance

1 Introduction

Corporate culture – patterns of thought, emotions, behaviour and beliefs – plays a crucial role in the creation and development of innovation within a company. Each company has its own culture which is the result of a complex dynamic where factors as diverse as the nature of the activity, the history of the organisation and the memory of its successes and failures, the personality of the leader, etc. play a role (Habhab-Rave 2011). Innovation, through its strategic importance as well as its impact on the overall performance of the company, constitutes a determining basis of the culture, around which the collective representations constituting the company's culture are shaped and arranged. Indeed, organisations whose culture emphasises innovation tend to implement more innovations and develop a competitive advantage).

This study examines the dimensions of innovation, culture and organisational performance. Managers need to be attentive and consistent in their means of intervention and leadership style to improve organisational performance. It is important to consider two important aspects of management: the constantly changing social values and the history of the company as it emerges from the social structure itself. In this context, a thorough understanding of corporate culture can improve company performance. Indeed, it is the shared beliefs, practices and values that define the organisational culture that provide the informal control mechanisms that coordinate the efforts of employees. By collaborating more quickly with their former colleagues, new recruits discover the company's objectives and practices that are an integral part of the company's culture. In this logic of exchange of practices shared by the employees, the company culture is the result of a social construction by the employees, and not of an imposition on them. In addition to the self- construction of the culture in question, previous research has shown that workers become more sensitive to the encouragement and consideration of their superiors, and are more motivated to produce more for the same pay. The savings achieved through a strong corporate culture therefore hold out hope for the performance of the company.

Corporate culture is both a motivating factor and a positive image to the outside world (Dezecot and Fleck 2021). Corporate culture is a complex, living and changing concept that has received much attention in today's business world (Gareth 2019). Many initiatives are aimed at building employee loyalty, fostering a sense of belonging or changing the organisation and methods. In this sense, organisational culture seems to have a direct impact on performance and value creation processes. By the same token, corporate culture reflects the correct approach of a company to its overall activities and is now considered an important and integral factor in supporting and optimising the value chain of a company. Similarly, a good corporate culture helps to ensure processes.

Innovation is a primary source of performance, being fundamental for organisations that want to remain competitive and have renewable sources of competitive advantage. It is implicit in the literature that one of the factors that can stimulate innovation is organisational culture (Martins and Terblanche 2003). Furthermore, the culture of innovation relies on an enabling environment that fosters a socially anchored perception of research and development, a joint involvement around the customer's goal and a design thinking philosophy based on organisational agility and flexibility.

In summary, innovation therefore acts as an intermediary between corporate culture and financial performance and can improve and strengthen corporate performance. Thus, innovation can act as an intermediary between corporate culture and financial performance.

Most management research has focused on the development of a link between organisation and corporate culture, emphasising the role of culture in improving the performance of organisations (Hofstede 1980; Schein 1990; Uhalde and Osty 2007). Little research has focused on the link between innovation and corporate culture (Alter 2000; Sainsaulieu 1994; Francfort et al. 1995). This research has examined only a limited aspect of the influence of culture on innovation. Thus, an examination of the intermediary role that innovation plays between culture and performance seems particularly appropriate. An in-depth understanding of the place of innovation in the organisation and its importance for the development of an innovative culture and innovation performance.

The aim of this paper is to analyse in depth the links between corporate culture, performance and innovation, and to go beyond the simplistic approach that addresses culture as a factor that conditions the action of innovation, but rather to focus on the mutual influence of the culture- innovation-performance trilogy and to characterise their interactions in a hyper-competitive and turbulent environment.

Based on the above, we can formulate the following question:

How can innovation mediate *the relationship between organisational culture and financial performance?*

We will present a review of the existing literature on relationship between organisational culture and financial performance in the first section. The second section will present the methodological choices. An empirical study has made it possible to analyse empirically these critical relationships between corporate culture, innovation and performance. The third section will present and discuss the results obtained. Finally, the conclusion will be devoted to a synthesis of the contribution of our research.

2   Literature Review and Study Hypotheses

Several studies have shown that factors can affect the financial performance of a company. These factors are Corporate culture and innovation.

2.1   The Influence of Corporate Culture on Company Performance

The link between culture and performance finds its development in the valorisation of the human factor, which is the cornerstone of any company and the basic fibre that guarantees its performance.

Companies with a strong culture perform better than those without. Companies with strong corporate cultures focus on all components of key human factors, including shareholders, employees and customers.

The term 'corporate culture' refers to the activities, operating rules and values (morals, ethics, environment, etc.) shared by all members of the company.

Working in a coherent, methodical and efficient way. It is its history, its project, its strategic vision. Generally carried by managers, the corporate culture is identified in the "DNA of the company".

The first step in building the best corporate culture is to define the company's main purpose in light of its history and ambition. This leads to a set of values, beliefs and rules that best achieve that purpose (Graham et al. 2017). After completing this stage, the results of the retrospective need to be effectively communicated to all employees. This role is delegated to managers. Because they embody the corporate culture and propagate it in their speeches, decisions and actions. They must ensure that it is communicated to all employees, including new ones, and create a healthy work environment that fosters trust and interaction between colleagues. Finally, in addition to the dissemination of the company's values, the corporate culture also includes symbols (office design, fittings, specific language, slogans, projects supported by the company, etc.) and rituals (welcome programme for each new recruit, employee). All these elements are also essential tools for the corporate culture and can be made visible and accessible.

According to Vayssade (2022), a culture is defined by five parameters, namely, a working environment, a sense of community, leadership involvement, investment in human capital, value systems and diversity. These parameters influence three factors other than financial performance which are: Effective levels of collaboration, customer satisfaction, employee engagement and motivation. Overall, a supportive corporate culture motivates employees to achieve their goals, thereby increasing the value and financial performance of the company. However, shareholders may not be able to evaluate corporate culture favourably as they see it as an avoidable expense that can lead to a loss of company value. Poor culture can also be a barrier to the realisation of business benefits.

For example, the study cites improved employee retention through a better corporate culture. Managers also generally seem to overestimate the importance of the work environment and underestimate the return on investment of training programmes. The impact of a good company culture is 1.5 times more likely to grow by more than 15% over the last 3 years and 2.5 times more likely to outperform (Djoumessi et al 2020). A study by Grant Thornton and Oxford Economics only partially and incompletely addresses the complex issue of the relationship between corporate culture and financial performance, but proposes a related methodology to help measure and quantify the relationship between culture and performance among managers. Building a culture that optimises financial performance is not an easy task. Humility, openness, perseverance and willingness are qualities that are hard to find in many organisations.

From the theoretical and empirical research that has been cited it seems that there is a consensus that there is a real impact of corporate culture on performance. Culture has a decisive impact on the economic results of companies. Indeed, companies that give primary importance to the human factor show better results than those that value these aspects less.

When a company succeeds in aligning its culture with its strategy and management, all the parameters are in place to obtain positive economic results. The company must develop a culture oriented towards learning, creativity and advanced onboarding.

On the basis of what has been said, we can formulate the following hypothesis:

Assumptions (H1): Corporate culture has a positive influence on financial performance.

2.2 The Influence of Corporate Culture on Innovation

Several elements characterise the innovative company: a strategy oriented towards open innovation, knowledge of customer requirements, a general policy based on investment in research and development. But most of all, there is the role of the thread played by the culture. (Jaruzelski and Katzenbach 2012).

Corporate culture has a special relationship with the concept of innovation. In the literature there are cultural drivers such as creativity and cultural brakes such as bureaucracy. Organisational creativity, which has its roots in the corporate culture, in particular the entrepreneurial culture, is a function of the ability to mobilise and combine skills and creativity effectively within groups of individuals, including entrepreneurs. A limited world of possibilities for creating useful new products, services or processes that create value for the company.

Bureaucracy, so prevalent in hierarchical and market cultures, can undermine an organisation's ability to innovate by slowing down the decision-making process, limiting the responsiveness of structures and creating an organisational environment that is not conducive to innovation.

The authors propose four cultural typologies. A hierarchical (or bureaucratic) culture is characterised by rigidity, an emphasis on control and efficiency, and a conservative leadership style with little or no room for innovative initiatives. It is structured around a set of conservative rules and values that emphasise the formalisation of production processes, control and domination of situations (Rabaud 2023). A market culture oriented towards rational decision- making, planning and construction of production activities. This culture refers to companies that are strongly market-oriented and whose functions are mainly based on transactions with external stakeholders. A group culture (or clan culture) which emphasises cohesion, team spirit and support. It is also characterised by a friendly atmosphere at work, interaction between members of the organisation and autonomy in making certain decisions. Ideocratic (entrepreneurial) culture, adaptability to change, risk-taking, innovation, culture of organisational creativity. Ougharbi and Achour (2020) conclude that this culture is characterised by dynamism, entrepreneurship, creativity and risk-taking, with leaders being visionaries, innovators and risk-takers, and employees creating new things. The primary objective of innovative and successful products and services.

According to Cameron and Quinn (2011), companies with an entrepreneurial culture define success as having innovative and unique products that enable the company to become a leader and innovator in the market. For a company to innovate, it must be creative, transformative and have a profile that allows it to produce products that are both new and appropriate to the situation in which it emerges (Amabile 1996; Bonnardel 2002).

A corporate culture that fosters innovation encourages creativity through the development of new products and the exploration of new avenues. Many organisational cultures (O'Reilly et al. 1989) establish norms that foster innovation processes (O'Reilly et al. 1989). Corporate culture also facilitates co-ordination and co-operation among employees. As mentioned earlier, corporate culture promotes employee interaction and commitment, improves the effectiveness of information sharing and results in business innovation.

At this level, innovation, understood as the process of creating and developing new products and services, is of strategic importance and represents one of the "pivots" of this corporate culture, of which it is the collective expression; (Habhab-Rave 2011). Thus, the study of corporate culture is a major advance in the analysis of the innovation process, but it should not be forgotten that the relationship between corporate culture and innovation is complex. In this sense, culture is based on symbols associated with the past, while innovation is the break between the past and tradition, considered as a fundamental element of culture (Pesqueux 2015). According to Plane (2017), the importance of organisational culture is to foster an entrepreneurial spirit among the members of the organisation and to develop long-term visions and strategic actions aimed at improving the quality of the goods and services to be promoted.

Although there is a lot of research dealing with corporate culture, much of it has focused on developing a link between organisation and culture with an emphasis on performance improvement (Hofstede 1980; Schein 1990; Sainsaulieu 1994; Uhalde and Osty 2007). Few studies have focused on the link between innovation and corporate culture (Alter 2000; Sainsaulieu 1994; Francfort et al. 1995).

Therefore, we can make the following hypothesis:

Assumptions (H2): Corporate culture has a positive influence on innovation

2.3 Innovation Has a Positive Influence on Financial Performance

Innovation has now become an inexhaustible source of competitive advantage and a key ideological reference insofar as it is put forward as the saviour of growth. Innovation is one of the main drivers of value creation in firms and appears to be one of the most effective bulwarks in the face of a changing and highly competitive market (Besbes et al. 2013; Hall et al. 2005). Moreover, innovation is widely recognised as one of the most important mechanisms for firms to sustain and stimulate growth in the dynamic, globalised and changing technological environment.

In this sense, the first to explain the notion of a positive relationship between innovation and performance was Schumpeter (1934). He argued that new innovative products in the market face limited direct competition, allowing firms to achieve relatively high profits. Subsequently, the literature on the relationship between innovation and performance has grown. Some research has argued that there is a positive relationship between innovation and performance (Geroski et al. 1993). Others try to prove and explain the absence of a direct link (Deltour and Lethiais 2014). Faced with these controversies we formulate the following hypothesis:

Assumptions (H3): Innovation has a positive influence on financial performance.

2.4 Innovation Mediates the Relationship Between Corporate Culture and Financial Performance

In a knowledge-based economy, innovation is critical to the success of companies, as it contributes to competitive advantage. As a result, intangible investments are now seen as a fundamental determinant of firm value. In fact, innovation influences economic activity and can lead to a more efficient allocation of the resources available to companies. Therefore, it is important that a wide range of users, including managers, investors, creditors and other stakeholders, evaluate innovation activities. Creativity is often seen as a prerequisite for technological innovation. Much research has focused on organisational contexts that foster creativity.

A mediating variable is an intermediate variable that describes the relationship between the independent and dependent variables. More precisely, it explains how and why the effect occurs (Jérolon et al. 2020). The level of innovation of a company is considered as a parameter in this study. The latter variable is a composite index calculated from a combination of several elements that reflect the level of innovation of a company. It is the sum of binary indicators (items) of innovation activities carried out by the company.

Assumptions (H4): Innovation mediates the relationship between corporate culture and financial performance.

The basis of our hypotheses, the conceptual framework of this study is based on modelling with parameters such as innovation. Our model therefore allows us to highlight the direct relationship between organisational culture and financial performance. Finally, our model also includes innovation as a mediating variable for the indirect relationship between organisational culture and financial performance (Fig. 1).

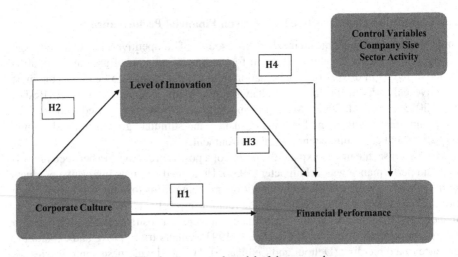

Fig. 1. Conceptual model of the research

3   Research Methodology

In the empirical part we first present a sample of empirical studies, data sources and models. We then define the different variables and their measures retained in this study. The dependent variable retained for our study is the financial performance of the company. The independent or explanatory variables of the study were: degree of innovation, size of the firm, field of activity.

3.1   Data Resources

Our survey sample consists of 70 Tunisian companies listed on the Tunis Stock Exchange (B.V.M.T). To test our hypothesis, we collected data on the dependent variable from the annual report and reference documents for that year (Graham et al. 2017). The data for the independent and control variables used in these papers were obtained from databases, annual reports and database reference documents (Graham et al. 2017). The annual reports and reference data were collected from company websites.

The descriptive analysis is the step that allows to describe the relationships between the characteristics of the sample and the variables. Table 1 below presents the descriptive statistics (number of observations, mean, standard deviation, minimum and maximum values) for the variables used in the analysis.

Table 1. Descriptive Statistics of the Sample

Variables	Mean	Std. deviation	Min	Max
CULT	0.765	0.182	0.30	1.00
ROE	0.241	0.173	0.004	0.609
SECT	0.763	0.428	00	1.00
FSIZE	4.198	3.913	–0.03	9.79
INNOV	0.025	0.041	00	0.21

- Descriptive statistics of the dependent variable:

The average financial performance (ROE) is 0.241 with a standard deviation of 0.173. Its minimum and maximum values are 0.004 and 0.609 respectively. "0.609". This means that the financial performance of the financial statements of the companies in the sample is very low. This result is consistent with those of Cheng and Courtenay (2006), Pateli and Prencipe (2007) and Fang et al. (2009), Xiaowen (2012), Russo et al. (2015), Mensah (2016), but disagree with the findings of Eng and Mak (2000), Leng and Ding (2011) and Hunziker (2013). Due to the low level of financial performance (0.241), it is very difficult for the company's stakeholders to judge the company's future performance.

- Descriptive statistics of independent variables:

The means of the corporate culture and innovation variables are 0.765 and 0.025 respectively. 0.025. The standard deviations are 0.182 and 0.041. Its minimum and maximum values are 0.30 and 1.00 respectively.

- Descriptive statistics of control variables:

The average firm size in this study (measured by total log assets) is approximately 4.198, with a minimum of –0.03 and a maximum of 9.79. In this case, the industry average is 0.763 and the standard deviation is 0.428. Its minimum and maximum values are 0 and 1.00 respectively.

3.2 The Variables

The content of the company's website included in the cultural proxy includes:

CEO speech, culture pages, employee engagement, social responsibility, employee training programmes, company news and media coverage. Create a dummy variable Speech that is 1 if the company's website has a section dedicated to CEO speech, 0 otherwise. We choose CEO speech because it is likely that companies choose their culture and CEOs feed it from above (Graham et al. 2017). A CEO speech is a direct way for all stakeholders to understand the culture promoted by the CEO of the company. A culture page is a direct way to show whether you are promoting the company culture.

Create a dummy variable culture page that will be 1 if your company website has its own culture page, otherwise null.

Employee training programmes not only improve employees' knowledge of the company's activities, but also establish a corporate culture promoted among employees. Employees can be an integral embodiment of the corporate culture that a company promotes. Employee training is about communicating the company's mission and code of conduct, explicitly and implicitly, to employees so that they can perform their duties. Therefore, we believe that employee training is an integral part of promoting the corporate culture. Furthermore, once the CEO sets the tone for the culture being promoted, employees are motivated to adopt that culture, thereby promoting coordination and collaboration among employees. Employee training programmes are one way to achieve this. Employee activities are another. Employee activities are created to match the number of employee activities on the company's website. Therefore, the measured value of this variable is the calculated result based on the measured value of this variable.

3.3 Econometric Models

Let us recall that our main objective is to test the impact of corporate culture on the social performance of Tunisian companies. Thus our model:

$$CC = \alpha 0 + \alpha 1 INT + FSIZE + SECT \tag{1}$$

$$INT = \alpha 0 + \alpha 1 FP + FSIZE + SECT \tag{2}$$

$$FP = \alpha 0 + \alpha 1 CC + \alpha 2 INT + FSIZE + SECT \tag{3}$$

With:

- FP: Financial Performance
- INT: Innovation
- CULT:Campany Culture
- FSIZE: Campany Size
- SECT: Sector of Activity

3.4 Explanation of Variables

Here we have tried to list different variables that can be categorised into dependent variables, i.e. financial performance, independent variables mainly related to corporate culture, control variables related to performance.

Check for mediation effects using hierarchical regression. Baron and Kenny (1986) propose four conditions for testing the perfect mediation of M in the X-Y relationship.

Condition (1): Variable X should have a large influence on variable Y.

Condition (2): The variable X should have a large influence on the variable M.

Condition (3): If the influence of variable X on Y is controlled, the putative mediator variable M should have a large influence on variable Y.

Condition (4): The significant effect of variable X on Y should disappear when the effect of M on Y is statistically controlled.

3.4.1 Measurement of the Dependent Variable

Financial performance was the dependent variable in this study, and to determine its measurement, data were manually extracted from the financial statements and registration records of the companies used in the study. Measured as average return on equity (ROE/Equity), average return on assets (*ROA/Total Assets*) and average return on equity (*ROE/Total Assets*).

ROE and ROA are two measures of financial performance that provide an internal assessment of a company's profitability (efficient use of equity and assets).

3.4.2 Measurement of Independent Variables

Les variables indépendantes de cette étude étaient: Culture d'entreprise et degré d'innovation.

Company Culture

A good company culture encourages good behaviour, increases employee happiness and productivity and reduces turnover. It also attracts loyal customers who value the services/products your company offers. All this contributes to the satisfaction and profitability of the company. Furthermore, several studies have undoubtedly shown that the quality of the company culture is directly linked to the company's performance. It is a variable that reflects several aspects. This includes the development of multi-element configurations.

Level of Innovation

Many researchers and practitioners consider research and development (R&D) to be synonymous with innovation. However, a review of the literature suggests that innovation is broader than R&D expenditure (Kirner et al. 2009). First, we present the methodological challenges of innovation research. Part 2 describes international efforts to measure innovation. The third point concerns the accounting of innovation activities by Tunisian accounting. Finally, the fourth point concerns the scale of innovation assumed in this research.

Table 2. Summary of the variables used in this study and their respective measures.

Types of variables	Variables	Code	Measures selected by reference to internal studies
Dependent variables	Financial Performance	FP	ROA: Return on assets = operating profit after tax/total assets ROE: Return on equity = net income/equity
Independent variables	Company culture	CULT	
Mediating variables	Level of Innovation	INT	Innovation index
Control variables	Company size	FSIZE	Logarithm of the company's total assets
	Sector of Activity	SECT	Company's sector of activity

Source: prepared by us.

3.4.3 Measurement of Control Variables

4 Empirical Results

After clarifying and justifying our methodological choices, we will now present the main results and how they confirm or clarify our hypotheses.

Multi-variety Analysis

To properly study the impact of organisational culture on financial performance, the validity of the models needs to be tested.

The multiple regression results for the model show the following indications. The Fisher statistic (F), which measures the overall significance of the model, is equal to 5.79, confirming the good quality of the model below the significance level above 1%. Therefore, the Fisher statistic is significant at the 1% level, so that the model seems reasonably explanatory. The model therefore has overall relevance and explains the phenomenon under study.

Testing the Research Hypotheses: Analysis of the Impact of Corporate Culture on Financial Performance

Recall that we formulated four hypotheses concerning organisational culture and financial performance, the level of innovation and the relationship between these two variables. These relationships were tested by multiple linear regression and the results are presented and interpreted in this final section. The following table shows the results of the multiple linear regression (Table 3).

Table 3. Multiple linear regression results of the first model

Explanatory variables	Coef.	T-Student	Sig.
Constant	0.355	3.115	0.003**
CULT	0.056	2.425	0.037**
SECT	−0.065	−1.140	0.260 (n.s)
FSIZE	0.005	1.832	0.064**
R2 = 0.382			
Adjusted R2 = 0.195			
F 12.662 Sig. 0.006			

***: significant at 1% level; **: significant at 5% level; *: significant at 10% level; n.s.: not significant in the following, we present the results of the first model:

Table 4. Multiple linear regression results of the second model

Explanatory Variables	Coef.	T-Student	Sig.
Constant		3.085	0.003***
CULT	0.059	1.662	0.097**
SECT	0.160	1.122	0.268(n.s)
FSIZE	−0.113	−0.763	0.449(n.s)
INNOV	0.014	3.097	0.003***

***: significant at 1% level; **: significant at 5% level; *: significant at 10% level;n.s.: not significant

The table above can be used to test hypotheses and provide corresponding explanations (Table 4).

First hypothesis (H1) is used to test whether corporate culture positively influences financial performance. The regression results presented in the table confirm that corporate culture appears to have a significant effect on financial performance. The results show that the coefficient of corporate culture is positive (0.056) and significant (Student's $t = 2.425$ and $p = 0.037$), which means that this variable has an effect on financial performance. These results confirm the first hypothesis (H1). This result confirms the work of (Graham et al. 2017), who confirm that corporate culture improves the effectiveness of an organisation by enhancing coordination and control within the company.

The second hypothesis (H2) indicates that corporate culture has a positive effect on innovation. The results show that the coefficient of innovation is positive (0.059) and significant (Student's $t = 1.662$ and $p = 0.097$ significant at 10%). This allows us to accept the second hypothesis (H2). Thus, the presence of the level of innovation plays a very important role in determining the effect of corporate culture. The study of corporate culture is a significant advance for the analysis of innovation processes (Schumpeter 1934; Habhab-Rave 2011). We predict that corporate culture has a positive relationship with the innovation outcome of a firm.

The third hypothesis (H3) indicates that innovation has a positive impact on financial performance. The examination of the statistical tests shows that this variable has a positive and statistical influence on the financial performance of companies. The examination of the causal effect shows that the statistical coefficient associated with the "Innov" variable has a positive value (0.014). The significance of this coefficient is determined using Student's t-test. The value of t = 3.097, p =0.003 significant at 5%). This means that innovation has a positive and significant effect on financial performance. This allows us to accept the predictions of hypothesis (H3). This is in line with the previous results of Hofstede et al (2010), which show that innovation is one of the main drivers of value creation for firms. At this level, innovation as a process of creating and developing new products and services is of strategic importance.

The fourth hypothesis (H4) states that innovation mediates the relationship between corporate culture and financial performance. The empirical results show that innovation has a positive effect on corporate culture and at the same time positively influences the company's financial performance. Thus, the coefficient of this variable is positive (0.014) and significant (Student's t =3.097, p =0.003 significant at 5%). These results confirm the fourth hypothesis (H4). The main result of model 2 (full model) indicates a complete mediation, i.e. the mediator (the level of innovation) fully explains the association between the explanatory variable and the variable to be explained.

Analysis of the Influence of Control Variables on Financial Performance

- **Company size:**

Our study shows that company size has a positive influence on financial performance. The examination of statistical tests shows that this variable has a positive and statistical influence on the financial performance of the company with a positive value (0.005). The significance of this coefficient is obtained using the student test. The value of (t = 1.832, p = 0.064 significant at 10%). This shows that company size has a positive and significant relationship on financial performance.

- **Sector of Activity:**

For this control variable, the results show that the coefficient on industry is negative (–0.065) and insignificant (–1.140) with p= 0.260, meaning that this variable has no effect on financial performance.

Having analysed the overall significance of the world, let's look at the individual meanings of the parameters. This test allows you to find variables that have a significant impact on the financial performance of a company and to eliminate explanatory variables that do not contribute significantly to the regression model. Finally, based on the results of the tests we conducted, we can present a validated model of the relationship between corporate culture and corporate financial performance in Tunisian firms.

$$Y = 0.059\text{CULT} + 0.014\text{INNOV} + 0.005\text{FSIZE} + (-0.065)\text{SECT} \qquad (4)$$

5 Discussion of the Results

The main objective of our study is to examine the relationship between corporate culture and financial performance in Tunisian firms. Several linear regression tests allowed us to identify the impact of organizational culture on financial performance.

By examining different linear regression results, we were able to confirm the importance of the cultural variables that had the most impact on financial performance. The positive relationship and impact of corporate culture on performance was clearly identified. Corporate culture is becoming an increasingly important issue for boards. It is our third priority after strategy and financial performance. The majority of managers interviewed agree that they are responsible for defining and promoting culture within their company. Corporate culture can be seen not only as a management tool, but also as a means of social control. As a management tool, it can contribute to improving company performance under certain conditions (Sarkis and Dhavale 2015). As a tool of social control, it requires members of the firm to conform to the expectations of management. Ultimately, it is the overall corporate culture that needs to be developed to improve the performance of the company. It is the precursor and prerequisite for any strategic thinking (January 2016).

As for the innovation variable, it is positively correlated with the financial performance of companies, as shown in the first part of the literature. Indeed, the results show that innovation is more important and impacts financial performance. This proves that innovation was previously thought to have a positive relationship and impact on firm performance. For example, Hall et al. (2005) Innovation is one of the main drivers of value creation in firms.

Contribution to Research

The contribution of this study lies in its ability to explain the impact of organisational culture on financial performance. From a theoretical point of view, this work confirms the conceptual research model. The latter is based on issues related to the identification and understanding of organisational culture as it relates to financial performance. At the practical level, this research identifies the strategies considered in the innovation process as key factors for improving financial performance.

On the other hand, at the theoretical level, we have focused on the concept of corporate culture and its relationship with financial performance. On the other hand, innovation plays an important role in the performance of a company. Based on these theories, four hypotheses were proposed. Empirical studies were used to test them in the Tunisian context.

Methodologically, hypothesis-driven research methodologies were used to test the hypotheses of quantitative studies.

The aim of this study was to examine the impact of corporate culture on financial performance. These concepts include innovation as a mediating variable. This study also adjusted for variables that previous studies have found to contribute significantly to organisational culture. Control variables included: company size and industry. Multiple regression was used to analyse the data collected. This study provides empirical evidence of the impact of these variables on financial performance.

Corporate culture contributes to:

- Ensuring group cohesion by improving communication (emphasising shared values rather than asserting different interests).
- Better adaptation to the environment, in particular to ensure the survival of the group by forming a more coherent group and responding more quickly to threats through a shared vision of the future.

    If all members of the company share common values, they will sympathise with their company. This leads to better motivation as employees integrate the company's objectives. Where internal control is difficult and self-management is important (qualitative rather than quantitative objectives), the presence of a corporate culture is even more necessary. A fundamental principle of corporate culture is that employees are more likely to defend the company when they see it as the community to which they belong.

- Corporate culture, in turn, increases the competitiveness and performance of a company. Indeed, a strong corporate culture improves the economic performance of a company by reducing its costs. The common beliefs, practices and myths that define the organisational culture provide an informal control mechanism for coordinating the efforts of employees. New employees are less likely to hear a different version of the company's goals and practices, so they are more quickly matched with existing employees. Moreover, this culture is socially constructed by employees rather than imposed on them. As a result, motivation and morale are better than when they are controlled by a boss. Labour costs are also cheaper. Therefore, the savings generated by a strong corporate culture can lead to improved financial performance of the company.

6 Conclusion

The main objective of our research was to analyse the impact of corporate culture on the financial performance of Tunisian listed companies (BVMT 70 companies).

At the theoretical level, we mobilized several theories to answer the question. In this respect, we have sought to develop a theoretical basis for the relationship between corporate culture and the financial performance of companies by relying on agency relationships or signal theory.

Our empirical study is based on a sample of 70 Tunisian firms. Manually collect data from company websites and perform statistical analyses. Models were estimated using multiple regression methods. The results of the survey show that corporate culture and innovation have a strong impact on firm performance. The hypothesis that corporate culture has a positive impact on company performance is confirmed by the results obtained. The results also allow us to understand how companies improve their performance, competitiveness and environmental capabilities.

It also contributes to the literature on corporate culture by suggesting that a particular corporate culture is less important than a chosen corporate culture commitment in relation to corporate performance such as value, financial performance and increased performance. A corporate culture tailored to your needs.

A corporate culture can improve performance more than a structured management style. First of all, the company can easily manage integration problems. H. A sense of interdependence, a common language to facilitate communication, etc. Secondly, it can improve compliance with the company's objectives. The achievement of goals, in turn, motivates company members to participate in the action.

The positive association between the promotion of organisational culture and innovation outcomes seems to be consistent with the previous arguments that organisational culture promotes coordination and collaboration among employees, thus fostering innovation. Furthermore, it is understood that the relationship between organisational culture and firm performance is more than a direct link and may depend on firm strategy and changes in the environment (Sørensen et al. 2002).

References

Alter, K.J.: The European Union's legal system and domestic policy: spillover or backlash? Int. Organ. **54**(3), 489–518 (2000)

Amabile, T.M.: Creativity and Innovation in Organizations, vol. 5. Harvard Business School, Boston (1996)

Baron, R.M., Kenny, D.A.: The moderator–mediator variable distinction in social psychological research: conceptual, strategic, and statistical considerations. J. Pers. Soc. Psychol. **51**(6), 1173 (1986)

Besbes, A., Aliouat, B., Gharbi, J.E.: L'impact de l'innovation managériale sur la performance: rôle de l'orientation marché et de l'apprentissage organisationnel. Rev. Fr. Gest. **6**, 161–174 (2013)

Bonnardel, N.: Entrée: Créativité. In: Tiberghien, G. (ed.), Dictionnaire des sciences cognitives, pp. 95– 97 (2002)

Deltour, F., Lethiais, V.: L'innovation en PME et son accompagnement par les TIC: quels effets sur la performance? Systèmes d'information et management **19**(2), 45–73 (2014)

Dezecot, J., Fleck, N.: Perceptions, freins et motivations des consommateurs à l'égard des artisans des métiers de bouche. Décis. Market. **3**, 55–81 (2021)

Djoumessi, F., Gonne, J., Djoutsa Wamba, L.: L'introduction en bourse améliore-t-elle la performance financière de l'entreprise? Une application au cas des entreprises cotées à la Douala Stock Exchange (DSX). Revue Congolaise de Gestion **1**, 101–133 (2020)

Francfort, H.P., et al.: Les pétroglyphes de Tamgaly. Bull. Asia Inst. **9**, 167–207 (1995)

Gareth, M. (2019). *Images de l'organisation*. Presses de l'Université Laval

Geroski, P., Machin, S., Van Reenen, J.: The profitability of innovating firms. RAND J. Econ. **24**(2), 198–211 (1993)

Graham, R.M., et al.: Increasing frequency and duration of Arctic winter warming events. Geophys. Res. Lett. **44**(13), 6974–6983 (2017)

Habhab-Rave, S.: Irrationalité de la décision: une approche par les préférences. Revue Sciences de Gestion (79) (2011)

Hall, A.: Capacity development for agricultural biotechnology in developing countries: an innovation systems view of what it is and how to develop it. J. Int. Dev. **17**(5), 611–630 (2005)

Hofstede, G.: Culture and organizations. Int. Stud. Manag. Organ. **10**(4), 15–41 (1980)

Jaruzelski, B., Katzenbach, J.: Building a culture that energizes innovation: creating an innovation culture is notoriously difficult. Here are some fresh insights and a roadmap for tackling the culture conundrum. Financ. Exe. **28**(2), 32–36 (2012)

Jérolon, A., Baglietto, L., Birmelé, E., Alarcon, F., Perduca, V.: Causal mediation analysis in presence of multiple mediators uncausally related. The Int. J. Biostat. **17**(2), 191–221 (2020)

Kirner, E., Kinkel, S., Jaeger, A.: Innovation paths and the innovation performance of low-technology firms—an empirical analysis of German industry. Res. Policy 38(3), 447–458 (2009)

Martins, E.C., Terblanche, F.: Building organisational culture that stimulates creativity and innovation. Eur. J. Innov. Manag. 6(1), 64–74 (2003)

O'Reilly III, C.A., Caldwell, D.F., Barnett, W.P.: Work group demography, social integration, and turnover. Admin. Sci. Q. 21–37 (1989)

Ougharbi, N.A., Achour, F.Z.: Dynamique intrapreneuriale: 'influence de la dimension organisationnelle. Revue du contrôle, de la comptabilité et de l'audit 4(3) (2020)

Pesqueux, Y.: Du changement organisationnel (2015)

Plane, J.M.: Théorie des organisations-5e éd. Dunod (2017)

Rabaud, M.: Congo Lucha–Tita Productions (2017)

Sainsaulieu, R.: L'identité en entreprise. J. Chevalier, Centre de relations internationales et de sciences politiques, et Centre universitaire de recherches sur l'action publique et le politique, épistémologie et sciences sociales (Amiens), L'identité politique, pp. 252–261 (1994)

Sarkis, J., & Dhavale, D. G. (2015). Supplier selection for sustainable operations: A triple-bottom-line approach using a Bayesian framework. *International Journal of Production Economics, 166*, 177–191

Schein, E.H.: Organizational Culture, vol. 45, no. 2, p. 109. American Psychological Association (1990)

Sørensen, N.N., Michelsen, J.A., Schreck, S.: Navier-Stokes predictions of the NREL phase VI rotor in the NASA Ames 80 ft× 120 ft wind tunnel. Wind Energy Int. J. Prog. Appl. Wind Power Conv. Technol. 5(2–3), 151–169 (2002)

Schumpeter, J.A.: The theory of economic development: an inquiry into profits, capital, credit, interest and the business cycle. Harvard Econ. Stud. 46 (1934)

Uhalde, M., Osty, F.: Les mondes sociaux de l'entreprise. Lectures, Publications reçues, Penser le développement des organisations (2007)

Vayssade, J.A., Jones, G., Gée, C., Paoli, J.N.: Pixelwise instance segmentation of leaves in dense foliage. Comput. Electron. Agric. 195, 106797 (2022)

A Forecast of Brent Prices in Times of Ukrainian Crisis Using ARFIMA Models

Adriana Anamaria Davidescu$^{(\boxtimes)}$, Eduard Mihai Manta, Margareta-Stela Florescu, and Maria Ruxandra Cojocaru

Calea Dudesti, 188, Complex IncityBl.B, Et.10, Ap.75Sector 3, Bucuresti, Romania
{adriana.alexandru,duard.manta}@csie.ase.ro,
margareta.florescu@ari.ase.ro, cojocaruruxandra19@stud.ase.ro

Abstract. The recent incursion of Russian military forces onto Ukrainian territory has sparked global apprehension regarding the stability of stock market prices. This paper forecasts the direction that Brent spot prices will take during the year following the 2022 Ukrainian conflict, using ARFIMA parametric and semiparametric methods. According to the series' long memory, prices will fall steeply during the next few months, reaching up to 80 or 75 dollars by the end of March 2023.

Keywords: Brent forecast · ARFIMA · Long-memory · Ukrainian crisis

1 Introduction

The current invasion of Russian forces on Ukrainian land, launched on 24th February 2022, has caused worldwide concerns in terms of stock market price stability. Since the very first day of the attack there have been serious repercussions on financial markets, especially in the case of commodity prices for petrol, gas, energy, and foods such as wheat, grain, and soybeans, which have raised significantly and are now the main focus of economic analysts.

Since Russia is a key exporter of oil-related products, providing up to 14% of global oil supply in 2021, the international response to Russia's military attack has consisted in waves of sanctions that led to an embargo on Russian oil. EU has announced that it will reduce Russian crude oil imports by 90% by 2023.

The Western countries are now facing incredibly high prices of petrol-related products, and the Brent spot price, Europe's benchmark for crude oil, is expected to reach 150 dollars/barrel according to The Washington Post and Bloomberg, some claiming that by the end of 2022 there will be prices as high as 180 dollars/barrel. The total spillover of volatility on markets increased from 35% to 85%, as crude oil has become a clear transmitter of contagion [15], yet the contagion effect of oil price is short-run and gradually attenuates [3]. Meanwhile, the Brent price for its futures contracts is going down, having been 123 dollars/barrel in May and only 110 dollars/barrel in June, showing that investors collectively believe that prices cannot stay up for too long. Reports done by the EIA offer further insight, estimating that if the price of spot Brent crude oil was 113 barrels in May, in the second half of 2022 it will average $ 108 / barrel, and it will drop to $ 97 / barrel by 2023 [10].

The forecasting of the evolution of Brent's price is thus an urgent problem in the given international context, and it represents a much-needed decision tool for investors on the oil market. This paper is proposing answers to the pressing question of whether prices will be further going up or they will start declining or persist at actual levels. The method which will be employed aims to consider the long memory of the observed Brent prices on the market to better predict the evolution of Brent price, using both ARFIMA parametric and semiparametric methods. The research's forecasts bring an element of novelty to the wider existing literature, by applying a complex and lesser- known model, such as ARFIMA, in both its parametric and semiparametric form, to recent Brent price data.

Therefore, our research focused on the following research question: Are the Brent prices expected to decrease in the period 2022–2023? Thus, the core hypothesis of the paper is the following:

Hypothesis 1 (H1). *The Brent prices are decreasing during the period 2022–2023.*

The paper is structured as follows. The second section provides an overview of the data and methodology used in the research, preparing the grounds for the case study presented in Sect. 3, where the empirical results of the ARFIMA model will be presented. The case study is followed by the conclusions section, where the most important results of the analysis will be highlighted.

2 Research Strategy and Methodology

The data used are the real monthly spot prices of Brent crude oil for 1988.01 - 2022.03, obtained by deflation with the US dollar consumer price index, base year 2015. Data on nominal prices and CPI were taken from the Federal Reserve economic data website based on their availability.

Fractal studies of Brent prices have been conducted before with favorable results. A recent overview of the existing literature on ARFIMA offers a foundation for subsequent research when the value of d is a non-integer number, concluding that the method serves the purpose of studying oil prices and other time series well. The value of the fractional difference (d) and other long memory parameters have been estimated using a variety of techniques and functions. These techniques and tools, which include the Geweke and Porter-Hudak (GPH) estimator, the smoothed periodogram (Sperio), the fractionally differenced (Fracdiff), and the Hurst exponent, can all be used successfully for our purposes [11].

According to a study, ARFIMA(1,0.47,2) and ARFIMA(2,0.09,0) are good semi-parametric models for the assessment and forecast of WTI and Brent weekly prices from 1987 - 2013, respecting all the assumptions on the residuals. The paper claims that the Brent data displayed three breaks, while the WTI series likewise revealed three of these breaks, centered around the years 1999, 2004 and 2009 [12].

A time series of Saudi Arabia's oil prices, which covered the period from November 1990 to December 2020, was shown to be unstable, until the first difference stabilized it.

It was determined that the series has long memory through the autocorrelation function analysis, that can give a preliminary indication about the presence of the long memory phenomenon. After analyzing various alternative ARMA models in Eviews10, the ARFIMA model (2, 0.469, 3) was found to be the best model to reflect the series, later used to forecast oil prices in 2021. According to the study, the model predicted a drop in oil price [1].

Gasoline prices in Southern Brazil are the subject of another paper, which makes use of data from January 1, 2002, to August 9, 2009, using ARFIMA (1, 0.3995, 0) as the model that best explains the series. The Akaike Information Criterion (AIC) was used to select the representative model of the series under investigation after estimation of all the competing models [14].

Crude oil price dynamics is further explored through support vector machine (SVM), feed-forward neural networks (FNN), auto-regressive integrated moving average (ARIMA), fractional integrated ARIMA (ARFIMA), Markov-switching ARFIMA (MS-ARFIMA), and random walk (RW), taking monthly data from January 1990 to July 2008 into consideration. In relation to ARFIMA, the paper discovers that MS-ARFIMA performs generally better than ARIMA and. In terms of forecasting Brent crude oil prices, the ARFIMA model is unable to outperform ARIMA, although that knowing that the ARFIMA model can capture the long memory characteristic gives it a theoretical advantage over the ARIMA model [16].

Evaluating and comparing the out-of-sample performances of diverse forecast methods is also the subject of a paper focusing on Brent oil price. It makes use of the GARCH-in-Mean model, several nonparametric data-driven methods, and ARIMA, ARFIMA, and AR, a nonlinear autoregressive artificial neural network and genetic programming. The findings indicate that none of the methods significantly differ in their ability to forecast the value and direction of the Brent oil price, all of them being equally good for forecasting [5].

In another study, monthly Brent prices from 1979 – 2019 are used in parametric models ARFIMA(2,0.3589648,2)-sGARCH(1,1) and ARFIMA(2,0.3589648,2)-fGARCH(1,1), which manage to capture the long-term price evolution, also taking into account volatility [4].

Another paper uses daily Brent prices from 2009 – 2017, and the resulting parametric model used was ARFIMA(1,0.4577, 2), which was surpassed in accuracy by the hybrid model constituted by the extension with ANFIS and Markov, which also takes into account the interdependencies between markets [2].

Similarly, the monthly West Texas Intermediate (WTI) oil price series from 2003 to 2021 can be fractionally represented using a long-memory data pattern, such as ARIFMA, which can be used to produce hybrid models. The new model of the hybrid ARFIMA with FTSMC, referred to as ARFIMA-FTSMC is a successful times series model of crude oil price. The hybrid ARFIMA-FTSMC model outperforms ARFIMA in terms of accuracy according to MAE, RMSE, and MAPE [7].

Data about Persian Gulf Gas-Oil prices were taken from the OPEC website and applied ARFIMA, covering the first week of 2009 through the first week of 2012 for model fitting and the second week of 2012 through the thirteenth week of 2012 for value prediction. The findings suggest that the ARFIMA(0,0.19,1) model is preferable to ARIMA (1,1,0) [6].

Lastly, others analyze the long memory property of realized volatility in Shanghai fuel oil market, modelling and forecasting realized volatility using ARFIMA models and comparing their performance with seminal GARCH-class models for daily returns. The conclusion is that ARFIMA has greater forecasting accuracy than the latter [13].

After viewing the existing literature on the topic of long memory modelling, it is clear that the model to be applied is the fractional ARIMA, which differentiates with a positive fractal number between 0 and 0.5 in order to achieve stationarity yet avoid over differentiation, as some series with long-term memory that are still differentiated at lag one may lose information useful for prediction [8, 9]. To identify whether a series has long memory the Hurst exponent can be calculated via R/S analysis, where values of H between 0.5 and 1 indicate long memory, while the ACF graph of the series should show a slow hyperbolic decrease.

Therefore, the methodology to be followed when constructing an ARFIMA model (p, d, q) is the following: checking the stationarity of the series with ADF, KPSS or PP tests, identifying the long memory characteristic of the series, estimating the parameters p, d and q by parametric or semiparametric methods, residue testing and selecting the optimal model, followed by accuracy analysis.

The parametric approach is based on estimating all parameters in one step through EML method, while the semiparametric method implies fixing the difference parameter first, then estimating p and q by looking at the ACF and PACF diagrams. The d parameter can be calculated using H as the Hurst exponent, or other estimators like GPH and Sperio: $d = H- 0.5$.

Models ARFIMA (p, d, q) can be expressed as:

$$\phi(B)(1 - B)^d (Y_t - \mu) = \theta(B)\varepsilon_t$$

$$\theta_q(B) = (1 - \theta_1 B - ... - \theta_q.B^q) \text{ is the polynomial operator MA(q),} \qquad (1)$$

$$\phi_q(B) = (1 - \phi_1 B - ... - \phi_p.B^p) \text{ is the polynomial operator AR(p),} \qquad (2)$$

$$d \text{ is the order of differenciation,} \qquad (3)$$

$$\varepsilon_t \text{ is white noise.} \qquad (4)$$

3 Empirical Results

The evolution of Brent prices since 1988 has been marked by numerous market shocks, such as the Iraqi invasion of Kuwait in 1990, the starting wars in the Levant in 2006, the financial crisis from 2008 and the demand crisis from 2015, followed by the Covid pandemics of 2020 and now the Russian invasion of Ukraine (Fig. 1).

The overall analysis was conducted in R software. Descriptive statistics show that the series is positively asymmetric and 13 change points in mean have been detected using

Fig. 1. Nominal price (in red) vs deflated real price of Brent (in black)

binary segmentation method, as well as 3 change points in variance according to Pelt method. The data displays variance fluctuations and was applied a log transformation.

Seasonality has been checked with Hegy and OCSB tests, the series having no seasonality, yet the tests for stationarity displayed in Table 1 have shown that it presents unitary roots, thus being non-stationary in mean. The long-term memory of the series is visible through the hyperbolic decrease of coefficients in ACF, as well as by looking at the values of Hurst exponent, between 0.5 and 1 (Fig. 2).

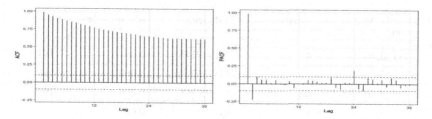

Fig. 2. Correlogram of series

Table 1. Hurst exponent calculation

Method applied	Value
Simple R/S Hurst estimation	0.848
Corrected R over S Hurst exponent	0.997
Empirical Hurst exponent	1.026
Corrected empirical Hurst exponent	0.993
Theoretical Hurst exponent	0.549

The non-stationary long memory process can then be reduced to stationarity by applying the ARFIMA model. For training the models, both a sample with data up to 2019 and the entire set of data were used (Table 2). The parametric method requires a first estimation of d, which is 0.499 for the training set consisting of all data. Applying the difference and visualizing the ACF and PACF diagrams led to the identification of the three potential models in Table 3. All parameters are estimated simultaneously while running the models.

Table 2. Analysis of unitary roots of monthly real Brent price

Unitary Root	T&C	C
ADF level	−3.265*	−2.397
PP level	0.255	0.267
KPSS level	0.660	3.661
ADF first difference	−13.889***	−13.905***
PP first difference	0.01***	0.01***
KPSS first difference	0.040***	0.043***

Note: ***, **, * means stationary at 1%, 5% and 10%; T&C is the most general model with a constant and trend; C is the model with a constant and no trend

Table 3. Potential models for parametric ARFIMA on all data

Nr	ARFIMA Model (p,d,q)	Parameter	Coefficient	Significance	AIC
1	(1, d, 0)	$\Phi 1$	0.7419992***	0.000	−1919.2
		d	0.4754367***	0.000	
2	(2, d, 0)	$\Phi 1$	0.8175293***	0.000	−1921.13
		$\Phi 2$	−0.0979939**	0.046	
		d	0.4725299***	0.000	
3	(3,d,0)	$\Phi 1$	0.8518480***	0.000	−1922.43
		$\Phi 2$	−0.1778635**	0.011	
		$\Phi 3$	0.0931303	0.073	
		d	0.4481110***	0.000	

Applying the AIC selection criterion, the optimal ARFIMA model (3, 0.448, 0) with the lowest AIC was chosen. The model's residuals pass the Ljung-Box test with p-value > 0.1, meaning they do not show autocorrelation, and don't present heteroscedasticity according to ARCH-LM. However, they aren't normally distributed according to Jarque-Berra test. The model can be written as:

$$(1 - 0.851 \cdot B^1 + 0.177 \cdot B^2 - 0.093 \cdot B^3)(1 - B)^{0.448} Y_t = \varepsilon_t$$

The semiparametric method makes use of the estimators shown in Table 4.

Table 4. Semiparametric estimators for d

Method	Value
Gweke dan Porte-Hudak (GPH)	0.82575
Smoothed GPH (Sperio)	0.75907
R/S	0.50848

The mean of estimators is 0.697, of which 0.5 is eliminated, obtaining the degree of fractal differentiation of 0.197 that will be applied in the modelling process. ACF and PACF charts of the series differentiated by 0.197 seem to indicate pure AR processes. From the potential models in Table 5, ARFIMA(3,0.197,0) is optimal due to having the lowest AIC. The model's residuals are then checked, and they are found to have no autocorrelation as specified by Ljung-Box test and no heteroscedasticity according to ARCH-LM, however they are not normally distributed.

Table 5. Potential models for semiparametric ARFIMA on all data

Nr	ARFIMA Model (p,d,q)	Parameter	Coefficient	Significance	AIC
1	(1, 0.197, 0)	$\Phi 1$	0.9989834***	0.000	−660.7
2	(2, 0.197, 0)	$\Phi 1$	1.201163***	0.000	−673.67
		$\Phi 2$	−0.202433***	0.000	
3	(3,0.197,0)	$\Phi 1$	1.220867***	0.000	−678.98
		$\Phi 2$	−0.364763***	0.000	
		$\Phi 3$	0.142839***	0.006	

The model ARFIMA(3,0.197,0) can be written as:

$$(1 - 1.22 \cdot B^1 + 0.364 \cdot B^2 - 0.142 \cdot B^3)(1 - B)^{0.197} Y_t = \varepsilon_t$$

The same procedures have been applied to a training set ending in 2019, with the results being visible in figure 3 alongside the forecasts resulted from the whole data analysis. The models fitted on the reduced training set could not capture the shock of the pandemic or that of the war, but those fitted on all data available predict an accentuated fall of prices in the 12 months following March 2022.

The RMSE favors the model built by the parametric method. This method indicates a downward trend of price in the next year, with a less steep slope than that associated with the semiparametric method for the first six months forecasted. After august, the semiparametric method suggests a decrease in the rate of price decline, which will lead to a stabilization of the price around $ 83. The forecast for March 2023, one year after the outbreak of the armed conflict in Ukraine, is $ 80.72. The parametric method, however, suggests a price decline up to $ 75 in March (figure 3) (Table 6).

Table 6. Accuracy indicators

Out-of-sample approach					In-sample approach	
Model	Parametric ARFIMA		Semiparametric ARFIMA		Parametric ARFIMA	Semiparametric ARFIMA
Indicators	Training	Test	Train ing	Test	All sample	All sample
RMSE	0.635	0.330	0.096	2.970	0.085	0.330
MAE	0.531	0.228	0.070	2.95	0.065	0.222
MAPE	1.727	0.056	5.795	2.906	0.009	6.104
MASE	6.913	2.015	0.994	26.080	0.265	0.896

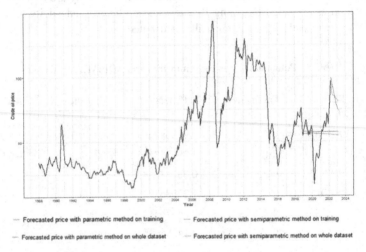

— Forecasted price with parametric method on training   — Forecasted price with semiparametric method on training

— Forecasted price with parametric method on whole dataset   — Forecasted price with semiparametric method on whole dataset

Fig. 3. Forecasts of parametric and semiparametric ARFIMA

4   Conclusions

Amid the 2022 Ukrainian crisis, the real price of Brent oil is a distressing topic for consumers worldwide as well for investors, who face incredible price volatility on the market. The evolution of the price is widely speculated, the paper at hand providing a useful forecast of real Brent prices in conformity to the methodology of ARFIMA modelling, thus capturing the long memory of the market to better predict prices.

The results of the analysis using the ARFIMA models, meaning both parametric ARFIMA(3, 0.448, 0) and semiparametric ARFIMA(3,0.197,0), show that the price of Brent follows a steep descending trend from April 2022 to April 2023, leading to prices of $80, respectively $75 dollars, after a year of war, in March 2023. The two models give overall similar results. The semiparametric technique's prediction for the first six months differs through its increased steepness, but takes on a milder slope after august, which will result in a stabilization of the price around $ 83. This might be either due to the international effort of producing more supply, or due to the reorientation of investors onto renewable resources of energy.

The paper brings an element of novelty to the existing literature from two points of view. Firstly, it compares two types of ARFIMA models, the parametric and semiparametric one respectively, to conclude on the differences in performance that these models can achieve. From this point of view, the models have turned out to perform similarly well on the dataset under study, a fact which was checked through the Diebol Mariano test as well. Secondly, the paper makes use of data from 1988 to 2022, being thus able to learn from recent events like the pandemic of COVID-19 and the Ukrainian crisis and to predict the evolution of the Brent oil price in the short term, in a time where such a forecast is much needed.

Further research on the topic of oil prices could extend the applicability of the ARFIMA parametric and semiparametric models through the construction of hybrid models to encourage non-linearity in forecasting. Other extensions could refer to the GARCH family models, to ensure a good incorporation of the volatility usually present on the oil market into the model.

References

1. Abdallah, B., Yassin, E.: Measuring the Impact of the COVID-19 Pandemic on Oil Prices Using Long Memory Models (November 1990 to December 2020). Global J. Econo. Bus. (GJEB) **12**(1), pp. 109–117 (2022). https://doi.org/10.31559/GJEB2022.12.1.6
2. Abdollahi, H., Ebrahimi, S.: A new hybrid model for forecasting Brent crude oil price. Energy **12**, 1–13 (2020). https://doi.org/10.1016/j.energy.2020.117520
3. Adekoya, O.B., Oliyide, J.A., Yaya, O.S., Al-Faryan, M.A. S.: Does oil connectdifferently with prominent assets during war? Analysis of intra-day data during the Russia- Ukraine saga. Resources Policy 77 (2022). https://doi.org/10.1016/j.resourpol.2022.102728
4. Al Gounmeein, R., Ismail, M.: Modelling and forecasting monthly Brent crude oil prices: a long memory and volatility approach. Statistics in Transition. Statistics in Transition. New Series **22**(1), 1–26 (2021). https://doi.org/10.21307/stattrans-2021-002
5. Álvarez-Díaz, M.: Is it possible to accurately forecast the evolution of Brent crude oil prices? An answer based on parametric and nonparametric forecasting methods. Empirical Economics **59**(3), 1285–1305 (2019). https://doi.org/10.1007/s00181-019-01665-w
6. Amadeh, H., Amini, A., Effati, F.: ARIMA and ARFIMA Prediction of Persian Gulf Gas-Oil F.O.B. Investment Knowledge 2(7), 2–21 (2013)
7. Devianto, D., et al.: The hybrid model of autoregressive integrated moving average and fuzzy time series Markov chain on long-memory data. Frontiers in Applied Mathematics and Statistics **8**, 1–15 (2022). https://doi.org/10.3389/fams.2022.1045241
8. Granger, C., Joyeux, R.: An introduction to long–memory time series and fractional differencing. Time Series Anal **1**(1), 15–30 (1980). https://doi.org/10.1111/j.1467-9892.1980.tb0 0297.x
9. Hosking, J.: Fractional differencing. Biometrika **68**(1), 165–176 (1981). https://doi.org/10. 2307/2335817
10. IEA (2022) www.iea.org. [Online] Available at: https://www.iea.org/articles/energy-fact-sheet-why-does-russian-oil-and-gas-matter
11. Ismail, M., Al-Gounmein, R.: Overview of long memory for economic and financial time series dataset and related time series models: a review study. Int. J. Appl. Math. **52**(2), 261–269 (2022)

12. Jibrin, S.A., Musa, Y., Zubair, U.A., Saidu, A.S.E.: ARFIMA modelling and investigation of structural break(s) in west texas intermediate and brent series. CBN Journal of Applied Statistics 6(2), 59–79 (2015)
13. Liu, L., Wan, J.: A study of Shanghai fuel oil futures price volatility based on high frequency data: Long-range dependence, modeling and forecasting. Econ. Model. 29(6), 2245–2253 (2012). https://doi.org/10.1016/j.econmod.2012.06.029
14. Souza, F.M., Almeida, S.G., Souza, A.M., Lopes, L.F.D., Zanini, R.R.: Gasoline price forecasting to southern region of Brazil. Iberoamerican J. Indus. Eng. 3(1), 234–248 (2011)
15. Wang, Y., Bouri, E., Fareed, Z., Dai, Y.: Geopolitical risk and the systemic risk in the commodity markets under the war in Ukraine. Finance research Letters, 1–29 (2022). https://doi.org/10.1016/j.frl.2022.103066
16. Yu, L., Zhang, X., Wang, S.: Assessing potentiality of support vector machine method in crude oil price forecasting. EURASIA J. Math. Sci. Technol. Educ. 13(12), 7893–7904 (2017). https://doi.org/10.12973/ejmste/77926

Cognitive Assessment Based on Skeleton-Based Action Recognition: Ball-Drop Case

Sayda Elmi[1,2]($\boxtimes$) and Morris Bell[2]

[1] University of New Haven, West Haven, USA
[2] School of Medicine, Yale University, New Haven, USA
{saida.elmi,morris.bell}@yale.edu

Abstract. Human action recognition aims at extracting features on top of human skeletons and estimating human pose. It has received increasing attention in recent years. However, existing methods capture only the action information while in a real world application such as cognitive assessment, we need to measure the executive functioning that helps psychiatrists to identify some mental disease such as Alzheimer, Schizophrenia and ADHD. In this paper, we propose a skeleton-based action recognition named Mind-In-Action (MIA) for cognitive assessment. MIA integrates a pose estimator to extract the human body joints and then automatically measures the executive functioning employing the distance and elbow angle calculation. Three score functions were designed to measure the executive functioning: the accuracy score, the rhythm score and the functioning score. We evaluate our model on two different datasets and show that our approach significantly outperforms the existing methods.

Keywords: Mental health · Embodied cognition · executive functioning · ADHD · Alzheimer · Action recognition · Skeleton extraction

1 Introduction

Human action recognition, as a central task in video analyses, becomes increasingly crucial and has received an important attention in recent years. Moreover, existing studies have shown promising progress on pose estimation [2,4]. To fully describe the spatial configurations and temporal dynamics in human actions, skeleton-based representations have been used for human action recognition, as human skeletons provide a compact data form to extract dynamic features in human body movements [9]. In practice, human skeletons in a video are mainly represented as a sequence of joint coordinate lists. Many action recognition techniques [13–16] have shown great performance on public benchmarks, where the body joint coordinates are extracted by pose estimators. However, such performance is not necessarily replicated in real-world scenarios, where the data

R. Jallouli et al. (Eds.): ICDEc 2023, LNBIP 485, pp. 425–435, 2023.
https://doi.org/10.1007/978-3-031-42788-6_26

comes from specific application requirements. The specific real-world application that we are focusing on in this paper is cognitive assessment in adults and children using cognitively demanding physical tasks. In addition, in the existing state-of the-art, only the pose information is extracted and skeleton sequences capture only action information, while in a real world application such as cognitive assessment, we need to measure executive functioning in addition to the pose estimation.

Cognitive impairments, represented by inattention, laziness, hyperactivity or acting impulsively, lack of motivation and being forgetful, are commonly found among children and adults. According to [3,17], Attention Deficit/Hyperactivity Disorder (ADHD) is a psychiatric neurodevelopmental disorder that is very hard to diagnose. In fact, symptoms for ADHD arise from a primary deficit in executive functions [11]. Embodied cognition is a well established construct [19], recognizing that mental functioning involves brain and body working together and cognition develops along with and by way of physical movement. Better measures of cognition that closely relate to individual functioning and predict disability are sorely needed to provide proper remedial intervention at the appropriate time [12]. As a measure of embodied cognition, the Traffic-Lights-Game (TLG), which is one of the core tasks with higher cognitive demand, is an attention and response inhibition task. It is similar to computerized continuous performance tests that assess sustained attention and response inhibition but is more complex and requires rhythmic upper body movement in response to commands. The participant is asked to pass a juggling ball (or any other object) from one hand to the other in rhythm to the words "Green Light", to move the ball up and down to the words "Yellow Light" and to not pass the ball when the participant hears "Red Light". The task is subsequently repeated at a faster pace in different trials. The participant is then presented with the same task but using a sequence of pictures of green, red, and yellow traffic lights as visual cues, rather than the spoken cues, thus allowing for comparison between sensory modalities in audio and visual trials. The Traffic-Lights-Game can provide sufficient psychometric observations and can be used as a measure of behavioral self-regulation. The game has four trials and the subjects are expected to perform the sequential movement for every count/beat provided by the therapist. Then, they are evaluated by three scores: (i) Action Score: helps to evaluate the working memory and represents the total number of correct actions, (ii) Rhythm Score: helps to evaluate the coordination and self-regulation and represents the total number of correct rhythms, accurately keeping the beat. Starting late and rushing to catch the beat is not correct and (iii) Functioning Score: helps to evaluate the executive functioning and represents the total number of correct actions in rhythm. Monitoring such a task and scoring it manually is tiresome and requires constant attention from the therapists.

In this paper, inspired by the success of the computer vision tools for action recognition and human skeleton extraction, we investigate how to apply a deep learning model to monitor cognitive abilities, which helps with identifying cognitive impairments. We propose an automated intelligent system called MIA, to monitor and assess cognitive behavior through physical tasks which are part of assessment and training for people with Executive Function Disorder.

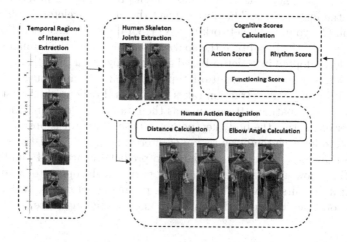

Fig. 1. Overview of the proposed architecture.

2   MIA: Model Overview

2.1   Problem Formulation

In this section, we first introduce the key data structures used in this paper and formally define our problem. Following the convention, we use capital letters (e.g., X) to represent both matrices and graphs, and use squiggle capital letters (e.g., $\mathcal{X}$) to denote sets. Human action recognition requires to temporally segment all frames of a given video. We first extract a set of temporal regions of interest $\mathcal{X}$ where $\mathcal{X} = X_{i,i\in\{1..K\}}$. Then, we predict the action in each temporal region of interest $X_{i,i\in\{1..K\}}$ and calculate a set of cognitive scores $\mathcal{S}$ where $\mathcal{S} = \{\varphi_A, \varphi_R, \varphi_F\}$ and $\varphi_A, \varphi_R, \varphi_F$ are the action, rhythm and functioning scores, respectively. The task can be formulated as follows:

Given K temporal regions of interest X, each $X_{i,i\in K}$ is a sequence of D-dimensional features where $X_{i,i\in K} = (x_1, \ldots, x_{|X_i|})$ and $x_{j,j\in\{1..|X_i|\}} \in \mathbb{R}^D$, the task is to infer the sequence of frame-wise action labels $Y_{i,i\in K} = (y_1, \ldots, y_{|Y_i|})$ and there are C action classes $\mathcal{C}$ where $\mathcal{C} = \{1, \ldots, C\}$ and $y_{j,j\in\{1..|Y_i|\}} \in \mathcal{C}$. A set of cognitive scores $\mathcal{S}$ is calculated for every Y_i for K temporal regions of interest.

2.2   Model Architecture

As shown in Fig. 1, the architecture of MIA comprises four major modules which are: (i) temporal regions of interest extraction, (ii) human skeleton joints extraction, (iii) human action recognition, i.e. the pose estimator and (iv) a cognitive scoring module.

For action recognition, researchers usually segment all frames of a given video. To efficiently segment the videos, our model proposes to extract the temporal regions of interest where the subject has a high probability to practice the task and follow the instructions. Then, we extract the human skeleton joints employing a Graph Convolutional Network (GCN) [13,14] since it has very deep structure that can effectively capture the spatial dynamics from the human skeleton. GCN is widely adopted in skeleton-based action recognition [13,14] and it models human skeleton sequences as spatio-temporal graphs. As an input, the module of human skeleton joints extraction takes K temporal regions of interest $X_{i,i\in K}$. GCN extracts the spatial patterns such as the human topology and the skeleton joints. After extracting the body key-points, a pose estimator is proposed to predict the action for each temporal region of interest $X_{i,i\in K}$. The distance between hands and the elbow angle are calculated to predict the action. In addition, we calculate the elbow angle between the body part and the opposite hand to have more accurate results. Finally, based on the predicted actions, we calculate the cognitive scores: action score, rhythm score and functioning score.

3   MIA: Methodology

3.1   Temporal Regions of Interest Extraction

The tasks are specifically designed to fit in the theory of embodied cognition, where cognition can be influenced through physical activities. A screen is used to display a music video where the host instructs the subjects to perform the task following the instructions. There are 4 trials overall and each trial has varying trial segments.

Definition 1 (Temporal Regions of Interest). *Given a trial video, a temporal region of interest (TRI) is defined as the trial segment where the subject is told to do an action. TRI is denoted by $X_{i,i\in K}$ where K in the total number of TRIs in the video.*

While action segmentation requires to temporally segment all frames of a given video [6], we extract K temporal regions of interest X to predict the action in each $X_{i,i\in K}$ as predicting the actions in all frames is more expensive and inefficient. The extraction of the TRIs can be done with the speech recognition to segment the video based on the played instructions. In this paper, the videos are segmented based on the time intervals when the subject is told to perform the action based on the announced instructions as shown in Fig. 1.

3.2   Human Skeleton Joints Extraction

Currently, skeleton-based representations have been very popular for human action recognition, as human skeletons provide a compact data form to depict dynamic changes in human body movements [13]. Skeleton data is a series of 3D coordinates of multiple skeleton joints, which can be estimated from 2D images [1]. For the joint localization problem on RGB data, we explored various existing state-of-the-art methods and decided on using the deep-learning architecture proposed in [14]. While some of the other pre-trained models works well with upper-body pose [7] and useful for certain other applications, our problem requires an efficient and accurate pose estimator for full-body human joint. In particular, we build upon the GCN model [14] providing highly accurate results regarding the relative position of human body-joints. We choose to use the pose estimator model stated above as it is the current state-of-the-art pose estimator for multi-person pose estimation and also provides competitive performance on single-person pose estimation as demonstrated by their results on popular datasets for these problems. The joints extraction component predicts the location of all human skeleton key-points as shown in Fig. 1. The tracker predicts the presence of the person on the current frame and the body joints coordinates.

3.3   Action Recognition

Human skeletons in a video are mainly represented as a sequence of joint coordinate lists. For the action recognition, we first monitor and analyze hands' positions.

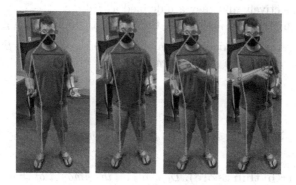

Fig. 2. Different classes that occur in the Traffic-Light task for its four trials.

Based on the Traffic-Lights task, there are a total of three classes, i.e., $|\mathcal{C}| = 3$, as represented in Fig. 2 where class1: hands are in the initial position at the same level, when the subject is told "Red-Light", class2: one hand goes up and down when the subject is told "Yellow-Light", class3: one hand is up and ready to pass the ball (or other object) to the other hand.

Then, we evaluate if the subject's action complies with the expected motion employing two main measures: **(i) Distance calculation**: the output of our pose tracker is pixel locations for the human body joints. We use these joint locations to measure the distance between hands and **(ii) Elbow angle calculation**: we calculate $\hat{r}$ and $\hat{l}$ as the elbow angles of right hand and left hand, respectively.

A given temporal region of interest X is a sequence of D-dimensional features, called frames, where $X_{i,i \in K} = (x_1, \ldots, x_{|X_i|})$ and $x_{j,j \in \{1..|X_i|\}} \in \mathbb{R}^D$. Action recognition for each temporal region of interest X requires to temporally segment all frames of a given $X_{i,i \in K}$, i.e., predicting the action in each frame $x_{j,j \in \{1..|X_i|\}}$.

The probability that a given frame $x_{j,j \in \{1..|X_i|\}}$ belongs to the gesture classes $\mathcal{C}$ is given as follow:

$$P(x_j \in \mathcal{C}) = \begin{cases} 1, & D \leq \alpha \text{ and } A \leq \beta \\ 0 \end{cases} \tag{1}$$

where α and β are the distance and angle thresholds. D is the euclidean distance between the hand position coordinates. A is the elbow angles where $A = \{\hat{r}, \hat{l}\}$.

The gesture classes obtained from the action recognition module are incorporated in the calculations for the cognitive scores in longer sequences of steps performed. The details about calculations of these scores for the steps and sequences that we record is specified in the next sections.

3.4 Cognitive Scoring Functions

The scoring protocol created by the psychologist experts specifies 3 cognitive scores $\mathcal{S} = \{\varphi_A, \varphi_R, \varphi_F\}$ where $\varphi_A, \varphi_R, \varphi_F$ represent action, rhythm and function scores, respectively and they are defined as follows:

Let Y be the predicted actions for the Traffic-Light task in a given video.

Definition 2 (Action Score). *Depends on the amount of times that the subject performs the correct action and defined as:*

$$\varphi_A(Y) = \sum_{i=1}^{K} y_i \in \mathcal{C} \tag{2}$$

where $\mathcal{C}$ is the set of classes and K is the number of predicted classes in K regions of interest.

Definition 3 (Rhythm Score). *Depends on the amount of times that the subject responds within one second after receiving the instruction and defined as:*

$$\varphi_F(Y) = \sum_{i=1}^{K} y_i \in X_i \tag{3}$$

where X is the set of different regions of interest.

Definition 4 (Function Score). *Represents the total number of actions that the subject performs the correct actions in the rhythm and defined as:*

$$\varphi_R(Y) = \sum_{k=1}^{C} \sum_{i=1}^{K} y \in \{X_i \cap C_k\} \tag{4}$$

where C is the number of classes, i.e., $C = |\mathcal{C}|$ and K is the number of temporal regions of interest, i.e., $K = |X|$.

Other distinguishing feature of our proposed model MIA, is that its cognitive scores can directly be translated to measure executive functioning which is one of the key factor to distinguish self-regulation, response inhibition, working memory, co-ordination and attention.

Table 1. Evaluation of MIA model in terms of RMSE and MAE

Method	Adult Data-set					
	Action Score		Rhythm Score		Function Score	
	RMSE	MAE	RMSE	MAE	RMSE	MAE
DTGRM	1.652	0.791	1.521	1.192	0.101	0.498
MSTCN++	1.532	0.738	1.422	1.132	0.925	0.412
ASRF	1.743	0.818	1.635	1.254	1.132	0.52
MSTCN	2.051	1.215	1.982	1.458	1.532	0.891
MIA	**1.312**	**0.635**	**1.198**	**0.912**	**0.707**	**0.250**

4 Experimental Evaluation

For our experiments, we collect data from participants and perform analysis of participants' performances using our MIA model. We then provide our evaluation measures that we use to calculate MIA accuracy.

4.1 Experimental Settings

Data Description. In our experiment, we used two data-sets to evaluate our MIA model. Details are given as follows:

- Adults data-set: it is important to collect data from a broad range of people who are healthy or clinically well characterized and when possible have had conventional cognitive assessments. The adult data collection covers the lifespan from 11 year to 90 years. We collected RGB data from 35 participants that are recruited to follow the instructions provided by the music video and perform the task sequences for 4 trials with a total of around 150 videos. All participants were required to perform all the four trials to the best of their cognitive abilities.
- Kids Data-set: Children (ages 5–10 years) were recruited from the community (N = 75). Each subject perform 4 different trials with a total of around 300 videos were collected.

Traffic-Light task was performed twice for a sub-sample, approximately 2 weeks apart. Motion capture data were collected and then converted into cognitive scores.

Evaluation Metrics. Our MIA model aims to predict three cognitive scores, i.e., φ_A, φ_R and φ_F. We measure our method by Root Mean Square Error (RMSE) and Mean Absolute Error (MAE) for each of our predicted cognitive scores as follows: $RMSE = \sqrt{\frac{1}{n}\Sigma_{t=1}^{n}\left(s - \varphi(Y)_t\right)^2}$ and $MAE = \frac{1}{n}\Sigma_{t=1}^{n}|s - \varphi(Y)_t|$ where $\varphi(Y)$ and s are the predicted score value and real score value, respectively; n is the number of all predicted score values.

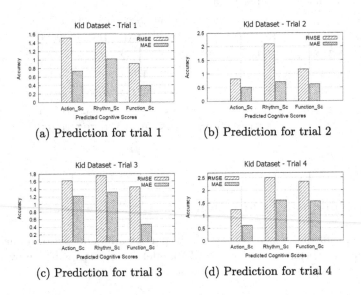

(a) Prediction for trial 1   (b) Prediction for trial 2

(c) Prediction for trial 3   (d) Prediction for trial 4

Fig. 3. Kid dataset: Prediction for different trials.

4.2   Model Performance

For the first three trials, the subjects are required to follow the audio instructions, but for the last trial, the challenge becomes cognitively demanding as they are told to follow visual instructions showing green, yellow and red traffic lights. In the following, we evaluate the performance of our MIA model in terms of accuracy of the predicted cognitive scores. The results on four trials were used to evaluate the accuracy, reported in Table 1.

MIA Performance. Four deep learning-based methods are used to evaluate our proposed model MIA:

- MSTCN [5]: introduces an auxiliary self-supervised task to find correct and in-correct temporal relations in videos using smoothing loss to avoid over-segmentation errors.
- DTGRM [18]: uses Graph Convolution Networks (GCN) and to model temporal relations in videos. It has the ability for efficient temporal reasoning.

- MSTCN++ [10]: is an improvement over MSTCN where the system generates frame level predictions using a dual dilated layer that combines small and large receptive field.
- ASRF [8]: alleviates over-segmentation errors by detecting action boundaries.

The Table 1 reports the RMSE and MAE of the above models as well as MIA model. In our experiment, we used two data-sets, i.e., Adult data-set and Kid data-set.

Table 1 shows the comparative performances for MSTCN, DTGRM, MSTCN++, ASRF and MIA for different predicted cognitive scores. On Adult data-sets, MSTCN++ shows a better performance against DTGRM and ASRF while MIA has the best performance comparing to other models, being immune to contextual nuisances, such as background variation and lighting changes.

However on kid data-sets, ASRF shows better results than MSTCN++. DTGRM shows stability on both data-sets and MSTCN did not perform well while MIA has the best performance comparing to other models, being immune to contextual nuisances, such as background variation and lighting changes.

Figure 3 shows the results on kid data-sets. We evaluate the accuracy (both RMSE and MAE are reported) of the different cognitive scores, i.e., action, rhythm and function scores, for the four trials. Results show that prediction for function score is highly related to action score prediction. That is because when the actions are mis-identified, both scores are impacted. Although the actions performed by children might be imprecise, results on Kid data-sets show similar variations over cognitive scores as reported in Fig. 3. That means that the two measures, distance and elbow angle calculation, both have an impact to deal with the fine-grained motions.

Parameters Evaluation. In this section, we evaluate the distance as well as the elbow angle thresholds, α and β, respectively. Experiments were on adult data-sets, evaluating the predicted action score varying different values of α and β.

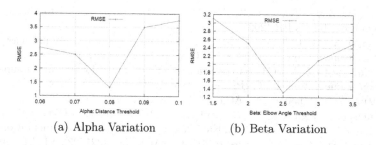

(a) Alpha Variation   (b) Beta Variation

Fig. 4. Parameters Evaluation.

As shown in Fig. 4, varying the parameters α and β, the action score has its best performance when α and β have the values 0.08 and 2.5, respectively. Thus, we set the default values to 0.08 and 2.5 for distance and elbow angle thresholds, respectively.

5 Conclusion

This paper proposes a deep learning based action recognition method for evaluating and monitoring cognitive abilities of human subjects. We deploy a deep learning architecture to analyze human activity and provide informative measures to the experts regarding the performance of the subject, i.e., cognitive scores. To evaluate our method, we created two data-sets with adult and kid subjects performing four different trials of the Traffic-Light task. We illustrate the accuracy of our method and we show detail results for each specific trial, achieving performances which are significantly beyond four existing methods, confirming that our model is applicable to the cognitive assessment problem. This can help to identify digital behavioral biomarkers of embodied cognition that relate to various neuro-developmental, neurological and neuro-psychiatric disorders. An interesting future direction is to analyse the effect of environmental and other external factors and model the temporal dependencies for recognizing activity. This later may provide knowledge that can have important impact on the activity evaluation.

References

1. Cao, Z., Hidalgo, G., Simon, T., Wei, S.-E., Sheikh, Y.: Openpose: realtime multi-person 2D pose estimation using part affinity fields. IEEE Trans. Pattern Anal. Mach. Intell. **43**(1), 172–186 (2021)
2. Chen, Y., Zhang, Z., Yuan, C., Li, B., Deng, Y., Hu, W.: Channel-wise topology refinement graph convolution for skeleton-based action recognition. In: ICCV, pp. 13359–13368 (2021)
3. Cormier, E.: Attention deficit/hyperactivity disorder: a review and update. J. Pediatr. Nurs. **23**(5), 345–357 (2008)
4. Duan, H., Zhao, Y., Chen, K., Lin, D., Dai, B.: Revisiting skeleton-based action recognition. In: CVPR (2022)
5. Farha, Y.A., Gall, J.: MS-TCN: multi-stage temporal convolutional network for action segmentation. In: IEEE CVPR, pp. 3575–3584 (2019)
6. Fayyaz, M., Gall, J.: SCT: set constrained temporal transformer for set supervised action segmentation. In: CVPR, pp. 498–507 (2020)
7. Gattupalli, S., Ghaderi, A., Athitsos, V.: Evaluation of deep learning based pose estimation for sign language recognition. In: PETRA, p. 12. ACM (2016)
8. Ishikawa, Y., Kasai, S., Aoki, Y., Kataoka, H.: Alleviating over-segmentation errors by detecting action boundaries. In: IEEE WACV, pp. 2321–2330. IEEE (2021)
9. Johansson, G.: Visual perception of biological motion and a model for its analysis. Percept. Psychophys. **14**(2), 201–211 (1973)
10. Li, S., Abu Farha, Y., Liu, Y., Cheng, M.-M., Gall, J.: MS-TCN++: multi-stage temporal convolutional network for action segmentation. CoRR, abs/2006.09220 (2020)

11. McClelland, M.M., Cameron, C.E.: Self-regulation in early childhood: improving conceptual clarity and developing ecologically valid measures. Child Dev. Perspect. **6**(2), 136–142 (2012)
12. McClelland, M.M., et al.: Predictors of early growth in academic achievement: the head-toes-knees-shoulders task. Front. Psychol. **5**(2), 599 (2014)
13. Song, Y.-F., Zhang, Z., Shan, C., Wang, L.: Stronger, faster and more explainable: a graph convolutional baseline for skeleton-based action recognition. In: MM, pp. 1625–1633. ACM (2020)
14. Song, Y.-F., Zhang, Z., Shan, C., Wang, L.: Constructing stronger and faster baselines for skeleton-based action recognition. IEEE Trans. Patterns Pattern Anal. Mach. Intell. **45**(2), 1474–1488 (2021)
15. Sun, K., Xiao, B., Liu, D., Wang, J.: Deep high-resolution representation learning for human pose estimation. In: CVPR, pp. 5693–5703 (2019)
16. Tran, D., Wang, H., Torresani, L., Feiszli, M.: Video classification with channel-separated convolutional networks. In: ICCV, pp. 5552–5561 (2019)
17. Tucha, O.: The history of attention deficit hyperactivity disorder. ADHD Atten. Defic. Hyperact. Disord. **2**(4), 241–255 (1999)
18. Wang, D., Hu, D., Li, X., Dou, D.: Temporal relational modeling with self-supervision for action segmentation. CoRR, abs/2012.07508 (2020)
19. Wilson, A.D., Golonka, S.: Embodied cognition is not what you think it is. Front. Psychol. **12**(2) (2013)

Author Index

Printed in the United States
by Baker & Taylor Publisher Services

Printed in the United States
by Baker & Taylor Publisher Services